Mathematics Probability

Mathematics — Mechanics and Probability

L. Bostock, B.Sc.

S. Chandler, B.Sc.

Stanley Thornes (Publishers) Ltd.

First published in 1984 by
Stanley Thornes (Publishers) Ltd
Ellenborough House
Wellington Street
CHELTENHAM GL50 1YD

Reprinted 1985
Reprinted 1987
Reprinted 1988
Reprinted 1989
Reprinted 1990
Reprinted 1991
Reprinted 1993

British Library Cataloguing in Publication Data

Bostock, L.
    Mathematics: mechanics and
    probability.
    1. Mathematics–1961–
    I. Title   II. Chandler, S.
    510   QA32.2

    ISBN 0-85950-141-8

Typeset by Tech-Set, Gateshead, Tyne & Wear.
Printed and bound in Great Britain at The Bath Press, Avon.

PREFACE

Many students who embark on an A-level course in Mathematics choose the combination of Pure Mathematics with applications to Mechanics. The Pure Mathematics content of most such syllabuses is covered in our book *Mathematics — The Core Course for A-level*, and this volume provides the companion Mechanics course. It also contains a section on Probability, a topic which some Examining Boards include in their Mathematics syllabus.

Combined with *Further Applied Mathematics*, this volume also provides for those who choose to study Applied Mathematics as a separate subject at A-level.

An appreciation of the properties of vectors is introduced at an early stage and, throughout the book, problems are solved using vector methods whenever this is appropriate.

Many worked examples are incorporated in the text to illustrate each main development of a topic and a set of straightforward problems follows each section. A selection of more challenging questions is given in the miscellaneous exercise at the end of most chapters. Multiple choice exercises are also included on most topics.

We are grateful to the following Examination Boards for permission to reproduce questions from past examination papers:

The Associated Examining Board   (AEB)
University of London Entrance and School Examination Council   (U of L)
University of Cambridge Local Examinations Syndicate   (C)
Joint Matriculation Board   (JMB)
Oxford Delegacy of Local Examinations   (O)
Welsh Joint Education Committee (WJEC)
Part question (p)

Responsibility for the answers to these questions is the authors' alone.

L. Bostock
S. Chandler

CONTENTS

Preface   v

Notes on Use of the Book   ix

Chapter 1.   **Introduction**   1

Basic concepts of force and motion.

Chapter 2.   **Vectors. Components and Resultants. Moment**   12

Vector representation. Properties of vectors. Resolution.
Resultant of concurrent coplanar forces. Vector equation
of a line. Vector equation of the path of a moving particle.
Position vector of the point of intersection of two lines.
Moment of a force. Resultant moment.

Chapter 3.   **Coplanar Forces in Equilibrium. Friction**   66

Equilibrium of three coplanar forces. Triangle of forces.
Lami's theorem. Contact forces between solid bodies.
Laws of friction. Equilibrium of more than three
concurrent forces.

Chapter 4.   **Velocity and Acceleration**   110

Motion in a straight line. Velocity. Acceleration.
Displacement-time and velocity-time graphs. Equations
of motion for constant linear acceleration. Vertical
motion under gravity. Motion with constant velocity.
Motion in a plane. Angular motion. Equations of
motion for constant angular acceleration.

Chapter 5.   **Newton's Laws of Motion**   149

The effect of a constant force on a body. Motion of
connected particles.

Chapter 6. **Work and Power**   181

Chapter 7. **Hooke's Law. Energy**   199

Properties of elastic strings and springs. Work done in
stretching a string. Mechanical energy. Conservation of
mechanical energy.

Chapter 8. **Momentum. Direct Impact**   232

Impulse. Inelastic impact. Conservation of linear
momentum. Elastic impact. Law of restitution.

Chapter 9. **Projectiles**   267

General equations of motion of a projectile. Equation
of the path of a projectile. Special properties.

Chapter 10. **Motion in a Circle**   293

Circular motion with constant speed. Conical
pendulum. Banked tracks. Motion in a vertical circle.

Chapter 11. **General Motion of a Particle**   338

Motion in a straight line with variable acceleration. The
effect of a variable force on a body. Graphical methods.
Forces producing motion in a plane. Motion in three
dimensions. Collision of moving particles. Distance
between moving particles. Scalar product of two vectors.
Work done by a constant force. Work done by a variable
force. Impulse of a variable force.

Chapter 12. **Simple Harmonic Motion**   382

Basic equations of linear and angular SHM. Associated
circular motion. Simple pendulum. Moving particle
attached to an elastic string or spring. Incomplete
oscillations.

Chapter 13. **Resultant Motion. Relative Motion**   420

Resultant velocity vectors. Resultant direction of
motion. Frames of reference. Relative velocity. Relative
position. Line of closest approach. Interception.

Chapter 14. **Resultants of Coplanar Forces. Equivalent Force Systems**   454

Coplanar forces reducing to a single force. Resultant of
parallel forces. Couple. Properties of a couple.
Resultant of forces represented by line segments.
Replacement force systems.

Chapter 15. **Centre of Gravity**   498

Uniform triangular lamina. Composite bodies. Methods
using integration. Body hanging freely. Body resting on
a plane.

Chapter 16. **Problems Involving Rigid Bodies**   545

Equilibrium of a rigid body under the action of
(a) three forces, (b) more than three forces. Sliding
and overturning. Composite bodies. Heavy jointed rods.

Chapter 17. **Frameworks**   570

Calculation of stress in light rods. Bow's notation.
Method of sections.

Chapter 18. **Probability**   587

Possibility space. Empirical probability. Mutually
exclusive events. Independent events. Conditional
probability. Tree diagrams. Sample points. Venn
diagrams. Expectation.

Appendix   632

Answers   634

Index   655

NOTES ON USE OF THE BOOK

1. Notation Used in Diagrams

Force

Velocity

Acceleration

Dimensions

Where components and resultant are shown in one diagram the resultant is denoted by a larger arrow-head thus:

2. Value of g

Throughout this book the value of g, unless stated otherwise, is taken as $9.8\,\mathrm{m\,s^{-2}}$.

3. Useful Pure Mathematics

In any triangle ABC

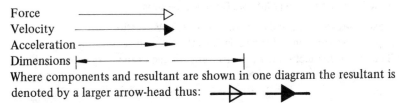

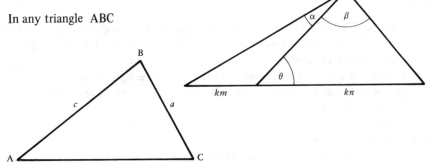

Sine Rule $\qquad \dfrac{\sin A}{a} = \dfrac{\sin B}{b} = \dfrac{\sin C}{c}$

Cosine Rule $\qquad a^2 = b^2 + c^2 - 2bc\cos A$

Cotangent Rule $\quad (m+n)\cot\theta = m\cot\alpha - n\cot\beta$

Compound Angle Formulae

$$\sin(A \pm B) = \sin A\cos B \pm \cos A\sin B$$

$$\cos(A \pm B) = \cos A\cos B \mp \sin A\sin B$$

ix

Small angles

$$\text{As} \quad \theta \to 0, \quad \frac{\sin \theta}{\theta} \to 1$$

Integrals

$$\int \frac{f'(x)}{f(x)} \, dx = \ln |kf(x)|$$

$$\int \frac{1}{\sqrt{(a^2 - b^2 x^2)}} \, dx = \frac{1}{b} \arcsin \frac{bx}{a} + k$$

4. Instructions for Answering Multiple Choice Exercises

These exercises are at the end of most chapters. The questions are set in groups, each group representing one of the variations that may arise in examination papers. The answering techniques are different for each type of question and are classified as follows:

TYPE I

These questions consist of a problem followed by several alternative answers, only *one* of which is correct.
Write down the letter corresponding to the correct answer.

TYPE II

In this type of question some information is given and is followed by a number of possible responses. *One or more* of the suggested responses follows directly from the information given.
Write down the letter(s) corresponding to the correct response(s).
A response is regarded as correct only if it *must* follow from the given data.
For example, in a triangle PQR:
(a) $\hat{P} + \hat{Q} + \hat{R} = 180°$.
(b) PQ + QR is less than PR.
(c) If $\hat{P}$ is obtuse, $\hat{Q}$ and $\hat{R}$ must both be acute.
(d) $\hat{P} = 90°$, $\hat{Q} = 45°$, $\hat{R} = 45°$.

The correct responses are (a) and (c).

(b) is definitely incorrect
(d) may or may not be true of the triangle PQR so is not regarded as correct.

TYPE III

Each problem contains two independent statements (a) and (b).
1) If (a) implies (b) but (b) does not imply (a)   write A.
2) If (b) implies (a) but (a) does not imply (b)   write B.

3) If (a) implies (b) *and* (b) implies (a)   write C.
4) If (a) denies (b) *and* (b) denies (a)   write D.
5) If none of the first four relationships apply   write E.

TYPE IV

A problem is introduced and followed by a number of pieces of information. You are not required to solve the problem but to decide whether:
1) the total amount of information given is insufficient to solve the problem. If so write I,
2) *all* the given information is needed to solve the problem. In this case write A,
3) the problem can be solved *without* using one or more of the given pieces of information. In this case write down the letter(s) corresponding to the item(s) not needed.

TYPE V

A single statement is made. Write T if the statement is always true and F if the statement is false (or true only in certain cases).

CHAPTER 1

INTRODUCTION

This book is about Mechanics and the solving of mechanical problems with the help of Pure Mathematics.

Mechanics, which deals with the effects that forces have on bodies, is a science. So the laws of Mechanics are scientific laws. They come from observation and experiments and so can never be considered as universally true. The most that can be said of several of these laws is that they agree with observed results to the extent that they are accurate enough for most purposes. Pure Mathematics, on the other hand, is an art and its theorems are universally true. When Pure Mathematics is used to solve a Mechanical problem it is important to distinguish clearly between the use of a scientific law and a mathematical theorem.

CONVENTIONS

Certain factors which have a negligible effect on a problem are often ignored. This has the advantage of simplifying the problem without sacrificing much accuracy, and is best illustrated by an example.
Consider a heavy bob suspended from a fixed point by means of a thin wire.

The weight of the wire is negligible compared with the weight of the bob, and can be ignored. In such a case it would be described as a *light* wire.

If the dimensions of the bob are small compared with the length of the wire, the bob can be considered as a point and will be described as a *particle*.

If the bob is swinging in still air, then *air resistance* to its motion will be negligible. In fact air resistance is ignored in all problems unless specific mention is made of it.

If the bob is in the shape of a flat disc, where the surface area is large compared to its thickness, the thickness is ignored and the bob is described as a circular *lamina*.

1

If the bob has a spherical shape and the thickness of the material it is made from is small compared to its surface area, this thickness is again ignored and the bob is described as a *hollow* sphere or *spherical shell*.

If the bob is made to slide across a table, then there will be some frictional resistance to its motion. Although it is rare to find a frictionless surface the amount of friction is often small enough to be ignored and such a surface is described as *smooth*.

Summary of Conventions

Light. . . . . Considered weightless
Particle . . . . Object having no dimensions (considered as a point)
Lamina . . . . Flat object, having dimensions of area only
Hollow . . . . 3-dimensional shell of no thickness
Smooth . . . . Frictionless
Air resistance . . . Ignored, unless mention is made of it.

UNITS

Most quantities used in this book are measured in the S.I. system of units. The three basic quantities are *mass*, *length* and *time*. All the other quantities are derived from these three but their definitions are left until the appropriate chapters.

Quantity	Unit	Symbol
mass	kilogram	kg
length	metre	m
time	second	s
force	newton	N
work	joule	J
power	watt	W

Mechanics deals with the effect of forces acting on bodies, and one effect is that motion is produced. Before the relationship between force and the resulting motion is discussed we will consider them separately.

MOTION

The following quantities are needed to describe the motion of a body: *Distance* is the *length of a given path*.

The *unit of distance* is the metre (m).

Displacement defines the *position* of one point relative to another point: displacement includes both the distance between two points and the direction of the first point from the second point.

Speed is the rate at which a moving body covers its path, no account being taken of the direction of motion.

The unit of speed. The unit of distance is the metre and the unit of time is the second, hence the unit of speed is the metre per second (m s^{-1}).

Velocity includes both the rate of motion *and* the direction of motion.

Acceleration. When a velocity changes, it is because either the speed changes, or the direction of motion changes, or both change. Acceleration measures this change in either speed, or direction of motion or both, i.e. acceleration involves direction as well as a magnitude.

The unit of acceleration. The unit of speed is the metre per second, so the unit of acceleration is the metre per second per second (m s^{-2}).

Note that distance and speed involve magnitude only, but displacement, velocity and acceleration involve direction as well as magnitude.

EXAMPLES 1a

1) A particle moves round a square ABCD in the sense indicated by the letters. B is due north of A and C is due west of B and the side of the square is 10 m. If the particle starts from A, what distance has it travelled when it is mid-way between B and C, and what is its displacement then from A?

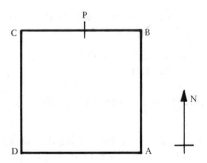

When the particle is at P, the distance travelled $=$ AB + PB $=$ 15 m

The distance between P and A $= \sqrt{(10^2 + 5^2)}$ m $= 5\sqrt{5}$ m
$\angle$BAP $=$ arc tan $\frac{5}{10}$ $= 26.6°$
Therefore the displacement of P from A is $5\sqrt{5}$ m in the direction $333.4°$

2) If the particle in Example 1 is covering its path at a constant rate of $2\,\mathrm{m\,s}^{-1}$, what is the speed when travelling along (a) AB, (b) BC?
State also its velocity when travelling along (a) AB, (b) BC.

Speed along AB $= 2\,\mathrm{m\,s}^{-1}$
Speed along BC $= 2\,\mathrm{m\,s}^{-1}$
Velocity along AB $= 2\,\mathrm{m\,s}^{-1}$ due north
Velocity along BC $= 2\,\mathrm{m\,s}^{-1}$ due west

Note that although the speed along AB is equal to the speed along BC, the velocity along AB is *not* equal to the velocity along BC.

3) If the particle in Example 1 moves so that when moving from C to D its speed increases at a rate of $2\,\mathrm{m\,s}^{-2}$, and when moving from D to A its speed decreases at a rate of $2\,\mathrm{m\,s}^{-2}$, what is its acceleration along CD and along DA?

When the particle is moving along CD (the direction of motion is given by the order of the letters, i.e. C to D) the speed is increasing at a rate of $2\,\mathrm{m\,s}^{-2}$. Therefore the acceleration is $2\,\mathrm{m\,s}^{-2}$ in the direction CD.

When the particle is moving along DA the speed is decreasing at a rate of $2\,\mathrm{m\,s}^{-2}$. Therefore the acceleration is $2\,\mathrm{m\,s}^{-2}$, but in the direction AD because the speed is decreasing.

or $-2\,\mathrm{m\,s}^{2}$
indicate opp. direction

EXERCISE 1a

1) A particle moves round the sides of a regular hexagon ABCDEF of side 3 m. The particle starts from A and moves in the sense ABC. What is the distance travelled by the particle and its displacement from A when it is:
(a) at C,   (b) at the midpoint of DE?

2) If the particle in Question 1 covers its path at the constant rate of $2\,\mathrm{m\,s}^{-1}$, what is its displacement from A after 12 s?

3) What is the velocity of the particle in Question 2 after:
(a) 5 s,   (b) 10 s?

4) A particle moves with constant speed on the circumference of a circle. Is the velocity constant?

5) A particle moves with a constant speed along the track shown in the diagram. For which sections of its journey is the velocity constant?

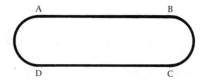

FORCE

Most people have an intuitive idea of force. Consider, for instance, a book lying on a horizontal table. We know that force must be applied to the book to move it along the table. Force may be applied directly to the book by pushing it, or indirectly by, for example, tying a string to the book and pulling the string. Obviously the movement of the book is related to the amount of force used. The direction in which the force is applied also affects the movement of the book: with the string horizontal the book will move along the table; with the string vertical the book will be lifted off the table. The point at which the force is applied to the book also affects the result. If the string is attached to one edge of the book and pulled vertically the book will tilt about the opposite edge, but if the string is attached to the middle of the book and pulled vertically no tilting will take place.

So three factors determine the effect that a force has on a body to which it is applied:

(a) The amount, or the *magnitude*, of the applied force. The unit of magnitude is the newton (N).

(b) The direction in which the force is applied.

(c) The point of application of the force. An alternative way of expressing the direction and point of application of a force is to give its *line of action* and the *sense* of the force along that line.

We also know that the book will not move on its own account. From many such observations it is deduced that: *force is necessary to make an object begin to move*. Conversely, if an object starts to move then a force must have caused that motion to start.

WEIGHT

If a body is dropped it will start to fall, so we deduce that there must be a force acting on that body which attracts it to the ground. This force is called the gravitational force or the *weight* of the body; thus the weight of a body is a force and is measured in force units (newtons).
If we hold a heavy object we can still feel this gravitational pull, even though the object is not moving, illustrating that the weight of a body acts on it at all times, regardless of whether the object is moving or not.

MASS

It is a well known phenomenon that the force with which an object is attracted to the surface of the moon is less than the force with which the same object is attracted to the surface of the earth. It is also found that the weight of an object varies slightly in different places on the surface of the earth. So, although the amount of matter which constitutes an object is an absolute property of that object, its weight is not absolute.

Mass is a measure of the matter contained in an object.

The unit of mass is the kilogram (kg).

Forces Acting on Bodies

Consider again a book lying on a horizontal table.

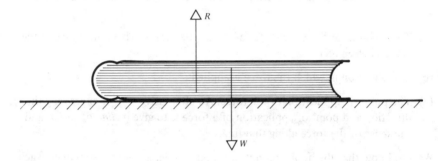

The book is not moving, but there is at least one force acting on it, i.e. its weight. If the table was not there the book would fall, so the table must be exerting an upward force on the book to counteract its weight. This force is called the reaction. A reaction force acts on a body whenever that body is in contact with another body which is supporting it.

Now consider the book being pulled along the table by a horizontal string attached to the book.

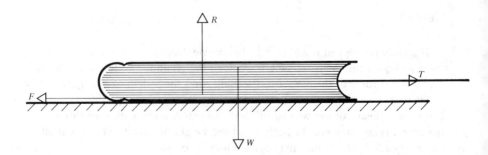

The weight and the reaction again act on the book, together with a pull from the string. The pull that the string is exerting on the book is referred to as the tension in the string. If there is friction between the book and the table there will be some resistance to the movement of the book along the table. This resistance is called the frictional force and it acts on a body whenever there is a tendency for that body to move over a rough surface.

SUMMARY

The forces which act on a body come mainly from three sources.

1) Gravitational pull (weight).

2) Contact with another body.

3) Attachment to another body.

(There are other sources, such as wind force, engines, etc., which we shall meet later on.)

DIAGRAMS

Before attempting the solution of any problem concerned with the action of forces on a body, it is important to draw a diagram which shows clearly all the forces acting on that body.

The points to remember are:

(a) A body is always acted on by its weight unless the body is described as light.

(b) If there is contact with another body there is a reaction and possibly some friction.

(c) If there is attachment to another body (by means of a string, hinge, pivot, etc.) there is a force acting on the body at the point of attachment.

(d) Check that there are no other sources of force.

(e) Only the forces which are acting on the body itself are considered.
A common fault is to include forces which are acting on an object with which the body is in contact.

(f) Do not make the diagram too small.

EXAMPLES 1b

1) Draw a diagram to show the forces acting on a block which is sliding down a smooth plane inclined at $20°$ to the horizontal.

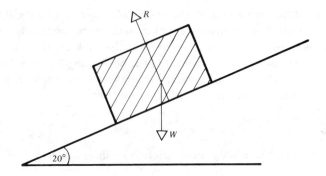

The plane is smooth so there is no friction.

2) Draw a diagram to show the forces acting on a block which is being pulled up a rough plane by a string attached to the block. The plane is inclined at $15°$ to the horizontal and the string is inclined at $30°$ to the horizontal.

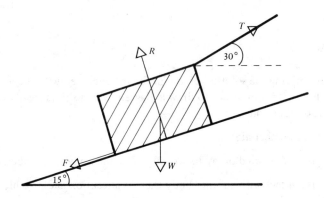

As the plane is rough there is a frictional force acting on the block down the plane (friction opposes motion).

3) A particle is suspended from a fixed point by a string and it is swinging in a horizontal circle below that point. Draw a diagram to show the forces which are acting on the particle.

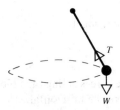

4) Draw a diagram showing the forces acting on a ladder which is standing with one end on rough horizontal ground and the other end against a rough, vertical wall.

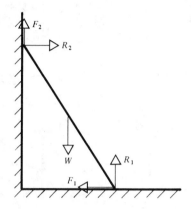

The lower end of the ladder has a tendency to slide away from the wall, so the frictional force acts towards the wall. The upper end of the ladder has a tendency to slide down the wall, so the frictional force acts upwards.

5) A cylindrical tin stands on a smooth table and two smooth spheres rest inside the tin as shown in the sketch.

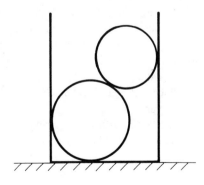

Draw diagrams to show (a) the forces acting on the large sphere, (b) the forces acting on the small sphere, (c) the forces acting on the tin.

(a)

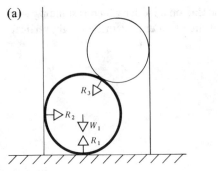

The forces acting on the large sphere.

(b)

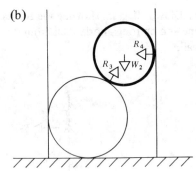

The forces acting on the small sphere.

(c)

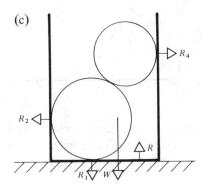

The forces acting on the tin.

EXERCISE 1b

1) Draw diagrams to show the forces that are acting on a block which is:

(a) at rest on a smooth horizontal surface,

(b) at rest on a rough horizontal surface,

(c) at rest on a rough surface inclined at an angle of $20°$ to the horizontal,

(d) sliding down a smooth surface inclined at an angle of $30°$ to the horizontal,

(e) sliding down a rough surface inclined at an angle of $30°$ to the horizontal,

(f) pulled down a smooth surface inclined at an angle of $10°$ to the horizontal by a string parallel to the plane,

(g) pulled down a rough surface inclined at an angle of $20°$ to the horizontal by a string parallel to the plane,

(h) pulled along a smooth horizontal surface by a string at an angle of $20°$ to the horizontal,

(i) pulled up a rough surface inclined at an angle of $20°$ to the horizontal by a string inclined at an angle of $40°$ to the horizontal.

2) Draw a diagram to show the forces acting on a ladder which is leaning with one end against a smooth vertical wall and the other end standing on rough horizontal ground.

3) Draw a diagram to show the forces acting on a particle which is suspended from a fixed point by a string when:
(a) it is hanging at rest,
(b) it is turning in a vertical circle about the fixed point,
(c) it is turning in a horizontal circle below the fixed point,
(d) the string has broken and it is falling.

4) A ball is thrown into the air. Draw a diagram to show the forces acting on it at any point in its flight.

5) A ladder rests in a vertical plane with one end against a rough vertical wall, and the other end on rough horizontal ground. There is a block tied to the ladder by a string one-third of the way up the ladder. Draw diagrams to show:
(a) the forces acting on the ladder,
(b) the forces acting on the block.

6) A plank is supported in a horizontal position by two vertical strings, one attached at each end. A block rests on the plank a quarter of the way in from one end. Draw diagrams to show:
(a) the forces acting on the plank,
(b) the forces acting on the block.

7) Two bricks, one on top of the other, rest on a horizontal surface. Draw diagrams to show:
(a) the forces acting on the bottom brick,
(b) the forces acting on the top brick,

8)

The diagram shows a rough plank resting on a cylinder with one end of the plank on rough ground.

Draw diagrams to show:
(a) the forces acting on the plank,
(b) the forces acting on the cylinder.

CHAPTER 2

VECTORS. COMPONENTS AND RESULTANTS. MOMENT

DEFINITIONS

Certain quantities are described completely when their magnitudes are stated in appropriate units:

e.g. a speed of $50 \, \text{km} \, \text{h}^{-1}$
a mass of $10 \, \text{kg}$
a temperature of $30°\text{C}$
a time of 3 seconds;

Such quantities are called *scalar* quantities.

Other quantities possess both magnitude and direction and are not completely defined unless both of these are specified:

e.g. a velocity of $5 \, \text{m} \, \text{s}^{-1}$ vertically upward
a force of $10 \, \text{N}$ vertically downward
a displacement of $8 \, \text{km}$ due East.

The name for this type of quantity is *vector*.

Vector Representation

Because a vector quantity has both magnitude and direction, it can be represented by a segment of a line. The *length* of the line represents the *magnitude* of the vector quantity and the *direction* of the line shows which way the quantity goes.

Thus the line AB can be used to represent a displacement vector of 3 m North East.

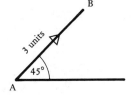

To indicate that a line segment represents a vector, any of the *vector symbols* AB, $\overrightarrow{AB}$, **r** may be used. In the first two cases the sense of the vector is given by the *order* of the letters but, as the single symbol **r** does not include any indication of sense, it must be accompanied by an arrow on the diagram.

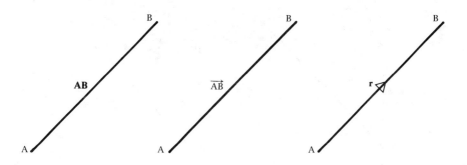

EQUAL VECTORS

Two vectors of *equal magnitude* and with the *same direction* are said to be equal.

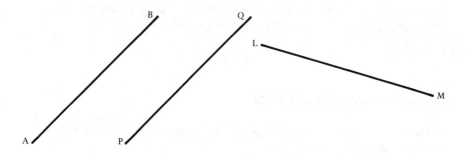

In the diagram, the lines AB and PQ are parallel and equal in length hence

$$\overrightarrow{AB} = \overrightarrow{PQ}.$$

Although LM is equal in length to AB, these lines are not parallel so

$$\overrightarrow{AB} \neq \overrightarrow{LM}.$$

It is, however, correct to write   AB = LM   since AB and LM are *scalar symbols* referring only to the magnitude of the lines and not to their direction.

PARALLEL VECTORS

Consider two parallel vectors which are in the same sense but have different magnitudes.

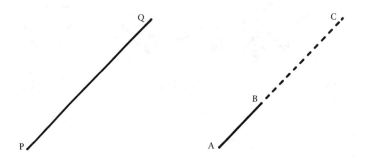

PQ is parallel to AB and the length (magnitude) of PQ is k times the length of AB.

If we produce AB to C so that   AC = PQ   then   AC = kAB.

But AC and PQ are identical in magnitude, direction and sense and therefore represent equal vectors.

Therefore $\overrightarrow{AC} = \overrightarrow{PQ}$

and $k\overrightarrow{AB} = \overrightarrow{PQ}$.

In general the equation $\mathbf{a} = k\mathbf{b}$ means that $\mathbf{a}$ and $\mathbf{b}$ are parallel vectors, the magnitude of $\mathbf{a}$ being k times the magnitude of $\mathbf{b}$.

EQUAL AND OPPOSITE VECTORS

Two parallel vectors of equal magnitude but opposite sense are said to be *equal and opposite*.

Considering a displacement vector $\overrightarrow{AB}$ and the equal and opposite vector $\overrightarrow{BA}$ it is clear that these two together result in zero displacement.

i.e. $\overrightarrow{AB} + \overrightarrow{BA} = \mathbf{0}$

or $\overrightarrow{AB} = -\overrightarrow{BA}$.

A negative sign in vector work therefore indicates a reversal of sense.

In general if $\mathbf{a} = -\mathbf{b}$ then $\mathbf{a}$ and $\mathbf{b}$ are parallel vectors of equal magnitude but opposite sense.

FREE VECTORS

The representation of a vector by a line segment includes magnitude and direction but not, in general, the actual location of the vector. So if a line AB represents a vector, then any line parallel and equal to AB represents the same vector.

Vectors represented in this way are *free vectors*.

In some circumstances it will be necessary to extend the linear representation of a vector to include its position.

In this case we shall be dealing with a *tied vector*.

EQUIVALENT VECTORS

Consider a displacement $\overrightarrow{AB}$ of 2 m due E followed by a displacement $\overrightarrow{BC}$ of 2 m due N.

The combined effect of these two displacements is the same as a single displacement $\overrightarrow{AC}$ of $2\sqrt{2}$ m NE.

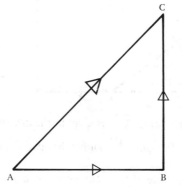

Hence $\overrightarrow{AB} + \overrightarrow{BC} = \overrightarrow{AC}$

In this vector equation

+   means '*together with*'

=   means '*is equivalent to*'.

We say that $\overrightarrow{AC}$ is the *resultant* of $\overrightarrow{AB}$ and $\overrightarrow{BC}$, or that $\overrightarrow{AB}$ and $\overrightarrow{BC}$ are the *components* of $\overrightarrow{AC}$. The triangle ABC is a vector triangle.

It is possible to find the resultant (or equivalent) vector of more than two components using a similar argument.

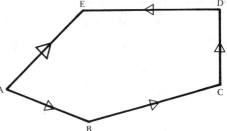

Displacements of $\overrightarrow{AB}, \overrightarrow{BC}, \overrightarrow{CD}$ and $\overrightarrow{DE}$ are equivalent to the single displacement $\overrightarrow{AE}$

i.e. $\overrightarrow{AE} = \overrightarrow{AB} + \overrightarrow{BC} + \overrightarrow{CD} + \overrightarrow{DE}$.

In this case the figure ABCDE is a vector polygon.

Note. A is the starting point and E is the end point both for the set of components and for the resultant.

In most of the illustrations so far, displacement vectors have been used because they are easy to visualise. Other vector quantities can, however, be dealt with in the same way. In fact it was from the results of experiments with force vectors that the concept of vector geometry and algebra first arose. Again it will be noticed that the vectors considered so far have always been in the same plane (coplanar vectors). The principles explained do, however, apply equally well to vectors in three dimensions but at this stage it is sufficient to understand how to add and subtract coplanar vectors using the concept of equivalent vectors, and to appreciate that, in the vector diagrams we draw, lines represent vectors in magnitude and direction but not necessarily in position.

EXAMPLES 2a

1) What is the resultant of displacements 2 m E, 3 m N and 6 m W?

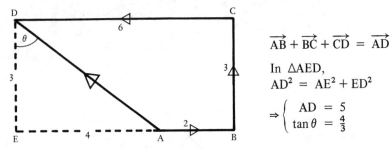

$$\overrightarrow{AB} + \overrightarrow{BC} + \overrightarrow{CD} = \overrightarrow{AD}$$

In $\triangle AED$,
$$AD^2 = AE^2 + ED^2$$

$$\Rightarrow \begin{cases} AD = 5 \\ \tan\theta = \frac{4}{3} \end{cases}$$

Therefore the resultant, $\overrightarrow{AD}$, is 5 m in the direction N arctan $\frac{4}{3}$ W.

2) A vector **a** of magnitude 8 units has two components. One is perpendicular to **a** and is of magnitude 6 units.
What is the magnitude of the other component?

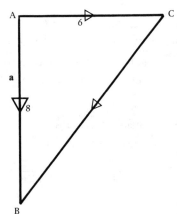

Let the given vector be represented by $\overrightarrow{AB}$ and the given component by $\overrightarrow{AC}$.
The second component is then $\overrightarrow{CB}$ and

$$\overrightarrow{AB} = \overrightarrow{AC} + \overrightarrow{CB}.$$

But $BC^2 = AB^2 + AC^2$

$\Rightarrow$ $BC^2 = 64 + 36$

$\Rightarrow$ $BC = 10.$

The magnitude of the other component is 10 units.

3) In a quadrilateral ABCD, the sides $\overrightarrow{AB}, \overrightarrow{BC}$ and $\overrightarrow{DC}$ represent vectors $\mathbf{p, q}$ and $\mathbf{r}$ respectively. Express in terms of $\mathbf{p, q}$ and $\mathbf{r}$ the vectors represented by $\overrightarrow{AC}, \overrightarrow{AD}$ and $\overrightarrow{DB}$.

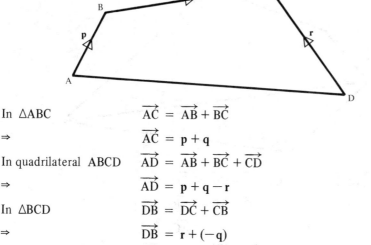

In △ABC	$\overrightarrow{AC} = \overrightarrow{AB} + \overrightarrow{BC}$
⇒	$\overrightarrow{AC} = \mathbf{p} + \mathbf{q}$
In quadrilateral ABCD	$\overrightarrow{AD} = \overrightarrow{AB} + \overrightarrow{BC} + \overrightarrow{CD}$
⇒	$\overrightarrow{AD} = \mathbf{p} + \mathbf{q} - \mathbf{r}$
In △BCD	$\overrightarrow{DB} = \overrightarrow{DC} + \overrightarrow{CB}$
⇒	$\overrightarrow{DB} = \mathbf{r} + (-\mathbf{q})$
So	$\overrightarrow{DB} = \mathbf{r} - \mathbf{q}$

4) ABCDEF is a regular hexagon in which AB represents a vector $\mathbf{p}$ and BC represents a vector $\mathbf{q}$.
Express in terms of $\mathbf{p}$ and $\mathbf{q}$ the vectors which the remaining sides represent.

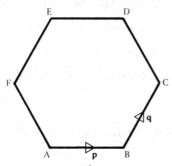

ED is equal and parallel to AB so $\overrightarrow{ED} = \mathbf{p}$

FE is equal and parallel to BC so $\overrightarrow{FE} = \mathbf{q}$

AD is twice as long as, and parallel to, BC so $\overrightarrow{AD} = 2\mathbf{q}$

But $\overrightarrow{CD} = \overrightarrow{CB} + \overrightarrow{BA} + \overrightarrow{AD}$

Therefore $\overrightarrow{CD} = -\mathbf{q} - \mathbf{p} + 2\mathbf{q} = \mathbf{q} - \mathbf{p}$

AF is equal and parallel to CD so $\overrightarrow{AF} = \mathbf{q} - \mathbf{p}$

5) In a pentagon ABCDE:
(a) find the resultant of (i) $\overrightarrow{AB}$, $\overrightarrow{BC}$ and $\overrightarrow{CD}$ (ii) $\overrightarrow{BC}$ and $\overrightarrow{AB}$ (iii) $\overrightarrow{AB} - \overrightarrow{AE}$,
(b) find two sets of components of $\overrightarrow{AD}$.

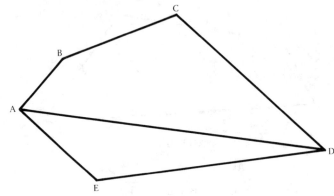

(a) (i) In ABCD $\qquad \overrightarrow{AB} + \overrightarrow{BC} + \overrightarrow{CD} = \overrightarrow{AD}$

(ii) In ABC $\qquad\qquad \overrightarrow{BC} + \overrightarrow{AB} = \overrightarrow{AB} + \overrightarrow{BC}$

$\qquad\qquad\qquad\qquad\qquad\qquad = \overrightarrow{AC}$

(iii) In ABE $\qquad\qquad \overrightarrow{AB} - \overrightarrow{AE} = \overrightarrow{AB} + \overrightarrow{EA}$

$\qquad\qquad\qquad\qquad\qquad\qquad = \overrightarrow{EA} + \overrightarrow{AB}$

$\qquad\qquad\qquad\qquad\qquad\qquad = \overrightarrow{EB}$

(b) In ABCD $\qquad\qquad \overrightarrow{AD} = \overrightarrow{AB} + \overrightarrow{BC} + \overrightarrow{CD}$

and in ADE $\qquad\qquad \overrightarrow{AD} = \overrightarrow{AE} + \overrightarrow{ED}$

These are both suitable sets of components for $\overrightarrow{AD}$.

(We could equally well have chosen the set $\overrightarrow{AB} + \overrightarrow{BD}$ or $\overrightarrow{AC} + \overrightarrow{CD}$.)

EXERCISE 2a

1) What is the resultant of the following vectors: 5 m N, 3 m E and 2 m S?

2) In a quadrilateral ABCD what is the resultant of:
(a) $\overrightarrow{AB} + \overrightarrow{BC}$ (b) $\overrightarrow{BC} + \overrightarrow{CD}$ (c) $\overrightarrow{AB} + \overrightarrow{BC} + \overrightarrow{CD}$ (d) $\overrightarrow{AB} + \overrightarrow{DA}$?

3) ABCDEF is a regular hexagon in which BC represents a vector **b** and FC represents a vector 2**a**. Express in terms of **a** and **b** the vectors represented by AB, CD and BE.

4) Draw diagrams illustrating the following vector equations:
(a) $\overrightarrow{AB} - \overrightarrow{CB} = \overrightarrow{AC}$ (b) $\overrightarrow{AB} = 2\overrightarrow{PQ}$ (c) $\overrightarrow{AB} + \overrightarrow{BC} = 3\overrightarrow{AD}$ (d) **a** + **b** = −**c**.

5) If $\overrightarrow{AB} = \overrightarrow{DC}$ and $\overrightarrow{BC} + \overrightarrow{DA} = \mathbf{0}$, prove that ABCD is a parallelogram.

6) ABCD is a rectangle. Which of the following statements are true?
(a) $\overrightarrow{BC} = \overrightarrow{DA}$ (b) $BD = AC$ (c) $\overrightarrow{AB} + \overrightarrow{CD} = \vec{0}$ (d) $\overrightarrow{AB} + \overrightarrow{BC} = \overrightarrow{CA}$
(e) $\overrightarrow{AC} + \overrightarrow{CD} = \overrightarrow{AD}$ (f) $\overrightarrow{AB} + \overrightarrow{BC} = \overrightarrow{AD} + \overrightarrow{DC}$.

7) In an isosceles triangle ABC in which AB = BC and D is the mid-point of AC, show that $\overrightarrow{BA} + \overrightarrow{BC} = 2\overrightarrow{BD}$.

RESOLVING A VECTOR

When a vector is replaced by an equivalent set of components, it has been *resolved*. One of the most useful ways in which to resolve a vector is to choose only two components which are at right angles to each other. The magnitude of these components can be evaluated very easily using trigonometry.

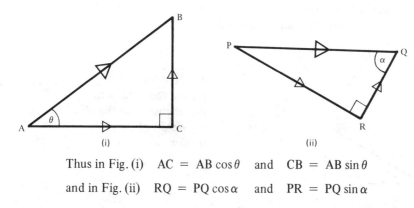

(i)   (ii)

Thus in Fig. (i) $AC = AB \cos\theta$ and $CB = AB \sin\theta$

and in Fig. (ii) $RQ = PQ \cos\alpha$ and $PR = PQ \sin\alpha$

Finding such components is referred to as

resolving in a pair of perpendicular directions.

Note that the components need not act along the actual lines AC, CB or PR, RQ. These lines give the directions of the components but not necessarily their position.

EXAMPLES 2b

1) Resolve a weight of 10 N in two directions which are parallel and perpendicular to a slope inclined at $30°$ to the horizontal.

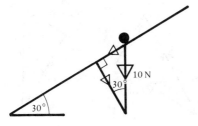

The component parallel to the slope is of magnitude $10 \sin 30°\text{N}$ i.e. $5\,\text{N}$. The magnitude of the component perpendicular to the slope is $10 \cos 30°\text{N}$ i.e. $5\sqrt{3}\,\text{N}$.

2) Resolve horizontally and vertically a force of 8 N which makes an angle of 45° with the horizontal.

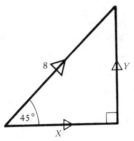

If X and Y are the magnitudes, in newtons, of the two components then

$$X = 8 \cos 45° = 4\sqrt{2}$$
$$Y = 8 \sin 45° = 4\sqrt{2}$$

3) A body is supported on a rough plane inclined at 30° to the horizontal by a string attached to the body and held at an angle of 30° to the plane. Draw a diagram showing the forces acting on the body and resolve each of these forces
(a) horizontally and vertically,
(b) parallel and perpendicular to the plane.

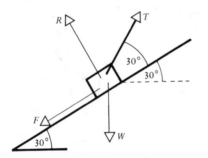

The forces are,

the tension in the string	T
the reaction with the plane	R
the weight of the body	W
friction	F

(a) Resolving horizontally and vertically:

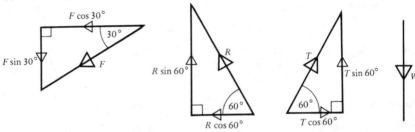

(b) Resolving parallel and perpendicular to the plane:

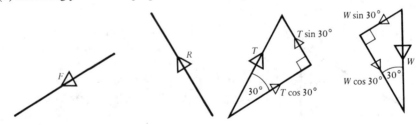

(**Note** that any force already in one of the directions specified is unchanged and has no component perpendicular to itself.)

Sense of Resolved Parts

In the answer to Example 3 above it is worth noticing that, without diagrams, the sense of each component would be unknown. This is because the specification of the required components was not precise enough. The description *parallel to the plane* does not differentiate between the uphill sense and the downhill sense. This ambiguity is avoided if the positive sense of the required components is stated at the outset. A component in the opposite sense is then negative. Using Example 3 to demonstrate this approach, the answer could be given as follows:

(a) Resolving horizontally and vertically in the senses Ox and Oy as shown, the components are:

Force	Components	
	Parallel to Ox	Parallel to Oy
F	$-F\cos 30°$	$-F\sin 30°$
R	$-R\cos 60°$	$R\sin 60°$
T	$T\cos 60°$	$T\sin 60°$
W	0	$-W$

(b) Resolving parallel and perpendicular to the plane in the senses Ox' and Oy' as shown:

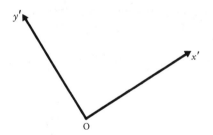

Force	Components	
	Parallel to Ox'	Parallel to Oy'
F	$-F$	0
R	0	R
T	$T\cos 30°$	$T\sin 30°$
W	$-W\sin 30°$	$-W\cos 30°$

CARTESIAN VECTOR NOTATION

Components in perpendicular directions can be expressed more simply if we use the symbols **i** and **j** where

i is a vector of magnitude one unit in the direction Ox
j is a vector of magnitude one unit in the direction Oy.

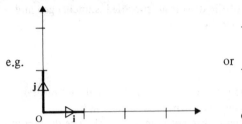

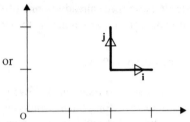

e.g.   or

Thus 3i means   a vector of magnitude 3 units in the direction Ox
and   4j means   a vector of magnitude 4 units in the direction Oy.

If a force vector **F** has components
parallel to Ox and Oy of magnitudes
3 and 4 units respectively then using
the symbols **i** and **j**, we can say
F has components 3**i** and 4**j**.
As **F** is equivalent to the vector sum
of its components,

$$\mathbf{F} = 3\mathbf{i} + 4\mathbf{j}.$$

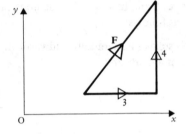

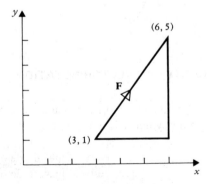

The *magnitude*, or *modulus*, of **F**
which we denote by $|\mathbf{F}|$, is
represented by the length of the
hypotenuse of the vector triangle,

i.e. $|\mathbf{F}| = \sqrt{(3^2 + 4^2)}$

In general, the modulus of a vector
$\mathbf{v} = a\mathbf{i} + b\mathbf{j}$ is given by

$$|\mathbf{v}| = \sqrt{(a^2 + b^2)}$$

A vector can be represented by a line
segment which is defined by the
coordinates of its end points. For
example, the force **F** in the diagram
above could be represented by the
line joining the point $(3, 1)$ to the
point $(6, 5)$. In this case

$$\mathbf{F} = (6-3)\mathbf{i} + (5-1)\mathbf{j}$$

and

$$|\mathbf{F}| = \{(6-3)^2 + (5-1)^2\}^{\frac{1}{2}}$$

In general, if a vector **v** is represented by a line joining the point (x_1, y_1) to the point (x_2, y_2) then

$$\mathbf{v} = (x_2 - x_1)\mathbf{i} + (y_2 - y_1)\mathbf{j}$$

Note. This notation is very easily extended to deal with vectors in 3 dimensions. A unit vector in the direction Oz, perpendicular to the xy plane, is represented by **k**.

For example, $2\mathbf{i} + 3\mathbf{j} + 5\mathbf{k}$ is a vector with three perpendicular components, parallel to Ox, Oy and Oz, of magnitudes $2, 3$ and 5 units respectively and its magnitude is $\sqrt{(2^2 + 3^2 + 5^2)}$.

EXAMPLES 2b (continued)

4) Forces $\mathbf{F_1}, \mathbf{F_2}, \mathbf{F_3}$ and $\mathbf{F_4}$ have magnitudes $6, 2, 3$ and $3\sqrt{2}\,\text{N}$ respectively and act in directions as shown in the diagram below. By finding the components of each force in the directions Ox and Oy, express each force in the form $a\mathbf{i} + b\mathbf{j}$.

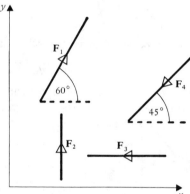

$\mathbf{F_1} = (6\cos 60°)\mathbf{i} + (6\sin 60°)\mathbf{j} = 3\mathbf{i} + 3\sqrt{3}\mathbf{j}$
$\mathbf{F_2} = 2\mathbf{j}$
$\mathbf{F_3} = -3\mathbf{i}$
$\mathbf{F_4} = (-3\sqrt{2}\cos 45°)\mathbf{i} + (-3\sqrt{2}\sin 45°)\mathbf{j} = -3\mathbf{i} - 3\mathbf{j}$

Note that, when force vectors are expressed in this form, the unit is understood to be the newton unless otherwise stated. It is not correct, however, to say $\mathbf{F} = (2\mathbf{i} + 3\mathbf{j})\text{N}$, as $2\mathbf{i} + 3\mathbf{j}$ includes both magnitude and direction.

EXERCISE 2b

1) Calculate the magnitude of the horizontal and vertical components of:
(a) a force of $6\,\text{N}$ inclined at $20°$ to the horizontal,
(b) a velocity of $20\,\text{m s}^{-1}$ inclined at $30°$ to the vertical,
(c) a tension of $8\,\text{N}$ in a string of length $10\,\text{m}$ which has one end fastened to the top of a flagpole of height $6\,\text{m}$ and the other end fixed to the ground.

2) What are the components, parallel and perpendicular to an incline of $30°$, of a weight of $4\,\text{N}$?

3) An object of weight W is fastened to one end of a string whose other end is fixed and is pulled sideways by a horizontal force P until the string is inclined at $20°$ to the vertical. Draw a diagram showing the forces acting on the object and resolve each force parallel and perpendicular to the string.

4) The diagram shows the forces acting on a body. Express each force in terms of $\mathbf{i}$ and $\mathbf{j}$ where $\mathbf{i}$ is a unit vector in the direction $\overrightarrow{AP}$ and $\mathbf{j}$ is a unit vector in the direction $\overrightarrow{AQ}$.

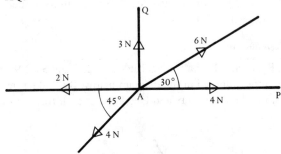

5) Using axes Ox and Oy , mark on a diagram the following force vectors.

$$\mathbf{F_1} = \mathbf{i} + \mathbf{j}; \quad \mathbf{F_2} = 2\mathbf{i} - \mathbf{j}; \quad \mathbf{F_3} = -3\mathbf{i} + 4\mathbf{j}; \quad \mathbf{F_4} = -\mathbf{i} - 3\mathbf{j}.$$

6) A boat is steering due North at $24 \, \mathrm{km\,h^{-1}}$ in a current running at $6 \, \mathrm{km\,h^{-1}}$ due West. A wind is blowing the boat North East at $10 \, \mathrm{km\,h^{-1}}$ (see diagram below). What are the components of each velocity in the directions East and North?

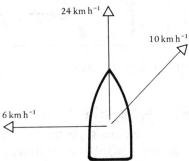

Unit Vectors

Any vector of magnitude 1 unit is a unit vector ($\mathbf{i}$ and $\mathbf{j}$ are unit vectors).

Consider a line OPQ where OP represents the vector $\mathbf{r}$ and OQ is of length 1 unit. Then $\overrightarrow{OQ}$ represents a unit vector in the direction of $\mathbf{r}$.

Such a unit vector is written $\hat{\mathbf{r}}$.

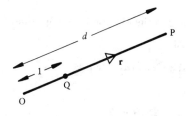

Now   OQ = 1   and,   if   OP = d,

then $\overrightarrow{OP} = d\,\overrightarrow{OQ}.$

But $d = |\mathbf{r}|$

Hence $\mathbf{r} = |\mathbf{r}|\,\hat{\mathbf{r}}$

This important property applies to all vectors, i.e.,

> any vector, **v**, can be expressed as the product of its magnitude and a unit vector in the same direction,
>
> i.e. $\mathbf{v} = |\mathbf{v}|\,\hat{\mathbf{v}}.$

Direction Vectors

A vector which is used to specify the direction of another vector can be called a *direction vector*.

If, for example, we are told that a vector **v**, of magnitude 26 units, is in the direction of the vector $5\mathbf{i} + 12\mathbf{j}$ then

> $5\mathbf{i} + 12\mathbf{j}$ is a direction vector for **v** and can be denoted by **d**

The unit direction vector $\hat{\mathbf{d}}$ is given by

$$\hat{\mathbf{d}} = \mathbf{d}/|\mathbf{d}| = \tfrac{1}{13}(5\mathbf{i} + 12\mathbf{j})$$

But we know that any vector is the product of its magnitude and a unit direction vector, so

$$\mathbf{v} = |\mathbf{v}|\,\hat{\mathbf{d}} = 26\{\tfrac{1}{13}(5\mathbf{i} + 12\mathbf{j})\}$$

$$= 10\mathbf{i} + 24\mathbf{j}$$

EXAMPLES 2c

1) A force **F** of magnitude 20 N acts in the direction $4i-3j$. Find **F**.

The direction vector for **F** is $d = 4i - 3j$

$\Rightarrow$ $\hat{d} = d/|d| = \frac{1}{5}(4i - 3j)$

But $F = |F|\hat{d} = 20\{\frac{1}{5}(4i - 3j)\}$

$\Rightarrow$ $F = 16i - 12j$

2) A particle whose speed is $50\,\mathrm{m\,s^{-1}}$ moves along the line from $A(2, 1)$ to $B(9, 25)$. Find its velocity vector.

The direction of motion of the particle is $\overrightarrow{AB}$ and this is therefore the direction vector, **d**, for the velocity of the particle.

Now $\overrightarrow{AB} = 9i + 25j - (2i + j) = 7i + 24j$

and $\hat{d} = \overrightarrow{AB}/|\overrightarrow{AB}| = \frac{1}{25}(7i + 24j)$

The speed of the particle is the magnitude of its velocity, so

$$v = |v|\hat{d} = 50\{\tfrac{1}{25}(7i + 24j)\}$$

$\Rightarrow$ $v = 14i + 48j$

EXERCISE 2c

Find in the form $ai + bj$,

1) a vector of magnitude 5 units, in the direction $3i + 4j$.

2) a vector of magnitude 39 units, in the direction $5i - 12j$.

3) a vector of magnitude 28 units, in the direction $-i + \sqrt{3}j$.

4) A force of 50 N parallel to the vector $24i - 7j$.

5) A force of 2 N parallel to the vector $-4i - 3j$.

6) A force of 13 N acting along the line from $A(1, -3)$ to $B(13, 2)$.

7) The velocity vector of a plane flying from $A(10, 50)$ to $B(130, -110)$ at a speed of $100\,\mathrm{m\,s^{-1}}$.

8) A vector whose magnitude is twice the magnitude of the vector $2i + j$ and which is parallel to the vector $6i - 12j$.

9) A force of 20 N parallel to the line PQ where P is $(-1, 7)$ and Q is $(1, 5)$.

10) The velocity vector of a boat moving in the direction $24i - 7j$ with a speed of $15\,\mathrm{m\,s^{-1}}$.

Position Vector

Cartesian vector notation, which we have already used to describe free vectors (e.g. velocity, acceleration) can also be used to describe the position of a point.

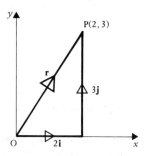

If a point P has coordinates (2,3) then the displacement of P *from the origin* has components 2i and 3j.

Thus   r = 2i + 3j

r is called the *position vector* of the point P.

Similarly, in three dimensions, a point with coordinates (1,2,3) has a position vector r where

$$r = i + 2j + 3k$$

The Vector Equation of a Line

Each point on a line has a position vector relative to an origin O. If we can find a way of describing the position vector of a *general* point on the line we are then defining the complete set of points on that line.

Consider a line in the *xy* plane whose direction vector is d and which passes through a point A with position vector a.

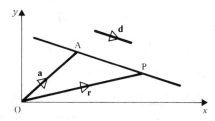

If P is any other point on the line then

$$AP \text{ is parallel to } d \Rightarrow \overrightarrow{AP} = \lambda d$$

and
$$\overrightarrow{OP} = \overrightarrow{OA} + \overrightarrow{AP} \Rightarrow r = a + \lambda d$$

Each value of λ (positive or negative) gives the position vector of one point on the specified line.

So $r = a + \lambda d$ is called the vector equation of the line.

For example, the vector equation of the line which is parallel to the vector
$i-4j$ and which passes through the point $(-5,7)$ is

$$r = -5i + 7j + \lambda(i - 4j)$$

Similarly, a line with direction vector $i-j+k$ and which passes through
$(5, 1, 3)$, has a vector equation

$$r = 5i + j + 3k + \lambda(i - j + k)$$

A Line Through Two Points

If we now consider a line which is known to pass through two points A and
B with position vectors **a** and **b** respectively we see that

{ either A or B can be used as a fixed point on the line
  the direction vector of the line is either $\overrightarrow{AB}$ or $\overrightarrow{BA}$.

So the vector equation of the line through A and B can be given as

$$r = a + \lambda(b \sim a)$$

or$$r = b + \lambda(b \sim a)$$

For example, the vector equation of the line passing through the points with
position vectors $2i + 5j$ and $4i - 3j$ can be given in any of the following
forms,

$$r = 2i + 5j + \lambda(2i - 8j)$$

$$r = 2i + 5j + \lambda(-2i + 8j)$$

$$r = 4i - 3j + \lambda(2i - 8j)$$

$$r = 4i - 3j + \lambda(-2i + 8j)$$

Recognising Direction and Finding Points from the Vector Equation of a Line

If $r = a + \lambda d$ is a vector equation of a line, then **d** is its direction vector
and **a** is the position vector of one point on the line.
Further points on the line can be found by giving λ various numerical values.

EXAMPLE 2d

A line has vector equation $r = 2i + 6j + \lambda(i - 3j)$.   State its direction vector
and the coordinates of three points on the line. Find the position vectors of the
points where this line crosses each of the coordinate axes.

The direction vector is $\mathbf{i}-3\mathbf{j}$
One point on the line is $(2,6)$
Another point on the line is given by $\lambda = 1$,   i.e. $(3,3)$
A third point on the line is given by $\lambda = -1$,   i.e. $(1,9)$

The line crosses the x axis where $y = 0$,   i.e. where the coefficient of $\mathbf{j}$ is zero

$$\Rightarrow \qquad 6 - 3\lambda = 0 \qquad \Rightarrow \qquad \lambda = 2$$

When $\lambda = 2$, $\mathbf{r} = 4\mathbf{i}$

The line crosses the y axis where $x = 0$

$$\Rightarrow \qquad 2 + \lambda = 0 \qquad \Rightarrow \qquad \lambda = -2$$

When $\lambda = -2$, $\mathbf{r} = 12\mathbf{j}$.

EXERCISE 2d

Find a vector equation for a line passing through the given point and with the given direction vector:

1) a point with position vector $3\mathbf{i}$; a direction vector $2\mathbf{i}+4\mathbf{j}$,

2) a point with position vector $\mathbf{i}-\mathbf{j}$;   a direction vector $5\mathbf{i}$,

3) a point with position vector $5\mathbf{j}$; a direction vector $\mathbf{i}-5\mathbf{j}$,

4) the origin; a direction vector $3\mathbf{i}+4\mathbf{j}+2\mathbf{k}$

5) a point with position vector $-4\mathbf{i}-\mathbf{j}+\mathbf{k}$;   parallel to a line with vector equation $\mathbf{r} = 2\mathbf{i}+3\mathbf{j}+\lambda(\mathbf{i}+\mathbf{j}-\mathbf{k})$.

Write down a vector equation for the line through A and B where the position vectors of A and B are:

6) $A(2\mathbf{i} + 3\mathbf{j})$, $B(\mathbf{i} - 7\mathbf{j})$

7) $A(3\mathbf{i})$, $B(7\mathbf{i}-9\mathbf{j})$

8) $A(\mathbf{i}-\mathbf{j})$, $B(3\mathbf{j})$

9) $A(5\mathbf{i} - 7\mathbf{j} + \mathbf{k})$, $B(2\mathbf{i}+\mathbf{j}-2\mathbf{k})$

10) $A(-\mathbf{j} + 2\mathbf{k})$, $B(\mathbf{i}-3\mathbf{k})$

Write down the direction vector and name the coordinates of the specified points on each of the following lines.

11) $\mathbf{r} = 4\mathbf{i} + \mathbf{j} + \lambda(3\mathbf{i} + 7\mathbf{j})$;   points of intersection with Ox and Oy.

12) $\mathbf{r} = (1 + \lambda)\mathbf{i} + (3 - 5\lambda)\mathbf{j}$;   point for which $x = 3$.

13) $\mathbf{r} = \lambda(\mathbf{i} - 7\mathbf{j})$;   any two points.

14) $\mathbf{r} = 2\mathbf{i} + \lambda\mathbf{j}$;   points of intersection with the lines $y = 1$ and $y = 4$.

15) $\mathbf{r} = 2\mathbf{i} + 2\mathbf{j} + \lambda(\mathbf{i}-\mathbf{j})$;   point of intersection with Oy and the point where $y = 4$.

THE LINE OF ACTION OF A FORCE

If a force is given in vector form, $a\mathbf{i} + b\mathbf{j}$, then $a\mathbf{i} + b\mathbf{j}$ is the direction vector of the force. To find the equation of the line of action of the force we need also a location — usually a point through which the force is known to pass. This position vector, together with the direction vector, gives the equation of the line of action. For example, if a force $3\mathbf{i} - 4\mathbf{j} + \mathbf{k}$ acts through a point with position vector $\mathbf{i} + \mathbf{j} + 2\mathbf{k}$, its line of action has a vector equation

$$\mathbf{r} = \mathbf{i} + \mathbf{j} + 2\mathbf{k} + \lambda(3\mathbf{i} - 4\mathbf{j} + \mathbf{k})$$

Note. The equation of the line of action of a force provides the *direction* of the force but this must not be taken as the actual force vector (although sometimes it may be). In addition to the equation of the line of action we need to know the magnitude of the force in order to find the force vector.

EXAMPLE 2e

A force, **F**, acts along the line $\mathbf{r} = \mathbf{i} - 3\mathbf{j} + \lambda(3\mathbf{i} + 4\mathbf{j})$ and its magnitude is 20 N. Find **F**.

We do not know *which way* the force acts along the line, so the direction vector, **d**, of the force is $\pm(3\mathbf{i} + 4\mathbf{j})$.

$$\Rightarrow \qquad\qquad \hat{\mathbf{d}} = \pm \frac{(3\mathbf{i} + 4\mathbf{j})}{5}$$

Hence $\quad \mathbf{F} = |\mathbf{F}|\hat{\mathbf{d}} = \dfrac{\pm 20(3\mathbf{i} + 4\mathbf{j})}{5} = \pm(12\mathbf{i} + 16\mathbf{j})$

EXERCISE 2e

Write down the equation of the line of action of each of the following forces.

1) $\mathbf{F} = 8\mathbf{i} - 7\mathbf{j}$ and passes through the point with position vector $(2\mathbf{i} - 3\mathbf{j})$.

2) $\mathbf{F} = 4\mathbf{i}$ and passes through the origin.

3) **F** passes through the points with position vectors $\mathbf{i} + \mathbf{j}$ and $5\mathbf{i} + 11\mathbf{j}$.

4) **F** is parallel to $\mathbf{i} - 2\mathbf{j}$ and passes through $(7, 8)$.

5) **F** acts through the origin and through $(11, -7, 3)$.

Find the position vector of the point where the line of action of the following force intersects (a) the x axis (b) the y axis

6) The force in Question 1.

7) The force in Question 3.

8) The force in Question 4.

9) Determine whether the line of action of the force in Question 1 passes through the point $(10,-4)$.

10) Does the line of action of the force in Question 3 pass through the point with position vector $6\mathbf{i} + 12\mathbf{j}$?

Find in the form $a\mathbf{i} + b\mathbf{j}$, a force:

11) of magnitude $65\,\text{N}$ acting along the line $\mathbf{r} = \mathbf{i} + \lambda(5\mathbf{i} - 12\mathbf{j})$.

12) of magnitude $4\,\text{N}$ acting along the line $\mathbf{r} = 7\mathbf{i} - 8\mathbf{j} + \lambda\mathbf{i}$.

13) of magnitude $8\sqrt{2}\,\text{N}$ acting along the line $\mathbf{r} = 3\mathbf{i} - \mathbf{j} + \lambda(\mathbf{i} + \mathbf{j})$.

14) of magnitude $20\,\text{N}$ passing through the points $(1,2)$ and $(2,5)$.

15) of magnitude $13\,\text{N}$ parallel to the line with equation $\mathbf{r} = 2\mathbf{i} + 5\mathbf{j} + \lambda(4\mathbf{i} - 7\mathbf{j})$.

THE EQUATION OF THE PATH OF A PARTICLE MOVING WITH CONSTANT VELOCITY

A particle whose constant velocity is $\mathbf{v}$ moves in the direction of this velocity vector so $\mathbf{v}$ is also a direction vector for the line along which the particle moves. If the particle passes through a particular point with position vector $\mathbf{a}$, the equation of the path of the particle is

$$\mathbf{r} = \mathbf{a} + \lambda\mathbf{v}$$

EXAMPLE 2f

A particle starts moving from the point $(2,7,1)$ with a velocity $6\mathbf{i} - 5\mathbf{j} + 3\mathbf{k}$. Find the equation of the line along which the particle moves.

The particle moves in the direction of its velocity, i.e. $6\mathbf{i} - 5\mathbf{j} + 3\mathbf{k}$ is the direction vector of the line of motion.
Now $2\mathbf{i} + 7\mathbf{j} + \mathbf{k}$ is the position vector of a point on this line so the equation of the line is

$$\mathbf{r} = 2\mathbf{i} + 7\mathbf{j} + \mathbf{k} + \lambda(6\mathbf{i} - 5\mathbf{j} + 3\mathbf{k})$$

EXERCISE 2f

Find the equation of the path of a particle:

1) passing through $(4,-1)$ with velocity $\mathbf{i} + 7\mathbf{j}$.

2) passing through $3\mathbf{i} - 2\mathbf{j} - \mathbf{k}$ with velocity $-5\mathbf{i} + 6\mathbf{j} + 8\mathbf{k}$.

3) passing through $\mathbf{i} + \mathbf{j}$ with speed $5\,\text{m s}^{-1}$ in the direction $4\mathbf{i} - 3\mathbf{j}$.

4) with velocity $8\mathbf{i} - 7\mathbf{j}$ and passing through the point where the line
$\mathbf{r} = 3\mathbf{i} - \mathbf{j} + \lambda(\mathbf{i} + 6\mathbf{j})$ meets the y-axis.

5) passing through the point of intersection of the lines $y = 4$ and
$\mathbf{r} = 3\mathbf{i} + 5\mathbf{j} + \lambda(\mathbf{i} - \mathbf{j})$,   with velocity $9\mathbf{i} - 2\mathbf{j}$.

DETERMINATION OF RESULTANT VECTORS

A single vector **R** equivalent to a set of vectors is the resultant of those
vectors (which are, themselves, the components of **R**). The method of
evaluating **R** depends upon the number and type of vectors in the given set.

The Resultant of Two Perpendicular Vectors

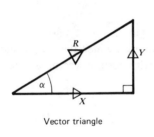

Vector triangle

If X and Y are the magnitudes of the
vectors then the magnitude, R, of the
resultant is given by

$$R^2 = X^2 + Y^2$$

The direction of the resultant is given by

$$\tan \alpha = \frac{Y}{X}$$

Therefore the resultant is of the magnitude $\sqrt{X^2 + Y^2}$ and makes $\arctan \dfrac{Y}{X}$
with the component of magnitude X.

The Resultant of Two Non-perpendicular Vectors

At this point it becomes important to understand what is meant by the angle
between two vectors. Suppose that, from a point O, two line segments are
drawn representing the vectors **P** and **Q**. Then if both vectors point away from
O as in Fig. (i), or both vectors point towards O as in Fig. (ii), the angle θ
between the lines at O is the angle between the vectors. But if one vector points
towards O and the other points away from O as in Fig. (iii) then the angle
between the lines at O is $(180° - \theta)$ where θ is the angle between the
vectors.

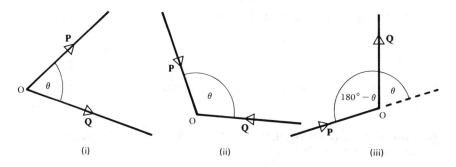

(i)   (ii)   (iii)

We are now ready to calculate the resultant of two such vectors.

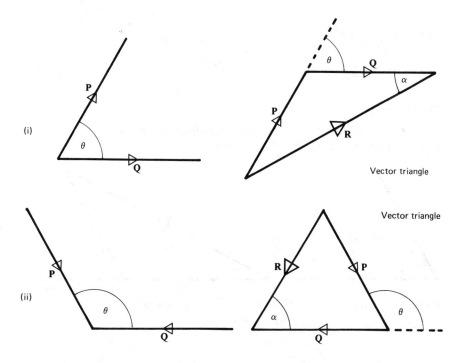

Vector triangle

Vector triangle

The resultant is represented, in magnitude and direction but not necessarily position, by the third side of a triangle formed by drawing a line representing the vector of magnitude P followed by a line representing the vector of magnitude Q (note that θ is an exterior angle of this triangle). Then the magnitude R of the resultant can be found using the cosine formula,

$$R^2 = P^2 + Q^2 - 2PQ \cos(180° - \theta)$$

or $$R^2 = P^2 + Q^2 + 2PQ \cos \theta$$

The direction of the resultant can next be determined by using the sine rule,

$$\frac{\sin \alpha}{P} = \frac{\sin(180° - \theta)}{R} \qquad \text{or} \qquad \sin \alpha = \frac{P \sin \theta}{R}$$

These formulae for calculating the values of R and α are valid whether θ is acute or obtuse.

Note that if P and Q are equal, the resultant bisects the angle between the forces and the value of R is $2P \cos \theta/2$.

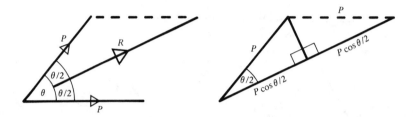

EXAMPLES 2g

1) Find the resultant of two vectors of magnitudes 8 units and 10 units if the angle between them is (a) 60° (b) 90° (c) 120°.

(a)

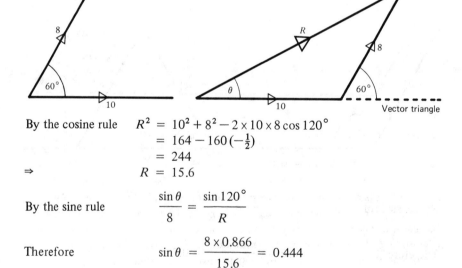

Vector triangle

By the cosine rule
$$\begin{aligned}
R^2 &= 10^2 + 8^2 - 2 \times 10 \times 8 \cos 120° \\
&= 164 - 160\left(-\tfrac{1}{2}\right) \\
&= 244
\end{aligned}$$

$\Rightarrow \qquad R = 15.6$

By the sine rule
$$\frac{\sin \theta}{8} = \frac{\sin 120°}{R}$$

Therefore
$$\sin \theta = \frac{8 \times 0.866}{15.6} = 0.444$$

$\Rightarrow \qquad \theta = 26.4°$

The resultant is of magnitude 15.6 units at an angle 26.4° with the vector of magnitude 10 units.

(b)

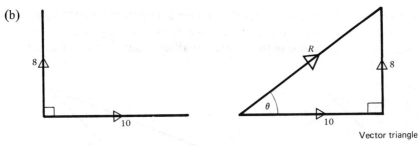

Vector triangle

Using Pythagoras' Theorem $\qquad R^2 = 8^2 + 10^2 = 164$

$\Rightarrow \qquad\qquad\qquad\qquad R = 12.8$

and $\qquad\qquad\qquad\qquad \tan \theta = \dfrac{8}{10}$

$\Rightarrow \qquad\qquad\qquad\qquad \theta = 38.7°$

The resultant is of magnitude 12.8 units at an angle 38.7° with the vector of magnitude 10 units.

(c)

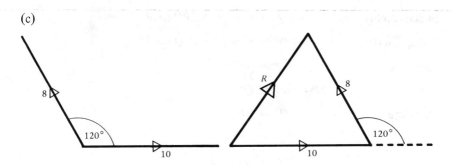

By the cosine rule $\qquad R^2 = 10^2 + 8^2 - 2 \times 8 \times 10 \cos 60°$

$\qquad\qquad\qquad\qquad\quad = 84$

$\Rightarrow \qquad\qquad\qquad R = 9.17$

By the sine rule $\qquad\qquad \dfrac{\sin \theta}{8} = \dfrac{\sin 60°}{R}$

Therefore $\qquad\qquad \sin \theta = \dfrac{8 \times 0.866}{9.17} = 0.756$

$\Rightarrow \qquad\qquad\qquad \theta = 49.1°$

The resultant is of magnitude 9.17 units at an angle 49.1° with the vector of magnitude 10 units.

2) When two vectors of magnitudes P and Q are inclined at an angle θ, the magnitude of their resultant is $2P$. When the inclination is changed to $(180° - \theta)$ the magnitude of the resultant is halved. Find the ratio of P to Q.

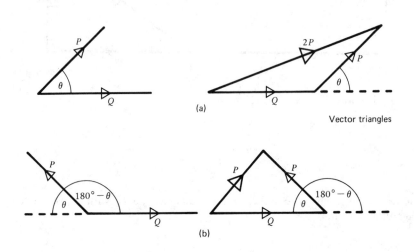

(a)

Vector triangles

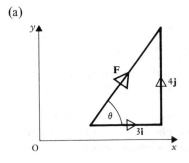

(b)

In diagram (a) $(2P)^2 = P^2 + Q^2 + 2PQ \cos \theta$

In diagram (b) $(P)^2 = P^2 + Q^2 - 2PQ \cos \theta$

Therefore $2PQ \cos \theta = 3P^2 - Q^2$

and $2PQ \cos \theta = Q^2$

Therefore $Q^2 = 3P^2 - Q^2$

$\Rightarrow$ $2Q^2 = 3P^2$

$\Rightarrow$ $P : Q = \sqrt{2} : \sqrt{3}.$

3) Find the magnitude and the inclination to Ox of a force vector $\mathbf{F}$ if
(a) $\mathbf{F} = 3\mathbf{i} + 4\mathbf{j}$ (b) $\mathbf{F} = -\mathbf{i} + \mathbf{j}$

(a)

Since $\mathbf{F}$ has components of 3 and 4 units in perpendicular directions the magnitude of $\mathbf{F}$ is given by

$$|\mathbf{F}| = \sqrt{(3^2 + 4^2)} = 5$$

The inclination of $\mathbf{F}$ to Ox is θ where $\tan \theta = 4/3$

(b)

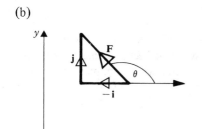

The magnitude of **F** is given by

$$|\mathbf{F}| = \sqrt{(1^2 + 1^2)} = \sqrt{2}$$

The inclination of **F** to Ox is θ where

$$\theta = 180° - \arctan(1/1)$$

i.e. $\theta = 180° - 45° = 135°$

EXERCISE 2g

1) The following pairs of forces are, in each case, perpendicular to each other. Find the magnitude and direction of the resultant force.
(a) 3 N and 4 N   (b) 24 N and 10 N   (c) 5 N and 5 N
(d) 2 N and 6 N   (e) 7 N and 24 N

2) If **i** and **j** represent forces of magnitude 1 N in the directions Ox and Oy respectively, find the magnitude and inclination to Ox of each of the following force vectors.
(a) $12\mathbf{i} + 5\mathbf{j}$ (b) $2\mathbf{i} + 2\mathbf{j}$ (c) $24\mathbf{i} - 7\mathbf{j}$
(d) $-4\mathbf{i} + 3\mathbf{j}$ (e) $-7\mathbf{i} - \mathbf{j}$.

3) Find the magnitude of the resultant of each of the following pairs of forces
(a) 10 N and 6 N inclined at $60°$ to each other
(b) 3 N and 5 N inclined at $150°$ to each other
(c) 2 N and 7 N in the same direction
(d) 2 N and 7 N in opposite directions
(e) 4 N and 6 N inclined at $45°$ to each other.

4) A force vector $\mathbf{F} = p\mathbf{i} + 12\mathbf{j}$ has a magnitude of 13 units. Find the two possible values of p and the corresponding inclinations of **F** to Ox.

5) An aircraft is flying with an engine speed of $400 \, \text{km h}^{-1}$ on a course due North in a wind of speed $60 \, \text{km h}^{-1}$ from the South West. At what speed is the aircraft covering the ground?

6) Two vectors have magnitudes of 4 units and 6 units. Find the angle between them if their resultant is of magnitude (a) 8 units   (b) 4 units.

7) A force of 8 N and a force P have a resultant of magnitude 17 N. Find P if the angle between the two forces is (a) $90°$ (b) $60°$.

8) Two forces of magnitudes P and $2P$ are inclined at an angle θ. Find θ if the resultant is of magnitude (a) $2P$ (b) $3P$ (c) P.
(It should not be necessary to use the cosine rule in all three cases.)

The Resultant of More than Two Coplanar Vectors

Consider a set of four vectors whose magnitudes and directions are shown in diagram (i). The resultant can be found by drawing consecutive lines representing the given vectors in magnitude and direction; the line which completes the polygon represents the resultant (diagram (ii)).

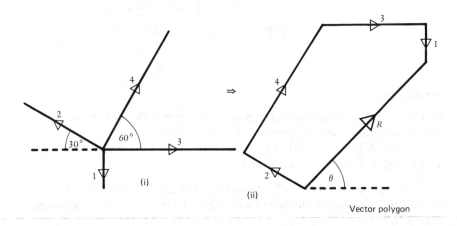

Vector polygon

Careful drawing to scale and measurement give values for the magnitude R and the direction θ of the resultant. The values obtained in this way however are only as accurate as the drawing; more precise values will be given by calculation as follows:

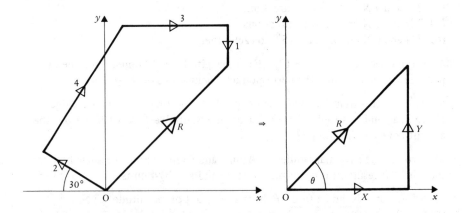

Suppose that the components of R in the directions Ox and Oy are X and Y. The value of X is the sum of the components of the original vectors in the direction Ox and the value of Y is their sum in the direction Oy.

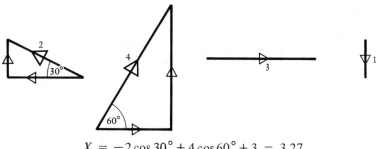

i.e.

$$X = -2\cos 30° + 4\cos 60° + 3 = 3.27$$
$$Y = 2\sin 30° + 4\sin 60° - 1 = 3.46$$

Now the resultant of X and Y (two perpendicular components) can be found using

$$R = \sqrt{X^2 + Y^2} = \sqrt{22.66} = 4.76$$

and

$$\tan\theta = \frac{Y}{X} = \frac{3.46}{3.27} = 1.06$$

Therefore the resultant of the given vectors is a vector of magnitude 4.76 units inclined at 46.7° to Ox.

X and Y are very easily found if the forces are expressed in the form

$$\mathbf{F} = p\mathbf{i} + q\mathbf{j}$$

since p and q represent the magnitudes of the components of $\mathbf{F}$ in the directions Ox and Oy.

Suppose, for instance, that forces $\mathbf{F_1}, \mathbf{F_2}, \mathbf{F_3}$ and $\mathbf{F_4}$ act on a particle P as shown in the diagram, and

$$\mathbf{F_1} = 2\mathbf{i} + \mathbf{j}$$
$$\mathbf{F_2} = \mathbf{i} - 3\mathbf{j}$$
$$\mathbf{F_3} = -3\mathbf{i} + 4\mathbf{j}$$
$$\mathbf{F_4} = 4\mathbf{i} + \mathbf{j}$$

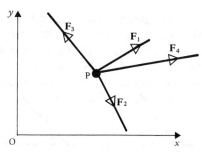

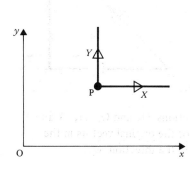

Their resultant can be expressed in the form $X\mathbf{i} + Y\mathbf{j}$ where

$$X = (2 + 1 - 3 + 4)$$
and $$Y = (1 - 3 + 4 + 1)$$

The resultant force can hence be represented by $4\mathbf{i} + 3\mathbf{j}$

EXAMPLES 2h

1) Find the resultant of five coplanar forces of magnitudes 5, 4, 3, 2 and 1 newton, the angle between consecutive pairs being 30°.

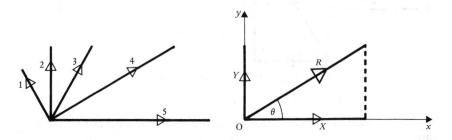

Let the resultant have components X and Y newtons parallel to Ox and Oy as shown. Resolving all forces along Ox and Oy we have:

$$X = 5 + 4\cos 30° + 3\cos 60° - 1\cos 60° = 9.46$$

$$Y = 4\sin 30° + 3\sin 60° + 2 + 1\sin 60° = 7.46$$

Then
$$R = \sqrt{X^2 + Y^2}$$

⇒
$$R = 12.1$$

and
$$\tan\theta = \frac{Y}{X} = 0.789$$

Therefore the resultant is a force of 12.1 N making an angle of 38.3° with the force of 5 N.

2) A river is flowing due East at a speed of $3\,\text{ms}^{-1}$. A boy in a rowing boat, who can row at $5\,\text{ms}^{-1}$ in still water, starts from a point O on the south bank and steers the boat at right angles to the bank. The boat is also being blown by the wind at $4\,\text{ms}^{-1}$ South West. Taking axes Ox and Oy in the directions East and North respectively find the velocity of the boat in the form $p\mathbf{i} + q\mathbf{j}$ and hence find its resultant speed.

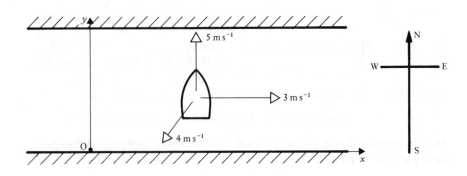

The velocity of the river can be written as $3\mathbf{i}$

The velocity due to rowing can be written as $5\mathbf{j}$

The velocity of the wind can be written as $-4\cos 45°\,\mathbf{i} - 4\cos 45°\,\mathbf{j}$

i.e. $-2\sqrt{2}\mathbf{i} - 2\sqrt{2}\mathbf{j}$

The resultant velocity $\mathbf{v}$ is then given by

$$\mathbf{v} = 3\mathbf{i} + 5\mathbf{j} + (-2\sqrt{2}\mathbf{i} - 2\sqrt{2}\mathbf{j})$$

i.e. $\mathbf{v} = (3 - 2\sqrt{2})\,\mathbf{i} + (5 - 2\sqrt{2})\,\mathbf{j}$

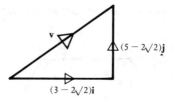

The resultant speed is the magnitude of the resultant velocity, i.e. $|\mathbf{v}|$, where

$$|\mathbf{v}| = \sqrt{(3 - 2\sqrt{2})^2 + (5 - 2\sqrt{2})^2} = \sqrt{50 - 32\sqrt{2}}$$

3) Three tugs are pulling a liner due North into a harbour. The ropes attaching the liner to the tugs are in the directions NE, N 10° E and N 30° W. If the tensions in the first two ropes are 2×10^5 N and 10^6 N, find the tension in the third rope and the resultant pull on the liner.

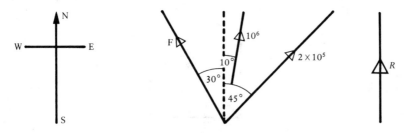

Since the liner is being moved due North, the resultant pull, R newton, is in that direction (i.e. there is no overall component in the East-West direction). Let the tension in the third rope be F newton.

Resolving all forces in the directions East and North we have

$\rightarrow$ $0 = 2 \times 10^5 \sin 45° + 10^6 \sin 10° - F \sin 30°$ [1]

$\uparrow$ $R = 2 \times 10^5 \cos 45° + 10^6 \cos 10° + F \cos 30°$ [2]

From [1] $\tfrac{1}{2}F = 10^5(2 \sin 45° + 10 \sin 10°)$

$F = 2 \times 10^5(1.414 + 1.736) = 10^5 \times 6.3$

From [2] $R = 10^5(2 \cos 45° + 10 \cos 10° + 6.3 \cos 30°)$

$= 10^5(1.414 + 9.848 + 5.456) = 10^5 \times 16.718$

Therefore the tension in the third rope is 6.3×10^5 N and the resultant pull on the liner is 1.67×10^6 N.

4) ABCDEF is a regular hexagon. Forces of magnitudes $3F, 4F, 2F, 6F$ act along $\overrightarrow{AB}, \overrightarrow{AC}, \overrightarrow{EA}, \overrightarrow{AF}$, respectively. Find the magnitude and direction of their resultant.

Note. *Only the direction* of the forces is denoted by $\overrightarrow{AB}$ etc. The magnitudes are given separately and are *not represented by the lengths* of the lines **AB**, etc.

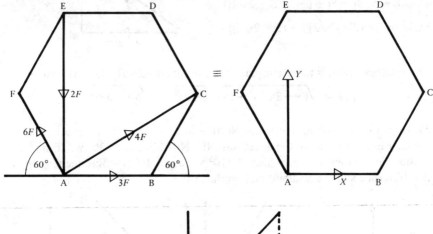

Let the resultant have components X and Y parallel to AB and AE as shown.

Resolving all forces along AB and AE we have:

$$X = 3F + 4F\cos 30° - 6F\cos 60° = 2\sqrt{3}F$$

$$Y = 4F\sin 30° - 2F + 6F\sin 60° = 3\sqrt{3}F$$

Then
$$R = \sqrt{X^2 + Y^2} = F\sqrt{3}\sqrt{2^2 + 3^2}$$

$\Rightarrow$
$$R = F\sqrt{39}$$

and
$$\tan\theta = \frac{Y}{X} = \frac{3\sqrt{3}}{2\sqrt{3}} = 1.5$$

Therefore the resultant is a force of magnitude $F\sqrt{39}$ which is inclined at an angle $\arctan 1.5$ to **AB**.

EXERCISE 2h

In Questions 1–4, find the magnitude and direction of the resultant of the given set of vectors.

1) Four forces, in newtons, represented by $3i - j$, $i + 7j$, $5j$ and $i + j$.

2) Three velocities, in metres per second, represented by $4i - 7j$, $-3i + 8j$ and $2i + 3j$.

3) The forces shown in the following diagrams:

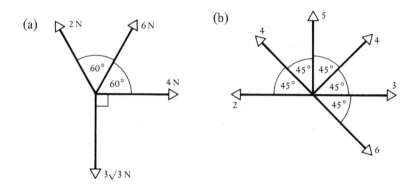

4) Forces of magntiudes $3 N$, $4 N$ and $5 N$ acting respectively along the lines $\overrightarrow{AB}$, $\overrightarrow{AC}$ and $\overrightarrow{DA}$ where ABCD is a rectangle in which $AB = 4 m$ and $BC = 3 m$.

5) Find the resultant of forces of magnitudes 4, 3 and 6 newton acting in the directions AB, BC and CA respectively, where ABC is an equilateral triangle.

6) Starting from O, a point P traces out consecutive displacement vectors of $2i + 3j$, $-i + 4j$, $7i - 5j$ and $i + 3j$.
What is the final displacement of P from O?

7) Three boys are pulling a heavy trolley by means of three ropes. The boy in the middle is exerting a pull of $100 N$. The other two boys, whose ropes both make an angle of $30°$ with the centre rope, are pulling with forces of $80 N$ and $140 N$. What is the resultant pull on the trolley and in what direction will it move?

8) A surveyor starts from a point O and walks $200 m$ due North. He then turns clockwise through $120°$ and walks $100 m$ after which he walks $300 m$ due West. What is his resultant displacement from O?

9) An object A is subjected to coplanar forces of $5 N, 2 N$ and $3 N$ inclined at $30°, 90°$ and $150°$ respectively to the line AB. Taking AB as the x axis, express their resultant in the form $ai + bj$.

10) A small boat is travelling through the water with an engine speed of $8 \, \text{km h}^{-1}$. It is being steered due East but there is a current running South at $2 \, \text{km h}^{-1}$ and wind is blowing the boat South West at $4 \, \text{km h}^{-1}$. Find the resultant velocity of the boat.

11) Rain, which is falling vertically, makes streaks on the vertical sides of a van travelling at $80 \, \text{km h}^{-1}$. If the streaks are at $30°$ to the vertical, calculate the speed of the raindrops.

12) Forces of magnitudes $2P, 3P, 4P$ and $5P$, act along $\overrightarrow{AB}, \overrightarrow{AC}, \overrightarrow{AD}$ and $\overrightarrow{AE}$, respectively. Find the magnitude and direction of their resultant if:
(a) ABCDEF is a regular hexagon,
(b) ABCDE is made up of a square ABCE together with an equilateral triangle CDE (D is outside the square).

THE POSITION OF A RESULTANT FORCE

When a number of forces act on a *particle*, their lines of action all pass through the point where the particle is located. Clearly, in this case, the resultant of the set of forces also acts on the particle and therefore passes through the point of intersection of these forces. This property applies to any set of concurrent forces whether they act on a particle or a bigger object, i.e.,

the resultant of a set of concurrent forces acts through their point of intersection.

(When the forces are not concurrent the location of their resultant is not obvious and methods for determining it are given later in Chapter 14.)

We will now consider the location of the resultant of two non-parallel forces whose lines of action are given in vector form.
The point through which the resultant passes has a position vector which satisfies the vector equations of both lines of action.
We now need a method for determining such a point.

Intersection of Two Lines in a Plane

Consider two lines whose vector equations are

$$r_1 = a_1 + \lambda d_1$$

and
$$r_2 = a_2 + \mu d_2$$

Unless $d_1 = d_2$ (i.e. the lines are parallel) the lines intersect at a point where $r_1 = r_2$.
When all the vectors involved are given in Cartesian form, this equation can be solved and the point of intersection determined.

EXAMPLES 2i

1) Find the position vector of the point of intersection of the lines whose vector equations are

$$\mathbf{r}_1 = \mathbf{i} + \mathbf{j} + \lambda(2\mathbf{i} - \mathbf{j})$$

and

$$\mathbf{r}_2 = 3\mathbf{i} + 4\mathbf{j} + \mu(2\mathbf{i} - 5\mathbf{j})$$

We see that $\mathbf{d}_1 \neq \mathbf{d}_2$ so the lines meet at a point where $\mathbf{r}_1 = \mathbf{r}_2$

i.e. where

$$\mathbf{i} + \mathbf{j} + \lambda(2\mathbf{i} - \mathbf{j}) = 3\mathbf{i} + 4\mathbf{j} + \mu(2\mathbf{i} - 5\mathbf{j})$$

$\Rightarrow$

$$(1 + 2\lambda)\mathbf{i} + (1 - \lambda)\mathbf{j} = (3 + 2\mu)\mathbf{i} + (4 - 5\mu)\mathbf{j}$$

Hence

$$\left.\begin{array}{r} 1 + 2\lambda = 3 + 2\mu \\ 1 - \lambda = 4 - 5\mu \end{array}\right\} \Rightarrow \lambda = 2, \ \mu = 1$$

and

Using either $\lambda = 2$ in $\mathbf{r}_1$ or $\mu = 1$ in $\mathbf{r}_2$ we see that the position vector of the point of intersection of the given lines is

$$\mathbf{r} = 5\mathbf{i} - \mathbf{j}$$

2) Two forces, $\mathbf{F}_1 = \mathbf{i} + 5\mathbf{j}$ and $\mathbf{F}_2 = 3\mathbf{i} - 2\mathbf{j}$, act through points with position vectors $\mathbf{i}$ and $-3\mathbf{i} + 14\mathbf{j}$ respectively. Find the point where their lines of action meet and hence write down the equation of the line of action of their resultant.

The vector equation of the line of action of $\mathbf{F}_1$ is

$$\mathbf{r}_1 = \mathbf{i} + \lambda(\mathbf{i} + 5\mathbf{j})$$

and, for $\mathbf{F}_2$, it is

$$\mathbf{r}_2 = -3\mathbf{i} + 14\mathbf{j} + \mu(3\mathbf{i} - 2\mathbf{j})$$

These lines meet at a point given by

$$\mathbf{r}_1 = \mathbf{r}_2$$

$\Rightarrow$

$$(1 + \lambda)\mathbf{i} + 5\lambda\mathbf{j} = (-3 + 3\mu)\mathbf{i} + (14 - 2\mu)\mathbf{j}$$

$\Rightarrow$

$$\left.\begin{array}{r} 1 + \lambda = -3 + 3\mu \\ 5\lambda = 14 - 2\mu \end{array}\right\} \Rightarrow \lambda = 2, \ \mu = 2$$

So the point of intersection has position vector $3\mathbf{i} + 10\mathbf{j}$.

Now the resultant of $\mathbf{F}_1$ and $\mathbf{F}_2$ is $\mathbf{F}_1 + \mathbf{F}_2$ and it passes through the point where $\mathbf{F}_1$ and $\mathbf{F}_2$ meet. So the equation of the line of action of the resultant is

$$\mathbf{r} = 3\mathbf{i} + 10\mathbf{j} + \lambda(4\mathbf{i} + 3\mathbf{j})$$

EXERCISE 2i

Find the position vectors of the points of intersection of the pairs of lines given in Questions 1-7.

1) $r_1 = i + j + \lambda(3i - 4j)$ and $r_2 = 2i - 4j + \mu(i + 6j)$.

2) $r_1 = i + 4j + \lambda(3i - j)$ and $r_2 = 2j + \mu(-7i)$.

3) $r_1 = 6j + \lambda(i - j)$ and the line through $(1, 0)$ and $(9, 2)$.

4) The lines through $(4, 2)$ and $(7, -4)$, and through $(3, 0)$ and $(-3, 4)$.

5) The lines of action of two forces F_1 and F_2 if $F_1 = 3i + 4j$ and passes through $(-2, -3)$, $F_2 = 2i - j$ and passes through $(-3, 3)$.

6) The lines of action of F_1 and F_2 if F_1 passes through $(-2, -3)$ and $(4, 5)$ and F_2 passes through $(-3, 3)$ and $(3, 0)$. Can you state the magnitudes of F_1 and F_2?

7) The lines of action of F_1 and F_2 if F_1 passes through $(5, 2)$ and is parallel to the line whose equation is $r = \lambda(i - j)$ and F_2 passes through the origin and has direction vector $6i + j$.

8) A force F_1 has magnitude 50 N, acts in the direction $24i - 7j$ and passes through O. A second force, F_2, is $-2i + j$ and passes through $(5, 0)$.
(a) Find the equations of the lines of action of F_1 and F_2.
(b) Find the resultant of F_1 and F_2.
(c) Find the equation of the line of action of the resultant.

THE TURNING EFFECT OF FORCES

(a) Consider two equal and opposite forces each of magnitude F acting at the centre of a rod AB.

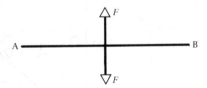

We know from experience that the rod will not move and this is consistent with the results of resolving the forces parallel and perpendicular to the rod.

Resolving parallel to AB gives $X = 0$
Resolving perpendicular to AB gives $Y = 0$
So the resultant force is zero.

(b) Now consider the same two forces, one acting at A and the other at B.

Resolving parallel to AB gives $X = 0.$
Resolving perpendicular to AB gives $Y = 0.$

So once again the resultant force is zero.

But this time we notice that the rod will rotate, so clearly the turning effect, if any, of a set of forces cannot be found by the method of resolving in two perpendicular directions.

In order to assess completely the effect that a set of forces has on the object to which they are applied, it is now clear that we must evaluate:
(a) the magnitude and direction of the resultant force,
(b) the magnitude of the turning effect of the set of forces.

The methods used for dealing with (a) have been explored in this chapter so we will now investigate the turning effect of sets of forces.

Most readers will, at some time, have attempted to loosen a tight nut by using a spanner. If the spanner is a short one it may be difficult to undo the nut at a first attempt. In this case we can either a) exert a greater pulling force on the short spanner or b) use the original pull on a longer spanner.

This simple example shows that the size of the turning effect, or *moment*, of a force depends both on the size of the force and on its distance from the centre, or axis, of rotation.

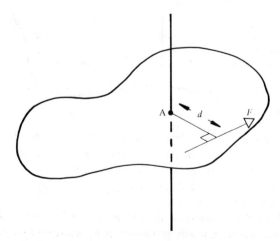

This property leads to the definition of the moment of a force.

MOMENT OF FORCE

The turning effect C of a force F is calculated by multiplying together the *magnitude* of the force and its perpendicular distance, d, from the axis of rotation.

i.e.

$$C = Fd$$

C is called the *moment of the force* about the specified axis and the unit in which it is measured is the newton metre, Nm.

Torque

We have just seen that one of the ways in which rotation can be caused is to apply a force at some distance from the axis, or pivot. But there are other means of producing rotation. To turn a door knob, for instance, we simply take hold of it and twist it. The general name given to any turning effect is *torque*. The magnitude of a torque of any type is measured in newton metres.

Direction of Torque

The angular direction of a torque is the sense of the rotation it would cause.

Consider a lamina that is free to rotate in its own plane about an axis perpendicular to the lamina and passing through a point A on the lamina.

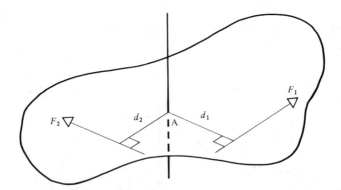

In the diagram the moment about the axis of rotation of the force F_1 is $F_1 d_1$ anticlockwise and the moment of the force F_2 is $F_2 d_2$ clockwise. A convenient way to differentiate between clockwise and anticlockwise torques is to allocate a positive sign to one sense (usually, but not invariably, this is anticlockwise) and a negative sign to the other.
With this convention, the moments of F_1 and F_2 are $+F_1 d_1$ and $-F_2 d_2$.
(When using a sign convention in any problem it is advisable to specify the chosen positive sense.)

Graphical Representation of Torque

A force **F**, distant d from an axis through **A**, can be represented in magnitude, direction and position (i.e. completely) by a line $\overrightarrow{PQ}$

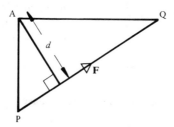

The magnitude of the torque about the axis is $|\mathbf{F}| \times d$ which is represented by $PQ \times d$. But $\frac{1}{2} \times PQ \times d$ is the area of triangle PAQ.

> The magnitude of the moment about an axis through **A** of a force represented completely by a line PQ is represented by twice the area of triangle PAQ.

Zero Moment

If the line of action of a force passes through the axis of rotation, its perpendicular distance from the axis is zero. Therefore its moment about that axis is also zero.

Terminology

Whenever we refer to the moment of a set of coplanar forces about an axis, at this stage it is implicit that the axis is perpendicular to the plane in which the forces act. In a diagram of the forces in their plane of action, the axis of rotation, being perpendicular to that plane, can be indicated only by a point (its point of intersection with the plane).

Because of this it is common to refer to the moment of a force about a point. This is, of course, inaccurate, because forces do not cause turning about a point, but about a line. It should always be appreciated therefore that an expression such as 'the moment of force F about **A**' really means 'the moment of force F about an axis through **A** and perpendicular to the plane in which F acts'.

Examples 2j

1) ABCD is a square of side 2 m and O is its centre. Forces act along the sides as shown in the diagram. Calculate the moment of each force about:
(a) an axis through A,
(b) an axis through O.

Taking anticlockwise moments as positive we have:

(a)

Magnitude of force Distance from A	2 N 0	5 N 2 m	4 N 2 m	3 N 0
Moment about A	0	− 10 Nm	+ 8 Nm	0

(b)

Magnitude of force Distance from O	2 N 1 m	5 N 1 m	4 N 1 m	3 N 1 m
Moment about O	+ 2 Nm	− 5 Nm	+ 4 Nm	− 3 Nm

2) Forces act as indicated on a rod AB which is pivoted at A. Find the anticlockwise moment of each force about the pivot.

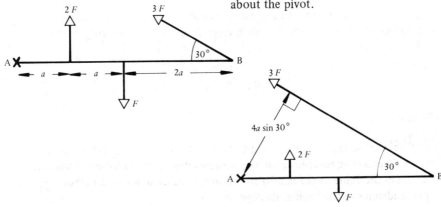

Magnitude of force Distance from A	2F a	F 2a	3F 4a sin 30°
Anticlockwise moment about A	+ 2Fa	− 2Fa	+ 6Fa

3) ABC is an equilateral triangle of side 2 m. Forces of magnitudes P, Q and R act along the sides AB, BC and CA respectively. If the anticlockwise moments about axes perpendicular to the triangle through A, B and C are $+2\sqrt{3}$ Nm, $-4\sqrt{3}$ Nm and $+\sqrt{3}$ Nm respectively, calculate P, Q and R.

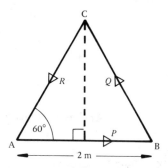

The altitude d of the triangle is $2 \sin 60°$ i.e. $d = \sqrt{3}$.

The anticlockwise torque about A is Qd

Therefore $Qd = +2\sqrt{3}$

$\Rightarrow$ $Q = +2$

About B the anticlockwise torque is Rd

Therefore $Rd = -4\sqrt{3}$

$\Rightarrow$ $R = -4$

(the negative sign shows that R is in the direction $\overrightarrow{AC}$ and not $\overrightarrow{CA}$).

Similarly about C $Pd = +\sqrt{3}$

$\Rightarrow$ $P = +1$

Therefore the forces are $\begin{cases} 1\,\text{N in the direction } \overrightarrow{AB} \\ 2\,\text{N in the direction } \overrightarrow{BC} \\ 4\,\text{N in the direction } \overrightarrow{AC} \end{cases}$

EXERCISE 2j

In Questions 1 to 4, calculate the anticlockwise torque of each of the forces acting in the plane of the lamina shown in the diagram, about an axis perpendicular to the lamina, through A.

1)

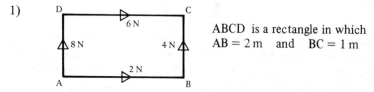

ABCD is a rectangle in which
AB = 2 m   and   BC = 1 m

2)

ABCDEF is a regular hexagon of side $2a$.

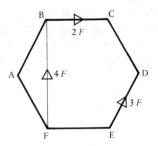

3)

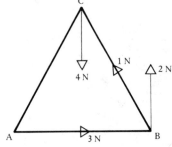

ABC is an equilateral triangle of side 2 m.

4)
BC is a rod pivoted about its
midpoint A
BM = MA = AN = NC = a.

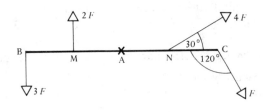

5)

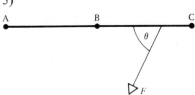

The moment of F about A is
3 Nm clockwise and about B
is 1 Nm clockwise.
If   AB = BC = 1 m   find the
moment of F about C.

6)

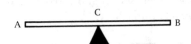

AB is a see-saw of length 4 m, pivoted at its midpoint C. Calculate the
anticlockwise moment, about a horizontal axis through C, of a child of weight
230 N who sits,
a) at A   b) 0.5 m from A   c) at B   d) at C.

RESULTANT TORQUE

When several coplanar forces act on an object, their resultant turning effect about a specified axis is the algebraic sum of the moments of the individual forces about that axis (i.e. the sum of the separate moments taking into account the sign which indicates the sense),

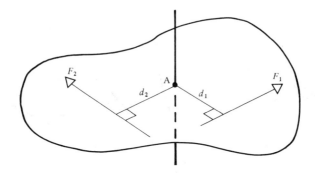

e.g. the resultant moment about the axis through A of forces F_1 and F_2 as shown in the diagram, is the sum of $+F_1 d_1$ and $-F_2 d_2$.
i.e. the torque about A is $F_1 d_1 - F_2 d_2$.

This important principle formulates the following property of forces:

The resultant moment of a set of forces is equal to the moment about the same axis of the resultant force.

A proof of this statement is given below but readers who have not yet done much trigonometry may prefer to leave this section until they are familiar with the factor formulae.

Consider two forces F_1 and F_2 which meet at a point O, enclosing an angle θ, and whose resultant is F_3.

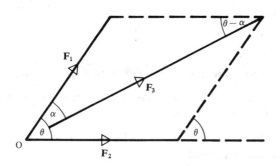

Using the sine rule gives

$$\frac{F_1}{\sin(\theta - \alpha)} = \frac{F_2}{\sin \alpha} = \frac{F_3}{\sin \theta} \qquad [1]$$

Now consider any point A in the plane of the forces, whose perpendicular distances from the lines of action of F_1, F_2 and F_3 are d_1, d_2 and d_3 respectively. AO is of length l and is inclined at an angle β to the line of action of F_1.

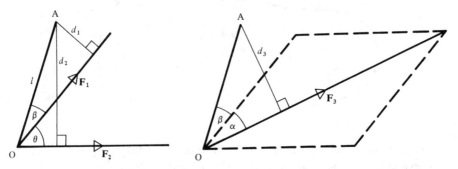

About an axis through A, perpendicular to the plane of the forces, the resultant moment of F_1 and F_2 is $F_1 d_1 + F_2 d_2$ anticlockwise, i.e.

$$F_1 l \sin \beta + F_2 l \sin (\theta + \beta)$$

$$= \frac{F_3 \sin (\theta - \alpha)}{\sin \theta} (l \sin \beta) + \frac{F_3 \sin \alpha}{\sin \theta} (l \sin (\theta + \beta)) \qquad \text{(from [1])}$$

$$= \frac{F_3 l}{\sin \theta} \left\{ \sin \beta \sin (\theta - \alpha) + \sin \alpha \sin (\theta + \beta) \right\}$$

$$= \frac{F_3 l}{2 \sin \theta} \left\{ \cos (\beta - \theta + \alpha) - \cos(\beta + \theta - \alpha) + \cos(\theta + \beta - \alpha) - \cos (\alpha + \theta + \beta) \right\}$$

$$= \frac{F_3 l}{2 \sin \theta} \left\{ 2 \sin (\alpha + \beta) \sin \theta \right\}$$

$$= F_3 l \sin (\alpha + \beta)$$

This is also the anticlockwise moment of F_3 about the same axis.

Therefore, for two forces, the torque about A of the resultant force is equal to the combined torque of the separate forces.

This argument can be applied successively to further forces in order to establish the general Principle of Moments.

EXAMPLES 2k

1) Forces of magnitudes 2 N, 3 N, 1 N and 5 N act along the sides $\overrightarrow{AB}, \overrightarrow{BC}, \overrightarrow{DC}$ and $\overrightarrow{AD}$ respectively of a square ABCD of side 1 m. What is their resultant moment about (a) an axis through A (b) an axis through C?

Giving a positive sign to a torque in the sense ABC (i.e. anticlockwise in the diagram) we have:

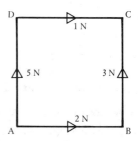

(a) About an axis through A:
   The individual moments are $+3$ Nm and -1 Nm (the forces of 5 N and 2 N pass through A so their moment is zero).

   Therefore the resultant moment is $(+3-1)$ Nm $= +2$ Nm
   i.e. 2 Nm in the sense ABC.

(b) About an axis through C:
   The individual moments are $+2$ Nm and -5 Nm

   Therefore the resultant moment is -3 Nm
   i.e. 3 Nm in the sense CBA.

Note. In this problem the diagram can be lettered correctly in several different ways. A force which in one diagram has an anticlockwise moment may cause clockwise rotation in another as the following example shows.

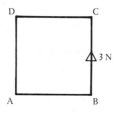

3 Nm anticlockwise about A

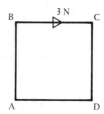

3 Nm clockwise about A

This ambiguity is avoided when the positive sense is specified by *letter order*. In either of the above diagrams the torque is 3 Nm in the sense ABC.

2) Two forces of magnitudes P and $\sqrt{3}P$ act in the plane of a square ABCD as shown in the figure. If $AB = a$ find the resultant moment about an axis perpendicular to the square, through A.

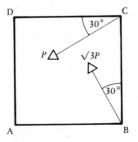

In this problem the perpendicular distance from A to the force P is not immediately obvious. On such occasions it is often better to resolve the force into components whose distances from the axis are more easily obtained.

Resolving the force P along $\overrightarrow{CD}$ and $\overrightarrow{CB}$ and the force $\sqrt{3}P$ along $\overrightarrow{BA}$ and $\overrightarrow{BC}$ we see that, about an axis through A, the individual moments are:

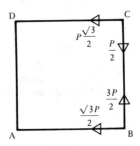

$$+Pa\frac{\sqrt{3}}{2}, \quad -\frac{Pa}{2}, \quad +\frac{3Pa}{2}, \quad \text{zero}$$

(anticlockwise moments are positive).

Therefore the resultant moment is $\frac{1}{2}Pa(\sqrt{3}-1+3)$

i.e. $\frac{1}{2}(2+\sqrt{3})Pa$ anticlockwise.

3) ABCD is a rectangle in which $AB = 2\,m$ and $BC = 1\,m$. A force of $2\,N$ acts along $\overrightarrow{BC}$. If the magnitude of the resultant torque about A is to be $6\,Nm$ in the sense ABC find the extra forces needed if:
(a) only one more force acts along CD,
(b) two more forces, of equal magnitude, act along BC and CD.

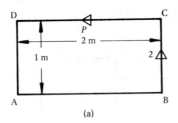

(a)

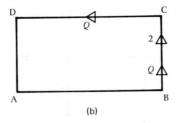

(b)

(a) If the one extra force along CD is of magnitude P newton then the individual moments about A in the sense ABC are $+4\,Nm$ and $+P$ newton metre. But the resultant moment is $+6\,Nm$

Therefore $4+P = 6$ $\Rightarrow$ $P = 2$.

Hence a force of $2\,N$ is required along $\overrightarrow{CD}$.

(b) If the two extra forces along BC and CD are each of magnitude Q newton, the individual moments are $+2Q$ newton metre and $+Q$ newton metre.

Therefore $2Q+4+Q=6 \Rightarrow Q=\frac{2}{3}$.

Hence forces of magnitude $\frac{2}{3}$ N are required along $\overrightarrow{BC}$ and $\overrightarrow{CD}$.

4) Find the resultant torque of the following forces, about an axis through the point with position vector $\mathbf{i}+\mathbf{j}$,

$\mathbf{F_1} = 4\mathbf{i}+7\mathbf{j}$ acting through the point $\mathbf{r_1} = -4\mathbf{i}+3\mathbf{j}$
$\mathbf{F_2} = -\mathbf{i}-2\mathbf{j}$ acting through the point $\mathbf{r_2} = \mathbf{i}-\mathbf{j}$
$\mathbf{F_3} = 6\mathbf{j}$ acting through the point $\mathbf{r_3} = 5\mathbf{i}$

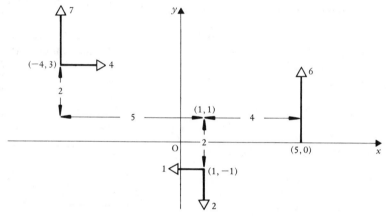

Taking the clockwise sense as positive, the moment of each force about the axis through $(1,1)$ is

for $\mathbf{F_1}$ $7 \times 5 \; + \; 4 \times 2 \; = \; +43$ units
for $\mathbf{F_2}$ $1 \times 2 \;\;\;\;\;\;\;\;\;\;\;\;\;\; = \; +2$ units
for $\mathbf{F_3}$ $-6 \times 4 \;\;\;\;\;\;\;\;\;\;\; = \; -24$ units

The resultant torque is therefore 21 units clockwise.

EXERCISE 2k

In Questions 1–4 all forces act in the plane of the lamina. Calculate the resultant torque about an axis through A perpendicular to the lamina, stating the sense in which it acts.

1)
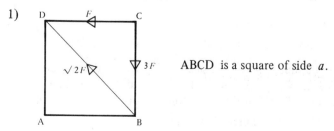

ABCD is a square of side a.

2) ABCDEF is a regular hexagon of side $2a$.

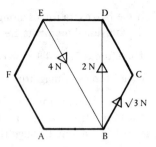

3)

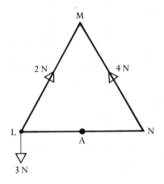

ABC is a metal rod bent at B to a right angle.
AB = $4a$ and BC = a.
M is the mid-point of AB.

4) LMN is an equilateral triangle of side 1 m and A bisects LN.

5) Forces represented by $5\mathbf{i}$, $4\mathbf{i}+2\mathbf{j}$, $-3\mathbf{j}$, $\mathbf{i}-6\mathbf{j}$ act respectively through points with position vectors $\mathbf{i}+\mathbf{j}$, $\mathbf{i}-\mathbf{j}$, $3\mathbf{j}$, $4\mathbf{i}$. Find their resultant moment about an axis through (a) the origin (b) the point $(-2, -1)$

6) Calculate the anticlockwise moment of each of the following forces about an axis through O.
$\mathbf{F}_1 = 4\mathbf{i}+2\mathbf{j}$ and acts through a point $\mathbf{r}_1 = \mathbf{i}+\mathbf{j}$
$\mathbf{F}_2 = 3\mathbf{i}-5\mathbf{j}$ and acts through a point $\mathbf{r}_2 = 2\mathbf{i}-\mathbf{j}$
$\mathbf{F}_3 = 4\mathbf{i}$ and acts through a point $\mathbf{r}_3 = 3\mathbf{j}$
$\mathbf{F}_4 = -6\mathbf{j}$ and acts through a point $\mathbf{r}_4 = \mathbf{i}-6\mathbf{j}$.

7) O is the centre of a square ABCD of side 1 m. Calculate the magnitudes of three forces which act along AB, BC and CD such that the resultant moment, in the sense ABC, about A is -1 Nm, about B is $+3$ Nm and about O is $+5$ Nm.

SUMMARY

1) When lines representing vectors in magnitude and direction are drawn consecutively, the line which completes the polygon represents the resultant vector in magnitude and direction but not necessarily in position.

2) The resultant of two vectors **P** and **Q** inclined at an angle θ has magnitude R given by $R^2 = P^2 + Q^2 + 2PQ \cos\theta$.

3) The resultant of more than two coplanar vectors is calculated by resolving in two perpendicular directions.

4) The moment of a force of magnitude F about an axis distant d from the line of action of F is given by Fd.

5) Two vectors **a** and **b** are parallel if $\mathbf{a} = \lambda\mathbf{b}$.

6) A vector of magnitude V in a direction **d** is given by $V\hat{\mathbf{d}}$.

7) A line through a point with position vector **a** and in a direction **d** has a vector equation $\mathbf{r} = \mathbf{a} + \lambda\mathbf{d}$.

MULTIPLE CHOICE EXERCISE 2
(The instructions for answering these questions are given on page x.)

TYPE I

1) The resultant of displacements 2 m South, 4 m West, 5 m North is of magnitude:
(a) 3 m (b) 7 m (c) 5 m (d) $\sqrt{65}$ m (e) 11 m.

2) If ABCD is a quadrilateral whose sides represent vectors, $\overrightarrow{AB}$ is equivalent to:
(a) $\overrightarrow{CA} + \overrightarrow{CB}$ (b) $\overrightarrow{CD}$ (c) $\overrightarrow{AD} + \overrightarrow{DC} + \overrightarrow{CB}$ (d) $\overrightarrow{AD} + \overrightarrow{BD}$ (e) $\overrightarrow{AC} - \overrightarrow{CB}$.

3) The horizontal component of a force of 10 N inclined at $30°$ to the vertical is:
(a) 5 N (b) $5\sqrt{3}$ N (c) 3 N (d) $\dfrac{10}{3}$ N (e) $\dfrac{10}{\sqrt{3}}$ N.

4) Two vectors inclined at an angle θ have magnitudes 3 N and 5 N and their resultant is of magnitude 4 N. The angle θ is:
(a) $90°$ (b) $\arccos \frac{4}{5}$ (c) $\arccos \frac{3}{5}$ (d) $\arccos -\frac{3}{5}$ (e) $60°$.

5) Two forces $\mathbf{F}_1$ and $\mathbf{F}_2$ have a resultant $\mathbf{F}_3$. If $\mathbf{F}_1 = 2\mathbf{i} - 3\mathbf{j}$ and $\mathbf{F}_3 = 5\mathbf{i} + 4\mathbf{j}$ then $\mathbf{F}_2$ is:
(a) $7\mathbf{i} + \mathbf{j}$ (b) $-3\mathbf{i} - 7\mathbf{j}$ (c) $3\mathbf{i} + 7\mathbf{j}$ (d) $7\mathbf{i} + 7\mathbf{j}$.

6)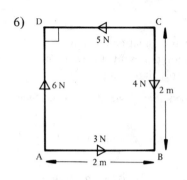

The forces in the diagram have a resultant anticlockwise torque about an axis through **B** of:

(a) 2 Nm   (b) 22 Nm

(c) −2 Nm   (d) −4 Nm.

7) A light rod, pivoted at **A**, has forces applied to it as indicated. The rod will:

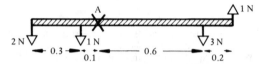

(a) rotate clockwise,

(b) rotate anticlockwise,

(c) remain horizontal.

8)

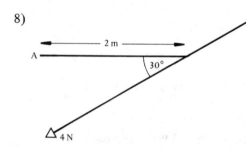

The moment of the force shown in the diagram, about a perpendicular axis through **A**, is of magnitude:

(a) 8 Nm   (b) −8 Nm

(c) −4 Nm   (d) 4 Nm.

TYPE II

9) $\overrightarrow{AB}$ and $\overrightarrow{PQ}$ are two vectors such that $\overrightarrow{AB} = 2\overrightarrow{PQ}$.

(a) AB is parallel to PQ.

(b) PQ is twice as long as AB.

(c) A, B, P and Q must be collinear.

10) The vector equation $\overrightarrow{AC} = \overrightarrow{AB} + \overrightarrow{BC}$ applies directly to:

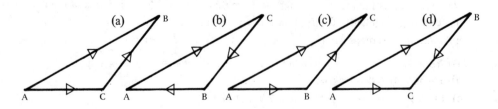

11) ABCD is a parallelogram.

(a) $\overrightarrow{AB} = \overrightarrow{CD}$ (b) $\overrightarrow{AD} = \overrightarrow{BC}$ (c) $\overrightarrow{AB} + \overrightarrow{BC} = \overrightarrow{CD} + \overrightarrow{DA}$
(d) $\overrightarrow{BC} + \overrightarrow{CD} = \overrightarrow{BA} + \overrightarrow{AD}$.

12) A force $F = 3i + 4j$.

(a) The magnitude of the force is 5 units.
(b) The force acts through the origin.
(c) The direction of the force is at $\arctan \frac{4}{3}$ to the x axis.

13) A force $F_1 = 2i - 3j$ acts through a point $i - 2j$ and a force
$F_2 = 4i + 5j$ acts through a point $2i + j$.

(a) The magnitude of F_1 is $\sqrt{13}$ units.
(b) The moment of F_1 about the origin is of magnitude 1 unit.
(c) The magnitude of F_2 is 3 units.

TYPE III

14)   (a) The moment of a force of magnitude k newtons, about an axis through
         A, is zero.
      (b) A force of magnitude k newtons acts through A.

15)   (a) A force $F = 2i + 3j$.
      (b) A force has perpendicular components of magnitudes 2 and 3 units.

16) AB and PQ are two lines in the same plane:

(a) AB = 3PQ.
(b) $\overrightarrow{AB} = 3\overrightarrow{PQ}$.

17) ABC is a triangle:

(a) $\overrightarrow{AC} = \overrightarrow{AB} + \overrightarrow{BC}$.
(b) $\overrightarrow{AB} = \overrightarrow{AC} + \overrightarrow{CB}$.

TYPE IV

18) Calculate the magnitude of the resultant of two forces F_1 and F_2.

(a) $F_1 = 3i + 7j$.
(b) $F_2 = i - 4j$.
(c) Both forces act at a point with position vector $2i + j$.

19) ABCDEF is a hexagon. Find, in terms of **a** and **b**, the vectors which the
remaining sides represent.

(a) $\overrightarrow{AB} = \mathbf{a}$.
(b) The hexagon is regular.
(c) $\overrightarrow{FC} = \mathbf{b}$.

20) Six forces acting on a particle have directions parallel to the sides AB, BC, CD, DE, EF, FA of a hexagon. Find the magnitude and direction of their resultant.
(a) The forces have magnitudes $F, 2F, 3F, 2F, 2F, F$ respectively.
(b) The sense of each force is indicated by the order of the letters.
(c) The hexagon is regular.

21) Express a force **F** in the form $a\mathbf{i} + b\mathbf{j}$.
(a) The magnitude of the force is 5 N.
(b) The force is inclined at $60°$ to the horizontal.
(c) **j** is in the direction of the upward vertical.

22) Calculate the moment of a force about an axis through a point A:
(a) the magnitude of the force is 10 N,
(b) the sense of rotation is clockwise,
(c) the axis is perpendicular to the force.

23) 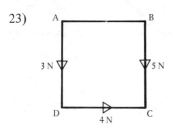 ABCD is a square of side 2 m. Find the position of the point X through which a perpendicular axis passes if, about that axis:
(a) the moment of the 3 N force is 4.5 Nm,
(b) the moment of the 4 N force is 2 Nm,
(c) the resultant moment is 4 Nm.

TYPE V

24) The resultant of $\overrightarrow{AB}$ and $\overrightarrow{BC}$ is $\overrightarrow{CA}$.

25) Two vectors of equal magnitude and which are in the same direction are equal vectors.

26) A particle of weight W is on a plane inclined at α to the horizontal. The component of the weight parallel to the plane is $W \cos \alpha$.

27) The resultant of two vectors of magnitudes P and Q and inclined at $60°$ is $\sqrt{P^2 + Q^2 - PQ}$.

28) If $\mathbf{F}_1 = 2\mathbf{i} + 3\mathbf{j}$ and $\mathbf{F}_2 = 2\mathbf{i} - 3\mathbf{j}$ then $\mathbf{F}_1$ and $\mathbf{F}_2$ are equal and opposite.

29) A square ABCD can be rotated in a vertical plane about the side AB.

30) The resultant moment of a set of forces about an axis is independent of the axis.

MISCELLANEOUS EXERCISE 2

1) A force of $30\,N$ is inclined at an angle θ to the horizontal. If its vertical component is $18\,N$, find the horizontal component and the value of θ.

2) Resolve a vector into two perpendicular components so that:
(a) the components are of equal magnitudes,
(b) the magnitude of one component is twice that of the other.

3) Forces of magnitudes $2, 3, 2$ and 5 newton act at a point. The angles between them are $30°, 60°$ and $30°$ respectively. Calculate their resultant and verify your results by drawing a suitable scale diagram.

4) Forces represented by $3i + 5j$, $i - 2j$ and $3i + j$ together with a fourth force **F** act on a particle. If the resultant force is represented by $4i + j$, find **F**.

5) ABCDEF is a regular hexagon. Forces acting along $\overrightarrow{CB}$, $\overrightarrow{CA}$, $\overrightarrow{CF}$ and $\overrightarrow{CD}$ are of magnitudes $2, 4, 5$ and 6 newton respectively. What is the inclination of their resultant to CF?

6) If **a** represents a velocity of $4\,m\,s^{-1}$ North East and **b** represents a velocity of $6\,m\,s^{-1}$ West, what velocities are represented by:
(a) $-2a$ (b) $a + b$ (c) $3b - a$?

7) In a regular pentagon ABCDE:
(a) what is the resultant of: (i) $\overrightarrow{AB} + \overrightarrow{BC}$ (ii) $\overrightarrow{EA} - \overrightarrow{BA}$,
(b) prove that $\overrightarrow{AD} + \overrightarrow{DC} = \overrightarrow{AB} - \overrightarrow{CB}$.

8) ABCD is a parallelogram. What represents the resultant of forces represented by $\overrightarrow{AB}$, $\overrightarrow{BC}$, $\overrightarrow{BD}$ and $\overrightarrow{CA}$?

9) ABC is an equilateral triangle and D is the mid-point of BC. Forces of $1, 2, 4$ and $3\sqrt{3}$ newton act along $\overrightarrow{BC}$, $\overrightarrow{BA}$, $\overrightarrow{CA}$ and $\overrightarrow{AD}$ respectively. Resolve each of the forces in the directions BC and DA and verify that the sum of the components in each direction is zero.

10) A force of $2\sqrt{2}\,N$ acts along the diagonal AC of a square ABCD and another force P acts along AD. If the resultant force is inclined at $60°$ to AB find the value of P.

11) Forces of magnitudes $2P, 4P, 3P$ and P act on a particle in directions parallel to the sides $\overrightarrow{AB}$, $\overrightarrow{BC}$, $\overrightarrow{CD}$ and $\overrightarrow{DE}$ of a regular hexagon. Find the magnitude and direction of their resultant.

12) Forces $2i - 3j$, $5i + j$, $-4i + 7j$ act through points with position vectors $i + j$, $-2i + 2j$, $3i - 4j$ respectively. Find their resultant moment about
(a) the origin,
(b) the point with position vector $i - j$.

13) Forces of magnitudes $2\,N$, $3\,N$, $4\,N$ and $5\,N$ act along the lines $\overrightarrow{AB}$, $\overrightarrow{BC}$, $\overrightarrow{ED}$ and $\overrightarrow{AD}$ respectively where ABCDEF is a regular hexagon of side $2\,m$. Find the resultant moment about
(a) the centre of the hexagon,
(b) the vertex F.

14) Forces of magnitudes $7\,N$, $4\,N$, $5\,N$ and $X\,N$ act respectively along the sides $\overrightarrow{AB}$, $\overrightarrow{CB}$, $\overrightarrow{CD}$ and $\overrightarrow{AD}$ of a rectangle ABCD in which $AB = 2AD$. If the resultant moment about the midpoint of AD is twice the resultant moment about the midpoint of AB, find X.

15) Forces of $9, 2, 5$ and 1 newton act along the sides OA, AB, BC and CO of a rectangle OABC and a force of 15 newtons acts along AC. $OA = 4a$ and $AB = 3a$. Taking OA and OC as x and y axes respectively find an expression for the resultant force vector in the form $Xi + Yj$.

16) A quadrilateral ABCD has opposite sides AB and DC parallel. Angle $ABC = 150°$ and angle $BAD = 60°$. Forces $2P, P, P, 2P$ act along $\overrightarrow{AB}$, $\overrightarrow{BC}$, $\overrightarrow{CD}$, $\overrightarrow{AD}$ respectively. Prove that the resultant has magnitude $P(8 + 3\sqrt{3})^{\frac{1}{2}}$ and find the tangent of the angle it makes with AB.

(U of L)

17) Two forces, F_1 and F_2, act through $A(1, 3)$ and $B(1, -2)$ respectively. $F_1 = 2i - j$ and F_2 is of magnitude 10 and acts in a direction $4i + 3j$. Find:
(a) a vector equation for the line of action of each force,
(b) the resultant of F_1 and F_2,
(c) a vector equation for the line of action of the resultant force.

18) Forces P and Q act along lines OA and OB respectively and their resultant is a force of magnitude P. If the force P along OA is replaced by a force $2P$ along OA, the resultant of $2P$ and Q is also a force of magnitude P. Find:
(a) the magnitude of Q in terms of P,
(b) the angle between OA and OB,
(c) the angles which the two resultants make with OA.

(O)

19) A plane lamina has perpendicular axes Ox and Oy marked on it, and is acted upon by the following forces:

$5P$ in the direction Oy,

$4P$ in the direction Ox,

$6P$ in the direction OA where A is the point $(3a, 4a)$,

$8P$ in the direction AB where B is the point $(-a, a)$.

Express each force in the form $p\mathbf{i} + q\mathbf{j}$ and hence calculate the magnitude and direction of the resultant of these forces.

20) The diagonals of the plane quadrilateral ABCD intersect at O, and X, Y are the mid-points of the diagonals AC, BD respectively. Show that:

(a) $\overrightarrow{BA} + \overrightarrow{BC} = 2\overrightarrow{BX}$

(b) $\overrightarrow{BA} + \overrightarrow{BC} + \overrightarrow{DA} + \overrightarrow{DC} = 4\overrightarrow{YX}$

(c) $2\overrightarrow{AB} + 2\overrightarrow{BC} + 2\overrightarrow{CA} = \mathbf{0}$

If $\overrightarrow{OA} + \overrightarrow{OB} + \overrightarrow{OC} + \overrightarrow{OD} = 4\overrightarrow{OM}$, find the location of M.   (AEB)

21) Given two vectors $\overrightarrow{OP}$ and $\overrightarrow{OQ}$ show how to construct geometrically the sum $(\overrightarrow{OP} + \overrightarrow{OQ})$ and the difference $(\overrightarrow{OP} - \overrightarrow{OQ})$.

If X, Y, Z are the mid-points of the lines BC, CA, AB respectively and O is any point in the plane of the triangle ABC, show that

$$\overrightarrow{OA} + \overrightarrow{OB} + \overrightarrow{OC} = \overrightarrow{OX} + \overrightarrow{OY} + \overrightarrow{OZ}$$

and find the position of the point D such that $\overrightarrow{OA} + \overrightarrow{OB} - \overrightarrow{OC} = \overrightarrow{OD}$.

(U of L)

22) Forces of magnitudes $1, 2, 3, 6, 5$ and 4 N act respectively along the sides $\overrightarrow{AB}, \overrightarrow{CB}, \overrightarrow{CD}, \overrightarrow{ED}, \overrightarrow{EF}$ and $\overrightarrow{AF}$ of a regular hexagon of side a. Find their resultant moment about axes perpendicular to the hexagon through

(a) A   (b) B   (c) the centre of the hexagon.

23) Forces of magnitudes $F, 2F, pF, 3\sqrt{2}F$ and $q\sqrt{2}F$ act along AB, BC, DC, AC and BD respectively, where ABCD is a square of side $2a$ (the order of the letters indicates the direction of each force).

If the magnitude of the resultant torque, in the sense DCB, about an axis through A perpendicular to ABCD is $4Fa$ and the resultant force is of magnitude $10F$, find p and q.

CHAPTER 3

COPLANAR FORCES
IN EQUILIBRIUM. FRICTION

THE STATE OF EQUILIBRIUM

A set of coplanar forces acting on an object can be reduced (using methods discussed in Chapter 2) to a single resultant force. The effect of this linear resultant on the object would be to move it in a straight line. In addition, the set of forces may have a resultant turning effect which would cause the object to rotate. Forces which have zero linear resultant and zero turning effect will not cause any change in the motion of the object to which they are applied.

Such forces (and the object) are said to be in *equilibrium*.

A set of concurrent forces has zero turning effect about the point of concurrence, so,

concurrent forces are in equilibrium if their linear resultant is zero.

It is important to remember, however, that non-concurrent forces with zero linear resultant are not necessarily in equilibrium.

Equilibrium of Concurrent Coplanar Forces

We have already seen that there are basically two ways of finding the linear resultant of a set of forces:
(a) by drawing a vector diagram in which lines representing the given forces form all but one side of a polygon. The last side then represents the resultant,
(b) by resolving and collecting the forces in each of two perpendicular directions.

When the forces are in equilibrium their resultant is zero and the above methods can be adapted as follows:

(a) The side representing the resultant is now of zero length, i.e. the given forces themselves can be represented by the sides of a closed polygon,

e.g. if the forces in diagram (i) are in equilibrium, the corresponding vector diagram will be as in diagram (ii).

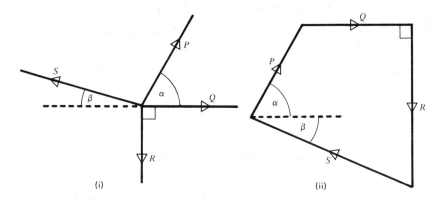

(i)   (ii)

(b) When the given forces are resolved and collected in two perpendicular directions, the magnitude of the resultant, F, is normally calculated using $F = \sqrt{(X^2 + Y^2)}$.

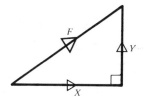

Neither X^2 nor Y^2 can ever be negative. So F is zero only if

$$X = 0 \quad \text{and} \quad Y = 0.$$

E.g. in diagram (i) above, resolving parallel and perpendicular to the force Q we have:

$\rightarrow$ $$X = Q + P\cos\alpha - S\cos\beta = 0$$

$\uparrow$ $$Y = P\sin\alpha + S\sin\beta - R = 0$$

These two equations give the condition for P, Q, R and S to be in equilibrium.

Either of the methods above can be used to solve problems where the forces are in equilibrium.

EXAMPLES 3a

1) ABCDEF is a regular hexagon and O is its centre. Forces of $1, 2, 3, 4, P, Q$ newton act at O in the directions OA, OB, OC, OD, OE, OF respectively. If the six forces are in equilibrium find the values of P and Q.

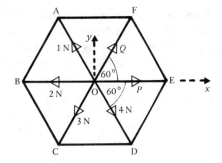

Resolving all forces in the directions
Ox and Oy and using $X = 0$ and
$Y = 0$ we have:

$\rightarrow \quad X = P + Q \cos 60° + 4 \cos 60° - 1 \cos 60° - 2 - 3 \cos 60° = 0 \qquad [1]$

$\uparrow \quad Y = Q \sin 60° + 1 \sin 60° - 4 \sin 60° - 3 \sin 60° = 0 \qquad [2]$

From [1] $P + \tfrac{1}{2}Q = 2$
From [2] $Q = 6$

Therefore the required values are $P = -1$ and $Q = 6$.
($P = -1$ indicates a force of 1 N along EO.)

2) Four forces of magnitudes 4 N, 3 N, 1 N and $3\sqrt{2}$ N act on a particle as
shown in the diagram. Prove, using a polygon of forces, that the particle is in
equilibrium.

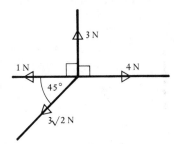

The polygon ABCDE is constructed so that AB, BC, CD and DE represent the
forces 4 N, 3 N, 1 N and $3\sqrt{2}$ N respectively in magnitude and direction.

But $DF = 3\sqrt{2} \cos 45° = 3$ units

and $EF = 3\sqrt{2} \sin 45° = 3$ units

Therefore $DF = CB$

Therefore E and F are both on AB.

Also $EF + DC = AB$

Therefore E coincides with A.

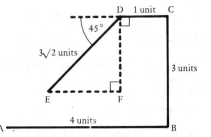

The four given concurrent forces therefore form a closed vector polygon and
so are in equilibrium.

Equilibrant

A set of forces which is not in equilibrium may be reduced to equilibrium by the introduction of one extra force. This force is then called the *equilibrant* of the original set. Since it counteracts the resultant effect of the original set of forces,

the equilibrant of a system is equal and opposite to the resultant of that system.

3) Four forces acting on a particle are represented by $2i + 3j$, $4i - 7j$, $-5i + 4j$ and $i - j$. Find the resultant force vector $\mathbf{F}$. A fifth force $pi + qj$ is added to the system which is then in equilibrium. Find p and q and check that $pi + qj = -\mathbf{F}$.

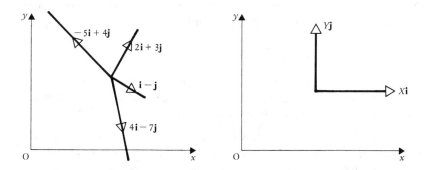

$$\mathbf{F} = X\mathbf{i} + Y\mathbf{j} = (4 + 1 + 2 - 5)\mathbf{i} + (-7 - 1 + 3 + 4)\mathbf{j}$$
$$\Rightarrow \qquad \mathbf{F} = 2\mathbf{i} - \mathbf{j}.$$

Now considering the set of five forces which are in equilibrium and hence have a resultant represented by $0\mathbf{i} + 0\mathbf{j}$ we have:

$$(2\mathbf{i} + 3\mathbf{j}) + (4\mathbf{i} - 7\mathbf{j}) + (-5\mathbf{i} + 4\mathbf{j}) + (\mathbf{i} - \mathbf{j}) + (p\mathbf{i} + q\mathbf{j}) = 0\mathbf{i} + 0\mathbf{j}$$

Therefore $2 + 4 - 5 + 1 + p = 0 \Rightarrow p = -2$

and $3 - 7 + 4 - 1 + q = 0 \Rightarrow q = +1$

The fifth force is therefore $-2\mathbf{i} + \mathbf{j} = -(2\mathbf{i} - \mathbf{j}) = -\mathbf{F}$

EXERCISE 3a

1) ABCD is a square. A force of 2 N acts along AB. Find the magnitude of forces acting along AC and AD if the three forces are in equilibrium.

2) In a regular hexagon ABCDEF, forces of magnitudes 2 N, 4 N, 3 N and 2 N act along the lines AB, AC, AD and AF respectively. Find the equilibrant of the given forces and verify that it is equal and opposite to their resultant.

3) Forces $2i + 3j$, $i - 7j$, $4i + j$ and $-3i - j$ act on a particle. Find the resultant force. What is its magnitude? What extra force would keep the particle in equilibrium?

4) Five forces are in equilibrium. Four of the forces are $9i - j$, $4i + 6j$, $-5i - 2j$ and $2i + j$. What is the fifth force?

5) Three forces, $2i + j$, $7i - 2j$ and $3i + 4j$ act on a particle. A fourth force **F** is introduced to keep the particle in equilibrium. Find **F**.

6) A ring of weight 2 N is threaded on to a string whose ends are fixed to two points A and B in a horizontal line. The ring is pulled aside by a horizontal force P newton parallel to AB. When the ring is in equilibrium the two sections of the string are inclined to the vertical at angles of $40°$ and $20°$. Find the two possible values of P.

7) ABCDEF is a regular hexagon. Forces represented by $\overrightarrow{AB}, \overrightarrow{FA}, \overrightarrow{BC}$ and $2\overrightarrow{DE}$ act on a particle. Prove that the particle is in equilibrium.

THREE FORCES IN EQUILIBRIUM

The methods already discussed can be applied to problems on any number of forces, including three. The situation where *just* three forces are in equilibrium, however, is of particular interest and special methods are applicable.

Consider three forces P, Q and R which are in equilibrium. Lines representing, in magnitude and direction, a set of vectors in equilibrium, form a closed polygon. In this case the polygon is a triangle and is often referred to as the *triangle of forces*.

The formal statement of this property is:

Three forces which are in equilibrium can be represented in magnitude, direction and sense by the sides of a triangle taken in order.

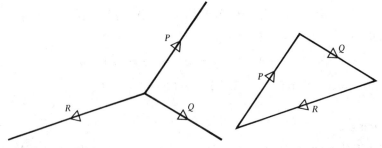

Conversely,

If a triangle can be found whose sides, in order, have the same directions as three concurrent forces in equilibrium, then the magnitudes of the forces are proportional to the sides of the triangle.

EXAMPLES 3b

1) One end of a string 0.5 m long is fixed to a point A and the other end is fastened to a small object of weight 8 N. The object is pulled aside by a horizontal force, P, until it is 0.3 m from the vertical through A. Find the magnitudes of the tension, T, in the string and the force P.

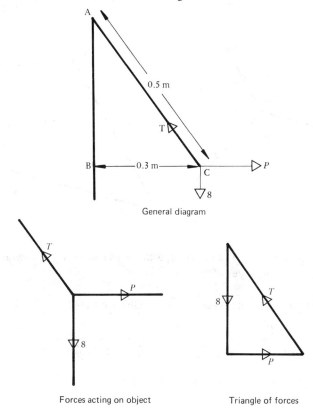

General diagram

Forces acting on object   Triangle of forces

Triangle ABC is a suitable triangle of forces since

AB is in the same direction as the weight
BC is in the same direction as P
CA is in the same direction as T

Then $\dfrac{8}{AB} = \dfrac{P}{BC} = \dfrac{T}{CA}$

But the length of AB is 0.4 m (Pythagoras).

Hence $\dfrac{8}{0.4} = \dfrac{P}{0.3} = \dfrac{T}{0.5}$

The tension in the string is therefore 10 N and the horizontal force is 6 N.

LAMI'S THEOREM

Consider again three forces P, Q and R which are in equilibrium, and the corresponding triangle of forces ABC.

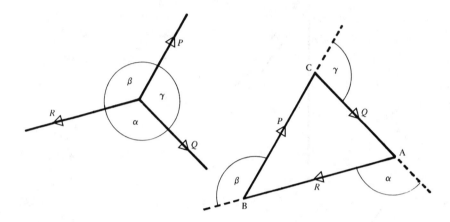

If the angles between P, Q and R are α, β and γ as shown in the diagram, then α, β and γ are exterior angles of triangle ABC.

Applying the sine rule to the vector triangle ABC we have

$$\frac{P}{\sin(180° - \alpha)} = \frac{Q}{\sin(180° - \beta)} = \frac{R}{\sin(180° - \gamma)}$$

But since $\sin(180° - \alpha) = \sin \alpha$, a simpler form is

$$\frac{P}{\sin \alpha} = \frac{Q}{\sin \beta} = \frac{R}{\sin \gamma}$$

This property of three forces in equilibrium is known as *Lami's Theorem* and is a very neat method of solving many *three force* problems.

EXAMPLES 3b (continued)

2) One end of a string is fixed to a point A and the other end is fastened to a small object of weight 8 N. The object is pulled aside by a horizontal force until the string is inclined at $30°$ to the vertical through A. Find the magnitudes of the tension in the string and the horizontal force.

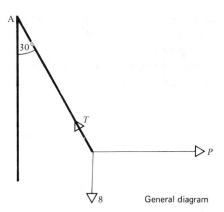

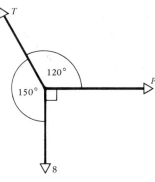

General diagram   Forces acting on object

Applying Lami's Theorem we have

$$\frac{8}{\sin 120°} = \frac{P}{\sin 150°} = \frac{T}{\sin 90°}$$

i.e.

$$\frac{8}{\sqrt{\frac{3}{2}}} = \frac{P}{\frac{1}{2}} = \frac{T}{1}$$

Therefore the tension is $\dfrac{16\sqrt{3}}{3}$ N   and the horizontal force is $\dfrac{8\sqrt{3}}{3}$ N.

Note the similarity between Examples 1 and 2.

The *lengths* given in Example 1 suggested using the triangle of forces method whereas the *angles* given in Example 2 suggested the use of Lami's Theorem. It is also interesting to observe that either problem could have been solved by resolving the forces horizontally and vertically as in the earlier examples.

Concurrence Property

If three non-parallel forces are in equilibrium their lines of action must be concurrent.

It is easy to see that this must be true by considering three forces P, Q and R which are known to be in equilibrium.

If P and Q meet at a point A, then their resultant, S, also passes through A.

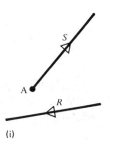

(i)

The original three forces have now been reduced to two and these two, shown in diagram (i), are to be in equilibrium. R and S therefore have zero linear resultant and zero turning effect.

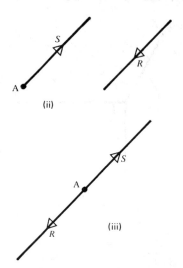

(ii)

Hence R and S are equal in magnitude and in opposite directions.
If the positions of R and S are as shown in diagram (ii) however, they have a turning effect.

This turning effect will be zero only when R and S are collinear, as in diagram (iii) and in this case R also passes through A.
Therefore in order that P, Q and R shall be in equilibrium, all three forces must pass through A.

(iii)

This property is of considerable value in solving problems where one of three forces in equilibrium would otherwise have an unknown direction.

EXAMPLES 3b (continued)

3) A uniform rod AB of weight $12\,\text{N}$ is hinged to a vertical wall at A. The end B is pulled aside by a horizontal force until it is in equilibrium inclined at $60°$ to the wall. Find the magnitude of the horizontal force and the direction of the force acting at the hinge.

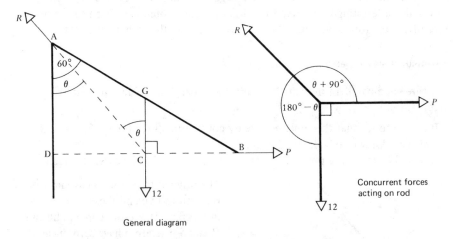

Concurrent forces acting on rod

General diagram

The rod is in equilibrium under the action of three forces only, so these three forces must be concurrent. The weight and the horizontal force P meet at C so the hinge force must also pass through C. But the hinge force acts at A so its direction must be CA produced.

First we deal with the mensuration of the general diagram.
G is the midpoint of AB and GC is parallel to AD so C is the midpoint of DB.

Now
$$\tan \theta = \frac{DC}{AD} = \frac{\frac{1}{2}DB}{AD} = \frac{1}{2}\tan 60° = \frac{\sqrt{3}}{2}$$

Hence
$$\theta = 40.9°$$

Applying Lami's Theorem we have

$$\frac{12}{\sin(\theta + 90°)} = \frac{P}{\sin(180° - \theta)} \left(= \frac{R}{\sin 90°} \text{ which is not needed} \right)$$

$$\Rightarrow \qquad P = \frac{12 \sin 139.1°}{\sin 130.9°} = 10.4$$

Therefore the horizontal force is of magnitude 10.4 N and the hinge force is inclined at 40.9° to the wall.

Problem Solving

The methods so far available for solving problems involving three concurrent forces in equilibrium, use
(a) the 'triangle of forces',
(b) Lami's Theorem,
(c) resolution in two perpendicular directions.

In attempting to select the best approach to a particular problem the following points should be noted.

1) A diagram including a suitable triangle whose sides are given (or are simple to calculate) suggests the use of method (a). It is not, however, worth introducing special construction to create a suitable triangle.

2) When the angles between pairs of forces are known, Lami's Theorem is often the best method.

3) If two of the three forces are in perpendicular directions, resolving in these directions gives a quick and easy solution.

It is important in all cases to remember that *three non-parallel forces in equilibrium must be concurrent*.

EXAMPLES 3b (continued)

4) A small block of weight 20 N is suspended by two strings of lengths 0.6 m and 0.8 m from two points 1 m apart on a horizontal beam. Find the tension in each string.

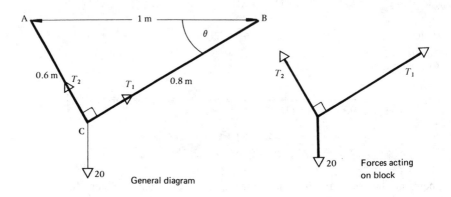

General diagram

Forces acting on block

Triangle ABC is easily recognised as being right-angled at C.

Hence $\cos \theta = 0.8$ and $\sin \theta = 0.6$

Resolving in the directions of T_1 and T_2 gives

$$T_1 - 20 \sin \theta = 0 \quad \Rightarrow \quad T_1 = 0.6 \times 20$$

$$T_2 - 20 \cos \theta = 0 \quad \Rightarrow \quad T_2 = 0.8 \times 20$$

So the tensions in the strings are 12 N and 16 N.

5) A particle of weight W rests on a smooth plane inclined at $30°$ to the horizontal and is held in equilibrium by a string inclined at $30°$ to the plane. Find, in terms of W, the tension in the string.

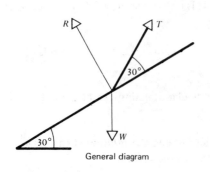

General diagram

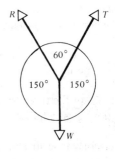

Applying Lami's Theorem we have:

$$\frac{W}{\sin 60^\circ} = \frac{T}{\sin 150^\circ} \left(= \frac{R}{\sin 150^\circ} \text{ which is not needed} \right)$$

Therefore

$$T = \frac{W \sin 150^\circ}{\sin 60^\circ} = \frac{W\sqrt{3}}{3}$$

6) A uniform rod AB of weight 10 N is hinged to a fixed point at A and maintained in a horizontal position by a string attached to B and to a point C vertically above A. If AC = AB = l, find the magnitude and direction of the force at the hinge and the tension in the string.

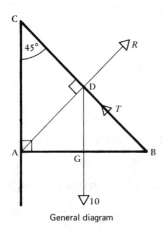

General diagram

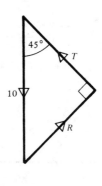

Triangle of forces

The lines of action of the weight of the rod and the tension in the string meet at D. Therefore the third force also passes through D.

D is the midpoint of CB (since AG = GB and DG is parallel to CA).
Therefore $A\hat{D}C = 90^\circ$.

In triangle CAD, $\overrightarrow{CA}$ is parallel to the weight
$\overrightarrow{AD}$ is parallel to the hinge force
$\overrightarrow{DC}$ is parallel to the tension.

Therefore

$$\frac{10}{CA} = \frac{R}{AD} = \frac{T}{DC}$$

But

$$AD = DC = l\cos 45^\circ$$

Therefore

$$R = 10\cos 45^\circ = T$$

The tension in the string is of magnitude 7.07 N and the reaction at the hinge, also of magnitude 7.07 N, is inclined at 45° to the vertical.

7) A point A on a sphere of radius a, weight W and centre O, rests in contact with a smooth vertical wall and is supported by a string of length a joining a point B on the sphere to a point C on the wall. Find the tension in the string in terms of W.

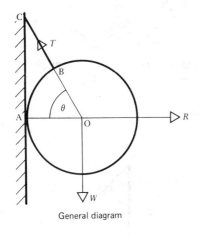

General diagram

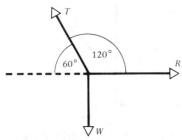

The reaction at the wall and the weight both pass through O, so the line of action of the tension in the string also passes through O. Thus OBC is a straight line and $OC = 2a$.

Hence $\cos\theta = \dfrac{a}{2a} = \dfrac{1}{2}$

$\Rightarrow \qquad \theta = 60°$

Using Lami's Theorem gives

$$\frac{T}{\sin 90°} = \frac{W}{\sin 120°} \left(= \frac{R}{\sin 150°} \right)$$

$\Rightarrow \qquad T = \dfrac{2W}{\sqrt{3}}$

EXERCISE 3b

1) A particle of weight 24 N is attached to one end of a string 1.3 m long whose other end is fastened to a point on a vertical pole. A horizontal force acting on the particle keeps it in equilibrium (a) 0.5 m from the pole (b) so that the string is inclined at $20°$ to the vertical. Calculate the tension in the string and the magnitude of the horizontal force in each case.

2) A small object of weight 10 N rests in equilibrium on a rough plane inclined at $30°$ to the horizontal. Calculate the magnitude of the frictional force.

3) A weight of 26 N is supported by two strings AB and AC of lengths 0.5 m and 1.2 m respectively. If BC is horizontal and of length 1.3 m, calculate the tension in AC and the angle BCA.

4) A small block of weight W rests on a smooth plane of inclination θ to the horizontal. Find the value of θ if:
(a) a force of $\frac{1}{2}W$ parallel to the plane is required to keep the block in equilibrium,
(b) a horizontal force of $\frac{1}{3}W$ keeps the block in equilibrium.

5) A uniform rod AB of weight 20 N is hinged to a fixed point at A. A force acts at B holding the rod in equilibrium at 30° to the vertical through A. Find the magnitude of this force if:
(a) it is perpendicular to AB,
(b) it is horizontal.

6) A uniform rod AB of weight W rests in equilibrium with the end A in contact with a smooth vertical wall and the end B in contact with a smooth plane inclined at 45° to the wall. Find the reactions at A and B in terms of W.

7) Three forces P, Q and R act on a particle. P and Q are perpendicular to each other and the angle between Q and R is 150°. If the magnitude of P is 12 N find the magnitudes of Q and R.

8) A uniform rod AB, hinged to a fixed point at A is held in a horizontal position by a string attached to B and to a point C vertically above A so that angle ACB is 45°. Find the magnitude and direction of the force acting at the hinge.

CONTACT FORCES

Two solid objects in contact exert equal and opposite forces upon each other. The two forces due to frictionless contact are each perpendicular to the common surface of contact and are known as *normal contact forces*, or *normal reactions*, or simply *normals*.
If however the objects are in rough contact and have a tendency to move relative to each other (without losing contact) then frictional forces arise which oppose such potential motion. Again each object exerts a frictional force on the other and the two forces are equal and opposite.

Consider two wooden blocks A and B being rubbed against each other.

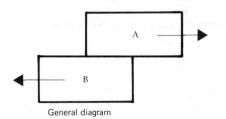

General diagram

In the diagram, A is being moved to the right while B is being moved leftward.

In order to see more clearly which forces act on A and which on B, a second diagram is drawn showing a space between the blocks but they are still supposed to be in contact.

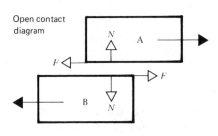

Open contact diagram

The two normal contact forces, each of magnitude N, are perpendicular to the surface of contact between the blocks.

The two frictional forces, each of magnitude F, act along that surface, each in a direction opposing the motion of the block upon which it acts.

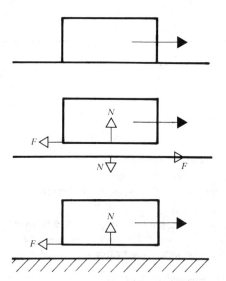

Now consider one block being pushed along the ground as shown. Again each solid object exerts a normal force and a frictional force on the other and these are marked separately on the second diagram. In this case however, the ground is *fixed* and the two forces which act upon it do not have any calculable effect on it. Consequently they are rarely included in the diagrams drawn to illustrate problems. The *fixed* surface is often indicated by shading.

Fixed Objects

The earth is our *frame of reference*, i.e. it is treated as absolutely stationary (fixed) and movement is observed relative to it. Other objects which are immovably attached to the earth become virtually part of its surface and are therefore also fixed. e.g. a wall built on the ground or a pole with its foot bedded in the ground.
A fixed object cannot be moved relative to the earth.
Contact between a moveable object and a fixed one is described as *external* contact and the contact force acting on the moveable object is an *external force*. Contact between two moveable objects is *internal* and the contact forces acting on both objects are *internal forces*.

EXAMPLES 3c

1) A block rests on a smooth horizontal plane and a smooth rod is placed against the block with one end on the ground. Draw diagrams showing the forces acting on the block and on the rod, indicating which contacts are internal and which are external.

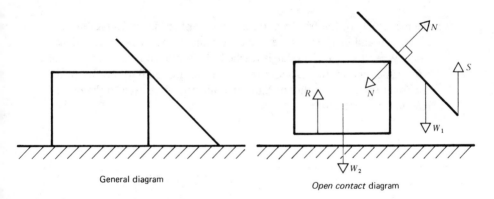

General diagram

Open contact diagram

The forces acting on the rod are
the weight W_1,
the normal reaction, S, with the plane (external contact),
the normal reaction, N, with the block (internal contact).

The forces acting on the block are
the weight W_2,
the normal reaction, R, with the plane (external contact),
the normal reaction, N, with the rod (internal contact).

Forces $R\downarrow$ and $S\downarrow$ which act on the fixed plane are disregarded.

Note that the line of action of N is perpendicular to the *rod*.

FRICTION

Friction is a property of contact between objects.
Two surfaces which can move one across the other without encountering any resistance are in frictionless contact, or *smooth* contact.
Conversely two objects whose relative surface movement is resisted have friction between them and their contact is *rough*.
It is now appreciated that the existence of friction between surfaces does not depend on their roughness or smoothness in the everyday sense of these words. In fact there can be very large frictional forces between two highly polished flat metal surfaces. Consequently it is important, in mechanics, to interpret smooth as *frictionless* rather than *free from projections*.
The results of experimental investigation into the behaviour of frictional forces confirm that:

(a) friction opposes the movement of an object across the surface of another with which it is in rough contact.

(b) the direction of the frictional force is opposite to the potential direction of motion.

(c) the magnitude of the frictional force is only just sufficient to prevent movement and increases as the tendency to move increases, up to a limiting value. When the limiting value is reached, the frictional force cannot increase any further and motion is about to begin (limiting equilibrium). When the frictional force, F, reaches its limit, its value then is related to the normal reaction N in the following way:

$F = \mu N$

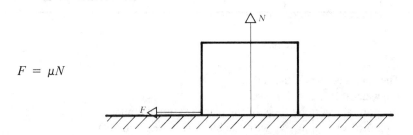

The constant μ is called the *coefficient of friction* and each pair of surfaces has its own value for this constant.

> In limiting equilibrium $F = \mu N$.
> In general $F \leqslant \mu N$.

The Angle of Friction

At a point of rough contact, where slipping is about to occur, the two forces acting on each object are the normal reaction N and frictional force μN.

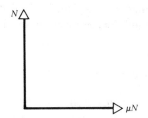
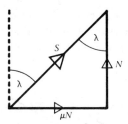

The resultant of these two forces is S, and S makes an angle λ with the normal, where

$$\tan \lambda = \frac{\mu N}{N} = \mu$$

The angle λ is called the angle of friction.

At a point of rough contact when slipping is about to occur we can therefore use either

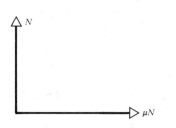

or

components N and μN at right angles to each other.

S at an angle λ to the normal where S is the resultant contact force or *total reaction* and λ is the angle of friction.

Note. The use of S instead of N and μN reduces the number of forces in a problem and can often lead to a *three force problem*.

SUMMARY

1) When the surfaces of two objects in rough contact tend to move relative to each other, equal and opposite frictional forces act on the objects, opposing the potential movement.

2) Up to a limiting value, the magnitude of a frictional force, F, is just sufficient to prevent motion.

3) When the limit is reached $F = \mu N$ where N is the normal reaction and μ is the coefficient of friction for the two surfaces in contact.

4) At all times $F \leqslant \mu N$.

5) The resultant of N and μN makes an angle λ with the normal, where $\tan \lambda = \mu$ and λ is the angle of friction.

EXAMPLES 3c (continued)

2) A particle of weight $10\,N$ rests in rough contact with a plane inclined at $30°$ to the horizontal and is just about to slip. Find the coefficient of friction between the plane and the particle.

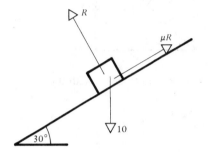

The particle tends to slide down the plane so the frictional force on the particle acts up the plane. Friction is limiting so $F = \mu R$.

Resolving in the directions of μR and R we have

$$\nearrow \quad \mu R - 10 \sin 30° \; = \; 0$$

$$\nwarrow \quad R - 10 \cos 30° \; = \; 0$$

Hence
$$\mu \; = \; \frac{10 \sin 30°}{10 \cos 30°} \; = \; \tan 30°$$

$\Rightarrow$
$$\mu \; = \; \frac{1}{\sqrt{3}}$$

3) A particle of weight W rests on a horizontal plane with which the angle of friction is λ.

A force P inclined at an angle θ to the plane is applied to the particle until it is on the point of moving. Find the value of θ for which the value of P will be least.

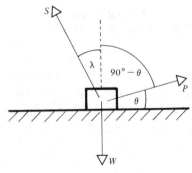

Using the total contact force S inclined at λ to the normal, only three forces act on the particle.

Then Lami's Theorem gives

$$\frac{P}{\sin(180° - \lambda)} = \frac{W}{\sin(90° - \theta + \lambda)} = \left[\frac{S}{\sin(90° + \theta)}\right]$$

$$\Rightarrow \qquad \frac{P}{\sin\lambda} = \frac{W}{\cos(\theta - \lambda)}$$

$$\Rightarrow \qquad P = \frac{W\sin\lambda}{\cos(\theta - \lambda)}$$

P will be least when $\cos(\theta - \lambda)$ is greatest, since W and $\sin\lambda$ are constant, i.e. when $\cos(\theta - \lambda) = 1$ and $\theta - \lambda = 0$.

Therefore P is least when $\theta = \lambda$ and its value then is $W\sin\lambda$.

4) A uniform ladder rests against a smooth vertical wall and on rough horizontal ground. The weight of the ladder is $10\,N$ and it is just about to slip when inclined at $30°$ to the vertical. Calculate the coefficient of friction.

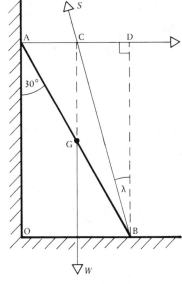

Three forces keep the ladder in equilibrium, the normal reaction R with the smooth wall,

the weight W,

the total reaction S with the rough ground.

The three forces must be concurrent, so S passes through C, the point of intersection of R and W.

S is inclined at λ to the normal BD and $\tan\lambda = \dfrac{CD}{DB}$.

But the coefficient of friction μ is equal to $\tan\lambda$.

Hence $\quad \mu = \dfrac{CD}{DB} = \dfrac{\frac{1}{2}AD}{DB}$ $\qquad$ (since CG is parallel to DB and $AG = GB$)

i.e. $\qquad\qquad \mu = \frac{1}{2}\tan 30° = \dfrac{1}{2\sqrt{3}}$

The coefficient of friction is therefore $\sqrt{3}/6$.

5) A small block of weight $10\,\text{N}$ rests on a rough plane inclined at $30°$ to the horizontal. The coefficient of friction is $\frac{1}{2}$. Find the horizontal force required:
(a) to prevent the block from slipping down,
(b) to make it just about to slide up the plane.

(a)

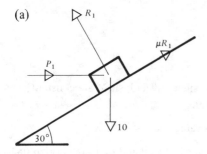

In this case, as the block is about to slip downward, friction on the block acts up the plane and is limiting.

Resolving parallel and perpendicular to the plane,

$$\nearrow \quad \tfrac{1}{2}R_1 + P_1\cos 30° - 10\sin 30° = 0$$

$$\nwarrow \quad R_1 - P_1\sin 30° - 10\cos 30° = 0$$

Hence $20\sin 30° - 2P_1\cos 30° = P_1\sin 30° + 10\cos 30°$

$\Rightarrow$ $10 - 1.73P_1 = 0.5P_1 + 8.66$

$\Rightarrow$ $1.34 = 2.23P_1$

So the required horizontal force is of magnitude $0.6\,\text{N}$.

(b)

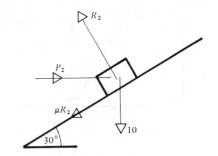

This time the block is about to slide upward and the limiting frictional force acts downward.

Resolving as before:

$$\nearrow \quad P_2\cos 30° - \tfrac{1}{2}R_2 - 10\sin 30° = 0$$

$$\nwarrow \quad R_2 - P_2\sin 30° - 10\cos 30° = 0$$

Hence $1.73P_2 - 10 = 0.5P_2 + 8.66$

$\Rightarrow$ $1.23P_2 = 18.66$

This time the magnitude of the horizontal force is $15.2\,\text{N}$.

Note. In examples 3 and 4, a phrase frequently encountered in examination questions is used, viz. 'a body rests on a rough plane . . .'.
This implies, incorrectly, that friction is a property of *one surface*.
The description 'a body rests in rough contact with a plane . . .' is better because it conveys the idea of friction *between two surfaces*.

EXERCISE 3c

1) A small block of weight W is placed on a plane inclined at an angle θ to the horizontal. The coefficient of friction between the block and the plane is μ.
(a) When $\theta = 20^{\circ}$ the block is in limiting equilibrium. Find μ.
(b) When $\mu = \frac{1}{3}$ and $\theta = 30^{\circ}$ a horizontal force of 6 N is required to prevent the block from slipping down the plane. What is the weight of this block?
(c) A force of 10 N up the plane causes the block to be on the point of sliding up. If $W = 20$ N and $\mu = \frac{1}{4}$ find θ.
(d) If $\theta = 40^{\circ}$ and $\mu = \frac{1}{2}$ find the magnitude and direction of the least force required to prevent the block from sliding down the plane when $W = 12$ N.

2) A block of weight 20 N rests on a rough plane of inclination 30°, the coefficient of friction being 0.25. Find what horizontal force will be required:
(a) just to prevent it from slipping down,
(b) to make it just begin to slide up.

3) A sledge whose weight is 4000 N is pulled at constant speed along level ground by a rope held at 30° to the ground. If $\mu = \frac{1}{4}$ find the pulling force required.

4) A uniform ladder rests on rough horizontal ground with its top against a smooth vertical wall. If the angle of friction is 15° find the least possible inclination of the ladder to the horizontal.

5) A small block of weight 8 N is standing on rough horizontal ground. A horizontal force P is applied to the block. If the coefficient of friction between block and ground is 0.5, what is the value of the frictional force when:
(a) $P = 1$ N   (b) $P = 4$ N   (c) $P = 5$ N
State in each case whether or not the block moves.

6) A crate of weight 4000 N is placed on a ramp inclined at 20° to the horizontal, and is just on the point of slipping down the ramp. A workman then attaches a rope to the crate, to haul it straight up the ramp. If the rope is parallel to the ramp, what is the least force with which the workman must pull the rope?

RESULTANT MOMENT OF COPLANAR FORCES IN EQUILIBRIUM

Consider a stationary object upon which a number of forces begin to act.
If, about a certain axis, the forces have a resultant anticlockwise moment, the
object will begin to rotate anticlockwise about that axis.
Similarly the object will begin to rotate clockwise if the forces acting on it have
a resultant clockwise moment.
If, however, the object does not begin to rotate at all, there can be no resultant
torque in either sense about any axis.
But one of the conditions necessary for a set of forces to be in equilibrium is
that they cause no change in rotation. It therefore follows that

if a set of forces is in equilibrium their resultant moment about any axis is zero.

This property can often be used to evaluate some of the unknown forces acting
on an object in equilibrium.

EXAMPLES 3d

1) A uniform rod AB of length 2 m and weight 20 N rests horizontally on
smooth supports at A and B. A load of 10 N is attached to the rod at a
distance 0.4 m from A. Find the forces exerted on the rod by the supports.

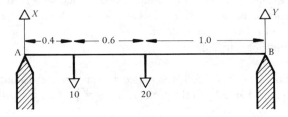

Let X and Y be the magnitudes (in newtons) of the supporting forces at A
and B respectively.
Because the rod is at rest, the resultant moment of the forces acting on it is zero
about any axis.
Using the symbol A⤴ to indicate that the resultant moment about an axis
through A is to be assessed in the sense indicated by the arrow, we have

$$A⤴ \qquad 10 \times 0.4 + 20 \times 1.0 - Y \times 2.0 = 0 \qquad [1]$$

$$B⤴ \qquad X \times 2.0 - 10 \times 1.6 - 20 \times 1.0 = 0 \qquad [2]$$

Hence $\qquad X = 18 \quad$ and $\quad Y = 12$

Therefore the supporting forces are 18 N at A and 12 N at B.

The sum of the supporting forces is equal to the sum of the loads, confirming
that the resultant of the vertical forces acting on the rod is zero.

2) A uniform plank AB of weight 100 N and length 4 m lies on a horizontal roof, perpendicular to the edge of the roof and overhanging by 1.5 m. If a load of 200 N is to be attached to the overhanging end A, what force must be applied at the opposite end B just to prevent the plank from overturning?

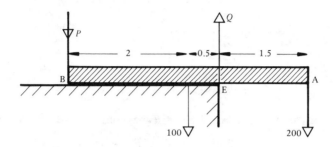

When the plank is just on the point of overturning it is in contact with the roof only at the edge E. The normal reaction therefore acts at E.
Let the normal reaction be Q and the force required at B be P (both in newtons).

Then,   E) $200 \times 1.5 - 100 \times 0.5 - P \times 2.5 = 0$

Hence $P = 100.$

Therefore a force of 100 N is needed at B.

Note. The unknown force Q, which is not required, is avoided by choosing to take moments about an axis through which Q passes.

3) A uniform rod AB of weight W is hinged to a fixed point at A. It is held in a horizontal position by a string, one end of which is attached to B and the other end to a fixed point C such that angle ABC is 30°. Find, in terms of W, the tension in the string.

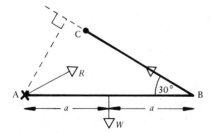

Let the length of the rod be $2a$.

A) $Wa - T \times 2a \sin 30° = 0$

i.e. $Wa - Ta = 0$

(The unknown force R at the hinge A is avoided by taking moments about an axis through A.)

Therefore the tension in the string is of magnitude W.

4) A non-uniform rod AB of length 2 m is suspended in a horizontal position by two vertical strings, one at each end. The weight of the rod acts at G where $AG = 1.1$ m and is of magnitude 60 N. A load of 20 N is placed on the rod at a variable point P. If either string snaps when the tension in it exceeds 42 N, find the section of the rod in which P can lie.

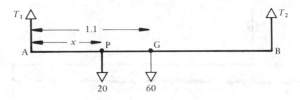

If the tensions at A and B are T_1 and T_2 newtons and $AP = x$ metres, then:

A) $20x + 60 \times 1.1 - 2T_2 = 0$

B) $2T_1 - 20(2 - x) - 60 \times 0.9 = 0$

Therefore $T_1 = 47 - 10x$

and $T_2 = 10x + 33$

But $T_1 \leqslant 42$ and $T_2 \leqslant 42$

Therefore $47 - 10x \leqslant 42$

and $10x + 33 \leqslant 42$

giving $x \geqslant 0.5$ and $x \leqslant 0.9$

The load can therefore be placed anywhere within the section $P_1 P_2$ without breaking either string, where $AP_1 = 0.5$ m   and $P_2 B = 1.1$ m.

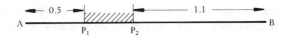

EXERCISE 3d

1) A uniform beam AB of length 1.6 m and weight 40 N rests on two smooth supports at C and D where $AC = BD = 0.3$ m. A load is attached to A so that the supporting force at C is twice the supporting force at D. Find the magnitude of the load.

2) A non-uniform rod of weight 40 N and length 1 m is suspended by a single string attached to the mid-point of the rod. If the rod is horizontal when a weight of 30 N is attached to one end of the rod, find the supporting force which would be required at the opposite end to keep the rod horizontal when the 30 N weight is removed.

3) A uniform beam 3 m long has weights 20 N and 30 N attached to its ends. If the weight of the beam is 50 N find the point on the beam where a support should be placed so that the beam will rest horizontally.

In Questions 4–8 each diagram shows an object in equilibrium. Using the principle of moments calculate the forces or distances indicated (units are newtons and metres throughout).

4) 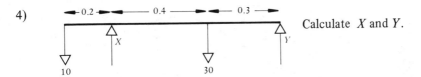 Calculate X and Y.

5) A rod is hinged at A. Calculate the distance AB if the smooth support at B exerts a force 25 N on the rod.

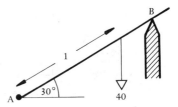

6) 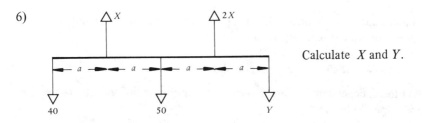 Calculate X and Y.

7) A plank AB weighs 100 N. Find the least force F required to prevent the plank overturning.

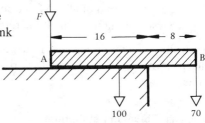

8) 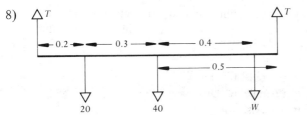 Find W so that the tensions are equal and find the tension.

THE EFFECT OF COPLANAR FORCES

We are now going to consider the general effect of a set of non concurrent coplanar forces acting on an object (the simplest object to visualise is a lamina in the plane of the forces).
For reference purposes let O be some point in the lamina and Ox, Oy be perpendicular lines through O in the plane of the lamina.

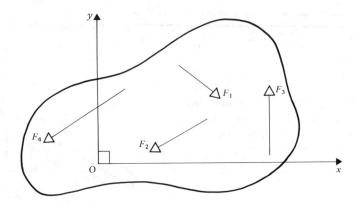

The movement of the lamina in its own plane can then be made up only of:
(a) linear movement parallel to Ox,
(b) linear movement parallel to Oy,
(c) rotation about some axis perpendicular to the lamina.

These three independent factors in the possible movement of the lamina are caused respectively by:
(a) the algebraic sum of the force components parallel to Ox,
(b) the algebraic sum of all the force components parallel to Oy,
(c) the resultant moment of all the forces about the axis of rotation.

The ability of a set of coplanar forces to generate movement made up of three independent factors is referred to as the *three degrees of freedom* of the force system.

Coplanar Forces in Equilibrium

When a stationary object is in equilibrium under the action of a set of coplanar forces, each of the three independent factors which comprise the possible movement of the object must be zero,
i.e. the object has:
(a) no linear movement parallel to Ox,
(b) no linear movement parallel to Oy,
(c) no rotation about any axis.

The set of forces must therefore be such that:
- (a) the algebraic sum of the components parallel to Ox is zero,
- (b) the algebraic sum of the components parallel to Oy is zero,
- (c) the resultant moment about any specified axis is zero.

The use in a particular problem of this set of conditions for equilibrium leads to the formation of *not more than three independent equations* relating the forces in the system.

EXAMPLES 3e

1) A rod AB rests with the end A on rough horizontal ground and the end B against a smooth vertical wall. The rod is uniform and of weight W. A mass also of weight W is attached at B. If the coefficient of friction at A is $\frac{3}{4}$ find the angle at which the rod is inclined to the vertical when it is just about to slip.

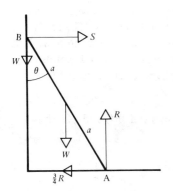

When the rod is about to slip the frictional force at A is $\frac{3}{4}R$.

Let the length of the rod be $2a$ and its inclination to the wall be θ.

Then, resolving parallel to the ground and to the wall and taking moments about an axis through A, we have:

$$\rightarrow \qquad S - \tfrac{3}{4}R = 0 \qquad\qquad [1]$$

$$\uparrow \qquad R - 2W = 0 \qquad\qquad [2]$$

$$\text{A} \!\rangle \qquad W \times a \sin\theta + W \times 2a \sin\theta - S \times 2a \cos\theta = 0 \qquad [3]$$

From [2] $\qquad\qquad R = 2W$

From [1] $\qquad\qquad S = \tfrac{3}{4}(2W) = \tfrac{3}{2}W$

From [3] $\qquad\qquad S = \tfrac{3}{2}W \tan\theta$

Therefore $\qquad\qquad \tfrac{3}{2}W = \tfrac{3}{2}W \tan\theta$

$\Rightarrow \qquad\qquad \tan\theta = 1$

The rod is therefore inclined at $45°$ to the vertical.

Alternative Conditions for Equilibrium of Coplanar Forces

When a stationary object is in equilibrium it is not rotating about *any* axis or moving linearly in *any* direction. There are consequently many more equations which could be formed by equating to zero the resultant moment about various different axes or the collected force components in various different directions. But, as the *total number of independent equations is limited to three*, the various groups of equations which may be used are based on:
(a) resolving in any two directions and taking moments about one axis,
(b) resolving in one direction and taking moments about two axes,
(c) taking moments about three axes (which must not be collinear or the third resultant moment would simply be the combination of the first two, giving no extra information).

EXAMPLES 3e (continued)

2) A uniform rod AB of length $2a$ and weight W is smoothly pivoted to a fixed point at A. A load of weight $2W$ is attached to the end B. The rod is kept horizontal by a string attached to the midpoint G of the rod and to a point C vertically above A. If the length of the string is $2a$ find, in terms of W, the tension in the string and the magnitude of the reaction at the pivot.

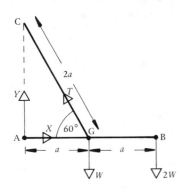

The given lengths of AG and CG show that

$$\cos A\widehat{G}C = \frac{a}{2a} = \tfrac{1}{2}$$

$$\Rightarrow \qquad A\widehat{G}C = 60°$$

More than three forces keep the rod in equilibrium, so they do not have to be concurrent. Consequently we have no way of deciding upon the direction of the hinge force. The easiest way of dealing with a force which is unknown both in magnitude and in direction is to introduce it as a pair of perpendicular components.
Using this technique for the hinge force, we have components X and Y acting horizontally and vertically at A.

Then, resolving horizontally and vertically and taking moments about an axis through A, we have:

$\rightarrow$ $\qquad\qquad\qquad\qquad X - T\cos 60° = 0$ $\qquad\qquad\qquad$ [1]

$\uparrow$ $\qquad\qquad\qquad\qquad\quad Y + T\sin 60° - 3W = 0$ $\qquad\qquad\quad$ [2]

A$\rangle$ $\qquad\qquad\qquad\quad Wa + 2W(2a) - Ta\sin 60° = 0$ $\qquad\qquad$ [3]

From [3] $\qquad\quad T = \dfrac{10W}{\sqrt{3}} = \dfrac{10\sqrt{3}}{3}W$

From [1] $\qquad\quad X = \left(\dfrac{10\sqrt{3}}{3}W\right)\left(\dfrac{1}{2}\right) = \dfrac{5\sqrt{3}}{3}W$

From [2] $\qquad\quad Y = 3W - \left(\dfrac{10\sqrt{3}}{3}W\right)\left(\dfrac{\sqrt{3}}{2}\right) = -2W$

The reaction at the hinge is of magnitude R where

$$R = \sqrt{X^2 + Y^2} = \sqrt{(\tfrac{25}{3}W^2 + 4W^2)} = W\sqrt{\tfrac{37}{3}}$$

The tension in the string is $\dfrac{10\sqrt{3}}{3}W$.

3) A ladder rests in limiting equilibrium against a rough vertical wall and with its foot on rough horizontal ground, the coefficient of friction at both points of contact being $\frac{1}{2}$. The ladder is uniform and weighs 300 N. Find the normal reaction at the wall and the angle θ which the ladder makes with the horizontal.

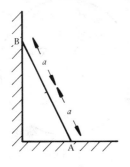
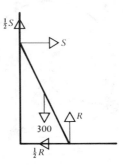

The rod is in limiting equilibrium, so the frictional forces at A and B are $\frac{1}{2}R$ and $\frac{1}{2}S$ where R and S respectively are the normal reactions.
Let $2a$ be the length of the rod.

Taking moments about two axes, through A and B, and resolving horizontally we have:

A)
$$300 \times a \cos\theta - S \times 2a \sin\theta - \tfrac{1}{2}S \times 2a \cos\theta = 0 \qquad [1]$$

B)
$$R \times 2a \cos\theta - \tfrac{1}{2}R \times 2a \sin\theta - 300 \times a \cos\theta = 0 \qquad [2]$$

→
$$S - \tfrac{1}{2}R = 0 \qquad [3]$$

From [1] and [2], first dividing each by $a \cos\theta$, we get

$$300 = S(2 \tan\theta + 1) = R(2 - \tan\theta)$$

But
$$R = 2S$$

Therefore
$$(2 \tan\theta + 1) = 2(2 - \tan\theta)$$

⇒
$$\tan\theta = \tfrac{3}{4}$$

Therefore the ladder is inclined at an angle $36.9°$ to the horizontal.

From equation [1]
$$S = \frac{300}{2 \tan\theta + 1} = \frac{300}{2.5}$$

Therefore the normal reaction at the wall is $120\,\text{N}$.

4) O is the centre of a circular disc of weight W which rests in a vertical plane on two rough pegs A and B, the coefficient of friction with each being 0.5. AO makes $60°$ and BO makes $30°$ with the vertical. Find, in terms of W, the maximum force which can be applied tangentially at the highest point of the disc without causing rotation in the sense from A to B.

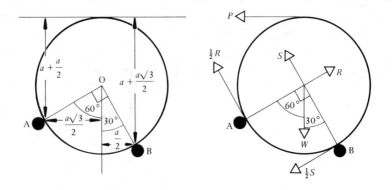

When P has its maximum value the frictional forces at A and B are $\tfrac{1}{2}R$ and $\tfrac{1}{2}S$. Let the radius of the disc be a.

Taking moments about axes through A, B and O (which are not collinear) we have:

A)
$$P \times \frac{3a}{2} + Sa - \tfrac{1}{2}Sa - W\frac{a\sqrt{3}}{2} = 0 \qquad [1]$$

B)
$$P\left(a + a\frac{\sqrt{3}}{2}\right) + W\frac{a}{2} - Ra - \tfrac{1}{2}Ra = 0 \qquad [2]$$

O)
$$Pa - \tfrac{1}{2}Ra - \tfrac{1}{2}Sa = 0 \qquad [3]$$

From [1] $\qquad S = \sqrt{3}W - 3P$

From [2] $\qquad 3R = W + P(2 + \sqrt{3})$

From [3] $\qquad 2P = R + S$

Therefore $\qquad 2P = \tfrac{1}{3}[W + 2P + \sqrt{3}P] + \sqrt{3}W - 3P$

$\Rightarrow \qquad (13 - \sqrt{3})P = (1 + 3\sqrt{3})W$

$\Rightarrow \qquad P = \left(\dfrac{1 + 3\sqrt{3}}{13 - \sqrt{3}}\right)W = \dfrac{(1 + 3\sqrt{3})(13 + \sqrt{3})}{166}W$

The greatest force is therefore $\dfrac{(11 + 20\sqrt{3})}{83}W$.

Note: The limitation to three independent equations is vital. If, mistakenly, a fourth equation is introduced (e.g. by resolving twice and taking moments twice) then, in the subsequent working, it will be found that everything cancels out and some useless result such as $P = P$ will emerge. If, in a problem, there seem to be four unknown quantities, so that three equations are not sufficient, the fourth necessary equation must come from a different source, e.g. mensuration.

EXERCISE 3e

In Questions 1-4 a uniform rod AB whose midpoint is M, is in equilibrium in a vertical plane as shown in each diagram.

1)

The rod rests on a rough peg at C and a force F acts at A as shown. If BC = CM and $\tan \alpha = \tfrac{4}{3}$ find the coefficient of friction at C and the force F.

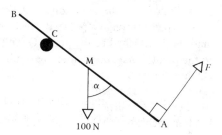

2)

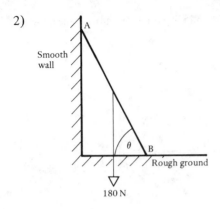

Smooth wall

180 N

Rough ground

If the coefficient of friction at the ground is $\frac{1}{3}$, calculate the normal reactions at A and B and find the angle θ.

3)

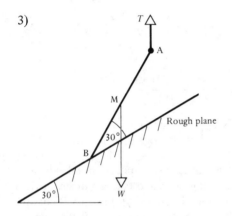

Rough plane

A vertical string is attached to A. Find T in terms of W and calculate the value of μ, the coefficient of friction at B.

4)

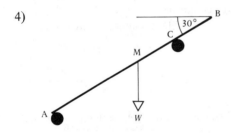

The rod rests on a rough peg at A and a smooth peg at C.
MC = CB
Find the coefficient of friction at A and the normal reaction at C (in terms of W).

5) A disc of mass m and radius a is free to turn in a vertical plane about a smooth pivot through a point P on the circumference. A particle, also of mass m is attached to the point Q on the rim of the disc diametrically opposite to the pivot. What force should be applied to the lowest point of the disc to keep PQ horizontal if:
(a) the force is tangential,
(b) the force is vertical.
Find, in each case, the magnitude of the reaction at the pivot.

Questions 6-8 show sets of coplanar forces which are in equilibrium.

6)

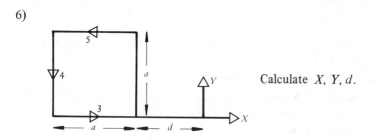

Calculate X, Y, d.

7)

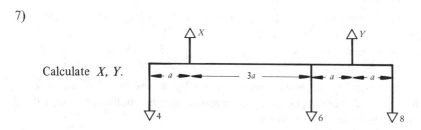

Calculate X, Y.

8)

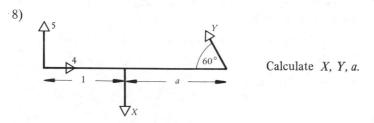

Calculate X, Y, a.

9) A uniform rod AB of length $2a$ and weight W is inclined at $30°$ to the horizontal with its lower end A on rough horizontal ground, the angle of friction being $30°$. The rod rests in contact with a smooth peg C (AC < AB). Calculate the height of the peg above the ground and the reaction at the peg if the rod is in limiting equilibrium.

10) A uniform ladder is placed with its foot on horizontal ground and its upper end against a vertical wall. The angle of friction at both points of contact is $30°$. Find the greatest possible inclination of the ladder to the vertical. (The ladder will not slip until limiting friction has been reached at both ends.)

11) A uniform rod AB of weight $200\,$N is lying on rough horizontal ground when a string attached to B begins to lift that end of the rod. When AB is inclined at $30°$ to the ground the end A is about to slip. If at this instant the string is inclined to the vertical at $30°$ calculate the tension in the string and the angle of friction between the rod and the ground.

MULTIPLE CHOICE EXERCISE 3

(The instructions for answering these questions are given on page x.)

TYPE I

1) Two perpendicular forces have magnitudes 5 N and 4 N. The magnitude of their resultant is:

(a) 3 N   (b) $\sqrt{11}$ N   (c) $\sqrt{41}$ N   (d) 1 N.

2) A block of weight 12 N rests in rough contact with a horizontal plane and $\mu = \frac{1}{3}$.   A force of 3 N is applied horizontally to the block. The frictional force acting on the block is:

(a) 4 N   (b) 3 N   (c) -4 N   (d) zero because the block does not move.

3) Forces represented by $2\mathbf{i} + 5\mathbf{j}$, $\mathbf{i} - 8\mathbf{j}$ and $p\mathbf{i} + q\mathbf{j}$ are in equilibrium, therefore:

(a) $p = 3$ and $q = -3$ (b) $p = -3$ and $q = 3$

(c) $p = -2$ and $q = 3$ (d) $p = 2$ and $q = -40$.

4) A light string is attached at one end to a point on a vertical wall and at the other end to a smooth sphere. When the sphere rests in equilibrium against the wall the direction of the string is:

(a) at $45°$ to the wall   (b) horizontal   (c) tangential to the sphere
(d) through the centre of the sphere.

5) A particle rests in equilibrium on a rough plane inclined at $30°$ to the horizontal therefore:

(a) $\mu = \dfrac{1}{2}$ (b) $\mu = \dfrac{1}{\sqrt{3}}$ (c) $\mu \leqslant \dfrac{1}{2}$ (d) $\mu \geqslant \dfrac{1}{\sqrt{3}}$

TYPE II

6) Three forces $\mathbf{F}_1$, $\mathbf{F}_2$ and $\mathbf{F}_3$ are in equilibrium, therefore,

(a) $\mathbf{F}_1 = \mathbf{F}_2 + \mathbf{F}_3$
(b) $\mathbf{F}_1 + \mathbf{F}_2 + \mathbf{F}_3 = 0$
(c) $\mathbf{F}_1 - \mathbf{F}_2 - \mathbf{F}_3 = 0$
(d) $-\mathbf{F}_1 = \mathbf{F}_2 + \mathbf{F}_3$.

7) Three concurrent forces represented by $2\mathbf{i} + 3\mathbf{j}$, $\mathbf{i} - 4\mathbf{j}$ and $-3\mathbf{i} + \mathbf{j}$:
(a) are in equilibrium,
(b) have zero linear resultant,
(c) have an equilibrant,
(d) exert a turning effect.

8) ABCD is a rectangle. Forces represented in magnitude and direction by $\overrightarrow{AB}$, $\overrightarrow{BC}$, $\overrightarrow{CD}$ and $\overrightarrow{DA}$:
(a) are in equilibrium,
(b) obey Lami's Theorem,
(c) have zero linear resultant,
(d) have a resultant $2\overrightarrow{AC}$.

9) A ladder is resting at $30°$ to a rough vertical wall with its foot on a horizontal plane.
(a) Friction acts on the ladder.
(b) The plane is smooth.
(c) The ladder is about to slip.
(d) Friction acts on the wall.

TYPE III

10) (a) Three non-parallel forces are concurrent.
    (b) Three non-parallel forces are in equilibrium.

11) (a) The resultant of a set of forces is **F**.
    (b) An extra force $-$**F** added to a set of forces produces a state of equilibrium.

12) (a) Two objects are in rough contact with each other.
    (b) Two objects are in contact and each exerts a frictional force on the other.

13) (a) A force of $2\,N$ is applied to a block of weight $4\,N$ in an attempt to move it across a rough table.
    (b) The coefficient of friction between a block and a table is $\frac{1}{2}$.

14) (a) A supporting force just prevents a particle from slipping down a rough inclined plane.
    (b) A particle is in a state of limiting equilibrium on an inclined plane.

15) (a) The resultant torque of a set of forces is zero.
    (b) A set of forces is in equilibrium.

16) (a) A rod AB whose midpoint is M is in equilibrium.
    (b) The forces acting on a rod AB have zero resultant torque about axes through each of the points A, B and the midpoint M of AB.

17) (a) The moment of a force F about an axis through A is zero.
    (b) A force F acts through a point A.

TYPE IV

18) Three forces P, Q and R act on a particle. Find the magnitude of P.
(a) P is inclined at $120°$ to R.
(b) P is inclined at $150°$ to Q.
(c) The magnitude of Q is $10\,N$.

19) A block rests on a rough inclined plane. Find the coefficient of friction between block and plane:
(a) the weight of the block is $8\,N$,
(b) the elevation of the plane is $30°$,
(c) friction is limiting.

20) Determine whether or not three forces are in equilibrium:
(a) the magnitudes of the forces are $P = 3$, $Q = 4$, $R = 5$,
(b) the angle between P and Q is $60°$,
(c) the angle between Q and R is $150°$.

21) A ladder is placed with its foot on horizontal ground and the other end leaning against a smooth vertical wall. Find the angle between the ladder and the wall when the ladder is about to slip:
(a) the weight of the ladder is 500 N,
(b) the ground is rough and $\mu = \frac{1}{2}$,
(c) the length of the ladder is 5 m.

22) A non-uniform rod AB rests horizontally on two supports at points C and D. Calculate the forces at the supports if:
(a) AC = 0.4 m,
(b) DB = 0.7 m,
(c) the weight of the rod is 40 N,
(d) the length of the rod is 2 m.

23) A uniform rod AB is hinged to a vertical wall at A. The midpoint is attached by an inelastic string to a point on the wall above A. Find the tension in the string if:
(a) the weight of the rod is 20 N,
(b) the rod and the string have the same length,
(c) the rod is horizontal,
(d) the string is inclined at $30°$ to the wall.

TYPE V

24) Three forces acting along the sides of a triangle are in equilibrium.

25) Lami's Theorem states that when three forces act on a particle each force is proportional to the sine of the angle between the other two forces.

26) If a frictional force acts on a body, it is not necessarily of value μR where R is the normal contact force.

27) The angle of friction is the angle between the frictional force and the normal reaction.

28) Three forces in equilibrium must be concurrent.

29) If a set of forces is in equilibrium the resultant moment about any two axes is zero.

30) If a body is kept in equilibrium by four unknown forces, these forces can be found by resolving in two perpendicular directions and taking moments about two different axes.

MISCELLANEOUS EXERCISE 3

1) ABCD is a square. CD is produced to E so that DE = CD.   Forces of magnitudes 2, 3√2, 4 and 2√2 units act along AB, AC, DA and AE respectively. Find the magnitude and direction of their resultant. A fifth force acting at A is added so that the system is in equilibrium. What is the magnitude and direction of the extra force?

2) O is any point in the plane of a regular hexagon ABCDEF. Prove that forces $\overrightarrow{OA}, \overrightarrow{OE}, \overrightarrow{CD}, \overrightarrow{CB}$ and $2\overrightarrow{FO}$ are in equilibrium.

3) A uniform rod AB of weight W is freely hinged at A. The rod is in equilibrium at an angle θ to the vertical when a horizontal force $\frac{1}{2}W$ acts at B. Calculate θ and the reaction of the hinge on the rod.

4) A small object of weight $4W$ in rough contact with a horizontal plane is acted upon by a force inclined at $30°$ to the plane. When the force is of magnitude $2W$ the object is about to slip. Calculate the magnitude of the normal reaction and the coefficient of friction between the object and the plane.

5) Three telegraph cables are attached to the top of a telegraph pole. Their tensions, in order, are 2500, 3000 and 3500 N and the cables are separated by angles of 20°. A fourth cable is to be attached to the same point on the post in order to ensure that the post is in equilibrium. Assuming that all the cables are horizontal find the tension which the fourth cable must take.

6) ABCDEF is a regular hexagon. Forces of 2, 4√3, 10 and 6 N act along AB, AC, DA and AF respectively. Show that these forces are in equilibrium.

7) A sphere of radius 9 cm rests on a smooth inclined plane (angle 30°). It is attached by a string fixed to a point on its surface to a point on the plane 12 cm from the point of contact and on the same line of greatest slope. Find the tension in the string if the weight of the sphere is 100 N.

8) Find the values of the unknown forces in each of the following cases. Each set of forces is in equilibrium.

(a)   (b)

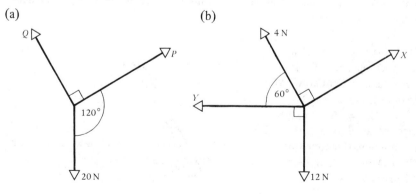

(c)   (d)

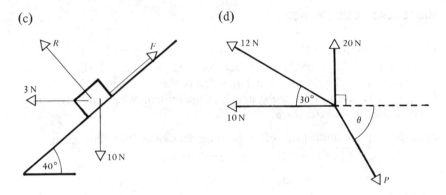

In each case use calculation to solve the problem but in addition sketch the vector polygon.

9) A weight W is suspended by two ropes which make $30°$ and $60°$ with the horizontal. If the tension in the first rope is $20\,N$, find the tension in the other and the value of W.

10) A uniform bar AB, $1\,m$ long can be balanced about a point $0.2\,m$ from A by hanging a weight of $5\,N$ at A. Find the weight of the bar. What additional weight should be hung from A if the point of support is moved $0.1\,m$ nearer to A?

11) A uniform rod BC, of length $0.6\,m$ and weight $2\,N$, is hinged to a fixed point at B. It is supported in equilibrium by a string $0.8\,m$ long attached to C and to a point A vertically above B. If $AB = 1\,m$ calculate the tension in the string.

12) A uniform plank AB rests on a horizontal roof and B overhangs by 2 m. If the length of the plank is $10\,m$ and its weight is $560\,N$, find how far a man of weight $1400\,N$ can walk along the overhanging section without causing the plank to tip up. Find also what weight should be placed at A to allow the man to walk to the end B in safety.

13) A loft door OA of weight $100\,N$ is propped open at $60°$ to the horizontal by a light strut AB. The door is hinged at O. If $OA = OB = 1.2\,m$ and the weight of the door acts through a point C on the door where $OC = 0.4\,m$, find the force in the strut.

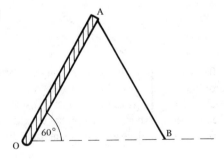

14) A uniform beam AB, 5 m long and of weight 60 N is supported in a horizontal position at A and at one other point. A load of 10 N is suspended from B and loads of 50 N and 40 N are suspended from points distant 1.8 m and 3 m respectively from B. If the supporting force at A is 40 N find the position of the other support.

15) A diving board of mass 150 kg is clamped at one end. A diver of mass 75 kg walks gently along the board which is 3 m long. What torque is exerted on the clamp when the diver is:
(a) 1 m from the free end,
(b) at the free end.

16) A rod XY is of length $(x+y)$ and its weight acts through a point distant x from X. It rests on two supports equidistant from X and Y and distant z apart. Prove that the forces exerted by the supports are in the ratio

$$(x-y+z):(y-x+z).$$

17) A uniform rod AB of weight 12 N is free to turn in a vertical plane about a smooth hinge at its upper end A. It is held at an angle θ to the vertical by a force P acting at B.
(a) P is 5 N applied horizontally. What is the force at the hinge?
(b) P is horizontal and θ is $\arctan\frac{3}{4}$. What is the force at the hinge?
(c) P is at right angles to AB and of magnitude 3 N. What is the force at the hinge?
(d) P is at right angles to AB and θ is $\arctan\frac{3}{4}$. Find P and the hinge force.

18) A cylinder of weight 100 N rests in the angle between a smooth vertical wall and a smooth plane inclined at $30°$ to the wall. Find the thrusts of the cylinder on the wall and the plane.

19) With reference to perpendicular axes Ox and Oy, A and B are points with coordinates $(2a,0)$ and $(2a,4a)$. A force with components X and Y parallel to Ox and Oy passes through a point P on the x axis. Its anticlockwise moments about axes perpendicular to the xy plane through O, A and B are respectively $+4Fa, -4Fa$ and $+10Fa$. Find, in terms of F and a, the magnitude and direction of the force and the distance OP.

20) A uniform rod AB, 2 m long and of weight 200 N, is suspended horizontally by two vertical ropes one attached 0.2 m from A and the other 0.3 m from B. If the first rope snaps when its tension exceeds 140 N and the second snaps when its tension exceeds 160 N find where on the rod a load of 100 N can be placed without snapping either rope.

21) A non uniform beam AB rests on two supports in a horizontal line, one at A and one at a point C. AB = 5 m,   AC = 4 m   and the weight of the beam is 350 N. If the supports exert equal forces on the beam find the point on the beam where the weight acts. If an extra weight W is then attached to B find the value of W if:
(a) the supporting force at C is twice the supporting force at A,
(b) the beam is just about to rotate.

22) A uniform plank of mass 80 kg and length 4 m overhangs a horizontal roof by 1.5 m. A man can walk to within 0.5 m of the overhanging end when a mass of 12 kg is placed on the opposite end. What is the mass of the man and how much bigger a load must be placed at the end of the plank to enable the man to walk right to the overhanging end.

23) The foot of a uniform ladder, of length l and weight W, rests on rough horizontal ground, and the top of the ladder rests against a smooth vertical wall. The ladder is inclined at $30°$ to the vertical. Find the magnitude of the force exerted by the ladder on the wall.
Given that the coefficient of friction between the ladder and the ground is $\frac{1}{4}\sqrt{3}$, show that a man of weight $4W$ cannot climb to the top of the ladder without the ladder slipping, and find the least weight which when placed on the foot of the ladder would enable the man to climb to the top of the ladder.
(U of L)

24) A uniform rod AB, of length $2a$ and weight W, is hinged to a vertical post at A and is supported in a horizontal position by a string attached to B and to a point C vertically above A, where $\angle ABC = \theta$.   A load of weight $2W$ is hung from B. Find the tension in the string and the horizontal and vertical resolved parts of the force exerted by the hinge on the rod. Show that, if the reaction of the hinge at A is at right angles to BC, then
$$AC = 2a\sqrt{5} \qquad\qquad \text{(U of L)}$$

25)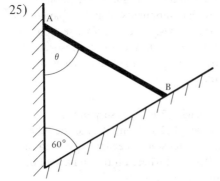

The diagram shows a uniform rod AB resting in the angle between a vertical plane and a plane inclined at $60°$ to the vertical. Find the angle θ if:
(a) both planes are smooth,
(b) the inclined plane is smooth but the vertical plane is rough,
     A is on the point of slipping down and $\mu = \frac{1}{2}$.

26) A uniform rod AB, of length $2l$ and weight W, is in equilibrium with the end A on a rough horizontal floor and the end B against a smooth vertical wall. The rod makes an angle $\tan^{-1}2$ with the horizontal and is in a vertical plane which is perpendicular to the wall. Find the least possible value of μ, the coefficient of friction between the floor and the rod.

Given that $\mu = 5/16$, find the distance from A of the highest point of the rod at which a particle of weight W can be attached without disturbing equilibrium.   (U of L)

27) A uniform ladder of weight W rests on rough horizontal ground against a smooth vertical wall. The vertical plane containing the ladder is perpendicular to the wall and the ladder is inclined at an angle α to the vertical. Prove that, if the ladder is on the point of slipping and μ is the coefficient of friction between it and the ground, then $\tan \alpha = 2\mu$.   (O)

28) A uniform rod AB of weight W is in limiting equilibrium at an angle of $45°$ to the horizontal with its end A on a rough horizontal plane and with a point C in its length against a horizontal rail. This rail is at right angles to the vertical plane containing AB. The coefficient of friction between the rod and the plane is $\frac{1}{2}$ and between the rod and the rail is $\frac{1}{3}$. Calculate the magnitude and direction of the resultant reaction at A.   (AEB)

29) A ladder rests with its foot on smooth horizontal ground and its upper end against a smooth vertical wall. The ladder is uniform, weighs $300\,N$ and is inclined to the wall at an angle θ. What horizontal force must be applied to the foot of the ladder to prevent it slipping if
(a) $\theta = 30°$
(b) $\theta = \arctan \frac{3}{4}$.

30) A uniform rod AB of length $2a$ and weight W has its lower end A on rough horizontal ground. It is supported at $60°$ to the horizontal by a string attached to its upper end B and at right angles to the rod. Find the tension in the string and the frictional and normal forces at the ground.

31) A uniform ladder of weight W rests inclined at an angle θ to the vertical, with one end against a smooth vertical wall and the other end on rough horizontal ground. Find, in terms of W, the magnitude of the frictional force when $\theta = \arctan \frac{12}{5}$. If the angle of friction between the ladder and the ground is $\arctan \frac{3}{8}$, find the value of θ when the ladder is about to slip.

32) A heavy uniform sphere of radius a has a light inextensible string attached to a point on its surface. The other end of the string is fixed to a point on a rough vertical wall. The sphere rests in equilibrium touching the wall at a point distant h below the fixed point. If the point of the sphere in contact with the wall is about to slip downwards and the coefficient of friction between the sphere and the wall is μ, find the inclination of the string to the vertical.

If $\mu = \dfrac{h}{2a}$ and the weight of the sphere is W, show that the tension in

the string is $\dfrac{W}{2\mu}(1+\mu^2)^{\frac{1}{2}}$.   (U of L)

33) The figure shows a uniform rod AB of weight W resting with one end A against a rough vertical wall. One end of a light inextensible string is attached at B and the other end is attached at a point C, vertically above A. The points A, B and C lie in the same vertical plane with $AB = BC = 4a$ and $AC = a$. If equilibrium is limiting, calculate:
(a) the tension in the string.
(b) the angle of friction between the rod and the wall.
(c) the magnitude of the resultant force acting at A.

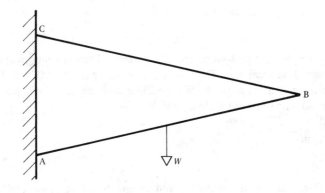

(AEB)

34) A particle rests on a rough plane inclined at an angle θ to the horizontal. The coefficient of friction between the particle and the plane is μ. When the weight of the particle is W, a horizontal force of magnitude P just prevents the particle from slipping down the plane. If however a force of magnitude $2P$ acts parallel to the plane, the particle is on the point of slipping up the plane. The same force acting on a particle of weight $2W$ just prevents it from slipping down the same plane. Find the values of θ and μ, and express P in terms of W.

35) A uniform rod AB, of weight W and length $2l$, rests in equilibrium with the end A on rough horizontal ground and with the end B in contact with a smooth vertical wall, which is perpendicular to the vertical plane containing the rod. If AB makes an angle α with the horizontal, where $\tan \alpha = 4/3$, find the least possible value of μ, the coefficient of friction between the rod and the ground, for equilibrium to be preserved.

If $\mu = \frac{1}{2}$, find the distance from A of the highest point of the rod at which a load of weight W can be attached without equilibrium being disturbed.

(U of L)

36) ABCDEF is a regular hexagon, lettered in an anticlockwise direction. A system of forces in the plane of the hexagon has total anticlockwise moment M_1 about A, M_2 about B and M_3 about C. Show that the moment of the system about D is $M_1 - 2M_2 + 2M_3$, and find the moments about E and F.

37) A uniform rod AB of weight W has its end A on rough horizontal ground and rests at $45°$ to the vertical against a small smooth peg at C, where $AC = \frac{3}{4}AB$. If the rod is on the point of slipping in the vertical plane containing the rod, calculate μ, the coefficient of friction between the rod and the ground. If $\mu = \frac{3}{4}$, calculate the largest vertical downward force which can be applied to the rod at C without disturbing the equilibrium.   (AEB)

CHAPTER 4

VELOCITY AND ACCELERATION

MOTION IN A STRAIGHT LINE

When a particle moves in a straight line its displacement, velocity and acceleration can have one of only two possible directions. Positive and negative signs are used to distinguish between the two directions by taking one sense as positive and the other as negative.

UNIFORM VELOCITY

In Chapter 1, speed was defined as the rate at which a moving body covers its path and velocity was defined as the speed of the body together with the direction in which the body is moving. So a particle moving with *uniform velocity* has a *constant speed in a fixed direction*.

Consider a particle moving with uniform velocity along a line as shown in the diagram, O being a fixed point on that line.

(a) If at some instant the particle is at A and 2 seconds later it is at B, it has covered a distance of 4 metres in 2 seconds. So its speed is $2\,\mathrm{m\,s^{-1}}$.
It is moving in the positive direction so its velocity is $+2\,\mathrm{m\,s^{-1}}$.

Alternatively the displacement from O has increased by $+4$ metres in 2 seconds.
Therefore its displacement from O is increasing at the rate of $+2\,\mathrm{m\,s^{-1}}$ and this is its velocity.

(b) If at some instant the particle is at B and 2 seconds later it is at A, it has again covered a distance of 4 metres in 2 seconds and its speed is therefore again $2\,\mathrm{m\,s^{-1}}$.
This time it is moving in the negative direction so its *velocity* is $-2\,\mathrm{m\,s^{-1}}$.
Alternatively the displacement from O has decreased by 4 m, or increased by -4 m, in 2 s.
Therefore its displacement from O is increasing at the rate of $-2\,\mathrm{m\,s^{-1}}$ and this is its velocity.

In both examples *velocity is the rate of increase of displacement* and the velocity of any moving object, whether uniform or not, is defined in the same way.

Displacement–Time Graph

When a particle is moving in a straight line, a graph of its displacement, s, from a fixed point on the line plotted against time, t, is often a useful way of representing the motion. When the velocity is uniform, equal distances are covered in equal intervals of time, so the graph is a straight line.

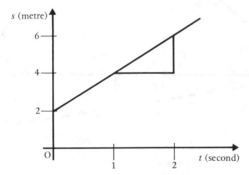

This is a displacement–time graph for the motion discussed in example (a). The gradient of the line is $+2$ and this is the velocity of the particle.

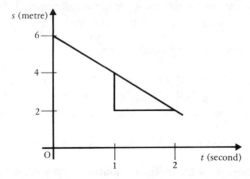

This is a displacement–time graph for the motion discussed in example (b).

The gradient of this line is -2 and this is the velocity of the particle. Thus in both examples the gradient of the line represents the velocity. In general, for uniform velocity,

> the gradient of the displacement–time graph represents the velocity.

Average Velocity

A cyclist starting from a point A travels $200\,\text{m}$ due North to a point B at a constant speed of $5\,\text{m}\,\text{s}^{-1}$. He rests at B for 30 seconds and then travels $300\,\text{m}$ due South to a point C at a constant speed of $10\,\text{m}\,\text{s}^{-1}$.

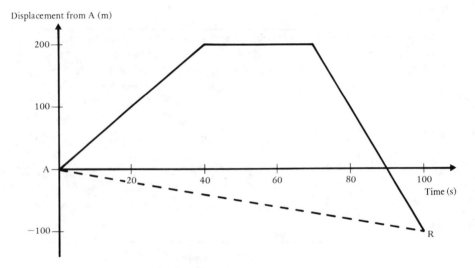

The time taken for the whole journey is $100\,\text{s}$.

The total distance travelled is $500\,\text{m}$.

The *average speed* for the whole journey is the constant speed that would be required to cover the total distance in the same time.

Thus the average speed for the journey is $\dfrac{500}{100}\,\text{m}\,\text{s}^{-1}$, i.e. $5\,\text{m}\,\text{s}^{-1}$.

The *average velocity* for the whole journey is the uniform velocity that would be required to achieve the final increase in *displacement* from A in 100 seconds. The increase in displacement from A after 100 seconds is $-100\,\text{m}$.

Thus the average velocity for the journey is $\dfrac{-100}{100}\,\text{m}\,\text{s}^{-1}$, i.e. $-1\,\text{m}\,\text{s}^{-1}$.

On the displacement–time graph for the journey, this average velocity is represented by the gradient of the chord AR.

In general, for any type of motion, over a given interval of time,

$$\text{Average speed} = \frac{\text{Distance covered in that interval of time}}{\text{Interval of time}}$$

$$\text{Average velocity} = \frac{\text{Increase in displacement in that interval of time}}{\text{Interval of time}}$$

In a displacement–time graph

the gradient of a chord represents the average velocity.

EXERCISE 4a

1) A cyclist rides his bicycle along a straight road for 30 minutes at $10\,\text{m s}^{-1}$ and then gets off and pushes his bicycle for 10 minutes at $1.5\,\text{m s}^{-1}$. Draw a displacement–time graph and find his average velocity for the whole journey.

2) A man walks up a hill at constant speed taking 10 minutes to cover a distance of 800 m. He rests for 2 minutes and then walks down again at constant speed in 6 minutes. Draw a displacement–time graph and find his average speed for the whole journey.

3) A ball is rolled along a line on the floor at a constant speed of $3\,\text{m s}^{-1}$, towards a wall which is 5 m from its starting point. It bounces on the wall and returns at a constant speed of $2\,\text{m s}^{-1}$ along the same line and is caught when it is 7 m from the wall. Draw a displacement–time graph showing the displacement of the ball from its starting point and find the average speed and the average velocity of the ball for its complete journey.

4) A particle is made to move along a straight line at constant speeds in such a way that, measuring from a fixed point O on the line, it goes forward a distance of 12 m at $1.5\,\text{m s}^{-1}$, then backwards a distance of 5 m at $2.5\,\text{m s}^{-1}$ and then forward again a distance of 3 m at $1\,\text{m s}^{-1}$. Draw a graph plotting the displacement of the particle from O against time and find the average speed and the average velocity of the particle for its complete journey.

5) A particle is moving along a straight line and O is a fixed point on that line. The table shows the displacement (s) of the particle from O at given instants of time (t)

t (second)	0	1	2	3	4	5	6
s (metre)	0	2	4	6	6	2	−2

Assuming that the particle has constant speeds over the intervals of time $t = 0$ to $t = 3$, $t = 3$ to $t = 4$, $t = 4$ to $t = 6$, draw a displacement–time graph and find the average velocity of the particle over the interval of time
(a) $t = 0$ to $t = 3$, (b) $t = 1$ to $t = 5$, (c) $t = 2$ to $t = 6$.

VELOCITY AT AN INSTANT

A particle is moving along a straight line where O is a fixed point on that line. The table below gives the displacement of the particle from O at given instants of time.

t (second)	0	1	2	3	4	5
s (metre)	0	1	4	9	16	25

The displacement–time graph is not a straight line as varying distances are covered in equal intervals of time.

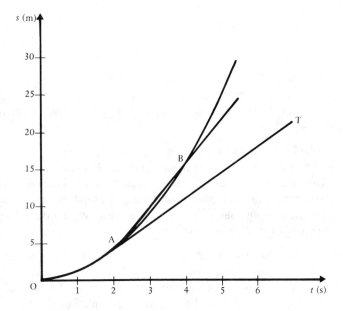

The gradient of the chord AB is 6 so the average velocity over the interval of time from $t = 2$ to $t = 4$ is $6 \, \text{m s}^{-1}$.
This can be taken as an approximate value for the actual velocity at the instant when $t = 2$. It is clearly not a very good approximation but better approximations can be found by taking smaller intervals of time.
The actual velocity at the instant when $t = 2$ is represented by the gradient of the tangent to the curve at A and this can be estimated from the graph.
From the graph, the gradient of AT is approximately $4 \, \text{m s}^{-1}$.
Therefore the velocity at the instant when $t = 2$ is approximately $4 \, \text{m s}^{-1}$.

In general, the velocity at an instant can be found by determining the gradient of the tangent to the displacement–time graph at that instant.

EXAMPLE 4b

A particle moves along a straight line and O is a fixed point on that line.
The displacement s metres of the particle from O at time t seconds is given by

$$s = (t-1)(t-5).$$

Draw a displacement-time graph for the interval of time from $t = 0$ to $t = 6$.
From the graph find:
(a) the average velocity over the interval from $t = 0$ to $t = 4$,
(b) the distance covered in the interval from $t = 0$ to $t = 4$,
(c) the time at which the velocity is zero.

Using $s = (t-1)(t-5)$ and taking $t = 0, 1, 2, 3, 4, 5, 6$, the following
table can be completed:

t (second)	0	1	2	3	4	5	6
s (metre)	5	0	-3	-4	-3	0	5

The displacement-time graph can then be drawn.

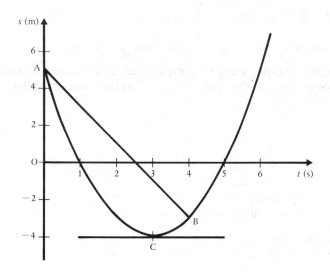

(a) the gradient of the chord AB is -2.
So the average velocity over the interval from $t = 0$ to $t = 4$ is $-2\,\mathrm{m\,s^{-1}}$.

(b) From $t = 0$ to $t = 3$ the particle is moving in the negative sense
along the line.
When $t = 0$, its displacement from O is $5\,\mathrm{m}$.
When $t = 3$, its displacement from O is $-4\,\mathrm{m}$.
Therefore the *distance* covered between $t = 0$ and $t = 3$ is $9\,\mathrm{m}$.

From $t = 3$ to $t = 4$ the particle moves in the positive sense along the line.
When $t = 3$ its displacement from O is $-4\,\text{m}$.
When $t = 4$ its displacement from O is $-3\,\text{m}$.
Therefore the distance covered between $t = 3$ and $t = 4$ is $1\,\text{m}$.
So the distance covered from $t = 0$ to $t = 4$ is $10\,\text{m}$.

(c) The gradient of the tangent to the curve represents the velocity at an instant. From the graph we see that the gradient of the tangent is zero at the point C where $t = 3$. Therefore the velocity is zero when $t = 3$.

EXERCISE 4b

1) A particle is moving along a straight line and O is a point on that line. The displacements, s, of the particle from O at given instants of time, t, are shown in the table.

t (second)	0	1	2	3	4	5	6
s (metre)	0	3	4	3	0	-5	-12

Draw a displacement–time graph and find the average velocity over the interval of time
(a) from $t = 0$ to $t = 2$,   (b) from $t = 0$ to $t = 6$.

2) A particle is moving along a straight line and O is a fixed point on the line. The displacement, s, of the particle from O at given instants of time, t, is shown in the table.

t (second)	0	1	2	3	4
s (metre)	0	2	2	0	-4

Draw a displacement–time graph.
Find the average velocity over the interval of time from $t = 1$ to $t = 2$ and estimate the velocity at the instant when $t = 1$.

3) A particle moves along a straight line and O is a fixed point on that line. The displacements from O at given instants of time are shown in the table.

t (second)	0	1	2	3	4	5
s (metre)	0	3	8	9	0	-25

Draw a displacement–time graph and find, over the interval of time from $t = 1$ to $t = 4$,
(a) the increase in displacement,   (b) the distance covered,
(c) the average speed,   (d) the average velocity,
Estimate the velocity when $t = 4$.

4) A particle is moving along a straight line. Its displacement, s, from a fixed point O on the line, at time t, is given by $s = t - 5t^2$.
Draw a displacement-time graph for the interval $t = 0$ to $t = 6$.
Measuring s in metres and t in seconds, use your graph to find
(a) the average velocity over the interval $t = 2$ to $t = 5$,
(b) the velocity when $t = 4$,
(c) the time at which the velocity is zero.

5) A particle is moving along a straight line and O is a fixed point on that line. Its displacement s metres from O at time t seconds is given by $s = 6 + t - t^2$.
Draw a displacement-time graph for the interval of time from $t = -1$ to $t = 5$. Use your graph to find:
(a) the distance travelled in the interval from $t = 0$ to $t = 2$,
(b) the displacement of the particle from O when $t = 0$.
(c) the velocity when $t = 0$,
(d) the time at which the velocity is zero.

MOTION OF A PARTICLE WITH CONSTANT VELOCITY

Consider a particle moving with constant velocity $\mathbf{v}$, which passes through a point A with position vector $\mathbf{p}$ when the time t is zero.
Because $\mathbf{v}$ is constant the particle is travelling along a straight line through A.

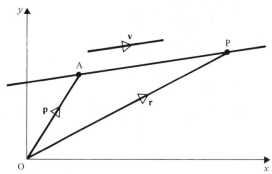

If the particle is at a point P, with general position vector $\mathbf{r}$, at a time t, then

$$\overrightarrow{AP} = t\mathbf{v}$$

But
$$\overrightarrow{OP} = \overrightarrow{OA} + \overrightarrow{AP}$$

Hence
$$\mathbf{r} = \mathbf{p} + t\mathbf{v}$$

This is the *equation of motion* of the particle.

Note it is also the equation of the path of the particle, each value of t gives the *actual position of the particle* at that time and not just any point on the line.

EXAMPLE 4c

A particle travels with speed $50 \, \text{m s}^{-1}$ from the point $(3, -7)$ in a direction $7\mathbf{i} - 24\mathbf{j}$. Find its position vector after
(a) t seconds
(b) 3 seconds.

The velocity vector of the particle is given by

$$\mathbf{v} = 50\left(\frac{7\mathbf{i} - 24\mathbf{j}}{25}\right) = 14\mathbf{i} - 48\mathbf{j}$$

So after t seconds the position vector of the particle is

$$\mathbf{r} = 3\mathbf{i} - 7\mathbf{j} + t(14\mathbf{i} - 48\mathbf{j})$$

After 3 seconds, $t = 3$, so

$$\mathbf{r} = 3\mathbf{i} - 7\mathbf{j} + 3(14\mathbf{i} - 48\mathbf{j})$$

$$= 45\mathbf{i} - 151\mathbf{j}$$

EXERCISE 4c

Find the position vector of an object with constant speed V in a direction $\mathbf{d}$ from a point with position vector $\mathbf{p}$, (a) at time t (b) when $t = 2$,   if

1) $V = 10$, $\mathbf{d} = 2\mathbf{i} + \mathbf{j}$, $\mathbf{p} = 4\mathbf{i}$

2) $V = 8$, $\mathbf{d} = \mathbf{i} + \mathbf{j}$, $\mathbf{p} = 3\mathbf{i} + \mathbf{j}$

3) $V = 40$, $\mathbf{d} = \mathbf{i} - 3\mathbf{j}$, $\mathbf{p} = \mathbf{j}$

4) $V = 5$, $\mathbf{d} = 4\mathbf{i}$, $\mathbf{p} = 2\mathbf{j}$

5) $V = 13$, $\mathbf{d} = 10\mathbf{i} - 24\mathbf{j}$, $\mathbf{p} = \mathbf{i} - \mathbf{j}$

ACCELERATION

If a particle moving in a straight line has a velocity of $2 \, \text{m s}^{-1}$ at one instant, and 4 seconds later it has a velocity of $10 \, \text{m s}^{-1}$, its velocity has increased by $8 \, \text{m s}^{-1}$ in 4 seconds.

If the velocity is increasing steadily, its rate of increase is $2 \, \text{m s}^{-1}$ each second (written $2 \, \text{m s}^{-2}$) and the particle is said to have a constant acceleration of $2 \, \text{m s}^{-2}$.

If, on the other hand, the particle has a velocity of $10 \, \text{m s}^{-1}$ at one instant and 4 seconds later it has a velocity of $2 \, \text{m s}^{-1}$, its velocity has decreased by $8 \, \text{m s}^{-1}$ in 4 seconds, or has increased by $-8 \, \text{m s}^{-1}$ in 4 seconds.

If this increase is steady then the rate of increase of velocity is $-2\,\mathrm{m\,s^{-1}}$ each second, so the acceleration is $-2\,\mathrm{m\,s^{-2}}$.

In general   acceleration is the rate of increase of velocity.

EXAMPLE 4d

A particle moving in a straight line has a constant acceleration of $-2\,\mathrm{m\,s^{-2}}$. If it has a velocity of $-4\,\mathrm{m\,s^{-1}}$ at one instant, find its velocity 3 seconds later.

The acceleration is $-2\,\mathrm{m\,s^{-2}}$.

Therefore the velocity is increasing at a rate of $-2\,\mathrm{m\,s^{-1}}$ each second.

Therefore the increase in velocity after 3 seconds is $-6\,\mathrm{m\,s^{-1}}$.

The initial velocity is $-4\,\mathrm{m\,s^{-1}}$.

So the velocity after 3 seconds is $-10\,\mathrm{m\,s^{-1}}$.

EXERCISE 4d

1) A particle moving in a straight line with constant acceleration has a velocity of $8\,\mathrm{m\,s^{-1}}$ at one instant and 3 seconds later it has a velocity of $2\,\mathrm{m\,s^{-1}}$. Find its acceleration.

2) A particle is moving in a straight line with a constant acceleration of $3\,\mathrm{m\,s^{-2}}$ and has a velocity of $2\,\mathrm{m\,s^{-1}}$ at one instant. Find its velocity 2 seconds later.

3) A particle moving in a straight line with a constant acceleration of $-3\,\mathrm{m\,s^{-2}}$ has a velocity of $15\,\mathrm{m\,s^{-1}}$ at one instant. Find its velocity:
(a) 4 seconds later,
(b) 5 seconds later,
(c) 6 seconds later.

4) A particle moving in a straight line with constant acceleration has a velocity of $-8\,\mathrm{m\,s^{-1}}$ at one instant. If the acceleration of the particle is $2\,\mathrm{m\,s^{-2}}$, find its velocity after 5 seconds.

5) A particle is moving in a straight line with constant acceleration. At one instant its velocity is $-10\,\mathrm{m\,s^{-1}}$ and 4 seconds later its velocity is $2\,\mathrm{m\,s^{-1}}$. Find its acceleration.

Velocity–Time Graph

A graph of velocity plotted against time is a useful way of representing motion in a straight line. When the acceleration is constant the increase in velocity is the same for equal intervals of time so the graph is a straight line.

Consider a particle, moving in a straight line with constant acceleration, which has a velocity of $2\,\mathrm{m\,s}^{-1}$ at one instant and 3 seconds later has a velocity of $8\,\mathrm{m\,s}^{-1}$.

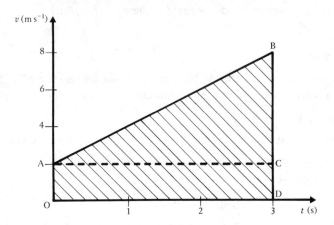

The acceleration is $\frac{6}{3}\,\mathrm{m\,s}^{-2}$ i.e. $2\,\mathrm{m\,s}^{-2}$.

This is represented on the graph by the fraction $\dfrac{BC}{AC}$ which is the gradient of the line AB.

In general, the gradient of the velocity–time graph represents the acceleration.

As the graph is a straight line the average velocity over the interval of three seconds is the numerical average of the initial velocity $2\,\mathrm{m\,s}^{-1}$ and the final velocity, $8\,\mathrm{m\,s}^{-1}$.
So the average velocity in the interval from $t = 0$ to $t = 3$
is $\frac{1}{2}(2+8)\mathrm{m\,s}^{-1} = 5\,\mathrm{m\,s}^{-1}$.

In general, when a particle is moving in a straight line with constant acceleration the average velocity over an interval of time is the average of the initial and final velocities in that interval of time.

Consider again the definition

$$\text{Average velocity} = \frac{\text{Increase in displacement}}{\text{Time}}$$

On the graph, the average velocity is represented by $\frac{1}{2}(AO + BD)$
and the interval of time is represented by OD.
Hence the increase in displacement is represented by $\frac{1}{2}(AO + BD)OD$.
But this is the area of the trapezium OABD.

In general, the area bounded by the velocity-time graph, the time axis and the ordinates at t_1 and t_2, represents the increase in displacement over the interval of time from $t = t_1$ to $t = t_2$.

EXAMPLES 4e

1) A car is moving along a straight line. It is taken from rest to a velocity of $20\,\mathrm{m\,s^{-1}}$ by a constant acceleration of $5\,\mathrm{m\,s^{-2}}$. It maintains a constant velocity of $20\,\mathrm{m\,s^{-1}}$ for 5 seconds and then is brought to rest again by a constant acceleration of $-2\,\mathrm{m\,s^{-2}}$. Draw a velocity-time graph and find the distance covered by the car.

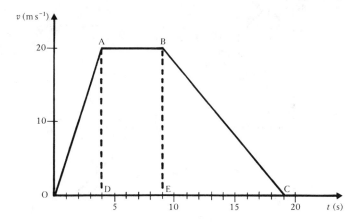

When velocity decreases, as happens in this case between $t = 9$ and $t = 19$, the acceleration is negative and is sometimes referred to as a *deceleration* or a *retardation*.

The increase in displacement while the car is accelerating is represented by the area of triangle OAD.

The increase in displacement at uniform velocity is represented by the area of rectangle ABED.

The increase in displacement while the car is decelerating is represented by the area of triangle BEC.

Therefore the total increase in displacement is represented by the area of the trapezium OABC

i.e. by $\qquad \tfrac{1}{2}(AB + OC)(AD) = \tfrac{1}{2}(5 + 19) \times 20 = 240$

So the increase in displacement is 240 m.

As the car is travelling in the same sense along the line at all times, the distance covered is equal to the increase in displacement.

Hence the distance covered is also 240 m.

2) A particle is travelling in a straight line. It has a velocity of $10\,\mathrm{m\,s}^{-1}$ when it is subjected to an acceleration of $-2\,\mathrm{m\,s}^{-2}$ for 8 seconds.
Draw a velocity–time graph for this interval of eight seconds and find:
(a) the increase in displacement,
(b) the distance covered for the interval of eight seconds.

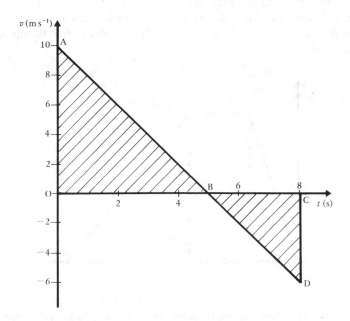

From $t = 0$ to $t = 5$ the velocity is positive, so the particle is travelling in a positive sense along the line.
So the area of triangle OAB represents an increase in displacement of 25 m.

From $t = 5$ to $t = 8$ the velocity is negative, so the particle is travelling in a negative sense along the line.
This time the area of triangle BCD represents a decrease in displacement of 9 m, or an increase in displacement of -9 m.
Therefore the increase in displacement from $t = 0$ to $t = 8$ is

$$(25 - 9)\,\mathrm{m} \;=\; 16\,\mathrm{m}$$

The distance covered from $t = 0$ to $t = 5$ is 25 m.
The distance covered from $t = 5$ to $t = 8$ is 9 m.
So the distance covered from $t = 0$ to $t = 8$ is $(25 + 9)\,\mathrm{m} = 34\,\mathrm{m}$.

EXERCISE 4e

1) A car accelerates uniformly from a velocity of $10 \, \text{m s}^{-1}$ to a velocity of $40 \, \text{m s}^{-1}$ in a time of $10 \, \text{s}$. Draw a velocity–time graph and find the acceleration and the distance covered by the car in this time of $10 \, \text{s}$.

2) A train is brought to rest from a velocity of $24 \, \text{m s}^{-1}$ by a constant acceleration of $-0.8 \, \text{m s}^{-2}$. Draw a velocity–time graph and find the distance covered by the train while it is decelerating.

3) A particle moving in a straight line moves from rest with a uniform acceleration of $4 \, \text{m s}^{-2}$ for 4 seconds. It is then brought to rest again by a uniform acceleration of $-2 \, \text{m s}^{-2}$. Draw a velocity–time graph and find the total distance covered by the particle.

4) A particle moves from rest in a straight line with an acceleration of $4 \, \text{m s}^{-2}$ for 3 seconds. It maintains a uniform velocity for 6 seconds and is then brought to rest again in a time of 4 seconds with a uniform retardation. Draw a velocity–time graph and find the final acceleration and the final displacement of the particle from its starting point.

5) A particle moves in a straight line with a constant velocity of $5 \, \text{m s}^{-1}$ for 2 seconds. It then moves with a constant accleration of $-2 \, \text{m s}^{-2}$ for 8 seconds. Draw a velocity–time graph for the interval of 10 seconds and find:
(a) the final velocity,
(b) the total distance covered by the particle,
(c) the increase in displacement of the particle.

6) A particle moves in a straight line. It has a velocity of $6 \, \text{m s}^{-1}$ when it is subjected to an acceleration of $-3 \, \text{m s}^{-2}$ for 3 seconds. It maintains a uniform velocity for 2 seconds and is then brought to rest in a time of 2 seconds. Draw a velocity–time graph and find, for the 7-second interval:
(a) the final acceleration,
(b) the distance covered,
(c) the increase in displacement.

EQUATIONS OF MOTION FOR A PARTICLE MOVING IN A STRAIGHT LINE WITH CONSTANT ACCELERATION

Motion in a straight line with constant acceleration occurs frequently enough to justify obtaining general equations which can then be applied to a particular problem, removing the need to go back to first principles each time.

Consider a particle which is moving in a straight line with a constant acceleration a and which has an initial velocity u and a final velocity v after an interval of time t.

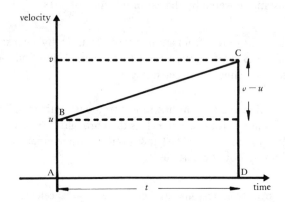

In the velocity–time graph the acceleration is represented by the gradient of the line BC so $\quad a = \dfrac{v - u}{t}$

$\Rightarrow$ $$v = u + at \qquad\qquad [1]$$

The increase in displacement, s, in time t is represented by the area of ABCD.

i.e. $$s = \tfrac{1}{2}(u + v)t \qquad\qquad [2]$$

Eliminating v from equations [1] and [2] gives $\quad s = \tfrac{1}{2}[u + (u + at)]t$

$\Rightarrow$ $$s = ut + \tfrac{1}{2}at^2 \qquad\qquad [3]$$

Eliminating u from equations [1] and [2] gives $\quad s = \tfrac{1}{2}[(v - at) + v]t$

$\Rightarrow$ $$s = vt - \tfrac{1}{2}at^2 \qquad\qquad [4]$$

Eliminating t from equations [1] and [2] gives $\quad s = \tfrac{1}{2}(u + v)(v - u)$

$\Rightarrow$ $$v^2 = u^2 + 2as \qquad\qquad [5]$$

Equations [1], [2], [3], [4], [5] can now be used for solving any problem involving motion in a straight line with constant acceleration and they should be memorised.

When deciding which of these equations to use in solving a particular problem it helps if a list is made of the information given and that required.

EXAMPLES 4f

1) A particle is moving along a straight line with a constant retardation of $3\,\mathrm{m\,s^{-2}}$. If initially it has a velocity of $10\,\mathrm{m\,s^{-1}}$ find the time when the velocity is zero.

Information given: $\quad u = 10$ ⎫⎪⎪⎬⎪⎪⎭ Using the equation $\quad v = u + at$

$\qquad\qquad\qquad\qquad v = 0 \qquad\qquad\qquad\quad \Rightarrow \quad 0 = 10 - 3t$

$\qquad\qquad\qquad\qquad a = -3 \qquad\qquad\qquad\quad \Rightarrow \quad t = 3\tfrac{1}{3}$

Information required: $\quad t$

Hence the velocity is zero after $3\tfrac{1}{3}$ seconds.

2) A particle is moving along a straight line with a constant acceleration of $-2\,\mathrm{m\,s^{-2}}$. It passes through a point A on the line with a velocity of $6\,\mathrm{m\,s^{-1}}$. Find the displacement from A of the particle after 5 seconds and the distance travelled by the particle in this time.

Given $\qquad\qquad\qquad u = 6$ ⎫⎪⎪⎬⎪⎪⎭ Using the equation $\quad s = ut + \tfrac{1}{2}at^2$

$\qquad\qquad\qquad\qquad a = -2 \qquad\qquad\qquad\quad \Rightarrow \quad s = 30 - 25$

$\qquad\qquad\qquad\qquad t = 5 \qquad\qquad\qquad\quad\; \Rightarrow \quad s = 5$

Required: $\qquad\qquad s$

Therefore the displacement of the particle from A after $5\,\mathrm{s}$ is $5\,\mathrm{m}$.

A velocity-time graph for a problem often leads to a quick solution, especially when distances or displacements are involved, so a sketch graph should always be drawn.

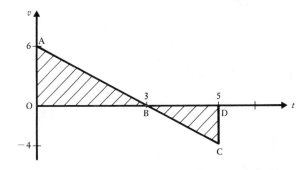

From the sketch we can see that the distance covered in $5\,\mathrm{s}$ is represented by

$$\text{area of } \triangle OAB + \text{area of } \triangle BDC$$

Therefore the distance covered in $5\,\mathrm{s}$ is $(9 + 4)\,\mathrm{m}$ or $13\,\mathrm{m}$.

(The increase in *displacement* is represented by area of $\triangle OAB - $ area of $\triangle BCD$)

3) A train travelling along a straight line with constant acceleration is observed to travel consecutive distances of 1 km in times of 30 s and 60 s respectively. Find the initial velocity of the train.

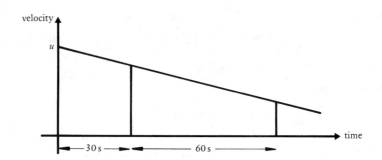

If we let u metre/second be the initial velocity then, as units must be consistent, the distance must be measured in metres.

Required: u

Given: when $s = 1000$, $t = 30$

             when $s = 2000$, $t = 90$

Using $s = ut + \frac{1}{2}at^2$ twice, we have

$$1000 = 30u + 450a \qquad\qquad [1]$$

$$2000 = 90u + 4050a \qquad\qquad [2]$$

Eliminating a from equations [1] and [2] gives

$$200 - 9u = 9(100 - 3u)$$

$\Rightarrow$ $u = 38.9$

The initial velocity of the train is $38.9 \, \mathrm{m\,s^{-1}}$.

Alternatively:

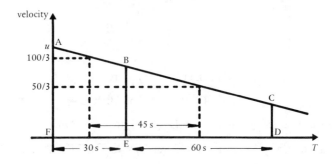

For the first 1000 m the average velocity is $\frac{1000}{30}$ m s^{-1}

Hence the velocity is $\frac{100}{3}$ m s^{-1} when $T = 15$.

For the second 1000 m the average velocity is $\frac{1000}{60}$ m s^{-1}

Hence the velocity is $\frac{50}{3}$ m s^{-1} when $T = 60$.

For the interval of time from $T = 15$ to $T = 60$,

$$t = 45, \quad u = \tfrac{100}{3} \quad \text{and} \quad v = \tfrac{50}{3}$$

Using $v = u + at$ gives $\quad \frac{50}{3} = \frac{100}{3} + 45a$

$\Rightarrow$
$$a = -\tfrac{10}{27}$$

For the interval of time from $T = 0$ to $T = 15$,

$$t = 15, \quad a = \tfrac{10}{27} \quad \text{and} \quad v = \tfrac{100}{3}$$

Using $v = u + at$ gives $\quad \frac{100}{3} = u - \frac{50}{9}$

$\Rightarrow$
$$u = 38.9$$

Therefore the initial velocity of the train is $38.9 \, \text{m s}^{-1}$.

4) A particle starts from a point O with an initial velocity of $2 \, \text{m s}^{-1}$ and travels along a straight line with a constant acceleration of $2 \, \text{m s}^{-2}$. Two seconds later a second particle starts from rest at O and travels along the same line with an acceleration of $6 \, \text{m s}^{-2}$. Find how far from O the second particle overtakes the first.

When the second particle overtakes the first they will both have the same displacement from O. Let that displacement be d metre.

If the first particle takes T seconds to reach this point the second particle takes $(T-2)$ seconds to reach the same point.

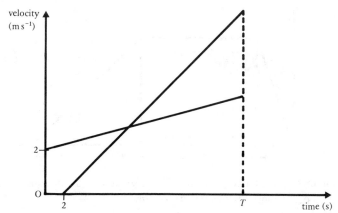

For the first particle $s = d$
$u = 2$
$t = T$ using $s = ut + \frac{1}{2}at^2$ gives
$a = 2$ $d = 2T + T^2$ [1]

For the second particle $s = d$
$u = 0$
$t = T - 2$ using $s = ut + \frac{1}{2}at^2$ gives
$a = 6$ $d = 3(T - 2)^2$ [2]

Eliminating d from equations [1] and [2] gives

$$2T + T^2 = 3(T - 2)^2$$

$\Rightarrow$ $T^2 - 7T + 6 = 0$

$\Rightarrow$ $(T - 6)(T - 1) = 0$

$(T \neq 1$ because this is before the second particle starts)

Therefore $T = 6$

and $d = 48$

Therefore the second particle overtakes the first 48 m from O.

5) A train takes 5 minutes to cover a distance of 3 km between two stations
P and Q. Starting from rest at P, it accelerates at a constant rate to a speed of
40 km h^{-1} and maintains this speed until it is brought uniformly to rest at Q.
If the train takes three times as long to decelerate as it does to accelerate, find
the time taken by the train to accelerate.

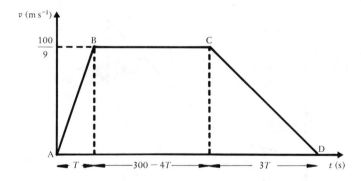

As the time involved is fairly small we will use seconds and, for consistency of
units, metres per second. So we convert 40 km h^{-1} to $\frac{100}{9}$ m s^{-1}.

Let the time taken to accelerate be T seconds so that the time taken to decelerate is $3T$ seconds.

Then the time for which the speed is constant is $(300-4T)$ seconds.

The area of trapezium ABCD represents the distance travelled by the train, so

$$\text{the area of ABCD} = \tfrac{1}{2}(300 + \{300-4T\})\left(\tfrac{100}{9}\right)$$

$$\Rightarrow \qquad 3000 = \tfrac{1}{2}(600-4T)\left(\tfrac{100}{9}\right)$$

$$\Rightarrow \qquad 540 = 600-4T$$

$$\Rightarrow \qquad T = 15$$

Therefore the time taken to accelerate is 15 s.

EXERCISE 4f

1) A particle with an initial velocity of $2\,\mathrm{m\,s^{-1}}$ moves in a straight line with a constant acceleration of $3\,\mathrm{m\,s^{-2}}$ for 5 seconds. Find the final velocity and the distance covered.

2) A particle is moving in a straight line with a constant acceleration of $-4\,\mathrm{m\,s^{-2}}$. If the initial velocity is $10\,\mathrm{m\,s^{-1}}$ find the increase in displacement after
(a) 2 s   (b) 4 s.

3) A particle moving in a straight line with constant acceleration has a velocity of $5\,\mathrm{m\,s^{-1}}$ at one instant and 4 seconds later it has a velocity of $15\,\mathrm{m\,s^{-1}}$. Find the acceleration and the distance covered by the particle in the 4 seconds.

4) A particle is moving in a straight line with constant acceleration. Initially it is at rest and after 6 seconds its velocity is $15\,\mathrm{m\,s^{-1}}$. Find the acceleration and the distance covered in the 6 seconds.

5) A particle which is moving in a straight line with constant acceleration $2\,\mathrm{m\,s^{-2}}$ is initially at rest. Find the distance covered by the particle in the third second of its motion.

6) A particle moving in a straight line with a constant acceleration $-5\,\mathrm{m\,s^{-2}}$ has an initial velocity of $15\,\mathrm{m\,s^{-1}}$. Find when the velocity is zero.

7) A particle moving in a straight line with a constant retardation of $3\,\text{m}\,\text{s}^{-2}$ has an initial velocity of $10\,\text{m}\,\text{s}^{-1}$. Find after what time it returns to its starting point.

8) A particle which is moving in a straight line with constant acceleration covers distances of $10\,\text{m}$ and $15\,\text{m}$ in two successive seconds. Find the acceleration.

9) A particle moving in a straight line with constant acceleration takes 3 seconds and 5 seconds to cover two successive distances of 1 m. Find the acceleration.

10) A particle moving in a straight line with constant acceleration of $-3\,\text{m}\,\text{s}^{-2}$ has an initial velocity of $15\,\text{m}\,\text{s}^{-1}$. Find the time at which its displacement from the starting point is   (a) $15\,\text{m}$ (b) $-15\,\text{m}$.

11) A particle starts from rest at a point O on a straight line and moves along the line with a constant acceleration of $2\,\text{m}\,\text{s}^{-2}$. Three seconds later a second particle starts from rest at O and moves along the line with constant acceleration $4\,\text{m}\,\text{s}^{-2}$. Find when the second particle overtakes the first particle.

12) Two particles are travelling along a straight line AB of length $20\,\text{m}$. At the same instant one particle starts from rest at A and travels towards B with a constant acceleration of $2\,\text{m}\,\text{s}^{-2}$ and the other particle starts from rest at B and travels towards A with a constant acceleration of $5\,\text{m}\,\text{s}^{-2}$. Find how far from A the particles collide.

13) A particle starts from rest and moves along a straight line with a constant acceleration until it reaches a velocity of $15\,\text{m}\,\text{s}^{-1}$. It is then brought to rest again by a constant retardation of $3\,\text{m}\,\text{s}^{-2}$. If the particle is then $60\,\text{m}$ from its starting point, find the time for which the particle is moving.

14) A car takes 60 seconds to travel between two sets of traffic lights, starting from rest at the first set and coming to rest again at the second set. It accelerates uniformly to a speed of $12\,\text{m}\,\text{s}^{-1}$ and then uniformly decelerates to rest. Find the distance between the two sets of lights.

15) A train stops at two stations P and Q which are $2\,\text{km}$ apart. It accelerates uniformly from P at $1\,\text{m}\,\text{s}^{-2}$ for 15 seconds and maintains a constant speed for a time before decelerating uniformly to rest at Q. If the deceleration is $0.5\,\text{m}\,\text{s}^{-2}$ find the time for which the train is travelling at a constant speed.

VERTICAL MOTION UNDER GRAVITY

Before the time of Galileo it was thought that if two objects of different masses were dropped the heavier object would fall faster than the light one. In a famous series of experiments Galileo showed that this was not true. (He allegedly dropped objects from the top of the leaning tower of Pisa and timed their descent by the Cathedral clock opposite.)

The results that Galileo observed are that if air resistance is ignored *all bodies (whatever their mass) have the same constant acceleration towards the centre of the earth when they are moving under the action of their weight only.*

This acceleration is denoted by the letter g, and a good approximation to its value is $9.8 \, \text{m s}^{-2}$.

When a body is thrown vertically upward, or is dropped, it moves in a vertical straight line. The only force acting on it is its weight, causing a constant vertical acceleration g, so the equations for motion in a straight line with constant acceleration apply. In some problems it is convenient to take the downward direction as positive, in which case the acceleration is $+g$, but in other problems it is convenient to take the upward direction as positive, in which case the acceleration is $-g$.

EXAMPLES 4g

1) A stone is thrown vertically upward from the top of a tower and hits the ground 10 seconds later with a speed of $51 \, \text{m s}^{-1}$. Find the height of the tower.

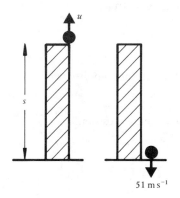

$51 \, \text{m s}^{-1}$

Taking the downward direction as positive we have,

given:
$$v = 51$$
$$a = 9.8$$
$$t = 10$$

required: s

Using $\quad s = vt - \tfrac{1}{2}at^2 \quad$ gives

$$s = 510 - (50 \times 9.8)$$

$\Rightarrow \qquad s = 20$

Therefore the tower is $20 \, \text{m}$ high.

2) A ball is thrown vertically upward from a point 0.5 m above ground level with a speed of $7\,\mathrm{m\,s^{-1}}$. Find the height above this point reached by the ball and the speed with which it hits the ground.

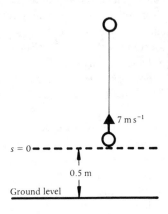

This time we will take the upward direction as positive. The velocity of the ball is zero when it reaches its greatest height above its initial position. So we have,

given: $u = 7$

                $v = 0$ Using $v^2 = u^2 + 2as$ gives

                $a = -9.8$ $0 = 49 - 19.6s$

required: s $\Rightarrow$ $s = 2.5$

Therefore the stone reaches a height of 2.5 m above its initial position.

When the stone hits the ground it is 0.5 m below its initial position.

Given $u = 7$

                $s = -0.5$ Using $v^2 = u^2 + 2as$ gives

                $a = -9.8$ $v^2 = 49 + 9.8$

Required: v $\Rightarrow$ $v = \pm 7.66$

When the stone reaches the ground it is travelling downwards, so $v = -7.66$; but the speed is the magnitude of the velocity,
therefore the stone hits the ground with a speed of $7.66\,\mathrm{m\,s^{-1}}$.

3) A ball is thrown vertically upward with a speed of $14 \, \text{m s}^{-1}$. Two seconds later a second ball is dropped from the same point. Find where the two balls meet.

The balls will meet when they have the same displacement (d metre) from the starting point.
If the time taken by the first ball to achieve this displacement is T second, the time taken by the second ball is $(T-2)$ second.

Taking the upward direction as positive, we have,

for the first ball:
$$\left. \begin{array}{l} u = 14 \\ a = -9.8 \\ t = T \\ s = d \end{array} \right\} \quad \text{Using} \quad s = ut + \tfrac{1}{2}at^2 \quad \Rightarrow \quad d = 14T - 4.9T^2 \qquad [1]$$

for the second ball:
$$\left. \begin{array}{l} u = 0 \\ a = -9.8 \\ t = T-2 \\ s = d \end{array} \right\} \quad \text{Using} \quad s = ut + \tfrac{1}{2}at^2 \quad \Rightarrow \quad d = -4.9(T-2)^2 \qquad [2]$$

Eliminating d from equations [1] and [2] gives
$$2T - 0.7T^2 = -0.7(T-2)^2$$

$\Rightarrow \qquad\qquad\qquad\qquad T = 3.5$

which gives $\qquad\qquad\qquad d = -11.0$

Therefore the balls meet $11.0 \, \text{m}$ below their initial position.

EXERCISE 4g

1) A stone is dropped from a cliff $100 \, \text{m}$ above the sea. Find the speed with which it hits the sea.

2) A stone is thrown vertically upward with a speed of $10 \, \text{m s}^{-1}$. Find the greatest height reached by the stone.

3) A ball is thrown vertically upward to a height of $10 \, \text{m}$. Find the time taken to reach this height and the initial speed of the ball.

4) A particle is projected vertically upward from ground level with a speed of $20 \, \text{m s}^{-1}$. Find the time for which the particle is in the air.

5) A stone is thrown vertically upward with a speed of $7 \, \text{m s}^{-1}$ from the top of a cliff which is $70 \, \text{m}$ above sea level. Find the time at which the stone hits the sea.

6) A stone is projected vertically upward with a speed of $21 \, \mathrm{m s^{-1}}$. Find the distance travelled by the stone in the first 3 seconds of its motion.

7) A ball is thrown vertically upward with a speed of $15 \, \mathrm{m s^{-1}}$ from a point which is $0.7 \, \mathrm{m}$ above ground level. Find the speed with which the ball hits the ground.

8) A particle is projected vertically upward from ground level with a speed of $50 \, \mathrm{m s^{-1}}$. For how long will it be more than $70 \, \mathrm{m}$ above the ground?

9) A falling stone takes 0.2 seconds to fall past a window which is $1 \, \mathrm{m}$ high. From how far above the top of the window was the stone dropped?

10) A stone is projected vertically upward with a speed of $7 \, \mathrm{m s^{-1}}$ and one second later a second stone is projected vertically upward from the same point with the same speed. Find where the two stones meet.

11) A stone is dropped from the top of a building and at the same time a second stone is thrown vertically upward from the bottom of the building with a speed of $20 \, \mathrm{m s^{-1}}$. They pass each other 3 seconds later. Find the height of the building.

INTRODUCTION TO MOTION IN A PLANE

Consider a particle P moving along a curve; the curve is called the path of the particle.

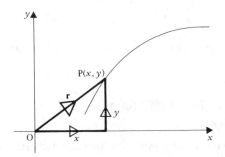

If the particle is at a point with coordinates (x, y) at time t, its displacement from O is $\overrightarrow{OP}$ or **r**.

$\overrightarrow{OP}$ has components $\begin{cases} x \text{ in the direction of } Ox \\ y \text{ in the direction of } Oy \end{cases}$

So we can say

$$\mathbf{r} = x\mathbf{i} + y\mathbf{j}$$

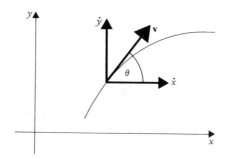

The velocity component in the direction Ox is $\dfrac{dx}{dt}$ (denoted by $\dot{x}$) and the velocity component in the direction Oy is $\dfrac{dy}{dt}$ or $\dot{y}$.

So, if $\mathbf{v}$ is the velocity of the particle at time t we can say

$$\mathbf{v} = \dot{x}\mathbf{i} + \dot{y}\mathbf{j}$$

$\Rightarrow$
$$\mathbf{v} = \frac{d\mathbf{r}}{dt}$$

Further, the components of the acceleration, $\mathbf{a}$, of the particle at time t are $\dfrac{d(\dot{x})}{dt}$ (denoted by $\ddot{x}$) in the direction Ox and $\dfrac{d(\dot{y})}{dt}$, or $\ddot{y}$, in the direction Oy, so that

$$\mathbf{a} = \ddot{x}\mathbf{i} + \ddot{y}\mathbf{j}$$

$\Rightarrow$
$$\mathbf{a} = \frac{d\mathbf{v}}{dt}$$

Note that, if θ is the angle between the direction of $\mathbf{v}$ and the x axis, then

$$\tan \theta = \frac{\dot{y}}{\dot{x}} = \frac{dy}{dt} \bigg/ \frac{dx}{dt} = \frac{dy}{dx} = \text{gradient of tangent at P}$$

Therefore the direction of $\mathbf{v}$ is the direction of the tangent at P to the path of the particle. This is the direction of motion of the particle.

EXAMPLE 4h

A particle moves in the xy plane such that, at time t, its displacement from a fixed point O is given by $\mathbf{r} = 2t\mathbf{i} + t^2\mathbf{j}$.   Show that its acceleration $\mathbf{a}$ is always $2\mathbf{j}$ and find its direction of motion when $t = 1$.

If $\mathbf{r} = 2t\mathbf{i} + t^2\mathbf{j}$,   the velocity $\mathbf{v}$ is given by

$$\mathbf{v} = \frac{d\mathbf{r}}{dt} = 2\mathbf{i} + 2t\mathbf{j}$$

Then $\mathbf{a} = \dfrac{d\mathbf{v}}{dt} = 2\mathbf{j}$

This does not depend on the value of t so the acceleration is always $2\mathbf{j}$.

From $\mathbf{v}$ we see that, when $t = 1$, $\dot{x} = 2$ and $\dot{y} = 2$.

The angle between the direction of motion and the x axis is therefore $\arctan\frac{2}{2}$,   i.e. $45°$.

EXERCISE 4h

In Questions 1–4 find $\mathbf{v}$ and $\mathbf{a}$ (a) at time t (b) when $t = 3$.
Find also the direction of motion when $t = 1$.

1) $\mathbf{r} = t^3\mathbf{i} + t^2\mathbf{j}$

2) $\mathbf{r} = 3\mathbf{i} - t^4\mathbf{j}$

3) $\mathbf{r} = (t + 2)\mathbf{i} + (1 - t^2)\mathbf{j}$

4) $\mathbf{r} = t^2\mathbf{i} - t^2\mathbf{j}$

5) A particle moves in the xy plane so that, at time t, its displacement from a fixed point O is given by $\mathbf{r} = 4t\mathbf{i} + (3t - 5t^2)\mathbf{j}$.   Find its velocity vector at time t and hence find the velocity components when $t = 0$.   Show that the acceleration is constant.
Do you notice anything significant about this acceleration?

ANGULAR VELOCITY

Consider a particle P which is moving round the circumference of a circle. It can rotate about O in only two senses, clockwise or anticlockwise. Positive and negative signs are used to differentiate between these two senses and it is customary to take the anticlockwise sense as positive.

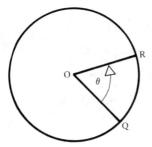

If, initially, the particle is at Q and after an interval of time it is at R, then if angle QOR is θ,

the angular velocity of P is defined as the rate of increase of θ.

Angular velocity is usually denoted by ω.

If θ is increasing at a constant rate then the angular velocity ω is uniform.

Angles are measured in radians so the unit of angular velocity is the radian per second (rad s^{-1}).

EXAMPLE 4i

The hour and minute hands of a clock coincide at exactly 12.00 hours. Find when they next coincide.

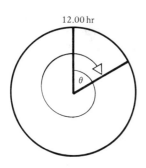

The hour hand rotates through 1 revolution in 12 hours, i.e. 2π rad in 12 hours. So the angular velocity of the hour hand is $\frac{\pi}{360}$ rad/min. (This is a more convenient unit than the rad s^{-1} in this problem.)

The minute hand rotates at the steady rate of 2π rad per hour. Therefore the angular velocity of the minute hand is $\frac{\pi}{30}$ rad/min.

If they next coincide after t minutes when they make an angle θ radians with their initial position, then the hour hand will have turned through an angle of θ radians and the minute hand through an angle of $(2\pi + \theta)$ radians.

For the hour hand $\qquad\qquad \dfrac{\pi}{360} t = \theta$ $\qquad\qquad\qquad$ [1]

For the minute hand $\qquad\qquad \dfrac{\pi}{30} t = \theta + 2\pi$ $\qquad\qquad\qquad$ [2]

[1] and [2] give

$$\frac{\pi}{30}t = \frac{\pi}{360}t + 2\pi$$

$\Rightarrow$ $\qquad\qquad 12t = t + 720$

$\Rightarrow$ $\qquad\qquad t = 65.45$

Therefore the hands next coincide 65.5 minutes after 12.00 hours
i.e. at 13.05 hours.

Relationship Between Angular Velocity and Linear Velocity

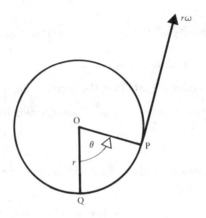

Consider a point P which is rotating in a circle of radius r with a constant
angular velocity ω. Its direction of motion at any instant is tangential,
as we saw on p. 135.

If P turns through an angle θ from its initial position Q in a time t then

$$\theta = \omega t \qquad\qquad [1]$$

The length of the arc PQ is $r\theta$, where θ is measured in radians, and this is the
distance covered by P in this time.

Therefore the speed of P is $\qquad\qquad \dfrac{r\theta}{t} \qquad\qquad [2]$

Substituting for θ from equation [1] shows that the speed of P is $r\omega$,
therefore

> the linear velocity is $r\omega$ in the direction of the tangent to the circle

Thus a point which is rotating in a circle of radius 2 m with an angular velocity
of $4\ \text{rad}\,\text{s}^{-1}$ has a speed of $8\ \text{m}\,\text{s}^{-1}$.

EXERCISE 4i

1) Find the angular velocity, in rad s^{-1}, of a record which is rotating at a rate of:
(a) 33 revolutions per minute,
(b) 45 revolutions per minute.

2) Find the angular velocity, in rad s^{-1}, of the second hand of a clock.

3) A wheel of radius $2\,\text{m}$ is rotating at the constant rate of $20\,\text{rad s}^{-1}$. Find the speed of a point on its circumference in m s^{-1}.

4) Find the speed, in km h^{-1}, of a point on the equator of the earth, assuming it to be a circle of radius $6400\,\text{km}$.

5) The minute and hour hand of a clock coincide exactly at 12 o'clock. Find the time between 3 o'clock and 4 o'clock when they coincide.

Constant Angular Acceleration

Angular acceleration is defined as the rate of increase of angular velocity.

The *unit* of angular acceleration is the radian per second per second (rad s^{-2}). When the angular velocity increases at a steady rate the angular acceleration is constant. In this case if angular velocity is plotted against time the graph is a straight line.

Consider a particle describing a circle with constant angular acceleration α.

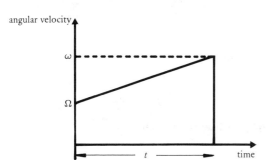 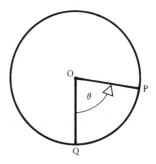

If, initially, the particle is at Q with an angular velocity Ω and, after an interval of time t, it is at P with angular velocity ω then

the increase in angular velocity is $\omega - \Omega$

So the rate of increase of angular velocity is $\dfrac{\omega - \Omega}{t}$

i.e. $$\alpha = \frac{\omega - \Omega}{t} \quad \Rightarrow \quad \omega = \Omega + \alpha t \tag{1}$$

As the angular acceleration is constant the average angular velocity for this interval of time is $\frac{1}{2}(\Omega + \omega)$.

So, if θ is the angle turned through by the particle in time t,

$$\theta = \tfrac{1}{2}(\Omega + \omega)t \tag{2}$$

Eliminating ω from [1] and [2] gives $\qquad \theta = \Omega t + \tfrac{1}{2}\alpha t^2 \tag{3}$

Eliminating Ω from [1] and [2] gives $\qquad \theta = \omega t - \tfrac{1}{2}\alpha t^2 \tag{4}$

Eliminating t from [1] and [2] gives $\qquad \omega^2 = \Omega^2 + 2\alpha\theta \tag{5}$

These five equations are the equations for circular motion with constant angular acceleration and can be quoted in any problem involving circular motion with constant acceleration.

(Note the similarity to the equations for motion in a straight line with constant acceleration. This should be a help in recalling them.)

EXAMPLE 4j

A wheel rotates with constant angular acceleration and, starting from rest, it is observed to make 5 complete revolutions in 3 seconds. What is the angular velocity in radians per second at the end of the 3 seconds?

The wheel makes 5 revolutions in 3 seconds, so it turns through an angle of 10π radians in this time.

Given: $\qquad \theta = 10\pi$

$\qquad\qquad\quad t = 3 \qquad$ Using $\qquad \theta = \tfrac{1}{2}(\Omega + \omega)t \quad$ gives

$\qquad\qquad\quad \Omega = 0 \qquad\qquad\qquad\qquad 10\pi = \tfrac{1}{2}\omega \times 3$

Required $\qquad \omega \qquad\qquad\qquad\qquad\quad \Rightarrow \quad \omega = \tfrac{20}{3}\pi$

Therefore the angular velocity of the wheel is $\tfrac{20}{3}\pi$ rad s^{-1}.

EXERCISE 4j

1) A wheel rotates with a constant angular acceleration of 3 rad s^{-2}. If it starts from rest find its angular velocity 2 seconds later.

2) A particle describes a circle with constant angular acceleration. It makes one complete revolution in 2 seconds starting from rest. What is its angular acceleration?

3) The angular velocity of a rotating wheel changes from $2\,\mathrm{rad\,s^{-1}}$ to $4\,\mathrm{rad\,s^{-1}}$ in 5 seconds. Assuming that the angular acceleration is constant find the angle the wheel turns through in this time and the angular acceleration.

4) A flywheel rotates with constant angular acceleration. If its angular velocity changes from 10 revolutions per second to 4 revolutions per second in one revolution of the flywheel find the angular acceleration.

5) A wheel makes 4 complete revolutions in 3 seconds. If at the end of the 3 seconds it has an angular velocity of $\pi\,\mathrm{rad\,s^{-1}}$, find its angular acceleration assuming this to be constant.

6) A particle starting from rest moves in a circle with a constant angular acceleration of $\frac{\pi}{4}\,\mathrm{rad\,s^{-2}}$. Find the angle it turns through in the third second of its motion.

SUMMARY

Velocity is the rate of increase of linear displacement.
Acceleration is the rate of increase of velocity.
Angular velocity is the rate of increase of angular displacement.
Angular acceleration is the rate of increase of angular velocity.

Equations of Motion with Constant Acceleration

Motion in a straight line:
$$v = u + at$$
$$s = \tfrac{1}{2}(u + v)t$$
$$s = ut + \tfrac{1}{2}at^2$$
$$s = vt - \tfrac{1}{2}at^2$$
$$v^2 = u^2 + 2as$$

Circular motion:
$$\omega = \Omega + \alpha t$$
$$\theta = \tfrac{1}{2}(\omega + \Omega)t$$
$$\theta = \Omega t + \tfrac{1}{2}\alpha t^2$$
$$\theta = \omega t - \tfrac{1}{2}\alpha t^2$$
$$\omega^2 = \Omega^2 + 2\alpha\theta.$$

General motion:
$$\mathbf{v} = \frac{d\mathbf{r}}{dt}$$
$$\mathbf{a} = \frac{d\mathbf{v}}{dt}$$

If the velocity is constant and the particle passes through **p** when $t = 0$,
$$\mathbf{r} = \mathbf{p} + t\mathbf{v}$$

MULTIPLE CHOICE EXERCISE 4

(The instructions for answering these questions are given on page x.)

TYPE I

1)

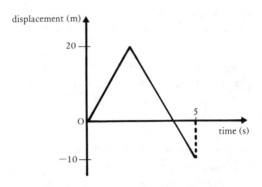

The diagram shows the displacement–time graph for a particle moving in a straight line. The average velocity for the interval from $t = 0$ to $t = 5$ is:

(a) 0   (b) $6 \, \mathrm{m \, s^{-1}}$ (c) $-2 \, \mathrm{m \, s^{-1}}$ (d) $2 \, \mathrm{m \, s^{-1}}$ (e) $-4 \, \mathrm{m \, s^{-1}}$

2)

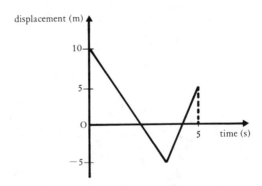

The diagram shows the displacement–time graph for a particle moving in a straight line. The distance covered by the particle in the interval from $t = 0$ to $t = 5$ is:

(a) $20 \, \mathrm{m}$ (b) $25 \, \mathrm{m}$ (c) $15 \, \mathrm{m}$ (d) $5 \, \mathrm{m}$ (e) $10 \, \mathrm{m}$

3)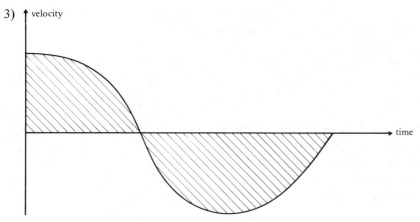

The diagram shows the velocity-time graph for a particle moving in a straight line. The sum of the two shaded areas represents:
(a) the increase in displacement of the particle,
(b) the average velocity of the particle,
(c) the average acceleration of the particle,
(d) the distance moved by the particle,
(e) the average speed of the particle.

4) A particle moving in a straight line with a constant acceleration of $3\,\mathrm{m\,s^{-2}}$ has an initial velocity of $-1\,\mathrm{m\,s^{-1}}$. Its velocity 2 seconds later is:
(a) $5\,\mathrm{m\,s^{-1}}$ (b) $6\,\mathrm{m\,s^{-1}}$ (c) $4\,\mathrm{m\,s^{-1}}$ (d) 0   (e) $-7\,\mathrm{m\,s^{-1}}$.

5) A particle moves in a straight line and passes through O, a fixed point on the line, with a velocity of $6\,\mathrm{m\,s^{-1}}$. The particle moves with a constant retardation of $2\,\mathrm{m\,s^{-2}}$ for 4 seconds and thereafter moves with constant velocity.
How long after leaving O does the particle return to O?
(a) 3 s   (b) 8 s   (c) never   (d) 4 s   (e) 6 s.

TYPE II

6) When a number of particles, all of different weights, are dropped, the acceleration of each particle:
(a) is constant but different for each particle, depending on its weight,
(b) is constant and the same for each particle,
(c) increases as the particle falls.

7) If a particle is moving in a straight line with constant acceleration and a velocity-time graph is drawn for the motion, the gradient of the graph represents:
(a) the acceleration,
(b) the rate of increase of velocity,
(c) the rate of decrease of velocity.

8) A particle is rotating in a circle with constant angular acceleration. With the usual notation, the speed of the particle at any time t is:

(a) $r(\Omega + \alpha t)$,

(b) $\dfrac{r\theta}{t}$,

(c) $r\omega$.

9) A particle passes through a point with position vector $\mathbf{i}+\mathbf{j}$ when $t = 0$ and moves with velocity $3\mathbf{i}-\mathbf{j}$

(a) its position vector at time t is $3\mathbf{i}-\mathbf{j}+t(\mathbf{i}+\mathbf{j})$,

(b) its speed is constant,

(c) it is accelerating.

TYPE III

10) (a) A particle is moving in a straight line with constant acceleration.

(b) The average velocity of a particle moving in a straight line is the average of the initial and final velocities.

11) (a) A particle is moving in a straight line with a constant acceleration of $2\,\mathrm{m\,s}^{-2}$.

(b) A particle moving in a straight line with a constant acceleration has a velocity of $2\,\mathrm{m\,s}^{-1}$ at one instant and a velocity of $8\,\mathrm{m\,s}^{-1}$ three seconds later.

12) Using the standard notation for a particle moving in a straight line with constant acceleration:

(a) The particle covers a distance s in time t where $s = ut + \frac{1}{2}at^2$.

(b) $u > 0$ and $v < 0$.

TYPE IV

13) A particle is moving in a straight line. Find when the particle returns to its initial position.

(a) The particle is thrown vertically upwards.

(b) The initial velocity of the particle is $10\,\mathrm{m\,s}^{-2}$.

(c) The weight of the particle is $20\,\mathrm{N}$.

14) A particle is moving in a circle. Find the speed of the particle when it returns to its initial position.

(a) The acceleration is constant and equal to α.

(b) The initial angular velocity is Ω.

(c) The radius of the circle is r.

15) Two particles A and B are moving along a straight line and initially B is behind A. Determine whether B overtakes A.
(a) B moves with a constant velocity of $6 \, \text{m s}^{-1}$.
(b) B is 4 m behind A initially.
(c) A moves with a constant acceleration of $3 \, \text{m s}^{-2}$.

16)

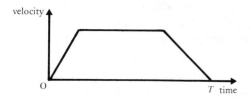

The diagram shows a sketch of a velocity-time graph for a particle moving in a straight line. Find the value of T.

(a) The distance covered is 100 m.
(b) The maximum velocity reached is $10 \, \text{m s}^{-1}$ and is maintained for five seconds.
(c) The acceleration is twice the retardation.

TYPE V

17) Velocity is the rate of increase of distance.

18) A particle moving in a straight line with a constant acceleration of $-2 \, \text{m s}^{-2}$ has a velocity of $3 \, \text{m s}^{-1}$ at one instant and a velocity of $-3 \, \text{m s}^{-1}$ three seconds later.

19) A particle moving under the action of its weight only has a constant acceleration g vertically downwards.

20) A particle is moving with constant acceleration in a straight line. At one instant it has a velocity u and t seconds later it has a velocity v.
Its acceleration is $(u-v)/t$.

21) A particle is moving in the positive sense on the circumference of a circle of radius 2 m. The particle has a constant angular acceleration of $3 \, \text{rad s}^{-2}$. At one instant the speed of the particle is $2 \, \text{m s}^{-1}$ and one second later it is $8 \, \text{m s}^{-1}$.

22) A particle is moving in a straight line. A displacement-time graph is drawn for its motion. The gradient of the tangent to the graph at time T represents the velocity of the particle at time T.

23) A car travels from A to B at a constant speed of $30 \, \text{km h}^{-1}$ and returns to A immediately at a constant speed of $40 \, \text{km h}^{-1}$. The average speed for the journey is $35 \, \text{km h}^{-1}$.

24) If a particle moving in a straight line has a negative acceleration then this always means that the speed is decreasing.

MISCELLANEOUS EXERCISE 4

1) A stone is dropped from the top of a building 20 m high. A second stone is dropped from half-way up the same building. Find the time that should elapse between the release of the two stones if they are to reach the ground at the same time.

2) A particle is describing a circle of radius 4 m with a constant angular acceleration. At one instant it has a speed of $2\,\mathrm{m\,s^{-1}}$ and 4 seconds later it has a speed of $10\,\mathrm{m\,s^{-1}}$. Find its angular acceleration and the distance it has travelled in this time.

3) A particle is describing a vertical circle of radius 2 m with a constant angular acceleration of $\frac{\pi}{6}\,\mathrm{rad\,s^{-2}}$. If it is initially at rest at the lowest point of the circle find its speed 2 seconds later and its displacement from its original position.

4) A toy train is moving along a straight length of track. It accelerates uniformly from rest to a velocity of $0.5\,\mathrm{m\,s^{-1}}$ and maintains this velocity for a time before decelerating uniformly to rest again. If the time taken for this journey is 2 seconds and it moves a distance of 0.8 m along the track, find the time for which the speed of the train is uniform.

5) A car has a maximum acceleration of $6\,\mathrm{m\,s^{-2}}$ and a maximum deceleration of $8\,\mathrm{m\,s^{-2}}$. Find the least time in which it can cover a distance of 0.2 km starting from rest and stopping again. What is the maximum speed reached by the car in this time?

6) A particle moving in a straight line covers distances of 90 m and 240 m in successive times of 2 seconds and 4 seconds. Show that the particle has a constant acceleration and find it.

7) A particle P moves along the x axis and a particle Q moves along the y axis. P starts from rest at the origin and moves with a constant acceleration of $2\,\mathrm{m\,s^{-2}}$. At the same time Q is at the point $(0, 3)$ with a velocity of $2\,\mathrm{m\,s^{-1}}$ and is moving with a constant acceleration of $-3\,\mathrm{m\,s^{-2}}$. Find the distance between P and Q 4 seconds later.

8) A particle P starts from rest from a point A and moves along a straight line with constant acceleration $2\,\mathrm{m\,s^{-2}}$. At the same time a second particle Q is 5 m behind A and is moving in the same direction as P with a speed of $5\,\mathrm{m\,s^{-1}}$. If Q has a constant acceleration of $3\,\mathrm{m\,s^{-2}}$ find how far from A it overtakes P.

9) A particle P which is moving along a straight line with a constant acceleration of $0.3\,\mathrm{m\,s^{-2}}$ passes a point A on the line with a velocity of $20\,\mathrm{m\,s^{-1}}$. At the time when P passes A a second particle Q is 20 m behind A and is moving with a constant velocity of $30\,\mathrm{m\,s^{-1}}$. Prove that the particles collide.

10) A bus moves away from rest at a bus stop with an acceleration of $1\,\mathrm{m\,s^{-2}}$. As the bus starts to move a man who is $4\,\mathrm{m}$ behind the stop runs with a constant speed after the bus. If he just manages to catch the bus find his speed.

11) A particle moves so that its position vector after t seconds is given by

$$\mathbf{r} = (3t^2 - 2t^3)\mathbf{i} - 2t\mathbf{j}$$

Find the acceleration of the particle when $t = 2$.

12) A model aeroplane is constrained to fly in a circle by a guide line which is $3\,\mathrm{m}$ long. It accelerates from a speed of $2\,\mathrm{m\,s^{-1}}$ with a constant angular acceleration of $\frac{\pi}{10}\,\mathrm{rad\,s^{-2}}$ for $2\frac{1}{2}$ revolutions. The guide line then breaks. Find the speed of the aeroplane when the guide line breaks.

13) A stone is thrown vertically upward with a speed of u metres per second. A second stone is thrown vertically upward from the same point with the same initial speed but T seconds later than the first one. Prove that they collide at a distance of $\left(\dfrac{4u^2 - g^2T^2}{8g}\right)$ metres above the point of projection.

14) A stone is dropped from the top of a tower. In the last second of its motion it falls through a distance which is a fifth of the height of the tower. Find the height of the tower.

15) A particle moving in a straight line OD with uniform retardation leaves point O at time $t = 0$, and comes to instantaneous rest at D. On its way to D the particle passes points A, B, C at times $t = T, 2T, 4T$, respectively after leaving O, where $AB = BC = l$. Find, in terms of l, (a) the length of CD and (b) the length of OA.   (JMB)

16) Three points A, B, C on a motor racing track are such that B is $1\,\mathrm{km}$ beyond A and C is $2\,\mathrm{km}$ beyond B. A car X, moving with uniform acceleration takes 1 minute to travel from A to B and $1\frac{1}{2}$ minutes to travel from B to C. Find its acceleration in km/h/min and show that its speed at C is $92\,\mathrm{km/h}$. Another car Y, which is moving with uniform acceleration of $8\,\mathrm{km/h/min}$. passes C 15 seconds earlier than X, and its speed is then $75\,\mathrm{km/h}$. Find where X passes Y.   (C)

17) In a motor race, a car A is $1\,\mathrm{km}$ from the finishing post, and is travelling at $35\,\mathrm{m\,s^{-1}}$ with a uniform acceleration of $\frac{2}{5}\,\mathrm{m\,s^{-2}}$. At the same instant a second car B is $200\,\mathrm{m}$ behind A and is travelling at $44\,\mathrm{m\,s^{-1}}$ with a uniform acceleration of $\frac{1}{2}\,\mathrm{m\,s^{-2}}$. Show that B passes A $220\,\mathrm{m}$ before the finish. Show also that, if these accelerations are maintained, B arrives at the finishing post 1 second before A.   (C)

18) A flywheel is brought to rest by a constant retarding torque. From the instant this torque is applied, the flywheel is observed to make 200 revolutions in the first minute and 120 revolutions in the next minute. Calculate how many more revolutions the wheel makes before coming to rest and the time taken to stop the wheel.   (AEB)

19) A flywheel starts from rest and is uniformly accelerated to an angular speed of 120 revolutions per minute. It maintains this speed until it is uniformly retarded to rest again. The magnitude of the retardation is three times the value of the starting acceleration. Between starting and coming to rest again the flywheel completes N revolutions in five minutes.
Sketch the angular speed–time graph and hence find, in terms of N, the time for which the flywheel is travelling at the maximum speed.
Show that $300 < N < 600$.
If $N = 480$, find the starting acceleration and the number of revolutions completed in the first two minutes.   (AEB)

20) Two trains, P and Q, travel by the same route from rest at station A to rest at station B. Train P has constant acceleration f for the first third of the time, constant speed for the second third and constant retardation f for the last third of the time. Train Q has constant acceleration f for the first third of the distance, constant speed for the second third and constant retardation f for the last third of the distance. Show that the times taken by the two trains are in the ratio $3\sqrt{3} : 5$.   (U of L)

21) The brakes of a train, which is travelling at $30\,\mathrm{m\,s^{-1}}$, are applied as the train passes point A. The brakes produce a constant retardation of magnitude $3\lambda\,\mathrm{m\,s^{-2}}$ until the speed of the train is reduced to $10\,\mathrm{m\,s^{-1}}$. The train travels at this speed for a distance and is then uniformly accelerated at $\lambda\,\mathrm{m\,s^{-2}}$ until it again reaches a speed of $30\,\mathrm{m\,s^{-1}}$ as it passes point B. The time taken by the train in travelling from A to B, a distance of 4 km, is 4 minutes. Sketch the speed–time graph for this motion and hence calculate
(a) the value of λ,
(b) the distance travelled at $10\,\mathrm{m\,s^{-1}}$.

22) A particle is uniformly accelerated from A to B, a distance of 192 m, and is then uniformly retarded from B to C, a distance of 60 m. The speeds of the particle at A and B are 4 m/s and V m/s respectively and the particle comes to rest at C. Express, in terms of V only, the times taken by the particle to move from A to B and from B to C.
Given that the total time taken by the particle to move from A to C is 22 seconds, find:
(a) the value of V,
(b) the acceleration and the retardation of the particle.

CHAPTER 5

NEWTON'S LAWS OF MOTION

The study of mechanics is based on three laws which were first formulated by Newton:

1. *Every body will remain at rest or continue to move with uniform velocity unless an external force is applied to it.*

2. *When an external force is applied to a body of constant mass the force produces an acceleration which is directly proportional to the force.*

3. *When a body A exerts a force on a body B, B exerts an equal and opposite force on A.*

NEWTON'S FIRST LAW

This law in effect defines force: it states that if a body is travelling with uniform velocity there is no external force acting on the body; conversely if there is an external force acting on the body its velocity changes: i.e. force is the quantity which, when acting on a body, changes the velocity of that body. There is often more than one external force acting on a body so, to cause the body to accelerate, there must be a resultant force acting on it. Conversely there will be no acceleration if the resultant force acting on the body is zero. Summing up:

1. If a body has an acceleration there is a resultant force acting on that body.
2. If a body has no acceleration the forces acting on the body are in equilibrium.

If a body has zero acceleration it can either be at rest *or* moving with uniform velocity. This should dispel the notion that because a body is moving with uniform velocity there is a force responsible for the maintenance of that velocity: there is not.

EXAMPLE 5a

1) The diagram shows the forces that are acting on a particle. Has the particle an acceleration?

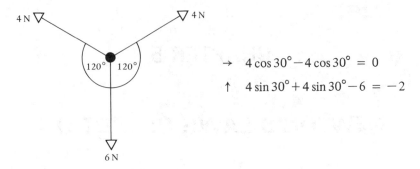

$$\rightarrow \quad 4\cos 30° - 4\cos 30° = 0$$

$$\uparrow \quad 4\sin 30° + 4\sin 30° - 6 = -2$$

We see that there is a resultant force acting on the particle.
Therefore it has an acceleration.

2) A particle of weight 4 N is attached to the end of a vertical string. If the particle is moving upwards with a uniform velocity find the tension in the string.

As the particle is moving with uniform velocity the forces acting on it are in equilibrium.

$$\uparrow \quad T - 4 = 0$$

$$\Rightarrow \quad T = 4$$

Therefore the tension is 4 N.

EXERCISE 5a

The diagram shows the forces acting on a particle. In Questions 1–4 determine whether or not the particle has an acceleration.

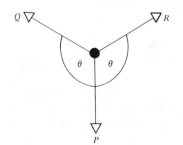

1) $P = Q = R = 6,$ $\theta = 120°$

2) $P = Q = R = 4,$ $\theta = 150°$

3) $P = 8, Q = R = 4,$ $\theta = 120°$

4) $P = Q = 3, R = 4,$ $\theta = 135°$

5) The diagram shows the forces acting on a particle:

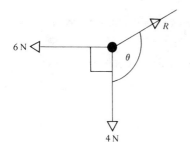

Find R and θ if the particle is moving with uniform velocity.

NEWTON'S SECOND LAW

This law gives the relationship between force, mass and acceleration. It states that when a force is applied to a body causing it to accelerate, the acceleration is directly proportional to the force. Experimental evidence also shows that the acceleration is inversely proportional to the mass of the body so, if the force is F the mass is m and the acceleration is a,

$$a \propto \frac{F}{m} \quad \text{or} \quad F \propto ma$$

Introducing a constant of proportion, k, this relationship becomes

$$F = kma$$

Now if $m = 1$ and $a = 1$ then $F = k$ so the amount of force needed to give 1 kg an acceleration of $1\,\mathrm{m\,s^{-2}}$ is equal to k.

If we choose this amount of force to be the unit of force, then $k = 1$ and the relationship above takes the simple form

$$F = ma$$

The *unit of force* is now defined as that force which gives a mass of 1 kg an acceleration of $1\,\mathrm{m\,s^{-2}}$. This unit of force is called a *newton* (N).

The equation $F = ma$ is the basic equation of motion and it is of fundamental importance to the study of the motion of a body with constant mass. It should be noted that, as force and acceleration are both vector quantities, the equation $F = ma$ is a vector equation: therefore as well as the magnitudes of both sides being equal, force and acceleration have the same direction. If the force is constant the acceleration will also be constant and, conversely, if the force varies so does the acceleration. There is often more than one force acting on a body and in this case F represents the resultant force acting on the body.

Summing up:

1. The resultant force acting on a body of constant mass is equal to the mass of the body multiplied by its acceleration:

$$F(\text{newton}) = m(\text{kilogram}) \times a(\text{metre/second}^2)$$

2. The resultant force acting on a body and the acceleration of the body are both in the same direction.

3. A constant force acting on a constant mass produces a constant acceleration.

Weight and Mass

Consider a body of mass m which is falling under the action of its weight only. It has an acceleration $g \, \text{m s}^{-2}$ downwards.

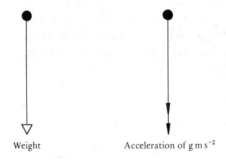

Weight   Acceleration of $g \, \text{m s}^{-2}$

Using $F = ma$ gives

$$\text{weight} = mg \text{ newton}$$

i.e. a body of mass m kilogram has a weight of mg newton

(It is interesting to note than an average sized apple has a mass of about 0.1 kg, so it has a weight of about 1 N!)

Problem Solving

When using Newton's Laws to solve a problem it is helpful to draw a diagram showing the forces that are acting on the body under consideration, and the acceleration of the body. It must also be remembered that:

(a) the resultant force and the acceleration are both in the same direction,

(b) if there is no acceleration the forces are in equilibrium.

In problems which involve a large body (as opposed to a particle) the body is, at present, treated as a particle of equal mass.

EXAMPLES 5b

1) A particle of mass 5 kg slides down a smooth plane inclined at $30°$ to the horizontal. Find the acceleration of the particle and the reaction between the particle and the plane.

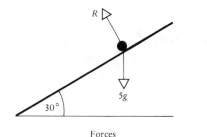

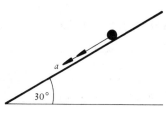

Forces

Acceleration

As the acceleration is down the plane, the resultant force is also down the plane. (It is the resultant force that causes the acceleration.)

The resultant force down the plane is $5g \sin 30°$

Using $F = ma$ gives $5g \sin 30° = 5a$

$\Rightarrow$ $a = \frac{1}{2}g$

Therefore the acceleration of the particle is $\frac{1}{2}g$ m s^{-2} down the plane.

There is no component of acceleration perpendicular to the plane, so there is no component of force perpendicular to the plane.

Resolving perpendicular to the plane gives,

$$R - 5g \cos 30° = 0$$

$\Rightarrow$ $$R = \frac{5g\sqrt{3}}{2}$$

Therefore the reaction between the particle and the plane is $\dfrac{5g\sqrt{3}}{2}$ N.

2) A block of mass 2 kg rests on the floor of a lift which has an acceleration of 5 m s^{-2} upwards. Find the reaction between the block and the lift.

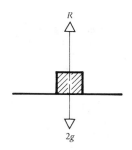

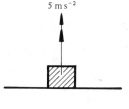

The resultant upward force on the block is $R - 2g$

Using $F = ma$ gives $R - 2g = 2 \times 5$

Hence $R = 10 + 2g$

$\Rightarrow$ $R = 29.6$

Therefore, the reaction between the block and the lift is $29.6\,\text{N}$.

3) A particle of mass 5 kg is pulled along a rough horizontal surface by a string which is inclined at $60°$ to the horizontal. If the acceleration of the particle is $\frac{1}{3}g\,\text{m s}^{-2}$ and the coefficient of friction between the particle and the plane is $\frac{2}{3}$, find the tension in the string.

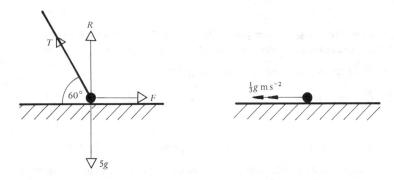

As there is no vertical component of acceleration, the vertical component of the resultant force is zero.

Resolving vertically gives

$$R + T\sin 60° - 5g = 0 \qquad\qquad [1]$$

The friction is limiting, so

$$F = \tfrac{2}{3}R \qquad\qquad [2]$$

The resultant horizontal force to the left is $T\cos 60° - F$

Using $F = ma$ gives

$$T\cos 60° - F = \tfrac{5}{3}g \qquad\qquad [3]$$

Eliminating F and R from equations [1], [2] and [3] gives,

$$T\cos 60° - \tfrac{2}{3}(5g - T\sin 60°) = \tfrac{5}{3}g$$

$\Rightarrow$ $T = 10g\sqrt{3}(2 - \sqrt{3})$.

4) A car of mass 1000 kg is brought to rest from a speed of $40\,\text{m s}^{-1}$ in a distance of 80 m. Find the braking force of the car assuming that it is constant and that there is a constant resistance to motion of 100 N.

As the braking force is constant the acceleration of the car is constant. Taking the direction of motion as positive we have

$$u = 40, \quad v = 0, \quad s = 80$$

Using $v^2 = u^2 + 2as$ gives $\quad 0 = 1600 + 160a$

$\Rightarrow$ $\qquad\qquad\qquad\qquad a = -10$

Therefore the car has an acceleration of $-10\,\mathrm{m\,s^{-2}}$.

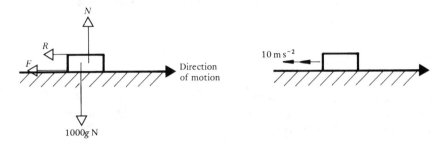

In the diagram F is the braking force and R is the resistance. So the resultant horizontal force is $F + R$.

Using Newton's Law gives $\quad F + R = 1000 \times 10$

But $R = 100$ so $\qquad\qquad F = 10\,000 - 100$

$\qquad\qquad\qquad\qquad\qquad = 9900$

Therefore the braking force of the car is $9900\,\mathrm{N}$.

EXERCISE 5b

1) A particle of mass $2\,\mathrm{kg}$ has an acceleration of $5\,\mathrm{m\,s^{-2}}$. Find the magnitude of the resultant force acting on the particle.

2) A particle has a resultant force of magnitude $8\,\mathrm{N}$ acting on it. If the mass of the particle is $3\,\mathrm{kg}$, find the magnitude of its acceleration.

3) A particle of mass $5\,\mathrm{kg}$ is pulled along a smooth horizontal surface by a horizontal string. If the acceleration of the particle is $3\,\mathrm{m\,s^{-2}}$ find the tension in the string.

4) A particle of mass $10\,\mathrm{kg}$ is pulled up a smooth slope inclined at $60°$ to the horizontal by a string parallel to the slope. If the acceleration of the particle is $\frac{g}{10}\,\mathrm{m\,s^{-2}}$ find the tension in the string.

5) A particle of mass $8\,\mathrm{kg}$ is pulled along a smooth horizontal surface by a string inclined at $30°$ to the horizontal. If the tension in the string is $10\,\mathrm{N}$ find the acceleration of the particle.

6) A particle of mass 4 kg is pulled along a rough horizontal surface by a string parallel to the surface. If the tension in the string is 20 N and the coefficient of friction between the particle and the plane is $\frac{1}{5}$ find the acceleration of the particle.

7) A particle of mass 8 kg slides down a rough plane which is inclined at arcsin $\frac{1}{6}$ to the horizontal. If the acceleration of the particle is $\frac{g}{10}$ find the coefficient of friction between the particle and the plane.

8) A block of mass 15 kg rests on the floor of a lift. Find the reaction between the block and the floor of the lift if the lift is accelerating down at $4\,\mathrm{m\,s^{-2}}$.

9) A block of mass 12 kg rests on the floor of a lift. If the reaction between the block and the lift floor is 20 N find the acceleration of the lift.

10) A bullet of mass 0.02 kg is fired into a wall with a velocity of $400\,\mathrm{m\,s^{-1}}$. If the bullet penetrates the wall to a depth of 0.1 m find the resistance of the wall assuming it to be uniform.

11) A lift of mass 500 kg is drawn up by a cable. It makes an ascent in three stages: it is brought from rest to its maximum speed by a constant acceleration of $\frac{1}{2}g$, it then moves with its maximum speed for an interval of time and is then brought to rest by a deceleration of g. Find the tension in the cable in each of the three stages.

12) A car of mass 300 kg is brought to rest in a time of 4 seconds from a speed of $20\,\mathrm{m\,s^{-1}}$. If there is no resistance to motion find the force exerted by the brakes assuming it to be constant.

13) A car of mass 500 kg is capable of braking with a deceleration of $\frac{g}{2}$. If the resistance to motion is constant and equal to 50 N find the braking force assuming this to be constant.

14) The diagram shows the forces that are acting on a wedge which is in contact with a rough horizontal table.

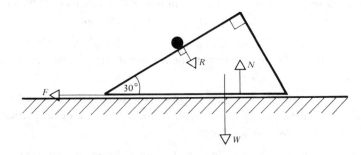

If the mass of the wedge is 10 kg, $R = 6g$ and the coefficient of friction between the wedge and the table is $\frac{1}{7}$ find the acceleration of the wedge.

NEWTON'S THIRD LAW

This states that action and reaction are equal and opposite:

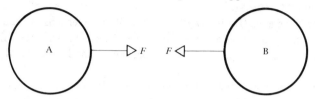

i.e. if a body A exerts a force on a body B then B exerts an equal and
opposite force on A. This is true whether A and B are in contact with each
other or if they are some distance apart; it is also true whether A and B are
moving or are stationary. However, we are mainly concerned with the forces
between two bodies which are in contact and the statements in Chapter 3 on
contact and internal forces are based on this law. A rigid body may be considered
as a collection of particles that are held together by forces of attraction between
the particles. Newton's Third Law states that these forces occur in equal and
opposite pairs; thus their net effect on the whole body is zero. This justifies the
fact that only the external forces acting on a body are considered.

Note. Most of us have an intuitive idea of what a force is and the effect that it
produces but it required Newton's genius to express these ideas in such basically
simple terms. Under normal conditions the results that are obtained from the
use of Newton's Laws agree very closely indeed with observed results and this
is justification enough for their use. Although it is now known that they do not
represent the whole truth, significant errors arising from their use cannot be
found unless conditions are extreme (very high temperatures, very small masses
such as atomic particles, etc.).

MOTION OF CONNECTED PARTICLES

Consider two particles, of unequal mass, connected by a light string passing
over a fixed pulley as shown in the diagram.

If the pulley is smooth the tension in the string is the same throughout its length.

If the pulley is rough the tensions in the portions of the string on either side of the pulley are different.

If the string is inelastic (i.e. its length does not alter under tension) the acceleration of the particles attached to it have the same magnitude. Also, at a given instant of time, the particles have equal speeds and have covered equal distances.

To analyse the motion of the system the forces acting on each particle must be considered separately and the equation $F = ma$ applied to each particle in turn.

EXAMPLES 5c

1) Two particles of mass $5\,\text{kg}$ and $3\,\text{kg}$ are connected by a light inelastic string passing over a smooth fixed pulley. Find the accelerations of the particles and the tension in the string when the system is moving freely.

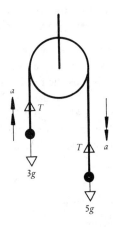

For the $3\,\text{kg}$ mass the resultant upward force is $T - 3g$

Applying $F = ma$ to the $3\,\text{kg}$ mass gives $T - 3g = 3a$ [1]

For the $5\,\text{kg}$ mass the resultant downward force is $5g - T$

Applying $F = ma$ to the $5\,\text{kg}$ mass gives $5g - T = 5a$ [2]

$[1] + [2] \quad \Rightarrow \qquad\qquad\qquad 2g = 8a$

$\Rightarrow \qquad\qquad\qquad\qquad\qquad a = \frac{1}{4}g$

Then, from [1], $T = \frac{3}{4}g + 3g = \frac{15}{4}g$

Therefore the acceleration of the system is $\frac{1}{4}g\,\text{m s}^{-2}$

and the tension in the string is $\frac{15}{4}g\,\text{N}$.

2) A particle of mass 2 kg rests on the surface of a rough plane which is inclined at $30°$ to the horizontal. It is connected by a light inelastic string passing over a light smooth pulley at the top of the plane, to a particle of mass 3 kg which is hanging freely. If the coefficient of friction between the 2 kg mass and the plane is $\frac{1}{3}$ find the acceleration of the system when it is released from rest and find the tension in the string. Find also the force exerted by the string on the pulley.

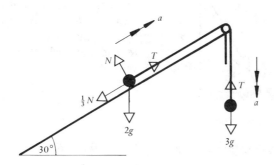

Consider the 2 kg mass.
There is no component of acceleration perpendicular to the plane.

Therefore resolving perpendicular to the plane gives

$$N - 2g \cos 30° = 0 \quad \Rightarrow \quad N = g\sqrt{3}$$

There is an acceleration a up the plane.
The resultant force parallel to the plane is $T - \frac{1}{3}N - 2g \sin 30°$

So applying $F = ma$ gives

$$T - \frac{1}{3}N - 2g \sin 30° = 2a$$

$\Rightarrow \qquad\qquad\qquad T - \frac{1}{3}g(\sqrt{3} + 3) = 2a$ [1]

For the 3 kg mass the resultant force is $3g - T$ vertically downwards.

So applying $F = ma$ gives $\qquad 3g - T = 3a$ [2]

Adding [1] and [2] $\quad \Rightarrow \quad 3g - \frac{1}{3}g(\sqrt{3} + 3) = 5a$

Hence $\qquad\qquad\qquad\qquad\qquad a = \frac{1}{15}(6 - \sqrt{3})g$

and, from [2], $\qquad\qquad\qquad\qquad T = \frac{1}{5}(9 + \sqrt{3})g$

Therefore the acceleration of the system is $\frac{1}{15}(6 - \sqrt{3})g \, \text{m s}^{-2}$ and the tension in the string is $\frac{1}{5}(9 + \sqrt{3})g \, \text{N}$.

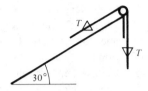

The forces acting on the pulley are
T acting down the plane and T
acting vertically downward.

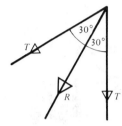

These two forces are equal so their
resultant, R, bisects the angle
between them, so
R acts at an angle of $30°$ to the
vertical.

Resolving in the direction of R gives $2T \cos 30° = R$

$\Rightarrow$ $R = T\sqrt{3} = \frac{3}{5}(3\sqrt{3}+1)g$

So the force acting on the pulley is $\frac{3}{5}(3\sqrt{3}+1)g\,\text{N}$ acting at $30°$ to the
vertical.

3)

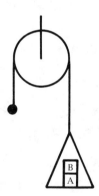

The diagram shows a particle of mass $8\,\text{kg}$ connected to a light scale pan by
a light inextensible string which passes over a smooth fixed pulley. The scale
pan holds two blocks A and B of masses $3\,\text{kg}$ and $4\,\text{kg}$ respectively,
with B resting on top of A. Find the acceleration of the system and the
reaction between A and B.

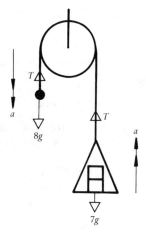

The reaction forces between A and B and between A and the scale pan are internal forces when considering the scale pan and its contents as one unit.

For the scale pan and its contents the resultant force upwards is $T - 7g$

$$F = ma \;\Rightarrow\; T - 7g = 7a \qquad\qquad [1]$$

For the 8 kg mass the resultant force downwards is $8g - T$

$$F = ma \;\Rightarrow\; 8g - T = 8a \qquad\qquad [2]$$

From [1] and [2] we get $\qquad\qquad a = \tfrac{1}{15}g$

To find the reaction between A and B, let us consider the forces that act on B.

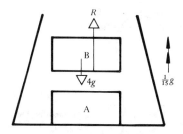

The upward acceleration of B is $\tfrac{1}{15}g\,\mathrm{m\,s^{-2}}$ and the upward resultant force is $R - 4g$

$$F = ma \;\Rightarrow\; R - 4g = \tfrac{4}{15}g$$
$$\Rightarrow\; R = \tfrac{64}{15}g$$

Therefore the reaction between A and B is $\tfrac{64}{15}g\,\mathrm{N}$.

4) Two particles of masses 5 kg and 8 kg are connected by a light inelastic string passing over a fixed pulley. The system is released from rest with both portions of the string vertical and both particles at a height of 3 m above the ground. In the subsequent motion the 8 kg mass hits the ground and does not rebound. Find the greatest height reached by the 5 kg mass if the pulley is of such height that the mass never reaches the pulley.

Before the 8 kg mass reaches the ground the two particles are moving as a connected system, but when the 8 kg mass hits the ground there is a sudden change in the conditions of the system. After the 8 kg mass has hit the ground the 5 kg mass is moving on its own with the string slack. These two conditions must be considered separately.

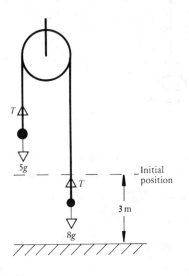

Using $F = ma$ we have,

for 5 kg mass: ↑ $T - 5g = 5a$
for 8 kg mass: ↓ $8g - T = 8a$

$\Rightarrow$ $a = 3g/13$

As the 8 kg mass moves 3 m down the 5 kg mass moves the same distance up.

Therefore considering the motion of the 5 kg mass we have:

$a = 3g/13, \quad u = 0, \quad s = 3$

Using $v^2 = u^2 + 2as$ gives

$$v^2 = 18g/13$$

So the 5 kg mass has an upward velocity of $\sqrt{18g/13}\,\mathrm{m\,s^{-1}}$ at the instant when the 8 kg mass hits the ground.

After that the string goes slack and the 5 kg mass moves under the action of its weight alone, so it has a downward acceleration of g. When it reaches its highest position its velocity is zero so we have

$v = 0, \quad u = \sqrt{18g/13}, \quad a = -g$

Using $v^2 = u^2 + 2as$ gives

$$0 = \tfrac{18}{13}g - 2gs$$

$\Rightarrow$ $s = \tfrac{9}{13}$

i.e the 5 kg mass rises a distance $\tfrac{9}{13}$ m after the 8 kg mass hits the ground.

Therefore it reaches a height of $6\tfrac{9}{13}$ m above the ground.

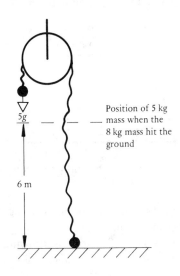

Position of 5 kg mass when the 8 kg mass hit the ground

EXERCISE 5c

1) Two particles of mass 5 kg and 10 kg are connected by a light inextensible string which passes over a smooth fixed pulley. Find the acceleration of the system and the tension in the string.

2) Two particles of mass 9 kg and 10 kg are connected by a light inelastic string which passes over a smooth fixed pulley. Find the acceleration of the system and the tension in the string.

3) Two particles of mass m and M are connected by a light inelastic string which passes over a smooth fixed pulley. Find the acceleration of the system and the tension in the string.

4) A particle of mass 4 kg rests on a smooth plane which is inclined at 60° to the horizontal. The particle is connected by a light inelastic string passing over a smooth pulley at the top of the plane to a particle of mass 2 kg which is hanging freely. Find the acceleration of the system and the tension in the string.

5) A particle of mass 4 kg rests on a smooth horizontal table. It is connected by a light inextensible string passing over a smooth pulley at the edge of the table to a particle of mass 2 kg which is hanging freely. Find the acceleration of the system and the tension in the string.

6) A particle of mass 5 kg rests on a rough horizontal table. It is connected by a light inextensible string passing over a smooth pulley at the edge of the table to a particle of mass 6 kg, which is hanging freely. The coefficient of friction between the 5 kg mass and the table is $\frac{1}{3}$. Find the acceleration of the system and the tension in the string.

7)

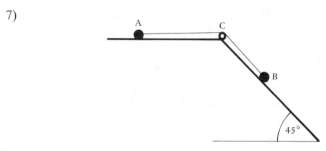

In the diagram particles A and B are of mass 10 kg and 8 kg respectively and rest on planes as shown. They are connected by a light inextensible string passing over a smooth fixed pulley at C. Find the acceleration of the system and the tension in the string if:

(a) the planes the particles are in contact with are smooth,
(b) the planes are rough and the coefficient of friction between each particle and the plane is $\frac{1}{4}$.

8) Two particles A and B of mass 10 kg and 5 kg are connected by a light inextensible string passing over a smooth fixed pulley C and rest on inclined planes as shown in the diagram. Find the acceleration of the system and the tension in the string if:
(a) both planes are smooth,
(b) both planes are rough and the coefficient of friction is $\frac{1}{10}$ for both particles.

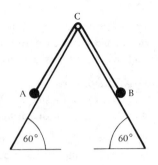

9)

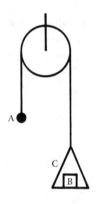

A particle A of mass 5 kg is connected by a light inextensible string passing over a smooth fixed light pulley to a light scale pan C as shown in the diagram. C holds a block B of mass 8 kg. Find the tension in the string and the reaction between B and C.

10) Two particles A and B rest on the inclined faces of a fixed triangular wedge as shown in the diagram.
A and B are connected by a light inextensible string which passes over a light smooth pulley at C. The faces of the wedge are smooth and A and B are both of mass 7 kg. Find the force exerted by the string on the pulley at C when the system is moving freely with both particles in contact with the wedge.

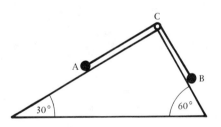

11) A particle of mass 10 kg lies on a rough horizontal table and is connected by a light inextensible string passing over a fixed smooth light pulley at the edge of the table to a particle of mass 8 kg hanging freely. The coefficient of friction between the 10 kg mass and the table is $\frac{1}{4}$. The system is released from rest with the 10 kg mass a distance of 1.5 m from the edge of the table. Find:
(a) the acceleration of the system,
(b) the resultant force on the edge of the table,
(c) the speed of the 10 kg mass as it reaches the pulley.

12) Two particles of mass 3 kg and 4 kg are connected by a light inextensible string passing over a smooth fixed pulley. The system is released from rest with the string taut and both particles at a height of 2 m above the ground. Find the velocity of the 3 kg mass when the 4 kg mass reaches the ground.

13) Two particles of mass 5 kg and 7 kg are connected by a light inelastic string passing over a smooth fixed pulley. The system is released from rest with the string taut and both particles at a height of 0.5 m above the ground. Find the greatest height reached by the 5 kg mass, assuming that the pulley is of such height that the 5 kg mass does not reach the pulley, and that the 7 kg mass does not rebound when it hits the ground.

14)

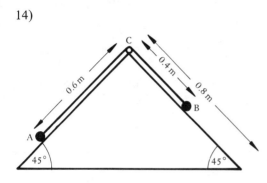

Two particles A and B of mass 5 kg and 9 kg respectively rest on the smooth faces of a fixed wedge as shown in the diagram. They are connected by a light inextensible string passing over a smooth pulley at C and are released from rest from the position shown in the diagram. In the subsequent motion B hits the ground and does not rebound.

Find:
(a) the speed of the particles when B hits the ground,
(b) the acceleration of A after B hits the ground,
(c) the distance of A from C when A first comes to rest.

Related Accelerations

In problems concerned with connected particles and moveable pulleys or bodies in contact where each body is free to move, the accelerations of different parts of the system will not necessarily have the same magnitude. However, a relationship between the accelerations can be found by considering the physical properties of the system. As before, Newton's Law must be applied to each body of the system. However, it is not always convenient to apply the law in the direction of the acceleration.

As $F = ma$ ⇒ $F \cos \theta = ma \cos \theta$, the equation can be applied in any direction in this form: i.e. the component of the resultant force in a chosen direction is equal to the mass multipled by the component of the acceleration in the same direction.

EXAMPLES 5d

1)

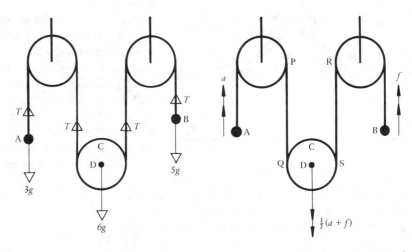

The diagram shows two particles A and B, of masses 3 kg and 5 kg, connected by a light inextensible string passing over two fixed smooth pulleys and under a light smooth moveable pulley C, which carries a particle D of mass 6 kg. The system is released from rest. Find:

(a) the acceleration of the particle A,

(b) the acceleration of the pulley C,

(c) the tension in the string.

If A moves up with an acceleration a and B moves up with an acceleration f
then   the portion of the string PQ moves down with acceleration a
and   the portion of the string RS moves down with acceleration f.

So the pulley C moves down with an acceleration which is equal to the average of a and f, i.e. $\frac{1}{2}(a+f)$

(If we are wrong about the directions we have chosen for the various accelerations, the answers we obtain will be negative.)

Applying $F = ma$ to each part of the system we have

for A: ↑ $T - 3g = 3a$ [1]

for B: ↑ $T - 5g = 5f$ [2]

for C: ↓ $6g - 2T = 3(a+f)$ [3]

$5 \times [1] + 3 \times [2] \Rightarrow \qquad 8T - 30g = 15(a+f)$ [4]

Eliminating T from [3] and [4] $-6g = 27(a+f)$

$\Rightarrow$ $\frac{1}{2}(a+f) = -\frac{1}{9}g$ [5]

Therefore the pulley C moves *up* with an acceleration of $\frac{1}{9}g\,\mathrm{m\,s^{-2}}$

Substituting [5] in [3] $\Rightarrow$ $6g - 2T = -\frac{2}{3}g$

$\Rightarrow$ $T = \frac{10}{3}g$ [6]

Therefore the tension in the string is $\frac{10}{3}g$ N.

Substituting [6] in [1] $\Rightarrow$ $\frac{10}{3}g - 3g = 3a$

$\Rightarrow$ $a = \frac{1}{9}g$

Therefore the mass A has an upward acceleration of $\frac{1}{9}g\,\mathrm{m\,s^{-2}}$

2) A particle A of mass 6 kg is connected by a light inextensible string passing over a fixed smooth pulley to a light smooth moveable pulley B. Two particles C and D of masses 2 kg and 1 kg are connected by a light inextensible string passing over the pulley B. When the system is moving freely find the acceleration of the 1 kg mass and the tensions in the strings.

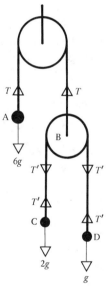 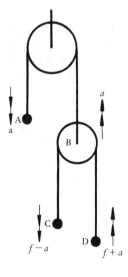

(There are two strings involved in this problem: their tensions are not necessarily the same.)

If A moves down with an acceleration a, B moves up with an acceleration a. If B were stationary, C would accelerate downwards and D would have an equal acceleration upwards. But as B has an acceleration a upwards then

D has an acceleration $(f+a)$ upward   and
C an acceleration $(f-a)$ downwards.

Applying $F = ma$ to each part of the system, we have

for A: ↓ $6g - T = 6a$ [1]

for B: ↑ $T - 2T' = 0$ (B has zero mass)   [2]

for C: ↓ $2g - T' = 2(f - a)$ [3]

for D: ↑ $T' - g = (f + a)$ [4]

[1] + [2]   ⇒ $6g - 2T' = 6a$

            ⇒ $T' = 3g - 3a$ [5]

[5] in [3] ⇒ $-g = 2f - 5a$ [6]

[5] in [4] ⇒ $2g = f + 4a$ [7]

Now from [6] and [7] $a = \frac{5}{13}g$ and $f = \frac{6}{13}g$,

Then [1] and [2] give $T = \frac{48}{13}g$ and $T' = \frac{24}{13}g$

Therefore D moves up with acceleration $\frac{11}{13}g\,\mathrm{m\,s^{-2}}$.
The tension in CD is $\frac{24}{13}g$ N and the tension in AB is $\frac{48}{13}g$ N.

3) A particle of mass m is in contact with a smooth sloping face of a wedge
which is itself standing on a smooth horizontal surface. If the mass of the wedge
is M and the sloping face of the wedge is inclined at an angle of $30°$ to the
horizontal find the acceleration of the wedge in terms of m and M.

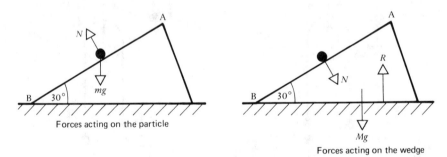

Forces acting on the particle   Forces acting on the wedge

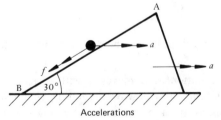

Accelerations

The wedge will move horizontally, so let it have a horizontal acceleration a.

The particle will move down the slope AB, so if the wedge were stationary it would have an acceleration in the direction AB. But as it remains in contact with the wedge as the wedge moves, the particle has

an acceleration of a horizontally
and an acceleration of f in the direction AB.

Applying $F = ma$ to each part of the system:

For the particle, in the direction perpendicular to AB,

$$mg \cos 30° - N = ma \sin 30° \qquad [1]$$

For the wedge, along the plane,

$$N \sin 30° = Ma \qquad [2]$$

Eliminating N gives $\quad \dfrac{1}{2}\left(\dfrac{mg}{2}\sqrt{3} - \dfrac{ma}{2}\right) = Ma$

$$\Rightarrow \qquad\qquad a = \frac{mg\sqrt{3}}{(m + 4M)}$$

Therefore the acceleration of the wedge is $\dfrac{mg\sqrt{3}}{(m+4M)}$ horizontally.

Note. Newton's Law can be applied in any direction: the direction perpendicular to AB was chosen so that f, which is not required, does not appear in any equation.

4) Two particles A and B of masses 3 kg and 2 kg are connected by a light inextensible string. The particles are in contact with the smooth faces of a wedge DCE of mass 10 kg resting on a smooth horizontal plane. When the system is moving freely find the acceleration of the wedge and the acceleration of B.

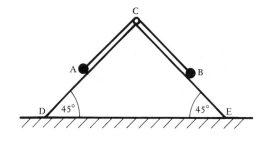

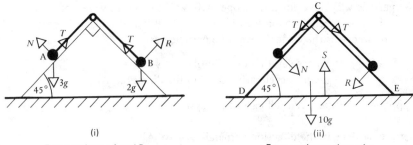

(i)

Forces acting on A and B

(ii)

Forces acting on the wedge

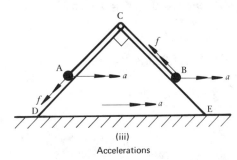

(iii)

Accelerations

If the wedge were stationary, A would have an acceleration down CD and, as A and B are connected by a string, B would have an equal acceleration up EC. But the wedge has an acceleration a horizontally, therefore the accelerations of A and B are made up of components as shown in diagram (iii).

Applying $F = ma$ to each part of the system we have:

for A,

$$\searrow \quad 3g\cos 45° - N = 3a\cos 45° \qquad \Rightarrow \qquad 3g - N\sqrt{2} = 3a \qquad [1]$$

$$\downarrow \quad 3g - N\cos 45° - T\cos 45° = 3f\cos 45° \quad \Rightarrow \quad 3g\sqrt{2} - N - T = 3f \qquad [2]$$

for B,

$$\nearrow \quad R - 2g\cos 45° = 2a\cos 45° \qquad \Rightarrow \qquad R\sqrt{2} - 2g = 2a \qquad [3]$$

$$\uparrow \quad T\cos 45° + R\cos 45° - 2g = 2f\cos 45° \quad \Rightarrow \quad T + R - 2g\sqrt{2} = 2f \qquad [4]$$

for the wedge,

$$\rightarrow \quad N\cos 45° + T\cos 45° - T\cos 45° - R\cos 45° = 10a$$

$$\Rightarrow \quad N - R = 10a\sqrt{2} \qquad [5]$$

Adding [1] and [3] $\qquad\qquad g - (N - R)\sqrt{2} = 5a$

Substituting from [5] $\qquad\qquad g - (10a\sqrt{2})\sqrt{2} = 5a$

Hence $\qquad\qquad\qquad\qquad a = \frac{1}{25}g$

Therefore the acceleration of the wedge is $\frac{1}{25}g\,\mathrm{m\,s}^{-2}$.

Adding [2] and [4] $g\sqrt{2}-(N-R) = 5f$

Substituting from [5] $g\sqrt{2} - 10a\sqrt{2} = 5f$

$\Rightarrow$ $g\sqrt{2} - \dfrac{10g\sqrt{2}}{25} = 5f$

Hence $f = \dfrac{3g\sqrt{2}}{25}$

The acceleration of B is composed of two components as shown.

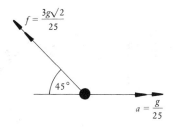

Resolving to find the magnitude and direction of the resultant we have

$\rightarrow \quad \dfrac{g}{25} - \dfrac{3g}{25} = -\dfrac{2g}{25}$

$\uparrow \quad \dfrac{3g}{25}$

So B has an acceleration of magnitude $\dfrac{g\sqrt{13}}{25}\,\mathrm{m\,s^{-2}}$ in a direction making arctan $\frac{3}{2}$ with ED.

EXERCISE 5d

For all questions in this exercise: all strings are light and inextensible, all pulleys are light and smooth, all surfaces are frictionless, the wedges are free to move.

Find, in each case, the acceleration of A and the tensions in the strings.

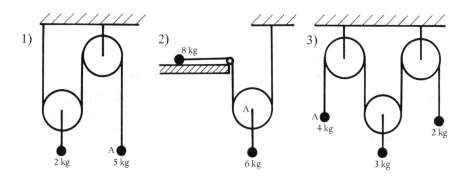

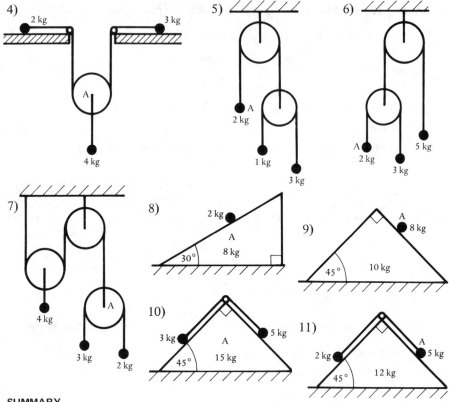

SUMMARY

Force is a quantity that changes the velocity of a body.

The resultant force acting on a body is equal to the mass of the body multiplied by the acceleration of the body: i.e. $F = ma$.

The resultant force and the acceleration are both in the same direction.

The weight of a body is its mass multipled by g.

To analyse the motion of a system of bodies which are not rigidly connected, Newton's Law $(F = ma)$ must be applied to each separate part of the system.

MULTIPLE CHOICE EXERCISE 5

(Instructions for answering these questions are given on page x.)

TYPE I

1) A particle of mass 5 kg is pulled along a smooth horizontal surface by a horizontal string. The acceleration of the particle is $10 \, \text{m s}^{-2}$. The tension in the string is:

(a) 2 N   (b) 50 N   (c) 5 N   (d) 15 N   (e) 10 N.

2) A particle of mass $3\,\mathrm{kg}$ slides down a smooth plane inclined at $\arcsin\frac{1}{3}$ to the horizontal. The acceleration of the particle is:
(a) $\frac{1}{3}g\,\mathrm{m\,s^{-2}}$ (b) $g\,\mathrm{m\,s^{-2}}$ (c) $1\,\mathrm{m\,s^{-2}}$ (d) $3g\,\mathrm{m\,s^{-2}}$ (e) 0.

3) A block of mass $10\,\mathrm{kg}$ rests on the floor of a lift which is accelerating upwards at $4\,\mathrm{m\,s^{-2}}$. The reaction of the floor of the lift on the block is:
(a) $104\,\mathrm{N}$ (b) $96\,\mathrm{N}$ (c) $60\,\mathrm{N}$ (d) $30\,\mathrm{N}$ (e) $140\,\mathrm{N}$.

4)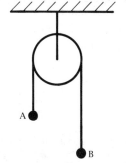

The pulley in the diagram is smooth and light. The masses of A and B are $5\,\mathrm{kg}$ and $2\,\mathrm{kg}$. The acceleration of the system is:

(a) g (b) $\frac{7}{3}g$

(c) $\frac{3}{7}g$ (d) $\frac{1}{7}g$

(e) $\frac{5}{2}g$

5) The pulleys in the diagram are all smooth and light. The acceleration of A is a upwards, the acceleration of C is f downwards. The acceleration of B is:
(a) $\frac{1}{2}(a-f)$ up
(b) $\frac{1}{2}(a+f)$ up
(c) $\frac{1}{2}(a+f)$ down
(d) $\frac{1}{2}(f-a)$ up.

6) The two pulleys in the diagram are smooth and light. The acceleration of B is a downwards. The acceleration of A is:
(a) a up
(b) $2a$ up
(c) a down
(d) $2a$ down
(e) 0.

TYPE II

7) A particle is moving with uniform velocity.
(a) The forces acting on the particle are in equilibrium.
(b) The particle has a zero acceleration.
(c) There is a resultant force acting on the body in the direction of the velocity.

8) A particle is moving horizontally with constant acceleration.
(a) The sum of the horizontal components of the forces acting on the particle is not zero.
(b) The sum of the vertical components of the forces acting is not zero.
(c) The forces acting on the particle are not in equilibrium.

9) A body of mass $10 \, \text{kg}$ has a resultant force of $20 \, \text{N}$ acting on it.
(a) The weight of the body is $10g \, \text{N}$.
(b) The acceleration of the body is $2 \, \text{m s}^{-2}$.
(c) The body is moving in a straight line.

10) Two particles A and B of masses 3 and $4 \, \text{kg}$ are connected by a light inelastic string passing over a smooth fixed pulley.
(a) The acceleration of A is $\frac{1}{7}g \, \text{m s}^{-2}$ upwards.
(b) The tension in the string is $\frac{24}{7}g \, \text{N}$.
(c) The acceleration of B is $-\frac{1}{7}g \, \text{m s}^{-2}$ upwards.

TYPE III

11) (a) A particle is moving with constant acceleration.
    (b) The resultant force acting on a particle is constant.

12) (a) A particle of mass $2 \, \text{kg}$ has a resultant force of $5 \, \text{N}$ acting on it.
    (b) A particle is moving with a constant acceleration of $5 \, \text{m s}^{-2}$.

13) (a) A particle is moving vertically downwards with a constant acceleration $g \, \text{m s}^{-2}$.
    (b) The only force acting on a particle is its weight.

14) (a) A particle is moving with a constant velocity.
    (b) The forces acting on a particle are in equilibrium.

TYPE IV

15) Two particles A and B are connected by a light inelastic string passing over a small smooth light fixed pulley. The particles are released from rest when both are at the same height above the ground. Find the speed of the particles when the heavier one hits the ground.
(a) The initial position of the particles is $1.5 \, \text{m}$ above the ground.
(b) The masses of A and B are $8 \, \text{kg}$ and $10 \, \text{kg}$ respectively.
(c) The length of the string is greater than $3 \, \text{m}$.

16) A ring is free to slide down a rough straight wire. Find the acceleration of the ring.
(a) The coefficient of friction between the wire and the ring is μ.
(b) The wire is inclined at an angle θ to the horizontal.
(c) The mass of the ring is m.

17) A particle is placed on the inclined face of a wedge which is itself resting on a horizontal surface. Find the acceleration of the particle when the system is moving freely.
(a) The sloping face of the wedge is inclined at $\alpha°$ to the horizontal.
(b) The contact between the wedge and the horizontal surface is smooth.
(c) The mass of the particle is m.

18) A particle slides down a rough plane. Find the coefficient of friction between the particle and the plane.
(a) The plane is inclined at $\alpha°$ to the horizontal.
(b) The mass of the particle is m.
(c) The acceleration of the particle is a.

19) Two particles A and B are connected by a light inelastic string passing over a smooth pulley. Find the acceleration of A if the pulley is moving upwards with an acceleration of $2\,\mathrm{m\,s^{-2}}$.
(a) The mass of A is $5\,\mathrm{kg}$.
(b) The mass of B is $4\,\mathrm{kg}$.
(c) The pulley is light.

20) A car is brought to rest by the action of its brakes which are assumed to exert a constant force on the car. Find the distance moved by the car before coming to rest.
(a) The mass of the car is $750\,\mathrm{kg}$.
(b) The initial velocity of the car is $40\,\mathrm{m\,s^{-1}}$.
(c) The time taken is 5 seconds.

21) A particle is projected up a rough plane. Find how far it moves up the plane.
(a) The mass of the particle is $2\,\mathrm{kg}$.
(b) The coefficient of friction between the particle and the plane is $\frac{1}{2}$.
(c) The initial velocity of the particle is $10\,\mathrm{m\,s^{-1}}$.

TYPE V

22) One newton is the force which will give a body of mass $1\,\mathrm{kg}$ an acceleration of $1\,\mathrm{m\,s^{-2}}$.

23) If a body has a resultant force acting on it the body will accelerate in the direction of the force.

24) Two bodies A and B are in contact. A exerts a force F on B and B exerts a force R on A. F and R are equal only if the bodies A and B are stationary.

25) A block A rests on a smooth horizontal table. It is pushed horizontally by another block B. B exerts a force F on A. By Newton's Third Law the block A exerts an equal and opposite force on B, so the total horizontal force acting on A is zero.

26) A particle is hanging freely attached to a light inextensible string. The string is made to accelerate vertically upward. The tension in the string is greater than the weight of the particle.

27) Two particles of masses 3 kg and 5 kg are connected by a light inextensible string passing over a fixed rough pulley. The acceleration of the system is $\frac{1}{5}g$.

MISCELLANEOUS EXERCISE 5

1) A bullet of mass $2m$ is fired horizontally into a fixed block of wood which offers a constant resistance R to the motion of the bullet. Find the deceleration of the bullet.

2) A ring of mass 2 kg slides down a wire which is inclined at $30°$ to the horizontal. If the ring has an acceleration of magnitude $\frac{1}{4}g$ find the coefficient of friction between the ring and the wire.

3) A particle of mass 5 kg is projected up a rough plane inclined at $45°$ to the horizontal. The coefficient of friction between the particle and the plane is $\frac{1}{3}$. If the initial speed of the particle is $7\,\mathrm{m\,s^{-1}}$, find how far it travels up the plane and the time it takes to return to its initial position.

4) A bullet of mass m is fired horizontally into a block of wood of mass M which is resting on a smooth horizontal surface. If the block offers a constant resistance R to the motion of the bullet, find the acceleration of the bullet and the acceleration of the block.

5) Two particles of mass 3 kg and 5 kg are connected by a light inextensible string passing over a smooth pulley which is fixed to the ceiling of a lift. Find the tension in the string when the system is moving freely and the lift has a downward acceleration $g\,\mathrm{m\,s^{-2}}$.

6) A particle P slides from rest down the rough surface of a plane inclined at $30°$ to the horizontal. If P travels a distance of 3.8 m down the plane in 2 s, find the coefficient of friction between P and the plane.

7) A heavy particle is suspended by a spring balance from the ceiling of a lift. When the lift moves up with constant acceleration f m/s^2 the balance shows a reading 1.8 kg. When the lift descends with constant acceleration $\frac{1}{3}f$ m/s^2 the balance shows a reading 1 kg. Find the mass of the particle and the value of f.

(U of L)p

8)

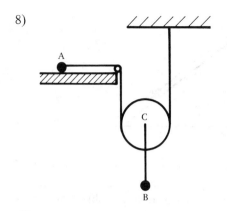

A particle A of mass m rests on a smooth horizontal table and is connected by a light inextensible string passing over a smooth fixed pulley at the edge of the table and under a smooth light pulley C to a fixed point on the ceiling as shown in the diagram. The pulley C carries a particle B of mass $2m$. Find the acceleration of C and the tension in the string.

9)

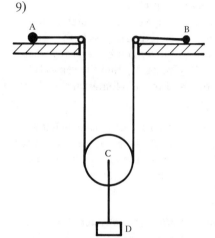

Particles A and B of mass 5 kg and 3 kg are connected by a light inextensible string passing under a smooth light pulley C which carries a particle D of mass 4 kg. A and B rest on horizontal rough surfaces as shown in the diagram. The coefficient of friction is the same for both A and B and is just sufficient to prevent A, but not B, from moving. Find the coefficient of friction.

10) Two particles of mass 8 kg and 3 kg are connected by a light inelastic string passing over a smooth fixed pulley. The system is held at rest with the string taut and the 8 kg mass at a height of 0.8 m above the ground. The system is then released and the 8 kg mass hits the ground and does not rebound. Find the time for which the string is slack.

11) A man of mass M carries in his hand a parcel of mass m. He stands in a lift of mass X which is descending with an acceleration $a\,(<g)$.
Find
(a) the reaction R_1 between his hand and the parcel;
(b) the reaction R_2 between his feet and the lift;
(c) the tension T in the cable supporting the lift.

If the man drops the parcel, find the values of R_2 and T during the period when the parcel is in the air, and also during the period after the parcel has hit the inelastic floor of the lift, assuming that the acceleration of the lift remains unchanged throughout these periods.   (C)

12)

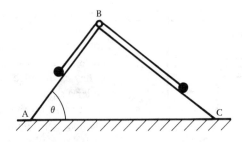

In the diagram, ABC is the right section of a prism; the angle BAC is $\theta\,(<45°)$ and the angle ABC is $90°$. Two particles, each of mass m, are on the smooth sloping faces of the prism and are connected by a light inextensible string which passes over a smooth pulley on the top edge of the prism.

The prism stands on a horizontal plane which is rough enough to prevent the prism moving. The system is released from rest when the string is in the plane ABC. Find the acceleration of the particles and the tension in the string when the particles are moving freely. If the prism is of mass M, find the vertical component of the reaction between the prism and the horizontal plane. (U of L)

13) A particle A of mass $2m$ is intially at rest on a smooth plane inclined at an angle α to the horizontal. It is supported by a light inextensible string which passes over a smooth light pulley P at the top edge of the plane. The other end of the string supports a particle B, of mass m, which hangs freely. Given that the system is in equilibrium, find α, and the magnitude and direction of the resultant force exerted by the string on the pulley.

A further particle of mass m is now attached to B and the system is released. Find, for the ensuing motion, the tension in the string, the acceleration of B, and the magnitude and direction of the resultant force exerted by the string on the pulley.   (U of L)

14) A light inextensible string passes over a smooth fixed pulley and has a particle of mass $5m$ attached to one end and a second smooth pulley of mass m attached to the other end. Another light inextensible string passes over the second pulley and carries a mass $3m$ at one end and a mass m at the other end. If the system moves freely under gravity, find the acceleration of the heaviest particle and the tension in each string.   (U of L)

15) One end of a light inextensible string is attached to a ceiling. The string passes under a smooth light pulley carrying a weight C and then over a fixed smooth light pulley. To the free end of the string is attached a light scale pan in which two weights A and B are placed with A on top of B as shown. The portions of the string not in contact with the pulleys are vertical.

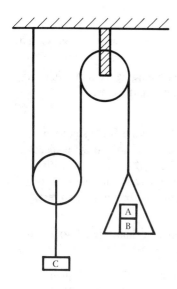

Each of the weights A and B has a mass M and the weight C has a mass kM. If the system is released from rest find the acceleration of the moveable pulley and of the scale pan and show that the scale pan will ascend if $k > 4$. When the system is moving freely find:

(a) the tension in the string,
(b) the reaction between the weights A and B.

(U of L)

16) An aeroplane is travelling horizontally at height 1200 m above horizontal ground when a parachutist of mass 80 kg steps out of the aeroplane and falls freely under gravity with negligible air resistance. After falling x m, he opens his parachute, and is then subject to a vertical resistive force of 1120 N. When the parachutist reaches the ground, the vertical component of his velocity is zero. Show that $x = 360$. Find also the total time taken for the fall.

17) A smooth plane and a rough plane, both inclined at $45°$ to the horizontal, intersect in a fixed horizontal ridge. A particle P of mass m is held on the smooth plane by a light string which passes over a small smooth pulley A on the ridge, and is attached to a particle Q of mass $3m$ which rests on the rough plane. The plane containing P, Q and A is perpendicular to the ridge. The system is released from rest with the string taut. Given that the acceleration of each particle is of magnitude $g/(5\sqrt{2})$, find

(a) the tension in the string,
(b) the coefficient of friction between Q and the rough plane,
(c) the magnitude and direction of the force exerted by the string on the pulley.

(U of L)

18) Two wooden discs X and Y of thickness $2a$ and $4a$ respectively are fixed at a small distance apart with their plane faces vertical and parallel. A small bullet of mass m is fired horizontally into X with initial speed u at right angles to the plane faces. It emerges from X with speed v and then enters Y into which it penetrates a distance a before being brought to rest. If the motion of a bullet through X and Y is opposed by constant forces R_1, R_2 respectively, find expressions for R_1 and R_2 in terms of u, v, a and m.

A second bullet of mass m is now fired horizontally into Y with initial speed u at right angles to the plane faces in a direction towards X. Show that this bullet will emerge from Y if $v < \frac{1}{2}u$.

If $v = \frac{1}{3}u$ and the second bullet enters X after emerging from Y, find the distance which it penetrates into X before being brought to rest.

(The effect of gravity may be ignored.)   (C)

19) Two points A and B on a rough horizontal table are at a distance a apart. A particle is projected along the table from A towards B with speed u, and simultaneously another particle is projected from B towards A with speed $3u$. The coefficient of friction between each particle and the table is μ. By considering the distance travelled by each particle before coming to rest, show that the particles collide if $u^2 \geqslant \frac{1}{5}\mu a g$.

If $u^2 = \frac{4}{7}\mu a g$, show that the collision occurs after a time $[a/(7\mu g)]^{\frac{1}{2}}$ and at a distance $\frac{3}{14}a$ from A.   (C)

20) A smooth wedge of mass $6m$ has a normal cross-section ABC such that AB = AC and the angle BAC is a right angle. The face containing BC is in contact with a horizontal plane, and a light taut string joining two particles of mass $3m$, m lies in the plane ABC so that each particle is in contact with one inclined face of the wedge. The centroid of the wedge lies in the plane ABC. If the system is released from rest, determine the acceleration of the wedge.

(U of L)

21) Three particles A, B, C are of masses 4, 4, 2 kg respectively. They lie at rest on a horizontal table in a straight line, with particle B attached to the mid-point of a light inextensible string. The string has particle A attached at one end and particle C at the other, and is taut. A force of 60 N is applied to A in the direction CA produced, and a force of 15 N is applied to C in the opposite direction. Find the acceleration of the particles and the tension in each part of the string

(a) if the table is smooth,

(b) if the coefficient of friction between each particle and the table is $\frac{1}{4}$.

[Take g as $10 \, \text{m/s}^2$.]   (U of L)

CHAPTER 6

WORK AND POWER

WORK

When a body moves under the action of a force it is useful to study the combination of the force and the distance moved by the body and from this study arises the following concept of work.

When a body is moved by the action of a constant force the work done by that force is the component of the force in the direction of motion multiplied by the distance moved by the point of application of the force.

So when a particle is moved from A to B by a constant force F

the work done by F is given by $(F \cos\theta)(AB)$

Note. This definition applies only to the work done by a *constant* force. The work done by variable forces is dealt with in the next volume.

The Unit of Work

The unit of force is the newton and the unit of distance is the metre so that the unit of work done by a force is the newton metre and is called the *joule*. (J)

When a body moves under the action of several forces, the work done by each force acting on the body can be found separately.

Consider a block which is pulled a distance s along a rough horizontal surface by a string inclined at an angle θ to the horizontal.

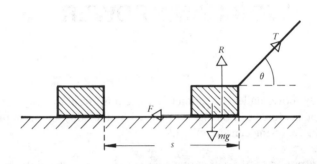

The point of application of each force moves a distance s.

The work done by the tension in the string $= T\cos\theta \times s = Ts\cos\theta$

The work done by the frictional force $\quad= -F \times s \quad= -Fs$

The work done by the weight $\quad= 0 \times s \quad= 0$

The work done by the normal reaction $\quad= 0 \times s \quad= 0$

These equations show that when an object moves under the action of several forces, not all of these forces do positive work. Those forces that have no component in the direction of motion (the weight and the normal reaction in this example) do no work.

When the work done by a force is negative, work is said to be done *against* that force, i.e. in this example, Fs is the work done against the frictional force.

Work Done against Gravity

Consider a body of mass m which is raised a vertical distance h.

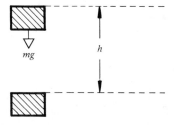

The work done by the weight is $-mgh$.

mgh is called the work done against gravity

If an agent, such as a crane, is responsible for lifting the body, then mgh is referred to as the work done by the crane against gravity.

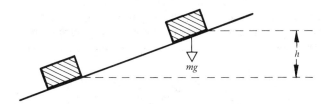

Similarly if a vehicle of mass m climbs a hill, and in doing so raises itself a vertical distance h, then mgh is called the work done by the vehicle against gravity.

Work Done by a Moving Vehicle

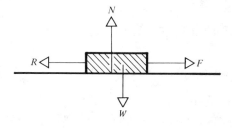

The diagram shows the forces that commonly act on a moving vehicle. R is the resistance to motion (this is always in the direction opposite to the direction of motion) and F is the driving force of the engine. The work done by F is referred to as the work done by the vehicle.

Note. If the vehicle is not accelerating, the forces acting on it are in equilibrium.

EXAMPLES 6a

1) A man lifts 20 boxes each of mass 15 kg to a height of 1.5 m. Find the work done by the man against gravity.

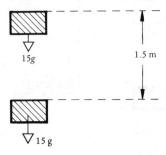

The work done against gravity in lifting one box $= 15g \times 1.5$ J
$\qquad\qquad\qquad\qquad\qquad\qquad\qquad\qquad\qquad\quad = 22.5g$ J
The work done against gravity in lifting 20 boxes $= 20 \times 22.5g$ J
$\qquad\qquad\qquad\qquad\qquad\qquad\qquad\qquad\qquad\qquad = 450g$ J.

2) A light tank, of mass 9 tonne, travels a distance of 10 m up a bank which is inclined at $\arcsin \frac{1}{3}$ to the horizontal. If the average resistance to motion is 200 N, find the total work done by the tank against the resistance and gravity.

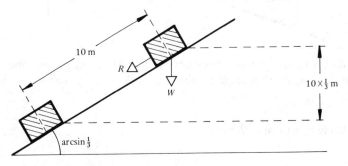

Representing the resistance by R and the weight by W we have

$R = 200$
So the work done against $R \qquad = 200 \times 10$ J $\qquad = 2000$ J
$W = 9000g$
Height risen by tank $= 10 \times \frac{1}{3}$ m
So the work done against gravity $= 9000g \times 10 \times \frac{1}{3}$ J $= 294\,000$ J
Therefore the total work done by the tank $\qquad\qquad = 296\,000$ J

3) A car of mass 1500 kg climbs a hill at a constant speed of 20 m s^{-1}. If the hill is inclined at $\arcsin \frac{1}{10}$ to the horizontal, find the work done by the car against gravity in one minute. If the total work done by the car in this time is 24×10^5 J, find the resistance to motion.

In one minute the distance moved up the slope by the car is 20×60 m

Therefore the vertical distance raised in one minute is $1200 \times \frac{1}{10}$ m $= 120$ m

So the work done against gravity in one minute $= 1500g \times 120$ J

$$= 1\,764\,000 \text{ J}$$

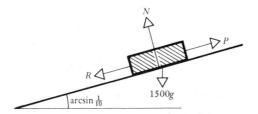

As the car is not accelerating, the forces acting on it are in equilibrium so, resolving parallel to the hill, we have

$$P = R + 1500g \times \tfrac{1}{10} = R + 1470$$

The work done by the car in one minute, i.e. the work done by P in one minute, is given by

$$P \times 1200 \text{ J}$$
$$= (R + 1470) \times 1200 \text{ J}$$

Therefore $\qquad 24 \times 10^5 = 1200(R + 1470)$

$\Rightarrow \qquad\qquad\qquad R = 530$

So the resistance to the motion of the car is 530 N.

EXERCISE 6a

1) A block is pulled a distance x along a rough horizontal table by a horizontal string. If the tension in the string is T, the weight of the block is W, the normal reaction is R and the frictional force is F, write down expressions for the work done by each of these forces.

2) A particle is pulled a distance l down a rough plane inclined at an angle α to the horizontal by a string inclined at an angle β to the horizontal $(\alpha + \beta < 90°)$. If the tension in the string is T, the normal reaction between the particle and the plane is R, the frictional force is F and the weight of the particle is W, write down expressions for the work done by each of these forces.

3) A block of mass 500 kg is raised a height of 10 m by a crane. Find the work done by the crane against gravity.

4) A block of mass 10 kg is pulled a distance 5 m up a plane which is inclined at $15°$ to the horizontal. Find the work done against gravity.

5) A train travels 6 km between two stations. If the resistance to motion averages 500 N, find the work done against this resistance.

6) A force $2\mathbf{i} - \mathbf{j}$ acts on a particle which undergoes a displacement of $3\mathbf{i}$. Find the work done by the force.

7) Two forces $\mathbf{F}_1$ and $\mathbf{F}_2$ act on a particle P causing it to move through a distance of $2\,\text{m}$. Find the work done by the resultant force if $\mathbf{F}_1 = \mathbf{i} - \mathbf{j}$ and $\mathbf{F}_2$ is of magnitude $10\,\text{N}$ and acts in the direction $4\mathbf{i} + 3\mathbf{j}$.

8) A cable car travelling at a steady speed moves a distance of $2\,\text{km}$ up a slope inclined at $20°$ to the horizontal. If the mass of the cable car is $1200\,\text{kg}$ and the resistance to motion is $400\,\text{N}$, find the work done by the tension in the cable.

9) A man climbs a mountain of height $2000\,\text{m}$. If the weight of the man is $700\,\text{N}$, find the work he does against gravity.

10) A man pushes his bicycle a distance of $200\,\text{m}$ up a hill which is inclined at $\arcsin\frac{1}{15}$ to the horizontal. If the man and his bicycle together weigh $850\,\text{N}$, find the work he does against gravity. If the average resistance to motion is $30\,\text{N}$, find the total work done by the man.

11) A block is pulled along a rough horizontal surface by a horizontal string. If the string pulls the block at a steady speed and does work of $100\,\text{J}$ in moving the block a distance of $5\,\text{m}$, find the tension in the string.

12) A block is pulled at a constant speed of $5\,\text{m s}^{-1}$ along a horizontal surface by a horizontal string. If the tension in the string is $5\,\text{N}$, find the work done by the string in ten seconds.

13) A block is pulled up an incline of $\arcsin\frac{1}{20}$ to the horizontal at a steady speed of $6\,\text{m s}^{-1}$. If the work done against gravity in one second is $400\,\text{J}$, find the weight of the block.

14) A particle of mass $5\,\text{kg}$ is pulled up a rough plane by a string parallel to the plane. If the plane is inclined at $30°$ to the horizontal, and if the work done by the tension in the string in moving the block a distance of $3\,\text{m}$ at a steady speed is $90\,\text{J}$, find the coefficient of friction between the block and the plane.

POWER

> Power is the rate at which a force does work.

If a force does $10\,\text{J}$ of work in five seconds, the average rate at which it is working is $2\,\text{J s}^{-1}$.

Unit of Power

The unit of power is the joule per second and this is called the watt (W). So the power of the force in the example above is $2\,\text{W}$. When large amounts of power are involved, a more convenient unit is the kilowatt (kW) where $1\,\text{kW} = 1000\,\text{W}$.

The Power of a Moving Vehicle

The power of a vehicle is defined as the rate at which the *driving force* is working.

Consider a vehicle moving at a constant speed v metres per second. The driving force is F newtons.

The distance moved in 1 second is v metres
The work done by the driving force in 1 second is Fv joules

Hence the power of the vehicle is Fv watts.

So, if P is the power, $$P = Fv$$

i.e. the power of a vehicle is given by multiplying the driving force by the velocity.

When the velocity is not constant this relationship gives the power at the instant when the velocity is v.

EXAMPLES 6b

1) A train has a maximum speed of $40\,\mathrm{m\,s^{-1}}$ on the level against resistive forces of magnitude $30\,000\,\mathrm{N}$. Find the maximum power of the engine.

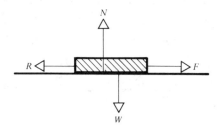

At the maximum speed there is no acceleration, so the forces acting on the train are in equilibrium.

Therefore $$F = R$$
$\Rightarrow$ $$F = 30\,000\,\mathrm{N}$$

At maximum speed the train is working at maximum power, so using $P = Fv$ we have

$$\text{maximum power} = 30\,000 \times 40\,\mathrm{W} = 1200\,\mathrm{kW}$$

2) A train of mass 200 tonne has a maximum speed of $20\,\mathrm{m\,s}^{-1}$ up a hill inclined at $\arcsin\frac{1}{50}$ to the horizontal when the engine is working at $800\,\mathrm{kW}$. Find the resistance to the motion of the train.

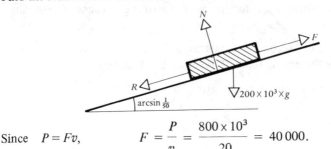

Since $P = Fv,$ $F = \dfrac{P}{v} = \dfrac{800 \times 10^3}{20} = 40\,000.$

At maximum speed, the forces acting on the train are in equilibrium.

Resolving parallel to the hill,

$$F = R + 200 \times 10^3 g \times \tfrac{1}{50}$$

$\Rightarrow$ $40\,000 = R + 39\,200$

Therefore the resistance is $800\,\mathrm{N}$.

3) A cyclist moves against a resistance to motion which is proportional to his speed. At a power output of $75\,\mathrm{W}$ he has a maximum speed of $5\,\mathrm{m\,s}^{-1}$ on a level road. If the cyclist and his machine together weigh $800\,\mathrm{N}$, find the maximum speed he reaches when travelling down a hill inclined at $\arcsin\frac{1}{40}$ to the horizontal when he is working at the rate of $25\,\mathrm{W}$.

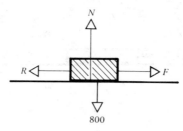

When travelling at any speed v, $F = \dfrac{P}{v}$ and $R = kv$

When travelling on the level $F = \frac{75}{5}$

As there is no acceleration $F = R$

But $R = k \times 5$

Therefore $15 = k \times 5 \Rightarrow k = 3$

$\Rightarrow$ $R = 3v$ at any velocity v

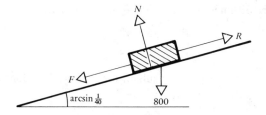

When travelling down the hill at maximum speed V,

$$F = \frac{P}{V} = \frac{25}{V} \quad \text{and} \quad R = 3V$$

There is no acceleration so, resolving parallel to the hill, we have

$$F + 800 \times \tfrac{1}{40} = R$$

$\Rightarrow$
$$\frac{25}{V} + 20 = 3V$$

$\Rightarrow$
$$3V^2 - 20V - 25 = 0$$

Hence $V = 7.7$ (the negative root is not applicable).

The maximum speed downhill is $7.7 \, \text{m s}^{-1}$

4) A car of mass $1500 \, \text{kg}$ has a maximum speed of $150 \, \text{km h}^{-1}$ on the level when working at its maximum power against resistances of $60 \, \text{N}$. Find the acceleration of the car when it is travelling at $60 \, \text{km h}^{-1}$ on the level with the engine working at maximum power assuming that the resistance to motion remains constant.

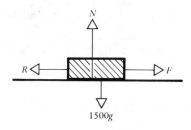

At maximum speed there is no acceleration.

So
$$F = R = 60$$

Also
$$P = Fv$$

$$= 60 \times 150 \times \tfrac{5}{18} = 2500$$

When the speed is $60 \, \text{km} \, \text{h}^{-1}$, i.e. $60 \times \frac{5}{18} \, \text{m} \, \text{s}^{-1}$, we have

$$F = \frac{P}{v} = \frac{2500 \times 18}{60 \times 5} = 150$$

As the car is accelerating, there is a resultant force in the direction of this acceleration of magnitude $F - R$ where

$$F - R = 90$$

If the acceleration is $a \, \text{m} \, \text{s}^{-2}$, Newton's Law gives

$$F - R = ma$$

Therefore

$$a = \frac{90}{1500} = 0.06$$

The acceleration is $0.06 \, \text{m} \, \text{s}^{-2}$.

5) An engine of mass 100 tonne pulls a train of mass 400 tonne. The resistance to motion of the engine is 1000 N and the resistance to motion of the train is 20 000 N. Find the tension in the coupling between the engine and the train at the instant when the speed of the train is $80 \, \text{km} \, \text{h}^{-1}$ and the engine is exerting a power of 4000 kW.

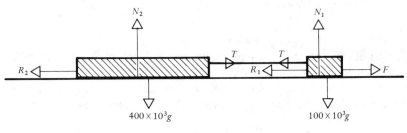

$$F = \frac{P}{V} \quad \Rightarrow \quad F = \frac{4000 \times 10^3 \times 18}{80 \times 5} = 180\,000$$

By considering the forces acting on the engine and train together, T is not brought into the calculations as it is an internal force.
The resultant force in the direction of motion is given by $F - (R_1 + R_2)$

i.e. $(180\,000 - 21\,000) \, \text{N} = 159\,000 \, \text{N}$

Therefore the train is accelerating.

If this acceleration is $a \, \text{m} \, \text{s}^{-2}$, Newton's Law gives

$$159\,000 = 500 \times 10^3 \times a$$

$\Rightarrow$

$$a = \frac{159\,000}{500 \times 10^3} = 0.318$$

Now that the acceleration of the engine and train is known, T can be found by considering the forces acting on either the train or the engine.

Considering the forces acting on the train, the resultant force in the direction of motion is $T - R_2$

So $\qquad\qquad T - R_2 = (400 \times 10^3 \times 0.318)$ $\qquad$ (Newton's Law)

$\Rightarrow \qquad\qquad\quad T = 400 \times 10^3 \times 0.318 + 20\,000$

Hence the tension in the coupling is $147\,200\,\text{N}$.

6) The resistance to motion of a car is proportional to the square of its speed. The car has a mass of $1000\,\text{kg}$ and can maintain a steady speed of $30\,\text{m}\,\text{s}^{-1}$ when travelling up a hill inclined at $\arcsin\frac{1}{20}$ to the horizontal with the engine working at $60\,\text{kW}$. Find the acceleration of the car when it is travelling down the same hill with the engine working at $40\,\text{kW}$ at the instant when the speed is $20\,\text{m}\,\text{s}^{-1}$.

The resistance to motion at any speed v is given by $R = kv^2$.

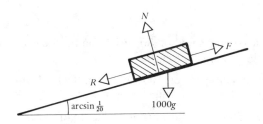

When the car is travelling up the hill $\quad F = \dfrac{P}{v}$

$$= \frac{60 \times 10^3}{30} = 2000$$

The forces acting on the car are in equilibrium so

$$F = R + 1000g \times \tfrac{1}{20}$$

$\Rightarrow \qquad\qquad R = 2000 - 490 = 1510$

But $\quad R = kv^2 \quad$ so $\qquad 1510 = k \times 900$

$\Rightarrow \qquad\qquad\qquad k = \dfrac{151}{90}$

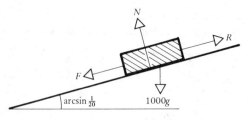

When the car is travelling down the hill $F = \dfrac{P}{v}$

$$= \frac{40 \times 10^3}{20} = 2000$$

The resultant force down the hill $= F + 1000g \times \frac{1}{20} - R$

$$= 2000 + 490 - \frac{151}{90} \times 20^2$$

$$= 1819$$

If the acceleration of the car is a, $1819 = 1000a$ (Newton's Law)

So the acceleration is $1.82 \, \mathrm{m\,s^{-2}}$

EXERCISE 6b

1) A train has a maximum speed of $80 \, \mathrm{km\,h^{-1}}$ on the level against resistance of $50\,000 \, \mathrm{N}$. Find the power of the engine.

2) A car has a maximum speed of $100 \, \mathrm{km\,h^{-1}}$ on the level with the engine working at $50 \, \mathrm{kW}$. Find the resistance to motion.

3) A train of mass 500 tonne has a maximum speed of $90 \, \mathrm{km\,h^{-1}}$ up an incline of $\arcsin \frac{1}{50}$ against frictional resistance of $100\,000 \, \mathrm{N}$. Find the power of the engine.

4) A cyclist working at $20 \, \mathrm{W}$ has a maximum speed of $30 \, \mathrm{km\,h^{-1}}$ down an incline of $\arcsin \frac{1}{20}$ to the horizontal. Find the frictional resistance to motion if the mass of the cyclist and his machine is $100 \, \mathrm{kg}$.

5) A car of mass $750 \, \mathrm{kg}$ has a maximum power of $30 \, \mathrm{kW}$ and moves against a constant resistance to motion of $800 \, \mathrm{N}$. Find the maximum speed of the car:
(a) on the level,
(b) up an incline of $\arcsin \frac{1}{10}$ to the horizontal,
(c) down the same incline.

6) An engine of mass 75 tonne moves against a resistance to motion which is proportional to its speed. It has a maximum speed of $40 \, \mathrm{m\,s^{-1}}$ on the level with the engine working at $1500 \, \mathrm{kW}$. Find the maximum speed of the engine up an incline of $\arcsin \frac{1}{50}$ to the horizontal with the engine working at the same power.

7) A hoist with a power input of 220 W can lift a block of weight 600 N to a height of 10 m in 30 seconds at a steady speed. Find the resistance to the motion of the hoist.

8) A constant force of 6 N moves a particle of mass 12 kg from rest through a distance of 30 m. Find the work done by the force and the maximum power achieved.

9) A car of mass 2000 kg has a constant frictional resistance to motion of 2000 N. Find the acceleration of the car when it has a speed of 20 km h^{-1} on a level road with the engine working at 100 kW.

10) A car of mass 1000 kg has a constant resistance to motion of 3000 N. If the maximum power of the car is 50 kW find the acceleration when travelling at 20 km h^{-1} up a hill inclined at arcsin $\frac{1}{20}$ to the horizontal.

11) A train of mass 400 tonne is travelling down an incline of arcsin $\frac{1}{50}$ to the horizontal against resistances of 30 000 N. Find the acceleration of the train when it is travelling at 20 m s^{-1} and the power output of the engine is 50 kW.

12) A car of mass 2000 kg pulls a caravan of mass 400 kg. The resistance to motion of the car is 1000 N and the resistance to motion of the caravan is 100 N. Find the acceleration of the car and the caravan at the instant when their speed is 40 km h^{-1} with the power output of the engine equal to 100 kW. Find also the tension in the coupling between the car and the caravan at this instant.

13) A cyclist moves against resistance to motion of $(3 + kv^2)$ N where k is a constant and his speed is v m s^{-1}. If his maximum speed on the level is 10 m s^{-1} when he is working at the rate of 75 W, find his acceleration on the level at the instant when his speed is 5 m s^{-1} and he is working at the same rate. The mass of the cyclist and his machine is 90 kg.

14) A car of mass 1500 kg tows another car of mass 1000 kg up a hill inclined at arcsin $\frac{1}{10}$ to the horizontal. The resistance to motion of the cars is 0.5 N per kg. Find the tension in the tow rope at the instant when their speed is 10 m s^{-1} and the power output of the towing car is 150 kW.

SUMMARY

Work: The work done by a constant force is the product of the component of the force in the direction of motion and the distance moved by the point of application of the force.

Power: Power is the rate at which a force does work.
The power of a vehicle is the rate at which the driving force works.
i.e. the power of a vehicle = driving force × velocity.

MULTIPLE CHOICE EXERCISE 6

(Instructions for answering these questions are given on page x.)

TYPE I

1)

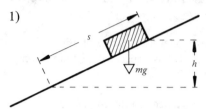

The work done against gravity in moving the block a distance s up the slope is:
(a) mh (b) mgs
(c) ms (d) mgh
(e) gh.

2) A block of weight W is pulled a distance l along a horizontal table. The work done by the weight is:

(a) Wl (b) 0   (c) Wgl (d) $\dfrac{Wl}{g}$ (e) W.

3) A child builds a tower from three blocks. The blocks are uniform cubes of side 2 cm. The blocks are initially all lying on the same horizontal surface and each block has a mass of 0.1 kg. The work done by the child is:
(a) 4 J   (b) 0.04 J   (c) 6 J   (d) 0.6 J   (e) 0.06 J.

4) A car is moving with a constant speed of $20 \, \mathrm{m\,s^{-1}}$ against a resistance of 100 N. The power exerted by the car is:
(a) 2 kW   (b) 5 W   (c) 200 W   (d) 1 kW   (e) 20 kW.

5) A particle of mass m moves from rest under the action of a constant force F which acts for two seconds. The maximum power attained is:

(a) $2Fm$ (b) $\dfrac{F^2}{m}$ (c) $\dfrac{2F}{m}$ (d) $\dfrac{2F^2}{m}$ (e) $\dfrac{F^2}{2m}$

TYPE III

6) (a) A train is moving with its engine working at constant power.
   (b) A train is moving with its engine exerting a constant driving force.

7) A particle is pulled by a string a distance s along a horizontal surface. The tension in the string is T.
(a) The work done by the tension in the string is Ts.
(b) The string is inclined at an angle θ to the horizontal.

TYPE IV

8) Find the work done by a forklift truck in lifting two uniform boxes which are stacked vertically.
(a) The boxes are cubes of side 0.6 m.

(b) The mass of each box is 20 kg.

(c) The boxes are lifted vertically a distance of 3 m.

9) A car tows a caravan. Find the tension in the coupling between the car and caravan at the instant when their speed is $15 \, \text{m s}^{-1}$.

(a) The mass of the car is 900 kg.

(b) The car is working at a steady rate of 50 kW.

(c) The resistance to motion of the car and caravan is 1000 N.

10) A car is climbing a hill against a resistance to motion which is proportional to its speed. Find the maximum power of the car.

(a) The car has a maximum speed of $20 \, \text{m s}^{-1}$ up the hill and a maximum speed of $40 \, \text{m s}^{-1}$ on the level.

(b) The inclination of the hill is $\arcsin \frac{1}{10}$ to the horizontal.

(c) The mass of the car is 1000 kg.

11) Find the maximum power at which a cyclist can work.

(a) The cyclist has a maximum speed of $70 \, \text{km h}^{-1}$ on the level.

(b) The resistance to the motion of the cyclist is constant at 10 000 N.

(c) The mass of the cyclist and his machine is 90 kg.

TYPE V

12) Work is a scalar quantity.

13) If the engine of a car is working at constant power the acceleration of the car must be constant.

14) The unit of work is the newton metre per second.

15) A car is towing a van at constant speed. The resistance to the motion of the car is R and the driving force of the car is F. F and R are in equilibrium.

16) A car is towing a van and is accelerating. The tension in the tow rope is greater than the resistance to the motion of the van.

17) A train covers a distance of 20 m in two seconds at a constant speed, with the engine exerting a driving force of 2000 N. The engine is working at the rate of 20 kW.

MISCELLANEOUS EXERCISE 6

1) A car of mass 900 kg accelerates uniformly from rest to a speed of 60 km/h in a time of two seconds when travelling on a level road. If there is a constant resistance to motion of 20 N find the maximum power of the engine.

2) A car of mass 1500 kg has a maximum speed of 150 km/h on a level road when the engine is exerting its maximum power of 200 kW. Find the resistance

to motion at this speed. If this resistance is proportional to the speed of the car find the maximum speed of the car up a road inclined at arcsin $\frac{1}{10}$ to the horizontal.

3) A car of mass 1000 kg has a maximum speed of 90 km/h up a slope inclined at arcsin $\frac{1}{7}$ to the horizontal and a maximum speed of 180 km/h down the same slope. If the resistance to motion varies as the speed of the car find the maximum power of the car.

4) A cyclist and his machine have a total mass of 100 kg. When travelling up a hill inclined at arcsin $\frac{1}{50}$ to the horizontal against a resistance to motion of 20 N the cyclist can maintain a speed of 12 km/h. Find the rate at which he is working. If the resistance to motion is unchanged, find the acceleration of the cyclist when travelling at 10 km/h on a level road and working at the same rate.

5) A car has a maximum power of 200 kW. Its maximum speed on a level road is twice its maximum speed up a hill inclined at arcsin $\frac{1}{15}$ to the horizontal against a resistance to motion of 1600 N in each case. Find the mass of the car. Find also the acceleration of the car at the instant when its speed is 30 km/h on the level with the engine working at full power, assuming the resistance to motion is unchanged.

6) A car of mass 1000 kg is travelling on a level road against a resistance to motion which varies as the square of its speed. If the maximum power of the engine is 60 kW and the car has a maximum speed of 150 km/h, find an expression for the resistance to motion at any speed. Find also the acceleration when the engine is working at three-quarters full power and the speed is 30 km/h.

7) An engine of mass 5 tonnes pulls a train of mass 50 tonnes against a constant resistance to motion of R newtons per tonne. The train has a maximum maximum speed of 110 km/h on the horizontal when the engine is working at its maximum power of 1500 kW. Find R.
Find also the tension in the coupling between the engine and the train at the instant when it is travelling at 30 km/h on the horizontal with the engine working at half power.

8) A car of mass 1200 kg tows another car of mass 800 kg, the frictional resistances being 120 N and 80 N respectively. If the tow rope has a breaking tension of 2000 N find the maximum acceleration possible, and the maximum power the towing car can use at the instant when the speed is 10 km/h.

9) A car of mass 1000 kg has a maximum speed of 15 m/s up a slope inclined at an angle θ to the horizontal where $\sin \theta = 0.2$. There is a constant frictional resistance equal to one tenth of the weight of the car. Find the maximum speed of the car on a level road.
If the car descends the same slope with its engine working at half its maximum power, find the acceleration of the car at the moment when its speed is 30 m/s.

(U of L)

10) A lorry of mass 10 000 kg has a maximum speed of 24 km/h up a slope of 1 in 10 against a resistance of 1200 newtons. Find the effective power of the engine in kilowatts.
If the resistance varies as the square of the speed, find the maximum speed on the level to the nearest km/h. (U of L)

11) A car of mass 1000 kg whose maximum power is constant at all speeds experiences a constant resistance R newtons. If the maximum speed of the car on the horizontal is 120 km/h and the maximum speed up a slope of angle θ where $\sin\theta = 1/100$ is 60 km/h, calculate the power of the car. Calculate also the maximum speed of the car (a) on the horizontal and (b) up the slope when it is pulling a caravan of mass 1000 kg if the total resistance to the motion of the car and the caravan is $3R$ newtons. (U of L)

12) At the instant a car of mass 840 kg passes a sign post on a level road its speed is 90 km/h and its engine is working at 70 kW. If the total resistance is constant and equal to 2100 N, find the acceleration of the car in m/s^2 at the instant it passes the sign post. Calculate the maximum speed in km/h at which this car could travel up an incline of $\arcsin(1/10)$ against the same resistance with the engine working at the same rate. (AEB)

13) A car of mass 1000 kg is moving on a level road at a steady speed of 100 km/h with its engine working at 60 kW. Calculate in newtons the total resistance to motion, which may be assumed to be constant.
The engine is now disconnected, the brakes are applied, and the car comes to rest in 100 metres. Assuming that the total resistance remains the same, show that the retarding force of the brakes is about 1700 newtons.
If the engine is still disconnected, find the distance the car would run up a hill of inclination $\arcsin\frac{1}{10}$ before coming to rest, starting at 100 km/h when the same resistance and braking force are operating. (C)

14) A car of weight W has maximum power H. In all circumstances there is a constant resistance R due to friction. When the car is moving up a slope of 1 in n ($\arcsin\frac{1}{n}$) its maximum speed is v and when it is moving down the same slope its maximum speed is $2v$. Find R in terms of W and n.
The maximum speed of the car on level road is u. Find the maximum acceleration of the car when it is moving with speed $\frac{1}{2}u$ up the given slope. (AEB)

15) The engine of a car, of mass M kg, works at a constant rate of H kW. The non-gravitational resistance to the motion of the car is constant. The maximum speed on level ground is V m/s. Find, in terms of M, V, H, α and g, expressions for the accelerations of the car when it is travelling at speed $\frac{1}{2}V$ m/s (a) directly up a road of inclination α, (b) directly down this road.

Given that the acceleration in case (b) is twice that in case (a), find $\sin\alpha$ in terms of M, V, H and g. Find also, in terms of V alone, the greatest steady speed which the car can maintain when travelling directly up the road.   (U of L)

16) A car of mass $1000\,\text{kg}$ moves with its engine shut off down a slope of inclination α, where $\sin\alpha = 1/20$, at a steady speed of $15\,\text{m s}^{-1}$. Find the resistance, in newtons, to the motion of the car. Calculate the power delivered by the engine when the car ascends the same inclination at the same steady speed, assuming that resistance to motion is unchanged.
[Take g as $10\,\text{m s}^{-2}$]   (U of L)

17) A locomotive of mass $20\,000\,\text{kg}$ is connected to carriages of total mass $130\,000\,\text{kg}$ by means of a coupling. The train climbs a straight track inclined at $\sin^{-1}(1/200)$ to the horizontal with the engine of the locomotive working at $350\,\text{kW}$. The non-gravitational resistances opposing this motion are constant and total $2000\,\text{N}$ for the locomotive and $8000\,\text{N}$ for the carriages. Given that, at a particular instant, the train is moving at $15\,\text{m/s}$, calculate
(a) the driving force produced by the engine of the locomotive,
(b) the acceleration of the train,
(c) the tension in the coupling between the locomotive and the carriages.
Show that the greatest steady speed that the train can achieve up this incline under the given conditions is $20\,\text{m/s}$. If the train sustains this speed for $2\,\text{km}$, measured along the track, calculate, in joules, the total work done by the engine of the locomotive in covering this distance.
[Take the acceleration due to gravity to be $10\,\text{m/s}^2$]   (AEB)

18) A car has an engine capable of developing $15\,\text{kW}$. The maximum speed of the car on a level road is $120\,\text{km/h}$. Calculate the total resistance in newtons at this speed.
Given that the mass of the car is $1000\,\text{kg}$ and that the resistance to motion is proportional to the square of the speed, obtain the rate of working, in kW to two decimal places, of the engine when the car is moving at a constant speed of $40\,\text{km/h}$ up a road of inclination θ, where $\sin\theta = 1/25$.   (U of L)

CHAPTER 7

HOOKE'S LAW. ENERGY

ELASTIC STRINGS

A string whose length changes when forces are applied to its ends is said to be *elastic*.

The length of the string when no forces are acting on it is its *natural length*.

In order to stretch an elastic string, equal and opposite extending forces must be applied outwards to the ends of the string. The string is then in tension and exerts an inward pull (tension) at each end, equal in magnitude to the extending force.

The difference between the natural length of the string and its stretched length is the *extension*.

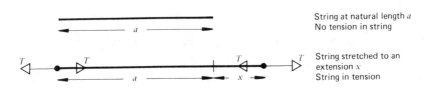

String at natural length a
No tension in string

String stretched to an extension x
String in tension

It can be shown experimentally that, up to a point, the tension in the string is directly proportional to the extension

i.e. $$T \propto x$$

This relationship, discovered in the seventeenth century, by Hooke, is known as *Hooke's Law* and is used in the form

$$T = \lambda \frac{x}{a}$$

where T is the tension in the string,

   a is the natural length,

   x is the extension,

and λ is the *modulus of elasticity* of the string.

Elastic Limit

If x is progressively increased, there comes a stage when the string becomes *overstretched* and will not return to its natural length when released. The string has then exceeded its *elastic limit* and no longer obeys Hooke's Law. In this state the string is no longer of any mathematical interest to us as, at this level, we study only those strings which have not reached their elastic limit and which do therefore obey Hooke's Law.

Modulus of Elasticity

For an elastic string of natural length a, Hooke's Law can be arranged in the form

$$\lambda = \frac{Ta}{x}$$

If $x = a$, i.e. the length of the string is doubled, then

$$\lambda = T$$

From this we see that λ, although a constant of proportion, has the dimensions of force and is equal to the tension in an elastic string whose length has been doubled.

Because λ has the dimensions of force it is measured in newtons.

SPRINGS

A spring is very similar to an elastic string with one important difference; a spring can be compressed as well as stretched.

When stretched, a spring behaves in exactly the same way as a stretched elastic string.

When the spring is compressed (i.e. has its length reduced from the natural length) the forces in the spring are an outward push (thrust) at each end. These forces again tend to restore the spring to its natural length and the spring is *in compression*

The reduction in length is the *compression*.

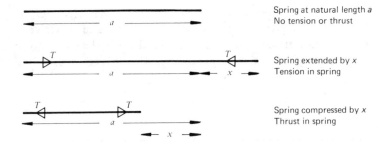

Spring at natural length *a*
No tension or thrust

Spring extended by *x*
Tension in spring

Spring compressed by *x*
Thrust in spring

In compression as well as in tension a spring obeys Hooke's Law

$$T = \lambda\frac{x}{a}$$

where T is now the thrust in the spring
and x is the compression.

SUMMARY

Elastic strings and springs obey Hooke's Law $T = \lambda\dfrac{x}{a}$

λ is the modulus of elasticity and has the dimensions of force.
λ is equal to the force required to double the length of the string or spring.

EXAMPLES 7a

1) An elastic string of natural length 2 m is fixed at one end and is stretched to
2.8 m in length by a force of 4 N. What is its modulus of elasticity?

$$\text{Tension} = \text{Extending Force}$$

$\Rightarrow$ $$T = 4$$

Using Hooke's Law gives

$$T = \lambda\left(\frac{0.8}{2.0}\right)$$

Therefore $$\lambda = 4\left(\frac{2.0}{0.8}\right)$$

So the modulus of elasticity is 10 N.

2) An elastic string of natural length $4l$ and modulus of elasticity $4mg$ is stretched between two points A and B which are on the same level, where $AB = 4l$. A particle attached to the midpoint of the string hangs in equilibrium with both portions of string making $30°$ with AB. What is the mass of the particle?

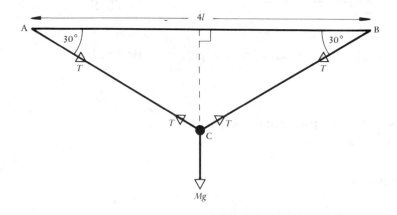

Let M be the mass of the particle and let C be the midpoint of the string.

Resolving vertically at C, $2T\sin 30° = Mg$

$\Rightarrow$ $T = Mg$

The stretched length of the string AC is $2l\sec 30°$

$\Rightarrow$ $AC = 2.31l$

The extension in the string is $AC - 2l = 0.31l$

Using Hooke's Law gives $T = \lambda\left(\dfrac{0.31l}{2l}\right)$

$\Rightarrow$ $Mg = 4mg\left(\dfrac{0.31l}{2l}\right)$

$\Rightarrow$ $M = 0.62m$

So the mass of the particle is $0.62m$

3) An elastic spring is fixed at one end. When a force of 4 N is applied to the other end the spring extends by 0.2 m. If the spring hangs vertically supporting a mass of 1 kg at the free end, the spring is of length 2.49 m. Find the natural length and modulus of elasticity of the spring.

Let the natural length of the spring be l m.

$$\text{Extending Force} = \text{Tension}$$

$$\Rightarrow \quad T_1 = 4$$

Hooke's Law gives $\quad T_1 = \lambda\left(\dfrac{0.2}{l}\right)$

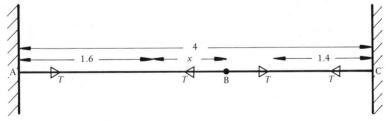

$$\Rightarrow \quad \lambda = \dfrac{4l}{0.2} = 20l$$

Now $T_2 = \lambda\left(\dfrac{2.49-l}{l}\right)$

and $\quad T_2 = (1)(g) = 9.8$

So $\quad 9.8 = 20l\left(\dfrac{2.49-l}{l}\right)$

$$\Rightarrow \quad 9.8 = 49.8 - 20l$$

$$\Rightarrow \quad l = 2$$

The natural length of the spring is 2 m and the modulus of elasticity is 40 N.

4) Two springs AB and BC are joined together end to end to form one long spring. The natural lengths of the separate springs are 1.6 m and 1.4 m and their moduli of elasticity are 20 N and 28 N respectively. Find the tension in the combined spring if it is stretched between two points 4 m apart.

Measuring all lengths in metres,

let the extension in spring AB be x $\qquad \Rightarrow \quad$ AB $= (1.6+x)$

then the length of spring BC is $4-(1.6+x)$ $\quad \Rightarrow \quad$ BC $= (2.4-x)$

But the natural length of spring BC is 1.4

So the extension in the spring BC is $(2.4-x-1.4) = (1-x)$

Because the point B is in equilibrium, the tensions in AB and BC are equal.

Using Hooke's Law for AB $\Rightarrow$ $$T = 20\frac{x}{1.6}$$ [1]

and for BC $\Rightarrow$ $$T = 28\frac{(1-x)}{1.4}$$ [2]

Hence $$\frac{20x}{1.6} = 28\frac{(1-x)}{1.4}$$

$\Rightarrow$ $$x = 1.6(1-x)$$

$\Rightarrow$ $$x = \frac{1.6}{2.6}$$

Then, in [1], $$T = \frac{20}{1.6}\left(\frac{1.6}{2.6}\right) = 7.69$$

So the tension in the spring is 7.69 N.

5) A rod AB of length $4a$ and weight W rests at $60°$ to a smooth vertical wall. It is supported with the end A in contact with the wall by an elastic string connecting a point C on the rod to a point D on the wall vertically above A. If the natural length of the string is $\frac{3}{4}a$ and the distances AC and AD are a, find the modulus of elasticity of the string.

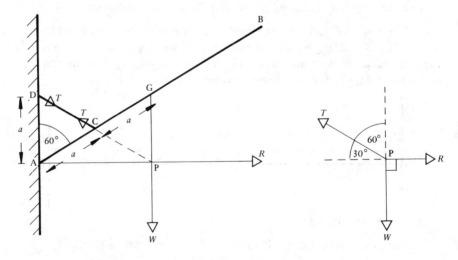

In $\triangle$DAC, DA = AC therefore $A\widehat{D}C = A\widehat{C}D$

But angle DAC is $60°$ so triangle DAC is equilateral.

Hence the string is at $60°$ to the wall and DC $= a$.

The rod is in equilibrium under the action of three forces which must therefore be concurrent. The line of action of the tension in the string must therefore pass through P, the point of intersection of R and W.

Lami's Theorem gives $$\frac{T}{\sin 90°} = \frac{W}{\sin 30°}$$

$\Rightarrow$ $$T = 2W$$

For the string, natural length $= \tfrac{3}{4}a$

stretched length $= a$

extension $= \tfrac{1}{4}a$

modulus $= \lambda$

Hooke's Law gives $$2W = \frac{\tfrac{1}{4}\lambda a}{\tfrac{3}{4}a} = \tfrac{1}{3}\lambda$$

So the modulus of elasticity is $6W$.

6) When an elastic string of natural length 2 m is fixed at one end and hangs vertically supporting a particle of mass 4 kg at the other end, it stretches to a length of 2.8 m. A horizontal force of 28 N is then applied gradually to the mass until it is once again in equilibrium. Calculate the length and the inclination to the vertical of the string in this position.

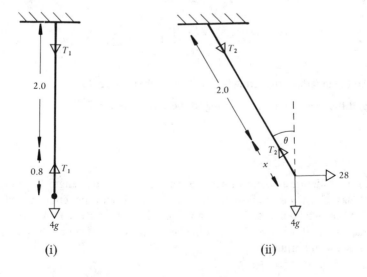

(i)   (ii)

In diagram (i) Hooke's Law gives

$$T_1 = \lambda \left(\frac{0.8}{2.0} \right)$$

The mass is in equilibrium so

$$T_1 = 4g$$

$\Rightarrow$
$$\lambda = 4g \left(\frac{2.0}{0.8} \right) = 98$$

In diagram (ii) Lami's Theorem gives

$$\frac{T_2}{\sin 90^\circ} = \frac{28}{\sin (180^\circ - \theta)} = \frac{4g}{\sin (90^\circ + \theta)}$$

or
$$\frac{T_2}{\sin 90^\circ} = \frac{28}{\sin \theta} = \frac{4g}{\cos \theta}$$

Hence
$$\tan \theta = \frac{28}{4g} = \frac{7}{9.8}$$

$\Rightarrow$
$$\theta = 35.5^\circ$$

Hence
$$T_2 = \frac{28}{\sin 35.5^\circ} = 48.17$$

Using Hooke's Law
$$T_2 = \lambda \frac{x}{2}$$

$\Rightarrow$
$$x = \frac{2T_2}{\lambda} = \left(\frac{2}{98} \right)(48.2) = 0.98$$

So the length of the string is $(2.0 + 0.98)\,\mathrm{m} = 2.98\,\mathrm{m}$

and the inclination of the string to the vertical is 35.5°

7) Two identical elastic strings AB and BC of natural length a and modulus of elasticity $2mg$ are fastened together at B. Their other ends A and C are fixed to two points $4a$ apart in a vertical line (A above C). A particle of mass m is attached at B. Find the height above C at which the particle rests in equilibrium.

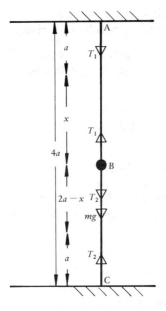

Let x be the extension in AB

Then the extension in BC is

$$(4a - 2a - x) = (2a - x)$$

The particle at B is in equilibrium

so $\qquad T_1 = T_2 + mg \qquad$ [1]

Using Hooke's Law gives

$$T_1 = \lambda \frac{x}{a} = 2mg \frac{x}{a} \qquad [2]$$

$$T_2 = \lambda \frac{(2a - x)}{a} = 2mg \frac{(2a - x)}{a} \qquad [3]$$

Combining [1], [2] and [3] gives

$$2mg \frac{x}{a} = 2mg \frac{(2a - x)}{a} + mg$$

$\Rightarrow \qquad\qquad 2\frac{x}{a} = 4 - 2\frac{x}{a} + 1$

$\Rightarrow \qquad\qquad 4\frac{x}{a} = 5$

$\Rightarrow \qquad\qquad x = \frac{5}{4}a$

So the height of B above C is $\quad 2a - x + a = \frac{7}{4}a$

i.e. the particle rests in equilibrium at a height $\frac{7}{4}a$ above C

EXERCISE 7a

1) An elastic string of natural length 3 m is fixed at one end. A force of 2 N is applied to the other end so as to stretch it. To what length will the string extend if its modulus of elasticity is:
(a) 0.3 N   (b) 2 N   (c) 4 N?

2) The length of an elastic spring whose modulus of elasticity is 25 N, which is fixed at one end, is reduced by 0.5 m when a force of 20 N compresses it. What is the natural length of the spring?

3) A string will break if the tension in it exceeds $10\,N$. If the maximum extension it can be given is $\frac{1}{4}$ of its natural length, find its modulus of elasticity.

4) A spring of unstretched length l and modulus λ hangs with a scale pan of mass m at its free end. If a mass M is placed gently on the scale pan find how far the new equilibrium position is below the old one.

5) What is the length and modulus of elasticity of an elastic string which has length a_1 when supporting a mass M_1 and length a_2 when supporting a mass M_2?

6) A spring is fixed at one end. When it hangs vertically, supporting a mass of 2 kilogram at the free end, its length is 3 metre. The mass of 2 kilogram is then removed and replaced by a particle of unknown mass. The length of the spring is then 2.5 metre. If the modulus of elasticity of the spring is 9.8 newton, find the mass of the second load.

7) A particle of mass M is attached to the midpoint of an elastic spring whose modulus is $2Mg$ and whose unstretched length is $2a$. One end P of the spring is attached to the ceiling, and the other end Q to the floor, of a room of height $4a$. If P is vertically above Q find the distance from the ceiling of the particle when it is in equilibrium.

8) A mass of 4 kilogram rests on a smooth plane inclined at $30°$ to the horizontal. It is held in equilibrium by a light elastic string attached to the mass and to a point on the plane. Find the extension in the string if it is known that a force of 49 newton would double the natural length of 1.25 metre.

9) The end A of an elastic string AB of natural length a and modulus of elasticity $2mg$ is fastened to one end of another elastic string AC of natural length $2a$ and modulus of elasticity $3mg$. The ends B and C are stretched between two points $6a$ apart in a horizontal line. Find the length of AB.

10) A light spring of natural length l is fixed at one end to a point O on a smooth horizontal table. The other end is attached to a particle P of mass m which rests on the table. The particle is pulled away from O until $OP = 5l/2$. If the modulus of elasticity of the spring is $2mg$ find the tension in the spring and the initial acceleration of the particle when released.

WORK DONE IN STRETCHING AN ELASTIC STRING

If a force is applied to the end of an elastic string so that the string stretches, the force is moving the object to which it is applied and is therefore doing work. Let us consider an elastic string of natural length a which is fixed at one end. A force is applied steadily to the other end until the extension in the string is x.

Calculation of the Amount of Work Done

The extending force will not be constant because it is always equal to the restoring tension in the string, which varies uniformly with the extension. The extending force is therefore directly proportional to the extension.

Consider the string when

    (a) the extension is x_1 and the extending force is T_1

    (b) the extension is x_2 and the extending force is T_2

While the extension increases from x_1 to x_2, the average extending force is $\frac{1}{2}(T_1 + T_2)$

The work done in stretching the string by $(x_2 - x_1)$ can be calculated using

$$\text{work done} = \text{average force} \times \text{extension} = \tfrac{1}{2}(T_1 + T_2)(x_2 - x_1)$$

If the string is initially unstretched, then $x_1 = 0$ and $T_1 = 0$ and we see that the amount of work then required to produce a general extension x,

is $\frac{1}{2}Tx$ where $T = \lambda\dfrac{x}{a}$.

Therefore, when the string is stretched from its natural length a to $a + x$,

$$\text{work done} = \frac{\lambda x^2}{2a}$$

Those students who are sufficiently familiar with calculus may prefer to derive the expression for the work done in stretching an elastic string by using integration, as follows:

When the extension is s the magnitude of the extending force is $\dfrac{\lambda s}{a}$.

The work done in producing a further small extension δs is therefore approximately $\left(\dfrac{\lambda s}{a}\right)(\delta s)$.

The total work done in stretching the string from a to $(a+x)$ is given by

$$\int_0^x \frac{\lambda s}{a}\,ds = \frac{\lambda x^2}{2a}.$$

Note. The work done when a spring of modulus λ and natural length a is compressed a distance x is also given by $\dfrac{\lambda x^2}{2a}$.

EXAMPLES 7b

1) An elastic string of natural length $2\,m$ and modulus of elasticity $6\,N$ is stretched until the extending force is of magnitude $4\,N$. How much work has been done and what is the final extension?

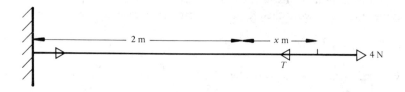

At maximum extension,   Tension = Extending Force = 4 N.

Using Hooke's Law, $T = \lambda\dfrac{x}{a}$, gives

$$4 = 6\frac{x}{2}$$

$\Rightarrow$ $x = \frac{4}{3}$

The average force is $\frac{1}{2}(0+4)\,N = 2\,N$

Hence   work done $= 2 \times \frac{4}{3}\,J = \frac{8}{3}\,J$.

So the work done $= 2\frac{2}{3}\,J$ and the maximum extension $= 1\frac{1}{3}\,m$

2) An elastic spring of modulus λ and natural length a is fixed at one end and is attached to a load of mass m at the other end. How much work is done in stretching the spring slowly from its natural length to the position of equilibrium of the load?

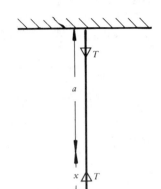

When the load is in equilibrium

$$T = mg$$

But using Hooke's Law gives

$$mg = \lambda \frac{x}{a}$$

$\Rightarrow$ $$x = \frac{mga}{\lambda}$$

Then the work done in stretching the spring is given by

$$\frac{\lambda x^2}{2a} = \frac{\lambda}{2a} \left(\frac{mga}{\lambda} \right)^2 = \frac{m^2 g^2 a}{2\lambda}$$

3) A spring of natural length $2l$ and modulus of elasticity mg is compressed to a length l and an elastic string of modulus $2mg$ is stretched to a length $\frac{3}{2}l$. If the work done in both cases is equal, find the natural length of the string.

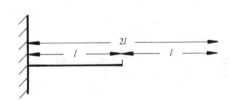

For the spring,

$$\lambda_1 = mg$$

$$\text{compression} = l$$

$$\text{work done} = \frac{\lambda_1 l^2}{2(2l)} = \frac{mgl}{4}$$

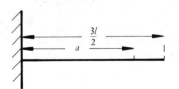

For the string,

$$\lambda_2 = 2mg$$

$$\text{natural length} = a$$

$$\text{extension} = \tfrac{3}{2}l - a$$

$$\text{Work done} = \lambda_2 \frac{(\frac{3}{2}l - a)^2}{2a} = \frac{2mg}{2a}(\tfrac{3}{2}l - a)^2$$

As equal work is done $\quad \dfrac{mgl}{4} = \dfrac{mg}{a}(\tfrac{3}{2}l-a)^2$

$\Rightarrow \qquad\qquad\qquad\qquad\qquad\qquad al = 4(\tfrac{3}{2}l-a)^2$

$\Rightarrow \qquad\qquad\qquad\qquad\qquad\qquad al = 9l^2 - 12al + 4a^2$

$\Rightarrow \qquad\qquad\qquad\qquad\qquad\qquad 0 = 4a^2 - 13al + 9l^2$

$\Rightarrow \qquad\qquad\qquad\qquad\qquad\qquad 0 = (4a - 9l)(a - l)$

Therefore $\qquad\qquad\qquad\qquad\qquad a = l \;$ or $\; \tfrac{9}{4}l$

But $\tfrac{9}{4}l$ cannot be the natural length of the string as it is greater than the stretched length $\tfrac{3}{2}l$.

So the natural length of the string is l.

EXERCISE 7b

1) An elastic string breaks if the tension in it exceeds 3 N. The unstretched length of the string is 4 m and its modulus of elasticity is 2 N. Find the work done in stretching it to breaking point and the length of the string at that moment.

2) If the work done in halving the length of a spring of modulus 4 N is 1.2 J what is the natural length?

3) Two elastic strings AB and CD are each fixed with one end fastened to the ceiling and the other to the floor of a room of height 2.6 m.
For AB $\quad \lambda = 2$ N $\quad$ and $\quad$ natural length $= 1.4$ m.
For CD $\quad \lambda = 3$ N $\quad$ and $\quad$ natural length $= 1.8$ m.
If both strings are vertical find the ratio of the work done in stretching them.

4) Find the work done in stretching a rubber band round a roll of papers of radius 4 centimetre if the band when unstretched will just go round a cylinder of radius 2 centimetre and its modulus of elasticity is 0.5 N.

5) The work done in compressing a spring of natural length $3l$ to a length $2l$ is twice as great as the work done in doubling the length of a string of natural length $2l$. Show that the moduli of elasticity are in the ratio $12:1$.

ENERGY

A body is said to possess energy if it has the capacity to do work.
When a body possessing energy does some work, part of its energy is used up.
Conversely if work is done to an object the object will be given some energy.
Energy and work are mutually convertible and are measured in the same unit,
the joule,

i.e.   Work done = Change in energy

There are various forms of energy. Heat, electricity, light, sound and chemical
energy are all familiar forms. In studying mechanics however we are concerned
chiefly with *mechanical energy*. This type of energy is a property of movement
or position.

Kinetic Energy

Kinetic Energy, (K.E.), is the capacity of a body to do work by virtue of its
motion.
If a body of mass m has a velocity v its kinetic energy is equivalent to the
work which an external force would have to do to bring the body from rest up
to its velocity v.
The numerical value of the kinetic energy can be calculated from the formula

$$\text{K.E.} = \tfrac{1}{2}mv^2$$

This formula can be derived as follows.
Consider a constant force F which, acting on a mass m initially at rest, gives
the mass a velocity v. If, in reaching this velocity, the particle has been moving
with an acceleration a and has been given a displacement s, then:

$F = ma$ (Newton's Law)

$v^2 = 2as$ (Motion of a particle moving with uniform acceleration.)

$Fs = $ Work done by the constant force

Combining these relationships we have:

$$\text{work done} = ma\left(\frac{v^2}{2a}\right)$$

$$= \tfrac{1}{2}mv^2$$

But the K.E. of the body is equivalent to the work done in giving the body its velocity.

Hence   K.E. $= \frac{1}{2}mv^2$

Note. Since both m and v^2 are always positive, K.E. is always positive and does not depend upon the direction of motion of the body.

Potential Energy

Potential energy is energy due to position.
If a body is in a position such that if it were released it would begin to move, it has potential energy.
There are two common forms of potential energy, gravitational and elastic.

Gravitational Potential Energy, (P.E.), is a property of height.

When an object is allowed to fall from one level to a lower level it gains speed due to gravitational pull, i.e. it gains kinetic energy. Therefore, in possessing height, a body has the ability to convert its height into kinetic energy, i.e. it possesses *potential* energy.
The magnitude of its gravitational potential energy is equivalent to the amount of work done by the weight of the body in causing the descent.
If a mass m is at a height h above a lower level the P.E. possessed by the mass is $(mg)(h)$.

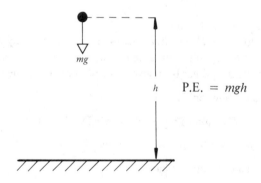

h P.E. $= mgh$

Since h is the height of an object *above* a specified level, an object *below* the specified level has negative potential energy.

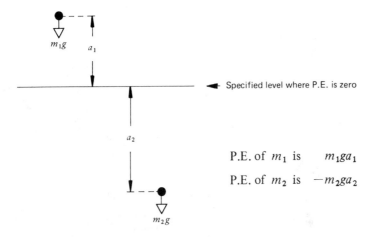

Specified level where P.E. is zero

P.E. of m_1 is $m_1 g a_1$

P.E. of m_2 is $-m_2 g a_2$

Note. The chosen level from which height is measured has no absolute position. It is important therefore to indicate clearly the zero P.E. level in any problem in which P.E. is to be calculated.

Elastic Potential Energy, (E.P.E.) is a property of stretched strings and springs or compressed springs.

The end of a stretched elastic string will begin to move if it is released. The string therefore possesses potential energy due to its elasticity.

The amount of elastic potential energy stored in a string of natural length a and modulus of elasticity λ when it is extended by a length x is equivalent to the amount of work necessary to produce the extension.

Earlier in the chapter we saw that the work done was $\dfrac{\lambda x^2}{2a}$ so

$$\text{E.P.E.} = \frac{\lambda x^2}{2a}$$

Note. E.P.E. is never negative whether due to extension or to compression.

SUMMARY

Energy is the ability to do work.

Energy and work are mutually convertible.

The *unit of energy* is the Joule.

Kinetic energy (K.E.) is given by $\frac{1}{2}mv^2$ and is never negative.

Gravitational Potential Energy (P.E.) is given by mgh. It is positive for objects above a specified level but negative for objects below this level.

Elastic Potential Energy (E.P.E.) is given by $\frac{1}{2}\lambda x^2/2a$ and is never negative.

EXAMPLES 7c

1) A body of mass 2 kg is held 3 m above the floor of a room. Find the potential energy of the body relative to:
(a) the floor,
(b) a table of height 0.8 m.

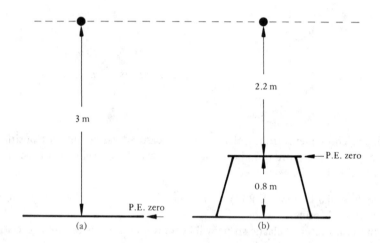

(a)

3 m

P.E. zero

(a)

2.2 m

—P.E. zero

0.8 m

(b)

(a)　　　　　　P.E. $= mgh_1$　and　$h_1 = 3$ m (relative to floor)
⇒　　　　　　P.E. $= (2)(9.8)(3)$ J $= 58.8$ J

(b)　　　　　　P.E. $= mgh_2$　and　$h_2 = 2.2$ m (relative to table)
⇒　　　　　　P.E. $= (2)(9.8)(2.2)$ J $= 43.12$ J.

2) A force acts on a body of mass 3 kilogram causing its speed to increase from 4 metre per second to 5 metre per second. How much work has the force done?

$$\text{Initial K.E.} = \tfrac{1}{2}mv_1{}^2 = \tfrac{1}{2}(3)(4)^2 \text{ J} = 24 \text{ J}$$

$$\text{Final K.E.} = \tfrac{1}{2}mv_2{}^2 = \tfrac{1}{2}(3)(5)^2 \text{ J} = 37.5 \text{ J}$$

$$\text{Work done} = \text{Change in energy}$$

Hence　work done by force $= (37.5 - 24)$ J $= 13.5$ J.

3) A stone of mass 3 kg is thrown so that it just clears the top of a wall 2 m high when its speed is 4 m s^{-1}. What is its total mechanical energy as it passes over the wall?

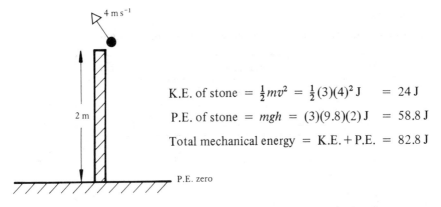

K.E. of stone $= \frac{1}{2}mv^2 = \frac{1}{2}(3)(4)^2$ J $\quad = 24$ J

P.E. of stone $= mgh = (3)(9.8)(2)$ J $\quad = 58.8$ J

Total mechanical energy $=$ K.E. $+$ P.E. $= 82.8$ J

4) Water is being raised by a pump from a storage tank 4 metre below ground and delivered at 8 metre per second through a pipe at ground level. If the cross-sectional area of the pipe is 0.12 square metre find the work done per second by the pump (1 cubic metre of water has a mass of 1000 kilogram).

Volume of water delivered per second $\quad = (8)(0.12)$ m^3 $= 0.96$ m^3

Mass of water delivered per second $\quad = (0.96)(10^3)$ kg $= 960$ kg

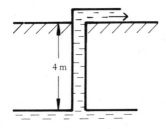

P.E. gained by water per second $(mgh) = (960)(9.8)(4)$ J $= 37\,632$ J

K.E. gained by water per second $(\frac{1}{2}mv^2) = \frac{1}{2}(960)(8^2)$ J $= 30\,720$ J

Total mechanical energy gained per second $=$ P.E. $+$ K.E. $= 68\,352$ J

Work done $=$ Change in energy
So the work done by the pump $= 68\,352$ joule per second.

Note. This is also the power of the pump because
change in energy per second $=$ work done per second $=$ power.

EXERCISE 7c

1) Complete the following table by calculating the missing items.

Mass	Velocity	Kinetic Energy
3 kg	$6\,\mathrm{m\,s^{-1}}$	
8 kg		100 J
	$4\,\mathrm{m\,s^{-1}}$	8 J

2) How much energy is stored in a spring if its natural length is 1 m and its modulus 2 N when it is:
(a) stretched to a length of 1.4 m,
(b) compressed to half its length?

3) An athlete of mass 80 kilogram starts from rest and sprints until his speed is 10 metre per second. He then takes off for a high jump and clears the bar when his body centre has risen 2.2 metre. How much work has he done up to the moment when he clears the bar?

4) An elastic string whose modulus is 4 N is stretched from 3 m to 4 m in length. What is its increase in energy if its natural length was 2 m?

5) A machine picks up a stationary block of mass m, lifts it through a height h and projects it with velocity v. This operation is carried out 20 times every minute. How much work does the machine do each minute?

CONSERVATION OF MECHANICAL ENERGY

Kinetic and Potential Energy are both forms of Mechanical Energy. The total mechanical energy of a body or system of bodies will be changed in value if:

(a) an external force other than weight causes work to be done (work done by weight is potential energy and is therefore already included in the total mechanical energy),

(b) some mechanical energy is converted into another form of energy (e.g sound, heat, light etc). Such a conversion of energy usually takes place when a sudden change in the motion of the system occurs. For instance, when two moving objects collide some mechanical energy is converted into sound energy which is heard as a *bang* at impact. Another common example is the conversion of mechanical energy into heat energy when two rough objects rub against each other.

If neither (a) nor (b) occurs then the total mechanical energy of a system remains constant. This is the *Principle of Conservation of Mechanical Energy* and can be expressed in the form:

The total mechanical energy of a system remains constant provided that no external work is done and no mechanical energy is converted into another form of energy.

When this principle is used in solving problems, a careful appraisal must be made of any external forces which are acting. Some external forces do work and hence cause a change in the total energy of the system. Others, however, can be present without doing any work and these will not cause any change in energy.

For example, consider a mass m moving along a rough horizontal surface.

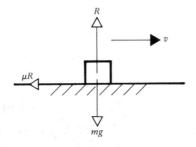

The normal reaction R is perpendicular to the direction of motion and does not do any work.
The frictional force μR, acting in the line of motion, *does* cause the velocity of the mass to change. The frictional force therefore does do work and the total mechanical energy will change.

The conservation of mechanical energy principle is a very powerful weapon to use in problem solving. It is applicable to any problem where the necessary conditions are satisfied and which is concerned with position and velocity.

Problems involving acceleration, however, are usually better approached by applying Newton's Law of Motion.

EXAMPLES 7d

1) A smooth heavy bead is threaded on to a wire in the shape of a circle of radius 0.6 m and centre C. The circular wire is fixed in a vertical plane with the bead at rest at the lowest point A. If the bead is projected from A with a velocity of $4.2\,\mathrm{m\,s^{-1}}$ find its height above A when it first comes to rest.

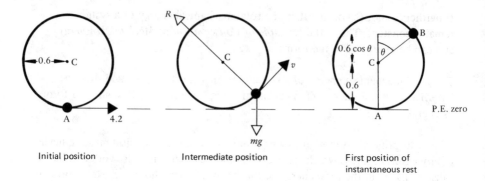

Initial position   Intermediate position   First position of
                                                                             instantaneous rest

Let the mass of the bead be m kg.

If the bead first comes to rest at B, let BC make an angle θ with the upward vertical, so that the height of B above A is $0.6 + 0.6 \cos\theta = 0.6(1 + \cos\theta)$

In the initial position   P.E. $= 0$

$$\text{K.E.} = \tfrac{1}{2}mv^2 = \tfrac{1}{2}m(4.2)^2$$

Total mechanical energy $=$ P.E. $+$ K.E. $= \tfrac{1}{2}m(4.2)^2$

In the first rest position   P.E. $= mgh = mg(0.6)(1 + \cos\theta)$

$$= m(9.8)(0.6)(1 + \cos\theta)$$

$$\text{K.E.} = 0$$

Total mechanical energy $=$ P.E. $+$ K.E. $= m(9.8)(0.6)(1 + \cos\theta)$

During the intermediate motion no work is done by the normal reaction because it is always perpendicular to the direction of motion so we can use conservation of mechanical energy,

Initial energy $=$ Final energy

Hence $\dfrac{m}{2}(4.2)^2 = m(9.8)(0.6)(1 + \cos\theta)$

$\Rightarrow$ $1 + \cos\theta = \dfrac{(4.2)(4.2)}{2(9.8)(0.6)} = \tfrac{3}{2}$

$\Rightarrow$ $\cos\theta = \tfrac{1}{2}.$

So   the height of B above A $= 0.6(1 + \tfrac{1}{2})\,\text{m}$

$$= 0.9\,\text{m}$$

2) Two particles of equal mass m are connected by a light inelastic string. One particle A rests on a smooth plane inclined at $30°$ to the horizontal. The

string passes over a smooth pulley at the top of the plane and then hangs vertically supporting the second particle. Initially particle A is held at a point A_1 on the plane and is released from this position. Find the speed of either particle when A has travelled a distance l up the plane.

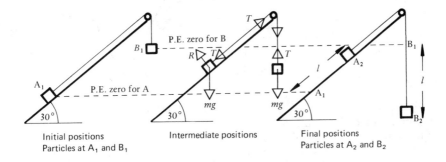

Initial positions — Particles at A_1 and B_1

Intermediate positions

Final positions — Particles at A_2 and B_2

Initial position   P.E. for A = 0
                           P.E. for B = 0
                           K.E. for A = 0
                           K.E. for B = 0
Total mechanical energy   = 0

Final position   P.E. for A = $mgl \sin 30° = \frac{1}{2} mgl$
                      P.E. for B = $-mgl$
                      K.E. for A = $\frac{1}{2} mv^2$
                      K.E. for B = $\frac{1}{2} mv^2$

Total mechanical energy   = $mv^2 - \frac{1}{2} mgl$

(No external work is done as R is always perpendicular to the direction of motion and T is an internal force)

Using conservation of mechanical energy gives

$$0 = mv^2 - \frac{1}{2} mgl$$

$\Rightarrow$ $v^2 = \frac{1}{2} gl$

Hence the velocity of either mass is $\sqrt{(\frac{1}{2} gl)}$

3) A light elastic string of natural length $2a$ has its ends fixed to two points A and B in a horizontal line where   AB = $2a$.   A particle P of mass m is fastened to the midpoint of the string and is held midway between A and B. When released, the particle first comes to instantaneous rest when both portions of string are at $60°$ to AB. Find the modulus of elasticity of the string.

(In this problem, the mechanical energy includes elastic potential energy.)

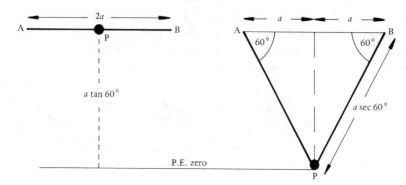

Initial position

P.E. $= mga \tan 60° = mga\sqrt{3}$

K.E. $= 0$

E.P.E. (string unstretched) $= 0$

Total mechanical energy $= mga\sqrt{3}$

First rest position

P.E. $= 0$

K.E. $= 0$

E.P.E. $= \dfrac{\lambda}{2(2a)}(2a \sec 60° - 2a)^2 = \lambda a$

Total mechanical energy $= \lambda a$

Using conservation of mechanical energy gives

$$mga\sqrt{3} = \lambda a$$

Therefore the modulus of elasticity of the string is $\sqrt{3}mg$.

4) An elastic string has one end fixed to a point A. The other end B, which is attached to a particle of mass 2 kg is pulled vertically down from A until AB is 3 m and then released. If the modulus of elasticity of the string is 21.6 N and its natural length is 1 m find:

(a) the velocity of the particle when the string first becomes slack,

(b) the distance from A of the particle when it first comes to rest.

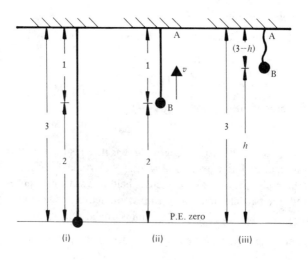

(i) Initial position   P.E. $= 0$

$$\text{K.E.} = 0$$

$$\text{E.P.E.} = \frac{\lambda}{2l}x^2 = \frac{(21.6)(2)^2}{2(1)} \text{ J}$$

Total mechanical energy $= 43.2$ J

(ii) String first slack   P.E. $= mgh = 2(9.8)(2)$ J

$$\text{K.E.} = \tfrac{1}{2}mv^2 = v^2 \text{ J}$$

$$\text{E.P.E.} = 0$$

Total mechanical energy $= (39.2 + v^2)$ J

(iii) Particle first at rest   P.E. $= mgh = 2(9.8)h$ J

$$\text{K.E.} = 0$$

$$\text{E.P.E.} = 0$$

Total mechanical energy $= 19.6h$ J

Using conservation of mechanical energy throughout gives

$$43.2 = 39.2 + v^2 = 19.6h$$

$\Rightarrow$ $v^2 = 43.2 - 39.2 = 4$

and $h = \dfrac{43.2}{19.6} = 2.2$

So the velocity of the particle when the string becomes slack is $2\,\text{m s}^{-1}$, and the depth of the particle below A when first at rest is 0.8 m.

EXERCISE 7d

1) A particle falls freely from rest until its speed is 7 metre per second. How far has it fallen?

2) A truck of mass M is pulled up a smooth track inclined at $30°$ to the horizontal. Its speed increases from u to $3u$ in a distance d. Find the work done by the engine.

3) One end of an elastic string is fixed to a point A on a smooth horizontal table. The other end is attached to a heavy particle P. The particle is pulled away from A until AP is of length $3l/2$ and is then released. If the natural length of the string is l and its modulus of elasticity is mg find the velocity of the particle when the string reaches its natural length, if the mass of the particle is m.

4) Two identical particles of mass m are connected by a light inelastic string of length $2l$. One particle A rests on a smooth horizontal table and the other particle B hangs freely over the edge. Initially A is held at a distance l from the edge of the table and the string attached to A is perpendicular to the edge. If A is released find its velocity when it reaches the table edge.

5) A particle of mass 0.5 kilogram is attached to a light elastic string of natural length 2 metre and modulus of elasticity 1 N. The other end of the string is fixed at point P on a smooth horizontal plane. The particle is projected from P along the plane with a velocity of 4 metre per second. Find its greatest distance from P during the following motion.

6) The end A of a light elastic string AB is fixed. A particle of mass m is attached to the end B. The particle is held as close as possible to A and is released from that position. Find the length of AB when the particle is in its lowest position if the natural length of the string is l and its modulus of elasticity is $2mg$.

7) A particle of mass m is suspended from a fixed point A by a light elastic string of natural length l and modulus of elasticity $4mg$. The particle is pulled down from its equilibrium position a distance d and then released. If the particle just reaches the height of A, find d.

8) Two equal scale pans each of mass M are connected by a light inelastic string which passes over a smooth pulley. The two pans are at the same level. If a load of mass $2M$ is gently placed on one pan and the system is released, find through what distance each pan has moved when their velocity is $2.1 \, \mathrm{m\,s^{-1}}$.

MULTIPLE CHOICE EXERCISE 7

(The instructions for answering these questions are given on page x.)

TYPE I

1) A force of 4 N is applied to an elastic string in order to stretch it. The string has natural length 3 m and modulus 12 N. The extension is:
(a) 9 m   (b) 3 m   (c) 1 m   (d) 4 m.

2) A spring is compressed to half its natural length by a force of 6 N. Its modulus of elasticity is:
(a) 12 N   (b) 3 N   (c) 6 N   (d) 4.5 N.

3) The potential energy of a body of mass m is mgh where h is:
(a) the distance from a chosen level,
(b) the height above the ground,
(c) the height above a chosen level,
(d) the vertical distance moved.

4) A particle of mass m slides a distance d down a plane inclined at θ to the horizontal. The work done by the normal reaction R is:
(a) Rd (b) $mgd \cos \theta$ (c) 0   (d) $mgd \sin \theta$.

5) A particle falls freely from rest through a distance d. Its speed is then:
(a) $\sqrt{gd}$ (b) $-\sqrt{2gd}$ (c) $-\sqrt{\tfrac{1}{2}gd}$ (d) $\sqrt{2gd}$.

TYPE II

6) A particle of mass $2m$ is attached to one end of an elastic string of modulus mg whose other end is fixed to a point P. The particle is dropped from P. It will first come to rest:
(a) when the tension in the string is $2mg$,
(b) when the kinetic energy is zero,
(c) below the equilibrium position,
(d) when the length of the string has doubled.

7) A particle travelling in a horizontal straight line has an acceleration of $+2 \, \mathrm{m\,s^{-2}}$.
(a) Its total mechanical energy is constant.
(b) The particle is doing work.
(c) Its potential energy is constant.
(d) Work is being done on the particle.

8) The modulus of elasticity of an elastic string is:
(a) the ratio of the extension to the natural length,
(b) equal to the force stretching the string,
(c) measured in joules,
(d) equal to the tension when the string is twice its natural length.

TYPE III

9) (a) The tension in a string of length 1 m is 2 N.
   (b) An elastic string of natural length 0.5 m and modulus of elasticity 2 N is extended by 0.5 m.

10) (a) The energy stored in an elastic string of natural length a and modulus λ is $\tfrac{1}{2}\lambda a$.
   (b) An elastic string of natural length a and modulus λ is stretched to a length $2a$.

11) (a) In a system the total work done, other than by weight, is zero.
   (b) The total mechanical energy of a system is constant.

12) (a) A block is set moving across a horizontal surface and as it moves the temperature of the block rises.

  (b) The kinetic energy of a block moving on a horizontal surface is constant.

TYPE IV

13) Calculate the extension in an elastic string:
(a) the natural length is 2 m,
(b) the elastic potential energy is 3J,
(c) the string is hanging vertically.

14) A particle is sliding down an inclined plane. Calculate its speed when it reaches the foot of the plane:
(a) the length of the plane is 4 m,
(b) contact is smooth,
(c) the inclination of the plane is 20°,
(d) the mass of the particle is 3 kg.

15) A particle is hanging in equilibrium at one end of an elastic string whose other end is fixed. Find the distance between the particle and the fixed end:
(a) the particle weighs 10 N,
(b) the modulus of elasticity is 8 N,
(c) the natural length of the string is 2 m.

16) A particle is released from rest at the top of a tower. Find its speed at the bottom:
(a) the tower is 50 m high,
(b) the mass of the particle is 2 kg,
(c) the particle moves vertically.

TYPE V

17) The energy stored in an elastic string is proportional to the extension.

18) As long as no external forces act on a system the kinetic energy must be constant.

19) Some external forces which act on a moving body do not do any work.

20) A spring obeys Hooke's Law when it is stretched but not when it is compressed.

MISCELLANEOUS EXERCISE 7

1) A body of mass m is released from rest and falls under gravity against air resistance. The body reaches a speed v after falling through a height h. Find the work done by the body against the air resistance.   (U of L)

2) An elastic string of natural length 1 m obeys Hooke's Law. When it is stretched to 1.2 m the energy stored in it is 16 J. Find the energy stored in the string when it is stretched to 1.5 m. (U of L)

3) A force, acting vertically upwards on a body of mass 10 kg, moves the body vertically from rest to a height 5 m above its starting point and gives it a speed of 6 m/s. Find the work done by the force.
[Take g as 10 m/s^2] (U of L)

4) Find the effective power, in watts, of a pump which raises 5 kg of water every second through a height of 10 m and ejects it at a speed of 20 m/s.
[Take g as 10 m/s^2] (U of L)

5) Two particles A and B are connected by a light inelastic string which passes over a smooth pulley. A is of mass m and B is of mass $2m$. Initially both particles are at rest at a depth $2l$ below the pulley. If they are released from rest find their velocity when each has moved a distance l.

6) Two springs AB and BC are fastened together at B. The ends A and C are fastened to two fixed points on a smooth horizontal table where AC is 2 m. AB and BC have natural lengths of 0.6 and 0.8 m and moduli of elasticity 2 and 4 N respectively. Find the stretched lengths of AB and BC.

7) A body of mass 2.5 kilogram is attached to the end B of a light elastic string AB of natural length 2 metre and modulus $5g$ newton. The mass is suspended vertically in equilibrium by the string whose other end A is attached to a fixed point.
(a) Find the depth below A of B when the body is in equilibrium.
(b) Find the distance through which the body must be pulled down vertically from its equilibrium position so that it will just reach A after release.

8) An engine is pumping water from a large tank and delivering it through a pipe of diameter 0.04 metre at a rate of 100 litre per second. Find the work done by the engine in one second.
[The mass of 1 litre of water is taken as 1 kilogram]

9) A ring is threaded on to a smooth wire in the form of a circle fixed in a vertical plane. The ring is projected from the lowest point on the wire with a velocity of 4.2 m s^{-1}. If the radius of the circular wire is 0.6 m, find the height above the centre at which the particle first comes to instantaneous rest. If, instead, the ring had been projected with a velocity of 5.6 m s^{-1}, describe its motion.

10) A light elastic string, of unstretched length a and modulus of elasticity W, is fixed at one end to a point on the ceiling of a room. To the other end of the string is attached a particle of weight W. A horizontal force P is applied to the particle and in equilibrium it is found that the string is stretched to three times its natural length. Calculate:

(a) the angle the string makes with the horizontal,

(b) the value of P in terms of W.

If, instead, P is not applied horizontally find the least value of P which in equilibrium will make the string have the same inclination to the horizontal as before. Deduce that the stretched length of the string is $\frac{3}{2}a$ in this case and find the inclination of P to the vertical.　　　　　　　　　(U of L)

11) Prove that the work done in stretching a light elastic string from its natural length a to a length $(a+x)$ is proportional to x^2.

One end of this string is fastened to a fixed point A, and at the other end a particle of mass m is attached. The particle is released from rest at A, and first comes to rest when it has fallen a distance $3a$. Show that at the lowest point of its path the acceleration of the particle is $2g$ upwards.

Find in terms of g and a the speed of the particle at the instants when the magnitude of its acceleration is $\frac{1}{2}g$.　　　　　　　　　(U of L)

12) In the diagram AC, BC and CD are three elastic strings with the same modulus of elasticity. The ends A and B are attached to a horizontal support and the end D of the string CD carries a particle of mass 2 kg hanging freely under gravity. The natural lengths of the strings AC and CD are 0.24 and 0.18 m respectively, and in the equilibrium position AC is extended by 0.03 m and the angles ACD and BCD are 120° and 150° respectively. Calculate:

(a) the modulus of elasticity of the strings,

(b) the natural length of BC,

(c) the depth of D below AB.

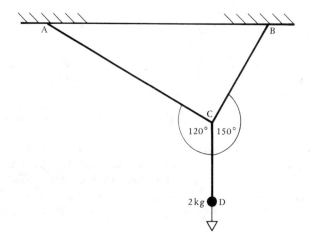

13) Two identical elastic strings of length 1 metre and modulus 4.9 N are each fastened to a particle of mass 0.5 kilogram. Their other ends are fixed to two points 4 metres apart in a vertical line. Find the height of the particle above the lower fixed point A in the equilibrium position. The particle is now pulled down to A and released from rest. Find the greatest height above A to which the particle rises.

14) A water pump raises 50 kg of water a second through a height of 20 m. The water emerges as a jet with speed 50 m/s. Find the kinetic energy and the potential energy given to the water each second and hence the effective power developed by the pump.
Given that the jet is directed vertically upwards, find the further height attained by the water.

15) Prove that the elastic energy of a light spring of natural length a and modulus of elasticity λ, stretched by an amount x, is $\lambda x^2/(2a)$.
A trolley of mass m runs down a smooth track of constant inclination $\pi/6$ to the horizontal, carrying at its front a light spring of natural length a and modulus mga/c, where c is constant. When the spring is fully compressed it is of length $a/4$, and it obeys Hooke's Law up to this point. After the trolley has travelled a distance b from rest the spring meets a fixed stop. Show that, when the spring has been compressed a distance x, where $x < 3a/4$, the speed v of the trolley is given by

$$cv^2/g = c(b+x) - x^2$$

Given that $c = a/10$ and $b = 2a$, find the total distance covered by the trolley before it momentarily comes to rest for the first time.   (U of L)

16) A ring of mass m can slide freely on a smooth wire in the shape of a circle of diameter $2a$, which is fixed in a vertical plane. The ring is fastened to one end of a light elastic string of natural length a and modulus of elasticity mg. The other end of the string is attached to the lowest point of the wire. The ring is held at the highest point of the wire and is slightly disturbed from rest. Find the velocity of the ring:
(a) when it is level with the centre of the circular wire,
(b) when the string first becomes slack,
(c) when the string makes an acute angle θ with the upward vertical.

17) A particle of weight W is attached by two light inextensible strings each of length a to two fixed points distant a apart in a horizontal line. Write down the tension in either string.

One of the strings is now replaced by an elastic string of the same natural length, and it is found that in the new position of equilibrium this string has stretched to a length $5a/4$. Prove that the modulus of elasticity of this string is $7W/\sqrt{39}$, and show that the tension in the other string has been increased in the ratio $5:\sqrt{13}$.   (U of L)

18) One end O of an elastic string OP is fixed to a point on a smooth plane inclined at $30°$ to the horizontal. A particle of mass m is attached to the end P and is held at O. If the natural length of the string is a and its modulus is $2mg$, find:

(a) the distance down the plane from O at which the particle first comes to instantaneous rest after being released from rest at O.

(b) the velocity of the particle as it passes through its equilibrium position.

19) In the diagram, BAC is a rigid fixed rough wire and angle BAC is $60°$. P and Q are two identical rings of mass m connected by a light elastic string of natural length $2a$ and modulus of elasticity mg. If P and Q are in equilibrium when $PA = AQ = 3a$ find the least coefficient of friction between the rings and the wire.

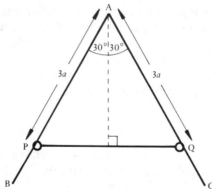

20) Water is pumped at the rate of 1.2 cubic metre per minute from a large tank on the ground, up to a point 8 metre above the level of the water in the tank. It emerges as a horizontal jet from a pipe with a cross-section of 5×10^{-3} square metre. If the efficiency of the apparatus is 60%, find the energy supplied to the pump per second.

21) A particle of weight W is attached to a point C of an unstretched elastic string AB, where $AC = 4a/3$, $CB = 4a/7$. The ends A and B are then attached to the extremities of a horizontal diameter of a fixed hemispherical bowl of radius a and the particle rests on the smooth inner surface, the angle BAC being $30°$. Show that the modulus of elasticity of the string is W and determine the reaction of the bowl on the particle.   (U of L)

22) Prove that the potential energy of a light elastic string of natural length l and modulus λ when stretched to a length of $(l+x)$ is $\frac{1}{2}\lambda x^2/l$.

Two points A and B are in a horizontal line at a distance $3l$ apart. A particle P of mass m is joined to A by a light inextensible string of length $4l$ and is joined to B by a light elastic string of natural length l and modulus λ. Initially P is held at a point C in AB produced such that $BC = l$, both strings being just taut, and is then released from rest. If $\lambda = \frac{1}{4}mg$ show that when AP is vertical the speed of the particle is $2\sqrt{gl}$ and find the instantaneous value of the tension in the elastic string in this position.   (JMB)

23) Two fixed points A and B on the same horizontal level are 20 cm apart. A light elastic string, which obeys Hooke's Law, is just taut when its ends are fixed at A and B. A block of mass 5 kg is attached to the string at a point P where AP = 15 cm. The system is then allowed to take up its position of equilibrium with P below AB and it is found that in this position the angle APB is a right angle. If $\angle BAP = \theta$, show that the ratio of the extensions of AP and BP is

$$\frac{4\cos\theta - 3}{4\sin\theta - 1}.$$

Hence show that θ satisfies the equation

$$\cos\theta\,(4\cos\theta - 3) = 3\sin\theta\,(4\sin\theta - 1).   \text{(U of L)}$$

24) A ring A of mass m is threaded on to a smooth fixed horizontal straight wire. The ring is attached to one end of a light elastic string whose other end is fixed to a point B at a height h above the wire. Initially the ring is vertically below B. In this position it is given velocity v along the wire. The string has a natural length h and modulus of elasticity mg. Show that the angle θ between AB and the wire when the ring first comes to instantaneous rest, is given by

$$\sin\theta\left(\frac{v}{\sqrt{gh}} + 1\right) = 1.$$

25) A mass of 3 kilogram is connected by an elastic string of natural length 1 metre and modulus of elasticity 14.7 N to a fixed point. A horizontal force equal to the weight of 1 kilogram acts on the mass maintaining it in equilibrium. Find the inclination of the string to the vertical. If the horizontal force is removed, what is the least force which must act on the particle to ensure that the string shall be inclined at the same angle as before. Calculate in each case the extension of the string.

CHAPTER 8

MOMENTUM. DIRECT IMPACT

The momentum of a body is the product of its mass and its velocity.

$$\text{Momentum} = mv$$

Because velocity is a vector quantity, momentum also is a vector whose direction is the direction of the velocity.

If a body is moving with constant velocity, its momentum is constant. In order to cause a change in velocity a force must act on the body. It follows, then, that a force must act in order to change momentum.

Properties of motion already established can be used to determine the relationship between a force applied to an object and the change in momentum which it produces. Consider a constant force F which acts for a time t on a body of mass m, thus changing its velocity from u to v. Because the force is constant the body will travel with constant acceleration a where:

$$F = ma$$

and

$$at = v - u$$

hence

$$\frac{F}{m}t = v - u$$

or

$$Ft = mv - mu$$

The product of a constant force F and the time t for which it acts is called the *impulse* of the force and the relationship above can be written:

The impulse of a force is equal to the change in momentum which it produces.

Unit. The unit of impulse is the newton second, $N\,s$.

Momentum can be measured in kilogram metre per second ($kg\,m\,s^{-1}$) units but the impulse unit, $N\,s$, can be used as the unit for momentum also.

INSTANTANEOUS IMPULSE

There are many occasions when a force acts for so short a time that the effect is instantaneous, e.g. a bat striking a ball. In such cases, although the magnitude of the force and the time for which it acts may each be unknown, there is, nevertheless, an instantaneous impulse whose value is equal to the change in momentum produced.

EXAMPLES 8a

1) A truck of mass $10^3\,$kg travelling at $3\,\mathrm{m\,s^{-1}}$ is brought to rest in 2 seconds when it strikes a buffer. What force (assumed constant) is exerted by the buffer?

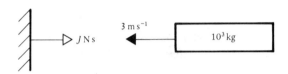

If the impulse exerted by the buffer is $+J$ newton second then the initial velocity of the truck is $-3\,\mathrm{m\,s^{-1}}$ and its final velocity is zero.

Then
$$J = mv - mu$$

$\Rightarrow$
$$J = 0 - 10^3(-3) = 3 \times 10^3$$

But
$$J = Ft = 2F$$

Hence
$$F = \frac{J}{2} = 1500$$

The force exerted by the buffer is $1500\,$N.

2) What constant force acting in the direction of motion of a particle of mass $2\,$kg will increase its speed from $4\,\mathrm{m\,s^{-1}}$ to $20\,\mathrm{m\,s^{-1}}$ in 4 seconds?

The constant force F, u and v are all in the same sense i.e. all are positive.

Since
$$Ft = mv - mu$$

$$F \times 4 = 2 \times 20 - 2 \times 4 = 8$$

The required force is $8\,$N.

3) A ball of mass m, travelling with velocity $2i+3j$, receives an impulse $-3mi$. What is the velocity of the ball immediately afterwards?

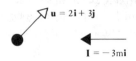

Using $I = m(v-u)$

gives $-3mi = m(v-\{2i+3j\})$

$\Rightarrow$ $v = -3i+\{2i+3j\}$

$= -i+3j$

Note that the velocity component in the direction of j is unchanged. This is because there is no impulse component in this direction.

4) A ball of mass $0.5\,kg$ is thrown towards a wall so that it strikes the wall normally with a speed of $10\,ms^{-1}$. If the ball bounces at right angles away from the wall with a speed of $8\,ms^{-1}$, what impulse does the wall exert on the ball?

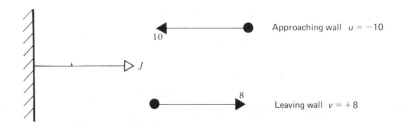

Taking the direction of the impulse J as positive and using

$$J = mv - mu$$

we have $J = \frac{1}{2} \times 8 - \frac{1}{2}(-10)$

$= 9$

Therefore the wall exerts an impulse of $9\,Ns$ on the ball.

5) A nozzle is discharging water at a rate of 200 litre per second, with a speed of 10 metre per second. If the water strikes a wall at right angles and does not bounce off the wall, find the force F newton exerted by the wall on the water. (The mass of 1 litre of water is 1 kilogram.)

Mass of water discharged per second $= 200\,\text{kg}$

Momentum destroyed per second $= 200 \times 10\,\text{kg}\,\text{m}\,\text{s}^{-1}$.

Impulse exerted by wall in one second $= F \times 1\,\text{N}\,\text{s}$

But   Impulse $=$ Change in momentum

Hence $F \times 1 = 2000$

$\Rightarrow$ $F = 2 \times 10^3$

Therefore the wall exerts a force of $2 \times 10^3\,\text{N}$ or $2\,\text{kN}$ on the water.

6) A bullet of mass m strikes an obstruction and ricochets off at $60°$ to its original direction. If its speed is also changed from u to v, find the magnitude of the impulse acting on the bullet.

This time the velocities before and after the impulse are not in line and it is necessary to consider components of impulse and velocities in two perpendicular directions. (Parallel and perpendicular to the initial velocity are convenient directions.)

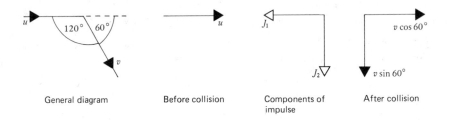

General diagram   Before collision   Components of   After collision
                                                   impulse

Consider components parallel to J_1 taking the sense of J_1 as positive

$$J_1 = m(-v\cos 60°) - m(-u)$$

Similarly, parallel to J_2 we have

$$J_2 = m(v\sin 60°) - 0$$

Hence $J_1 = m(u - \tfrac{1}{2}v)$

and $J_2 = \tfrac{1}{2}mv\sqrt{3}$

The magnitude of the resultant impulse is given by $\sqrt{J_1{}^2 + J_2{}^2}$

$$= m\sqrt{(u - \tfrac{1}{2}v)^2 + (\tfrac{1}{2}v\sqrt{3})^2}$$

$$= m\sqrt{u^2 - uv + v^2}$$

EXERCISE 8a

1) A constant force of $12\,\text{N}$ acts on a particle of mass $4\,\text{kg}$ whose initial speed is $8\,\text{m s}^{-1}$, the direction of the force being in the direction of motion. Find its speed at the end of 3 seconds.

2) In what time will a force of $8\,\text{N}$ reduce the speed of a particle of mass $3\,\text{kg}$ from $21\,\text{m s}^{-1}$ to $6\,\text{m s}^{-1}$?

3) A hammer of mass $1.2\,\text{kg}$ travelling at $15\,\text{m s}^{-1}$ is brought to rest when it strikes a nail. What impulse acts on the hammer?

4) A dart of mass $0.12\,\text{kg}$ flying at a speed of $20\,\text{m s}^{-1}$ hits the dartboard and comes to rest in 0.1 seconds. What is the average force exerted by the dartboard on the dart?

5) A batsman strikes a cricket ball at right angles to the bat so that its direction is reversed. If the ball approaches the bat with a speed of $30\,\text{m s}^{-1}$ and leaves it at $50\,\text{m s}^{-1}$, what is the magnitude of the impulse exerted by the bat on the ball if the mass of the ball is $0.13\,\text{kg}$?

6) A ball of mass m receives a blow which changes its velocity instantaneously from $5\mathbf{i}-2\mathbf{j}$ to $\mathbf{i}+7\mathbf{j}$. What is the impulse of the blow?

7) A sphere of unit mass is travelling with a speed of $10\,\text{m s}^{-1}$ in a direction $-3\mathbf{i}+4\mathbf{j}$ when it collides with a pole which changes the velocity of the sphere to $-2\mathbf{i}+\mathbf{j}$. What impulse is given to the sphere by the pole?

8) An impulse $4\mathbf{i}-7\mathbf{j}$ given to a moving particle of mass $2\,\text{kg}$ changes its velocity to $5\mathbf{i}+\mathbf{j}$. What was the velocity just beforehand?

9) Sand falls steadily through a hole on to a conveyor belt moving horizontally. $4\,\text{kg}$ of sand falls every second, striking the belt at $10\,\text{m s}^{-1}$. Find the vertical force exerted by the belt on the sand (assuming that the sand does not bounce on impact).

10) An object of mass $2\,\text{kg}$ is diverted from its path through $90°$ by collision with a solid obstruction. Find the magnitude and direction of the impulse incurred at impact if the speed is changed from $20\,\text{m s}^{-1}$ to $10\,\text{m s}^{-1}$.

11) A football of mass $0.4\,\text{kg}$ travels horizontally at $12\,\text{m s}^{-1}$ towards a player who diverts its path through $60°$ horizontally and passes it at $18\,\text{m s}^{-1}$ to a team mate. Find the impulse given to the ball:
(a) if it is passed horizontally,
(b) if it is kicked at an angle of $30°$ to the ground (consider three mutually perpendicular directions).

12) A jet of water travelling with a speed of $12\,\text{m s}^{-1}$ impinges on a plane at right angles to the jet. If the force (assumed constant) exerted by the water on the plane is $400\,\text{N}$, calculate the volume of water being discharged per minute. (The water does not bounce off the plane and its mass per litre is $1\,\text{kg}$.)

CONSTANT MOMENTUM

When a force affects the velocity of an object, momentum changes in the direction of that force.

It follows that, if in a certain direction *no* force affects the motion, there is no change in momentum in that direction.

Consider, for example, a football which is travelling along the ground at $16\,\mathrm{m\,s^{-1}}$. A player kicks the ball at right angles to its direction of motion. The impulse of the kick changes the momentum in the direction of the kick but the ball continues with an unchanged velocity component of $16\,\mathrm{m\,s^{-1}}$ in the original direction since no impulse has acted in this direction.

THE PRINCIPLE OF CONSERVATION OF LINEAR MOMENTUM

Internal Impact

Whenever two solid objects are in contact they exert *equal and opposite forces* on each other (Newton's Law).

It is clear that, regardless of the length of time for which they are in contact, each is in contact with the other for the *same time*.

Consequently they exert *equal and opposite impulses* on each other.

Since change in momentum is equal to the impulse which produces the change, it follows that equal and opposite impulses produce equal and opposite changes in momentum. The resultant change in momentum of two objects which are free to move is therefore zero and their *total* momentum remains constant although internal forces have affected the individual motion of each object.

This property can be combined with our earlier observations to form the following principle.

If, in a specified direction, no external force affects the motion of a system, the total momentum in that direction remains constant.

This very important relationship is known as the principle of conservation of linear momentum. It plays a vital part in the solution of problems where there are internal impulses, such as those involving a collision.

EXAMPLES 8b

1) A truck of mass 1200 kg is moving with a speed of $7\,\mathrm{m\,s^{-1}}$ when it collides with a second truck of mass 1600 kg which is stationary. If the two trucks are automatically coupled together at impact, with what speed do they move on together?

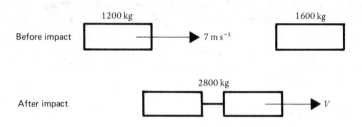

Let the velocity of the coupled trucks (total mass 2800 kg) be V. In the direction of motion,

$$\text{momentum before impact} = 1200 \times 7 + 1600 \times 0$$

$$\text{momentum after impact} = 2800\,V$$

A pair of equal and opposite internal impulses act at impact, therefore, using conservation of linear momentum we have

$$1200 \times 7 = 2800\,V$$

$$\Rightarrow \qquad\qquad V = 3$$

Therefore the speed of the coupled trucks is $3\,\mathrm{m\,s^{-1}}$.

2) A bullet of mass 0.04 kg travelling horizontally at $100\,\mathrm{m\,s^{-1}}$ hits a stationary block of wood of mass 8 kg, passes through it and emerges horizontally with a speed of $40\,\mathrm{m\,s^{-1}}$. If the block is free to move on a smooth horizontal plane find the speed with which it is moving after the bullet has passed through it.

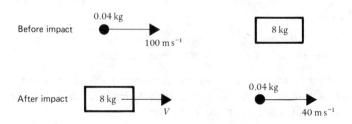

If the speed of the block is V then, using conservation of linear momentum (in the direction of motion) we have

$$0.04 \times 100 = (8V) + (0.04 \times 40)$$

$$\Rightarrow \qquad V = \frac{2.4}{8} = 0.3$$

Therefore the block has a speed of $0.3 \, \mathrm{m \, s^{-1}}$.

3) Two particles, each of mass m, collide head on when their speeds are $2u$ and u. If they stick together on impact, find their combined speed in terms of u.

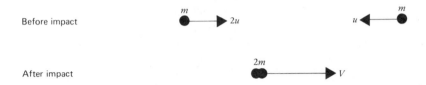

Before impact

After impact

Using conservation of linear momentum (in the direction of the velocity $2u$) we have

$$(m)(2u) - mu = 2m \times V$$

$$\Rightarrow \qquad V = \tfrac{1}{2}u$$

The combined mass will travel at speed $\tfrac{1}{2}u$.

(Note that the momentum of the second particle before impact is negative because its sense is opposite to that specified as positive.)

4) A gun of mass M fires a shell of mass m and recoils horizontally. If the shell travels *along the barrel* with speed v find the speed with which the barrel begins to recoil if:
(a) the barrel is horizontal,
(b) the barrel is inclined at an angle $30°$ to the horizontal.
State in each case the constant force required to bring the gun to rest in 2 seconds.

(a)

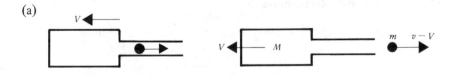

The speed of the shell is $v - V$ as it leaves the barrel, because the barrel is recoiling with speed V.

Before firing the shell, the gun is at rest and the total momentum is zero.
Using conservation of linear momentum (in the direction of the shell's motion)

$$0 = m(v-V) - MV$$

$\Rightarrow$
$$(M+m)V = mv$$

Therefore the initial velocity of recoil is $\dfrac{mv}{M+m}$

If a constant force F_1 brings the gun to rest it must exert, in 2 seconds, an impulse equal to the initial momentum of the gun

i.e.
$$2F_1 = M\left(\frac{mv}{M+m}\right)$$

So the force required is $\dfrac{Mmv}{2(M+m)}$

(b)

This time the shell leaves the barrel with a velocity which is the resultant of two components inclined at $150°$.
Using conservation of linear momentum in the direction of recoil gives

$$0 = MV + m(V - v\cos 30°)$$

$\Rightarrow$
$$\tfrac{1}{2}mv\sqrt{3} = (M+m)V$$

$\Rightarrow$
$$V = \frac{mv\sqrt{3}}{2(M+m)}$$

Therefore the initial velocity of recoil is $\dfrac{mv\sqrt{3}}{2(M+m)}$

and the force, F_2, required to stop the gun in two seconds is given by

$$2F_2 = M\left(\frac{mv\sqrt{3}}{2(M+m)}\right)$$

So the required force is $\dfrac{Mmv\sqrt{3}}{4(M+m)}$

Note that momentum is *not* conserved in the vertical direction because the impulse exerted by the ground on the gun is an external impulse which *does* change the total momentum.

Note that the speed of the shell as it *leaves* the gun is sometimes called the *muzzle speed*. It is *not* equal to the speed of the shell relative to the barrel.

EXERCISE 8b

1) Two particles A and B of equal mass are travelling along the same line with constant speeds $4\,\text{m}\,\text{s}^{-1}$ and $3\,\text{m}\,\text{s}^{-1}$ respectively. If they collide and coalesce find their common speed just after impact:
(a) if they collide head-on,
(b) if they were originally travelling in the same sense.

2) A truck of mass $400\,\text{kg}$ runs at a speed of $2\,\text{m}\,\text{s}^{-1}$ into a stationary truck. They become coupled together and move on with speed $0.8\,\text{m}\,\text{s}^{-1}$. What is the mass of the second truck.

3) A gun of mass $2000\,\text{kg}$ fires horizontally a shell of mass $25\,\text{kg}$. The gun's horizontal recoil is controlled by a constant force of $8000\,\text{N}$ which brings the gun to rest in 1.5 seconds. Find the initial velocity of the shell:
(a) relative to the gun,
(b) in the air.

4) A boy of mass $40\,\text{kg}$ is on a sledge of mass $10\,\text{kg}$ travelling at $5\,\text{m}\,\text{s}^{-1}$ when another boy comes from behind moving three times as fast as the sledge and jumps on to the sledge. What is the second boy's mass if the speed of the sledge is doubled?

5) A gun of mass km fires a shell of mass m. The barrel of the gun is elevated at an angle α and the gun recoils horizontally. Show that the shell leaves the barrel at an angle β to the horizontal where $\tan\beta = \dfrac{k+1}{k}\tan\alpha.$

6) A bullet of mass m is fired with a horizontal speed $2u$ into a stationary block of wood of mass $50m$ which is free to move horizontally. Find the velocity of the block if:
(a) the bullet goes right through it and emerges with speed u,
(b) the bullet becomes embedded in the block.

7) A vertical post of mass M is to be driven into the ground. A pile-driver of mass m strikes the post vertically with a velocity v. Assuming that the pile-driver does not bounce off the post, find the velocity with which the post enters the ground. If the combined mass comes to rest when the post has been driven into the ground to a depth h find the constant force with which the ground resists penetration.

8) A particle travelling horizontally with speed u collides and coalesces with a particle of equal mass hanging at rest at the end of a light inextensible string of length $2l$. If the string rotates through an angle of $60°$ before first coming to rest, show that $u^2 = 8gl$.

IMPULSIVE TENSIONS

When a string jerks, equal and opposite tensions act suddenly at each end. Consequently equal and opposite impulses act on the objects to which the two ends of the string are attached. There are two cases to consider.

(a) *One end of the string is fixed.*
The impulse which acts at the fixed end of the string cannot affect the momentum of the fixed object there. A moveable object attached to the free end however will undergo a change in momentum equal to the impulsive tension. In such cases the momentum of the system *does* change in the direction of the string but is unchanged in the perpendicular direction where no impulse acts.

(b) *Both ends of the string attached to moveable objects.*
In this case equal and opposite impulses act on the two objects, producing equal and opposite changes in momentum.
The total momentum of the system therefore remains constant, although the momentum of each individual object is changed in the direction of the string. Perpendicular to the string however, no impulse acts and the momentum of *each* particle in this direction is unchanged.
The velocities of two objects moving at the ends of a taut string are not independent. The important relationship between them can be illustrated as follows:

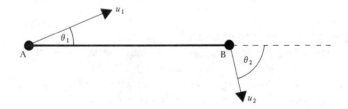

AB is a taut string. Particles A and B are moving with velocities as shown in the diagram.

Resolving the velocities along and perpendicular to AB we have

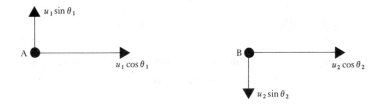

The noteworthy components are those along AB since:

$$\text{if} \quad u_1\cos\theta_1 > u_2\cos\theta_2 \quad \text{the string is not taut,}$$

$$\text{if} \quad u_2\cos\theta_2 > u_1\cos\theta_1 \quad \text{the string has snapped.}$$

Hence for the string to remain taut and unbroken, $u_1\cos\theta_1 = u_2\cos\theta_2$.

> So the two ends of a taut string have equal velocity components in the direction of the string.

EXAMPLES 8c

1) A string AB of length $2l$ is fixed at A to a point on a smooth horizontal table. A particle of mass m attached to B is initially at a point C distant l from A. The particle is projected horizontally with speed u at right angles to AC. Find the impulsive tension in the string when it becomes taut and the velocity of the particle immediately afterwards.

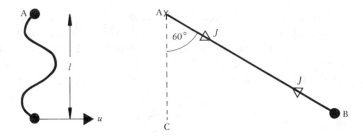

When the string becomes taut $AB = 2l$

$$\text{and} \quad \cos C\widehat{A}B = \tfrac{1}{2}$$

Hence $C\widehat{A}B = 60°$ when the instantaneous impulses act.

Just before the string jerks taut, the particle has velocity components parallel and perpendicular to AB of $u\sin 60°$ and $u\cos 60°$ respectively.

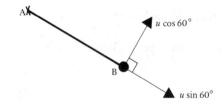

When the string becomes taut the length of AB is fixed and B can no longer travel in the direction $\overrightarrow{AB}$. After the jerk the velocity of the particle is therefore perpendicular to AB

Using   Impulse = Change in momentum

(a) along BA $J = 0 - (-mu \sin 60°)$

$\Rightarrow$ $J = \frac{1}{2}mu\sqrt{3}$

(b) perpendicular to BA (no impulse component)

$$0 = mv - mu \cos 60°$$

$\Rightarrow$ $v = \frac{1}{2}u$ (showing that the velocity in this direction does not change.)
Therefore, the velocity of the particle just after the string jerks taut is $\frac{1}{2}u$ perpendicular to the string.

2) A particle of mass m is attached to each end of a string AB of length $2l$. The whole system lies on a smooth horizontal table with B initially at a point C distant l from A. The particle at the end B is projected across the table with speed u perpendicular to AC. Find the velocity with which each particle begins to move after the jerk and the magnitude of the impulsive tension.

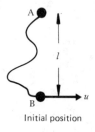

Initial position

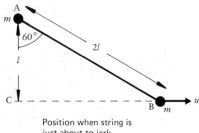

Position when string is
just about to jerk

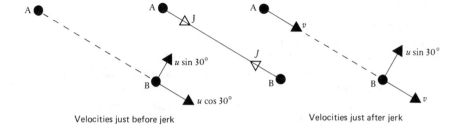

Velocities just before jerk   Velocities just after jerk

When the string jerks tight, both particles begin to move with equal velocity components, v, in the direction AB.

Perpendicular to AB there is no impulse on either particle; velocity components in this direction are therefore unchanged.

Using Conservation of Momentum in the direction AB:

$$0 + mu \cos 30° = mv + mv$$

giving $$v = \tfrac{1}{4}u\sqrt{3}$$

Just after the jerk therefore

the velocity of the mass at A $= \tfrac{1}{4}u\sqrt{3}$ along AB

the velocity of the mass at B $= \sqrt{(\tfrac{1}{2}u)^2 + (\tfrac{1}{4}u\sqrt{3})^2}$

$$= \tfrac{1}{4}u\sqrt{7}$$

in a direction inclined to AB at $\arctan\left(\dfrac{u \sin 30°}{v}\right)$

i.e.   at $\arctan\dfrac{2}{\sqrt{3}}$

The magnitude of J can be calculated by considering the change in momentum of *one* of the particles.
For the mass at A, in the direction AB,

$$J = mv - 0$$

Therefore $$J = \tfrac{1}{4}mu\sqrt{3}$$

It is important to appreciate that, in analysing the effect of an instantaneous impulse, the velocities involved are those *immediately* before and *immediately* after the impact or jerk. The subsequent motion depends, not on the impulse, but upon whatever forces act *after* the impulse has taken place.

SUMMARY

1) Momentum = mass × velocity
2) Impulse = change in momentum
3) Momentum increases in the direction of the impulse.
4) In a direction where no external force acts, the momentum of a system remains constant.
5) Particles moving at the ends of a taut string have equal velocity components in the direction of the string.

EXAMPLES 8c (continued)

3) Three equal particles A, B and C lie on a smooth horizontal table. Light inextensible strings which are just taut connect AB and BC and $\angle ABC$ is $135°$. An impulse J is applied to the particle C in the direction BC. Find the initial speed of each particle.

The external impulse applied to C causes both strings to jerk exerting internal impulses J_1 and J_2.

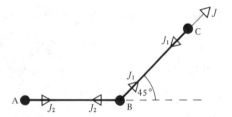

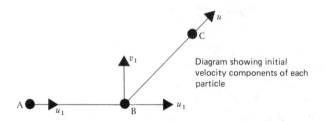

Diagram showing initial velocity components of each particle

Using impulse = change in momentum in the directions parallel and perpendicular to AB we have:

For particle A $J_2 = mu_1$ [1]

For particle B $J_1 \cos 45° - J_2 = mu_1$ [2]

                                            $J_1 \sin 45° = mv_1$ [3]

For particle C along BC $J - J_1 = mu$ [4]

Also the velocities of B and C along BC are equal, i.e.

$$v_1 \cos 45° + u_1 \cos 45° = u$$ [5]

Equations [1] and [2] give $\dfrac{1}{\sqrt{2}}J_1 - mu_1 = mu_1$

$$\Rightarrow \quad J_1 = 2\sqrt{2}mu_1$$

Equation [3] gives $mv_1 = 2\sqrt{2}mu_1 \dfrac{1}{\sqrt{2}}$

$$\Rightarrow \quad v_1 = 2u_1$$

Equation [5] gives $\dfrac{1}{\sqrt{2}}v_1 + \dfrac{1}{\sqrt{2}}u_1 = u$

i.e. $\dfrac{1}{\sqrt{2}}2u_1 + \dfrac{1}{\sqrt{2}}u_1 = u$

$$\Rightarrow \quad u = \dfrac{3}{\sqrt{2}}u_1$$

Equation [4] gives $J - 2\sqrt{2}mu_1 = \dfrac{3}{\sqrt{2}}mu_1$

$$J = \left(\dfrac{3\sqrt{2}}{2} + 2\sqrt{2}\right)mu_1$$

i.e. $\Rightarrow \quad J = \dfrac{7\sqrt{2}}{2}mu_1$

Hence   the initial speed of A $= \dfrac{2J}{7\sqrt{2}m} = \dfrac{J\sqrt{2}}{7m}$

the initial speed of C $= \left(\dfrac{3}{\sqrt{2}}\right)\left(\dfrac{2J}{7\sqrt{2}m}\right) = \dfrac{3J}{7m}$

and   the initial speed of B $= \sqrt{u_1^2 + v_1^2} = \dfrac{2J\sqrt{5}}{7\sqrt{2}m} = \dfrac{J\sqrt{10}}{7m}$

4) A mass $2m$ rests on a horizontal table. It is attached to a light inextensible string which passes over a smooth pulley and carries a mass m at the other end. If the mass m is raised vertically through a distance h and is then dropped, find the speed with which the mass $2m$ begins to rise.

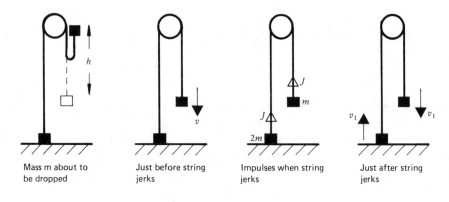

| Mass m about to be dropped | Just before string jerks | Impulses when string jerks | Just after string jerks |

When mass m falls vertically under gravity we have $u = 0$, $a = g$, $s = h$

Using $$v^2 - u^2 = 2as$$

gives $$v = \sqrt{2gh}$$

Using impulse = change in momentum for each mass gives,

for mass $2m$ $\qquad\qquad J = 2mv_1 - 0$

for mass m $\qquad\qquad J = mv - mv_1$

From these equations $\qquad v_1 = \tfrac{1}{3}v$

Hence the particle of mass $2m$ begins to rise with speed $\tfrac{1}{3}\sqrt{2gh}$.

EXERCISE 8c

1) Two particles, each of mass m, are connected by a light inextensible string of length $2l$. Initially they lie on a smooth horizontal table at points A and B distant l apart. The particle at A is projected across the table with velocity u. Find the speed with which the second particle begins to move if the direction of u is,

(a) along BA,

(b) at an angle of $120°$ with AB,

(c) perpendicular to AB.

In each case calculate (in terms of m and u) the impulsive tension in the string.

2) A particle A of mass 2 kg lies on the edge of a table of height 1 m. It is connected by a light inelastic string of length 0.65 m to a second particle B of mass 3 kg which is lying on the table 0.25 m from the edge (AB is perpendicular to the edge). If A is pushed gently over the edge find the velocity with which B begins to move. Find also the impulsive tension in the string.

3) Three particles A, B and C all of mass m rest on a smooth horizontal plane so that angle ABC is $120°$. B is connected to both A and C by light inextensible strings which are initially just taut. An impulse J is then applied to particle B in a direction making an angle of $150°$ with BC and $90°$ with BA. Find the impulsive tension in each string and the initial velocity of each particle.

4) Two particles, A of mass $2m$ and B of mass m, are connected by a light inextensible string which passes over a smooth fixed pulley. Initially the particles are held so that they are both at a height $0.81\,m$ above a fixed horizontal plane, and the string is just taut. The system is then released from rest. Find:

(a) the impulse exerted by the plane when A strikes it (without bouncing),

(b) the velocity with which A next leaves the plane.

5) Three identical particles A, B and C lie close together on a smooth plane. A is connected to B and to C by light inextensible strings. If B is set moving with velocity v across the plane find:

(a) the first impulsive tension in the string AB,

(b) the initial velocity of A,

(c) the initial velocity of C.

6)

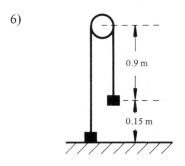

The illustration shows two particles connected by a light inextensible string passing over a pulley fixed at a height of $1.05\,m$ above a horizontal plane. A is of mass $2\,kg$ and is initially at rest on the plane. B is of mass $1\,kg$ and hangs at a depth of $0.9\,m$ below the pulley. B is then raised to the height of the pulley and released from rest from that position.

Calculate:

(a) the speed of B when the string is about to tighten,

(b) the impulsive tension in the string,

(c) the speed with which A leaves the plane,

(d) the speed of either particle when B reaches the plane,

(e) the impulse which B exerts when it strikes the plane (without bouncing).

Is there an impulsive tension in the string when B hits the plane?

DIRECT ELASTIC IMPACT

When two objects collide and *bounce*, the impact between them is *elastic*.
If, instead, they coalesce upon collision, the impact is *inelastic*.
(A reader who is studying Physics may find that these terms are defined
differently in that subject.)
A pair of equal and opposite impulses act at the moment of impact. If, just
before impact, the objects were moving along the line of action of these
impulses, the impact is *direct*, e.g.

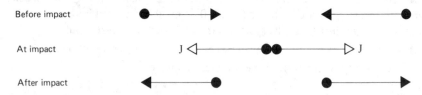

After impact the particles again begin to move along the line of action of the
impulses since, at impact, no impulse acted in the perpendicular direction.

NEWTON'S LAW OF RESTITUTION

When two objects are in direct elastic impact the speed with which they
separate after impact is usually less than their speed of approach before impact.

Experimental evidence suggests that the ratio of these relative speeds is constant.
This property, formulated by Newton, is known as the *law of restitution* and
can be written in the form

$$\text{separation speed : approach speed} \ = \ e$$

The ratio e is called the *coefficient of restitution* and is constant for two
particular objects.

Impact between objects which do not bounce is *inelastic* and in this case $e = 0$.

A collision between two objects whose relative speed is unchanged by the impact
is said to be *perfectly elastic*. For two such objects $e = 1$

In general $\qquad\qquad 0 \leqslant e \leqslant 1.$

Direct impact can occur between two moveable objects or between one fixed
and one moveable object. In both cases the law of restitution is valid.
The principle of conservation of linear momentum applies to impact between
two moveable objects (equal and opposite internal impulses) but not when one
of the objects in collision is fixed (external impulse).

EXAMPLES 8d

1) A smooth sphere of mass 0.5 kg moving with horizontal speed 3 m s⁻¹ strikes at right angles a vertical wall and bounces off the wall with horizontal speed 2 m s⁻¹. Find the coefficient of restitution between the sphere and the wall and the impulse exerted on the wall at impact.

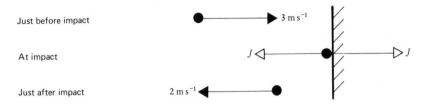

$$e = \text{separation speed : approach speed } = 2:3$$

Therefore the coefficient of restitution is $\frac{2}{3}$.

Using impulse = change in momentum for the sphere we have:

$$J = 0.5 \times 2 - 0.5(-3) = 2.5$$

The equal and opposite impulse acting on the wall is therefore 2.5 N s.

2) A smooth sphere of mass 2 kg is moving with speed 3 m s⁻¹ on a horizontal plane when it collides with a stationary smooth sphere of equal size but mass 4 kg. If the coefficient of restitution between the spheres is $\frac{1}{2}$ find the velocities of both spheres after impact.

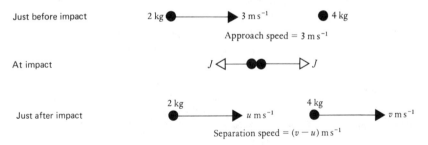

Using the law of restitution in the form

$$e \times \text{approach speed } = \text{separation speed}$$

and the principle of conservation of linear momentum we have:

$$\frac{1}{2} \times 3 = v - u \qquad\qquad [1]$$

and $\qquad\qquad 2 \times 3 = 2u + 4v \qquad\qquad [2]$

Hence $\quad v = \frac{3}{2}\quad$ and $\quad u = 0$

After impact the 2 kg mass is at rest and the 4 kg mass has a speed of 1.5 m s⁻¹.

3) Two identical smooth spheres of mass m collide directly head-on with speeds of $6\,\text{m}\,\text{s}^{-1}$ and $2\,\text{m}\,\text{s}^{-1}$. If the coefficient of restitution is $\frac{1}{4}$ find the speed of both spheres after impact.

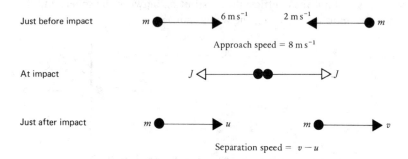

Law of restitution gives $\hspace{4cm} \frac{1}{4} \times 8 = v - u$

Conservation of linear momentum gives $\hspace{1cm} 6m - 2m = mu + mv$

These equations become $\hspace{1cm} \left.\begin{array}{l} 2 = v - u \\[1em] 4 = u + v \end{array}\right\}$ giving $v = 3$ and $u = 1$

and

Therefore the speeds after collision are $3\,\text{m}\,\text{s}^{-1}$ and $1\,\text{m}\,\text{s}^{-1}$.

4) Two identical smooth spheres A and B are free to move on a horizontal plane. B is at rest and A is projected with velocity u to strike B directly. B then collides with a vertical wall which is perpendicular to the direction of motion of the spheres. After rebounding from the wall B again collides with A and is brought to rest by this impact. If the coefficient of restitution has the same value at all impacts prove that $e = 1$.

First Impact: between A and B.

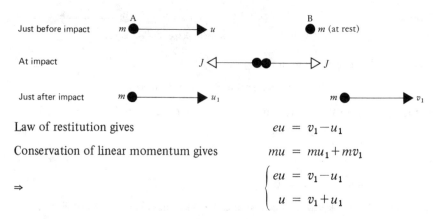

Law of restitution gives $\hspace{3cm} eu = v_1 - u_1$

Conservation of linear momentum gives $\hspace{1cm} mu = mu_1 + mv_1$

$\Rightarrow \hspace{4cm} \left\{\begin{array}{l} eu = v_1 - u_1 \\[1em] u = v_1 + u_1 \end{array}\right.$

hence $$(1+e)u = 2v_1 \qquad [1]$$

and $$(1-e)u = 2u_1 \qquad [2]$$

Second Impact: between B and the wall.

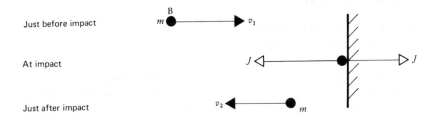

(This time, since the impact is external, momentum is not conserved.)

Law of restitution gives $$ev_1 = v_2 \qquad [3]$$

Third Impact: between A and B.

Just before impact

Just after impact

Law of restitution gives $\qquad e(u_1+v_2) = u_3$

Conservation of linear momentum gives $\quad mu_1 - mv_2 = -mu_3$

or $$v_2 - u_1 = u_3$$

Eliminating u_3 gives $$v_2 - u_1 = e(u_1 + v_2)$$

i.e. $$v_2(1-e) = u_1(e+1) \qquad [4]$$

But from [3] and [1] $\qquad v_2 = ev_1 = e(1+e)(\tfrac{1}{2}u)$

and from [2] $\qquad u_1 = (1-e)(\tfrac{1}{2}u)$

So [4] becomes $\qquad e(1+e)(\tfrac{1}{2}u)(1-e) = (1-e)(\tfrac{1}{2}u)(e+1)$

$\Rightarrow \qquad e = 1$

Note: Example 4, which involved several impacts, introduced a form of notation which helps to clarify the solution.

At every impact the symbol u was used for A's speed and v for that of B. The suffix used indicated which impact was being analysed e.g. u_3 represented the speed of A after the third impact; u_2 was never used because A was not involved in the second impact.

A problem involving three particles and multiple impacts can be similarly treated using u, v, w for speed symbols.

Loss in Mechanical Energy

In practice the total mechanical energy of a system is reduced by a collision or a jerk. The explanation for this loss can usually be *heard*, i.e. some mechanical energy is converted into the sound energy of the *bang* at impact.

Mechanical energy may also be transformed into heat or light energy.

Perfectly elastic impact however, in which there is no change in relative speed, is not accompanied by any mechanical energy loss.

EXAMPLES 8d (continued)

5) A and B are smooth spheres of equal size. A is stationary on a horizontal plane and B is moving on that plane with speed $2u$ when it collides directly with A. If the coefficient of restitution is $\frac{1}{2}$, A is of mass m and B of mass $2m$, find the loss in kinetic energy at impact.

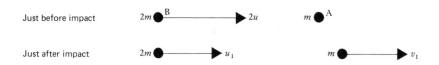

| Just before impact | $2m$ ● B ⟶ $2u$ | m ● A |
| Just after impact | $2m$ ● ⟶ u_1 | m ● ⟶ v_1 |

Law of restitution: $\frac{1}{2} \times 2u = v_1 - u_1$

Conservation of linear momentum: $2m \times 2u = 2mu_1 + mv_1$

hence $u = v_1 - u_1$

and $4u = v_1 + 2u_1$

giving $3u = 3u_1$ and $6u = 3v_1$

Original K.E. $= \frac{1}{2}(2m)(2u)^2 = 4mu^2$

Final K.E. $= \frac{1}{2}(2m)u_1^2 + \frac{1}{2}mv_1^2$

                       $= \frac{1}{2}(2m)u^2 + \frac{1}{2}m(2u)^2 = 3mu^2$

Therefore loss in K.E. $= 4mu^2 - 3mu^2 = mu^2$

6) Repeat Example 5 with a coefficient of restitution of 1 instead of $\frac{1}{2}$.

Law of restitution: $1 \times 2u = v_1 - u_1$

Conservation of linear momentum: $2m \times 2u = 2mu_1 + mv_1$

hence $2u = v_1 - u_1$

and $4u = v_1 + 2u_1$

giving $2u = 3u_1$ and $8u = 3v_1$

Original K.E. $= 4mu^2$

Final K.E. $= \frac{1}{2}(2m)(\frac{2}{3}u)^2 + \frac{1}{2}(m)(\frac{8}{3}u)^2$

$= \frac{1}{2}m(\frac{1}{9}u^2)(8 + 64) = 4mu^2$

Therefore loss in K.E. $= 4mu^2 - 4mu^2 = 0$

(This confirms that perfectly elastic impacts involve no loss in mechanical energy.)

Note. In problems on elastic impact, a particle A may catch up with, and collide with, another particle B moving less quickly in the same direction. In this situation A is said to *overtake* B.

EXERCISE 8d

In all questions involving spheres, these will be smooth and of equal size.

1) A sphere of mass 10 kg moving at 16 m s^{-1} impinges directly on another sphere of mass 5 kg moving in the opposite direction at 4 m s^{-1}. If $e = \frac{1}{2}$ find the speeds of both spheres after impact and the magnitude of the instantaneous impulses.

2) A ball of mass 2 kg moving at 6 m s^{-1} collides directly with another ball of mass 3 kg moving in the same direction at 4 m s^{-1}. Find the speed of each ball after impact and the loss in kinetic energy if $e = \frac{3}{4}$.

3) When two spheres of equal mass collide directly at speeds of 4 m s^{-1} and 8 m s^{-1} in opposite senses, half the original kinetic energy is lost upon impact. Prove that $e = \frac{2}{3}$.

4) A sphere A of mass 0.1 kg is moving with speed 5 m s^{-1} when it collides directly with a stationary sphere B. If A is brought to rest by the impact and $e = \frac{1}{2}$, find the mass of B, its speed just after impact and the magnitude of the instantaneous impulses.

5) Three perfectly elastic spheres A, B and C have masses $3m$, $2m$, m respectively. They are lying in a straight line on a horizontal plane and A is projected with speed u to collide directly with B which goes on to collide directly with C. Find the speed of each sphere after the second impact. Explain why there will be no further impacts.

6) Find, in terms of M, m, e, V and v, the instantaneous impulses which act when two spheres of masses M and m collide directly with speeds V and v respectively:
(a) if they collide head-on,
(b) if they are travelling in the same sense $(V > v)$.
The coefficient of restitution between the spheres is e.

7) A sphere of mass $2\,kg$ falls from rest at a height $10\,m$ above an elastic horizontal plane. Find the height to which the sphere will rise again after its first bounce, if the coefficient of restitution is $\frac{1}{2}$.

8) A small sphere which is dropped from a height of $1.2\,m$ on to a horizontal plane rebounds to a height of $1.0\,m$. Find the value of e and the loss in mechanical energy caused by the impact, if the mass of the sphere is $2\,kg$.

9) A light inextensible string AB has the end A fixed to a vertical wall. The end B is attached to a small elastic object which is drawn aside, from the wall, until the string makes an angle of $60°$ with the wall. The particle is then released from rest. Find the angle which the string makes with the wall when the particle next comes to instantaneous rest if the value of e is $\frac{3}{4}$.

10) A small sphere is dropped on to a horizontal plane from a height h. If the coefficient of restitution between the sphere and the plane is e find, in terms of h and e, the height to which the particle rises after each of the first, second and third impacts, showing that these heights are in geometric progression. Deduce the total distance travelled by the sphere before it comes to rest.

MULTIPLE CHOICE EXERCISE 8

(The instructions for answering these questions are given on page x.)

TYPE I

1) A ball of mass $0.4\,kg$ hits a wall at right angles with a speed of $12\,m\,s^{-1}$ and bounces off, again at right angles to the wall, with a speed of $8\,m\,s^{-1}$. The impulse exerted by the wall on the ball is:
(a) $1.6\,N\,s$ (b) $20\,N\,s$ (c) $4\,N\,s$ (d) $8\,N\,s$.

2) Two masses collide and coalesce as shown in the diagram. What is the speed V of the combined mass just after impact?

(a) $3v$ (b) $\frac{3}{5}v$ (c) v (d) $\frac{5}{3}v$.

3)

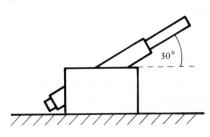

A gun which is free to recoil horizontally fires a bullet when the barrel is inclined at $30°$ to the horizontal. When the bullet leaves the barrel it will be travelling at an angle to the horizontal of:
(a) $30°$
(b) a little less than $30°$
(c) a little more than $30°$
(d) zero.

4) Two smooth objects, with a coefficient of restitution e, collide directly and bounce as shown

Newton's law of restitution gives:
(a) $e \times 4u = v_2 + v_1$
(b) $e \times 2u = v_1 - v_2$
(c) $e \times 2u = v_2 - v_1$
(d) it cannot be applied as the masses are not known.

5) A particle of mass $2\,\text{kg}$ moving with speed $4\,\text{m s}^{-1}$ is given a blow which changes the speed to $1\,\text{m s}^{-1}$ without deflecting the particle from a straight line. The impulse of the blow is:
(a) $10\,\text{N s}$
(b) $6\,\text{N s}$
(c) we do not know whether it is $10\,\text{N s}$ or $6\,\text{N s}$.

TYPE II

6) A body of mass m is moving with speed v when a constant force F is applied to it in the direction of motion for a time t:
(a) The impulse of the force is Ft.
(b) $Ft = mv$.
(c) The body loses an amount of kinetic energy equal to Ft.
(d) The final speed of the body is $v + \dfrac{Ft}{m}$.

7) When a particle P of mass $2m$ collides with a particle Q of mass m:
(a) P exerts an impulse on Q,
(b) the mechanical energy of the system is unchanged,
(c) the impulse which P exerts on Q is twice the impulse which Q exerts on P.
(d) Q exerts an impulse on P.

8) Two moving particles are attached, one to each end of a string AB. If the string jerks tight, then immediately afterwards:
(a) both particles have the same speed,
(b) the particles have the same speed if they are of equal mass.
(c) the particles have equal velocity components in the direction AB.

9) A sphere A of mass m, travelling with speed v, collides directly with a stationary sphere B. If A is brought to rest by the collision and B is given a speed V, then:

(a) $e = \dfrac{v}{V}$,   (b) the mass of B is $\dfrac{mv}{V}$,

(c) $e = \dfrac{V}{v}$,   (d) the particles are of equal mass.

10) A particle of mass 1 kg is dropped from a height of 3 m on to a horizontal plane where it bounces and rises to a height of 2 m above the plane.
(a) the coefficient of restitution is $\frac{2}{3}$,
(b) just before striking the plane the speed is $\sqrt{6g}$ m s^{-1},
(c) the coefficient of restitution is $\sqrt{\frac{2}{3}}$,
(d) just after striking the plane, the speed of the particle is $\sqrt{\dfrac{8g}{3}}$ m s^{-1}.

TYPE III

11) (a) In a specified direction a body has a constant speed.
    (b) No resultant force acts on a body.

12) (a) The coefficient of restitution between two colliding objects is < 1.
    (b) Mechanical energy is lost when two objects collide.

13) (a) Two spheres collide directly.
    (b) Two spheres are travelling towards each other in the same straight line.

14) (a) Two spheres collide directly without loss of momentum.
    (b) Two perfectly elastic spheres collide directly.

15) (a) When two spheres collide directly half the original kinetic energy is lost.
    (b) Two spheres have a coefficient of restitution of $\frac{1}{2}$.

TYPE IV

16) Two particles A and B collide directly head-on and bounce. Find their speeds immediately after impact.
(a) The mass of A is twice the mass of B.
(b) Just before impact the speed of A is 4 m s^{-1} and that of B is 3 m s^{-1}.
(c) No kinetic energy is lost by the impact.

17) A ball moving on a horizontal floor hits a smooth vertical wall normally. Calculate the speed with which it leaves the wall if:

(a) the speed when approaching the wall is $3 \, m \, s^{-1}$,

(b) the coefficient of restitution is $\frac{1}{2}$,

(c) the mass of the ball is $0.4 \, kg$.

18) A ball falls vertically on to a horizontal plane and bounces. Find the impulse the ball exerts on the plane if:

(a) the ball is initially $2 \, m$ above the plane,

(b) it rises after bouncing to a height $1.2 \, m$,

(c) the coefficient of restitution is $\sqrt{\frac{3}{5}}$,

(d) the mass of the ball is $0.5 \, kg$.

19) Two particles A and B are travelling on the same straight line when they collide. Find the loss in kinetic energy due to impact if:

(a) A and B have equal mass,

(b) just before impact the speed of A is three times the speed of B,

(c) the coefficient of restitution is $\frac{2}{3}$.

20) An inelastic string has a particle A attached to one end and a particle B attached to the other end. If A is projected in the direction $\overrightarrow{BA}$ find the initial speed of B if:

(a) initially the string is slack,

(b) the speed of projection of A is $4 \, m \, s^{-1}$,

(c) the particles are of equal mass.

(d) the string is $2 \, m$ long.

TYPE V

21) The law of restitution applies to an elastic impact between a moving object and a fixed surface.

22) The coefficient of restitution is given by: relative speed before impact divided by relative speed after impact.

23) A perfectly elastic impact does not cause a loss in mechanical energy.

24) The momentum of a system remains constant in any direction in which no external force acts.

25) Impulse means an impact between moving bodies.

MISCELLANEOUS EXERCISE 8

1) A force of $10\,N$ acts on a mass of $2\,kg$ for three seconds. If the initial velocity was $50\,m\,s^{-1}$ what is the final velocity?

2) A stone weighing $5\,N$ is thrown vertically upwards, with velocity $80\,m\,s^{-1}$. What is its velocity after two seconds and after twenty seconds?
[Take $g = 10\,m\,s^{-2}$.]

3) Water issues from a pipe, whose cross section is $c\,m^2$, in a horizontal jet with velocity $v\,m\,s^{-1}$. What force must be exerted by a shield placed perpendicular to the jet to bring the water to a horizontal stop?
[The mass of $1\,m^3$ of water is $10^3\,kg$.]

4) Two masses of 20 and 10 units, moving in the same direction at speeds of 16 and 12 units respectively collide and stick together. Find the velocity of the combined mass immediately afterwards.

5) A gun of mass $1000\,kg$ can launch a shell of mass $1\,kg$ with a horizontal velocity of $1200\,m\,s^{-1}$. What is the horizontal velocity of recoil of the gun?

6) A sphere of mass m falls from rest at a height h above a horizontal plane and rebounds to a height $\frac{1}{2}h$. Find the coefficient of restitution, the impulse exerted by the plane and the loss in K.E. due to impact.

7) A particle of mass m moving with speed V strikes a particle of mass $2m$ at rest and coalesces with it. Express the final kinetic energy as a fraction of the original kinetic energy.

8) An inelastic pile driver of mass $4000\,kg$ falls freely from a height of $5\,m$ on to a pile of mass $1000\,kg$ driving the pile $20\,cm$ into the ground. Find the speed with which the pile starts to move into the ground and also the average resistance to penetration of the ground in newtons.
[Take g as $10\,m/s^2$.]   (U of L)p

9) Two particles P and Q, of mass $2m$ and $3m$ respectively, are connected by a light inelastic string which passes over a smooth fixed pulley. The system is released from rest with the string taut and the hanging parts vertical. After time t, the particle P picks up a stationary particle of mass m. Show that the loss of kinetic energy of the system due to the impulse is $mg^2t^2/60$.   (U of L)

10) A sphere A, of mass $2m$ and velocity $2u$, overtakes and collides with sphere B, of mass m and velocity u travelling in the same line which is perpendicular to a vertical smooth wall. After being struck by A, sphere B goes on to strike the wall. If the coefficient of restitution between A and B is $\frac{1}{2}$ and that between B and the wall is $\frac{3}{4}$ show that there is a second collision between A and B and describe what happens after the second impact.

11) A sphere A, of mass m_1, and velocity u, collides with a stationary sphere B of mass m_2. If sphere A is brought to rest by the collision, find the velocity of B after impact, and the coefficient of restitution. If sphere B now collides with a stationary sphere C and is brought to rest find the mass of sphere C assuming the same coefficient of restitution between A and B, and between B and C.

12) A smooth sphere A of mass $2m$, moving on a horizontal plane with speed u collides directly with another smooth sphere B of equal radius and of mass m, which is at rest. If the coefficient of restitution between the spheres is e, find their speeds after impact.
The sphere B later rebounds from a perfectly elastic vertical wall, and then collides directly with A. Prove that after this collision the speed of B is $\frac{2}{9}(1+e)^2 u$ and find the speed of A. (U of L)

13) State the law of conservation of linear momentum for two interacting particles. Show how the law of conservation of linear momentum applied to two particles which collide directly follows from Newton's laws of motion.
Three smooth spheres A, B, C, equal in all respects, lie at rest and separated from one another on a smooth horizontal table in the order A, B, C with their centres in a straight line. Sphere A is projected with speed V directly towards sphere B. If the coefficient of restitution at each collision is e, where $0 < e < 1$, find the velocity of each of the spheres just after C is set in motion. Show that A strikes B a second time. (JMB)

14) A pump raises water from a depth of 10 m and discharges it horizontally through a pipe of 0.1 m diameter at a velocity of 8 m s^{-1}. Calculate the work done by the pump in one second. If the water impinges directly with the same velocity on a vertical wall, find the force exerted by the water on the wall if it is assumed that none of the water bounces back. [Take g as 9.81 m s^{-2}, π as 3.142 and the mass of 1 m^3 of water as 1000 kg.) (U of L)

15) Two equal spheres B and C, each of mass $4m$, lie at rest on a smooth horizontal table. A third sphere A, of the same radius as B and C but of mass m, moves with velocity V along the line of centres of B and C. The sphere A collides with B which then collides with C. If A is brought to rest by the first collision show that the coefficient of restitution between A and B is $\frac{1}{4}$. If the coefficient of restitution between B and C is $\frac{1}{2}$ find the velocities of B and C after the second collision. Show that the total loss of kinetic energy due to the two collisions is $\dfrac{27mV^2}{64}$. (JMB)

16) Three smooth spheres A, B, C, of equal radii and masses m, λm, $\lambda^2 m$ respectively, where λ is a constant, are free to move along a straight horizontal groove with B between A and C. When any two spheres collide the impact is direct and the coefficient of restitution is e. Spheres B and C are initially at

rest and sphere A is projected towards sphere B with speed u. Show that the velocities of A and B after the first impact are

$$\frac{1-\lambda e}{1+\lambda}u \quad \text{and} \quad \frac{1+e}{1+\lambda}u \quad \text{respectively.}$$

Find the velocities of B and C after the second impact.

Given that $\lambda e < 1$, show that there is a third impact if $e < \lambda$.   (U of L)

17) (a) A sphere of mass m moving along a smooth horizontal table with speed V collides directly with a stationary sphere of the same radius and of mass $2m$. Obtain expressions for the speeds of the two spheres after impact, in terms of V and the coefficient of restitution e.

Half of the kinetic energy is lost in the impact. Find the value of e.

(b) A particle of mass m moving in a straight line with speed u receives an impulse of magnitude I in the direction of its motion. Show that the increase in kinetic energy is given by

$$I(I + 2mu)/(2m).$$ (U of L)

18) A particle of mass m is projected vertically upward with speed u and when it reaches its greatest height a second particle, of mass $2m$, is projected vertically upward with speed $2u$ from the same point as the first. Prove that the time that elapses between the projection of the second particle and its collision with the first is $\dfrac{u}{4g}$, and find the height above the point of projection at which the collision occurs.

If, on collision, the particles coalesce, prove that the combined particle will reach a greatest height of $\dfrac{19u^2}{18g}$ above the point of projection.   (JMB)

19)

Two particles, each of mass m, are connected by a light inextensible string which passes over a smooth pulley at the top of a fixed plane inclined at an angle $\arctan\frac{5}{12}$ to the horizontal. The particle A is on the plane and the particle B hangs freely (see figure). The system is released from rest with the string in a vertical plane through a line of greatest slope of the plane. The coefficient of friction between A and the plane is $\frac{1}{3}$. When B has fallen a distance h the string breaks. A comes to rest after travelling a further distance

s up the plane. B falls a further distance h to strike a horizontal plane and rises to a height h above that plane. Find:

(a) the speed of the particles when the string breaks,

(b) the value of s,

(c) the coefficient of restitution between B and the horizontal plane and the impulse of the blow when the particle B strikes this plane. (AEB)

20) Three particles A, B, C of masses m, $2m$, $3m$ respectively lie at rest in that order in a straight line on a smooth horizontal table. The distance between consecutive particles is a. A slack light inelastic string of length $2a$ connects A and B. An exactly similar slack string connects B and C. If A is projected in the direction CBA with speed V, find the time which elapses before C begins to move. Find also the speed with which C begins to move. Show that the ratio of the impulsive tensions in BC and AB when C is jerked into motion is $3:1$. Find the total loss of kinetic energy when C has started to move. (JMB)

21) A smooth plane is fixed at an inclination $30°$ with its lower edge at a height a above a horizontal table. Two particles P and Q, each of mass m, are connected by a light inextensible string of length $2a$, and P is held at the lower edge of the inclined plane while Q rests on the table vertically below P. The particle P is then projected with velocity u $(u > \sqrt{ga})$ upwards along a line of greatest slope of the plane. Find the impulsive tension in the string when Q is jerked into motion. Determine the magnitude of u if Q just reaches the lower edge of the plane, and the tension in the string while Q is moving. (JMB)

22) A hammer of mass $5m$, moving horizontally with velocity V, strikes a stationary horizontal nail of mass m. If the coefficient of restitution between the hammer and the nail is $\frac{3}{5}$ find the velocity of the nail just after the blow. Immediately after the blow the nail begins to penetrate a block of mass nm which is free to move on a smooth horizontal table. Penetration is resisted by a constant force R. Find the common velocity of the block and the nail when the nail ceases to penetrate the block. Show that penetration ceases at a time

$$\frac{4mnV}{3(n+1)R}$$ after the blow (it may be assumed that there is only one blow

between the hammer and the nail). (JMB)

23) Two particles of masses m and $3m$ are connected by a light inelastic string of length $2l$ which passes over a small smooth fixed peg. The particles are held in contact with the peg and then allowed, at the same instant, to fall from rest under gravity, one on either side of the peg. Prove that:

(a) the speed of each particle just after the string tightens is $\sqrt{(gl/2)}$,

(b) the sudden tightening of the string causes a loss of energy equal to $3mgl$,

(c) the lighter particle reaches the peg again after a total time $\sqrt{6l/g}$. (JMB)

24) A sphere A of mass m is moving with speed V on a smooth horizontal floor when it collides directly with a stationary sphere B of the same radius but of mass λm. The coefficient of restitution between the spheres is $\frac{2}{3}$. Find expressions for the speeds of A and B after impact.

Sphere B then strikes normally a vertical wall and rebounds. The coefficient of restitution between B and the wall is also $\frac{2}{3}$. If A and B do not collide again, show that $\lambda \geqslant 19/6$. Show that, when $\lambda = 6$, the kinetic energy lost when A strikes B is $5mV^2/21$. (U of L)

25) A small smooth sphere moves on a horizontal table and strikes an identical sphere lying at rest on the table at a distance d from a vertical wall, the impact being along the line of centres and perpendicular to the wall. Prove that the next impact between the spheres will take place at a distance

$$2de^2/(1 + e^2)$$

from the wall, where e is the coefficient of restitution for all impacts involved. (U of L)

26) Two particles A and B, of mass $2m$ and m respectively, are attached to the ends of a light inextensible string of length $4a$ which passes over a small smooth peg fixed at a height $3a$ above an inelastic table. The system is released from rest with each particle at a height a above the table.

Write down the equation of motion for each of the particles and hence determine the common magnitude of their accelerations. Show that, at the instant when A is first brought to rest by hitting the table, B has a speed V given by

$$V = \left(\frac{2ga}{3}\right)^{\frac{1}{2}}$$

Determine, in terms of V and g,
(a)   the time that elapses before A first hits the table,
(b)   the time that A is resting on the table after the first collision before it is first jerked off.
(c)   the speed with which A is first jerked off the table,
(d)   the time that elapses between A being first jerked off the table and A hitting the table again. (AEB)

27) Two small spheres of masses m and $2m$ are connected by a light inextensible string of length $2a$. When the string is taut and horizontal, its mid-point is fixed and the spheres are released from rest. The coefficient of restitution between the spheres is $\frac{1}{2}$. Show that the first impact brings the heavier sphere to rest, and that the second impact brings the lighter sphere to rest.

Find the velocity of each sphere immediately after the third impact. (U of L)

28) Two particles A and B of masses $2m$ and $3m$ respectively are placed on a smooth horizontal plane. The coefficient of restitution between A and B is $\frac{1}{2}$. The particle A is made to move with speed u directly towards B which is at rest. Calculate the speeds of A and B after their collision, the impulse of the force transmitted from A to B and the loss in kinetic energy due to the collision.

The particles A and B are now connected by a light inextensible string and are placed side by side on the smooth horizontal plane. The particle A is given a horizontal velocity v directly away from B. Calculate the impulse of the tension in the string at the instant when the string tightens. Calculate also the resulting common velocity of the two particles and show that the loss in kinetic energy due to the tightening of the string is $0.6\,mv^2$.   (AEB)

29) Two scale pans, each of mass m, are connected by a light inelastic string which passes over a small smooth fixed light pulley. On one scale pan there is an inelastic particle A of mass $2m$. The system is released from rest with the hanging parts of the string vertical. Find the tension in the string and the acceleration of either scale pan.

At the instant when motion begins, a particle of mass $3m$ is allowed to fall from rest and after t seconds it strikes, and adheres to, A. Find the impulsive tension in the string and the velocity of either scale pan immediately after the impact.   (JMB)

30) Two particles each of mass m are connected by a light inextensible string and a particle of mass M is attached to the midpoint of the string. The system is at rest on a smooth horizontal table with the string just taut and in a straight line. The particle M is given a velocity V along the table perpendicular to the string. Prove that, when the two end particles are about to collide:
(a) the velocity of M is $VM/(M+2m)$,
(b) the speed of each of the other particles is $V\{2M(M+m)\}^{\frac{1}{2}}/(M+2m)$.   (O)

31) Three particles A, B and C, each of mass m, lie at rest on a smooth horizontal table. Light inextensible strings connect. A to B and B to C. The strings are just taut with $\angle ABC = 135°$, when a blow of impulse J is applied to C in a direction parallel to $\overrightarrow{AB}$. Prove that A begins to move with speed $(J/7)m$ and find the impulsive tension in the string BC.   (U of L)

32) A bullet of mass m is fired with speed u into a fixed block of wood and emerges with speed $2u/3$. When the experiment is repeated with a block free to move the bullet emerges with speed $u/2$ *relative* to the block. Assuming the same constant resistance to penetration in both cases, find the mass and the final speed of the block in the second case. (Neglect the effect of gravity throughout.)   (U of L)

33) The masses of three perfectly elastic spheres A, B and C are M, M and m respectively $(M > m)$. The spheres are initially at rest with their centres in a straight line, C lying between A and B. If C is given a velocity towards A along the line of centres, show that after colliding first with A and then with B it will not collide a second time with A if $M < (\sqrt{5} + 2)m$. Find the ratios of the kinetic energies of the three spheres after the second collision and verify that no energy has been lost. (U of L)

CHAPTER 9

PROJECTILES

A projectile is a particle which is given an initial velocity and then moves under the action of its weight alone. In this chapter we analyse the motion of projectiles while they are in flight. For example, a ball which is thrown is a projectile and we are concerned with its flight from the moment it leaves the thrower's hand until its flight is interrupted.

If the initial velocity of a projectile is vertical it moves in a straight line (see Chapter 4).

If the initial velocity is not vertical the particle moves in a curve and its flight can be analysed by considering the vertical and horizontal components of its acceleration, velocity and displacement.

Consider a ball which is thrown with an initial velocity V at an angle α to the horizontal.

We will take horizontal and vertical axes Ox and Oy through O, the point of projection. With this frame of reference, the horizontal components of displacement, velocity and acceleration at any time during the flight are x, $\dot{x}$, $\ddot{x}$ and the vertical components are y, $\dot{y}$, $\ddot{y}$.

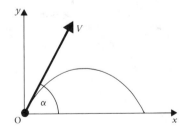
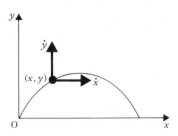

Throughout the flight the only force acting on the ball is its own weight, so its acceleration is g vertically downwards

i.e. $$\ddot{x} = 0 \quad \text{and} \quad \ddot{y} = -g$$

Hence the horizontal velocity component is constant and vertically there is motion with constant acceleration.

Initially the horizontal and vertical velocity components are $V\cos\alpha$ and $V\sin\alpha$. Hence, at any time t during the flight,

$$\begin{cases} \dot{x} = V\cos\alpha \\ \dot{y} = V\sin\alpha - gt \end{cases} \qquad \text{(using } v = u + at\text{)}$$

Further, since the ball starts from O, using $s = ut$ and $s = ut + \frac{1}{2}at^2$ gives

$$\begin{cases} x = Vt\cos\alpha \\ y = Vt\sin\alpha - \frac{1}{2}gt^2 \end{cases}$$

These expressions for displacement and velocity components can be used to determine all the information that might be required about the flight of a projectile.

EXAMPLES 9a

1) A ball is thrown with an initial velocity of $20\,\mathrm{m\,s^{-1}}$ at an angle of $30°$ above the horizontal. Find:
(a) the speed of the ball 2 seconds after projection,
(b) the distance of the ball from its point of projection 1 second after being thrown.
[Take $g = 10\,\mathrm{m\,s^{-2}}$.]

(a)

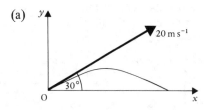 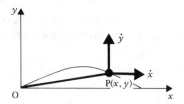

In this problem $V = 20$, $\alpha = 30°$, $g = 10$, $t = 2$

So $\dot{x} = V\cos\alpha$

$\Rightarrow$ $\dot{x} = 20\cos 30° = 10\sqrt{3}$

and $\dot{y} = V\sin\alpha - gt$

$\Rightarrow$ $\dot{y} = 20\sin 30° - (10)(2) = -10$

Note that when $\dot{y}$ is negative the ball has passed its highest point and is falling.

Now the speed of the particle is given by

$$v = \sqrt{\dot{x}^2 + \dot{y}^2}$$
$$= \sqrt{300 + 100} = 20$$

So the speed after 2 seconds is $20 \, \text{m s}^{-1}$

(b) When $t = 1$, $x = Vt \cos \alpha = (20)(1)(\sqrt{3}/2)$
$$= 10\sqrt{3}$$

and $y = Vt \sin \alpha - \frac{1}{2}gt^2 = (20)(1)(\frac{1}{2}) - \frac{1}{2}(10)(1)$
$$= 5$$

Then $OP = \sqrt{x^2 + y^2}$
$$= \sqrt{300 + 25} = 5\sqrt{13}$$

So after 1 second the ball is $5\sqrt{13}$ m from O.

2) A stone is thrown from the top of a tower which is 11 m high and stands on horizontal ground. The speed of projection is $12 \, \text{m s}^{-1}$ and the initial direction of motion is at $60°$ to the downward vertical. Find the time taken for the stone to reach the ground. Find also the direction of motion just before it hits the ground.
[Take g as $10 \, \text{m s}^{-2}$.]

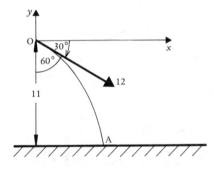

If we wish to use the same expressions in this problem, the origin, O, is at the top of the tower and the angle of projection is below the x axis.
So $\alpha = -30°$ and, at the foot of the tower, $y = -11$

Then $y = Vt \sin \alpha - \frac{1}{2}gt^2$

$\Rightarrow$ $-11 = (12t)(-\frac{1}{2}) - 5t^2$

$\Rightarrow$ $5t^2 + 6t - 11 = 0$

$\Rightarrow$ $t = 1$ or -2.2

Taking the positive value, the stone reaches the ground after 1 second.

The negative value represents the time *before* projection when the stone could have been at ground level.

Just before the stone hits the ground,

$$\dot{x} = 12 \cos(-30°) = 6\sqrt{3}$$

and
$$\dot{y} = 12 \sin(-30°) - (10)(1) = -16 \quad \text{(i.e. downwards)}$$

So, at A, the velocity components of the stone are as shown in the diagram. If the direction of motion is at an angle ϕ below the horizontal then

$$\tan \phi = \frac{16}{6\sqrt{3}} \quad \Rightarrow \quad \phi = 57°$$

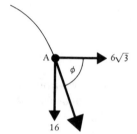

EXERCISE 9a

[Take g as $10 \, \text{m s}^{-2}$.]

In Questions 1–5, V is the speed of projection, α is the angle of projection, t is the time after projection and d is the distance of the projectile P from the point of projection at time t when the coordinates of P are (x, y).

1) $V = 12$, $\alpha = 60°$, $t = 2$; find d.

2) $V = 20$, $\alpha = 45°$, $t = 1$; find x and y.

3) $V = 10$, $\alpha = 30°$, $x = 10\sqrt{3}$; find t and y.

4) $\alpha = 60°$, $x = 30$, $t = 3$; find V and y.

5) $V = 12$, $x = 24$, $t = 4$; find α and d.

6) A particle is projected with a velocity of $40 \, \text{m s}^{-1}$ at an angle of $60°$ to the horizontal. Find its velocity $1\frac{1}{2}$ seconds later.

7) A particle is projected with a velocity of $10 \, \text{m s}^{-1}$ at an angle of $30°$ to the horizontal. Find its distance from the point of projection $\frac{1}{2}$ second later.

8) A particle is projected from a point on level ground with a velocity of $20 \, \text{m s}^{-1}$ and hits the ground $\frac{2}{3}$ of a second later. Find the angle of projection.

9) A particle is projected from a point O at an angle of $-30°$. ($30°$ below the horizontal). If the particle hits the ground, which is $50 \, \text{m}$ below the level of O, 2 seconds later find the initial speed of the particle.

THE EQUATION OF THE PATH

The path of a projectile (sometimes referred to as the trajectory) is a curve which is the locus of the set of points whose coordinates are given by

$$\begin{cases} x = Vt \cos \alpha \\ y = Vt \sin \alpha - \tfrac{1}{2}gt^2 \end{cases}$$

These are the parametric equations of the curve (t is the parameter) and the Cartesian equation can be obtained by eliminating t to give

$$y = x \tan \alpha - \frac{gx^2 \sec^2 \alpha}{2V^2}$$

or

$$y = x \tan \alpha - \frac{gx^2(1 + \tan^2 \alpha)}{2V^2}$$

Note that y is a quadratic function of x so

the path of a projectile is a parabola.

From the equation of the path we can find the value of $\dfrac{dy}{dx}$ for any particular value of x.

We saw in Chapter 4 that the direction of motion is along the tangent to the curve. Using $\dfrac{dy}{dx}$ therefore provides an alternative method for calculating the direction of motion at a particular *point* on the path rather than at a particular *time*.

PROBLEM SOLVING

The formulae that can be used to solve projectile problems are

$$\begin{cases} \dot{x} = V \cos \alpha & [1] \\ \dot{y} = V \sin \alpha - gt & [2] \end{cases}$$

$$\begin{cases} x = Vt \cos \alpha & [3] \\ y = Vt \sin \alpha - \frac{1}{2}gt^2 & [4] \end{cases}$$

$$y = x \tan \alpha - \frac{gx^2 \sec^2 \alpha}{2V^2} \qquad [5]$$

$$\frac{dy}{dx} = \tan \alpha - \frac{gx \sec^2 \alpha}{V^2} \qquad [6]$$

Note that equation [6] need not be memorised as it can easily be obtained from equation [5].

Problems involving velocity require the use of equations [1] and [2].

Problems involving position can be dealt with in two ways:

(a) by using equations [3] and [4] if the coordinates are required separately *at a given time*,

(b) by using equation [5] to *relate the coordinates* and to avoid introducing the time t.

Problems involving direction of motion can also be dealt with in two ways:

(a) by using $\dfrac{\dot{y}}{\dot{x}}$ to give the direction of motion at a *particular time*,

(b) by using $\dfrac{dy}{dx}$ to give the direction of motion at a *particular point*.

It is much better to select the most appropriate formulae for solving a particular problem, than to risk using all of them at some stage. This is fatal, as equation [5] is equivalent to the *pair* of equations [3] and [4]; the use of all three of these equations leads to an infuriating result such as $0 = 0$!

EXAMPLES 9b

1) A particle is projected with a speed of $20\,\mathrm{m\,s^{-1}}$ and reaches its greatest height above the point of projection $\frac{1}{3}$ of a second later. Find the angle of projection.

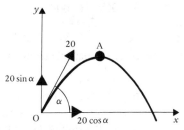

If A is the highest point on the path then, when the particle is at A it is travelling horizontally, i.e.

$$\dot{y} = 0$$

This occurs when

$$t = \tfrac{1}{3}$$

At any time t,

$$\dot{y} = 20 \sin\alpha - gt$$

So, at A,

$$0 = 20 \sin\alpha - (9.8)(\tfrac{1}{3})$$

Hence

$$\sin\alpha = \frac{9.8}{60} = 0.1633$$

$\Rightarrow$

$$\alpha = 9.4°$$

Therefore the angle of projection is $9.4°$.

2) A particle is projected from a point which is 2 m above ground level with a velocity of $40\,\mathrm{m\,s^{-1}}$ at an angle of $45°$ to the horizontal. Find its horizontal distance from the point of projection when it hits the ground.

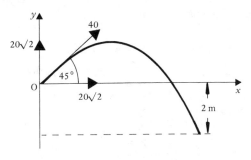

Using the equation of the path

$$y = x \tan\alpha - \frac{gx^2\sec^2\alpha}{2V^2}$$

gives

$$y = x - \frac{gx^2}{1600}$$

We require the value of x when $y = -2$

So $-2 = x - \dfrac{gx^2}{1600}$

$\Rightarrow$ $49x^2 - 8000x - 16\,000 = 0$

$\Rightarrow$ $x = 165$

Therefore the horizontal distance of the particle from O when it hits the ground is 165 m.

3) A stone is thrown from the top of a cliff 70 m high at an angle of $30°$ below the horizontal and hits the sea 20 m from the bottom of the cliff. Find the initial speed of the stone and the direction in which it is moving when it hits the sea.

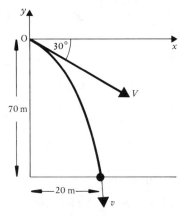

Let the initial speed by V m s^{-1}

Using the equation of the path $y = x \tan(-30°) - \dfrac{x^2 g}{2V^2} \sec^2(-30°)$

The stone hits the sea when $y = -70$ and $x = 20$

Therefore $-70 = \dfrac{-20}{\sqrt{3}} - \dfrac{400 \times 9.8}{2V^2} \times \dfrac{4}{3}$

$\Rightarrow$ $V^2 = 44.7$

$\Rightarrow$ $V = 6.7$

Therefore the initial speed of the stone is 6.7 m s^{-1}.

To find the direction of motion of the stone we can use

$$\dfrac{dy}{dx} = \tan(-30°) - \dfrac{xg \sec^2(-30°)}{V^2}$$

When the stone hits the sea, $x = 20$

So at that point
$$\frac{dy}{dx} = \frac{-1}{\sqrt{3}} - \frac{20 \times 9.8 \times 4}{44.7 \times 3}$$

$$= -6.42$$

Therefore the stone hits the sea at $81°$ to the horizontal.

4) A particle P is projected from a point O with an initial velocity of $60\,\mathrm{m\,s^{-1}}$ at an angle $30°$ to the horizontal. At the same instant a second particle Q is projected in the opposite direction with initial speed $50\,\mathrm{m\,s^{-1}}$ from a point level with O and $100\,\mathrm{m}$ from O. If the particles collide find the angle of projection of Q and find when the collision occurs.

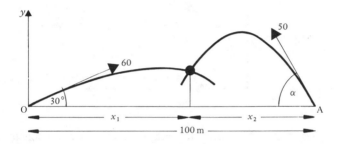

If the particles collide they must be at the *same point* at the *same time* so, as time is an important consideration, we do not use the equation of the path.

Let t be the time interval from projection to collision.

For P we use O as origin and the x axis along OA giving
$$x_P = (60 \cos 30°)t$$
$$y_P = (60 \sin 30°)t - \tfrac{1}{2}gt^2$$

For Q we use A as origin and its x axis along AO giving
$$x_Q = (50 \cos \alpha)t$$
$$y_Q = (50 \sin \alpha)t - \tfrac{1}{2}gt^2$$

But
$$x_P + x_Q = 100$$

$\Rightarrow$
$$t(30\sqrt{3} + 50 \cos \alpha) = 100 \qquad [1]$$

Also
$$y_P = y_Q$$

$\Rightarrow$
$$30 = 50 \sin \alpha$$

$\Rightarrow$
$$\sin \alpha = \tfrac{3}{5} \qquad [2]$$

Hence, from equation [2], $\cos\alpha = \frac{4}{5} \Rightarrow \alpha = 36.9°$

Therefore Q is projected at $36.9°$ to the horizontal.

Then equation [1] gives

$$t(30\sqrt{3} + 40) = 100$$

$\Rightarrow \qquad\qquad t = 1.09$

Therefore the particles collide 1.09 seconds after projection.

5) A particle is projected from a point O with initial velocity $3\mathbf{i} + 4\mathbf{j}$.
Find vector expressions for the velocity and position of the projectile at time t.

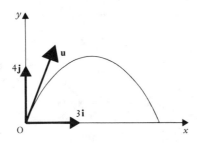

The magnitudes of the initial horizontal and vertical velocity components are
3 and 4 respectively, i.e. $V\cos\alpha = 3$ and $V\sin\alpha = 4$.

At time t, $\qquad\qquad \dot{x} = V\cos\alpha = 3$

and $\qquad\qquad\qquad \dot{y} = V\sin\alpha - gt = 4 - gt$

So $\qquad\qquad\qquad \mathbf{v} = 3\mathbf{i} + (4 - gt)\mathbf{j}$

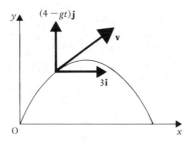

Similarly at time t, $\qquad x = Vt\cos\alpha = 3t$

and $\qquad\qquad\qquad y = Vt\sin\alpha - \frac{1}{2}gt^2 = 4t - \frac{1}{2}gt^2$

So the displacement vector, $\mathbf{r}$, is given by

$$\mathbf{r} = 3t\mathbf{i} + (4t - \tfrac{1}{2}gt^2)\mathbf{j}$$

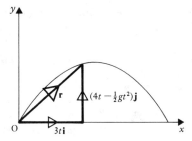

In general if a particle is projected with initial velocity $a\mathbf{i}+b\mathbf{j}$, then its velocity at any time t can be expressed in the form

$$\mathbf{v} = a\mathbf{i}+(b-gt)\mathbf{j}$$

and its position at any time t can be expressed in the form

$$\mathbf{r} = at\mathbf{i}+(bt-\tfrac{1}{2}gt^2)\mathbf{j}.$$

Any problem on projectiles may be solved using vector methods but in general it is unwise to do so unless the problem is phrased in vector terms.

EXERCISE 9b

In this exercise take g as $10\,\mathrm{m\,s^{-2}}$.

1) A particle is projected with a velocity of $30\,\mathrm{m\,s^{-1}}$ at an angle $\arctan\tfrac{3}{4}$ to the horizontal. It hits the ground at a point which is level with its point of projection. Find the time for which it is in the air.

2) A particle is projected with a velocity of $10\,\mathrm{m\,s^{-1}}$ at an angle of $45°$ to the horizontal. It hits the ground at a point which is $3\,\mathrm{m}$ below its point of projection. Find the time for which it is in the air and the horizontal distance covered by the particle in this time.

3) A ball is thrown from ground level with a velocity of $15\,\mathrm{m\,s^{-1}}$ at an angle of $60°$ to the horizontal. Find when the ball hits the ground and the time at which it reaches its greatest height above the point of projection.

4) A particle is projected with a velocity of $70\,\mathrm{m\,s^{-1}}$ at an angle of $20°$ to the horizontal. Find the greatest height reached by the particle above its point of projection.

5) A ball is thrown with a velocity of $15\,\mathrm{m\,s^{-1}}$ at an angle of $30°$ to the horizontal from a point which is $1.5\,\mathrm{m}$ above ground level. Find when the ball hits the ground and the direction in which it is moving just before it hits the ground.

6) A ball is thrown from ground level so that it just clears a wall $3\,\mathrm{m}$ high when it is moving horizontally. If the initial speed of the ball is $20\,\mathrm{m\,s^{-1}}$, find the angle of projection.

7) A particle is projected at an angle of $30°$ to the horizontal and 2 seconds later is moving in the direction $\arctan \frac{1}{4}$ to the horizontal. Find its initial speed.

8) In Question 7, if the direction of motion is $\arctan(-\frac{1}{4})$, 2 seconds after projection, what is the initial speed?
Also what is the significance of $\arctan(-\frac{1}{4})$?

9) A particle is projected from ground level with an initial velocity of 35 m s^{-1} at an angle of $\arctan \frac{3}{4}$ to the horizontal. Find the time for which the particle is more than 20 m above the ground.

10) A particle is projected from a point O which is 100 m above ground level. The initial velocity is 40 m s^{-1} horizontally. Find the time at which the particle hits the ground and the horizontal distance of this point from the point of projection.

11) A particle is projected from a point O with initial velocity vector $\mathbf{i} + 2\mathbf{j}$. Find the velocity vector and position vector of the particle (a) after t seconds, (b) after $1\frac{1}{2}$ seconds.

12) A particle is projected from a point O and $1\frac{1}{2}$ seconds later it passes through the point whose position vector is $4\mathbf{i} + \mathbf{j}$. Find the initial velocity of the particle.

13) Two seconds after projection from a point O a projectile P passes through a point with position vector $8\mathbf{i} - 12\mathbf{j}$. Find the initial velocity vector of P. Find also the position vector of P after 3 seconds.

14) A particle is projected from a point O with initial velocity vector $3\mathbf{i} - \mathbf{j}$. Find the direction in which it is moving 2 seconds later. Find also the Cartesian equation of its path.

15) A particle is projected from a point O with velocity vector $20\mathbf{i} + 30\mathbf{j}$. 2 seconds later a second particle is projected from O with velocity vector $60\mathbf{i} + 50\mathbf{j}$. Prove that the particles collide 1 second after the projection of the second particle.

16) Two particles are projected simultaneously from a point O in the same vertical plane with angles of projection $30°$ and $60°$ and with the same initial speed of $2\sqrt{3} \text{ m s}^{-1}$. Find the positions of the particles t seconds after projection and hence find the distance between them when $t = 2$.

17) A and B are two points on level ground, 60 m apart. A particle is projected from A towards B with initial velocity 30 m s^{-1} at $45°$ to the horizontal. At the same instant a particle is projected from B towards A with the same initial velocity. Find when the particles collide and the height above the level of AB at which they collide.

18) A particle is projected from a point O with an initial velocity of $20\,\mathrm{m\,s^{-1}}$ and at $\arctan\frac{3}{4}$ to the horizontal. 2 seconds later a second particle is projected from O and it collides with the first particle 1 second after leaving O. Find the initial velocity of the second particle.

19) A particle is projected from a point O with an initial velocity of $21\,\mathrm{m\,s^{-1}}$ at an angle of $\arctan\frac{4}{3}$ to the horizontal and 1 second later another particle is projected from a point 0.3 m below O with an initial velocity of $31.5\,\mathrm{m\,s^{-1}}$ at an angle $\arctan\frac{3}{4}$ to the horizontal. Prove that the particles collide and find when this occurs. Find also the direction in which each particle is moving when they collide.

PARTICULAR PROPERTIES OF PARABOLIC FLIGHT

Certain information about projectiles is required frequently enough to justify obtaining this in general terms.

Consider a particle which is projected from a point O on level ground with a velocity V at an angle α to the horizontal, reaching ground level again at a point A.

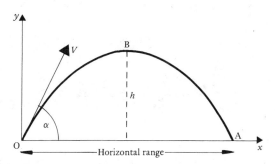

The Time of Flight

This is the time taken for the particle to travel along its path from O to A.

At any time t, $\qquad\qquad y = (V\sin\alpha)t - \tfrac{1}{2}gt^2$

When the particle is at A, $\qquad y = 0$

Therefore $\qquad\qquad (V\sin\alpha)t - \tfrac{1}{2}gt^2 = 0$

$\Rightarrow \qquad\qquad t = 0 \quad\text{or}\quad t = \dfrac{2V\sin\alpha}{g}$

> i.e. the time of flight is $\dfrac{2V\sin\alpha}{g}$

The Greatest Height

This is h in the diagram and is the height at the midpoint of the path.

At any time t, $\qquad\qquad\qquad\qquad \dot{y} = V \sin\alpha - gt$

When the particle is at B, it is moving horizontally, i.e. $\dot{y} = 0$

So $\qquad\qquad V \sin\alpha - gt = 0 \qquad \Rightarrow \qquad t = \dfrac{V \sin\alpha}{g}$

(**Note** that this is half the total time of flight.)

Then $\quad y = V \sin\alpha t - \frac{1}{2}gt^2 \qquad$ gives $\qquad h = \dfrac{V^2 \sin^2\alpha}{g} - \dfrac{V^2 \sin^2\alpha}{2g}$

i.e. the greatest height is given by $\quad h = \dfrac{V^2 \sin^2\alpha}{2g}$

The Horizontal Range

This is the distance from the initial position to the final position on a horizontal plane through the point of projection, i.e. OA.

At any time t, $\quad x = Vt \cos\alpha \qquad$ but, at A, $\qquad t = \dfrac{2V \sin\alpha}{g}$

So, for OA, $\qquad\qquad x = \dfrac{2V^2 \sin\alpha \cos\alpha}{g} = \dfrac{V^2 \sin 2\alpha}{g}$

i.e. the range is $\quad \dfrac{V^2 \sin 2\alpha}{g}$

The Maximum Horizontal Range

For a given value of V, the horizontal range is maximum when the value of $\dfrac{V^2 \sin 2\alpha}{g}$ is greatest. This occurs when $\sin 2\alpha = 1$ i.e. when $\alpha = 45°$.

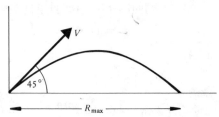

The maximum horizontal range is given by $\dfrac{V^2}{g}$ and it occurs when the angle of projection is $45°$.

Determination of the Angle of Projection

If the projectile has to pass through a particular point with coordinates (a, b) then we use the equation of the path in the form

$$y = x \tan \alpha - \frac{gx^2(1 + \tan^2 \alpha)}{2V^2}$$

giving

$$b = a \tan \alpha - \frac{ga^2(1 + \tan^2 \alpha)}{2V^2}$$

This is a quadratic equation in $\tan \alpha$ so, provided it has two different positive roots, there are two angles of projection for which the path of the projectile will pass through a given point, with a given speed of projection.

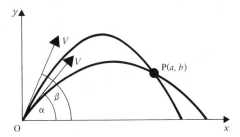

EXAMPLES 9c

[Take g as $10 \, \text{m s}^{-2}$ unless otherwise specified.]

1) A gun has a muzzle velocity of $200 \, \text{m s}^{-1}$ (i.e. a shell leaves the gun with an initial speed of $200 \, \text{m s}^{-1}$). Find the horizontal range of the gun when the angle of projection is $30°$. Find also the maximum horizontal range of the gun.

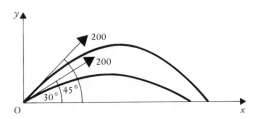

The horizontal range is $\dfrac{V^2 \sin 2\alpha}{g}$

When $\alpha = 30°$, the range is $\dfrac{(200)^2 \sin 60°}{g} = 3460$

The maximum horizontal range occurs when $\alpha = 45°$

Therefore the maximum range is $\dfrac{V^2}{g} = \dfrac{(200)^2}{10} = 4000$

Therefore the horizontal range of the gun is $3460\,\text{m}$ when the angle of projection is $30°$ and the maximum horizontal range is $4000\,\text{m}$.

2) A particle is projected from a point O with an initial speed of $30\,\text{m s}^{-1}$ to pass through a point which is $40\,\text{m}$ from O horizontally and $10\,\text{m}$ above O. Show that there are two angles of projection for which this is possible. If these angles are α and β show that $\tan(\alpha+\beta) = -4$.

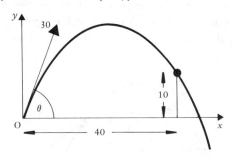

Let the angle of projection of the particle be θ.
The path of the particle has to pass through the point where $x = 40$, $y = 10$.

Using the equation of the path of the projectile in the form

$$y = x\tan\alpha - \frac{x^2 g}{2V^2}(1 + \tan^2\alpha)$$

gives

$$y = x\tan\theta - \frac{x^2}{180}(1 + \tan^2\theta)$$

The point $(40, 10)$ lies on this path so

$$10 = 40\tan\theta - \frac{80}{9}(1 + \tan^2\theta)$$

$\Rightarrow$ $8\tan^2\theta - 36\tan\theta + 17 = 0$ [1]

This is a quadratic equation in $\tan\theta$ with two positive roots. Therefore there are two values of θ less than $90°$, so there are two possible angles of projection.

Now we are asked to calculate $\tan(\alpha+\beta)$ which is equal to $\dfrac{\tan\alpha + \tan\beta}{1 - \tan\alpha\tan\beta}$

where $\tan\alpha$ and $\tan\beta$ are the roots of equation [1].

Hence $\tan\alpha + \tan\beta = \frac{36}{8} = \frac{9}{2}$ (sum of roots)

and $\tan\alpha\tan\beta = \frac{17}{8}$ (product of roots)

Therefore $\qquad\qquad \tan(\alpha+\beta) = \dfrac{\frac{9}{2}}{1-\frac{17}{8}} = -4$

3) An arrow which has an initial speed of $40\,\mathrm{m\,s^{-1}}$ is aimed at a target which is level with it at a distance of $100\,\mathrm{m}$ from the point of projection. Find the least time of flight for the arrow to hit the target.

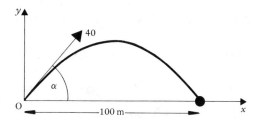

The horizontal range of a projectile is $\dfrac{V^2\sin 2\alpha}{g}$

As the horizontal range is to be $100\,\mathrm{m}$,

$$100 = 160\sin 2\alpha$$

$\Rightarrow \qquad\qquad \sin 2\alpha = \tfrac{5}{8}$

$\Rightarrow \qquad\qquad \alpha = 19.3° \quad \text{or} \quad \alpha = 70.7°$

Therefore there are two possible angles of projection for which the arrow hits the target.

The time of flight is $\qquad \dfrac{2V\sin\alpha}{g} = 8\sin\alpha$

This is least when $\sin\alpha$ has the smaller of its two values, i.e. when $\alpha = 19.3°$

When $\alpha = 19.3°$ the time of flight is $8\sin 19.3°$

Therefore the least time of flight is $2.6\,\mathrm{s}$.

4) In example 3, if the target is a strip which is $3.75\,\mathrm{m}$ high, find the possible values of the angle of projection if the arrow is to hit the target.

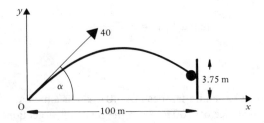

The equation of the path of the arrow is $\quad y = 10^2 \tan\alpha - \dfrac{10^4(1 + \tan^2\alpha)}{320}$

For the arrow to hit the target, $\quad 0 \leqslant y \leqslant 3.75 \quad$ when $\quad x = 100$

i.e. $\qquad\qquad 0 \leqslant 100\tan\alpha - \dfrac{1000}{32}(1 + \tan^2\alpha) \leqslant 3.75$

$\Rightarrow \qquad\qquad 0 \leqslant 800\tan\alpha - 250(1 + \tan^2\alpha) \leqslant 30$

If $\quad 800\tan\alpha - 250(1 + \tan^2\alpha) \leqslant 30 \quad$ we get $\quad 25\tan^2\alpha - 80\tan\alpha + 28 \geqslant 0$

$\Rightarrow \quad (25\tan\alpha - 14)(5\tan\alpha - 2) \geqslant 0 \quad \Rightarrow \quad \tan\alpha \leqslant \frac{2}{5} \quad$ or $\quad \tan\alpha \geqslant \frac{14}{5}$

$\Rightarrow \quad \alpha \leqslant 21.8° \quad$ or $\quad \alpha \geqslant 70.3°$

If $\quad 800\tan^2\alpha - 250\sec^2\alpha \geqslant 0 \quad$ we get $\quad 5\tan^2\alpha - 16\tan\alpha + 5 \leqslant 0$

$\Rightarrow \quad 19.3° \leqslant \alpha \leqslant 70.7°.$

Therefore to hit the target $\quad 19.3° \leqslant \alpha \leqslant 21.8° \quad$ or $\quad 70.3° \leqslant \alpha \leqslant 70.7°$

EXERCISE 9c

[Take g as $10\,\mathrm{m\,s^{-2}}$]

1) A gun has a maximum range of $200\,\mathrm{m}$ on the horizontal. Find the velocity of a shell as it leaves the muzzle of the gun.

2) The maximum range of a gun is $150\,\mathrm{m}$. What is the muzzle velocity and what is the greatest height reached by the shot?

3) A particle is projected from a point O to pass through a point level with O and $50\,\mathrm{m}$ from O. Find the minimum velocity of projection for this to be possible and the greatest height reached with this velocity.

4) A particle is projected at $20°$ to the horizontal and just clears a wall which is $10\,\mathrm{m}$ high and $30\,\mathrm{m}$ from the point of projection. Find the initial speed of the particle.

5) A ball is thrown with an initial velocity of $30\,\mathrm{m\,s^{-1}}$ at $30°$ to the horizontal. It just clears a wall, the foot of which is $25\,\mathrm{m}$ from the point of projection. Find the height of the wall.

6) A particle is projected from a point O with an initial speed of $30 \, \text{m s}^{-1}$ to hit a target which is level with O and 60 m from O. Show that there are two possible angles of projection for which this is possible and find them.

7) A particle is projected from a point O with an initial speed of $50 \, \text{m s}^{-1}$. The particle just clears a wall which is 50 m high and 100 m horizontally from O. Find the two possible angles of projection of the particle.

8) A particle is projected with an initial speed of $60 \, \text{m s}^{-1}$ towards a wall which is 100 m horizontally from the point of projection and 20 m high. Find the least angle of projection for which the particle will pass over the wall.

9) A particle is projected with an initial speed u to pass through a point which is $5u$ horizontally and u vertically from the point of projection. Show that if there are two angles of projection for which this is possible $u^2 > 20(u + 125)$. Find the value of u for which there is only one angle of projection.

10) A gun with a muzzle velocity of $100 \, \text{m s}^{-1}$ is fired from the floor of a tunnel which is 4 m high. Find the maximum angle of projection possible if a bullet is not to hit the roof, and the range of the gun with this angle of projection.

11) A gun is fired to hit a target level with it but 1000 m away. If the muzzle velocity of the gun is $200 \, \text{m s}^{-1}$ and the shell it fires has to pass over a tree 15 m high and 50 m from the gun, find the angle of projection necessary.

12) Show that, with an initial speed u, the maximum horizontal distance that a particle can travel from its point of projection is twice the maximum height it can reach above the point of projection.

13) A particle is projected from a point O with an angle of projection α. Find α if the horizontal range of the particle is five times the greatest height reached by it.

14) A particle is projected inside a tunnel which is 2 m high. If the initial speed is u show that the maximum range inside the tunnel is $4\sqrt{\left(\dfrac{u^2 - 4g}{g}\right)}$.

15) A particle is projected from a point O on level ground towards a smooth vertical wall which is 20 m from O. The particle hits the wall when travelling horizontally. If the speed of projection is $25 \, \text{m s}^{-1}$ find the two possible angles of projection. If the coefficient of restitution between the particle and the wall is $\frac{1}{2}$, find the distance from the foot of the wall of the point where the particle hits the ground.

16) A particle is projected from a point O on level ground towards a smooth vertical wall 30 m from O. The particle hits the wall when travelling horizontally with a speed of $15 \, \text{m s}^{-1}$. Find the initial velocity of the particle.

Show that the time taken by the particle to reach the ground again is independent of the coefficient of restitution between the particle and the wall.

17) A bomb is to be dropped from an aeroplane which is flying steadily at $1000\,\text{m}$ with a speed of $200\,\text{m s}^{-1}$. How far (horizontally) should the plane be from the target before it releases the bomb and how long will it take the bomb to hit the target which is on the ground.

18) Two particles P and Q are fired simultaneously from two points A and B on level ground with speeds of projection u and $2u$ respectively. P is projected so as to achieve its maximum range which is AB. If the particles collide, find the angle of projection of Q. Find also, in terms of u and g, the height at which the particles collide.

19) Two particles are projected simultaneously from two points A and B on level ground and a distance of $150\,\text{m}$ apart. The first particle is projected vertically upwards from A with an initial speed of $u\,\text{m s}^{-1}$ and the second particle is projected from B towards A with an angle of projection α. If the particles collide when they are both at their greatest height above the level of AB, prove that $\tan\alpha = \dfrac{u^2}{150g}$.

20) Two particles are projected simultaneously from a point O with the same initial speed but with angles of elevation α and $90° - \alpha$. Prove that the range of the two particles is the same and show that at any time during their flight the line joining them is inclined at $45°$ to the horizontal.

MULTIPLE CHOICE EXERCISE 9

(Instructions for answering these questions are given on page x.)

TYPE I

1) A ball is thrown with a speed of $20\,\text{m s}^{-1}$ at an angle $\arctan\frac{3}{4}$ to the horizontal. Its horizontal component of velocity two seconds later is:
(a) $4\,\text{m s}^{-1}$ (b) $32\,\text{m s}^{-1}$ (c) 0   (d) $12\,\text{m s}^{-1}$ (e) $16\,\text{m s}^{-1}$.

2) A projectile is given an initial velocity of $\mathbf{i} - 2\mathbf{j}$. Its horizontal component of velocity three seconds later is:
(a) $\sqrt{5}\,\text{m s}^{-1}$ (b) $-2\,\text{m s}^{-1}$ (c) $1\,\text{m s}^{-1}$ (d) $-1\,\text{m s}^{-1}$ (e) $-29\,\text{m s}^{-1}$.

3) A projectile is thrown from a point which is $1\,\text{m}$ above ground level. Taking Oy vertically upward it hits the ground when:
(a) $\dot{x} = 0$ (b) $y = -1$ (c) $y = 1$ (d) $\dot{y} = 0$ (e) $\dot{y} = 1$.

4) A projectile is thrown from ground level with an initial velocity $4\mathbf{i} + 3\mathbf{j}$. It reaches its greatest height above ground level after:
(a) $0.24\,\text{s}$ (b) $0.3\,\text{s}$ (c) $0.18\,\text{s}$ (d) $3\,\text{s}$ (e) $5\,\text{s}$.

5) A projectile is thrown with initial speed of $30\,\mathrm{m\,s^{-1}}$. Its maximum horizontal range is:
(a) $900\,\mathrm{m}$ (b) $30\,\mathrm{m}$ (c) $300\,\mathrm{m}$ (d) $90\,\mathrm{m}$ (e) $9\,\mathrm{m}$.

6) A projectile is given an initial velocity of $\mathbf{i} + 2\mathbf{j}$. The cartesian equation of its path is:
(a) $y = 2x - 5x^2$ (b) $4y = 2x - 5x^2$ (c) $3y = 6x - 25x^2$
(d) $y = 2x + 5x^2$ (e) $4y = 2x + 5x^2$.

7) A stone is thrown from a height of $10\,\mathrm{m}$ above the ground with an initial velocity of $10\,\mathrm{m\,s^{-1}}$ at $30°$ below the horizontal. Taking Oy vertically downward, it hits the ground when:
(a) $\dot{y} = 5$ (b) $\dot{y} = -5$ (c) $\dot{y} = 15$ (d) $\dot{y} = -15$ (e) $\dot{y} = 0$.

TYPE II

8) A particle is projected from ground level. Oy is taken vertically upward. When the particle reaches its greatest height above ground level:
(a) $\ddot{y} = -g$ (b) $\dot{y} = 0$ (c) $\dot{x} = 0$.

9) A projectile is fired with initial speed u so as to achieve the maximum horizontal range.
(a) The equation of its path is $y = x - \dfrac{10x^2}{u^2}$.
(b) The horizontal component of its velocity is $\tfrac{1}{2}u$.
(c) The angle of projection is $45°$.

10) A particle is projected from a point A with initial speed u at an angle α to the horizontal. Its horizontal range is R.
(a) The particle would have the same horizontal range if the angle of projection was $90° - \alpha$.
(b) The time of flight is $\dfrac{R}{u\cos\alpha}$.
(c) The particle reaches a maximum height of $\dfrac{u^2\sin^2\alpha}{2g}$ above A.

11) A projectile is projected from a point O on level ground with initial velocity u at $45°$ to the horizontal. When it hits the ground:
(a) $y = 0$,
(b) It has been in the air for a time $\dfrac{u\sqrt{2}}{10}$,
(c) $x = 0$.

TYPE IV

12) A particle is projected from a point O on level ground towards a wall which it hits normally. Find how far from O the particle hits the ground again.
(a) The coefficient of restitution between the particle and the wall is $\frac{1}{3}$.
(b) The horizontal component of initial velocity is $10\,\text{m s}^{-1}$.
(c) The distance of the wall from O is $30\,\text{m}$.

13) A particle is projected from a point O to hit a target which is level with O. Find the two possible angles of projection.
(a) The target is $100\,\text{m}$ from O.
(b) The mass of the projectile is $0.005\,\text{kg}$.
(c) The initial speed of the projectile is $35\,\text{m s}^{-1}$.

14) A particle is projected towards a wall which it hits normally. Find the time taken by the particle to reach ground level again.
(a) The wall is $20\,\text{m}$ from the point of projection.
(b) The initial speed of the projectile is $30\,\text{m s}^{-1}$.
(c) The coefficient of restitution between particle and wall is $\frac{1}{2}$.

15) A particle is projected so that it just clears a wall. Find the initial velocity of the projectile.
(a) The wall is $5\,\text{m}$ high.
(b) The foot of the wall is $30\,\text{m}$ horizontally from the point of projection.
(c) The particle is moving at an angle of $\arctan\frac{1}{2}$ to the downward vertical as it passes over the wall.

16) Two particles A and B are fired simultaneously towards each other from two points on level ground. Determine whether the particles collide.
(a) The two points of projection are $50\,\text{m}$ apart.
(b) The initial speed of A is $15\,\text{m s}^{-1}$.
(c) The initial speed of B is $30\,\text{m s}^{-1}$.

17) A stone is thrown into the sea from the top of a cliff. Find how far from the base of the cliff the stone hits the sea.
(a) The stone is in the air for 1.5 seconds.
(b) The cliff is $20\,\text{m}$ high.
(c) The initial horizontal component of velocity is $10\,\text{m s}^{-1}$.

MISCELLANEOUS EXERCISE 9

1) A tile slides down a roof inclined at $20°$ to the horizontal starting $3\,\text{m}$ from the edge of the roof. Assuming that the roof is smooth find the horizontal distance from the edge of the roof that the tile hits the ground if the edge of the roof is $8\,\text{m}$ above ground level.

2) Two particles are projected simultaneously from the same point with angles of projection α and β and initial speeds u and v. Show that at any time during their flight the line joining them is inclined to the horizontal at

$$\arctan \frac{u \sin \alpha - v \sin \beta}{u \cos \alpha - v \cos \beta}$$

3) At what point during its flight is the speed of a projectile minimum? A particle is projected from a point O on a horizontal plane with an angle of projection α. Show that the ratio of the greatest speed to the least speed during the flight is $1 : \cos \alpha$.

4) A projectile is fired from a point O. The speed of the projectile when at its greatest height h above O is $\sqrt{(2/5)}$ times its speed when at height $h/2$ above O. Show that the initial angle which the velocity of the projectile makes with the horizontal is $\pi/3$. (U of L)p

5) A ball is projected with speed $20\,\text{m/s}$ at an angle of $60°$ to the horizontal. Find the time taken for the ball to travel $10\,\text{m}$ horizontally. Find also the height of the ball above the level of the point of projection when it has travelled a horizontal distance of $10\,\text{m}$.
[Take g as $10\,\text{m/s}^2$.] (U of L)

6) A particle is projected from a point O with initial speed u to pass through a point which is at a horizontal distance a from O and a distance b vertically above the level of O. Show that there are two possible angles of projection. If these angles are α_1 and α_2 prove that $\tan(\alpha_1 + \alpha_2) = -(a/b)$.

7) A particle is projected with speed $u\,\text{m s}^{-1}$ at an angle α to the horizontal. Find the direction in which it is moving after t seconds. A particle is projected from a point O and after t seconds passes through a point P travelling in a direction perpendicular to the direction of projection. Prove that $OP = \frac{1}{2}gt^2$.
(AEB)

8) A stone thrown upwards from the top of a vertical cliff $56\,\text{m}$ high falls into the sea 4 seconds later, $32\,\text{m}$ from the foot of the cliff. Find the speed and direction of projection. (The stone moves in a vertical plane perpendicular to the cliff.) A second stone is thrown at the same time, in the same vertical plane, at the same speed and at the same angle to the horizontal, but downwards. Find how long it will take to reach the sea and the distance between the points of entry of the stones into the water.
[Take g to be $10\,\text{m/s}^2$.] (U of L)

9) A particle is projected from a point on horizontal ground with velocity V and angle of elevation α. Prove that the greatest height reached above the ground is $\dfrac{V^2}{2g} \sin^2 \alpha$.

A bowler bowls a ball at the wicket which is 20 metres away from him

measured horizontally. The ball leaves his hand 2 metres above the ground and without hitting the ground, passes through a point which is vertically above the wicket and $\frac{3}{4}$ metre vertically above the ground. The highest point reached by the ball is 3 metres above the ground. Find the angle of elevation at which the ball is projected. Show that the angle made with the horizontal by the direction of motion of the ball when it passes over the wicket is arctan $\frac{3}{8}$.
Find the time between the instant when the ball leaves the bowler's hand and the instant when it passes over the wicket.   (C)

10) A particle is projected under gravity with speed V from the point O, the angle of projection being α above the horizontal. The particle rises to a vertical height H above O and its range on the horizontal plane through O is R. Prove that

(a) $H = \dfrac{V^2}{2g} \sin^2 \alpha$ (b) $R = \dfrac{V^2}{g} \sin 2\alpha$

Deduce that $16H^2 - 8R_0 H + R^2 = 0$ where R_0 is the maximum range for the given speed of projection.
Given that $R_0 = 200$ m   and $R = 192$ m,   find the two possible values of H, and the corresponding values of α.   (JMB)

11) A particle is projected with speed u at an elevation α to the horizontal. Calculate the greatest height reached and the horizontal range.
The maximum horizontal range a particle can achieve with an initial speed u is R. If a particle projected with speed u has a horizontal range $\frac{3}{5}R$, calculate the two possible angles of projection. Show that the difference in the maximum heights attained with these angles of projection is $\frac{2}{5}R$.   (AEB)

12) A particle is projected from the origin O with velocity V at an angle of elevation θ to the horizontal. Show that its height y above O when it has travelled a distance x horizontally is given by $y = x \tan \theta - \dfrac{gx^2 \sec^2 \theta}{2V^2}$.

A ball thrown from O with speed 1400 cm/s is caught at a point P, which is 1000 cm horizontally from O and 187.5 cm above the level of O. Find the two possible angles of projection. If the ball is thrown from O with the same initial speed to pass through a point 562.5 cm vertically above P, show that there is only one possible angle of projection.   (U of L)

13) A particle is projected with speed V at an angle α to the horizontal. Show that its greatest height above the point of projection during its flight is $(V^2 \sin^2 \alpha)/(2g)$.   A ball is projected from a point at a height a above horizontal ground, with speed V at an angle α to the horizontal. At the highest point of its flight it impinges normally on a vertical wall and rebounds.
Show that the horizontal distance from the point of projection to the wall is $(V^2 \sin \alpha \cos \alpha)/g$ and that the time taken by the ball to reach the ground after the impact is $\sqrt{(V^2 \sin^2 \alpha + 2ga)/g}$.   (U of L)

14) If a particle is projected with speed u at an angle of elevation α show that the horizontal range is $(u^2 \sin 2\alpha)/g$ and the maximum height attained is $(u^2 \sin^2 \alpha)/2g$.

A golf ball is struck so that it leaves a point A on the ground with speed 49 m/s at an angle of elevation α. If it lands on the green which is the same level as A, the nearest and furthest points of which are 196 m and 245 m respectively from A, find the set of possible values of α. Find also the maximum height the ball can reach and still land on the green.

There is a tree at a horizontal distance 24.5 m from A and to reach the green the ball must pass over this tree. Find the maximum height of the tree if this ball can reach any point on the green.

(Assume the point A, the green and the base of the tree to be in the same horizontal plane.)   (AEB)

15) The height of a vertical mast OP is h high and it stands with O on the horizontal ground.

(a) Two particles are projected simultaneously from P in the same vertical plane with the same speed, but with different angles of projection. Show that the distance between the particles increases uniformly with time.

(b) If a particle is projected vertically upwards from O with velocity V and a second particle is projected at the same instant from P with velocity V and angle of projection θ show that they are at their shortest distance apart after time $h/(2V)$, and find this shortest distance.   (C)

16) A boy throws a ball with initial speed $2\sqrt{(ag)}$ at an angle θ to the horizontal. It strikes a smooth vertical wall and returns to his hand. By considering the vertical motion show that the time of flight is $4(a/g)^{\frac{1}{2}} \sin \theta$. By considering the horizontal motion, show that if the boy is standing at a distance a from the wall the coefficient of restitution between the ball and the wall equals

$$1/(4 \sin 2\theta - 1).$$

Deduce that the angle θ cannot be less than $15°$.   (U of L)

17) Two boys stand on horizontal ground at a distance a apart. One throws a ball from a height $2h$ with velocity V and the other catches it at height h. If θ is the inclination above the horizontal at which the first boy throws the ball, show that $ga^2 \tan^2 \theta - 2V^2 a \tan \theta + ga^2 - 2V^2 h = 0$.

When $a = 2\sqrt{2}h$ and $V^2 = 2gh$, calculate:

(a) the value of θ,

(b) the greatest height attained by the ball above the ground, in terms of h.

                                                                                    (AEB)

18) Two particles are projected with the same speed from the same point. The angles of projection are 2α and α and a time T elapses between the instants of projection. If the particles collide in flight, find the speed of projection in terms of T and α.
If the collision occurs when one of the particles is at its greatest height, show that α is given by $4\cos^4\alpha - \cos^2\alpha - 1 = 0$.   (AEB)

19) Two equal particles are projected at the same instant from points A and B at the same level, the first from A towards B with velocity u at $45°$ above AB, and the second from B towards A with velocity v at $60°$ above BA. If the particles collide directly when each reaches its greatest height, find the ratio $v^2:u^2$ and prove that $u^2 = ga(3 - \sqrt{3})$, where a is the distance AB. After the collision the first particle falls vertically. Show that the coefficient of restitution between the particles is $(\sqrt{3} - 1)(\sqrt{3} + 1)$.   (JMB)

20) A particle is projected with speed V and angle of elevation α from a point O. Show that the equation of the path of the particle, referred to horizontal and vertical axes Ox and Oy respectively in the plane of the path, is

$$y = x\tan\alpha - (g/2V^2)x^2\sec^2\alpha.$$

A particle is projected at an elevation α, where $\tan\alpha = 3$, from a point A on a horizontal plane distant 100 m from the foot of a vertical tower of height 50 m. The particle just clears the tower and lands at a point B on the horizontal plane. Determine the initial speed of the particle and the distance AB. Find also the greatest height reached by the particle above the plane.
[Take g as $10\,\text{m/s}^2$.]   (U of L)

21) A particle is projected with speed u at an angle of elevation α, where $\tan\alpha = 3$. Find, in terms of u and g, the height of the particle when its speed is $\frac{1}{2}u$. Find also the directions in which the particle is moving at this height.
If the velocity of the particle makes an angle of $45°$ with the horizontal at times t_1 and t_2 (where $t_2 > t_1$) after projection, show that $t_2 = 2t_1$.
                                                                                      (U of L)

22) An aircraft is flying with speed V in a direction inclined at an angle α above the horizontal. When the aircraft is at height h, a bomb is dropped. Show that the horizontal distance R, measured from the point vertically below the point at which the bomb is released to the point where the bomb hits the ground, is given by

$$gR = \tfrac{1}{2}V^2\sin 2\alpha + V(2gh + V^2\sin^2\alpha)^{\frac{1}{2}}\cos\alpha.$$ (U of L)

CHAPTER 10

MOTION IN A CIRCLE

TYPES OF ACCELERATION

A body has an acceleration whenever its velocity is not constant. Velocity is a vector quantity however and may change either in magnitude (i.e. speed) or in direction or both. In all cases a force must act on the body to produce an acceleration, the direction of the force determining the particular type of acceleration.

(a) A *change in speed* occurs when a force acts *in the direction of motion* of the body to which it is applied. Such a force cannot cause any change in the direction of the velocity.

(b) A *change in direction* at constant speed is caused by a force *perpendicular to the direction of motion* of the body. Such a force will push or pull the body off its previous course but will not affect the speed since there is no force component in the direction of motion.

(c) If both speed and direction of motion are to be changed a force with components both parallel and perpendicular to the direction of motion is required.

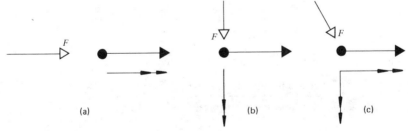

(a)   (b)   (c)

Type (a) Acceleration of this type has already been studied in Chapter 4 and needs no further analysis here.

Types (b) and (c) A body whose direction of motion is not constant traces out a curved path of some sort. The curve described depends upon the forces which are acting on the body.

In this chapter our analysis is concentrated on motion in one particular curve, the circle.

MOTION IN A CIRCLE WITH CONSTANT SPEED

Consider a particle P describing a circle, centre O and radius r, at constant speed v.
As there is no change in speed, no force component acts in the direction of motion, which is tangential at any instant.
A force must be acting on the particle however as the direction of motion is not constant.
This force must therefore act along the radius, producing a radial acceleration.

The Magnitude of the Radial Acceleration

Suppose that the particle travels from a point P_1 to an adjacent point P_2 in time δt and that the angle P_1OP_2 is $\delta\theta$.

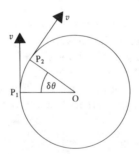

In the direction of $\overrightarrow{P_1O}$, the acceleration is given approximately by

$$\frac{\text{increase in velocity along } \overrightarrow{P_1O} \text{ from } P_1 \text{ to } P_2}{\text{time taken to travel from } P_1 \text{ to } P_2}$$

i.e.

$$\frac{v \sin \delta\theta}{\delta t}$$

Now as $\delta\theta \to 0$, $\sin \delta\theta \to \delta\theta$ and $\dfrac{\delta\theta}{\delta t} \to \dfrac{d\theta}{dt}$

So the acceleration at P_1 towards O is $v\dfrac{d\theta}{dt}$

But $\dfrac{d\theta}{dt}$ is the angular velocity of the particle, which we will denote by ω

and we know from Chapter 4 that $v = r\omega$ or $\omega = \dfrac{v}{r}$.

Hence $v\dfrac{d\theta}{dt} = v\omega = (r\omega)\omega$ or $v\left(\dfrac{v}{r}\right)$,

i.e. the radial acceleration of a particle travelling with constant speed v in a circle of radius r is towards the centre and is of magnitude

$$\frac{v^2}{r} \quad \text{or} \quad r\omega^2$$

It therefore follows that a particle can describe a circle with constant speed only when it is acted upon by a *force of constant magnitude towards the centre* producing a radial acceleration whose constant magnitude is $\dfrac{v^2}{r}$ or $r\omega^2$.

Note that it is only the *magnitude* of the acceleration that is constant. The acceleration itself is not constant as its direction is continuously changing.

EXAMPLES 10a

1) A particle of mass m is attached by a light inextensible string of length l to a fixed point A on a smooth horizontal table. If it is travelling with constant angular velocity ω in a circle what is the tension in the string and the reaction with the table?

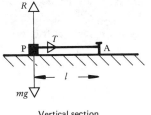 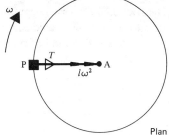

Vertical section
Plan

In this problem the force acting on the particle towards the centre is T, the tension in the string. As the particle is travelling in a horizontal circle, its vertical acceleration is zero.

Vertically   (zero acceleration) $R = mg$

Horizontally   (Force = mass × acceleration) $T = ml\omega^2$

Therefore $\begin{cases} \text{Tension} = ml\omega^2 \\ \text{Reaction} = mg \end{cases}$

2) A car of mass M is turning a corner of radius r. The coefficient of friction between the wheels and the horizontal road surface is μ. What is the maximum speed at which the car can turn the corner without skidding?

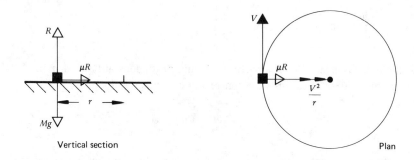

Vertical section   Plan

At maximum speed the central acceleration is also greatest and requires the maximum frictional force. Hence, at maximum speed V, friction is limiting.

Vertically   (zero acceleration) $R = Mg$

Horizontally   (Force = mass × acceleration) $\mu R = \dfrac{MV^2}{r}$

Eliminating R gives $\mu = \dfrac{MV^2}{rMg} = \dfrac{V^2}{rg}$

Therefore at maximum speed $V = \sqrt{\mu rg}$

Note. The frictional forces associated with the motion of a vehicle are quite complex. At this stage we are considering only the friction that acts perpendicular to the direction of motion; this is called the *lateral* friction.

EXERCISE 10a

1) A particle of mass m kg is travelling at constant speed v m s^{-1} round a circle of radius r m.
(a) If $v = 8$ and $r = 2$ find the magnitude of the central acceleration.
(b) If the force acting towards the centre of the circle is of constant magnitude 6 N, $m = 4$ and $v = 3$, find the value of r.

2) A circular tray of radius 0.2 m has a smooth vertical rim round the edge. The tray is fixed on a horizontal table and a small ball of mass 0.1 kg is set moving round the inside of the rim of the tray with speed 4 m s^{-1}. Calculate the horizontal force exerted on the ball by the rim of the tray.

3) A car of mass $400\,\text{kg}$ can turn a corner at $40\,\text{km h}^{-1}$ without skidding but at $50\,\text{km h}^{-1}$ it does skid. If the corner is an arc of a circle of radius $20\,\text{m}$, find values between which μ, the coefficient of friction between the wheels and the road surface, can lie.

4) A disc is free to rotate in a horizontal plane about an axis through its centre O. A small object P is placed on the disc so that $OP = 0.2\,\text{m}$. Contact between the particle and the disc is rough and the coefficient of friction is 0.5. The disc then begins to rotate. Find the angular velocity of the disc when the particle is about to slip.

5) A particle of mass $0.4\,\text{kg}$ is attached to one end of a light inextensible string of length $0.6\,\text{m}$. The other end is fixed to a point A on a smooth horizontal table. The particle is set moving in a circular path.
(a) If the speed of the particle is $8\,\text{m s}^{-1}$ calculate the tension in the string and the reaction with the table.
(b) If the string snaps when the tension in it exceeds $50\,\text{N}$, find the greatest angular velocity at which the particle can travel.

Conical Pendulum

Consider an inextensible string of length l which is fixed at one end, A. At the other end is attached a particle P of mass m describing a circle with constant angular velocity ω in a horizontal plane.

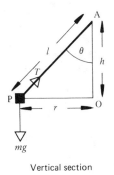

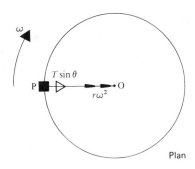

Vertical section   Plan

As P rotates, the string AP traces out the surface of a cone. Consequently the system is known as a *conical pendulum*.

Vertically $T \cos\theta = mg$ [1]

Horizontally $T \sin\theta = mr\omega^2$ [2]

In triangle AOP $\qquad\qquad r = l \sin\theta$ [3]

and $\qquad\qquad\qquad\qquad h = l \cos\theta$ [4]

Several interesting facts can be deduced from these equations:

(a) It is impossible for the string to be horizontal.

This is seen from equation [1] in which $\cos\theta = \dfrac{mg}{T}$ which cannot be zero.

Hence θ cannot be $90°$.

(b) The tension is always greater than mg.
This also follows from equation [1] as $\cos\theta < 1$ (θ is acute but not zero).

Hence $\qquad\qquad\qquad\qquad T > mg$

(c) The tension can be calculated without knowing the inclination of the string since, from equations [2] and [3]

$$T \sin\theta = ml \sin\theta\, \omega^2$$

$\Rightarrow \qquad\qquad\qquad T = ml\, \omega^2$

(d) The vertical depth h of P below A is independent of the length of the string since from equations [1] and [4]

$$T\frac{h}{l} = mg \quad\Rightarrow\quad T = \frac{lmg}{h}$$

But $\qquad\qquad\qquad\qquad T = ml\omega^2$

Therefore $\qquad\qquad\qquad ml\omega^2 = \dfrac{mlg}{h}$

$\Rightarrow \qquad\qquad\qquad h = \dfrac{g}{\omega^2} \qquad$ which is independent of l

EXAMPLES 10b

1) An inextensible string of length 2 m is fixed at one end A and carries at its other end B a particle of mass 3 kg which is rotating in a horizontal circle whose centre is 1 m vertically below A. Find the angular velocity of the particle and the tension in the string.

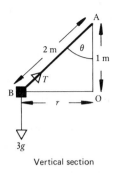

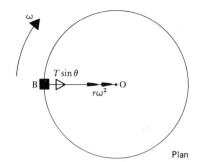

Vertical section   Plan

Vertically	(zero acceleration)	$T \cos \theta = 3g$	[1]
Horizontally	(Newton's Law)	$T \sin \theta = 3r\omega^2$	[2]

In triangle AOB $\begin{cases} \cos \theta = \frac{1}{2} & [3] \\ r = 2 \sin \theta & [4] \end{cases}$

[3] and [4] give $\qquad \theta = \frac{1}{3}\pi; \quad r = \sqrt{3}$

[2] ÷ [1] gives $\qquad \tan \theta = r\omega^2/g$

Hence $\qquad \sqrt{3} = \sqrt{3}\omega^2/g \; \Rightarrow \; \omega^2 = g$

In [1] $\qquad T \times \frac{1}{2} = 3g \qquad \Rightarrow \qquad T = 6g$

The angular velocity is $\sqrt{g}\,\mathrm{m\,s^{-1}}$ and the tension in the string is $6g$ N.

2) Two light inextensible strings AB and BC each of length l are attached to a particle of mass m at B. The other ends A and C are fixed to two points in a vertical line such that A is distant l above C. The particle describes a horizontal circle with constant angular velocity ω.

Find (a) the tension in AB,
      (b) the least value of ω so that both strings shall be taut.

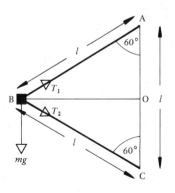

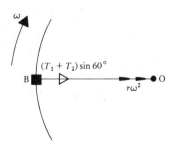

Vertically $\qquad\qquad T_1 \cos 60° = T_2 \cos 60° + mg$ $\qquad$ [1]

Horizontally $\qquad (T_1 + T_2) \sin 60° = mr\omega^2$ $\qquad$ [2]

In triangle AOB $\qquad\qquad r = l \sin 60°$ $\qquad$ [3]

Simplifying [1] gives $\qquad\quad T_1 - T_2 = 2mg$ $\qquad$ [4]

[2] and [3] give $\qquad\qquad T_1 + T_2 = ml\omega^2$ $\qquad$ [5]

[4] and [5] give $\qquad\qquad 2T_1 = 2mg + ml\omega^2$

So the tension in AB is $\quad mg + \frac{1}{2}ml\omega^2$

The string AB can never be slack but the string BC could become slack.
In order that it shall remain taut, T_2 must not become negative, i.e. $T_2 \geqslant 0$

[4] and [5] give $\qquad\qquad\qquad 2T_2 = ml\omega^2 - 2mg$

If $T_2 \geqslant 0$, then $ml\omega^2 \geqslant 2mg$.

Therefore in order that both strings shall be taut, $\omega^2 \geqslant \dfrac{2g}{l}$.

3) A light inextensible string of length $3l$ is threaded through a smooth ring
and carries a particle at each end. One particle A of mass m is at rest at a
distance l below the ring. The other particle B of mass M is rotating in a
horizontal circle whose centre is A. Find the angular velocity of B and find
m in terms of M.

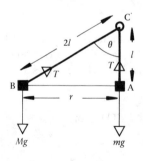
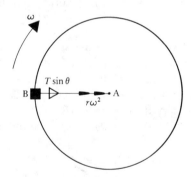

Since two separate particles are involved we must analyse the state of each.
As the ring is smooth, the tension is the same in both sections, BC and AC, of
the string.

For mass A (in equilibrium): $\qquad\qquad T = mg$ $\qquad$ [1]

For mass B:

$\quad$ Vertically $\qquad\qquad\qquad T \cos \theta = Mg$ $\qquad$ [2]

$\quad$ Horizontally $\qquad\qquad\qquad T \sin \theta = Mr\omega^2$ $\qquad$ [3]

In triangle ABC

$$\left\{ \begin{array}{l} \cos\theta = l/2l = \tfrac{1}{2} \qquad\qquad [4] \\ \quad\; r = 2l\sin\theta \qquad\qquad\quad [5] \end{array} \right.$$

[4] and [5] give $\theta = 60°$ and $r = \sqrt{3}l$

In [2] $T(\tfrac{1}{2}) = Mg$ $\Rightarrow$ $T = 2Mg$

But $T = mg$

Therefore $m = 2M$

In [3] $T\dfrac{\sqrt{3}}{2} = M\sqrt{3}l\omega^2$

But $T = 2Mg$ so $Mg\sqrt{3} = M\sqrt{3}l\omega^2$

Therefore $\omega = \sqrt{g/l}$

4) The base of a hollow right cone of semi vertical angle $30°$, is fixed to a horizontal plane. Two particles each of mass m are connected by a light inextensible string which passes through a small smooth hole in the vertex V of the cone. One particle, A, hangs at rest inside the cone. The other particle B moves on the outer smooth surface of the cone at a distance l from V, in a horizontal circle with centre A. Find the tension in the string, the angular velocity of B and the normal reaction between B and the cone.

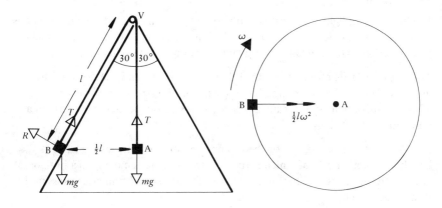

The tension is the same in both portions of string since the hole is smooth.

If the portion BV is of length l, the radius of B's circular path is $l\sin 30° = \dfrac{1}{2}$

For particle A (in equilibrium) $T = mg$ [1]

For particle B

vertically $T \cos 30° + R \sin 30° = mg$ [2]

horizontally $T \sin 30° - R \cos 30° = m\dfrac{l}{2}\omega^2$ [3]

Simplifying, we have: $T = mg$ [1]

$$\sqrt{3}T + R = 2mg$$ [2]

$$T - \sqrt{3}R = ml\omega^2$$ [3]

Eliminating R from [2] and [3] $\Rightarrow$ $4T = 2\sqrt{3}mg + ml\omega^2$

From [1] $4mg = 2\sqrt{3}mg + ml\omega^2$

$\Rightarrow$ $\omega^2 = (4 - 2\sqrt{3})\dfrac{g}{l}$

From [1] and [2] $R = 2mg - \sqrt{3}mg$

$\Rightarrow$ $R = (2 - \sqrt{3})mg$

Therefore the tension in the string is mg,

the angular velocity of B is $\left[\dfrac{2g}{l}(2 - \sqrt{3})\right]^{\frac{1}{2}}$,

and the normal reaction at B is $(2 - \sqrt{3})mg$.

EXERCISE 10b

1) One end of a light inextensible string of length 1 m is fixed. The other end is attached to a particle of mass 0.6 kg which is travelling in a horizontal circular path of radius 0.8 m. What is the angular speed of the particle?

2) A light inelastic string of length 1.2 m, fixed at one end, carries a particle P of mass 2 kg at the other end. If the tension in the string is not to exceed 40 N, what is the maximum angular speed at which the particle can travel in a horizontal circle?

3) A particle of mass m is attached to one end of a light inelastic string of length l the other end of which is fixed. If the particle is moving in a horizontal circle with the string inclined at an angle θ to the vertical find an expression for its angular velocity.

4) A ring of mass 0.6 kg is attached to a point P on a string AB of length 1.4 m, where AP is 0.8 m. The ends A and B are attached to two points 1.0 m apart in a vertical line, A being above B. The ring is made to travel in a horizontal circle with speed $v\,\mathrm{m\,s^{-1}}$.
(a) What is the smallest possible value of v if neither portion of string is slack?
(b) If $v = 4.2\,\mathrm{m\,s^{-1}}$ calculate the tension in the portion AP of the string.

5) A particle of mass m, attached to the end A of a light inextensible string describes a horizontal circle on a smooth horizontal plane. The string is of length $2l$ and the other end B is fixed,

(a) to a point on the plane.

(b) to a point which is at a height l above the plane.

If the angular velocity of the particle is ω, find, in each case, the tension in the string and the reaction between the particle and the plane, giving your answers in terms of m, l and ω.

6) Two particles A and B of masses m and M respectively are connected by a light inelastic string of length $3l$ which passes through a smooth swivel at a fixed height. If A can be made to perform horizontal circles about B as centre while B is at rest at a depth l below the swivel, find the value of $M:m$ and find, in terms of l an expression for the angular velocity of A.

7) Two particles of equal mass are connected by a light inextensible string of length 1 m which passes through a small smooth-edged hole in a smooth horizontal table. One particle hangs at rest at a depth 0.5 m below the hole. The other particle describes a horizontal circle on the table. What is its angular velocity?

8) A smooth ring of mass m is threaded on to a light inelastic string of length $8l$ whose ends are fixed to two points A and B distant $4l$ apart in a vertical line (A above B). Calculate the tension in the string when the ring describes horizontal circles about B as centre.

It is impossible for the ring to describe horizontal circles mid-way between the levels of A and B. Explain why this is so.

9) An elastic string AB of natural length a and modulus of elasticity $2mg$, has one end, A, fixed. A particle of mass m is attached to the end B and performs horizontal circles with angular velocity $\sqrt{3g/4a}$. Find the extension in the string and the cosine of the angle between the string and the vertical.

Banked Tracks

A vehicle which travels round a bend on horizontal ground relies entirely on the frictional force at the wheel base to provide the necessary central force. Because the magnitude of the frictional force is limited, the central acceleration, $\dfrac{v^2}{r}$, and hence the speed of the vehicle, are also limited (see Examples 10a).

If, however, the road surface is not horizontal, this limitation can be overcome to some extent.

Consider a vehicle of mass m travelling at speed V round a bend of radius r on a road which is banked at an angle θ.

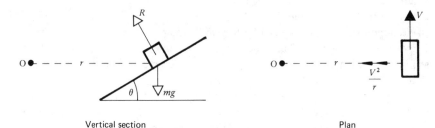

Vertical section   Plan

A force of $R \sin \theta$ acts towards O, the centre of the circular path.

Therefore $\qquad\qquad\qquad\qquad R \sin \theta = \dfrac{mV^2}{r}$ $\qquad\qquad$ [1]

Vertically (no acceleration) $\qquad R \cos \theta = mg$ $\qquad\qquad$ [2]

By eliminating R we see that $\qquad V^2 = rg \tan \theta$

So the vehicle can travel at a speed $V = \sqrt{rg \tan \theta}$ without any tendency to side-slip and V is called the design speed of the track.
The greater the value of θ, the faster the vehicle can round the bend without tending to slip.

If a speed v_1, greater than the design speed, is used then the force $R_1 \sin \theta$ is insufficient to provide the necessary central acceleration. The vehicle will tend to slip outwards from the circular path and a frictional force will oppose this tendency, up to its maximum value of μR_1.

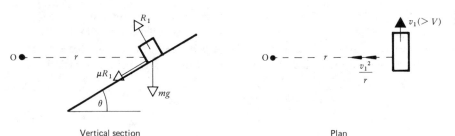

Vertical section   Plan

Towards O (Newton's law) $\qquad\qquad R_1 \sin \theta + \mu R_1 \cos \theta = \dfrac{mv_1^2}{r}$ $\qquad\qquad$ [1]

Vertically (no acceleration) $\qquad\qquad R_1 \cos \theta - \mu R_1 \sin \theta = mg$ $\qquad\qquad$ [2]

Dividing [1] by [2] gives $\qquad\qquad v_1^2 = rg \left(\dfrac{\sin \theta + \mu \cos \theta}{\cos \theta - \mu \sin \theta} \right)$

The vehicle can therefore travel without slipping round the bend at a speed v_1, greater than the design speed $\sqrt{rg\tan\theta}$, when both friction and the banking of the track contribute to the central force.

At a speed v_2, less than $\sqrt{rg\tan\theta}$, the component of reaction, $R_2\sin\theta$, causes an acceleration greater than is required to keep the vehicle on a circular path. In this case the vehicle tends to slip down the banked track; this tendency is opposed by a frictional force acting outwards.

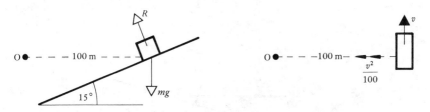

Vertical section   Plan

Towards O (Newton's law) $\qquad R_2\sin\theta - \mu R_2\cos\theta \;=\; \dfrac{mv_2^{\,2}}{r}$ [1]

Vertically (no acceleration) $\qquad R_2\cos\theta + \mu R_2\sin\theta \;=\; mg$ [2]

Dividing [1] by [2] gives $\qquad v_2^{\,2} \;=\; rg\!\left(\dfrac{\sin\theta - \mu\cos\theta}{\cos\theta + \mu\sin\theta}\right)$

This gives the speed v_2 which is the lowest possible speed at which the vehicle can travel round the track without slipping downwards.

EXAMPLES 10c

1) A car is travelling round a section of a race track which is banked at an angle of $15°$. The radius of the track is $100\,\text{m}$. What is the speed at which the car can travel without tending to slip?

If there is no tendency to slip there will be no lateral frictional force.

Horizontally (Newton's law) $\qquad R\sin 15° \;=\; \dfrac{mv^2}{100}$

Vertically (no acceleration) $\qquad R\cos 15° \;=\; mg.$

Hence
$$\tan 15° = \frac{v^2}{100g}$$

i.e.
$$v^2 = 100 \times 9.8 \times 0.2679$$

Therefore the design speed is $16.2 \, \mathrm{m\,s^{-1}}$.

2) A car travelling at $28 \, \mathrm{m\,s^{-1}}$ has no tendency to slip on a track of radius $200 \, \mathrm{m}$ banked at an angle θ. When the speed is increased to $35 \, \mathrm{m\,s^{-1}}$ the car is just on the point of slipping up the track. Calculate the coefficient of friction between the car and the track.

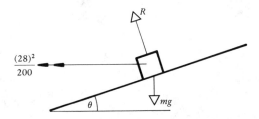

When there is no tendency to slip, no lateral frictional force acts.

Horizontally
$$R \sin \theta = m \frac{(28)^2}{200} \qquad [1]$$

Vertically
$$R \cos \theta = mg \qquad [2]$$

Dividing [1] by [2] gives
$$\tan \theta = \frac{(28)^2}{200 \times 9.8}$$

$\Rightarrow$
$$\tan \theta = 0.4$$

$\Rightarrow$
$$\theta = 21.8°$$

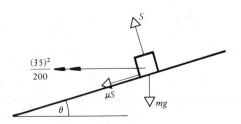

At a speed higher than $28 \, \mathrm{m\,s^{-1}}$ the car tends to slip outwards and friction acts down the slope.

Horizontally $\qquad\qquad S \sin\theta + \mu S \cos\theta = m\dfrac{(35)^2}{200}$ [3]

Vertically $\qquad\qquad\quad S \cos\theta - \mu S \sin\theta = mg$ [4]

Dividing [3] by [4] gives $\qquad \dfrac{\sin\theta + \mu\cos\theta}{\cos\theta - \mu\sin\theta} = \dfrac{(35)^2}{200 \times 9.8}$

Dividing by $\cos\theta$ gives $\qquad \dfrac{\tan\theta + \mu}{1 - \mu\tan\theta} = \dfrac{35 \times 35 \times 10}{200 \times 98}$

But $\quad \tan\theta = 0.4 \quad$ hence $\qquad \dfrac{0.4 + \mu}{1 - 0.4\mu} = \dfrac{5}{8}$

$\Rightarrow \qquad\qquad\qquad\qquad\qquad 3.2 + 8\mu = 5 - 2\mu$

$\Rightarrow \qquad\qquad\qquad\qquad\qquad\quad 10\mu = 1.8$

The coefficient of friction between car and track is 0.18.

3) A railway line is taken round a circular arc of radius $1000\,\mathrm{m}$, and is banked by raising the outer rail $h\,\mathrm{m}$ above the inner rail. If the lateral pressure on the inner rail when a train travels round the curve at $10\,\mathrm{m\,s^{-1}}$ is equal to the lateral pressure on the outer rail when the train's speed is $20\,\mathrm{m\,s^{-1}}$, calculate the value of h. (The distance between the rails is $1.5\,\mathrm{m}$.)

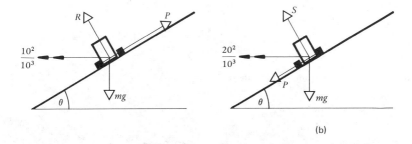

(b)

Let m be the mass of the train and θ the angle at which the rail track is banked.

(a) Horizontally $\qquad R \sin\theta - P \cos\theta = m\dfrac{10^2}{10^3}$ [1]

$\quad$ Vertically $\qquad\quad R \cos\theta + P \sin\theta = mg$ [2]

$\quad$ [1] gives $\qquad\qquad\quad R \sin\theta = \tfrac{1}{10}m + P \cos\theta$

$\quad$ [2] gives $\qquad\qquad\quad R \cos\theta = mg - P \sin\theta$

Dividing gives

$$\frac{\sin\theta}{\cos\theta} = \frac{\frac{1}{10}m + P\cos\theta}{mg - P\sin\theta}$$

Hence $\qquad mg\sin\theta - P\sin^2\theta = \frac{1}{10}m\cos\theta + P\cos^2\theta$

$\Rightarrow \qquad mg\sin\theta - \frac{1}{10}m\cos\theta = P \qquad\qquad (\cos^2\theta + \sin^2\theta = 1)$

(b) Horizontally $\qquad S\sin\theta + P\cos\theta = m\dfrac{20^2}{10^3}$ $\qquad\qquad$ [3]

Vertically $\qquad S\cos\theta - P\sin\theta = mg$ $\qquad\qquad$ [4]

[3] gives $\qquad\qquad S\sin\theta = \frac{4}{10}m - P\cos\theta$

[4] gives $\qquad\qquad S\cos\theta = mg + P\sin\theta$

Dividing gives $\qquad \dfrac{\sin\theta}{\cos\theta} = \dfrac{\frac{4}{10}m - P\cos\theta}{mg + P\sin\theta}$

Hence $\qquad mg\sin\theta + P\sin^2\theta = \frac{4}{10}m\cos\theta - P\cos^2\theta$

$\Rightarrow \qquad\qquad P = \frac{4}{10}m\cos\theta - mg\sin\theta$

Now from part (a) $\qquad P = mg\sin\theta - \frac{1}{10}m\cos\theta$

Therefore $\qquad \frac{4}{10}m\cos\theta - mg\sin\theta = mg\sin\theta - \frac{1}{10}m\cos\theta$

giving $\qquad\qquad \frac{1}{2}m\cos\theta = 2mg\sin\theta$

hence $\qquad\qquad \tan\theta = \dfrac{1}{4g} = 0.0255$

But the distance between the rails is 1.5 m.

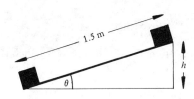

Hence $\qquad h = 1.5\sin\theta$

$\qquad\qquad = 1.5 \times 0.0255 \qquad\qquad (\sin\theta \simeq \tan\theta$ because θ is small)

So the outer rail is raised 0.0383 m above the inner rail.

EXERCISE 10c

1) A road banked at $10°$ goes round a bend of radius 70 m. At what speed can a car travel round the bend without tending to side-slip?

2) At what angle should an aircraft be banked when flying at $100 \, \text{m s}^{-1}$ on a horizontal circle of radius 3000 m?

3) A motor car describes a curve of 120 m radius on a road sloping downwards towards the inside of the curve at $\arctan \frac{1}{5}$. At what speed can the car travel with no tendency to side-slip?

4) On a level race track a car can just go round a bend of radius 80 m at a speed of $20 \, \text{m s}^{-1}$ without skidding. At what angle must the track be banked so that a speed of $30 \, \text{m s}^{-1}$ can just be reached without skidding, the coefficient of friction being the same in both cases? [Take g as $10 \, \text{m s}^{-2}$.]

5) A circular race track is banked at $45°$ and has a radius of 200 m. At what speed does a car have no tendency to side-slip? If the coefficient of friction between the wheels and the track is $\frac{1}{2}$, find the maximum speed at which the car can travel round the track without skidding.

6) An engine of mass 80 000 kg travels at $40 \, \text{km h}^{-1}$ round a bend of radius 1200 m. If the track is level, calculate the lateral thrust on the outer rail. At what height above the inner rail should the outer rail be raised to eliminate lateral thrust at this speed if the distance between the rails is 1.4 m?

7) A bend on a race track is designed with variable banking so that cars on the inside of the track can corner at $80 \, \text{km h}^{-1}$ and those on the outside at $160 \, \text{km h}^{-1}$ without lateral friction. If the inner radius is 150 m and the outer radius 165 m, find the difference between the angles of banking at the inside and outside of the track.

8) The sleepers of a railway track which is turning round a bend of radius 60 m are banked so that a train travelling at $40 \, \text{km h}^{-1}$ exerts no lateral force on the rails. Find the lateral force exerted on the rails by an engine of mass $10^5 \, \text{kg}$:
(a) travelling at $30 \, \text{km h}^{-1}$,
(b) travelling at $50 \, \text{km h}^{-1}$,
(c) at rest.
State in each case whether the force acts on the inner or outer rail.

MOTION IN A CIRCLE WITH VARIABLE SPEED

The velocity of a particle P travelling on a circular path with varying speed, is changing both in magnitude and direction. The particle therefore has *two* acceleration components:

(a) towards the centre of the circle, a component which is the rate of change of direction of the velocity.

Its magnitude at any instant is $\dfrac{v^2}{r}$ (or $r\omega^2$) but it is not constant when v varies.

(b) in the direction of motion, i.e. along the tangent to the circle at P, a component $\dfrac{dv}{dt}$ which is the rate of increase of magnitude of the velocity.

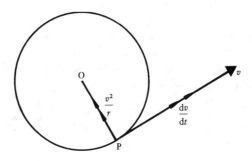

Motion of this type will result when the forces acting on the particle have both radial and tangential components. This situation arises when a particle is describing a circular path in a vertical plane.

MOTION IN A VERTICAL CIRCLE

A particle can be made to travel in a vertical circular path in a variety of ways. Some of these involve driving mechanisms and can be fairly complex. Our study however is limited to simple cases in which the *speed* of the particle, once it is set moving, is not affected by any external force other than weight.
In problems of this type the total mechanical energy of the system remains constant.

Consider the motion of a small bead of mass m threaded on to a smooth wire in the shape of a circle of radius a and centre O. The circle is fixed in a vertical plane and the bead passes the lowest point A on the wire with speed u. It subsequently passes with speed v through another point B where angle BOA is θ.

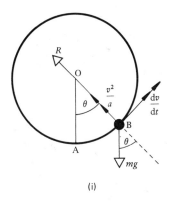

(i)

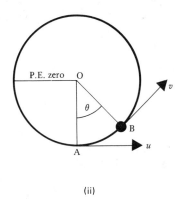

(ii)

Diagram (i) shows the forces acting on the bead, and its acceleration components at B.

The normal reaction R is always perpendicular to the wire and is therefore perpendicular to the direction of motion and does no work. Consequently the total mechanical energy remains constant.

Diagram (ii) shows the velocities and positions of the bead.

Applying Newton's law along radius and tangent at B (diagram (i)) we have:

Radially
$$R - mg\cos\theta = m\frac{v^2}{a} \qquad [1]$$

Tangentially
$$mg\sin\theta = -m\frac{dv}{dt} \qquad [2]$$

Using conservation of mechanical energy (diagram (ii)):

Total M.E. at A is $\frac{1}{2}mu^2 - mga$

Total M.E. at B is $\frac{1}{2}mv^2 - mga\cos\theta$

Therefore $\frac{1}{2}mu^2 - mga = \frac{1}{2}mv^2 - mga\cos\theta$ [3]

Equation [1] shows that R has its greatest value at A,

since $\quad R = mg\cos\theta + \dfrac{mv^2}{a}, \quad \cos\theta \leqslant 1 \quad$ and $\quad v \leqslant u.$

Equation [3] gives, in terms of u, the speed v at any specified position.

Using this expression in equation [1] gives the value of R at that position.

Equation [2] gives the tangential acceleration at a specified position.

These three equations can be used to analyse the motion of a particle describing a vertical circle in slightly different circumstances:

1) A particle attached to one end of a light rod which is free to rotate about a smooth fixed axis through the other end of the rod. In this case, the force, T, in the rod acts in the same way as the reaction, R, between the wire and the bead.

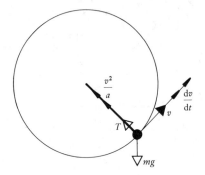

2) A particle rotating on the inside of a smooth circular surface. Again we have a normal reaction R between the surface and the particle.

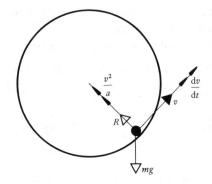

3) A particle rotating at the end of a light string whose other end is fixed. The tension, T, in the string helps to provide the force towards the centre of the circle in this case.

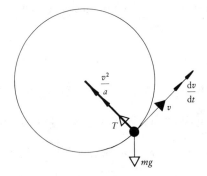

4) A particle moving on the outside of
a smooth circular surface. This case is
rather different from all the others,
since the normal reaction, R, exerted
on the particle always acts outward
from the centre. Hence only the weight
of the particle can provide any force
towards the centre and clearly this can
happen only in the upper part of the
circle. So the particle can remain in
contact with the *upper section only*
of the surface. Equations similar to
those already derived can be found
to analyse this form of circular motion,
as shown below.

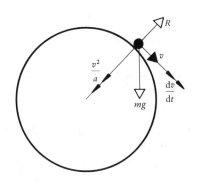

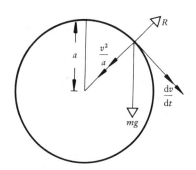

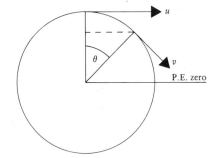

Newton's Law: ↙ $mg \cos\theta - R = \dfrac{mv^2}{a}$ [1]

              ↘ $mg \sin\theta = m\dfrac{dv}{dt}$ [2]

Conservation of M.E. $\tfrac{1}{2}mu^2 + mga = \tfrac{1}{2}mv^2 + mga \cos\theta$ [3]

Although the general analysis of all these cases is similar, there are in fact two
different groups of problems which must now be considered separately:

(a) those in which the particle cannot move off the circular path, e.g. the bead
threaded on the wire and the particle attached to the light rod;

(b) those in which the particle can leave the circular path and travel in some
other way, e.g. the particle at the end of a string or moving on a circular
surface. For these, circular motion is performed only while the string is taut
or the particle is in contact with the surface.

Motion Restricted to a Circular Path

Using the case of the bead threaded on the wire, we see that the bead may:

(a) pass through the highest point of the wire and go on to describe complete circles,

(b) come momentarily to rest before reaching the highest point and subsequently oscillate.

(a) If the bead passes through the highest point, then $v > 0$ at the top.

Using conservation of ME gives

$$\tfrac{1}{2}mu^2 = \tfrac{1}{2}mv^2 + 2mga$$

$$\Rightarrow \quad v^2 = u^2 - 4ga$$

But $\quad v > 0$

Hence $\quad u^2 > 4ga$

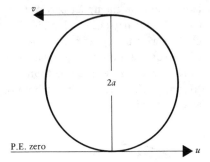

(b) If the bead comes momentarily to rest at some point A, then

$v = 0$ when $\theta = \alpha$

Using conservation of M.E. gives

$$\tfrac{1}{2}mu^2 = mga(1 - \cos\alpha)$$

$$\Rightarrow \quad \cos\alpha = 1 - \frac{u^2}{2ga}$$

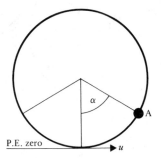

Note: *Because the bead cannot leave the wire,* the only condition necessary for it to describe complete circles is that *its velocity is greater than zero at the highest point.* If the velocity were to become zero at the top, the particle would remain there in unstable equilibrium.

EXAMPLES 10d

1) A particle of mass 2 kg is attached to the end B of a light rod AB of length 0.8 m which is free to rotate in a vertical plane about the end A. If the end B, when vertically below A, is given a horizontal velocity of 3 m s^{-1} show that the particle will not describe complete circles. Find the angle through which it oscillates and the greatest stress in the rod during the motion.

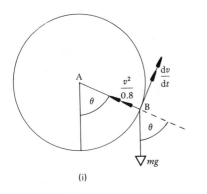

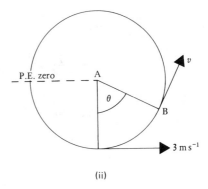

(i) (ii)

Using conservation of mechanical energy (diagram (ii)) gives

$$\tfrac{1}{2} \times 2 \times 3^2 - 2g(0.8) = \tfrac{1}{2} \times 2 \times v^2 - 2g(0.8)\cos\theta$$

If $v = 0$, $\qquad 2g(0.8)\cos\theta = 2g(0.8) - 9$

$$\Rightarrow \qquad\qquad \cos\theta = \frac{15.68 - 9}{15.68} = 0.425$$

Therefore $v = 0$ when $\theta = 64.8°$ and the particle comes to rest before it reaches the top of the circular path. So the particle oscillates through $129.6°$

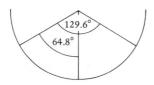

Applying Newton's law towards the centre (diagram (i)) gives

$$T - 2g\cos\theta = \frac{2 \times v^2}{0.8}$$

T is greatest when $\theta = 0$ and $v = 3$.

Therefore the maximum tension is $\left(\dfrac{18}{0.8} + 2g\right) N = 42.1\ N$

2) A small bead of mass $2\ kg$ is threaded on to a smooth circular wire of radius $0.6\ m$, which is fixed in a vertical plane. If the bead is slightly disturbed from rest at the highest point of the wire, find its speed when it reaches the lowest point. Find also the height above the centre, of the point at which the reaction between the bead and the wire becomes zero.

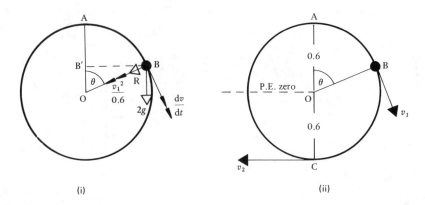

(i)   (ii)

Using conservation of mechanical energy from A to C gives

$$0 + 2g(0.6) = \tfrac{1}{2}(2v_2{}^2) - 2g(0.6) \tag{1}$$

$\Rightarrow$ $$v_2 = 4g(0.6)$$

Therefore the speed at the lowest point is $4.84\,\mathrm{m\,s^{-1}}$.

Applying Newton's law radially at B gives

$$R + 2g\cos\theta = \frac{2v_1{}^2}{0.6} \tag{2}$$

Using conservation of mechanical energy from A to B gives

$$0 + 2g(0.6) = \tfrac{1}{2}(2v_1{}^2) + 2g(0.6\cos\theta) \tag{3}$$

If B is the point where the reaction becomes zero, [2] gives

$$v_1{}^2 = 0.6g\cos\theta$$

Then [3] becomes

$$2g(0.6) = 0.6g\cos\theta + 1.2g\cos\theta$$

$\Rightarrow$ $$\cos\theta = \tfrac{2}{3}$$

Hence $$OB = \tfrac{2}{3}(0.6)\,\mathrm{m} = 0.4\,\mathrm{m}$$

The point where the reaction is zero is $0.4\,\mathrm{m}$ above the centre.

Note. Below the level of B the reaction between the bead and the wire acts towards the centre but above this level, where $\cos\theta > \tfrac{2}{3}$, R is negative showing that the reaction acts outwards, away from the centre.

3) A light rod of length l is free to rotate in a vertical plane about one end. A particle of mass m is attached to the other end.
When the rod is hanging at rest vertically downward, an impulse is applied to the particle so that it travels in complete vertical circles. Find the range of possible values of the impulse and the tangential acceleration when the rod is inclined at $60°$ to the downward vertical.

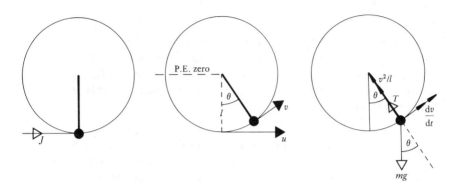

First, using   impulse $=$ change in momentum we have

$$J = mu \qquad\qquad [1]$$

Using conservation of mechanical energy gives

$$\tfrac{1}{2}mu^2 - mgl = \tfrac{1}{2}mv^2 - mgl \cos\theta \qquad\qquad [2]$$

Applying Newton's law tangentially gives

$$-mg \sin\theta = m\frac{dv}{dt} \qquad\qquad [3]$$

If the particle is to describe complete circles, $v > 0$ when $\theta = 180°$

When $\theta = 180°$,   [2] gives $v^2 = u^2 - 2gl + 2gl \cos 180°$

$\Rightarrow$ $\qquad\qquad\qquad\qquad\qquad v^2 = u^2 - 4gl$

But $v > 0$ therefore $u^2 > 4gl$

$\Rightarrow$ $\qquad\qquad\qquad\qquad\qquad u > 2\sqrt{gl}$ $\qquad\qquad$ (u cannot be negative)

Hence, from [1] $\qquad\qquad\qquad J > 2m\sqrt{gl}$

Therefore the value of the impulse must exceed $2m\sqrt{gl}$

When $\theta = 60°$,   equation (3) becomes $mg\dfrac{\sqrt{3}}{2} = m\dfrac{dv}{dt}$

So the tangential acceleration is $\tfrac{1}{2}g\sqrt{3}$

EXERCISE 10d

1) A light rod of length 1 m is smoothly pivoted about a horizontal axis through one end A. A particle of mass 2 kg attached to the other end B is released from the position when B is vertically above A. Find the tension in the rod and the velocity of the particle when AB makes an angle with the upward vertical of:
(a) 90°   (b) 120°   (c) 180°.

2) A bead of mass 1.5 kg is threaded on to a smooth circular wire of radius 1.5 m fixed in a vertical plane. The bead is projected from the lowest point on the wire with speed (a) $\sqrt{4g}$ m s^{-1} (b) $\sqrt{6g}$ m s^{-1} (c) $\sqrt{8g}$ m s^{-1}.
In each case determine in what way the bead moves on the wire (giving particular care to part (a)) and calculate the greatest value of the reaction between the bead and the wire.

3) A particle of mass m is attached to the end A of a light rod AB of length l, free to rotate in a vertical plane about the end B. The rod is held with A vertically above B and the particle is projected from this position with a horizontal velocity u. When the particle at A is vertically below B it collides with a stationary particle of mass $2m$ and coalesces with it. If the rod goes on to perform complete circles find the range of possible values of u.

4) A small bead of mass m is free to slide on a smooth circular wire of radius a fixed in a vertical plane. If the bead is slightly disturbed from rest at the highest point of the wire, find the reaction between the bead and the wire, the velocity of the bead and the resultant acceleration of the bead, when the bead has rotated through
(a) 90°   (b) 120°   (c) 180°.

5) A light rod AB of length 1 m is free to rotate in a vertical plane about an axis through A. A particle of mass 1 kg is attached to B. If the particle is projected from its lowest position with speed $3\sqrt{4.9}$ m s^{-1}, show that the particle describes complete circles. Find the vertical height above A of the end B when the stress in the rod is zero.

6) Two beads A and B of masses m and $2m$ respectively are free to slide in a vertical plane round a smooth circular wire of radius a and centre O. The bead A is at rest at the lowest point C of the wire while B is released from rest at a point on the same level as O. If the coefficient of restitution between the beads is $\frac{1}{2}$, find the height above C to which each particle rises after impact.

Motion not Restricted to a Circular Path

As an example of this case let us consider the motion of a particle rotating at one end of a light string fixed at its other end.

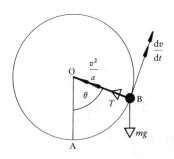
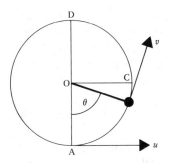

This time the particle can travel in one of three ways. It may:

(a) pass through D while the string is still taut and go on to describe complete circles;
(b) oscillate below the level of O, the string always being taut within this lower semi-circle;
(c) cease to travel on the circle at some point between C and D when the string becomes slack, subsequently moving as a projectile until the string becomes taut again.

Using Newton's law and conservation of mechanical energy in the diagrams above we get

$$T - mg \cos\theta \ = \ \frac{mv^2}{a} \qquad\qquad [1]$$

and $\qquad \frac{1}{2}mu^2 - mga \ = \ \frac{1}{2}mv^2 - mga \cos\theta \qquad\qquad [2]$

Hence $\qquad\qquad T \ = \ mg \cos\theta + \frac{mv^2}{a}$

$\Rightarrow \qquad\qquad T \ = \ mg \cos\theta + \frac{m}{a}(u^2 - 2ga + 2ga \cos\theta)$

$\Rightarrow \qquad\qquad T \ = \ m\left(\frac{u^2}{a} - 2g + 3g \cos\theta \right)$

(a) For complete circles, *the string must be taut* in the highest position
   i.e. $T \geqslant 0$ when $\theta = 180°$.

Hence $\qquad\qquad \frac{u^2}{a} \ \geqslant \ 2g - 3g \cos 180°$

$\Rightarrow \qquad\qquad u^2 \ \geqslant \ 5ga$

Note: It is not sufficient in this case that $v > 0$ at the highest point, as the particle could be moving *inside* the circle with velocity v when $\theta = 180°$.

The essential condition is $T \geqslant 0$ when $\theta = 180°$

(b) For oscillations the particle comes momentarily to rest at a point on, or below, the level of the centre O, i.e. $v = 0$ when $\theta \leqslant 90°$.

In equation [2] $\cos\theta = 1 - \dfrac{u^2}{2ga}$ when $v = 0$

But $\theta \leqslant 90°$ so $\cos\theta \geqslant 0$ hence $u^2 \leqslant 2ga$.

In both (a) and (b), the string is always taut.

If u is the velocity at the lowest point, the ranges of values for which the string never goes slack, and the particle therefore never leaves a circular path, are:

$$u \leqslant \sqrt{2ga} \quad \text{and} \quad u \geqslant \sqrt{5ga}$$

(c) Circular motion ceases at the instant when the string becomes slack, i.e. when $T = 0$. The angle θ at this instant is given by using

$$T = m\left(\frac{u^2}{a} - 2g + 3g\cos\theta\right) = 0$$

$$\Rightarrow \qquad \cos\theta = \frac{2ga - u^2}{3ga}$$

Once the string is slack, the only force acting on the particle is its own weight and the motion continues as that of a projectile.

This situation arises only if $90° < \theta < 180°$ (i.e. above the level of the centre).

In this case $0 > \cos\theta > -1$

giving $0 > \dfrac{2ga - u^2}{3ga} > -1$

Hence the range of values of u for which the string *does* go slack is

$$\sqrt{2ga} < u < \sqrt{5ga}$$

Note. It is most important, when tackling a problem on vertical circular motion, to decide whether or not the particle can leave the circular path or is restricted to it. The special conditions that can be applied are different in these two cases.

EXAMPLES 10e

1) A particle of mass 2 kg is moving on the inside surface of a smooth hollow cylinder of radius 0.2 m whose axis is horizontal. Find the least speed which the particle must have at the lowest point of its path if it travels in complete circles.

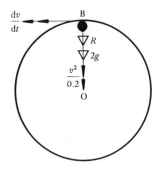
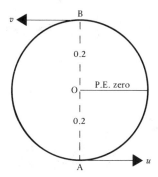

Applying Newton's law along BO we have

$$R + 2g = 2\left(\frac{v^2}{0.2}\right) \qquad [1]$$

Conservation of mechanical energy from A to B gives

$$(\tfrac{1}{2})(2u^2) - 2g(0.2) = (\tfrac{1}{2})(2v^2) + 2g(0.2) \qquad [2]$$

From [1] and [2] $R + 2g = 10(u^2 - 0.8g)$

or $R = 10u^2 - 10g$

But, for complete circles, $R \geqslant 0$ at B (i.e. contact is not lost at any point).

Therefore $10u^2 - 10g \geqslant 0 \Rightarrow u^2 \geqslant g$

Hence the least value of u is $\sqrt{g} = \sqrt{9.8}$

So the least speed at A is $3.1\,\mathrm{m\,s^{-1}}$

2) A particle of mass $\tfrac{1}{2}$ kg is suspended from a fixed point A by a light inelastic string of length 1 m. When in its lowest position it is given a horizontal speed of $8\,\mathrm{m\,s^{-1}}$.
(a) Prove that it performs complete circles.
(b) Find the ratio of the greatest to the least tension in the string.
(c) Calculate the tangential acceleration of the particle when the string is horizontal.

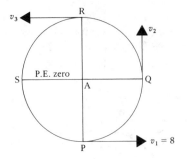

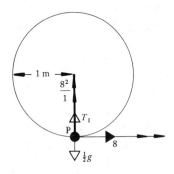

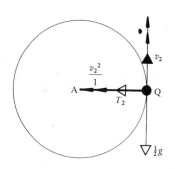

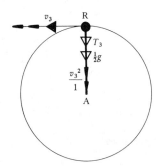

(a) Applying Newton's law radially at R we have

$$T_3 + \tfrac{1}{2}g = \tfrac{1}{2}\left(\frac{v_3{}^2}{1}\right)$$ [1]

Conservation of mechanical energy from P to R gives

$$(\tfrac{1}{2})(\tfrac{1}{2})(8^2) - (\tfrac{1}{2})(g)(1) = (\tfrac{1}{2})(\tfrac{1}{2})(v_3{}^2) + (\tfrac{1}{2})(g)(1)$$ [2]

Hence $T_3 + \tfrac{1}{2}g = 32 - 2g$

$\Rightarrow$ $T_3 = 32 - (\tfrac{5}{2})(9.8) > 0$

Therefore the string is taut at the highest point on the circle and the particle will describe complete circles.

(b) Maximum tension, T_{max}, occurs at P (i.e. T_1)
    and minimum tension, T_{min}, occurs at R (i.e. T_3)

Applying Newton's law radially at P gives

$$T_1 - \tfrac{1}{2}g = \tfrac{1}{2} \times \frac{8^2}{1}$$

Therefore $T_{max} = (32 + 4.9) = 36.9$

We already know that $\qquad T_{min} = (32 - 24.5) = 7.5$

Therefore $\qquad T_{max} : T_{min} = 36.9 : 7.5 \simeq 5 : 1$

(c) Applying Newton's law tangentially at Q gives

$\uparrow$ $$-\tfrac{1}{2}g = \tfrac{1}{2}\frac{dv}{dt}$$

Hence $$\frac{dv}{dt} = -g$$

The tangential acceleration when the string is horizontal is of magnitude g.

3) A particle of mass m rests at the highest point of the outer surface of a smooth cylinder of radius a whose axis is horizontal. If the particle is slightly disturbed from rest so that it begins to travel in a vertical circle find the vertical distance travelled by the particle before it leaves the surface of the cylinder. After leaving the cylinder how far does the particle fall while travelling a distance a horizontally?

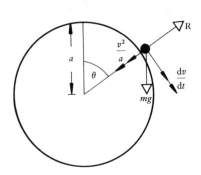 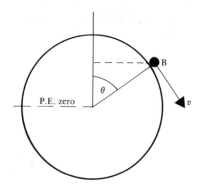

Applying Newton's law radially at B we have

$$mg\cos\theta - R = \frac{mv^2}{a} \qquad [1]$$

Conservation of mechanical energy from A to B gives

$$0 + mga = \tfrac{1}{2}mv^2 + mga\cos\theta \qquad [2]$$

From [1] and [2] $\qquad R = mg\cos\theta - \frac{m}{a}(2ga - 2ga\cos\theta)$

The particle is about to leave the surface at C, when $R = 0$ and $\theta = \alpha$

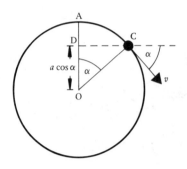

i.e. when $\quad 0 = 3mg \cos \alpha - 2mg$

$\Rightarrow \qquad \cos \alpha = \frac{2}{3}$

Then $\quad AD = a - a \cos \alpha = \frac{1}{3}a$

So the particle descends a vertical distance $\frac{1}{3}a$ before leaving the cylinder.

The velocity of the particle at the instant when it leaves the surface is given by using $\cos \alpha = \frac{2}{3}$ in equation 2,

i.e. $\qquad\qquad v^2 = 2ga(1 - \frac{2}{3}) = \frac{2}{3}ga$

The particle now begins to travel as a projectile from C with initial horizontal and vertical velocity components of $\quad v \cos \alpha \quad$ and $\quad v \sin \alpha$

But $\quad \cos \alpha = \frac{2}{3} \quad$ so $\quad \sin \alpha = \sqrt{(1 - \frac{4}{9})} = \frac{1}{3}\sqrt{5}$

Hence the velocity components at C are $\qquad \frac{2}{3}\sqrt{\frac{2}{3}ga} \quad$ and $\quad \frac{1}{3}\sqrt{\frac{10}{3}ga}$

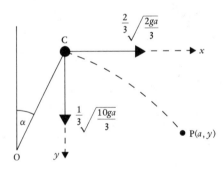

If the particle, travelling as a projectile, reaches a point $P(a, y)$ in time t then:

$$a = \frac{2}{3}t\sqrt{\frac{2}{3}ga} \qquad \text{and} \qquad y = \frac{1}{3}t\sqrt{\frac{10}{3}ga} + \frac{1}{2}gt^2$$

Hence $\qquad y = \frac{1}{3}\sqrt{\frac{10}{3}ga}\left(\frac{3}{2}a\sqrt{3/2ga}\right) + \frac{1}{2}g\left(\frac{3}{2}a\sqrt{3/2ga}\right)^2$

or $\qquad y = (\frac{\sqrt{5}}{2} + \frac{27}{16})a$

The particle therefore travels a vertical distance $\frac{1}{16}a(8\sqrt{5} + 27)$ while moving a horizontal distance a from C.

4) A particle P of mass m is attached by a light inextensible string of length $2a$ to a fixed point O. When vertically below O, P is given a horizontal velocity u. When OP becomes horizontal the string hits a small smooth rail, Q, distant a from O and the particle continues to rotate about Q as centre. If the particle just describes complete circles about the rail, find the value of u.

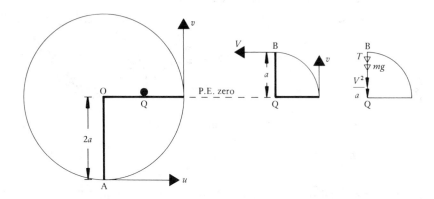

There is no loss in mechanical energy when the string hits the rail Q because the sudden change in tension is perpendicular to the direction of motion of the particle and therefore has no effect on its speed.

Conservation of mechanical energy from A to B gives

$$\tfrac{1}{2}mu^2 - mg(2a) = \tfrac{1}{2}mV^2 + mga \qquad [1]$$

Applying Newton's law radially at B we have

$$T + mg = m\frac{V^2}{a} \qquad [2]$$

Hence

$$T + mg = \frac{m}{a}(u^2 - 6ga)$$

$$\Rightarrow \qquad T = \frac{m}{a}(u^2 - 7ga)$$

For complete circles about Q, $\quad T \geqslant 0$ at B

i.e. $\qquad u^2 \geqslant 7ga$

If the particle *just* describes complete circles

$$u = \sqrt{7ga}$$

5) A smooth hollow cylinder of radius a and centre O, is fixed with its axis horizontal. A particle P of mass m is projected from a point on the inside surface of the cylinder, level with O, with speed $\sqrt{14ga}$ vertically downward. When P reaches the lowest point of the surface it collides with and adheres to a stationary particle Q also of mass m. Find the height above the centre of the cylinder at which the combined mass loses contact with the surface.

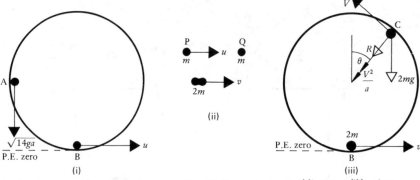

(ii)

(i)

(iii)

Conservation of mechanical energy for P from A to B (diagram (i)) gives

$$\tfrac{1}{2}m(14ga) + mga = \tfrac{1}{2}mu^2$$

$\Rightarrow$ $$u = 4\sqrt{ga}$$

At impact between P and Q, we use conservation of linear momentum

(diagram (ii))

$\Rightarrow$ $$m(4\sqrt{ga}) + 0 = 2mv$$

$\Rightarrow$ $$v = 2\sqrt{ga}$$

Now for the particle of mass $2m$ (diagram (iii)) conservation of mechanical energy from B to C gives

$$\tfrac{1}{2}(2m)(2\sqrt{ga})^2 = \tfrac{1}{2}(2m)V^2 + 2mga + 2mga \cos\theta$$

Applying Newton's Law radially at C we have

$$2mg \cos\theta + R = 2mV^2/a \qquad\qquad [2]$$

The particle leaves the surface when $R = 0$

so that $$2mg \cos\theta = 2mV^2/a$$

In equation [1] $$4mga = m(ag \cos\theta) + 2mga + 2mga \cos\theta$$

$\Rightarrow$ $$\cos\theta = \tfrac{2}{3}$$

The particle leaves the cylinder at a height $a \cos\theta$ above the centre,

i.e. $\tfrac{2}{3}a$ above the centre.

SUMMARY

1) A particle travelling in a vertical circle of radius r has two acceleration components:

$$\frac{v^2}{r} \text{ towards the centre and } \frac{dv}{dt} \text{ along the tangent.}$$

2) A particle which is restricted to the circular path will travel in complete circles if the velocity u at the lowest point satisfies $u^2 > 4gr$.

3) A particle which is free to leave the circular path must satisfy a condition which will ensure that the particle is always at a distance r from the centre of the circle, for example contact with the inside of a circular surface must not be lost. In this case $u^2 \geqslant 5gr$.

EXERCISE 10e

1) A particle of mass $2\,\text{kg}$ is attached to the end A of a light inextensible string AB fixed at B. Initially AB is horizontal and the particle is projected vertically downward from this position with velocity v. If the particle describes complete circles, find the possible values of v if the length of the string is $1\,\text{m}$.

2) A particle of mass m is projected horizontally from the highest point of a smooth solid sphere. If the particle loses contact with the surface after descending a vertical distance of one quarter of the radius a of the sphere, find the speed of projection.

3) A smooth hollow cylinder of radius $0.5\,\text{m}$ is fixed with its axis horizontal. A particle of mass $1.2\,\text{kg}$ is projected from the lowest point on the inner surface with speed (a) $3\,\text{m s}^{-1}$ (b) $4\,\text{m s}^{-1}$ (c) $5\,\text{m s}^{-1}$. Determine in each case whether the particle will oscillate, describe complete circles or lose contact with the cylinder.

4) A particle of mass m is free to rotate at the end of a light inextensible string fixed at its other end. If the length of the string is l and the particle is projected horizontally from its lowest position with speed $\sqrt{6gl}$, find the greatest and least tensions in the string during the ensuing motion. Find also the *resultant* acceleration of the particle when it is:
(a) at its lowest position,
(b) at its highest position,
(c) level with the fixed end of the string.

5) A particle of mass $1.5\,\text{kg}$ is lying at the lowest point of the inner surface of a hollow sphere of radius $0.5\,\text{m}$ when it is given a horizontal impulse. Find the magnitude of the impulse:
(a) if the particle subsequently describes complete vertical circles,
(b) if the particle loses contact with the sphere after rotating through $120°$.

6) A light inextensible string AB of length l is fixed at A and is attached to a particle of mass m at B. B is held a distance l vertically above A and is projected horizontally from this position with speed $\sqrt{2gl}$. When AB is horizontal, a point C on the string strikes a fixed smooth peg so that the radial acceleration of the particle is instantaneously doubled. Express the length of AC in terms of l.

The particle continues to describe vertical circles about C as centre. Compare the greatest and least tensions in the string during this motion.

MULTIPLE CHOICE EXERCISE 10

(The instructions for answering these questions are given on page x.)

TYPE I

1) A particle of mass m is travelling at constant speed v round a circle of radius r. Its acceleration is:

(a) rv^2 (b) $\dfrac{mv^2}{r}$ (c) $\dfrac{v^2}{r}$ (d) mrv^2.

2) A string of length l has one end fixed and a particle of mass m attached to the other end travels in a horizontal circle of radius r. The tension in the string is:

(a) mg (b) $\dfrac{mgl}{\sqrt{l^2-r^2}}$ (c) $mg\dfrac{r}{l}$ (d) $mg\dfrac{l}{r}$.

3) A bead is threaded on to a circular wire fixed in a vertical plane. The bead travels round the wire. The acceleration of the bead is:
(a) towards the centre and constant,
(b) towards the centre and varies,
(c) made up of two components one radial and one tangential,
(d) away from the centre and varies.

4) A vehicle can travel round a curve at a higher speed when the road is banked than when the road is level. This is because:
(a) banking increases the friction,
(b) banking increases the radius,
(c) the normal reaction has a horizontal component,
(d) when the track is banked the weight of the car acts down the incline.

5) A particle hanging at the end of a string of length a is given a horizontal velocity V so that it begins to travel in a vertical circle. The particle will describe complete circles if:

(a) $V \geqslant \sqrt{4ga}$ (b) $V < \sqrt{5ga}$ (c) $V > \sqrt{2ga}$ (d) $V \geqslant \sqrt{5ga}$.

TYPE II

6) A string of length l has one end fixed and a particle of mass m is attached to the other end. If the particle describes a horizontal circle at an angular speed ω:
(a) the tension in the string $= m/\omega^2$,
(b) the speed of the particle is $l\omega$,
(c) the resultant force acting on the particle has no vertical component.

7) A particle of mass m travelling in a vertical circle at the end of an inelastic string of length l will perform complete circles provided that:
(a) the kinetic energy at the lowest point is at least $2mgl$,
(b) the speed is zero only at the highest point,
(c) the string never goes slack,
(d) the string does not break until its tension exceeds $6mg$.

8) A bead is travelling on a smooth circular wire in a vertical plane and has a speed V at the lowest point.
(a) The mechanical energy of the bead is constant.
(b) No external forces on the bead.
(c) The bead will oscillate if $V < 2\sqrt{ga}$.
(d) The bead will oscillate only if $V < \sqrt{2ga}$.

9) A particle of mass m is on a smooth table travelling with angular speed ω in a horizontal circle at the end of a string of length l whose other end is fixed. T is the tension in the string.
(a) T is constant.
(b) $T = ml\omega^2$.
(c) $T = mg$.
(d) T is the resultant force acting on the particle.

TYPE III

10) (a) A particle is travelling in a circle.
    (b) A particle is travelling with constant velocity.

11) A particle is describing a vertical circle of radius a and the speed V at the lowest point is such that $\sqrt{4ga} < V < \sqrt{5ga}$.
(a) The particle is not free to leave the circular path.
(b) Complete circles are described.

12) A light rod of length l is rotating in a vertical plane about an axis through one end. A particle is attached to the other end.
(a) The rod is at all times in tension.
(b) The greatest speed of the particle is between $\sqrt{2gl}$ and $\sqrt{5gl}$.

TYPE IV

13) A particle at the end of a string is travelling as a conical pendulum. Calculate the tension in the string if:
(a) the angular velocity is $2 \, \text{rad s}^{-1}$,
(b) the length of the string is 1.5 m,
(c) the inclination of the string to the vertical is $30°$.

14) Find the angle at which a race track should be banked to enable a car to go round at a speed V without tendency to side-slip.
(a) The radius of the track is r,
(b) the mass of the car is m,
(c) the coefficient of friction is μ.

15) A particle is moving in a vertical plane on the inside of a smooth hollow cylinder. Determine where the particle loses contact with the cylinder.
(a) The velocity at the lowest point is $4 \, \text{m s}^{-1}$,
(b) the mass of the particle is 2 kg,
(c) the radius of the cylinder is 1 m.

TYPE V

16) A particle travelling in a circle of radius r has an acceleration of constant magnitude $\dfrac{v^2}{r}$ towards the centre. Therefore the particle has a constant velocity.

17) A particle travelling in a vertical plane must either oscillate or describe complete circles.

18) Every particle describing a circle has a resultant acceleration towards the centre.

19) One end A of a light inextensible string is attached to a fixed point. A particle suspended at the other end B can describe horizontal circles about A as centre.

MISCELLANEOUS EXERCISE 10

1) A race track has a circular bend of radius 50 m and is banked at $40°$ to the horizontal. If the coefficient of friction between the car wheels and the track is $\frac{3}{5}$, find within what speed limits a car can travel round the bend without slipping either inwards or outwards.

2) A particle of mass m is connected by an inextensible light string of length l to a fixed point on a smooth horizontal table. The string breaks when subject to a tension whose magnitude exceeds mg. Find the maximum number of revolutions per second that the particle can make without breaking the string.

(U of L)p

3) A particle, moving on the smooth inside surface of a fixed spherical bowl of radius 2 m, describes a horizontal circle at a distance $8/5$ m below the centre of the bowl. Prove that the speed of the particle is $3\,\text{m}\,\text{s}^{-1}$.
[Take g as $10\,\text{m}\,\text{s}^{-2}$.]   (U of L)p

4) A car moves with constant speed in a horizontal circle of radius r on a track which is banked at an angle α to the horizontal, where $\tan\alpha = \frac{3}{4}$. The coefficient of friction between the tyres and the track is $\frac{1}{2}$. Find, in terms of r and g, the range of speeds at which the car can negotiate this bend without the tyres slipping on the road surface. Show that the greatest possible speed is $\sqrt{11}$ times the least possible speed. (It may be assumed that the car will not overturn at these speeds.)   (U of L)

5) A particle is held at a point P on the surface of a smooth fixed sphere of radius $2a$ and centre O, where PO makes an angle $30°$ with the upward vertical. If the particle is released from rest at P find the height above O of the point where the particle loses contact with the sphere. Find also the horizontal distance of the particle from O when it is level with O.

6) A particle A of mass m is held on the surface of a fixed smooth solid sphere centre O and radius a at a point P such that OP makes an acute angle $\arccos\frac{3}{4}$ with the upward vertical, and is then released. Prove that, when OA makes an angle θ with the upward vertical, the velocity v of the particle is given by

$$v^2 = \tfrac{1}{2}ga(3 - 4\cos\theta)$$

provided that the particle remains on the surface of the sphere, and find the normal reaction on the particle at this time.
Deduce that the particle leaves the surface when OA makes an angle $\frac{1}{3}\pi$ with the upward vertical.   (O)

7) A light inextensible string AB has length $7a$ and breaking tension $4mg$. A particle of mass m is fastened to the string at a point P, where AP $= 4a$. The ends A and B are secured to fixed points, A being at a height $5a$ vertically above B. If the particle is revolving in a horizontal circle with both portions of the string taut, show that the time of one revolution lies between

$$3\pi\sqrt{\frac{a}{5g}} \quad \text{and} \quad 8\pi\sqrt{\frac{a}{5g}} \qquad \text{(U of L)}$$

8) A light inextensible string of length l is threaded through a smooth bead of mass m and has one end fixed at a point A on a smooth horizontal table and the other at a point B at a height $\frac{1}{2}l$ vertically above A. The bead is projected so as to describe a circle in contact with the table with angular velocity ω. Find the radius of the circle. Prove that the tension in the string is $\frac{15}{64}ml\omega^2$, and that ω must not exceed a certain value. Find this value.   (JMB)

9) A heavy particle is projected horizontally with speed u from the lowest point on the inside of a hollow smooth sphere of internal radius a. Show that the least value of u for the particle to complete a vertical circle is $\sqrt{5ga}$. The particle projected with this velocity, hits a rubber peg after travelling a distance $\frac{3}{2}\pi a$, the coefficient of restitution between the peg and the particle being $\frac{1}{2}$. Calculate the vertical height of the particle above the point of projection at the moment when it leaves the surface of the sphere. (AEB)

10) A particle A of mass m hangs by a light inextensible string of length a from a fixed point O. The string is initially vertical and the particle is then given a horizontal velocity $\sqrt{(nga)}$. Show that it will move round a complete circle in a vertical plane provided $n \geqslant 5$.
If when the string OA reaches the horizontal the particle A collides and coalesces with a second particle at rest also of mass m, find the least value of n for the vertical circle to be completed. (U of L)

11) A light inelastic string of length a has one end fixed at O and a particle of mass m attached to the other end. The particle describes a circle in a horizontal plane below O with constant angular velocity ω so that the string makes an angle θ with the vertical through O. Write down the equations of motion and show that $\cos\theta = g/a\omega^2$.
The string is now replaced with an elastic string of unstretched length a and modulus λmg and the particle is set in motion so that it rotates in a horizontal circle with the same angular velocity ω as before. Prove that, if the string is inclined at an angle α to the vertical, then

$$\cos\alpha = (\lambda g - a\omega^2)/\lambda a\omega^2$$

12) Two light inelastic strings AP and BP connect a particle P to fixed points A and B. The point B is vertically above A and $AB = AP = l$ and $BP = l\sqrt{3}$. The particle P moves in a horizontal circle with constant speed. The least angular speed of P for both strings to be taut is ω. At this speed calculate the angle between the strings and the value of ω. When the angular speed of P is ω_1 ($> \omega$) the tensions in the string are equal. Show that $\omega_1^2 = 2g/(l\sqrt{3})$. (AEB)

13) The sleepers on a railway line which rounds a circular bend are banked so that at speed V an engine would exert no lateral thrust on the rails. The thrust on the inner rail when the engine's speed is v_1 is equal to the thrust on the outer rail when the speed is v_2 ($v_2 > V > v_1$). Show that $2V^2 = v_1^2 + v_2^2$.

14) A particle moves in a vertical circle on the smooth inner surface of a fixed hollow sphere of radius a and centre O, the plane of the circle passing through O. The particle is projected from the lowest point of the sphere with initial velocity u, and leaves the surface of the sphere at a point P, where OP makes an angle θ with the upward vertical through O. Show that

$$\cos\theta = \frac{u^2 - 2ga}{3ga}$$

If $\cos\theta = \frac{4}{5}$, show that after leaving the sphere the particle will pass the vertical line through O at a distance above O of $\frac{115}{128}a$.   (C)

15) One end of a light inelastic string is attached to a point A vertically above a point O on a smooth horizontal plane and at a height h above it. The string carries a particle P of mass m at its other end. When just taut the string is inclined to the vertical at an angle α.
(a) If P moves in a horizontal circle, centre O, with speed v, show that
   $v^2 \leqslant hg \tan^2\alpha$.
(b) One end of a light elastic string of natural length h and modulus of elasticity $\frac{1}{4}mg$ is now attached to a fixed point below the plane at a distance h from O. The other end is passed through a small smooth hole at O and is attached to P. If P describes a circle on the plane with both strings taut, and if the reaction of P on the plane is $\frac{1}{2}mg$, find an expression for the speed v of P in terms of h, g and α.

16) Two rigid, light rods AB, BC, each of length $2a$, are smoothly jointed at B, and the rod AB is smoothly jointed at A to a fixed smooth vertical rod. The joint at B carries a particle of mass m. A small ring, also of mass m, is smoothly jointed to BC at C and can slide on the vertical rod below A. The ring rests on a smooth horizontal ledge fixed to the vertical rod at a distance $2a$ below A, as shown in the diagram.

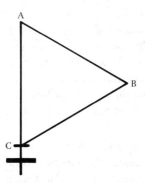

The system rotates about the vertical rod with constant angular velocity ω. Find the force exerted by the ledge on the ring, and deduce that if the ring remains on the ledge, then $a\omega^2 \leqslant 3g$.   (JMB)

17) A smooth hemispherical bowl with centre O and of radius a is fixed with its rim upwards and horizontal. A particle P of mass $3m$ describes a horizontal circle on the inner surface of the bowl with angular velocity ω. This mass is attached to one end of a light inextensible string of length $2a$. The string passes through a smooth hole at the lowest point of the bowl. At the other end of the string is attached a particle of mass m which moves as a conical pendulum in a horizontal circle with angular velocity ω. By considering the motion of the second particle show that the motion is possible only if $\omega^2 > g/b$, where b is the length of string outside the bowl.

If the angle made by OP with the vertical is $60°$, show that $\omega^2 = 6g/a$, and find, as a multiple of mg, the reaction between the first particle and the bowl.

(C)

18) A particle of mass m is attached to one end of a light inelastic string of length l. The other end of the string is held at a height h (less than l) above a smooth horizontal table. If the particle is held on the table with the string taut and is projected along the table so that it moves in a horizontal circle with uniform speed v, prove that the force that it exerts on the table is given by

$$m\left(g - \frac{v^2 h}{l^2 - h^2}\right)$$

Find an expression for T, the tension in the string, in terms of m, v, l, h.
If $h = 0.3$ m   and $l = 0.5$ m   and $m = 2$ kg,
(a) find the force exerted on the table when the speed is $1 \, \mathrm{m\,s^{-1}}$
(b) find the maximum velocity for which the particle will remain on the table and the corresponding tension of the string.

19) One end of a light inextensible string of length l is attached to a fixed point A and the other end to a particle B of mass m which is hanging freely at rest.

The particle is then projected horizontally with velocity $\sqrt{7gl/2}$. Calculate the height of B above A when the string goes slack.

The procedure is repeated but this time a small smooth peg C is placed at the same level as A so that when the string is horizontal it comes into contact with the peg. If the particle then describes a complete circle about C, find the least value of AC. When AC has this least value find the tension in the string immediately before and after the string strikes the peg.   (U of L)

20) A particle moves with constant speed v in a circle of radius r. Show that the acceleration of the particle is v^2/r directed towards the centre of the circle.

A rough horizontal plate rotates with constant angular velocity ω about a fixed vertical axis. A particle of mass m lies on the plate at a distance $5a/4$ from this axis. If the coefficient of friction between the plate and the particle is $\frac{1}{3}$ and the particle remains at rest relative to the plate, show that $\omega \leqslant \sqrt{4g/15a}$

The particle is now connected to the axis by a horizontal light elastic string, of natural length a and modulus $3mg$. If the particle remains at rest relative to the plate and at a distance $5a/4$ from the axis, show that the greatest possible angular velocity of the plate is

$$\sqrt{\left(\frac{13g}{15a}\right)}$$

and find the least possible angular velocity. (JMB)

21) One end of a light inelastic string of length a is attached to a fixed point A and a particle of mass m is attached to the other end, B. The particle is held at the same level as A, at a distance of $a \sin \alpha$ away from A, and released. Find:
(a) the impulse in the string when it becomes taut,
(b) the speed of the particle immediately after the string becomes taut,
(c) the cosine of the angle between the string and the vertical when the particle first comes to instantaneous rest.

22) A particle P of mass m moves in a vertical circle along the smooth inner surface of a fixed hollow sphere of internal radius a and centre O, the plane of the circle passing through O. The particle is projected from the lowest point of the sphere with a horizontal velocity u, where $u^2 > 2ga$. When OP makes an angle θ with the upward vertical, the velocity of the particle is v and the normal reaction between the particle and the sphere is R. Find expressions for v and R in terms of m, a, u, θ and g.
Show that if $u^2 < 5ga$ the particle leaves the sphere where

$$\cos \theta = \frac{u^2 - 2ga}{3ga}$$

If the particle leaves the sphere at a point A and its trajectory meets the sphere again at a point B such that AB is a diameter of the sphere, show that OA makes an angle of $45°$ with the vertical, and find the requisite value of u. (C)

23) Particles P and Q of equal mass are connected by a light inelastic string of length l threaded through a small hole O in a smooth horizontal table. The particle P is free to move on the table and describes a horizontal circle so that OP rotates with constant angular velocity ω. The particle Q moves below the table, with the string taut, in a horizontal circle with the same angular velocity ω. Prove that $OP = l/2$. Find the angle which OQ makes with the vertical and show that $\omega^2 > 2g/l$. (U of L)

24) A particle moves with constant speed v in a circle of radius r. Show that the acceleration of the particle is v^2/r directed towards the centre of the circle. A particle P of mass $2m$ is attached by a light inextensible string of length a to a fixed point O and is also attached by another light inextensible string of length a to a small ring Q of mass $3m$ which can slide on a fixed smooth vertical wire passing through O. The particle P describes a horizontal circle with OP inclined at an angle $\frac{1}{3}\pi$ with the downward vertical.
(a) Find the tensions in the strings OP and PQ.
(b) Show that the speed of P is $(6ga)^{\frac{1}{2}}$.
(c) Find the period of revolution of the system.   (JMB)

25) A smooth, hollow circular cone of semi-angle α, is fixed with its axis vertical and its vertex A downwards. A particle P, of mass m, moving with constant speed V, describes a horizontal circle on the inner surface of the cone in a plane which is at a distance b above A.
(a) Show that $V^2 = gb$.
(b) If P is attached to one end of a light elastic string PQ of natural length a and modulus of elasticity mg, find V^2 if (i) Q is attached to A;
    (ii) Q is passed through a small hole at A and is attached to a particle of mass m hanging freely in equilibrium.

26) A smooth wire bent into the form of a circle of radius a is fixed with its plane vertical. A small ring of mass m which can slide freely on the wire is attached to one end of a light elastic string of natural length a and modulus $4mg$, the other end of the string being tied to the highest point of the wire. The ring is held at the lowest point of the wire with the string taut and is then slightly displaced. Write down the equation of energy when the radius to the ring makes an angle θ with the downward vertical and deduce that the maximum velocity occurs when $\cos\theta = -1/9$.
Find the velocity of the ring when the string first becomes slack.   (U of L)

27) Prove that the potential energy of a light elastic string of natural length l and modulus λ when stretched to a length $(l+x)$ is $\frac{1}{2}\lambda x^2/l$.
A bead of mass m can slide without friction along a circular hoop of radius a which is fixed in a vertical plane. The bead is connected to the highest point of the hoop by a light elastic string of natural length a and modulus $3mg$. Initially the bead is moving with speed u through the lowest point of the hoop. Given that $u^2 = ag$, show that the bead just reaches the highest point of the hoop. Show that the speed was u at the instant when the string first went slack and find the reaction of the hoop on the bead at that instant.   (JMB)

28) The ends of a light string are fixed to two points A, B in the same vertical line, with A above B, and the string passes through a small smooth ring of mass m. The ring is fastened to the string at a point P, and when the string is taut the angle APB is a right angle, the angle BAP is θ and the distance of P from AB is r. The ring revolves in a horizontal circle with constant angular velocity ω and with the string taut. Find the tensions in the two parts of the string in terms of r, ω, m, g and θ.
Given that   AB $= 5a$,   AP $= 4a$,   show that

$$16a\omega^2 > 5g$$

If the ring is free to move on the string, instead of being fastened, show that it will remain in the same position on the string as before if the angular velocity Ω satisfies the equation

$$12a\Omega^2 = 35g$$

In this case give the period of the motion in terms of a, g and π.   (JMB)

29) A car undergoing trials is moving on a horizontal surface around a circular bend of radius 50 m at a steady speed of $14 \, \mathrm{m \, s^{-1}}$. Calculate the least value of the coefficient of friction between the tyres of the car and the surface.
Find the angle to the horizontal at which this bend should be banked in order that the car can move in a horizontal circle of radius 50 m around it at $14 \, \mathrm{m \, s^{-1}}$ without any tendency to side-slip.
Another section of the test area is circular and is banked at $30°$ to the horizontal. The coefficient of friction between the tyres of the car and the surface of this test area is 0.6. Calculate the greatest speed at which the car can move in a horizontal circle of radius 70 m around this banked test area.
[Take the acceleration due to gravity to be $10 \, \mathrm{m \, s^{-2}}$.]   (AEB)

30) A light inextensible string of length $3a$ has one end fixed at a point A and the other end fixed at a point B which is vertically below A and at a distance $2a$ from it. A small ring R of mass m is threaded on the string.
(a) If R is fixed to the mid-point of the string and moves in a horizontal circle with speed $\sqrt{(5ga)}$, find the tensions in the parts AR and BR of the string.
(b) If R is free to move on the string and moves in a horizontal circle centre B with the string taut, show that $BR = 5a/6$ and find the speed of R.
    (U of L)

31) A particle P, of mass m, is suspended from a fixed point O by a light elastic string of natural length l. In equilibrium, P hangs at a depth $3l/2$ below O. Find the modulus of elasticity of the string.
The particle P is set in motion and describes a horizontal circle with uniform angular speed and with the string inclined at $60°$ to the vertical. Find the tension in the string, the radius of the circle and the angular speed.   (U of L)

CHAPTER 11

GENERAL MOTION OF A PARTICLE

MOTION IN A STRAIGHT LINE

Consider a particle moving in a straight line such that, at time t, its displacement from a fixed point on that line is s, its velocity is v and its acceleration is a.

Now acceleration is the rate of increase of velocity so we can say

$$a = \frac{dv}{dt}$$

Also velocity is the rate of increase of displacement, so

$$v = \frac{ds}{dt}$$

Conversely

$$v = \int a\,dt \quad \text{and} \quad s = \int v\,dt$$

When a is constant these equations give rise to the formulae derived in Chapter 4, which can be used to analyse the motion of the particle but it is essential to appreciate that these formulae apply only to *constant* acceleration. In all cases where the acceleration is variable, calculus must be used to solve the appropriate differential equations.

The relationships defined above can be used directly to solve problems in which acceleration, velocity and displacement vary with time.

Consider, for instance, a particle moving along a straight line with an acceleration of $a\,\mathrm{m\,s^{-2}}$ at time t seconds where $a = 3t^2 - 2$. If initially the particle is at O, a fixed point on the line, with a velocity $2\,\mathrm{m\,s^{-1}}$ then

using $\qquad a = 3t^2 - 2 \quad$ and $\quad v = \displaystyle\int a\,dt$

we have $\qquad\qquad\quad v = \displaystyle\int (3t^2 - 2)\,dt = t^3 - 2t + c$

but $\quad v = 2 \quad$ when $\quad t = 0,\quad$ therefore $\quad c = 2$

$\Rightarrow \qquad\qquad\qquad\quad v = t^3 - 2t + 2$

Also $\qquad\qquad\qquad\quad s = \displaystyle\int v\,dt$

$\Rightarrow \qquad\qquad\quad s = \displaystyle\int (t^3 - 2t + 2)\,dt = \frac{t^4}{4} - t^2 + 2t + c_1$

$s = 0 \quad$ when $\quad t = 0,\quad$ therefore $\quad c_1 = 0$

$\Rightarrow \qquad\qquad\qquad\quad s = \tfrac{1}{4}t^4 - t^2 + 2t$

An alternative way of expressing this solution is given below.

Using $\quad a = 3t^2 - 2 \quad$ and $\quad a = \dfrac{dv}{dt}$

we have $\qquad\qquad\quad \dfrac{dv}{dt} = 3t^2 - 2$

Separating the variables gives

$$\int dv = \int (3t^2 - 2)\,dt$$

Now starting with $\quad v = 2 \quad$ and $\quad t = 0 \quad$ and moving to a general time t and a general velocity v, a definite integral can be produced, i.e.

$$\int_2^v dv = \int_0^t (3t^2 - 2)\,dt$$

$\Rightarrow \qquad\qquad\qquad v - 2 = t^3 - 2t$

$\Rightarrow \qquad\qquad\qquad v = t^3 - 2t + 2$

Then, using $\quad v = \dfrac{ds}{dt},\qquad \dfrac{ds}{dt} = t^3 - 2t + 2$

$\Rightarrow \qquad\qquad\quad \displaystyle\int_0^s ds = \int_0^t (t^3 - 2t + 2)\,dt$

$\Rightarrow \qquad\qquad\qquad s = \tfrac{1}{4}t^4 - t^2 + 2t$

EXAMPLES 11a

1) A particle moving in a straight line has an acceleration of $(3t-4)\,\mathrm{m\,s^{-2}}$ at time t seconds. The particle is initially 1 m from O, a fixed point on the line, with a velocity of $2\,\mathrm{m\,s^{-1}}$. Find the times when the velocity is zero. Find also the displacement of the particle from O when $t = 3$.

Using $a = \dfrac{dv}{dt}$ gives

$$\frac{dv}{dt} = 3t - 4$$

$\Rightarrow$
$$\int_0^v dv = \int_0^t (3t - 4)\,dt$$

$\Rightarrow$
$$v - 2 = \frac{3t^2}{2} - 4t$$

$\Rightarrow$
$$v = \frac{3t^2}{2} - 4t + 2$$

The velocity is zero when $\quad \dfrac{3t^2}{2} - 4t + 2 = 0$

i.e. when $\quad\quad (3t - 2)(t - 2) = 0$

$\Rightarrow$
$$t = \tfrac{2}{3} \quad \text{or} \quad 2$$

Using $\dfrac{ds}{dt} = v$ we have $\quad \dfrac{ds}{dt} = \dfrac{3t^2}{2} - 4t + 2,$

$\Rightarrow$
$$\int_1^s ds = \int_0^3 \left(\frac{3t^2}{2} - 4t + 2 \right) dt$$

$\Rightarrow$
$$s - 1 = \left[\frac{t^3}{2} - 2t^2 + 2t \right]_0^3 = 1\tfrac{1}{2}$$

$\Rightarrow$
$$s = 2\tfrac{1}{2}$$

Therefore the particle is $2\tfrac{1}{2}$ m from O when $t = 3$.

2) A particle starts from rest and travels in a straight line with an acceleration $\cos \pi t$ where t is the time. Find the distance covered by the particle in the interval of time from $t = 2$ to $t = 3$.

$$a = \frac{dv}{dt} = \cos \pi t \quad \Rightarrow \quad \int_0^v dv = \int_0^t \cos \pi t \, dt$$

Hence
$$v = \frac{1}{\pi} \sin \pi t$$

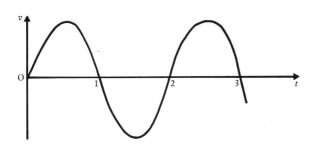

From the sketch of the velocity–time graph it can be seen that the velocity is never negative for the interval of time from $t = 2$ to $t = 3$:
i.e. the particle is moving in the same direction throughout this interval of time. Therefore if s_2 is the displacement of the particle from its initial position when $t = 2$ and s_3 is its displacement when $t = 3$, then $s_3 - s_2$ is the *distance* travelled by the particle in the interval $t = 2$ to $t = 3$.

$$v = \frac{ds}{dt} = \frac{1}{\pi} \sin \pi t \quad \Rightarrow \quad \int_{s_2}^{s_3} ds = \int_2^3 \frac{1}{\pi} \sin \pi t \, dt$$

$$\Rightarrow \quad s_3 - s_2 = \left[-\frac{1}{\pi^2} \cos \pi t \right]_2^3 = \frac{2}{\pi^2}$$

So the particle travels a distance of $\dfrac{2}{\pi^2}$ units between $t = 2$ and $t = 3$.

3) A particle moves in a straight line with an acceleration which is inversely proportional to t^3 where t is the time, measured in seconds. If the particle has a velocity of $3 \, \text{m s}^{-1}$ when $t = 1$ and the velocity approaches a limiting value of $5 \, \text{m s}^{-1}$, find an expression for the velocity at any time t.

$$a = \frac{k}{t^3} \quad \text{where } k \text{ is a constant.}$$

Using
$$\frac{dv}{dt} = \frac{k}{t^3} \quad \Rightarrow \quad \int_3^v dv = \int_1^t \frac{k}{t^3} dt$$

Hence
$$v - 3 = -\frac{k}{2t^2} + \frac{k}{2}$$

$\Rightarrow$
$$v = 3 + \frac{k}{2} - \frac{k}{2t^2}$$

The limiting value of the velocity is the value approached as the time increases indefinitely.

As $\quad t \to \infty, \quad \dfrac{k}{2t^2} \to 0, \quad$ therefore $\quad v \to 3 + \dfrac{k}{2}$

$\Rightarrow$
$$3 + \frac{k}{2} = 5$$

$\Rightarrow$
$$k = 4$$

$\Rightarrow$
$$v = 5 - \frac{2}{t^2}$$

EXERCISE 11a

1) A particle moving in a straight line starts from rest at a point O on the line and t seconds later has an acceleration $(t-6)\,\text{m s}^{-2}$. Find expressions for the velocity and displacement of the particle from O at time t and 6 seconds after leaving.

2) A particle moves in a straight line with an acceleration $2t\,\text{m s}^{-2}$ at time t. If it starts from rest at a point O on the line, find its velocity and displacement from O at time t.

3) A particle moves in a straight line with an acceleration $(3t-1)\,\text{m s}^{-2}$ where t is the time. If the particle has a velocity of $3\,\text{m s}^{-1}$ when $t = 2$ find its velocity at time t and when $t = 5$.

4) A particle moves in a straight line with velocity $v\,\text{m s}^{-1}$ at time t seconds where $v = 3t^2 - 1$. Find the increase in displacement of the particle for the interval $t = 2$ to $t = 3$.

5) A particle moves in a straight line with an acceleration $(6t-2)\,\text{m s}^{-2}$ at time t seconds. If the particle has an initial velocity of $3\,\text{m s}^{-1}$ find the distance travelled by the particle in the first second of its motion.

6) A particle moves in a straight line with acceleration $\dfrac{1}{t^3}\,\text{m s}^{-2}$ at time t seconds. If the particle is at rest at O, a fixed point on the line, when $t = 1$, find expressions for its velocity and displacement from O at time t and when $t = 2$.

7) A particle moves in a straight line with velocity $v\,\mathrm{m\,s^{-1}}$ where $v = \dfrac{1}{t^2} + 2$ at time t seconds. Show that the velocity approaches a limiting value and find an expression for the displacement of the particle at time t.

8) A particle moves in a straight line with acceleration $\sin 2t\,\mathrm{m\,s^{-2}}$ at time t seconds. If the particle is initially at rest when its displacement is $\frac{1}{2}\,\mathrm{m}$ from a fixed point O on the line find its velocity and displacement from O at any time t. Find also the time that elapses before the particle again comes to rest.

9) A particle moves in a straight line with an acceleration $a\,\mathrm{m\,s^{-2}}$ at time t seconds where $a = -\dfrac{1}{t^2}$. If when $t = 1$ the particle has a velocity of $3\,\mathrm{m\,s^{-1}}$ find the velocity when $t = 4$ and show that the velocity approaches $2\,\mathrm{m\,s^{-1}}$ as t increases.

10) A particle starts from rest at a point A and moves along a straight line AB with an acceleration $(8 - 2t^2)\,\mathrm{m\,s^{-2}}$ at time t seconds. Find the greatest speed of the particle in the direction AB and the distance covered by the particle in the first two seconds of its motion.

11) A particle moves from rest in a straight line with an acceleration $\cos \omega t\,\mathrm{m\,s^{-2}}$ at time t seconds. Find the maximum velocity of the particle and show that this maximum velocity occurs periodically at equal intervals of $\dfrac{2\pi}{\omega}$ seconds.

12) A particle moves in a straight line with an acceleration $\cos \pi t\,\mathrm{m\,s^{-2}}$ at time t seconds. If the particle is initially at rest find the velocity of the particle when $t = 1$ and $t = 2$ and the distance travelled by the particle in the interval of time from $t = 1$ to $t = 2$.

13) A particle moves from rest in a straight line with acceleration $a\,\mathrm{m\,s^{-2}}$ at time t seconds. If a is proportional to t and the particle has a velocity of $2\,\mathrm{m\,s^{-1}}$ when $t = 3$, find an expression for its velocity at any time t.

14) A particle moves in a straight line with an acceleration which is inversely proportional to $(t + 1)^3$ where t is the time. Initially the particle is at rest at O and 3 seconds later it has a velocity of $2\,\mathrm{m\,s^{-1}}$. Find the displacement of the particle from O at time t.

Acceleration as a Function of Velocity

Consider a particle which moves along a straight line with an acceleration $\dfrac{1}{v}$ where v is its velocity.

Since $a = \dfrac{1}{v}$ $\qquad\qquad \dfrac{dv}{dt} = \dfrac{1}{v}$ $\qquad\qquad$ [1]

This can be integrated with respect to time by separating the variables, i.e.

$$\int v\,dv = \int dt$$

$\Rightarrow$ $\qquad\qquad\qquad v^2 = 2t + c$

giving a relationship between velocity and time.

Although it is possible to continue as before, i.e. by using $v = \dfrac{ds}{dt}$, there is an alternative way of introducing the displacement. This relies on finding another form for the acceleration, as follows:

$$a = \lim_{t \to 0} \frac{\delta v}{\delta t} = \lim_{t \to 0} \frac{\delta s}{\delta t} \times \frac{\delta v}{\delta s} = \frac{ds}{dt} \times \frac{dv}{ds} = v\frac{dv}{ds}$$

i.e. $\qquad\qquad\qquad\qquad a = v\dfrac{dv}{ds}$

So, in this problem, we can use

$$v\frac{dv}{ds} = \frac{1}{v}$$

Separating the variables gives $\quad \displaystyle\int v^2\,dv = \int ds$

$\Rightarrow$ $\qquad\qquad\qquad\qquad \dfrac{v^3}{3} = s + c$

In general, if $a = f(v)$ then a relationship between v and t can be found by using $\displaystyle\int \frac{1}{f(v)}\,dv = \int dt$ and a relationship between v and s can be found by using $\displaystyle\int \frac{v}{f(v)}\,dv = \int ds$, both of these relationships coming directly from the acceleration.

EXAMPLES 11b

1) A particle moves in a straight line with acceleration $-\dfrac{1}{3v^2}$ where v is its velocity at time t. Initially the particle is at O, a fixed point on the line, with velocity u. Find in terms of u the time at which the velocity is zero and the displacement of the particle from O at this time.

First we need a relationship between v and t

$$a = \frac{dv}{dt} = -\frac{1}{3v^2}$$

$\Rightarrow$
$$\int_u^v -3v^2\,dv = \int_0^t dt$$

$\Rightarrow$
$$u^3 - v^3 = t$$

The particle is at rest when $v = 0$ and this occurs when $t = u^3$.

Now we will find an expression for the displacement by using

$$a = v\frac{dv}{ds} = -\frac{1}{3v^2}$$

$\Rightarrow$
$$\int_u^v -3v^3\,dv = \int_0^s ds$$

$\Rightarrow$
$$\tfrac{3}{4}(u^4 - v^4) = s$$

So the displacement from O when $v = 0$ is $\tfrac{3}{4}u^4$.

Note. A relationship between s and t can usually be found from the relationship between v and s by using $v = \dfrac{ds}{dt}$ and separating the variables.

Acceleration as a Function of Displacement

Consider a particle moving along a straight line with acceleration s^2 where s is its displacement from a fixed point on the line, i.e. $a = s^2$.

A relationship between v and s can be found by writing a as $v\dfrac{dv}{ds}$

i.e.
$$v\frac{dv}{ds} = s^2$$

Separating the variables gives
$$\int v\,dv = \int s^2\,ds$$

$\Rightarrow$
$$\frac{v^2}{2} = \frac{s^3}{3} + c$$

EXAMPLES 11b (continued)

2) A particle moves in a straight line with an acceleration which is proportional to its distance from a fixed point, O, on the line, and is directed towards O. Initially the particle is at rest when its displacement from O is l. Show that the particle has a maximum velocity when passing through O and zero velocity when its displacement from O is $+l$ or $-l$.

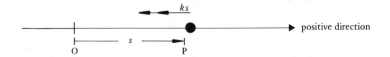

When the particle is at P, with a displacement s from O, it has an acceleration of magnitude ks where k is a positive constant.
Now the velocity is maximum when a is zero, i.e. when $s = 0$.
Therefore the velocity is maximum when the particle is at O.

Returning to the acceleration we see that it is in the negative direction so, using $a = v\dfrac{dv}{ds}$, we have

$$v\frac{dv}{ds} = -ks$$

$\Rightarrow$

$$\int_0^v v\,dv = \int_l^s -ks\,ds$$

$\Rightarrow$

$$v^2 = -ks^2 + kl^2$$

$\Rightarrow$

$$v^2 = k(l^2 - s^2)$$

when $v = 0$,

$$l^2 - s^2 = 0 \quad \Rightarrow \quad s = \pm l$$

Therefore the particle is at rest when its displacement from O is $+l$ or $-l$.

EXERCISE 11b

1) A particle moves along a straight line with an acceleration $a\,\mathrm{m\,s^{-2}}$ where $a = \dfrac{3}{v}$, $v\,\mathrm{m\,s^{-1}}$ being the velocity of the particle at time t seconds. Initially the particle is at rest at O, a fixed point on the line. Find expressions for the velocity and displacement of the particle from O at time t, and find the velocity of the particle when its displacement from O is $5\,\mathrm{m}$.

2) A particle moves in a straight line with acceleration $a\,\mathrm{m\,s^{-2}}$ where $a = -3v^3$, $v\,\mathrm{m\,s^{-1}}$ being the velocity of the particle at time t seconds. Initially the particle is at O, a fixed point on the line, with a velocity $2\,\mathrm{m\,s^{-1}}$. Find the velocity of the particle 3 seconds later and the displacement of the particle from O at this time.

3) A particle moves in a straight line with an acceleration $\dfrac{1}{4v^2}\,\mathrm{m\,s^{-2}}$ when the velocity of the particle is $v\,\mathrm{m\,s^{-1}}$. The particle has a velocity $1\,\mathrm{m\,s^{-1}}$ as it passes through O, a fixed point on the line. Find the displacement of the particle from O when the velocity was zero.

4) A particle moves in a straight line with an acceleration $(12s^2)\,\mathrm{m\,s^{-2}}$ where s metre is the displacement of the particle from O, a fixed point on the line, at time t seconds. The particle has zero velocity when its displacement from O is $-2\,\mathrm{m}$. Find the velocity of the particle as it passes through O.

5) A particle moves in a straight line and at time t its displacement from O, a fixed point on the line, is s. The acceleration of the particle is $-4s$, and the velocity is zero when $s = a$. Show that the velocity of the particle is $2\sqrt{(a^2-s^2)}$ when its displacement from O is s.

6) A particle moves in a straight line with an acceleration which is proportional to its velocity. The particle has a velocity of $20\,\mathrm{m\,s^{-1}}$ when it passes through O, a fixed point on the line, and a velocity of $4\,\mathrm{m\,s^{-1}}$ when its displacement from O is $4\,\mathrm{m}$. Show that subsequently the particle is always less than $5\,\mathrm{m}$ from O.

Motion Under the Action of a Variable Force

Note. Examples in this section involve integration leading to logarithmic and inverse trigonometric functions.

Relationship between Force and Acceleration

Newton's Law of Motion applies to any motion, however it is caused. It applies whether the force causing the motion is variable or constant. Thus if a body of constant mass m is moving under the action of a force and, at time t,

$$\left.\begin{array}{l}\text{the force is } F \\[4pt] \text{and the acceleration is } a\end{array}\right\} \quad \text{then} \quad F = ma$$

When F varies in a specific way, a differential equation can be formed by choosing the appropriate form for a.

If F is a function of time, so that $F = f(t)$, then using $a = \dfrac{dv}{dt}$ gives

$$f(t) = m\,\frac{dv}{dt}$$

$\Rightarrow$
$$\int f(t)\,dt = \int m\,dv$$

If F is a function of velocity, i.e. $F = f(v)$, then we can use either
$a = \dfrac{dv}{dt}$ or $a = v\dfrac{dv}{ds}$ giving

$$f(v) = m\frac{dv}{dt} \quad\Rightarrow\quad \int dt = \int \frac{m}{f(v)}\, dv$$

or

$$f(v) = mv\frac{dv}{ds} \quad\Rightarrow\quad \int ds = \int \frac{mv}{f(v)}\, dv$$

If F is a function of displacement, i.e. $F = f(s)$, then we use $a = v\dfrac{dv}{ds}$

so that

$$f(s) = mv\frac{dv}{ds}$$

$\Rightarrow$

$$\int f(s)\, ds = \int mv\, dv$$

Note. The expression for a is chosen so that not more than two variables are present in the resulting differential equation.

EXAMPLES 11c

1) A particle of mass m moves in a straight line under the action of a variable force such that at time t the displacement of the particle is $\cos 2t$ from O, a fixed point on the line. Show that the force varies as the displacement of the particle from O.

If s is the displacement from O at time t we have

$$s = \cos 2t$$

then

$$v = -2\sin 2t$$

and

$$a = -4\cos 2t$$

If the force is F at time t, applying Newton's Law gives

$$F = -4m\cos 2t$$

$\Rightarrow$

$$F = -4ms$$

But $-4m$ is constant, so the force varies as the displacement.

2) A particle of mass m falls from rest through a resisting medium where the resistance to motion is kv, where v is the velocity of the particle at time t, and k is a positive constant. Find the velocity of the particle at time t and show that the velocity approaches a limiting value of $\dfrac{mg}{k}$.

At time t the resultant downward force acting on the particle is

$$mg - kv$$

Newton's Law gives $$mg - kv = ma$$

Using $a = \dfrac{dv}{dt}$ gives $$mg - kv = m\frac{dv}{dt}$$

$\Rightarrow$ $$\int_0^v \frac{m\,dv}{mg - kv} = \int_0^t dt$$

$\Rightarrow$ $$-\frac{m}{k}\ln(mg - kv) + \frac{m}{k}\ln mg = t$$

$\Rightarrow$ $$-\frac{m}{k}\ln\left(\frac{mg - kv}{mg}\right) = t$$

$\Rightarrow$ $$\frac{mg - kv}{mg} = e^{-kt/m}$$

Hence $$v = \frac{mg}{k} - \frac{mg}{k}e^{-kt/m}$$

As $t \to \infty$, $e^{-kt/m} \to 0$, therefore $v \to \dfrac{mg}{k}$

Therefore the velocity approaches a limiting value of $\dfrac{mg}{k}$.

EXERCISE 11c

1) A particle P of unit mass is moving along a straight line Ox. The force acting on P is towards O and is of variable magnitude λx^2. If P starts from rest at the point where $x = a$, find its speed when it first reaches O.

2) The force acting in a straight line on a particle of mass m is of magnitude $km/(v + 1)$ where k is a constant and v is the speed of the particle when it has travelled a distance x. Find the distance moved by the particle when its speed increases from 0 to u.

3) A particle of mass m moves in a straight line under the action of a resistive force of magnitude $ke^{v/u}$ where u and k are constants. When $t = 0$ the speed of the particle is u. Find
(a) the time during which the speed decreases to $\frac{1}{2}u$,
(b) the further time taken for the particle to come to rest,
(c) the distance travelled by the particle from speed u to rest.

4) A particle of unit mass moving in a straight line is subjected to a variable resistive force which is proportional to the cube of the speed of the particle at any instant. The initial speed of the particle is $2\,\mathrm{m\,s}^{-1}$ and the initial retardation is $1\,\mathrm{m\,s}^{-1}$. Show that the speed $v\,\mathrm{m\,s}^{-1}$ of the particle after t seconds is given by

$$v^2 = \frac{4}{t+1}$$

Find, in joules, the change in kinetic energy between the instants when $t = 0$ and when $t = 10$.
Find also the distance covered by the particle between the instants when $t = 0$ and $t = 8$.

5) A particle falls from rest in a medium in which the resistance is proportional to the speed. If the velocity approaches a limiting value of gT, find the velocity, v, at time t and show that the distance, r, fallen in time t is given by

$$r = gtT - gT^2(1 - e^{-t/T})$$

Find the distance fallen when the acceleration is of value $\frac{1}{2}g$. Sketch graphs to show how v and r vary with t.

GRAPHICAL METHODS

Velocity–time Graph

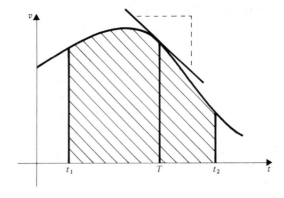

If a particle has an acceleration a, then $a = \dfrac{dv}{dt}$.

But $\dfrac{dv}{dt}$ is the gradient of the graph.

Thus the acceleration can be estimated at time T by drawing the tangent to the velocity–time graph at that point and finding its gradient.

Note that the tangent is drawn by observation, so the curve must be well drawn.

Note also that, in calculating the gradient of the tangent, the lengths of the sides of the triangle used must be taken from the scales on the two axes.

Also since $s = \displaystyle\int v\,dt$ the increase in displacement in the interval of time

from $t = t_1$ to $t = t_2$ is $\displaystyle\int_{t_1}^{t_2} v\,dt$. This is the area shaded in the diagram.

Therefore the increase in displacement over an interval of time $(t_2 - t_1)$ can be estimated by finding the area bounded by the velocity–time graph, the time axis and the ordinates at t_1 and t_2.

Velocity–displacement Graphs

A set of corresponding values of displacement and velocity can be used in a variety of ways to plot graphs from which can be found:

(a) the acceleration at a particular velocity or displacement,
(b) the time taken to achieve a given increase in displacement,

(a) To find the acceleration we can use $a = \dfrac{dv}{dt} = v\dfrac{dv}{ds}$

But $v\dfrac{dv}{ds} = \dfrac{d}{ds}(\tfrac{1}{2}v^2)$ i.e. $a = \dfrac{d}{ds}(\tfrac{1}{2}v^2)$

Now $\dfrac{d}{ds}(\tfrac{1}{2}v^2)$ is the gradient of the graph given by plotting $(\tfrac{1}{2}v^2)$

against s.

Therefore the acceleration at a given displacement can be estimated by drawing the tangent to the curve of $\tfrac{1}{2}v^2$ plotted against s and finding its gradient.

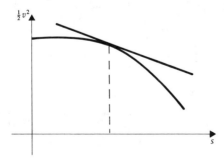

(b) To find the time taken for a given increase in displacement we can use

$$v = \frac{ds}{dt} \quad \Rightarrow \quad \int dt = \int \frac{1}{v}\,ds \quad \Rightarrow \quad t = \int \frac{1}{v}\,ds$$

But $\displaystyle\int_{s_1}^{s_2} \frac{1}{v}\,ds$ is the area shaded in the diagram.

Therefore the time taken for an increase in displacement from s_1 to s_2 can be found by estimating the area bounded by the graph of $\dfrac{1}{v}$ plotted against s, the s axis and the ordinates at s_1 and s_2.

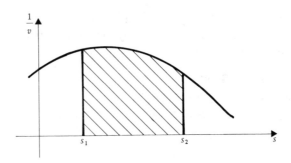

EXAMPLES 11d

Corresponding values of velocity and displacement for a particle moving in a straight line are given in the table

s (m)	0	2	4	6	8
$v\,(\mathrm{m\,s^{-1}})$	2	3	5	8	12

Draw a suitable graph to find the time taken to cover a distance of 6 m from the initial position.

The time can be found by plotting $\dfrac{1}{v}$ against s

s	0	2	4	6	8
$1/v$	0.5	0.33	0.2	0.13	0.08

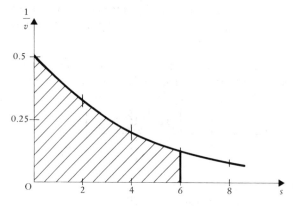

The time taken for the particle to travel 6 m from its initial position is $\int_0^6 \frac{1}{v}\, ds$

which is the area shaded in the diagram.

From the graph this area is approximately 1.63 units.

Therefore the particle takes 1.63 seconds to travel 6 m from its initial position.

Note. The answer above was obtained by using Simpson's Rule with three ordinates but any method for finding the approximate area under a curve can be used (see *The Core Course*).

EXERCISE 11d

1) A particle moves in a straight line. Its velocity v (m s^{-1}) at given times t (seconds) is shown in the table.

t	0	1	2	3	4	5	6
v	5	10.5	14.5	16.5	13	5	0

Draw a velocity-time graph and find
(a) the acceleration when $t = 3$,
(b) the distance moved by the particle between $t = 2$ and $t = 5$.

2) The diagram shows the velocity-time graph for a particle which is moving in a straight line.

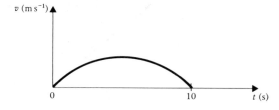

The scale for one unit is the same on both axes and the curve is exactly one quarter of the circumference of a circle. Use the graph to find the time at which the acceleration is zero and the distance moved by the particle in the time of 10 seconds.

3) A particle moves in a straight line and O is a fixed point on that line. The velocity $v(\mathrm{m\,s^{-1}})$ of the particle at given displacements s (metre) from O is shown in the table.

s	0	5	10	15	20	25
v	3	7	11	13	12	8

Draw suitable graphs to find:
(a) the acceleration when $s = 10$,
(b) the time taken to move a distance of 20 m from O.

4) The velocity of a particle moving in a straight line increases uniformly with the distance moved by the particle. The particle has an initial velocity of $2\,\mathrm{m\,s^{-1}}$ and a velocity of $12\,\mathrm{m\,s^{-1}}$ when it is 20 m from its initial position. Draw suitable graphs to estimate:
(a) the acceleration of the particle when it is 10 m from its initial position,
(b) the time taken to cover the distance of 20 m.

5) Show that the area represented by $\displaystyle\int_0^t a\,dt$ represents the velocity at time t. A particle moves in a straight line and its acceleration $a(\mathrm{m\,s^{-2}})$ at given times t (seconds) is shown in the table.

t	0	1	2	3	4	5
a	0	0.6	1.3	2.4	4	8

Draw a graph of a plotted against t and use it to find the velocity of the particle when $t = 2$ and when $t = 4$.

6) A particle moves in a straight line starting from rest. The diagram shows an acceleration-time graph for the first 10 seconds of its motion: both sections of the graph are straight lines.

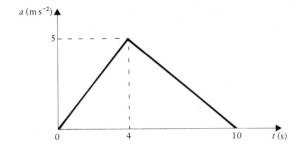

From the graph find the velocity of the particle at times $t = 2, 4, 6, 8, 10$ and hence draw a velocity-time graph for these 10 seconds. Use the velocity-time graph to find the distance travelled by the particle in the first 10 seconds of its motion.

MOTION IN TWO DIMENSIONS

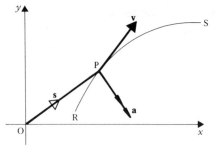

If a particle P is free to move in a plane then at any time its displacement, velocity and acceleration are likely to have different directions as well as different magnitudes. By taking the components of each of these quantities parallel to axes Ox and Oy we can use the methods for motion in a straight line in each of these directions.

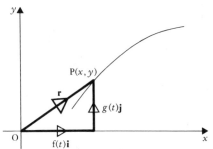

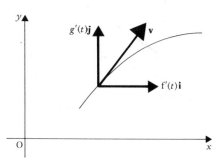

If the components of displacement are both functions of time

$$x = f(t) \quad \text{and} \quad y = g(t)$$

thus

$$\mathbf{r} = f(t)\mathbf{i} + g(t)\mathbf{j}$$

Using $f'(t)$ to denote $\dfrac{d}{dt}[f(t)]$, the velocity components of P are

$$\dot{x} = f'(t) \quad \text{and} \quad \dot{y} = g'(t)$$

so that

$$\mathbf{v} = f'(t)\mathbf{i} + g(t)\mathbf{j}$$

It can be now be seen that

$$\mathbf{v} = \frac{d}{dt}(\mathbf{r})$$

Similarly by writing the acceleration components of P as

$$\ddot{x} = f''(t) \quad \text{and} \quad \ddot{y} = g''(t)$$

we get $\mathbf{a} = f''(t)\mathbf{i} + g''(t)\mathbf{j}$ showing that

$$\mathbf{a} = \frac{d}{dt}(\mathbf{v}) = \frac{d^2}{dt^2}(\mathbf{r})$$

EXAMPLES 11e

1) A particle moves in the xy plane such that its position vector at time t is given by $\mathbf{r} = (3t^2 - 1)\mathbf{i} + (4t^3 + t - 1)\mathbf{j}$.   Find vector expressions for the velocity and acceleration of the particle at time t and when $t = 2$.

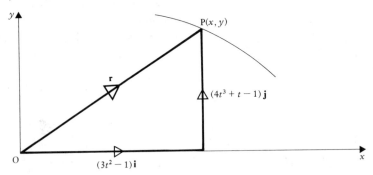

At time t $\mathbf{r} = (3t^2 - 1)\mathbf{i} + (4t^3 + t - 1)\mathbf{j}$

Using $\mathbf{v} = \dfrac{d\mathbf{r}}{dt}$ gives $\mathbf{v} = 6t\mathbf{i} + (12t^2 + 1)\mathbf{j}$

When $t = 2$ $\mathbf{v} = 12\mathbf{i} + 49\mathbf{j}$

Using $\mathbf{a} = \dfrac{d\mathbf{v}}{dt}$ gives $\mathbf{a} = 6\mathbf{i} + 24t\,\mathbf{j}$

When $t = 2$ $\mathbf{a} = 6\mathbf{i} + 48\mathbf{j}$

2)

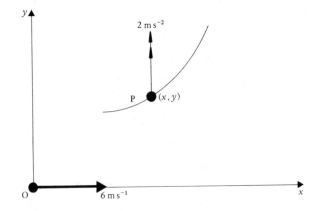

A particle moves in a plane with a constant acceleration of $2\,\mathrm{m\,s^{-2}}$ in the direction Oy. Initially it is at the origin with a velocity of $6\,\mathrm{m\,s^{-1}}$ in the direction Ox. Show that the path of the particle is a parabola.

As the components of acceleration at time t are $\ddot{x} = 0$ and $\ddot{y} = 2$, the acceleration can be written in the form

$$\mathbf{a} = 2\mathbf{j}.$$

Using $\mathbf{v} = \displaystyle\int \mathbf{a}\,dt$ gives

$$\mathbf{v} = c\,\mathbf{i} + (2t + k)\mathbf{j} \quad \text{where } c \text{ and } k \text{ are constants of integration.}$$

When $t = 0$, $\mathbf{v} = 6\mathbf{i}$, giving $c = 6$ and $k = 0$

Hence $\mathbf{v} = 6\mathbf{i} + 2t\mathbf{j}$

Using $\mathbf{r} = \displaystyle\int \mathbf{v}\,dt$ gives $\mathbf{r} = (6t + c')\mathbf{i} + (t^2 + k')\mathbf{j}$

When $t = 0$, $\mathbf{r} = 0$, giving $c' = 0$ and $k' = 0$

Hence $\qquad\qquad\qquad \mathbf{r} = 6t\mathbf{i} + t^2\mathbf{j}$

But $\qquad\qquad\qquad \mathbf{r} = x\mathbf{i} + y\mathbf{j}$

So $\qquad\qquad\qquad x = 6t \quad \text{and} \quad y = t^2$

Hence at time t the coordinates of P are $(6t, t^2)$.

Eliminating t gives $36y = x^2$ which is the equation of a parabola.

Note that $x = 6t$ and $y = t^2$ are the parametric equations of the path.

3) A particle moves in the xy plane and at time t is at the point $(t^2, t^3 - 2t)$. Find the time at which the directions of the velocity and acceleration of the particle are perpendicular.

At time t,

the components of displacement are $\qquad\qquad x = t^2, \qquad y = t^3 - 2t$

Therefore the components of velocity are $\qquad\qquad \dot{x} = 2t, \qquad \dot{y} = 3t^2 - 2$

and the components of acceleration are $\qquad\qquad \ddot{x} = 2 \qquad \ddot{y} = 6t$

so the direction of the velocity has gradient $\qquad\qquad \dfrac{\dot{y}}{\dot{x}} = \dfrac{3t^2 - 2}{2t}$

and the direction of the acceleration has gradient $\qquad \dfrac{\ddot{y}}{\ddot{x}} = \dfrac{6t}{2} = 3t$

When these are perpendicular, the product of their gradients is -1

i.e. $\qquad\qquad\qquad \left(\dfrac{3t^2 - 2}{2t}\right)(3t) = -1$

$\Rightarrow$ $$t(9t^2 - 4) = 0$$

$\Rightarrow$ $$t = \pm\tfrac{2}{3} \quad \text{or} \quad 0$$

EXERCISE 11e

1) A particle moves in the xy plane such that its displacement from O at time t is given by $\mathbf{r} = 3t^2\mathbf{i} + (4t - 6)\mathbf{j}$. Find vector expressions for the velocity and acceleration of the particle at time t and when $t = 4$.

2) A particle moves in the xy plane such that it has an acceleration $\mathbf{a}$ at time t where $\mathbf{a} = 2\mathbf{i} - \mathbf{j}$. Initially the particle is at rest at the point whose position vector is $3\mathbf{i} + \mathbf{j}$. Find the position vector of the particle at time t.

3) A particle moves in the xy plane such that its velocity at time t is given by $\mathbf{v} = 3t^2\mathbf{i} + (t - 1)\mathbf{j}$. Find the acceleration vector and position vector of the particle when $t = 3$ if, initially, the particle is at the origin.

4) The position vector of a particle at time t is given by $\mathbf{r} = \cos\omega t\,\mathbf{i} + \sin\omega t\,\mathbf{j}$. Show that the speed of the particle is constant.

5) A particle moves in a plane with a constant acceleration vector. The velocity vector is zero when $t = 0$ and equal to $3\mathbf{i} - 2\mathbf{j}$ when $t = 1$. Find an expression for the velocity vector at any time t.

6) A particle moves in the xy plane and at time t has acceleration components $\ddot{x} = 2$, $\ddot{y} = 0$. Initially the particle is at the origin with a velocity of $1\,\text{m s}^{-1}$ in the direction Oy. Find the velocity of the particle when $t = 1$ and show that the path of the particle is a parabola.

7) A particle moves in the xy plane and at time t is at the point $(\cos\omega t, \sin\omega t)$. Show that the path is a circle and find the velocity and acceleration of the particle at time t. Prove that the velocity and acceleration are always perpendicular.

8) A particle moves in the xy plane and at time t is at the point $(3t^2 + 2, t - t^2)$. Prove that the particle has a constant acceleration and find it.

9) At time t the position vector $\mathbf{r}$ of the point P with respect to the origin O is given by $\mathbf{r} = (\lambda \sin\omega t)\mathbf{i} + \lambda\mathbf{j}$, where λ and ω are constants. Show that the vector $\mathbf{a} + \omega^2\mathbf{r}$ is constant during the motion where $\mathbf{a}$ is the acceleration vector.

10) A particle moves in the xy plane and at time t it is at the point (x, y) with components of acceleration $\ddot{x}$ and $\ddot{y}$ where $\ddot{x} = x$ and $\ddot{y} = 2$.

Initially the particle is at rest at the point $(1, 0)$.

By writing $\ddot{x}$ as $\dot{x}\dfrac{d\dot{x}}{dx}$ and $\ddot{y}$ as $\dot{y}\dfrac{d\dot{y}}{dy}$ find the components of velocity at time t in terms of x and y respectively. Hence show that the particle moves on a curve whose equation can be derived from $\dfrac{dy}{dx} = \dfrac{2\sqrt{y}}{\sqrt{(x^2-1)}}$.

11) A particle moves in the xy plane and at time t its acceleration components are $\ddot{x}$ and $\ddot{y}$ where $\ddot{x} = \dfrac{2}{x}$ and $\ddot{y} = \dfrac{9}{y^2}$. Initially the particle is at rest at the origin. Find the velocity components $\dot{x}$ and $\dot{y}$ as functions of t and hence show that the equation of the path is $(\tfrac{3}{4}x)^8 = (\tfrac{4}{9}y)^9$.

FORCES PRODUCING MOTION IN A PLANE

Consider a particle of mass m whose acceleration under the action of a force $\mathbf{F}$ is $\ddot{x}\mathbf{i} + \ddot{y}\mathbf{j}$.

If the components of $\mathbf{F}$ are $F_x\mathbf{i}$ and $F_y\mathbf{j}$ then

$$F_x = m\ddot{x} \quad \text{and} \quad F_y = m\ddot{y}$$

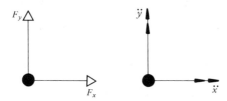

So we can write

$$F_x\mathbf{i} + F_y\mathbf{j} = m(\ddot{x}\mathbf{i} + \ddot{y}\mathbf{j})$$

i.e. $$\mathbf{F} = m\mathbf{a}$$

EXAMPLE 11f

At time t the force acting on a particle P of unit mass is $4\mathbf{i} - t\mathbf{j}$. P is initially at rest at the point with position vector $\mathbf{i} - 6\mathbf{j}$. Find the position vector of P when $t = 2$.

Using $\mathbf{F} = m\mathbf{a}$ gives

$$4\mathbf{i} - t\mathbf{j} = (1)(\mathbf{a})$$

$\Rightarrow$ $$\mathbf{a} = 4\mathbf{i} - t\mathbf{j}$$

Then using $\quad \mathbf{v} = \displaystyle\int \mathbf{a}\, dt \quad$ gives

$$\mathbf{v} = 4t\mathbf{i} - \tfrac{1}{2}t^2\mathbf{j} + \mathbf{V}$$

(where $\mathbf{V}$ is a constant of integration).

But $\quad \mathbf{v} = 0 \quad$ when $\quad t = 0 \quad \Rightarrow \quad \mathbf{V} = \mathbf{0}$

So $$\mathbf{v} = 4t\mathbf{i} - \tfrac{1}{2}t^2\mathbf{j}$$

The position vector of P is $\mathbf{r}$ where

$$\mathbf{r} = \int \mathbf{v}\, dt$$

$\Rightarrow$ $$\mathbf{r} = 2t^2\mathbf{i} - \tfrac{1}{6}t^3\mathbf{j} + \mathbf{R}$$

Now $\quad \mathbf{R} = \mathbf{i} - 6\mathbf{j} \quad$ when $\quad t = 0 \quad \Rightarrow \quad \mathbf{R} = \mathbf{i} - 6\mathbf{j}$

So $$\mathbf{r} = (2t^2 + 1)\mathbf{i} - (\tfrac{1}{6}t^3 + 6)\mathbf{j}$$

When $\quad t = 2 \quad$ the position vector of P is $\quad 9\mathbf{i} + \tfrac{22}{3}\mathbf{j}$

EXERCISE 11f

In questions 1-4 a force $\mathbf{F}$ acts on a particle of mass m, whose acceleration, velocity and position vector at time t are $\mathbf{a}$, $\mathbf{v}$ and $\mathbf{r}$. When $\quad t = 0 \quad$ the particle is at a point with position vector $\mathbf{r_0}$ with velocity $\mathbf{v_0}$.

1) $\mathbf{F} = 3\mathbf{i} + 4\mathbf{j}$, $\quad m = 1$, $\quad \mathbf{r_0} = \mathbf{0}$, $\quad \mathbf{v_0} = \mathbf{0}$. Find $\mathbf{a}$, $\mathbf{v}$ and $\mathbf{r}$.

2) $\mathbf{F} = 3t\mathbf{i} - \mathbf{j}$, $\quad m = 2$, $\quad \mathbf{r_0} = \mathbf{i} + \mathbf{j}$, $\quad \mathbf{v_0} = \mathbf{0}$. Find $\mathbf{r}$ at time t when $\quad t = 3$.

3) $\mathbf{F} = (\sin t)\mathbf{i} + (\cos t)\mathbf{j}$, $\quad m = 1$, $\quad \mathbf{r_0} = -\mathbf{j}$, $\quad \mathbf{v_0} = \mathbf{i}$. Find $\mathbf{v}$ and $\mathbf{r}$.

4) $\mathbf{r} = t^3\mathbf{i} - t^4\mathbf{j} + 3t\mathbf{i} - t\mathbf{j} + 2\mathbf{i} - 3\mathbf{j}$, $\quad m = 4$. Find $\mathbf{r_0}$, $\mathbf{v}$, $\mathbf{v_0}$, $\mathbf{a}$ and $\mathbf{F}$.

5) A particle P of mass 1 kg is at rest at the point A whose position relative to a fixed point O is $\mathbf{i} - 4\mathbf{j}$. If a constant force $\quad 3\mathbf{i} - \mathbf{j} \quad$ acts on the particle, find its velocity and displacement from A after time t. What is the position vector of P relative to O when $\quad t = 2$?

6) At time t the position vector of a particle of mass m is $\quad (\cos t)\mathbf{i} + t^2\mathbf{j}$. Find the resultant force acting on the particle when $\quad t = \pi$.

MOTION IN THREE DIMENSIONS

When the motion of a particle is not restricted to a plane, three axes are needed for a frame of reference. The most convenient axes are a set of three mutually perpendicular lines Ox, Oy and Oz.

We use **i**, **j** and **k** to represent unit vectors in the directions Ox, Oy and Oz. Hence if the particle is at a point (x, y, z), its displacement from O is given by

$$\mathbf{r} = x\mathbf{i} + y\mathbf{j} + z\mathbf{k}$$

It then follows that

$$\begin{cases} \mathbf{v} = \dot{x}\mathbf{i} + \dot{y}\mathbf{j} + \dot{z}\mathbf{k} \\ \mathbf{a} = \ddot{x}\mathbf{i} + \ddot{y}\mathbf{j} + \ddot{z}\mathbf{k} \end{cases}$$

So, in three dimensions as well as in two dimensions we have

$$\left. \begin{aligned} \mathbf{v} &= \frac{d\mathbf{r}}{dt} \\[2mm] \mathbf{a} &= \frac{d\mathbf{v}}{dt} \end{aligned} \right\} \qquad \text{and} \qquad \left\{ \begin{aligned} \mathbf{r} &= \int \mathbf{v}\, dt \\[2mm] \mathbf{v} &= \int \mathbf{a}\, dt \end{aligned} \right.$$

EXAMPLE 11g

A particle is moving so that at any instant its velocity vector, **v**, is given by $\mathbf{v} = 3t\mathbf{i} - 4\mathbf{j} + t^2\mathbf{k}$.

When $t = 0$ it is at the point $(1, 0, 1)$. Find the position vector when $t = 2$. Find also the magnitude of the acceleration when $t = 2$

$$\mathbf{v} = 3t\mathbf{i} - 4\mathbf{j} + t^2\mathbf{k} \qquad\qquad [1]$$

$$\Rightarrow \qquad \mathbf{r} = \int (3t\mathbf{i} - 4\mathbf{j} + t^2\mathbf{k})\, dt$$

$$= \tfrac{3}{2}t^2\mathbf{i} - 4t\mathbf{j} + \tfrac{1}{3}t^3\mathbf{k} + \mathbf{R}$$

(where **R** is a vector constant of integration).

But $\mathbf{r} = \mathbf{i} + \mathbf{k}$ when $t = 0$ so $\mathbf{R} = \mathbf{i} + \mathbf{k}$

$$\Rightarrow \qquad \mathbf{r} = (\tfrac{3}{2}t^2 + 1)\mathbf{i} - 4t\mathbf{j} + (\tfrac{1}{3}t^3 + 1)\mathbf{k}$$

When $t = 2$, $\mathbf{r} = 7\mathbf{i} - 8\mathbf{j} + \tfrac{11}{3}\mathbf{k}$

From [1], $$\mathbf{a} = \frac{d\mathbf{v}}{dt} = 3\mathbf{i} + 2t\mathbf{k}$$

When $t = 2$ $$\mathbf{a} = 3\mathbf{i} + 4\mathbf{k}$$

$$\Rightarrow \qquad |\mathbf{a}| = \sqrt{(3^2 + 4^2)} = 5$$

When $t = 2$, the position vector is $7\mathbf{i} - 8\mathbf{j} + \tfrac{11}{3}\mathbf{k}$ and the magnitude of the acceleration is 5.

EXERCISE 11g

A force $\mathbf{F}$ acts on a particle of mass m, whose acceleration, velocity and position vector at time t are $\mathbf{a}$, $\mathbf{v}$ and $\mathbf{r}$. When $t = 0$ the particle is at a point with position vector $\mathbf{r_0}$ with velocity $\mathbf{v_0}$.

1) $\mathbf{r} = t^3\mathbf{i} - (t^2 + 2t)\mathbf{j} + 3t\mathbf{k}$. Find $\mathbf{r_0}$, $\mathbf{v}$, $\mathbf{v_0}$ and $\mathbf{a}$.

2) $\mathbf{a} = (\sin t)\mathbf{i} + \mathbf{j}$, $\mathbf{v_0} = -\mathbf{i} + \mathbf{k}$, $\mathbf{r_0} = \mathbf{0}$. Find $\mathbf{v}$ and $\mathbf{r}$.

3) $\mathbf{F} = \mathbf{i} + 2\mathbf{j} + 3\mathbf{k}$, $m = 1$. Find $\mathbf{a}$, $\mathbf{v}$ and $\mathbf{r}$ if $\mathbf{v_0} = \mathbf{0} = \mathbf{r_0}$. Find also the speed when $t = 1$.

4) $\mathbf{v} = e^t\mathbf{i} + \mathbf{j} + t\mathbf{k}$, $\mathbf{r_0} = \mathbf{i}$, $m = 2$. Find $\mathbf{r}$, $\mathbf{a}$ and $\mathbf{F}$.

5) $\mathbf{r} = 6t\mathbf{i} - t^3\mathbf{j} + (\cos t)\mathbf{k}$, $m = 3$. Find $\mathbf{F}$, the magnitude of $\mathbf{a}$ when $t = \frac{1}{2}\pi$ and the speed when $t = \pi$.

COLLISION OF MOVING PARTICLES

Consider two particles whose position vectors at time t are $\mathbf{r_1}$ and $\mathbf{r_2}$.

If these particles collide, they are in the same place at the *same time*, i.e. there is a value of t for which $\mathbf{r_1} = \mathbf{r_2}$.

It is important to appreciate that their paths may cross without a collision taking place; this is because they can be at the point of intersection of the paths at different times.

EXAMPLES 11h

1) Two particles, A and B, have position vectors at time t given by $\mathbf{r_A} = 3\mathbf{i} - t\mathbf{j} + t^2\mathbf{k}$ and $\mathbf{r_B} = (t^2 - 1)\mathbf{i} + 2\mathbf{j} - 2t\mathbf{k}$. Find the value(s) of t for which A and B could collide, giving the position vectors of the point(s) of collision.

If A and B collide there is a value of t for which $\mathbf{r_A} = \mathbf{r_B}$.

Equating the coefficients of $\mathbf{i}$ (making the x coordinates equal) gives

$$3 = t^2 - 1 \quad \Rightarrow \quad t = \pm 2$$

When $t = 2$
$$\begin{cases} \mathbf{r_A} = 3\mathbf{i} - 2\mathbf{j} + 4\mathbf{k} \\ \mathbf{r_B} = 3\mathbf{i} + 2\mathbf{j} - 4\mathbf{k} \end{cases}$$

$\mathbf{r_A} \neq \mathbf{r_B}$ so the particles do not collide when $t = 2$.

When $t = -2$
$$\begin{cases} \mathbf{r_A} = 3\mathbf{i} + 2\mathbf{j} + 4\mathbf{k} \\ \mathbf{r_B} = 3\mathbf{i} + 2\mathbf{j} + 4\mathbf{k} \end{cases}$$

$\mathbf{r_A} = \mathbf{r_B}$ so, when $t = -2$, the particles *do* collide at the point with position vector $3\mathbf{i} + 2\mathbf{j} + 4\mathbf{k}$.

2) A particle A moves with velocity $2i - 3j$ from a point $(4, 5)$. At the same instant a particle B, moving in the same plane with velocity $4i + j$, passes through a point C. Find whether A and B collide given that
(a) C is $(2, -1)$ (b) C is $(0, -3)$.

(a) The equation of motion of A is $r_1 = 4i + 5j + t(2i - 3j)$.
   The equation of motion of B is $r_2 = 2i - j + t(4i + j)$.

   If $r_1 = r_2$ equating coefficients of i gives

$$4 + 2t = 2 + 4t \quad \Rightarrow \quad t = 1$$

   When $t = 1$ $r_1 = 6i + 2j$ and $r_2 = 6i$.

   So r_1 and r_2 cannot be equal for any value of t and the particles do not collide.

(b) This time $r_2 = -3j + t(4i + j)$ and equating coefficients of i gives
   $4 + 2t = 4t \quad \Rightarrow \quad t = 2$.

   When $t = 2$, $r_1 = 8i - j$ and $r_2 = 8i - j$.

   So the particles *do* collide, when $t = 2$, at the point with position vector $8i - j$.

EXERCISE 11h

In each of the following problems, r_1 and r_2 are the position vectors of two particles at time t. Determine whether the particles collide and, if they do, give the value of t when this occurs and the position vector of the point of collision.

1) $r_1 = 4i + j + t(2i + 3j)$
   $r_2 = 2i - 3j + t(6i + 11j)$

2) $r_1 = 2i + j + (\cos \pi t)i + (\sin \pi t)j + tk$
   $r_2 = i + 2j + k + (\sin 2\pi t)i - (\cos 2\pi t)j$

3) $r_1 = (3 + t^2)i + (7 + t)j + (1 - t)k$
   $r_2 = (11 + 2t)i + 11j + (11 - t^2)k$

4) $r_1 = -5i + 2j + 9k + t(5i - j + 2k)$
   $r_2 = i + 2j + 3k + t(3i - j + 4k)$

Further problems on collision (interception) will be found in Chapter 13.

DISTANCE APART

Consider again two particles P_1 and P_2 whose displacements at time t from a fixed point O, are r_1 and r_2.

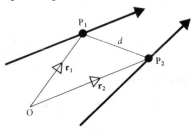

At any time t, the line joining P_1 to P_2 represents the vector $r_2 - r_1$.   The distance, d, between the particles is the length of the line P_1P_2,

i.e. $$d = |r_2 - r_1|$$

Unless the particles collide there is a time when they are closest together. This time can be found by calculating when $|r_2 - r_1|$ is least.

EXAMPLES 11i

1) Two particles A and B have position vectors r_A and r_B at time t, where $r_A = (1+t^2)i + j$ and $r_B = 3i - t^2 j$.   Both particles start moving when $t = 0$.   Find the subsequent time when they are closest together.

$$\overrightarrow{AB} = r_B - r_A = (2-t^2)i + (-t^2 - 1)j$$

The distance, d, between A and B is given by

$$d^2 = (2-t^2)^2 + (-t^2 - 1)^2$$
$$= 2t^4 - 2t^2 + 5$$

d^2 has stationary values when $8t^3 - 4t = 0 \Rightarrow t = 0, \pm \dfrac{1}{\sqrt{2}}$

The graph of d^2 against t shows that d^2 is minimum when $t = \pm \dfrac{1}{\sqrt{2}}$

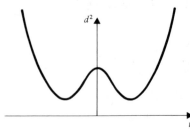

So, after they start moving, A and B are closest together when $t = \dfrac{1}{\sqrt{2}}$.

2) Two particles A and B start simultaneously from points A_0 and B_0 and move with constant velocities v_A and v_B. Find the time, and their distance apart when they are closest together, if A_0 is $(-1, -1)$, B_0 is $(4, 4)$, $v_A = 2i + j$ and $v_B = i - 2j$.

$$r_A = -i - j + t(2i + j)$$
$$r_B = 4i + 4j + t(i - 2j)$$
$$r_B - r_A = 5i + 5j + t(-i - 3j)$$

If d is the distance between A and B, we have

$$d^2 = (5 - t)^2 + (5 - 3t)^2$$

⇒
$$d^2 = 10t^2 - 40t + 50 \qquad\qquad [1]$$

$$\tfrac{1}{10}d^2 = t^2 - 4t + 5$$

$$= (t - 2)^2 + 1$$

But $(t - 2)^2 + 1$ is least when $t = 2$ and then $\tfrac{1}{10}d^2 = 1$.

So A and B are closest together when $t = 2$ and are then distant $\sqrt{10}$ units apart.

Note. The least value of d can also be found from equation [1] by using calculus. The algebraic method introduced above can be used only when d^2 is a quadratic function.

EXERCISE 11i

Find the shortest distance between A and B given r_A and r_B, which are the position vectors of A and B at time t.

1) $r_A = 2i - j + 5tj$
   $r_B = i + t(2i + 4j)$

2) $r_A = i + (\sin t)j$
   $r_B = (\cos t)i + j$

3) $r_A = 3(1 + t)i - (7 - 2t)j$
   $r_B = 2(4 + t)i - (6 - t)j$

4) $r_A = (3 - t^2)i + (1 + t)j$
   $r_B = (2 + t)i - t^2 j$

Further problems involving shortest distance apart (closest approach) are given in Chapter 13.

WORK DONE BY A CONSTANT FORCE

Consider a constant force **F**,
inclined at an angle θ to a given line,
which moves a particle through a
displacement **d** along this line.

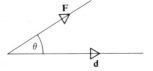

The work done by the force in causing this displacement is given by

$$(|F|\cos\theta)(|d|) \ = \ |F||d|\cos\theta$$

This rather clumsy expression can be recognised as the scalar product **F.d**

At this point the reader is recommended to revise the section in the *Core Course* on the scalar product of two vectors and is also reminded that the word *product* used in this context should not be confused with the more usual concept of multiplication. The scalar product of two vectors is an *operation carried out* on those two vectors and the dot indicates the operation.

In general, for any two vectors **a** and **b** which enclose an angle θ, the scalar product of **a** and **b** is denoted by **a.b**

where
$$\mathbf{a.b} \ = \ |a||b|\cos\theta \ = \ ab\cos\theta$$

If $\mathbf{a} = a_1\mathbf{i} + a_2\mathbf{j} + a_3\mathbf{k}$ and $\mathbf{b} = b_1\mathbf{i} + b_2\mathbf{j} + b_3\mathbf{k}$

then
$$\mathbf{a.b} \ = \ a_1b_1 + a_2b_2 + a_3b_3$$

For example, if $\mathbf{a} = 2\mathbf{i} + 3\mathbf{j} - 2\mathbf{k}$ and $\mathbf{b} = \mathbf{i} + \mathbf{j} - 3\mathbf{k}$

then
$$\mathbf{a.b} \ = \ (2)(1) + (3)(1) + (-2)(-3) \ = \ 11$$

Similarly, if $\mathbf{F} = 2\mathbf{i} + 5\mathbf{j}$ and $\mathbf{d} = 13\mathbf{i} - 4\mathbf{j}$, the work done by **F** in producing a displacement **d** is

$$\mathbf{F.d} \ = \ (2\mathbf{i} + 5\mathbf{j}).(13\mathbf{i} - 4\mathbf{j})$$
$$= \ (2)(13) + (5)(-4) \ = \ 6$$

Kinetic Energy Using Scalar Product

The kinetic energy of a particle of mass m moving with velocity **v** is
$$\tfrac{1}{2}mv^2 \ = \ \tfrac{1}{2}m\,\mathbf{v.v}$$

For example, if a particle of mass m has a velocity $2\mathbf{i} + \mathbf{j} - \mathbf{k}$, its kinetic energy is given by

$$\text{K.E.} \ = \ \tfrac{1}{2}mv^2 \ = \ \tfrac{1}{2}m(2\mathbf{i} + \mathbf{j} - \mathbf{k}).(2\mathbf{i} + \mathbf{j} - \mathbf{k})$$
$$= \ \tfrac{1}{2}m\{2^2 + 1^2 + (-1)^2\}$$
$$= \ 3m$$

EXAMPLES 11j

1) A force of magnitude 20 N, acting in the direction of $3i - 4j$, moves a particle from $A(-1, 5)$ to $B(7, 10)$. Calculate the work done by the force.

The force F is given by using   magnitude × unit direction vector

i.e.
$$F = 20\left(\frac{3i - 4j}{5}\right) = 12i - 16j$$

The displacement vector is $\overrightarrow{AB} = 8i + 5j$

The work done is given by $F.d = 12 \times 8 - 16 \times 5 = 16$

Hence the work done = 16 J.

2) Calculate the kinetic energy of a particle of mass 4 kg moving with a velocity vector $i - 2j$,   the unit being $m\,s^{-1}$

$$\text{Kinetic energy} = \tfrac{1}{2}(\text{mass})(\text{speed})^2$$
$$= \tfrac{1}{2}m\mathbf{v}.\mathbf{v} \qquad (\text{where } \mathbf{v} = i - 2j)$$
$$= 2(1^2 + 2^2)$$

Hence the kinetic energy is 10 J.

EXERCISE 11j

In each of the following questions units are N, m, s, kg.

Calculate the work done by a force F where:

1) F is of magnitude 52 N and it moves an object through a displacement vector $7i - 2j$. The direction of F is:
(a) $12i - 5j$ (b) $i + j$.

2) F is $8i + 5j$ and it moves a particle from $(1, 3)$ to $(7, -12)$.

3) F is the resultant of two forces, $4i + j$ and $7i - 6j$, and acts on an object which moves 20 cm in a direction $4i - 3j$.

4) F is of magnitude 50 N and acts in a direction $6i - 8j$. It acts on a particle which moves 75 m along the line whose vector equation is
$r = 2i + 9j + \lambda(24i - 7j)$.

Calculate the kinetic energy of a particle of mass m and velocity $\mathbf{v}$ where:

5) $m = 3$, $\mathbf{v} = 3i - 5j$.

6) $m = 7$, $\mathbf{v}$ is of magnitude 8 and is in the direction of the line with vector equation $r = 9i - 4j + \lambda(i - j)$.

The Impulse of a Force of Variable Magnitude

Consider a particle of mass m moving in a straight line under the action of a variable force. If, at a time t, the particle has an acceleration a and the force acting on it is F, then

$$F = ma$$

$\Rightarrow$ $$F = m\frac{dv}{dt} \qquad [1]$$

If the particle has a velocity u when $t = 0$ and a velocity v at time t then, by separating the variables, equation [1] becomes

$$\int_0^t F \, dt = \int_u^v m \, dv$$

$$= mv - mu$$

Now $mv - mu$ is the increase in momentum of the particle over the interval of time t.

The quantity $\displaystyle\int_0^t F \, dt$ is called the *impulse* of the force over the interval of time t.

Thus the impulse of a force (constant or variable) is equal to the increase in momentum.

For a constant force: Impulse $= Ft$

For a variable force: Impulse $= \displaystyle\int_0^t F \, dt$

Work Done by a Force of Variable Magnitude

If we write equation [1] above in the form

$$F = mv\frac{dv}{ds}$$

then, by separating the variables, we get

$$\int_0^s F \, ds = \int_u^v mv \, dv$$

where s is the increase in displacement of the particle in time t.

Therefore
$$\int_0^s F \, ds = \tfrac{1}{2}mv^2 - \tfrac{1}{2}mu^2$$

Now $\tfrac{1}{2}mv^2 - \tfrac{1}{2}mu^2$ is the increase in the kinetic energy of the particle.

The quantity $\int_0^s F \, ds$ is called the work done by the force causing an increase in displacement of s.

Thus the work done by a force (constant or variable) is equal to the change in kinetic energy.

For a constant force: Work done $= Fs$

For a variable force: Work done $= \int F \, ds$

The concepts of work and impulse sometimes lead to neat solutions although the methods given earlier can also be used.

EXAMPLES 11k

1) A particle of mass m moves in a straight line under the action of a force F where $F = 2t$ at time t. If the particle has a velocity u when $t = 0$, find the velocity when $t = 3$.

If v is the velocity when $t = 3$ then, by considering the impulse of F from $t = 0$ to $t = 3$, we have

$$mv - mu = \int_0^3 F \, dt$$

$$= \int_0^3 2t \, dt$$

$$= 9$$

Therefore
$$v = \frac{9 + mu}{m}$$

2) A particle of mass m slides from rest down a plane inclined at $30°$ to the horizontal. The resistance to the motion of the particle is ms^2 where s is the displacement of the particle from its initial position. Find the velocity of the particle when $s = 1$.

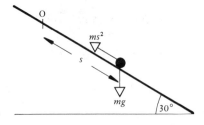

The resultant force down the plane is $\dfrac{mg}{2} - ms^2$.

By considering the work done by this force in displacing the particle 1 unit from O we have

$$\int_0^1 F \, ds = \tfrac{1}{2} mv^2 - 0$$

$\Rightarrow$ $$\int_0^1 \left(\frac{mg}{2} - ms^2 \right) ds = \tfrac{1}{2} mv^2 .$$

$\Rightarrow$ $$\frac{mg}{2} - \frac{m}{3} = \tfrac{1}{2} mv^2$$

Therefore $$v = \sqrt{\tfrac{1}{3}(3g - 2)}$$

EXERCISE 11k

1) Find the work done by a force F N which moves a particle from the origin O along the x axis to the point 5 m from O if:
(a) F is of constant magnitude 10,
(b) $F = x^2$.

2) A body of mass 4 kg falls from rest for 2 seconds in a medium whose resistance is $(2 + 15t)$ N. Find the velocity at the end of this time.
[Take g as $10 \, \mathrm{m\,s^{-2}}$]

3) A body of mass m falls from rest against a resistive force equal to $\tfrac{1}{10}s$ where s is the distance fallen. Find the work done by the resistance when the body has fallen a distance d. What is the kinetic energy of the body in this position?

4) A force acts on a particle of mass m causing its speed to increase from u to $2u$ in T seconds. The force acts in a straight line in the direction of motion and is of magnitude kt where $t = 0$ when the speed is u. Find T in terms of m, u and k.

5) A particle P of mass m passes through the origin O with speed V and moves along the positive x axis. It is subjected to a retarding force R which causes an acceleration of magnitude kx towards O. When P reaches the point where $x = 4$ find:
(a) the work done by R
(b) the speed of P, giving your answers in terms of m, k and V.

SUMMARY

1) Motion in a Straight Line:

If $a = f(t)$,

$$\int dv = \int f(t) \, dt$$

If $a = f(v)$

$$\int \frac{dv}{f(v)} = \int dt \quad \text{or} \quad \int \frac{v \, dv}{f(v)} = \int ds$$

If $a = f(s)$,

$$\int v \, dv = \int f(s) \, ds$$

2) General Motion:

If the position vector of a particle at time t is $\mathbf{r} = f(t)\mathbf{i} + g(t)\mathbf{j} + h(t)\mathbf{k}$

then $\mathbf{v} = \dfrac{d\mathbf{r}}{dt}$ and $\mathbf{a} = \dfrac{d\mathbf{v}}{dt}$

If a particle moves in a curved path, the velocity at time t is in the direction of the tangent to the path at time t.

If a particle moves under the action of a resultant force which is $\mathbf{F}$ at time t, and has an acceleration $\mathbf{a}$ at time t and a constant mass m then $\mathbf{F} = m\mathbf{a}$.

Two objects with position vectors $\mathbf{r_1}$ and $\mathbf{r_2}$ at time t (a) collide if a value of t exists for which $\mathbf{r_1} = \mathbf{r_2}$ (b) are closest together when $|\mathbf{r_1} - \mathbf{r_2}|$ is least.

The work done by a constant force $\mathbf{F}$ in producing a displacement $\mathbf{d}$ is $\mathbf{F.d}$.

The kinetic energy of a mass m with velocity $\mathbf{v}$ is $\frac{1}{2}m\mathbf{v.v}$.

The impulse of a constant force F acting for time t is Ft.

The impulse of a variable force F acting for time t is $\displaystyle\int_0^t F \, dt$.

The impulse of any force is equal to the increase in momentum produced.

The work done by a constant force F causing a displacement s along its line of action is Fs.

The work done when the force F is variable is $\displaystyle\int_0^s F \, ds$.

The work done by any force is equal to the change in mechanical energy produced.

MULTIPLE CHOICE EXERCISE 11

(Instructions for answering these questions are given on page x.)

TYPE 1

1) A particle moves along a straight line Ox such that $\ddot{x} = (6t-4)\,\mathrm{m\,s^{-2}}$ at time t. Initially the particle is at O with a velocity of $-2\,\mathrm{m\,s^{-1}}$. The displacement of the particle from O at time t is:
(a) $t^3 - 2t^2 - 2t$ (b) $t^3 - 2t^2$ (c) 6 (d) $t^3 - 2t^2 + 2$ (e) 0.

2) A particle moves along a straight line such that at time t its displacement from a fixed point O on the line is $3t^2 - 2$. The velocity of the particle when $t = 2$ is:
(a) $8\,\mathrm{m\,s^{-1}}$ (b) $4\,\mathrm{m\,s^{-1}}$ (c) $12\,\mathrm{m\,s^{-1}}$ (d) $6t$ (e) $t^3 - 2t$.

3) A particle of mass $3\,\mathrm{kg}$ moves along a straight line Ox under the action of a force F such that a time t, $x = t^2 + 3t$. The magnitude of F at time t is given by:
(a) 0 (b) $2\,\mathrm{N}$ (c) $3(2t+3)$ (d) $6\,\mathrm{N}$ (e) $-6\,\mathrm{N}$.

4) A particle moves along a straight line with acceleration $a \sin \omega t$ at time t. Initially the particle is at rest at O, a fixed point on the line. The displacement of the particle from O at time t is given by:

(a) $\dfrac{a}{\omega^2} \sin \omega t + \dfrac{a}{\omega} t$ (b) $\dfrac{-a}{\omega^2} \sin \omega t + \dfrac{a}{\omega} t$ (c) $a\omega^2 \cos \omega t$

(d) $-a\omega^2 \sin \omega t$ (e) $-\dfrac{a}{\omega^2} \sin \omega t + \dfrac{a}{\omega^2} \cos \omega t$.

5) A particle moves along a straight line with an acceleration of $\dfrac{2}{v}$ where v is the velocity at any instant. Initially the particle is at rest. The velocity of the particle at time t is:

(a) $2t$ (b) $4t$ (c) $\dfrac{2t}{v}$ (d) $2\sqrt{t}$ (e) $2\sqrt{t} + 2$.

6) A particle moves in a straight line with an acceleration $2s$ where s is its displacement from a fixed point on the line, and $v = 0$ when $s = 0$. Its velocity when its displacement is s is:
(a) s (b) s^2 (c) $-s\sqrt{2}$ (d) $s\sqrt{2}$ (e) $\sqrt{2s}$.

7) A particle moves in the xy plane such that at time t it is at the point $(2t^2,\ 3t-1)$. At time t the acceleration components are given by:

(a) $\ddot{x} = 4t,\ \ddot{y} = 3$ (b) $\ddot{x} = \frac{2}{3}t^3,\ \ddot{y} = \dfrac{3t^2}{2} - t$ (c) $\ddot{x} = 4,\ \ddot{y} = 3$

(d) $\ddot{x} = 0,\ \ddot{y} = 0$ (e) $\ddot{x} = 4,\ \ddot{y} = 0$.

8) A particle moves in the xy plane such that at time t its displacement from O is $(3t-1)\mathbf{i}+(2t^2+1)\mathbf{j}$. The acceleration vector of the particle at time t is given by:

(a) $4\mathbf{i}$ (b) $3\mathbf{i}+4t\mathbf{j}$ (c) $4\mathbf{j}$ (d) $-\mathbf{i}+\mathbf{j}$ (e) $\mathbf{i}+4\mathbf{j}$.

9) A particle of mass $2\,\mathrm{kg}$ moves in the xy plane under the action of a constant force $\mathbf{F}$ where $\mathbf{F}=\mathbf{i}-\mathbf{j}$. Initially the velocity of the particle is $2\mathbf{i}$. The velocity of the particle at time t is:

(a) $\frac{1}{2}(t+4)\mathbf{i}-\frac{1}{2}t\mathbf{j}$ (b) $t(\mathbf{i}-\mathbf{j})$ (c) $\frac{1}{2}t(\mathbf{i}-\mathbf{j})$ (d) $\frac{1}{2}t\mathbf{i}+\frac{1}{2}(t+4)\mathbf{j}$

(e) $2\mathbf{i}$

10) A particle moves in the xy plane such that at time t its velocity vector is $(3t^2-1)\mathbf{i}+2\mathbf{j}$. Initially the particle is at the origin. The position vector of the particle at time t is:

(a) $6\mathbf{i}$ (b) $6t\mathbf{i}$ (c) $(t^3-t-1)\mathbf{i}+(2t+1)\mathbf{j}$ (d) $(t^3-t)\mathbf{i}+2t\mathbf{j}$ (e) $(3t^2)\mathbf{i}$.

TYPE II

11) A particle moves along a straight line Ox. Its velocity at time t is given by:

(a) $\dot{x}$ (b) $\dfrac{dx}{dt}$ (c) $\displaystyle\int_0^t \ddot{x}\,dt$.

12) A particle moves on the curve $y=f(x)$. If the particle is at the point $P(x,y)$ on the curve at time t, the direction of its velocity is given by:

(a) $\dfrac{d^2y}{dx^2}$ (b) $\dfrac{dy}{dt}\Big/\dfrac{dx}{dt}$ (c) $\dfrac{dy}{dx}$.

13) The area shaded in the graph represents:

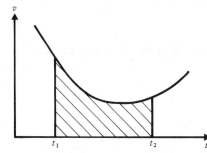

(a) the distance travelled in the time interval (t_2-t_1),

(b) the increase in the displacement in the time interval (t_2-t_1),

(c) the acceleration at time t_2.

14) A resultant force F of varying magnitude acts on a particle. The work done by F in moving the particle a distance s is:

(a) $\displaystyle\int_0^s F\,dt$,

(b) the increase in kinetic energy,

(c) $\displaystyle\int_0^s F\,ds$.

15) A particle moves along a straight line such that at time t its velocity is v and its displacement from a fixed point on the line is s. Its acceleration at time time t is:

(a) $\dfrac{dv}{dt}$ (b) $v\dfrac{dv}{ds}$ (c) $\displaystyle\int v\,dt$.

16) The speed of a particle of mass m increases from u to v in time t under the action of a force $\mathbf{F}$. In the same time the particle undergoes a displacement $\mathbf{d}$.
(a) The work done by the force is $\mathbf{F.d}$.
(b) The impulse of the force is $\mathbf{F.}t$.
(c) The work done by the force is $\frac{1}{2}m(v^2-u^2)$.
(d) $|\mathbf{F}|t = m(v-u)$.

TYPE III

17) (a) At time t the acceleration of a particle is given by $a = \dfrac{2}{v}$.

(b) The velocity of a particle at time t is given by $v = 2t^{\frac{1}{2}}$.

18) (a) $a = f(s)$ (b) $\displaystyle\int v\,dv = \int f(s)\,ds$.

19) (a) $\mathbf{v} = (2t-1)\mathbf{i} + 3t\mathbf{j}$ (b) $\mathbf{a} = 2\mathbf{i} + 3\mathbf{j}$.

20) (a) The impulse of a force F acting for a time t is Ft.
(b) F is a constant force.

21) (a) $\mathbf{r} = (3t^2+2)\mathbf{i} - (t+1)\mathbf{j} - t^3\mathbf{k}$ (b) $\mathbf{v} = 6t\mathbf{i} - \mathbf{j} - 3t^2\mathbf{k}$.

TYPE IV

22) A particle moves in a straight line. Find the distance covered by the particle in the third second of its motion.
(a) $s = 0$ when $t = 0$.
(b) $a = 3t-4$ at time t.
(c) $v = 0$ when $t = 0$.

23) A particle moves on the line Ox with an acceleration which is proportional to $-x$. Find the maximum velocity of the particle.
(a) $v = 0$ when $t = 0$.
(b) $x = a$ when $t = 0$.
(c) $\ddot{x} = 3$ when $t = 1$.

24) A particle moves under the action of a force $\mathbf{F}$. Find $\mathbf{F}$ in terms of t.
(a) $\ddot{x} = 3t^2 - 4$.
(b) $\ddot{y} = 6t + 3$.
(c) the mass of the particle is 2 kg.

25) A particle moves in the xy plane under the action of a force $\mathbf{F}$. Find the position vector of the particle at time t.
(a) $\mathbf{F} = 3\mathbf{i} - 2\mathbf{j}$.
(b) $\mathbf{v} = \mathbf{i}$ when $t = 0$.
(c) $\mathbf{r} = \mathbf{0}$ when $t = 0$.

26) A particle moves in a straight line under the action of a force F. Find the impulse of F over the interval $t = 0$ to $t = t_1$.
(a) the mass of the particle is 5 kg.
(b) $t_1 = 3$.
(c) the initial velocity is 0 and the velocity when $t = t_1$ is $4\,\mathrm{m\,s}^{-1}$.

TYPE V

27) A particle is moving along a straight line with variable acceleration. If, at some instant, the particle has a maximum velocity, the acceleration at that instant is zero.

28) If a particle has a constant acceleration it must be moving in a straight line.

29) If a particle moves in a straight line and the acceleration is plotted against the time, this graph can be used to find the velocity of the particle at any instant.

30) A particle moves in a plane under the action of a force $\mathbf{F}$, where $\mathbf{F} = a(\cos \omega t\, \mathbf{i} + \sin \omega t\, \mathbf{j})$ at time t, so the speed of the particle is constant.

31) The work done by any force F in moving an object a distance d is Fd.

MISCELLANEOUS EXERCISE 11

1) A particle of mass m moves in a straight line under the action of a force F where $F = -mk \sin 3t$ at time t and k is a positive constant. The particle is at O, a point on the line, when $t = 0$, with a velocity u. Find expressions for the acceleration, velocity and displacement from O at time t.

2) A particle of mass m moves in a straight line under the action of a force F where $F = ms$, s being the displacement of the particle from O, a fixed point on the line. When $s = -a$ the velocity of the particle is u. Find the velocity of the particle when $s = 0$.

3) A particle of mass m moves in the xy plane such that its position vector at time t is $\mathbf{r} = (3t^2 + 2)\mathbf{i} + (4 - 6t)\mathbf{j}$. Prove that the particle is moving under the action of a constant force and find it.

4) A particle of mass 2 kg moves in the xy plane under the action of a force $\mathbf{F}$ where $\mathbf{F} = 2\mathbf{i} - 6\mathbf{j} + \mathbf{k}$. Initially the particle is at the point whose position vector is $\mathbf{i} + \mathbf{j} - 2\mathbf{k}$ with a velocity vector $\mathbf{i} - 2\mathbf{j} + 3\mathbf{k}$. Find the position vector of the particle at any time t.

5) A particle of mass 3 kg moves so that its position vector after t seconds is given by

$$\mathbf{r} = (3t^2 - 2t^3)\mathbf{i} - 2t\mathbf{j}.$$

Find the force acting on the particle at time $t = 2$ s. (U of L)

6) A particle moves in a straight line so that its speed is inversely proportional to $(t+1)$, where t is the time in seconds for which it has been moving. After 2 seconds, the particle has a retardation of $10/9 \text{ m s}^{-2}$. Calculate the distance moved in the first second of the motion. (U of L)

7) A particle P moves along Ox with variable velocity $v \text{ m s}^{-1}$. When $OP = x$ m, the acceleration of P in the direction of x-increasing is $-v \text{ m s}^{-2}$. Given that $v = 10$ when $x = 0$, find v in terms of x. (U of L)

8) A particle moves along the x-axis. For all values of x its retardation is $1/(2v^2) \text{ m s}^{-2}$ where $v \text{ m s}^{-1}$ is its speed. At time $t = 0$ seconds the particle is projected from the origin with speed $u \text{ m s}^{-1}$ in the direction x increasing. Show that the speed is halved when $t = 7u^3/12$ seconds and find the value of x in terms of u at this instant. (U of L)

9) At time t, the position vector $\mathbf{r}$ of a particle P is given by

$$\mathbf{r} = \mathbf{u}t + \tfrac{1}{2}\mathbf{g}t^2,$$

where $\mathbf{u}$ and $\mathbf{g}$ are constant vectors. Find the velocity and the acceleration of P at time t. Obtain also the change in the velocity of P between time t_1 and time t_2. (U of L)

10) A particle of mass 4 kg moves from rest at the origin under the action of two forces each of magnitude 40 N. One force acts parallel to the vector $4\mathbf{i} - 3\mathbf{j}$, and the other parallel to the vector $-3\mathbf{i} + 4\mathbf{j}$. Find the acceleration of the particle.

11) A particle of mass m moves in a straight line against a resistance of $(mv + k)$ where v is the velocity of the particle and k is a positive constant. Initially the particle has a velocity of u. Find an expression for the velocity of the particle at any time t and show that the greatest displacement from the initial position occurs when $t = \ln\left(\dfrac{mu + k}{k}\right)$.

12) By writing a as $\dfrac{dv}{dt}$ show that $\displaystyle\int \frac{1}{a}\, dv = t$. Hence show that if $\dfrac{1}{a}$ is plotted against v, the area between the graph, the v axis and the ordinates $v = 0$, $v = V$ gives the time at which the velocity is V, if $t = 0$ when $v = 0$. A particle moves in a straight line with acceleration which decreases uniformly with the velocity. If the acceleration is 10 m s^{-2} when the velocity is zero and 4 m s^{-2} when the velocity is 6 m s^{-1}, find the times at which the velocity is 2 m s^{-1}, 8 m s^{-1}, if $t = 0$ when $v = 0$.

13) By writing a as $v\dfrac{dv}{ds}$ show that $\displaystyle\int a\,ds = \tfrac{1}{2}v^2$.

The table gives corresponding values of acceleration a ($\mathrm{m\,s^{-2}}$) and displacement s (metre) for a particle moving in a straight line.

s	0	2	4	6	8
a	0	0.4	1.6	3.6	6.4

Draw a graph of a plotted against s and use it to find the velocity when $s = 4$ and when $s = 8$.

14) The figure shows the velocity–time graph of a particle which moves along a straight line from rest to rest in 30 seconds. The parts OA and AB are straight lines and the curve BC is an arc of the circle whose radius is equal to the chord BC. Find:
(a) the acceleration during the stages OA and AB,
(b) the greatest and least retardation during the stage BC,
(c) the total distance covered by the particle.

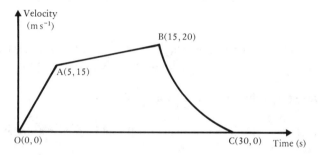

(AEB)

15) As a car of mass 1000 kg travels along a level road its motion is opposed by a constant resistance of 100 N. The values of the pull of the engine for given values of the time, t seconds, are as follows:

Time t (seconds)	0	1	2	3	4	5	6
Pull (newtons)	1100	1200	1350	1550	1850	2300	3100

Find the acceleration of the car at each of the given values of t. When $t = 0$ the speed of the car is $50\,\mathrm{km\,h^{-1}}$. Find graphically the speed of the car in $\mathrm{km\,h^{-1}}$ when $t = 6$.
State how you would find graphically the distance travelled by the car in the period from $t = 0$ to $t = 6$. (AEB)

16) A particle moves along a horizontal straight line with acceleration proportional to $\cos \pi t$, where t is the time. When $t = 0$ the velocity of the particle is u, and when $t = \tfrac{1}{2}$ its velocity is $2u$. Find the distance that the

particle has travelled when $t = 2$, and draw the velocity–time graph for the interval $0 \leqslant t \leqslant 2$. (U of L)

17) A point P is travelling in the positive direction on the x-axis with acceleration proportional to the square of its speed v. At time $t = 0$ it passes through the origin with speed gT and with acceleration g. Show that

$$dv/dx = v/(gT^2),$$

and hence obtain an expression for v in terms of x, g and T. Prove that, at time t,

$$x = gT^2 \ln \left(\frac{T}{T-t} \right).$$

Sketch the graph of x against t for $0 \leqslant t < T$. (U of L)

18) A particle moving along a straight line starts at time $t = 0$ seconds with a velocity $4 \, \mathrm{m \, s^{-1}}$. At any subsequent time t seconds the acceleration of the particle is $(6t - 8) \, \mathrm{m \, s^{-2}}$.

Find
(a) the distance the particle moves before first coming to instantaneous rest,
(b) the total time T seconds taken by the particle to return to the starting point,
(c) the greatest speed of the particle for $0 \leqslant t \leqslant T$. (U of L)

19) A particle starts from rest at time $t = 0$ and moves in a straight line with variable acceleration $f \, \mathrm{m \, s^{-2}}$; where

$$f = \frac{t}{5} \qquad (0 \leqslant t < 5)$$

$$f = \frac{t}{5} + \frac{10}{t^2} \qquad (t \geqslant 5)$$

t being measured in seconds. Show that the velocity is $2\frac{1}{2} \, \mathrm{m \, s^{-1}}$ when $t = 5$ and $11 \, \mathrm{m \, s^{-1}}$ when $t = 10$.
Show also that the distance travelled by the particle in the first 10 seconds is $(43\frac{1}{3} - 10 \ln 2) \, \mathrm{m}$. (U of L)

20) A parachutist of mass m falls freely until his parachute opens. When it is open, he experiences an upward resistance kv where v is his speed and k is a positive constant. Prove that, after time t from the opening of his parachute, $m(dv/dt) = mg - kv$. Prove also that, irrespective of his speed when he opens his parachute, his speed approaches a limiting value mg/k, provided that he falls for a sufficiently long time.

The parachutist falls from rest freely under gravity for a time $m/2k$ and then opens his parachute. Prove that the total distance he has fallen when his velocity is $3mg/4k$ is $\dfrac{m^2 g}{8k^2}(8\ln 2 - 1)$. (O)

21) A particle leaves a point A at time $t = 0$ with speed u and moves towards a point B with a retardation λv, where v is the speed of the particle at time t. The particle is at a distance s from A at time t. Show that:
(a) $v = u - \lambda s$,
(b) $\ln(u - \lambda s) = \ln u - \lambda t$.
At $t = 0$ a second particle starts from rest at B and moves towards A with acceleration $2 + 6t$. The particles collide at the mid-point of AB when $t = 1$. Find the distance AB and the speeds of the particles on impact. (AEB)

22) A particle is projected horizontally with speed u across a smooth horizontal plane from a point O in the plane. The particle is subjected to a retardation of magnitude k times the speed of the particle. Find the distance of the particle from O and also its speed at time t after projection.
Another particle is projected vertically upwards with speed u. In addition to the retardation due to gravity this particle is also subjected to a retardation of k times its speed. Find the time this particle takes to reach its greatest height.
(AEB)

23) A particle moves in the xy plane such that the acceleration of the particle at time t is $3\mathbf{i}$. At time $t = 0$ the particle is at the origin with velocity vector $-2\mathbf{j}$. Find the position vector of the particle at time t and hence find the cartesian equation of its path.

24) A particle is acted upon by two forces $\mathbf{F_1}$ and $\mathbf{F_2}$ where $\mathbf{F_1} = 2\mathbf{i} - t\mathbf{k}$ and $\mathbf{F_2} = \mathbf{i} + 4t\mathbf{j} + 3t\mathbf{k}$ at time t. The particle is initially at rest. Find the momentum of the particle 5 seconds later.

25) A particle of mass m moves under the action of a force $\mathbf{F}$ where $\mathbf{F} = m\cos t\,\mathbf{i} + m\sin t\,\mathbf{j}$. Initially the particle is at the point $-\mathbf{i}$ with velocity vector $-\mathbf{j}$. Prove that the path of the particle is a circle whose cartesian equation is $x^2 + y^2 = 1$.

26) A particle of unit mass is acted upon by a force which at time t is $4\mathbf{i} + 12t^2\mathbf{j}$. At time $t = 0$ the particle is at rest at the point $-\mathbf{i} + \mathbf{j}$. Find the position vector of the particle at time $t = T$, and deduce that the path of the particle is a parabola with vertex at the point $-\mathbf{i} + \mathbf{j}$. At time $t = 1$ the force acting on the particle becomes $4\mathbf{i}$. Find the position vector of the particle when $t = 2$. (U of L)

27) The resultant force acting on a train of mass m starting from rest on a level track is a constant P for speeds less than V. For speeds greater than V the power exerted by the resultant force has a constant value PV. Find the time taken to reach a speed $2V$ from rest, and the corresponding distance travelled.   (U of L)

28) With the usual notation, prove that $\dfrac{dv}{dt} = v\dfrac{dv}{ds}$

A particle P of mass m moves in a straight line and starts from a point O with velocity u. When $OP = x$, where $x \geqslant 0$, the velocity v of P is given by $v = u + \dfrac{x}{T}$, where T is a positive constant. Show that, at any instant, the force acting on P is proportional to v.

Given that the velocity of P at the point A is $3u$, calculate
(a) the distance OA in terms of u and T,
(b) the time, in terms of T, taken by P to move from O to A,
(c) the work done, in terms of m and u, in moving P from O to A. (AEB)

29) A particle moves in the xy plane such that at time t it is at the point (x, y) where $x = 2 \cos \omega t$, $y = 2 \sin \omega t$. Prove that the particle moves in a circular path with constant angular velocity. Prove that the acceleration of the particle at time t is in the direction of the radius from the particle to the centre of its path.

30) A disc is set spinning and turns through $\theta°$ in t seconds, where $\theta = 120t - 6t^2$. Calculate the rate, in revolutions per minute, at which the disc is rotating when $t = 6$.   (U of L)

31) A particle moves in the xy plane with acceleration components $\ddot{x}$ and $\ddot{y}$ where $\ddot{x} = (\dot{x})^2$ and $\ddot{y} = (\dot{y})^2$. Initially the particle is at the point $(1, 0)$ with velocity components $\dot{x} = 3$, and $\dot{y} = 3$. Find the direction of the velocity at time t and hence show that the particle moves in a straight line whose equation is $x - y - 1 = 0$.

32) If an engine works at a constant rate, show that the driving force P is inversely proportional to the velocity v at time t.

A car moves along a straight road against a resistance to motion which is ten times the speed of the car. The car has a mass of $800\,\text{kg}$ and the engine is working at the constant rate of $5\,\text{kW}$. Find an expression for the acceleration of the car as a function of the velocity at any time t. Hence find the distance covered by the car as its velocity increases from $5\,\text{m s}^{-1}$ to $10\,\text{m s}^{-1}$.

33) A car of mass m is moving in a straight line on a rough horizontal plane. At time t the car is moving with velocity v and the resistance to motion is kv where k is a constant. If the car works at a constant rate h, show that

$$mv\frac{dv}{dt} + kv^2 = h$$

If the car starts from rest, show that v is always less than $\left(\dfrac{h}{k}\right)^{\frac{1}{2}}$ and find the time taken for the car to reach the speed $\frac{1}{2}\left(\dfrac{h}{k}\right)^{\frac{1}{2}}$. (O)

34) A mass m hangs at the end of a light string and is raised vertically by an engine working at a constant rate kmg. Derive the equation of motion of the mass in the form

$$v^2\frac{dv}{dx} = (k-v)g$$

where v is the upward velocity of the mass and x is its displacement measured upwards.
Initially the mass is at rest and when it has risen to a height h its speed is u. Show that

$$gh = k^2\ln\left(\frac{k}{k-u}\right) - ku - \frac{1}{2}u^2$$

Without further integration find, in terms of m, k and u, the increase in the total energy of the mass due to this motion and hence, by considering the work done by the engine, deduce that the time taken is

$$\frac{1}{g}\left\{k\ln\left(\frac{k}{k-u}\right) - u\right\}$$ (JMB)

CHAPTER 12

SIMPLE HARMONIC MOTION

DEFINITIONS

Simple Harmonic Motion (SHM) is a particular type of oscillatory motion. It is defined in one of the following ways.

(a) A particle moving in a straight line with a linear acceleration proportional to the linear displacement from a fixed point, always directed towards that fixed point, is travelling with linear SHM.

(b) A particle which oscillates on a circular arc with angular acceleration which is proportional to the angular displacement from a fixed line and always directed towards that fixed line, is travelling with angular SHM.

BASIC EQUATIONS OF SHM

1. LINEAR SHM

Given a fixed point O and a particle P distant x from O at any time, the linear acceleration of P is $\dfrac{d^2x}{dt^2}$, or $\ddot{x}$, in the direction $\overrightarrow{OP}$.

But, by definition, the acceleration of P is proportional to x and towards O. Using n^2 as a constant of proportion,

the acceleration is n^2x in the direction $\overrightarrow{PO}$

Hence

$$\ddot{x} = -n^2x$$

This differential equation is the basic equation of linear SHM.

2. ANGULAR SHM

Given a fixed line OA and a particle P where OP is at an angular displacement θ from OA at any time t, the angular acceleration of P is $\dfrac{d^2\theta}{dt^2}$ or $\ddot{\theta}$ away from OA.

But by definition the angular acceleration of P is proportional to θ and towards OA.

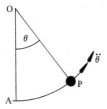 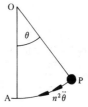

Hence $\ddot{\theta} = -n^2\theta$ is the basic equation of angular SHM.

By integrating either basic equation it is possible to derive further relationships involving velocity, displacement and time.

Linear SHM

The acceleration of P can be taken as $\dfrac{d^2x}{dt^2}$, $\dfrac{dv}{dt}$, or $v\dfrac{dv}{dx}$ (see Chapter 11), where v is the velocity of P at any time t.

Because the acceleration is a function of x we can use the form $v\dfrac{dv}{dx}$ giving

$$v\frac{dv}{dx} = -n^2x$$

$\Rightarrow$
$$\int v\frac{dv}{dx} = -n^2 \int x\,dx$$

$\Rightarrow$
$$\tfrac{1}{2}v^2 = -\tfrac{1}{2}n^2x^2 + K_1$$

If P is momentarily at rest at a point A where $OA = a$,   then $K_1 = \tfrac{1}{2}n^2a^2$

so that
$$v^2 = n^2(a^2 - x^2)$$

But
$$v = \frac{dx}{dt}$$

Therefore
$$\frac{dx}{dt} = n\sqrt{a^2 - x^2}$$

$\Rightarrow$
$$\int \frac{dx}{\sqrt{a^2 - x^2}} = n \int dt$$

$\Rightarrow$
$$\arcsin \frac{x}{a} = nt + K_2$$

If we choose to begin our analysis from point A so that $t = 0$ when $x = a$, then $K_2 = \frac{\pi}{2}$.

Hence
$$\arcsin \frac{x}{a} = nt + \frac{\pi}{2}$$

or
$$\frac{x}{a} = \sin\left(nt + \frac{\pi}{2}\right) = \cos nt$$

$\Rightarrow$
$$x = a \cos nt$$

Summarising our results so far we have

$$\frac{d^2 x}{dt^2} = -n^2 x \tag{1}$$

$$v = n\sqrt{a^2 - x^2} \tag{2}$$

$$x = a \cos nt \tag{3}$$

Now equation [2] shows that $v = 0$ when $x = \pm a$ confirming that the particle oscillates between two points A and A′ on opposite sides of O and equidistant from O.

The distance OA is called the *amplitude* of the SHM.

The point O is the *centre* or *mean position* of the motion.

The time taken to travel from A to O is obtained by using $x = 0$ in equation [3] giving $nt = \frac{\pi}{2}$ or $t = \frac{\pi}{2n}$.

It will take four times as long to travel from A to A' and back to A, i.e. to describe one complete oscillation.

This is the *periodic time* (or period of oscillation), T, and

$$T = \frac{2\pi}{n} \qquad \qquad [4]$$

Several interesting properties of SHM can be observed from the four standard formulae which have just been derived.

(a) The periodic time is independent of the amplitude of the motion
equation [4].

(b) The greatest speed is na, occuring when $x = 0$ i.e. at the centre of the path. The speed is zero when $x = \pm a$ i.e. at the ends of the path.

(c) The greatest acceleration is of magnitude n^2a, occuring when $x = \pm a$ while, when $x = 0$ at the centre of the path, the acceleration is zero.

Angular SHM

Using $\theta = \phi$ when $t = 0$ and the angular velocity $\omega = 0$, a similar set of relationships can be obtained for angular SHM. They are:

$$\frac{d^2\theta}{dt^2} = -n^2\theta \qquad \qquad [1]$$

$$\omega = n\sqrt{\phi^2 - \theta^2} \qquad \qquad [2]$$

$$\theta = \phi \cos nt \qquad \qquad [3]$$

$$T = \frac{2\pi}{n} \qquad \qquad [4]$$

Note. Unless their derivation is specifically asked for, the standard formulae can be quoted when solving problems on SHM whether linear or angular.

EXAMPLES 12a

1) A particle is describing linear SHM of amplitude 2 m. If its speed is $3\,\mathrm{m\,s^{-1}}$ when the particle is 1 m from the centre of the path find:
(a) the periodic time,
(b) the maximum velocity,
(c) the maximum acceleration.

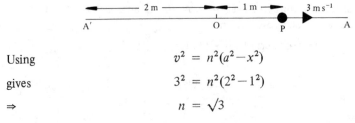

Using
$$v^2 = n^2(a^2 - x^2)$$

gives
$$3^2 = n^2(2^2 - 1^2)$$

$$\Rightarrow \qquad n = \sqrt{3}$$

(a) $T = \dfrac{2\pi}{n}$ gives the periodic time as $\dfrac{2\pi}{3}\sqrt{3}$ seconds.

(b) The velocity is greatest when $x = 0$ giving $v = na$.
Therefore the maximum velocity is $2\sqrt{3}\ \mathrm{m\,s^{-1}}$

(c) The acceleration is greatest when x is greatest i.e. when $x = a$.
Therefore the magnitude of the maximum acceleration is $6\ \mathrm{m\,s^{-2}}$.

2) A particle is travelling in a straight line with SHM of period 4 seconds. If the greatest speed is $2\ \mathrm{m\,s^{-1}}$, find the amplitude of the path and the speed of the particle when it is $3/\pi$ m from the centre.

The period of oscillation is 4 $\Rightarrow$ $4 = \dfrac{2\pi}{n}$

Therefore $n = \dfrac{\pi}{2}$

Then $v_{max} = na = 2$

Therefore $a = \dfrac{4}{\pi}$

The amplitude is $\dfrac{4}{\pi}$ m.

Also $v = n\sqrt{a^2 - x^2}$

When $x = 3/\pi$ $v = \dfrac{\pi}{2}\sqrt{\left(\dfrac{4}{\pi}\right)^2 - \left(\dfrac{3}{\pi}\right)^2}$ $\Rightarrow$ $v = \dfrac{\sqrt{7}}{2}$

The required speed is $\frac{1}{2}\sqrt{7}\ \mathrm{m\,s^{-1}}$.

3) A particle passes through three point, A, B, C in that order, with velocity 0, $2\ \mathrm{m\,s^{-1}}$ and $-1\ \mathrm{m\,s^{-1}}$ respectively. The particle is moving with SHM in a straight line. What is the period and amplitude of the motion if $AB = 2\ \mathrm{m}$ and $AC = 8\ \mathrm{m}$?

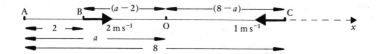

Since at A, $v = 0$, A must be one end of the path. Let O be the centre of the path where AO $= a$. The velocities at B and C, being opposite in sign, are in opposite directions. Therefore B and C are on opposite sides of O.

Measuring x from O in the direction $\overrightarrow{AO}$ we have

$$v = 2 \quad \text{when} \quad x = -(a-2)$$

$$v = -1 \quad \text{when} \quad x = (8-a)$$

Using $\qquad\qquad v^2 = n^2(a^2 - x^2)$

gives $\qquad\qquad 4 = n^2(a^2 - [2-a]^2)$ $\qquad\qquad$ [1]

and $\qquad\qquad 1 = n^2(a^2 - [8-a]^2)$ $\qquad\qquad$ [2]

Equation [2] $\div$ [1] gives

$$\frac{1}{4} = \frac{16a - 64}{4a - 4} = \frac{4(a-4)}{(a-1)}$$

Therefore $\qquad a = 4.2$

From [1] $\qquad 4 = n^2[(4.2)^2 - (-2.2)^2]$

$\Rightarrow \qquad\qquad 4 = n^2(6.4 \times 2.0)$

Hence $\qquad\qquad n = \dfrac{\sqrt{5}}{4}$

The periodic time is given by $\quad T = \dfrac{2\pi}{n}$ and is $\dfrac{8\pi\sqrt{5}}{5}$ seconds

and the amplitude is 4.2 m.

Summary of Formulae and Terms Used in Linear SHM

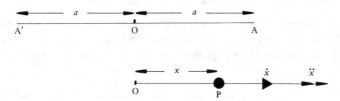

AA′ is the path
O   is the centre or mean position
a is the amplitude

For a particle at a general point P

$$\ddot{x} = -n^2 x \qquad \text{where } n \text{ is a constant}$$

$$\dot{x} = n\sqrt{a^2 - x^2}$$

$$x = a \cos nt$$

$$T = \frac{2\pi}{n} \qquad \text{where } T \text{ is the period of an oscillation}$$

The maximum acceleration has magnitude $n^2 a$ and occurs at A and A′.
The maximum speed is na and occurs at O.

EXERCISE 12a

1) A particle moves in a straight line with SHM. Find the periodic time if:
(a) the acceleration is of magnitude $2 \, \mathrm{m \, s^{-2}}$ when the particle is 1 m from the centre of oscillation,
(b) the maximum velocity is $4 \, \mathrm{m \, s^{-1}}$ and the maximum acceleration is $6 \, \mathrm{m \, s^{-2}}$.

2) The amplitude of oscillation of a particle describing linear SHM is 1.5 m. The speed at a distance $\sqrt{2}$ m from the mean position is $2 \, \mathrm{m \, s^{-1}}$. Find:
(a) the velocity of the particle at the mean position,
(b) the maximum acceleration,
(c) the period of one oscillation.

3) A particle describing angular SHM passes through its mean position with angular velocity 4 radians per second. If the amplitude is $\pi/6$ radians, find the angular velocity when the angular displacement from the mean position is $\pi/12$ radians.

4) A point is moving in a straight line with SHM about a fixed point A. The point has speeds v_1 and v_2 when its displacements from A are x_1 and x_2 respectively. Find, in terms of x_1, x_2, v_1 and v_2 the periodic time of one oscillation.

5) A particle is describing angular SHM of period π seconds. Its maximum angular acceleration is $4\pi/3 \, \mathrm{rad \, s^{-2}}$. Find the maximum angular displacement of the particle from its mean position and the angular velocity of the particle when its angular displacement is half the maximum value.

6) A piston performing SHM has a maximum speed of $0.5 \, \mathrm{m \, s^{-1}}$ and describes four oscillations in one minute. Find the amplitude of the motion and the velocity and acceleration of the piston when it is 1 m from the centre of oscillation.

7) A particle performs two SHM oscillations each second. Its speed when it is 0.02 m from its mean position is half the maximum speed. Find the amplitude of the motion, the maximum acceleration and the speed at a distance 0.01 m from the mean position.

ASSOCIATED CIRCULAR MOTION

A particle P is describing circular motion of radius a with constant angular velocity ω and Q is the foot of the perpendicular from P on to a diameter AA'. The velocity of P is $a\omega$ along the tangent and the acceleration of P is $a\omega^2$ towards the centre O of the circle.

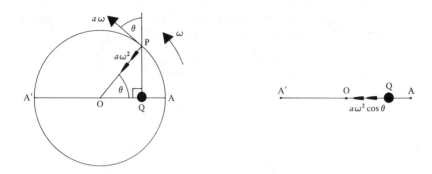

The components, parallel to AA', of the velocity and acceleration of P give the velocity and acceleration of Q.

Therefore, for Q, $\qquad$ velocity $= a\omega \sin\theta \quad$ along $\overrightarrow{QO}$

$$\text{acceleration} = a\omega^2 \cos\theta \quad \text{along } \overrightarrow{QO}$$

If the distance OQ is x, then $\quad \cos\theta = \dfrac{x}{a}$

Therefore Q has an acceleration $\quad a\omega^2 \left(\dfrac{x}{a}\right) = \omega^2 x \quad$ towards O.

But ω^2 is constant so the acceleration of Q is proportional to the distance of Q from O and is always towards O.

Therefore Q describes SHM about O as centre and with amplitude a.

The equations of SHM can now be derived by considering the associated circular motion of P (an alternative to the derivation in which calculus was used).

The velocity, v, of Q is $a\omega \sin\theta$

But $\qquad\qquad\qquad\qquad \sin\theta = \dfrac{\sqrt{a^2 - x^2}}{a}$

Therefore $\qquad\qquad\qquad v = \omega\sqrt{a^2 - x^2} \qquad\qquad$ [2a]

The period, T, of one oscillation of Q is the time taken for P to perform one revolution at angular velocity ω.

Therefore
$$T = \frac{2\pi}{\omega} \qquad [4a]$$

Comparing equations [2a] and [4a] with equations [2] and [4] (pages 384–5) derived earlier by integration, we see that ω represents the same constant of proportion as n, and, in fact, the symbol ω is frequently used instead of n. The time taken by Q to travel over any section of the diameter AA' is equal to the time taken by P to travel round the corresponding arc,

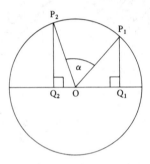

In the diagram above

the time, t, taken to move from Q_1 to Q_2 with SHM is the same as the time taken to move from P_1 to P_2 with constant angular velocity ω

i.e.
$$t = \frac{a}{\omega} \quad \text{where } \alpha \text{ is measured in radians}$$

EXAMPLES 12b

1) A particle is performing linear SHM about a centre O and with amplitude OA $= 4d$. B and C are two points on the path such that OB $= 2d$, OC $= d$. Find the time taken to travel (a) from A to B, (b) from A to C, if one oscillation is completed in π seconds.

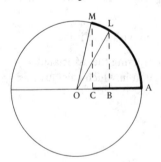

Project B and C on to the associated circle at L and M.

Let the constant angular speed round the associated circle be ω rad s^{-1}.

As $T = \dfrac{2\pi}{\omega} = \pi$ then $\omega = 2$.

$$\cos \widehat{LOA} = \frac{2d}{4d} = \tfrac{1}{2} \;\Rightarrow\; \widehat{LOA} = \frac{\pi}{3}$$

$$\cos \widehat{MOA} = \frac{d}{4d} = \tfrac{1}{4} \;\Rightarrow\; \widehat{MOA} = 1.32^c$$

(a) If t_1 seconds is the time from A to L at $2\,\text{rad s}^{-1}$ then $t_1 = \dfrac{\pi}{3} \div 2$.

So the time from A to B is $\frac{1}{6}\pi$ seconds.

(b) Similarly, if t_2 seconds is the time from A to M, $t_2 = 1.32 \div 2$.
So the time from A to C is 0.66 seconds.

Alternatively, having evaluated ω as above, the problem can then be solved by using the formula $x = a \cos \omega t$.

(a) At B, $x = 2d$ and the time from A to B is given by

$$2d = 4d \cos 2t_1$$

i.e.

$$2t_1 = \arccos \tfrac{1}{2} = \pi/3$$

$\Rightarrow$

$$t_1 = \pi/6$$

(b) At C, $x = d$ and the time from A to C is given by

$$d = 4d \cos 2t_2$$

i.e.

$$2t_2 = \arccos \tfrac{1}{4} = 1.32$$

$\Rightarrow$

$$t_2 = 0.66$$

2) A particle travelling with linear SHM of period T starts from the centre O of its path which is of length $2a$. The particle travels for a time t and is then at a point P. Find the distance OP if (a) $t = \frac{1}{6}T$ (b) $t = \frac{1}{3}T$.

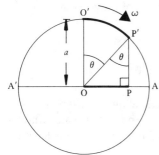

As P travels along AA′ with SHM its projection P′ on the associated circle travels with constant angular velocity.

$$T = \frac{2\pi}{\omega}$$

Hence

$$\omega = \frac{2\pi}{T}$$

The time, t, taken to travel from O to P with SHM is equal to the time taken to traverse the arc O′P′ with constant angular velocity

i.e.

$$t = \frac{\theta}{\omega} \quad \text{or} \quad \theta = \omega t$$

But

$$OP = a \sin \theta = a \sin \omega t = a \sin \frac{2\pi t}{T}$$

(a) If $t = \frac{1}{6}T$ $OP = a \sin\frac{\pi}{3} = a\frac{\sqrt{3}}{2}$

(b) If $t = \frac{1}{3}T$ $OP = a \sin\frac{2\pi}{3} = a\frac{\sqrt{3}}{2}$

Therefore P is at the same distance from O when $t = \frac{1}{6}T$ and $t = \frac{1}{3}T$, but is travelling in the first case away from O and in the second case toward O.

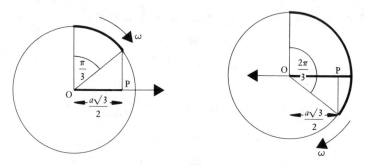

EXERCISE 12b

(The solutions to this exercise may be based either on the standard formulae for SHM or on the use of the associated circular motion.)

1) A particle is travelling between two points P and Q with linear SHM. If the distance PQ is 6 m and the maximum acceleration of the particle is $16\,\mathrm{m\,s^{-2}}$, find the time taken to travel:
(a) a distance 1.5 m from P,
(b) from P to the midpoint O of PQ,
(c) from the midpoint of PO to the midpoint of OQ.

2) A particle describes linear SHM of amplitude a about a fixed point O. The period of one complete oscillation is T seconds. If the particle passes through a point P, t seconds after passing through O, find in terms of a the length of OP if:
(a) $t = \frac{1}{6}T$ (b) $t = \frac{1}{12}T$ (c) $t = \frac{1}{3}T$.

3) A particle starts from rest at A and moves in a straight line with SHM of periodic time $12T$. If the length of the path is $4l$ find the time taken to travel a distance l from A. Show that the velocity at a time T after leaving A is half the maximum velocity.

4) A particle is performing linear SHM of amplitude 0.8 m about a fixed point O. A and B are two points on the path of the particle such that

$AO = 0.6$ m   and $OB = 0.4$ m.   If the particle takes 2 seconds to travel from A to B find, correct to one decimal place, the periodic time of the SHM:
(a) if A and B are on the same side of O,
(b) if A and B are on opposite sides of O.

5) A particle describes linear SHM between two points A and B. The period of one oscillation is 12 seconds. The particle starts from A and after 2 seconds has reached a point distant 0.5 m from A. Find:
(a) the amplitude of the motion,
(b) the maximum acceleration,
(c) the velocity 4 seconds after leaving A.

The Simple Pendulum

Probably the commonest example of angular simple harmonic motion is that of a heavy particle oscillating through a small angle at the end of a light string fixed at its other end, a system known as a simple pendulum.

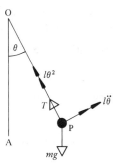

The particle P has mass m and the string, of length l, is fixed at O.
OA is vertical and the angle made by the string to the vertical at any time t is θ.

The angular acceleration of P is $\dfrac{d^2\theta}{dt^2}$ *away* from OA, the sense in which θ

increases. P also has an acceleration $l\dot{\theta}^2$ towards O because it is travelling in a circular path.

Applying Newton's law along the tangent gives

$$mg \sin \theta = -ml\ddot{\theta}$$

Now the angle θ is always very small, so

$$\sin \theta \simeq \theta$$

Hence $$mg\theta \simeq -ml\ddot{\theta}$$

$$\Rightarrow \qquad \ddot{\theta} \simeq -\frac{g}{l}\theta$$

But this is the basic equation of angular SHM. Therefore a particle oscillating through *small* angles at the end of a light string performs angular SHM (to a good approximation).

The period, T, of such oscillations is $\dfrac{2\pi}{n}$ where $n^2 = \dfrac{g}{l}$

Therefore
$$T = 2\pi\sqrt{l/g}$$

Note: T depends upon the length of the string and the value of gravitational acceleration but not upon the mass of the particle (often called the pendulum *bob*).

The Seconds Pendulum

A simple pendulum which swings from one end of its path to the other end in exactly one second is called a *seconds pendulum* and is said to *beat seconds*.

Since each half oscillation takes 1 second, the period of oscillation is 2 seconds,

i.e. $$T = 2$$

The length of string, l, required for a seconds pendulum can then be calculated using

$$T = 2\pi\sqrt{l/g} \qquad \Rightarrow \qquad 2 = 2\pi\sqrt{l/g}$$

giving $$l = \frac{g}{\pi^2}$$

EXAMPLES 12c

1) A simple pendulum which is meant to beat seconds (i.e. each *half oscillation* takes 1 second) gains 1 minute per day. By what percentage of its length should it be lengthened to make it accurate?

The pendulum makes $(24 \times 60 \times 60 + 60)$ half oscillations in 24 hours.

The time for half an oscillation is $\dfrac{24 \times 60 \times 60}{60(24 \times 60 + 1)}$ seconds

The time for one oscillation is $2\pi\sqrt{l/g}$ where l is the length of the pendulum.

Therefore $\dfrac{24 \times 60}{1441} = \pi \sqrt{\dfrac{l}{g}}$ [1]

Let kl be the *extra* length required for an accurate 1 second beat

Then $1 = \pi\sqrt{(l+kl)/g} = \pi\sqrt{l/g}\,\sqrt{1+k}$ [2]

Equation [2] $\div$ [1] gives $\sqrt{1+k} = \dfrac{1441}{1440}$

Hence $k = \left(\dfrac{1441}{1440}\right)^2 - 1$

$= 0.0014$

The percentage increase in length is given by $\left(\dfrac{kl}{l}\right)(100)\%$

The length should be increased by 0.14%

2) At ground level where $g = 9.81\,\mathrm{m\,s^{-2}}$ a simple pendulum beats exact seconds. If it is taken to a place where $g = 9.80\,\mathrm{m\,s^{-2}}$ by how many seconds per day will it be wrong?

If l is the length of the pendulum then

$$\pi\sqrt{\dfrac{l}{9.81}} = 1 \quad \text{giving} \quad \sqrt{l} = \dfrac{\sqrt{9.81}}{\pi}$$

When $g = 9.80$ the time, t, of one beat is given by $\pi\sqrt{\dfrac{l}{9.8}}$ and is

therefore $\sqrt{\dfrac{9.81}{9.8}}$ seconds.

The number of beats in 24 hours is now $(24 \times 60 \times 60) \div \sqrt{\dfrac{9.81}{9.8}}$

The number of beats lost in 24 hours is therefore

$$24 \times 60 \times 60 \left(1 - \sqrt{\dfrac{9.8}{9.81}}\right) = 24 \times 60 \times 60(0.0005)$$

$$= 44$$

Therefore, where $g = 9.80$ the pendulum will lose 44 seconds per day.

EXERCISE 12c

1) By what length should a simple pendulum be shortened if it is meant to beat seconds but loses 40 seconds in 12 hours?

2) A pendulum which beats seconds where $g = 9.81 \text{ m s}^{-2}$ is taken up a mountain to a place where it loses 30 seconds per day. What is the value of g at the new location?

3) If a simple pendulum which beats exact seconds has its length changed by 1%, find the number of seconds by which it will be inaccurate if:
(a) the length is increased,
(b) the pendulum is shortened.

FORCES WHICH PRODUCE SHM

Since linear SHM is motion in which the acceleration is proportional to the distance from, and directed towards, a fixed point, such motion will be produced by the action of *a force directed towards a fixed point and proportional to the distance from that point.*

If an elastic string is stretched, the tension in it is proportional to the extension and always acts to restore the string to its natural length.
Consequently we would expect a moving particle attached to a stretched elastic string to perform SHM when released and we will verify that this is so in several different cases.

EXAMPLES 12d

1) An elastic string, of natural length a and modulus of elasticity λ, is stretched between two points A and B distant $2a$ apart on a smooth horizontal table. A particle of mass m, fastened to the mid-point M of the string, is pulled towards A through a distance less than $a/2$ and is then released. Analyse the subsequent motion.

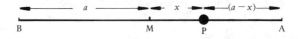

Consider the motion of the particle as it passes through a general point P which is distant x from M.
For the portion of string AP,

$$\text{stretched length} = a - x \qquad \text{and} \qquad \text{natural length} = \tfrac{1}{2}a$$

$\Rightarrow \qquad\qquad \text{extension} = (a - x) - \tfrac{1}{2}a = \tfrac{1}{2}a - x$

Therefore the tension, T_A, in AP $\quad = \dfrac{2\lambda}{a}\left(\dfrac{a}{2}-x\right)$ $\qquad$ (Hooke's Law)

$$= \frac{\lambda}{a}(a-2x).$$

Similarly we can show that, for the portion of string BP in which the extension is $\left(\dfrac{a}{2}+x\right)$,

the tension, $\quad T_B = \dfrac{\lambda}{a}(a+2x)$

The particle will never be further from M than its initial displacement. Since this distance is less than $\frac{1}{2}a$, neither string will ever go slack during the subsequent motion.

Therefore, for all positions of P, applying Newton's law in the direction $\overrightarrow{MP}$ gives

$$T_A - T_B = m\ddot{x}$$

Therefore $\qquad \dfrac{\lambda}{a}(a-2x) - \dfrac{\lambda}{a}(a+2x) = m\ddot{x}$

Hence $\qquad -\dfrac{4\lambda x}{a} = m\ddot{x}$

or $\qquad \ddot{x} = -\left(\dfrac{4\lambda}{ma}\right)x$

Comparing with $\ddot{x} = -n^2 x$ we see that the particle performs SHM about M as centre (M being the fixed point from which x is measured).

The period of oscillation, $\dfrac{2\pi}{n}$, is $2\pi\sqrt{\dfrac{ma}{4\lambda}} = \pi\sqrt{\dfrac{ma}{\lambda}}$

2) One end of an elastic string of natural length l is fixed to a point A on a smooth horizontal table. A particle of mass m is attached to the other end of the string. The particle is pulled away from A and is then released. Investigate the subsequent motion.

Consider the motion of the particle as it passes through a general point P which is distant x from B where $AB = l$.

The tension in the string is $\lambda \dfrac{x}{l}$

Applying Newton's Law in the direction $\overrightarrow{BP}$ gives

$$-\lambda \frac{x}{l} = m\ddot{x}$$

$\Rightarrow$
$$\ddot{x} = -\frac{\lambda}{ml}x$$

This is the basic equation of linear SHM where $n^2 = \dfrac{\lambda}{ml}$

The particle therefore initially performs SHM with B as centre.

But as the particle passes through B the string becomes slack and no horizontal force then acts on the particle. It will therefore travel with constant speed until the string becomes taut again at B′ where $AB' = l$.

Once beyond B′ the string again has a tension $\dfrac{\lambda x}{l}$ towards B′ where $B'P' = x$.

The particle again moves with SHM where $n^2 = \dfrac{\lambda}{ml}$ but about centre B′.

	B′		A		B	
◄ SHM ►◄		Constant speed			►◄ SHM ►	

The particle therefore performs half an oscillation with SHM at each end of its journey and covers the section between B and B′ with constant speed.

3) Consider an elastic string of natural length a and modulus $2mg$ attached at one end to a fixed point A and hanging vertically with a particle of mass m at the other end. If the particle is pulled vertically downward a distance d below its equilibrium position and then released, investigate the subsequent motion if $d < a/2$.

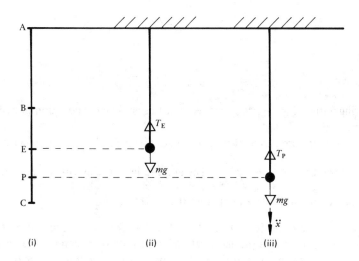

In diagram (i)   AB is the natural length of the string
                    E is the position of equilibrium of the particle
                    P is a general point through which the particle passes
                    C is the lowest position of the particle.

In diagram (ii)   where the extension in the string is e,

the tension $$T_E = \frac{\lambda e}{a} = \frac{2mge}{a} \qquad \text{(Hooke's Law)}$$

But the particle is in equilibrium

therefore $$T_E = mg \quad \Rightarrow \quad e = \frac{a}{2}$$

In diagram (iii) where the extension is $(e+x)$ and the acceleration of the particle is $\ddot{x}$ in the direction EP,

the tension $$T_P = \frac{\lambda}{a}(e+x) = \frac{2mg}{a}(e+x)$$

The maximum distance from E of the paricle is the initial displacement d which is less than $a/2$. The particle therefore never rises above the level of B and the string never goes slack. For all positions of P, then, applying Newton's law vertically downward at P gives

$$mg - \frac{2mg}{a}(e+x) = m\ddot{x}$$

Therefore $$mg - \frac{2mg}{a}\frac{a}{2} + x = m\ddot{x}$$

$$\Rightarrow \qquad\qquad -\frac{2mgx}{a} = m\ddot{x}$$

$$\Rightarrow \qquad\qquad \ddot{x} = -\frac{2g}{a}x$$

Comparing with $\ddot{x} = -n^2x$, we see that this is the basic equation of SHM with centre E.

The particle therefore travels throughout with linear SHM about E as centre and with periodic time $2\pi\sqrt{\dfrac{a}{2g}}$. The amplitude of the motion is d since this is the maximum displacement from the centre E.

Note. We chose to measure x from E rather than from B because at E the resultant force, and hence the acceleration, is zero. Zero acceleration being a property of the centre point of the path of any SHM, we anticipated that E was a likely centre.

EXERCISE 12d

1) A particle of mass 2 kg is attached to one end of an elastic string of natural length 1 m whose other end is fixed to a point A on a smooth horizontal plane. The particle is pulled across the plane to a point C where AC = 1.5 m and is released from rest at C. B is a point on AC such that AB = 1 m. If the modulus of the string is 10 N show that:

(a) from C to B the particle performs SHM with centre B (remember to analyse a general position),

(b) the time taken to travel from B to C is $\dfrac{\pi\sqrt{5}}{10}$ s,

(c) the speed at B is $\dfrac{\sqrt{5}}{2}$ m s^{-1},

(d) the particle then travels for $\frac{4}{5}\sqrt{5}$ s with constant speed.

2) A particle of mass 4 kg hangs at the end of a light elastic string of natural length 1 m attached at the other end to a fixed point A. The particle hangs in equilibrium at E where AE = 1.4 m. Calculate the modulus of elasticity of the string. If the particle is then pulled down to C where EC = 0.2 m and is released from rest at C prove that it performs SHM. State the centre and the period of the oscillations. What is the speed of the particle as it passes through E and what is the greatest height above E reached by the particle?

3) A particle P of mass m is attached to one end of each of two light elastic strings. The other ends are attached to two fixed points A and B on a smooth horizontal table. The natural length of AP is $2a$ and its modulus is mg. The natural length of BP is a and its modulus is $2mg$.

If the distance AB is $8a$ find the distance from A of the point E at which the particle will rest in equilibrium.
When the particle is pulled a short distance towards A and is then released, show that it performs SHM and find the periodic time.

4) A particle of mass $4m$ is attached to the midpoint of a light spring of modulus $2mg$ whose ends are attached to two fixed points distant $8a$ apart in a vertical line. If the spring is of natural length $2a$, find the depth below the upper fixed point, A, of the position of equilibrium of the particle. When the particle is slightly disturbed from rest in a vertical direction show that it performs SHM of periodic time $2\pi\sqrt{(a/g)}$.

5) A particle of mass 2 kg lies on a smooth horizontal table attached to one end of a light elastic spring whose other end is fixed to the table at a point A. The particle is at rest at E with the spring just taut when it is suddenly given a velocity of $4\,\text{m s}^{-1}$ towards A. The particle next comes to instantaneous rest at a point B where $AB = 0.8\,\text{m}$. If the natural length of the spring is 1 m find its modulus of elasticity. Prove that the particle performs SHM and find:
(a) its maximum acceleration,
(b) the time taken to travel from E to B,
(c) the velocity half way between E and B.

6) Prove that a particle of mass m, hanging from a fixed point at the end of a light elastic string, performs SHM when given a vertical displacement from its equilibrium position. Find the period of oscillation in terms of m, l and λ where l and λ are the natural length and modulus of elasticity of the string. What is the maximum vertical displacement which the particle can be given if its subsequent motion is entirely SHM?

INCOMPLETE OSCILLATIONS

There are some occasions when a particle begins to move with SHM but, before it reaches the end of its path, the character of its motion changes so that the simple harmonic oscillations are never completed, as we saw in Ex. 12d No. 2. Another way in which this can happen is described in the following case.

Consider an elastic string of natural length a and modulus $4mg$ which is fixed at one end to a point A and hangs vertically with a mass m attached to the other end. If the particle is pulled down a distance a below its equilibrium position and is then released, we will show that the particle describes partial SHM and we will investigate the subsequent motion.

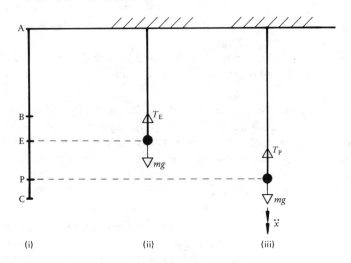

(i)   (ii)   (iii)

In diagram (i)   AB is the natural length of the string
                  E is the equilibrium position of the particle
                  P is a general position of the particle
                  C is the lowest position of the particle

In diagram (ii) where the extension is e, $T_E = \dfrac{4mge}{a}$

But the particle is in equilibrium so

$$\frac{4mge}{a} = mg \quad \Rightarrow \quad e = \frac{a}{4}$$

In diagram (iii) the extension is $(e+x)$ so $T_P = \dfrac{4mg}{a}(e+x)$

But the string is in tension *only* while the particle is *below the level of* B.
Provided, then, that P is below B, applying Newton's law vertically downwards
gives

$$mg - \frac{4mg}{a}(e+x) = m\ddot{x}$$

$$-\frac{4mg}{a}x = m\ddot{x}$$

$$\ddot{x} = -\frac{4g}{a}x$$

Comparing with $\ddot{x} = -n^2x$ we see that the particle performs SHM about E
as centre, but only while the string is taut. As the particle passes through B the
string becomes slack. The only force then acting on the particle is its own weight.

Above B, then, SHM ceases and the particle travels with vertical motion under gravity.

In order to investigate this second type of motion in detail, the velocity at B, v_B, is required and can be calculated using

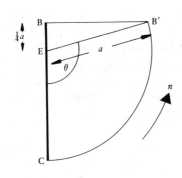

$$v^2 = n^2(a^2 - x^2)$$

$$\Rightarrow \quad v_B{}^2 = \frac{4g}{a}\left(a^2 - \left[\frac{a}{4}\right]^2\right)$$

$$\Rightarrow \quad v_B = \tfrac{1}{2}\sqrt{15ga}$$

This is the initial velocity for the motion under gravity above B.

The oscillations performed by the particle are compound and the periodic time of one oscillation can be determined in two parts.

(a) Time, t_1, taken from C to B with SHM.

t_1 is equal to the time taken to describe the arc CB$'$ with constant angular velocity n.

i.e. $\quad t_1 = \dfrac{\theta}{n}$

But $\quad \theta = \pi - B\widehat{E}B'$

or $\quad \theta = \pi - \arccos\tfrac{1}{4}$

So $\quad t_1 = \sqrt{\dfrac{a}{4g}}\left(\pi - \arccos\tfrac{1}{4}\right)$

(b) Time, t_2, taken to rise above B to instantaneous rest, moving under gravity.

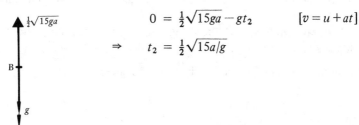

$$0 = \tfrac{1}{2}\sqrt{15ga} - gt_2 \qquad [v = u + at]$$

$$\Rightarrow \quad t_2 = \tfrac{1}{2}\sqrt{15a/g}$$

Now one complete oscillation will take a time of $2(t_1 + t_2)$.
Therefore the period of compound oscillations is

$$\sqrt{\frac{a}{g}\left(\pi - \arccos \tfrac{1}{4} + \sqrt{15}\right)}$$

Solutions to problems of this type are inevitably rather complex. It is essential to deal systematically with the various sections of the motion, avoiding the temptation to take unsound 'short cuts'.
Further problems which illustrate the need for patience when working through such solutions are given in Examples 12e, below.

Fewer complications occur when analysing *oscillating springs*, because a spring never becomes slack. When it is compressed to less than its natural length it continues to obey Hooke's Law exerting an outward push at each end. A particle attached to one end of the spring will therefore continue to travel with SHM even when the spring is reduced below its natural length.

EXAMPLES 12e

1) A particle of mass 2 kg lies, on a smooth horizontal table, at one end of an elastic string of length 1 m and modulus of elasticity 8 N. The other end of the string is attached to a fixed point A on the table. Initially the particle is at B where $AB = 1$ m. It is then pulled in the direction $\overrightarrow{AB}$ to a point C such that $AC = 2AB$, and is then released from rest. Show that, as the particle moves back towards A, its motion is of two different types. Determine each type of motion and find the time taken to travel from C to A.

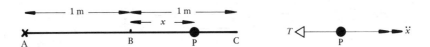

Consider the motion of the particle as it passes through a general point P distant x from B.
If P is between B and C the string is taut and the tension in the string is $8x$ (Hooke's Law).

Applying Newton's Law in the direction $\overrightarrow{BC}$ gives

$$-8x = 2\ddot{x}$$

$\Rightarrow \qquad\qquad\qquad \ddot{x} = -4x$

Comparing with $\ddot{x} = -n^2x$, we see that this is the basic equation of SHM about B as centre and for which $n = 2$. Also the amplitude, a, of the motion is BC i.e. $a = 1$.

Now C is the end of the path and B is the centre so BC is one quarter of a complete oscillation.

Therefore the time taken to travel from C to B is $\frac{1}{4}\left(\dfrac{2\pi}{n}\right) = \dfrac{\pi}{4}$

As the particle passes through B with velocity v_B, the string becomes slack. The particle no longer has any horizontal force acting on it and its horizontal velocity will therefore be constant.

Using $v^2 = n^2(a^2 - x^2)$ at B where $x = 0$, gives $v_B = na$

So the speed at B is $2\,\mathrm{m\,s^{-1}}$

The time taken to travel from B to A at this speed is therefore $\frac{1}{2}$ second.

The two types of motion are (a) SHM from C to B

(b) constant velocity from B to A.

The total time taken to travel from C to A is $(\frac{1}{4}\pi + \frac{1}{2})\,\mathrm{s}$.

2) A particle of mass 2 kg is attached to one end of a light elastic string of natural length 1 m whose modulus of elasticity is $4g$ N. The other end of the string is fastened to a fixed point O. The particle is held at O and is then released from that position. Find the depth below O of the level where the particle first comes to instantaneous rest. Find also the period of oscillation of the subsequent motion.

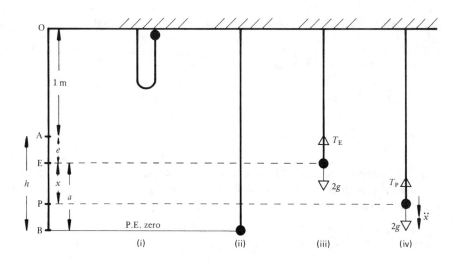

(i)   (ii)   (iii)   (iv)

In the diagram OA is the natural length of the string

E is the equilibrium position of the particle

B is the lowest position of the particle

P is a general position of the particle

From position (i) to (ii) we can use conservation of mechanical energy (an elastic string does not 'jerk' when it becomes taut, since it immediately begins to stretch).

$$(PE + KE + EPE)_{(i)} = (PE + KE + EPE)_{(ii)}$$

Therefore

$$2g(1+h) + 0 + 0 = 0 + 0 + \frac{4g}{2}(h)^2$$

giving

$$h^2 - h - 1 = 0$$

$\Rightarrow$

$$h = \tfrac{1}{2}(1 \pm \sqrt{5})$$

As B is below A we take h to be positive

i.e.

$$h = \tfrac{1}{2}(1 + \sqrt{5})$$

When the particle first comes to instantaneous rest, at B, its depth below A is $1 + h$

i.e.

$$\tfrac{3}{2} + \tfrac{1}{2}\sqrt{5}$$

When the particle is in equilibrium at E (diagram (iii))

$$T_E = \frac{4ge}{1} = 2g$$

$\Rightarrow$

$$e = \tfrac{1}{2}$$

In a general position P where the extension is $e + x$ (diagram (iv))

$$T_P = \frac{4g}{1}(e + x) = 4g(\tfrac{1}{2} + x)$$

While the particle is below A applying Newton's Law gives

$$2g - 4g(\tfrac{1}{2} + x) = 2\ddot{x}$$

$\Rightarrow$

$$\ddot{x} = -2gx$$

This is the equation of linear SHM about E as centre and for which $n^2 = 2g$, showing the particle moves with SHM while it is below A.

The amplitude of the motion, EB, is $(h - e)$, i.e. $\tfrac{1}{2}\sqrt{5}$

For the SHM between B and A, using the associated circular motion and the equation $v^2 = n^2(a^2 - x^2)$, we have

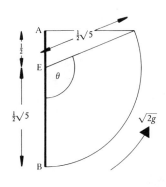

$$\theta = \pi - \arccos\frac{1}{\sqrt{5}}$$

The time taken from B to A is $\dfrac{\theta}{n}$

which is $\dfrac{\pi - \arccos\frac{1}{\sqrt{5}}}{\sqrt{2g}}$

Also $v_A{}^2 = 2g\left[\left(\frac{1}{2}\sqrt{5}\right)^2 - \left(\frac{1}{2}\right)^2\right]$

$\Rightarrow$ $v_A = \sqrt{2g}$

Above A the time, t, taken before next coming to rest is given by

$$0 = \sqrt{2g} - gt \qquad \text{(using } v = u + at)$$

$\Rightarrow$ $t = \sqrt{\dfrac{2}{g}} = \dfrac{2}{\sqrt{2g}}$

So the total time for one compound oscillation is

$$\frac{2}{\sqrt{2g}}\left[\pi - \arccos\frac{1}{\sqrt{5}} + 2\right]$$

3) A particle of mass m is attached to one end of a light elastic string whose other end is fixed to a point A on a smooth plane inclined at $30°$ to the horizontal. The length of the string is l and its modulus of elasticity is $2mg$. The particle is pulled down the line of greatest slope through A, to a point C where it is released from rest. If the particle just reaches A, find the time taken to travel from C to A.

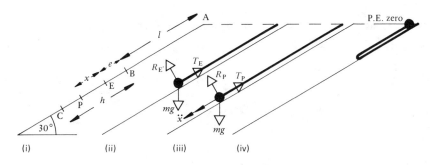

In diagram (i)   AB is the natural length of the string
                    E is the equilibrium position of the particle
                    C is the lowest position of the particle
                    P is a general position of the particle

In diagram (ii)   the particle is in equilibrium

Resolving parallel to the plane

$$T_E = mg \sin 30°$$

But
$$T_E = \frac{2mg}{l} e$$

Therefore
$$e = \tfrac{1}{4} l$$

In diagram (iii)
$$T_P = \frac{2mg}{l}(e + x)$$

Applying Newton's Law down the plane gives

$$mg \sin 30° - \frac{2mg}{l}(x + e) = m\ddot{x}$$

hence
$$\frac{mg}{2} - \frac{2mg}{l}(x + \tfrac{1}{4} l) = m\ddot{x}$$

giving
$$\ddot{x} = -\frac{2g}{l} x$$

This is the basic equation of SHM about E as centre. It is valid while the string is taut, i.e. below B.

Using conservation of mechanical energy between C and A using diagrams (i) and (iv), we have:

Total ME at A $= 0$

Total ME at C $= -mg(h + l) \sin 30° + \frac{2mg}{2l} h^2$

Therefore
$$0 = -\frac{mg}{2}(h + l) + \frac{mg}{l} h^2$$

Hence
$$0 = 2h^2 - hl - l^2$$

$\Rightarrow$
$$0 = (2h + l)(h - l)$$

Therefore
$$h = -\tfrac{1}{2} l \quad \text{or} \quad l$$

Taking the positive value since h is an extension, $h = l$.

The amplitude of the SHM is then $h - e = \tfrac{3}{4} l$

Now, for the SHM between C and B $(x = -\frac{1}{4}l$ at B) we first find the velocity, v_B, at B using $v^2 = n^2(a^2 - x^2)$

i.e. $v_B{}^2 = \dfrac{2g}{l}\left(\dfrac{9l^2}{16} - \dfrac{l^2}{16}\right)$

$\Rightarrow$ $v_B = \sqrt{gl}$

Using $x = a \cos nt$, the time t_1 taken to travel from C to B is given by

$$-\tfrac{1}{4}l = \tfrac{3}{4}l \cos t_1 \sqrt{2g/l}$$

$\Rightarrow$ $t_1 = \sqrt{l/2g} \ \text{arcos}\left(-\tfrac{1}{3}\right)$

$\Rightarrow$ $t_1 = \sqrt{l/2g} \ (\pi - \text{arcos} \ \tfrac{1}{3}).$

Above B there is a constant acceleration $g \sin 30°$ down the slope so we have:

initial velocity at B $= \sqrt{gl}$

final velocity at A $= 0$

acceleration $= -\tfrac{1}{2}g$

time from B to A $= t_2$

Using $v = u + at$ gives $0 = \sqrt{gl} - \tfrac{1}{2}gt_2$

$\Rightarrow$ $t_2 = 2\sqrt{l/g}$

The total time taken to travel from C to A is $t_1 + t_2$ where

$$t_1 + t_2 = \sqrt{l/g} \ (\pi - \text{arcos} \ \tfrac{1}{3} + 2\sqrt{2})$$

4) A light vertical spring is fixed at its lower end O. A platform of mass m is attached to the upper end of the spring and a particle, also of mass m, rests on the platform. The length of the spring is $4a$ and its modulus of elasticity is $8mg$. If the platform together with the particle is gently depressed through a distance $2a$ below the equilibrium position and is then released from rest, show that the particle performs partial SHM but also appears to bounce off the platform at some stage. Find the height above O when this occurs.

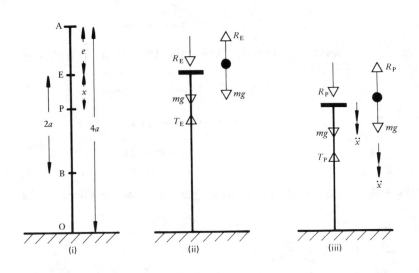

In diagram (i)   OA is the natural length of the spring
               E is the equilibrium position
               B is the lowest position
               P is a general position

In diagram (ii)   both the platform and the particle are in equilibrium and there is a pair of normal reactions, R_E, between them.

The compression in the spring, T_E, is $\dfrac{8mg}{4a}e$.

Because the platform is in equilibrium $T_E = R_E + mg$

Because the particle is in equilibrium $mg = R_E$

Therefore $2mg = \dfrac{8mg}{4a}e$

$\Rightarrow$ $e = a$

In diagram (iii) $$T_P = \frac{8mg}{4a}(e+x) = \frac{2mg}{a}(a+x)$$

Applying Newton's Law vertically downward we have:

for the platform $mg + R_P - T_P = m\ddot{x}$

for the particle $mg - R_P = m\ddot{x}$

As long as the particle is in contact with the platform, these equations can be combined to give

$$2mg - \frac{2mg}{a}(a+x) = 2m\ddot{x}$$

$\Rightarrow$ $$\ddot{x} = -\frac{g}{a}x$$

This basic equation of SHM about E as centre represents the motion of both the particle and the platform so long as they are in contact.

The maximum downward acceleration of the particle is g, since the maximum downward force acting on it is mg. The platform has acceleration g downward when $x = -a$ i.e. at a position D of height a above E.

But the amplitude of the motion of the platform is $2a$ (the initial displacement from E). The platform will therefore rise above D where its downward acceleration will exceed g.

Above D, then, the retardation of the platform is greater than that of the particle. Contact between them will be lost and the particle, as it continues to move under gravity, will appear to bounce off the platform (in fact it is the platform which withdraws from underneath the particle).

This apparent bounce occurs at D whose height above O is $4a$.

Note. Remember that some problems about particles moving on elastic strings or springs can be solved without using the equations of SHM. When considering only velocity and position, the principle of conservation of mechanical energy provides the best solution. Examples of this type were given in Chapter 7.

EXERCISE 12e

1) A particle of mass 1 kg is attached to one end of a light elastic string whose other end is fixed to a point O. The length of the string is 1 m and the particle hangs in equilibrium 1.2 m below O. If the particle is then pulled down a further 0.4 m and released show that it performs partial SHM and find the time which elapses before the particle next comes to instantaneous rest.

2) A particle of mass m is attached to the midpoint of a light elastic string of length $2a$ and modulus mg whose ends are attached to two fixed points A and B on a smooth horizontal table distant $4a$ apart. The particle is drawn aside until it is at the point A and is then released from rest. Show that, as the particle moves from A to the midpoint of AB it performs SHM of two different characteristics. Use the principle of conservation of mechanical energy to find the speed of the particle:

(a) when it is $\frac{1}{4}$ of the way from A to B,

(b) when it is halfway between A and B.

3) A particle of mass 2g hangs in equilibrium at the end of a light elastic string of length 1 m and modulus 10 N. The particle is projected vertically upwards from this position and just reaches the fixed upper end, A, of the string. Find the velocity of projection and time taken to rise to A. [Take $g = 10\,\mathrm{m\,s^{-2}}$.]

4) A particle of mass m rests on a smooth table, and is attached to one end of a light elastic string of natural length a and modulus mg. The other end of the string is attached to a fixed point O on the table. The particle is pulled away from O to a point B where $OB = 2a$ and is then released from rest. Find the time taken:

(a) to reach the point A where $OA = a$,

(b) to reach O,

(c) to return to B.

5) A particle of mass m hangs at the end of a light elastic string attached at the other end to a fixed point A. If the natural length of the string is a and its modulus is $4mg$, find the depth below A at which the particle rests in equilibrium. The particle is pulled down a further distance d below the equilibrium position and is released from rest. What is the greatest possible value of d if the particle's subsequent motion is entirely SHM? If d is given twice this value find the period of the compound oscillations which the particle will then perform.

SUMMARY

1) A particle whose acceleration is directed towards a fixed origin and is proportional to the distance from that origin, moves with SHM.

2) The basic equation of SHM is

$$\ddot{x} = -n^2 x \quad \text{or} \quad \ddot{\theta} = -n^2\theta$$

3) Further relationships, which can usually be quoted, are:

$$v^2 = n^2(a^2 - x^2) \quad \text{where } a \text{ is the amplitude}$$

$$x = a\cos nt$$

$$T = \frac{2\pi}{n} \qquad \text{where } T \text{ is the periodic time.}$$

4) The projection on a diameter of a point describing a circle with constant angular velocity ω, travels with SHM in which $\ddot{x} = -\omega^2 x$.
This concept can be used to advantage if the time taken to travel *part* of the path is required.

5) The motion of a particle moving on a stretched elastic string can be shown to be SHM during the time that the string is taut. Attached to an oscillating spring however a particle always performs SHM since the spring never becomes slack.

6) Remember that some problems about particles moving on elastic strings or springs can be solved without using the equations of SHM. When considering only velocity and position, the principle of conservation of mechanical energy provides the best solution.

MULTIPLE CHOICE EXERCISE 12
(The instructions for answering these questions are given on page x.)

TYPE I

1) A particle P describes SHM of amplitude 1 m. In performing one complete oscillation, P travels a distance:
(a) 2 m   (b) 0   (c) 4 m   (d) -2 m.

2) A particle performing SHM has a speed of $4\,\mathrm{m\,s^{-1}}$ when it is 1 m from the centre. If the amplitude is 3 m what is the period of oscillation?

(a) $\sqrt{2}\pi$ (b) $\dfrac{\pi}{\sqrt{2}}$ (c) $\dfrac{\pi}{2}$ (d) $\dfrac{\pi}{2\sqrt{2}}$.

3)

A particle travels between A and A′ with SHM of period 24 seconds. O is the centre and B is the midpoint of AO.
The time taken to travel from A to B is:
(a) 3 s   (b) 8 s   (c) 6 s   (d) 4 s.

TYPE II

4) A particle is travelling with SHM of amplitude 1 m and period π s.
(a) Its maximum velocity is $2\,\mathrm{m\,s^{-1}}$.
(b) Its maximum acceleration is $2\,\mathrm{m\,s^{-2}}$.
(c) The acceleration at a distance d from the centre is $4d$.

5) A particle of mass m is oscillating vertically at the end of an elastic string of length l and modulus $2mg$. The motion of the particle will be entirely simple harmonic if:
(a) the amplitude is less than l,
(b) the particle never rises above its equilibrium position,
(c) the string never goes slack,
(d) the amplitude is less than $\frac{1}{2}l$.

6) When a particle performs small oscillations at the end of a spring, the period depends upon:
(a) the mass of the particle,
(b) the modulus of elasticity of the spring,
(c) the natural length of the spring,
(d) the maximum extension of the spring.

TYPE IV

7) A particle P is moving with linear SHM about a point O. Find the period of oscillation if:
(a) the acceleration is $6\,\mathrm{m\,s^{-1}}$ when $OP = 2m$,
(b) the amplitude is $5\,\mathrm{m}$,
(c) the mass of the particle is $3\,\mathrm{kg}$.

8) Find the amplitude of the SHM described by a particle if:
(a) its maximum velocity is $8\,\mathrm{m\,s^{-1}}$,
(b) its maximum acceleration occurs at O,
(c) the periodic time is $4\,\mathrm{s}$.

9) A particle is attached to a fixed point by an elastic string and is performing small vertical oscillations. Find the period if:
(a) the natural length of the string is l,
(b) the modulus of elasticity is $2mg$,
(c) the particle is of mass m.

TYPE V

10) A particle whose acceleration is proportional to its displacement from a fixed point is moving with SHM.

11) A particle hanging at the end of an elastic string is pulled down and then released. The motion of the particle must be entirely SHM.

12) A particle describing linear SHM on a path AB with midpoint O has its greatest acceleration at either A or B.

13) A particle travelling in a circle with constant angular velocity ω is moving with SHM.

14) The period of oscillation of a particle travelling with angular SHM is $\dfrac{2\pi}{\omega}$ therefore ω is the angular velocity at the centre of the path.

15) A particle which is oscillating is not necessarily performing SHM.

MISCELLANEOUS EXERCISE 12

1) A particle P moves with an acceleration which is proportional to its distance from rest at a point A distant d from C, where the magnitude of its acceleration is $\lambda^2 d$, find an expression for the velocity of P when it is distant x from C.
After what time does P next come to instantaneous rest? In what time does P travel from A to a point Q where $AQ = \frac{1}{2}d$?

2) A particle of mass 1 kg is attached to the midpoint of a light elastic string of natural length 1 m and modulus of elasticity $4g$ N. The ends of the string are stretched between two points P and Q, 2 m apart in a vertical line (P above Q). Find the height above Q of the position of equilibrium of the particle. Find also the period of *small* vertical oscillations when the particle is disturbed from rest.

3) A particle is moving with linear simple harmonic motion. Its speed is maximum at a point C and is zero at a point A. P and Q are two points on CA such that $4CP = CA$ while the speed at P is twice the speed at Q. Find the ratio of the accelerations at P and Q.
If the period of one oscillation is 10 seconds find, correct to the first decimal place, the least time taken to travel between P and Q.

4) Prove that, if a particle moving with linear simple harmonic motion of amplitude a has velocity v when distant x from the centre of its path, then $v = \omega\sqrt{a^2 - x^2}$ where ω is a constant.
A point travelling with linear SHM has speeds $3\,\mathrm{m\,s^{-1}}$ and $2\,\mathrm{m\,s^{-1}}$ when distant 1 m and 2 m respectively from the centre of oscillations. Calculate the amplitude, the periodic time and the maximum velocity.

5) A particle of mass 10 kg is moving along a straight line with simple harmonic motion. The particle has speeds of $9\,\mathrm{m\,s^{-1}}$ and $6\,\mathrm{m\,s^{-1}}$ at P and Q respectively, whose distances from the centre of oscillation are 1 m and 2 m respectively. Calculate the greatest speed and the greatest acceleration of the particle.
If the points P and Q are on the same side of the centre of oscillation, calculate:
(a) the shortest time taken by the particle to move from P to Q,
(b) the work done during this displacement.

6) A particle P moves in a straight line so that its acceleration is always directed towards a point O in its path and is of magnitude proportional to the distance OP. When P is at the point A, where $OA = 1\,\mathrm{m}$, its speed is $3\sqrt{3}$ m/s and when P is at the point B, where $OB = \sqrt{3}\,\mathrm{m}$, its speed is 3 m/s. Calculate the maximum speed attained by P and the maximum value of OP.
Show that P takes $\pi/18$ seconds to move directly from A to B. Find, in m/s correct to 2 significant figures, the speed of P one second after it passes O.

(U of L)

7)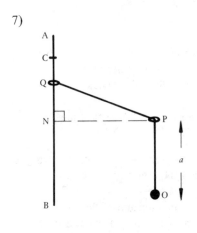

The diagram shows an elastic string OPQ of modulus λ and natural length a, one end of which is attached to a fixed point O. The string passes through a small smooth fixed ring at P, where OP $= a$. The other end of the string is attached to a small ring Q of mass m which can move on a smooth vertical wire AB. The perpendicular from P on to AB is PN. The ring is held at C, where NC $= c$, and is then released. Prove that the ring performs simple harmonic motion about a point on the wire distant mag/λ below N.

Find also the period of the motion and the speed of the ring when it passes through N.   (C)

8) A small sphere of mass m is suspended from a fixed point A by a light elastic string of modulus mg and natural length l. The sphere is pulled down to a point $\frac{1}{2}l$ vertically below its equilibrium position, and released from rest. As it passes through its equilibrium position it picks up a rider, also of mass m, previously at rest, which adheres to the sphere. Find the depth below A at which the sphere and rider next come to rest.   (U of L)

9) One end of a light elastic string, of natural length a and modulus of elasticity kmg, is attached at a fixed point on a frictionless plane inclined at an angle θ to the horizontal. A heavy particle is attached to the other end of the string. The particle is at rest on the plane with the string along a line of greatest slope and extended by a length b. The particle is then pulled down a distance d in the line of the string and released. Show that the period of the simple harmonic motion with which the particle starts to move is independent of θ.
If $d = 2b$, find the time from release to the string going slack and find also the speed of the particle at the instant when the string goes slack.   (AEB)

10) A particle of mass m is suspended from a ceiling by a light elastic string, of natural length a and modulus $12mg$. When the particle hangs at rest find the extension in the string. The particle is then pulled down vertically a distance x and released. If the particle just reaches the ceiling, find:
(a) the value of x,
(b) the maximum speed and the maximum acceleration during the motion.
                                                                                     (U of L)

11) A particle of mass m moves in a straight line in simple harmonic motion of period 4π s about a point O. It starts from rest at a point P, 4 m from O, and π s later a particle of mass $2m$ is released from rest at P and describes an exactly similar simple harmonic motion. Show that the two particles will collide $\frac{3}{2}\pi$ s after the second particle is released, and find how far from O the collision will occur.
Draw a rough graph of distance against time to illustrate your results.
If on colliding the two particles coalesce, find the magnitude and direction of the velocity of the composite particle immediately after the impact.   (C)

12) A light elastic spring, of modulus $8mg$ and natural length l, has one end attached to a ceiling and carries a scale pan of mass m at the other end. The scale pan is given a vertical displacement from its equilibrium position and released to oscillate with period T.

Prove that
$$T = 2\pi \sqrt{\left(\frac{l}{8g}\right)}$$

A weight of mass km is placed in the scale pan and from the new equilibrium position the procedure is repeated. The period of oscillation is now $2T$. Find the value of k.
Find also the maximum amplitude of the latter oscillations if the weight and the scale pan do not separate during the motion.   (AEB)

13) A particle P, of mass m, is suspended from a fixed point O by an elastic string. When the particle is in equilibrium the extension of the string is a.
Assuming that the string remains taut during the motion, prove that the period of vertical oscillations of P is $2\pi \sqrt{\left(\frac{a}{g}\right)}$.
A second particle Q, of mass $2m$, is attached to P. Find the extension of the string in the new equilibrium position and prove that, if Q now drops off, the string becomes slack after a time $\frac{2}{3}\pi \sqrt{\left(\frac{a}{g}\right)}$.   (O)

14) The end A of a light elastic string AB, obeying Hooke's Law and of natural length 0.5 m, is fixed. When a particle of mass 2 kg is attached to the string at B and hangs freely under gravity, the extension of the string in the equilibrium position is 0.075 m. Calculate, in newtons, the modulus of elasticity of the string.
The particle is now pulled down vertically a further 0.1 m and released. Show that, until the string becomes slack, the motion of the particle is simple harmonic. Show that the time that elapses before the particle first passes through the equilibrium position is $(\pi\sqrt{3})/40$ s and find the speed of the particle when it is in this position.
[Take g as $10\,\text{m/s}^2$.]   (U of L)

15) A light elastic spring AB of natural length b and modulus $2mg$ is secured to the floor at A. A light elastic string BC of natural length $4b$ and modulus mg is attached to the spring at B and to a point C vertically above A, where AC = $5b$. When a particle of mass m is attached at B, find:
(a) the depth below C of its position of equilibrium,
(b) the period of its small vertical oscillations about the position of equilibrium.

(U of L)

16) A light spring obeys Hooke's Law. A force of 20 N extends the spring by 0.01 m. Show that the work done in extending the spring by b m from the unstretched state is $10^3 b^2$ J.
This spring is placed in a long smooth straight cylindrical tube with one end fixed to the tube. The tube is fixed in a vertical position with the free end of the spring uppermost. The dimensions of the tube and of the spring are such that the spring can only move vertically and the spring always remains inside the tube. A particle of mass 4 kg is firmly attached to the free end of the spring. The particle is held so that the spring is compressed a distance of 0.1 m from its uncompressed state. The particle is then released. Show that subsequently

$$v^2 = 3 + 20y - 500y^2$$

where $v\,\mathrm{m\,s^{-1}}$ is the speed of the particle and y m is the compression of the spring.
Find (a) v^2 when the *extension* of the spring is 0.01 m,
(b) the value of y when the speed is a maximum,
(c) the maximum extension of the spring.
[Take g to be $10\,\mathrm{m\,s^{-2}}$.]

(AEB)

17) A particle P of mass m lies on a smooth horizontal table and is attached by two light elastic strings, of natural lengths $3a$, $2a$ and moduli λ, 2λ to two fixed points, S, T respectively, on the table. If ST = $7a$, show that, when the particle is in equilibrium, SP = $\dfrac{9a}{2}$.
The particle is held at rest at the point in the line ST where SP = $5a$, and then released. Show that the subsequent motion of the particle is simple harmonic of period $\pi\sqrt{(3ma/\lambda)}$. Find the maximum speed of the particle during this motion.

18) One end of a light elastic string, of natural length l and modulus of elasticity $4mg$, is fixed to a point A and a particle of mass m is fastened to the other end. The particle hangs in equilibrium vertically below A. Find the extension of the string.

The particle is now held at the point B at a distance l vertically below A and projected vertically downwards with speed $\sqrt{(6gl)}$. If C is the lowest point reached by the particle, prove that the motion from B to C is simple harmonic of amplitude $\frac{5}{4}l$. Prove also that the time taken by the particle to move from B to C is

$$\frac{1}{2}(\frac{1}{2}\pi + \arcsin \frac{1}{5})\sqrt{l/g}.$$

(You may quote a solution of the equation of simple harmonic motion.)   (JMB)

19) A particle is attached to one end of a light elastic string, the other end of which is fastened to a fixed point A on a smooth plane inclined at an angle arcsin $\frac{1}{4}$ to the horizontal. The particle rests in equilibrium at a point O on the plane with the string stretched along a line of greatest slope and extended by an amount c. If the particle is released from rest at a point P on AO produced, show that so long as the string remains taut the particle will oscillate in simple harmonic motion about O as centre, and state the periodic time.

If OP = 2c, find the velocity of the particle when it first reaches O after leaving P.   (U of L)

20) Two points A and B on a smooth horizontal table are at a distance $8l$ apart. A particle of mass m between A and B is attached to A by means of a light elastic string of modulus λ and natural length $2l$, and to B by means of a light elastic string of modulus 4λ and natural length $3l$. If M is the midpoint of AB, and O is the point between M and B at which the particle would rest in equilibrium, prove that MO = $\frac{2}{11}l$.

If the particle is held at M and then released, show that it will move with simple harmonic motion, and find the period of the motion.

Find the velocity V of the particle when it is at a point C distant $\frac{3}{11}l$ from M, and is moving towards B.   (C)

21) A light elastic spring, of natural length a, and modulus $8mg$, stands vertically with its lower end fixed and carries a particle of mass m fastened to its upper end. This particle is resting in equilibrium when a second particle, also of mass m, is dropped on to it from rest at a height $3a/8$ above it. The particles coalesce on impact. Show that the composite particle oscillates about a point which is at a height $\frac{3}{4}a$ above the lower end of the spring and that the equation of motion is

$$\frac{d^2x}{dt^2} = -\frac{4gx}{a}$$

where x is the displacement, at time t, of the composite particle from its centre of oscillation. State the period and find the amplitude of the resulting motion. (Standard formulae for simple harmonic motion may be quoted without proof.)
(JMB)

CHAPTER 13

RESULTANT MOTION. RELATIVE MOTION

RESULTANT VELOCITY VECTORS

It frequently happens that the motion of an object is made up of a number of components. For instance, a motor boat can be moving under the effect both of its engine and of a current in the water; or an aeroplane's movement in the sky can depend both on its engines and on the wind. The actual motion of such an object is the resultant of the various components involved.

So, if a boat has an engine whose velocity vector is v_e and it is being carried along by a current whose velocity vector is v_c, the velocity of the boat, v_b, is given by

$$v_b = v_e + v_c$$

Note that the velocity v_e, which the boat possesses regardless of the current, is often referred to as 'the velocity of the boat in still water'. Similarly the engine velocity of an aircraft can be called 'its velocity in still air'.

The resultant velocity of such moving objects can be found by any of the methods that were demonstrated in Chapter 2, i.e.,

(a) drawing and measurement,

(b) trigonometry,

(c) the use of Cartesian vector components, i and j.

The reader is recommended to revise this work before attempting the next revision exercise.

EXAMPLES 13a

1) A boat is drifting in the sea where the velocity of the current is $2i + 3j$. The wind blowing the boat has a velocity $i - 5j$. What is the velocity of the boat.

Velocity of boat = velocity of current + velocity of wind

$$= (2\mathbf{i} + 3\mathbf{j}) + (\mathbf{i} - 5\mathbf{j})$$

$$= 3\mathbf{i} - 2\mathbf{j}$$

2) A passenger walks directly across the deck of a ship from starboard to port at a speed of $6 \, \text{km h}^{-1}$. The ship which is travelling through the water at $20 \, \text{km h}^{-1}$ is steering due north in a current running south east at $4 \, \text{km h}^{-1}$. In what direction is the passenger actually moving? (Starboard is the right-hand side.)

Let the passenger's velocity have components $u \, \text{km h}^{-1}$ and $v \, \text{km h}^{-1}$ in the directions east and north respectively so that

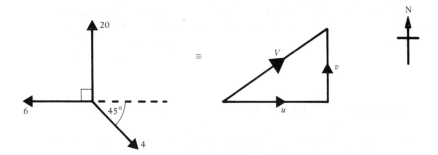

Resolving in the east and north directions we have

$\rightarrow$ $\qquad u = 4\cos 45° - 6 = -3.17$

$\uparrow$ $\qquad v = 20 - 4\sin 45° = 17.17$

Now a velocity of $-3.17 \, \text{km h}^{-1}$ eastward is really a velocity of $3.17 \, \text{km h}^{-1}$ westward, so the components of the passenger's velocity are as shown below.

$$\Rightarrow \qquad \begin{cases} \tan\theta = \dfrac{3.17}{17.17} = 0.184 \\[2mm] \theta = 10.4° \end{cases}$$

So the passenger moves in a direction $349.6°$ (N $10.4°$ W).

EXERCISE 13a

1) A plane whose velocity in still air is $10\mathbf{i} - 12\mathbf{j}$ is flying in a wind with velocity $-2\mathbf{i} + 3\mathbf{j}$. With what velocity is the plane flying?

2) A ship is travelling at $10\,\mathrm{m\,s^{-1}}$ in a direction $4\mathbf{i}-3\mathbf{j}$ in a wind with velocity $7\mathbf{i}-\mathbf{j}$. What is the speed of the ship in still water?

3) Rain is falling vertically at $8\,\mathrm{m\,s^{-1}}$. If a wind springs up, blowing horizontally at $6\,\mathrm{m\,s^{-1}}$ at what angle to the vertical will the rain fall?

4) A model boat with a speed in still water of $3\,\mathrm{m\,s^{-1}}$ is steered due north across a river flowing due east at $4\,\mathrm{m\,s^{-1}}$. Wind is blowing south-east at $2\,\mathrm{m\,s^{-1}}$. In what direction and at what speed will the boat move?

5) A boat whose speed in still water is $12\,\mathrm{m\,s^{-1}}$ is being steered on a bearing $030°$ in a current flowing on a bearing $060°$ at $5\,\mathrm{m\,s^{-1}}$. What is the speed of the boat relative to the earth? A passenger walks with a speed of $2\,\mathrm{m\,s^{-1}}$ across the deck in a direction such that, relative to the earth, he is moving north-east. Find the bearings of the two possible directions in which he could have been facing as he walked.

RESULTANT DIRECTION OF MOTION

When the motion of an object is made up of a number of velocities, the direction in which it moves is the direction of the resultant velocity.
Consider an aircraft, whose speed in still air is $\mathbf{v_e}$, flying in a wind of velocity $\mathbf{v_w}$, from airport A to airport B. The required direction of flight is along $\overrightarrow{AB}$. The direction of motion of the plane is given by the direction of its resultant velocity. Therefore $\mathbf{v_e}+\mathbf{v_w}$ and $\overrightarrow{AB}$ have the same direction. This fact is of fundamental importance in solving problems.

EXAMPLES 13b

1) An aircraft has to fly from an airport A to another airport B which is 240 km from A on a bearing of $120°$ from A. A wind with a speed of $15\,\mathrm{km\,h^{-1}}$ is blowing due north throughout the flight. If the speed of the plane in still air is $300\,\mathrm{km\,h^{-1}}$, find:
(a) the direction in which the plane should steer,
(b) the time for the flight.

The plane has to fly in the direction $\overrightarrow{AB}$ relative to the earth's surface, so this is the direction of the *resultant* velocity.

The information we have can be summarised as follows:

Velocity	Magnitude	Direction
Engine component, $\mathbf{v_e}$	$300\,\mathrm{km\,h^{-1}}$	Unknown
Wind component, $\mathbf{v_w}$	$15\,\mathrm{km\,h^{-1}}$	N
Resultant, V	Unknown	$120°$

A velocity vector triangle PQR can now be drawn and, from it, the magnitude of the resultant velocity and the direction in which the plane must steer, $\overrightarrow{PR}$, can be measured to scale or calculated.

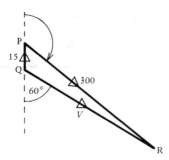

(a) Using calculation,

$$\sin P\widehat{R}Q = \frac{15 \sin 120°}{300}$$

$\Rightarrow \qquad P\widehat{R}Q = 2.5°$

$\Rightarrow \qquad Q\widehat{P}R = 57.5°$

Hence the plane must steer on a course $122.5°$.

(b) $\qquad V^2 = 15^2 + 300^2 - 2(15)(300) \cos 57.5°$

$\Rightarrow \qquad V = 292.2$

The time of flight, T, is given by

$$T = \frac{\text{distance AB}}{\text{speed along AB}} = \frac{240}{292.2}$$

So the time of flight is 0.821 hours, or 49.3 minutes.

2) A girl can paddle her canoe at $4 \, \text{m s}^{-1}$ in still water. She wishes to cross a straight river which is flowing at $6 \, \text{m s}^{-1}$. At what angle to the river bank should she steer to cross: (a) as quickly as possible, (b) by the shortest route?

(a) She will cross in the shortest time when the velocity component directly across the river is greatest and this is when the canoe is steered at right angles to the bank.

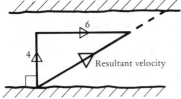

If the width of the river is d, the time taken to cross is $\frac{1}{4}d$.

(b) The river is crossed by the shortest route when α is as large as possible.

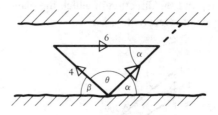

Now $\sin \alpha = (4 \sin \theta)/6$ and is greatest when $\theta = 90°$ i.e. the canoe should be steered at right angles to the resultant direction.

In this case $\alpha = 41.8°$ so the canoe should be steered upstream at $58.2°$ to the bank.

Note. Problems of this type should be studied carefully and individually as the angle called θ is not always $90°$. If, for instance, in the example above the speeds were interchanged we would have

$$\sin \alpha = \frac{6 \sin \theta}{4}$$

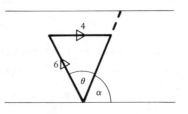

But $\sin \alpha \not> 1$ so this time θ cannot be $90°$ and the greatest value of $\sin \alpha$ occurs when $\alpha = 90°$
(i.e. when $\sin \theta = \frac{4}{6}$)

Note. While studying this topic the reader will find that the word 'course' has different meanings in different contexts. If this fact is appreciated, it should not be too difficult to take the appropriate meaning in each case.

E.g., a ship 'steers on a course' or 'sets a course' — this gives the direction of the velocity of the ship in still water.

the 'true course' of an aircraft — this is the direction of the resultant velocity.

three buoys, A, B and C, 'mark a course' for a race — this time 'course' simply means the path ABCA.

EXERCISE 13b

1) A boy can swim in still water at $v\,\text{ms}^{-1}$. He swims across a river flowing at $1.2\,\text{m s}^{-1}$ which is 368 m wide. Find the time he takes if he travels the shortest possible distance if (a) $v = 1$, (b) $v = 2$.

2) A helicopter flies with constant airspeed $200\,\text{km h}^{-1}$ from position **A** to position **B**, which is 100 km north east of **A**, and then flies back to **A**. Throughout the whole flight the wind velocity is $60\,\text{km h}^{-1}$ from the west. Find, by drawing or calculation, the course set for each of the two legs of the flight. Find also the total time of flight from **A** to **B** and back.

3) A river flows at a constant speed of $4\,\mathrm{m\,s^{-1}}$ between straight parallel banks which are $225\,\mathrm{m}$ apart. A boat, which has a maximum speed of $2.6\,\mathrm{m\,s^{-1}}$ in still water, leaves a point P on one bank and sails in a straight line to the opposite bank. Find graphically or otherwise, the least time the boat can take to reach a point Q on the opposite bank where $PQ = 375\,\mathrm{m}$ and Q is downstream from P. Find also the least time the boat can take to cross the river. Find the time taken to sail from P to Q by the slowest boat capable of sailing directly from P to Q.

4) A speedboat which can travel at $40\,\mathrm{km\,h^{-1}}$ in still water starts from the corner X of an equilateral triangle XYZ of side $20\,\mathrm{km}$ and describes the complete course XYZX in the least possible time. A tide of $10\,\mathrm{km\,h^{-1}}$ is running in the direction $\overrightarrow{ZX}$. Find:
(a) the speed of the boat along XY,
(b) to the nearest minute the time taken by the speedboat to traverse the complete course XYZX.

5) A destroyer is travelling north-west at a constant speed of $5\,\mathrm{m\,s^{-1}}$. A gun mounted on the ship can fire a shot with a horizontal muzzle velocity of $25\,\mathrm{m\,s^{-1}}$. If the target to be hit is due east of the ship find the direction in which the gun should be aimed. (Ignore the vertical motion of the shot.)

FRAMES OF REFERENCE

Most of the time we judge the position or the movement of an object with reference to the earth's surface, i.e. the earth's surface is our basic frame of reference.

Sometimes, however, we 'see' motion that is not relative to the earth. For instance, if an observer B, sitting in a moving railway carriage, looks out of the window at a passenger A who is in another train travelling on a parallel line at the same speed in the same direction, A *appears* to be stationary. Relative to the earth, of course, A is moving but, *relative to the observer B*, A is stationary. If B's train is travelling at $90\,\mathrm{km\,h^{-1}}$ and A's train at $100\,\mathrm{km\,h^{-1}}$ then A passes B at $10\,\mathrm{km\,h^{-1}}$. Relative to the earth, A's speed is $100\,\mathrm{km\,h^{-1}}$ but relative to B it is $(100-90)\,\mathrm{km\,h^{-1}}$.

In these two examples, B has become the fixed point in the frame of reference. The velocity of B relative to the earth is thus discounted i.e. B's velocity vector is subtracted from the velocity vector of A relative to the earth. In general

the velocity of A relative to B is $\mathbf{v_A} - \mathbf{v_B}$

where $\mathbf{v_A}$ and $\mathbf{v_B}$ are the velocities of A and B relative to the earth's surface.

Note that the term 'relative motion' is usually used only in cases where the frame of reference is not the earth's surface.

Relative Velocity

The main methods used to find $v_A - v_B$ are, once again,

(a) drawing and measurement,
(b) trigonometry,
(c) the use of Cartesian vector components.

EXAMPLES 13c

1) A man on a ship whose velocity is $20i - 30j$ is watching a yacht whose velocity is $5i + 4j$.   What does the velocity of the yacht appear to be to the man?

The velocity of the ship is v_S $\Rightarrow$ $v_S = 20i - 30j$.
The velocity of the yacht is v_Y $\Rightarrow$ $v_Y = 5i + 4j$.

The apparent velocity is $v_Y - v_S$

$$= (5i + 4j) - (20i - 30j)$$

$$= -15i + 34j$$

To the man on the ship, the velocity of the yacht appears to be $-15i + 34j$.

2) The driver of a car travelling due east on a straight road at $40 \, \text{km h}^{-1}$ observes a train moving due north at $75 \, \text{km h}^{-1}$. What is the apparent speed and direction of motion of the train?
If the velocity of the car is v_C and the velocity of the train is v_T,
the velocity of the train relative to the car (which is the apparent velocity of the train) is

$$v_T - v_C = v_T + (-v_C)$$

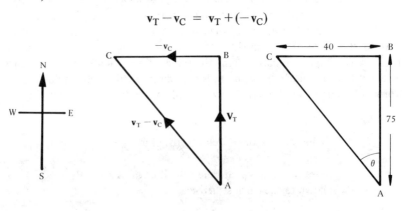

In triangle ABC, AB represents $\mathbf{v_T}$ to scale
and   BC represents $-\mathbf{v_C}$ to scale
so   AC represents $\mathbf{v_T} - \mathbf{v_C}$ to the same scale.

Measurement gives   AC = 85   and $\theta = 28°$.

So the apparent speed of the train is 85 km h^{-1} and the apparent direction of motion is 332° (N 28°W).

Alternatively we could use Pythagoras and trigonometry to calculate AC and θ.

3) To an observer in a boat moving north east at 20 km h^{-1} an aeroplane appears to be flying due west at 100 km h^{-1}. What is the true course and speed of the aeroplane?

We will sketch a triangle PQR in which
    PQ represents $\mathbf{v_A}$, the velocity of the plane
    QR represents $-\mathbf{v_B}$, where $\mathbf{v_B}$ is the velocity of the boat
    PR represents $\mathbf{v_A} + (-\mathbf{v_B})$ which is the apparent velocity of the plane.

The sides of the triangle that are known are QR and PR.

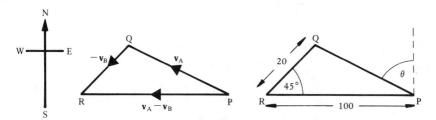

Using the cosine rule in triangle PQR gives

$$PQ^2 = 100^2 + 20^2 - 2 \times 100 \times 20 \cos 45°$$

$\Rightarrow$ $PQ = 87.02$

Then the sine rule gives

$$\frac{\sin Q\widehat{P}R}{20} = \frac{\sin 45°}{87.02}$$

Hence $Q\widehat{P}R = 9.35°$ $\Rightarrow$ $\theta = 80.65°$

So the true speed (i.e. relative to the earth) of the plane is 87.02 km h^{-1} on a course 279.35° (N 80.65°W).

4) To a cyclist riding due south at 20 km h^{-1} a steady wind appears to be blowing in the direction 240°. When he reduces his speed to 15 km h^{-1}, without changing direction, the wind appears to blow in the direction 210°. Find the true wind velocity.

(In a problem involving two cases of relative motion with a common unknown velocity — that of the wind in this case — it often helps to express all the velocities in $\mathbf{i}, \mathbf{j}$ form.)

Taking $\mathbf{i}$ and $\mathbf{j}$ to represent unit velocity vectors east and north respectively we have,

first velocity of cyclist is $\qquad \mathbf{v_A} = -20\mathbf{j}$
second velocity of cyclist is $\qquad \mathbf{v_B} = -15\mathbf{j}$
unknown wind velocity is $\qquad \mathbf{v_w}$

At first the apparent wind velocity has a *direction* $\quad -\sin 60°\mathbf{i} - \cos 60°\mathbf{j}$,
i.e. $\quad -\frac{1}{2}\sqrt{3}\mathbf{i} - \frac{1}{2}\mathbf{j}$, but its magnitude is not known.

So $\qquad\qquad\qquad \mathbf{v_w} - \mathbf{v_A} = \lambda(-\frac{1}{2}\sqrt{3}\mathbf{i} - \frac{1}{2}\mathbf{j})$ $\qquad$ [1]

Similarly for the second case

$$\mathbf{v_w} - \mathbf{v_B} = \mu(-\frac{1}{2}\mathbf{i} - \frac{1}{2}\sqrt{3}\mathbf{j}) \qquad\qquad [2]$$

Eliminating the unknown wind velocity from these equations gives

$$\mathbf{v_B} - \mathbf{v_A} = (\tfrac{1}{2}\mu - \tfrac{1}{2}\sqrt{3}\lambda)\mathbf{i} + (\tfrac{1}{2}\sqrt{3}\mu - \tfrac{1}{2}\lambda)\mathbf{j}$$

But $\qquad\qquad \mathbf{v_B} - \mathbf{v_A} = -15\mathbf{j} - (-20\mathbf{j}) = 5\mathbf{j}$

Therefore $\qquad\qquad (\tfrac{1}{2}\mu - \tfrac{1}{2}\sqrt{3}\lambda)\mathbf{i} + (\tfrac{1}{2}\sqrt{3}\mu - \tfrac{1}{2}\lambda)\mathbf{j} = 5\mathbf{j}$

Equating coefficients of $\mathbf{i}$ and $\mathbf{j}$ gives

$$\tfrac{1}{2}\mu - \tfrac{1}{2}\sqrt{3}\lambda = 0 \quad \text{and} \quad \tfrac{1}{2}\sqrt{3}\mu - \tfrac{1}{2}\lambda = 5$$

$\Rightarrow \qquad\qquad\qquad \lambda = 5 \quad \text{and} \quad \mu = 5\sqrt{3}$

From equation [1] we now have

$$\mathbf{v_w} = \mathbf{v_A} + 5(-\tfrac{1}{2}\sqrt{3}\mathbf{i} - \tfrac{1}{2}\mathbf{j}) = -\tfrac{5}{2}\sqrt{3}\mathbf{i} - \tfrac{45}{2}\mathbf{j}$$

i.e.

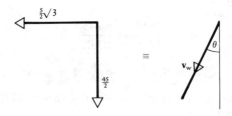

Hence $\qquad\qquad |\mathbf{v_w}| = \{(\tfrac{5}{2}\sqrt{3})^2 + (\tfrac{45}{2})^2\}^{\frac{1}{2}} = 5\sqrt{21}$

and $\qquad\qquad \tan\theta = \sqrt{3}/9 \quad \Rightarrow \quad \theta = 10.9°$

So the true wind velocity is $5\sqrt{21}\,\text{km h}^{-1}$ in a direction $190.9°$.

Note. Wind direction can be defined in two ways. In this problem we were told that 'the wind appears to be blowing in the direction $240°$. This information could equally well be expressed in the form 'the wind appears to be blowing *from* $060°$. Great care must always be taken, when reading questions involving wind direction, to interpret correctly the information given, since the two modes of expression are so similar.

5) From two reconnaissance vessels **A** and **B** observation is being kept on a foreign ship **C**.
To **A**, which is moving at 10 knots on a course $030°$ the ship **C** appears to be travelling in a direction $120°$. When viewed from **B** whose speed is 12 knots on a course $150°$, **C** appears to be travelling due east. What is the true velocity of the foreign ship?

Let **C** have velocity components u and v to the east and south respectively. Then, resolving the velocities $\mathbf{v}_A$, $\mathbf{v}_B$ and $\mathbf{v}_C$ of the three ships, in the directions east and south we have:

	$\mathbf{v}_A$	$\mathbf{v}_B$	$\mathbf{v}_C$	$\mathbf{v}_C - \mathbf{v}_A$	$\mathbf{v}_C - \mathbf{v}_B$
	$30°$	$30°$		$60°$	
Component →	5	6	u	$u-5$	$u-6$
Component ↓	$-5\sqrt{3}$	$6\sqrt{3}$	v	$v-(-5\sqrt{3})$	$v-6\sqrt{3}$

The direction of $\mathbf{v}_C - \mathbf{v}_A$ is $120°$

i.e.

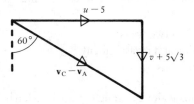

Therefore $$\tan 60° = \frac{u-5}{v+5\sqrt{3}}$$

$\Rightarrow$ $$\sqrt{3}(v+5\sqrt{3}) = u-5$$

$\Rightarrow$ $$\sqrt{3}v = u-20 \qquad [1]$$

The direction of $\mathbf{v_C} - \mathbf{v_B}$ is due east

i.e.

Hence $$v - 6\sqrt{3} = 0$$

$\Rightarrow$ $$v = 6\sqrt{3}$$

Then equation [1] gives $u = 38$

The speed of $C = \sqrt{(u^2 + v^2)} = 39.4$

The direction of C's motion is $S\alpha°E$ where $\tan\alpha = \dfrac{38}{6\sqrt{3}}$

The true velocity of the foreign ship C is therefore 39.4 knots on a course $105.3°$.

EXERCISE 13c

1) A particle A moves with a velocity $6(\mathbf{i} - \mathbf{j})$ and a particle B moves with a velocity $5\mathbf{i} - 7\mathbf{j}$. What is the velocity of:
(a) B relative to A, (b) A relative to B?

2) A particle A moves with velocity $14(\mathbf{i} + \mathbf{j})$ relative to a particle B which moves with velocity $2(-\mathbf{i} + \mathbf{j})$. Find the magnitude of the velocity of A.

3) A ship P is moving due east at $15\,\text{km h}^{-1}$. The velocity of a second ship Q relative to P is $12\,\text{km h}^{-1}$ in a direction $030°$. Find the velocity of the ship Q.

Answer Questions 4-7 in two ways:
   (a) by scale drawing and measurement,
   (b) by calculation.

4) A girl is riding a horse along a straight path at $5\,\text{km h}^{-1}$. A second rider is moving at $3\,\text{km h}^{-1}$ along a perpendicular straight path. What is the velocity of the second rider relative to the first?

5) A passenger in a train travelling north east at $100\,\text{km h}^{-1}$ watches a car moving on a straight road. The car seems to be travelling in the direction $210°$ at $125\,\text{km h}^{-1}$. What is the true velocity of the car?

6) Two aircraft are flying at the same height on straight courses. The first is flying at $400 \, \text{km h}^{-1}$ due north. The true speed of the second is $350 \, \text{km h}^{-1}$ and it appears, to the pilot of the first aircraft, to be on a course $220°$. Find the true course of the second aircraft.

7) A, B and C are three objects each moving with constant velocity. A's speed is $10 \, \text{m s}^{-1}$ in a direction $\overrightarrow{PQ}$. The velocity of B relative to A is $6 \, \text{m s}^{-1}$ at an angle of $70°$ to PQ. The velocity of C relative to B is $12 \, \text{m s}^{-1}$ in the direction $\overrightarrow{QP}$. Find the velocity of B and of C.

8) When a motorist is driving with velocity $6\mathbf{i} + 8\mathbf{j}$ the wind appears to come from the direction $\mathbf{i}$. When he doubles his velocity the wind appears to come from the direction $\mathbf{i} + \mathbf{j}$.
Prove that the true velocity of the wind is $4\mathbf{i} + 8\mathbf{j}$.
The motorist changes his speed but still drives in the same direction. If the wind appears to come from the direction $2\mathbf{i} + \mathbf{j}$, calculate the motorist's speed.

9) A boy is walking due north along a straight road and the wind appears to be blowing south west. When he turns right at a cross roads the wind appears to be blowing in the direction $260°$. If the boy walks at a constant $6 \, \text{km h}^{-1}$ and the two roads cross at right angles, find the true wind velocity.

10) Two aircraft, A and B, are flying at the same height. Both have speed $400 \, \text{km h}^{-1}$; A is flying on a bearing $330°$ and B is flying due east. A third aircraft, also flying at the same height, appears to the pilot of A to be on a course due south while to the pilot of B its course seems to be $240°$. In what direction is the third aircraft actually flying?

11) A boat A is sailing due east at $18 \, \text{km h}^{-1}$ and a second boat B is sailing on a bearing of $030°$ at $12 \, \text{km h}^{-1}$. At a certain instant a third boat C appears to an observer on A to be sailing due south and appears to an observer on B to be sailing on a bearing of $150°$. Find the speed of the boat C and the bearing on which it is sailing.

12) During a race between two yachts, A and B, there is a wind of $18 \, \text{km h}^{-1}$ blowing from due north. The resultant velocity of A is $12 \, \text{km h}^{-1}$ on a bearing of $060°$. Find the direction of the wind relative to A.
At the same time, the resultant velocity of B is $12 \, \text{km h}^{-1}$ on a bearing of $300°$. Find, correct to the nearest degree, the direction of the wind relative to B and, in km h^{-1} correct to one decimal place, the velocity of A relative to B.

RELATIVE POSITION

When one moving object, A, is viewed from another moving object, B, we usually choose a frame of reference in which B is regarded as fixed. In this case displacement as well as velocity is measured relative to B. Hence, if in a certain time A undergoes an actual displacement (i.e. relative to earth) of r_A and B has an actual displacement of r_B, then the displacement of A relative to B is $r_A - r_B$.

We also know that, relative to B, A has a velocity $v_A - v_B$ so, when B is taken as the fixed point in the frame of reference,

B does not move from its original position

A has a displacement $r_A - r_B$ and a velocity $v_A - v_B$.

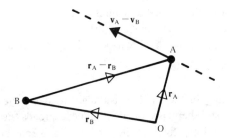

It follows that A's motion relative to B is in the direction of $v_A - v_B$ and that A and B are closest together when $|r_A - r_B|$ is least.

In some problems involving relative position, the given data is in Cartesian vector form and the methods used in Chapter 11 can be applied. When the information is given in other forms, problems can be solved by calculation or by drawing and measurement. If the latter method is chosen, two different scales are needed, one for speed and one for distance. It is safer to draw separate figures, one to each scale, the property they have in common being the *direction* of the relative motion.

EXAMPLES 13d

1) An object P passes through a point whose position vector is $3i - 2j$, with constant velocity $i + j$. At the same instant an object Q, moving with constant velocity $4i - 2j$ passes through the point with position vector $i + 4j$. Find the displacement of P relative to Q after t seconds and the time when P and Q are closest together. How far apart are they at that time? (Units are $m\,s^{-1}$ and m.)

If r_P and r_Q are the position vectors of P and Q at time t, then

$$r_P = 3i - 2j + t(i + j) \quad \text{and} \quad r_Q = i + 4j + t(4i - 2j)$$

The displacement of Q from P is $r_Q - r_P$ where

$$r_P - r_Q = 2i - 6j + t(-3i + 3j) = (2 - 3t)i + (3t - 6)j$$

The distance, d, between P and Q is $|r_P - r_Q|$

$$\Rightarrow \qquad d^2 = (2 - 3t)^2 + (3t - 6)^2 = 18t^2 - 48t + 40$$

If d is least, d^2 is also least and $\dfrac{d}{dt}(18t^2 - 48t + 40) = 0$,

i.e. $\qquad\qquad 36t - 48 = 0 \qquad \Rightarrow \qquad t = \frac{4}{3}$

When $t = \frac{4}{3}$, $d^2 = 8$, so the objects are closest together after $1\frac{1}{3}$ seconds and are then $2\sqrt{2}$ metres apart.

2) An aircraft P is 8000 m due north of another aircraft Q. Both are flying at the same height with constant velocities 150 m s^{-1} due west and 200 m s^{-1} in a direction $330°$. After what time will the aircraft be closest together and how far apart will they then be?

Choosing Q as the fixed point in our frame of reference, the direction of motion of P is $v_P - v_Q$.
Q remains stationary at its initial position Q_0 and P moves from its initial position, P_0, in the direction of $v_P - v_Q$, i.e. along the line P_0N in the diagram. (P_0N is parallel to AC.)

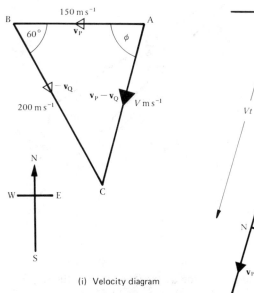

(i) Velocity diagram

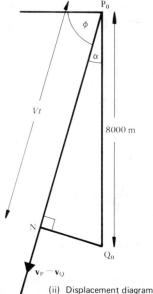

(ii) Displacement diagram

The shortest distance from Q_0 to the relative line of motion of P is Q_0N where Q_0N is perpendicular to P_0N.

P travels the distance P_0N at the relative speed V in a time t so $P_0N = Vt$. This relationship allows the value of t to be calculated.

The method described and explained above can be carried out quickly and easily by drawing and measurement *except* for evaluating t. It is recommended that the reader draws the two diagrams illustrated, to two *separate* scales, and so finds V, P_0N and Q_0N by measurement. Finally t can be evaluated.

Measurements from accurate drawings give

$$V \simeq 180; \quad P_0N \simeq 7690; \quad Q_0N \simeq 2200$$

Then $\quad t = \dfrac{P_0N}{V} \simeq 43$.

So the aircraft are closest together after 43 seconds and are then 2200 metres apart.

3) A ship moving at a speed of $15 \, \text{km h}^{-1}$, sights an enemy destroyer 10 km due south. The destroyer is travelling at $20 \, \text{km h}^{-1}$ north west. The captain of the ship is ordered to steer as far west of north as possible but the ship will be in range of the destroyer's guns if it approaches closer than 2 km. On what bearing can the ship steer so that it just stays out of range?

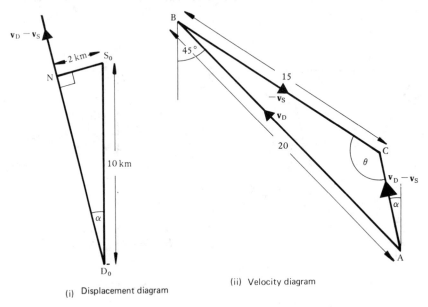

(i) Displacement diagram

(ii) Velocity diagram

In diagram (i) D_0N represents the path of the destroyer relative to the ship and is on a bearing $(360° - \alpha)$ where $\alpha = \arcsin \frac{2}{10} = 11.5°$.
In diagram (ii) the side AC of the velocity triangle represents the velocity of the destroyer relative to the ship.

Both D_0N and AC represent the direction of motion of the destroyer relative to the ship. So D_0N and AC are parallel.

In triangle ABC $\dfrac{\sin\theta}{20} = \dfrac{\sin(45°-\alpha)}{15}$

Therefore $\sin\theta = \frac{20}{15}\sin 33.5°$

$\Rightarrow$ $\theta = 132.7°$ (θ is known to be obtuse)

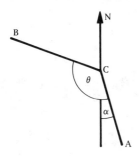

The angle between BC and the north is $180°-(\theta-\alpha)$

i.e. $58.9°$

The ship must not travel further to the west than $58.9°$ west of north.

Note. When graphical solutions are offered, explanation similar to that given in these examples should be included. *Only the trigonometric calculations should be replaced by measurement.*

Closest Approach (Choice of Course)

We have so far been considering the relative motion of two objects A and B, both of which are moving with specified velocities, and have found that the shortest distance between them is $d\sin\alpha$ where d is the initial distance apart and α is the angle between the relative path and the initial line.

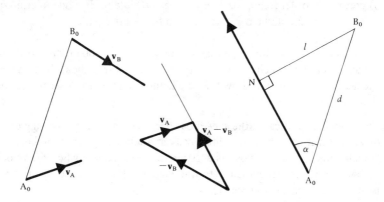

Suppose now that, while the speeds of both objects are fixed and **B** moves in a specified direction, **A** is free to choose its bearing.

The angle α is no longer fixed and, as α varies, the shortest distance l, between **A** and **B**, also varies.

If it is impossible for **A** to intercept **B**, i.e. l cannot be zero, then **A** will pass as close to **B** as possible when l, and hence α, takes its smallest possible value.

Consider first a general case where the relative path makes angles β and γ with the directions of motion of **B** and **A** respectively.

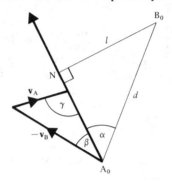

In this diagram, quantities which are constant are:

the magnitudes of v_A, v_B and d,

the directions of v_B and $\overrightarrow{A_0B_0}$,

the compound angle $(\alpha + \beta)$.

Quantities which vary as **A**'s bearing varies are: α, β, γ and l.

If α is to be as small as possible, β must be as large as possible because $\alpha + \beta$ is constant. By applying the sine rule in the velocity triangle we see that β is greatest when $\gamma = 90°$.

Therefore, in order to approach as close as possible to **B**, the direction of motion of **A** should be perpendicular to the relative path.

4) A speedboat travelling due east at $100 \, \text{km h}^{-1}$ is $500 \, \text{m}$ due north of a launch when the launch sets off to try to catch the speedboat. If the speed of the launch is $60 \, \text{km h}^{-1}$ show that the launch cannot get closer to the speedboat than $400 \, \text{m}$.

The launch cannot catch the speedboat because even when travelling due east at $60 \, \text{km h}^{-1}$ the speedboat is pulling away at a relative speed of $40 \, \text{km h}^{-1}$. The launch will approach as close as possible to the speedboat when the velocity of the launch v_A is perpendicular to the relative velocity $v_A - v_B$ (where v_B is the velocity of the speedboat).

If A_0 and B_0 are the initial positions of the launch and the speedboat, then:

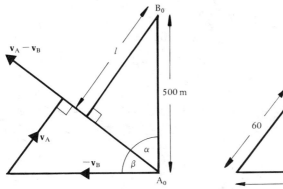
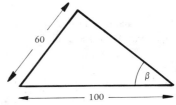

$$\sin \beta = \tfrac{60}{100} = \tfrac{3}{5}$$

Therefore $\sin \alpha = \sin(90° - \beta) = \cos \beta = \tfrac{4}{5}$.

The shortest distance l between the launch and the speedboat is therefore

given by $\qquad\qquad l = 500 \sin \alpha \quad$ and is $\quad 400\,\text{m}$

5) A motorboat with a speed of $5\,\text{m s}^{-1}$ sets out at 12.00 from a point with position vector $-11\mathbf{i} + 16\mathbf{j}$ with the aim of getting as close as possible to a yacht owned by a famous filmstar. At 12.00 the yacht is at the point $4\mathbf{i} + 36\mathbf{j}$ and is moving with constant velocity $10\mathbf{i} - 5\mathbf{j}$. Find the direction in which the motorboat must steer and show that the motorboat cannot ever reach the yacht.

Let the optimum velocity of the motorboat, $\mathbf{v_B}$, be $a\mathbf{i} + b\mathbf{j}$
The velocity of the yacht, $\mathbf{v_Y}$, is $10\mathbf{i} - 5\mathbf{j}$
The path of the motorboat relative to the yacht is $\mathbf{v_B} - \mathbf{v_Y}$

where $\qquad\qquad \mathbf{v_B} - \mathbf{v_Y} = a\mathbf{i} + b\mathbf{j} - (10\mathbf{i} - 5\mathbf{j})$

The best direction for the motorboat to steer is perpendicular to the relative path, i.e. $\mathbf{v_B}$ is perpendicular to $\mathbf{v_B} - \mathbf{v_Y}$

Therefore $\qquad\qquad\qquad\qquad \mathbf{v_B} \cdot (\mathbf{v_B} - \mathbf{v_Y}) = 0$

$\Rightarrow \qquad\qquad (a\mathbf{i} + b\mathbf{j}) \cdot (\{a - 10\}\mathbf{i} + \{b + 5\}\mathbf{j}) = 0$

$\Rightarrow \qquad\qquad\qquad a(a - 10) + b(b + 5) = 0 \qquad\qquad\qquad [1]$

But we also know that the speed of the motorboat is $5\,\text{m s}^{-1}$ so

$$a^2 + b^2 = 25 \qquad\qquad\qquad [2]$$

From [1] and [2], $\qquad 25 - 10a + 5b = 0$

$\Rightarrow \qquad\qquad\qquad\qquad\qquad b = 2a - 5$

Then [2] becomes $\qquad a^2 + (2a - 5)^2 = 25$

$\Rightarrow \qquad\qquad\qquad\qquad\qquad a = 0 \quad \text{or} \quad 4$

When $a = 0$, $b = -5$ and when $a = 4$, $b = 3$.

These solutions give $\qquad v_B = -5j \quad \text{or} \quad v_B = 4i + 3j$

However a diagram shows that when $v_B = -5j$ the motorboat is moving further away from the yacht.

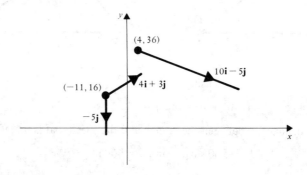

So $v_B = 4i + 3j$ and this gives the direction in which the motorboat should steer.

Now at time t, $\qquad\qquad r_B = -11i + 16j + t(4i + 3j)$

$$r_Y = 4i + 36j + t(10i - 5j)$$

If the motorboat can reach the yacht there is a value of t for which $r_B = r_Y$.

Equating the **i** terms gives

$$4t - 11 = 10t + 4 \quad \Rightarrow \quad t = -\tfrac{5}{2}$$

As this indicates a time before the motorboat started, we can see that the boat cannot reach the yacht. (Even if the significance of the negative value for t was not recognised, taking $t = -\tfrac{5}{2}$ gives $r_B = -21i + \tfrac{17}{2}j$ and $r_Y = -21i + \tfrac{97}{2}j$ so the two vessels are never in the same place at the same time.)

EXERCISE 13d

In Questions 1-3, complete the table as indicated, given that A and B are two objects moving with constant velocities v_A and v_B from initial positions A_0 and B_0 respectively. A and B are closest together when a time t has elapsed after passing through A_0 and B_0. The distance AB is then of magnitude l.

Question	1	2	3
v_A magnitude direction	$3\,m\,s^{-1}$ due S	$10\,m\,s^{-1}$ perpendicular to $\overrightarrow{A_0B_0}$	$20\,km\,h^{-1}$ NE
v_B magnitude direction	$4\,m\,s^{-1}$ due W	$20\,m\,s^{-1}$	$30\,km\,h^{-1}$ due N
$\overrightarrow{A_0B_0}$ magnitude direction	$20\,m$ due S	$40\,m$ any convenient direction	SE
$v_A - v_B$ magnitude direction			
t			15 minutes
l		$20\,m$	

4) Two straight paths, inclined to one another at $60°$, intersect at a point O. A boy A is on one path $300\,m$ from O, while a boy B is on the other path $400\,m$ from O. Angle $AOB = 60°$. Simultaneously the boys begin to run towards O, A with speed $15\,km\,h^{-1}$ and B with speed $12\,km\,h^{-1}$. What is the shortest distance between the two boys.

5) At noon an observer on a ship travelling due east at $20\,km\,h^{-1}$ sees another ship $20\,km$ due north which is travelling $S\,30°\,E$ at $8\,km\,h^{-1}$. At what time are the ships nearest together?

6) Two aircraft P and Q are flying at the same height at $300\,km\,h^{-1}$ on a bearing $135°$ and $350\,km\,h^{-1}$ on a bearing $060°$ respectively. If P is initially $10\,km$ north of Q, how close do they get to one another?

7) Two cyclists are riding one along each of two perpendicular roads which meet at A. At one instant both cyclists are $500\,m$ from A and both are approaching A. If the speed of one cyclist is $8\,m\,s^{-1}$ and the shortest distance between the cyclists is $50\,m$, find the two possible speeds of the second rider.

8) At time $t = 0$ a ship A is at the point O and a ship B is at the point with position vector $10j$ referred to O. The velocities of the two ships are constant. Ship A sails at $34\,km\,h^{-1}$, in the direction of the vector $8i + 15j$ and ship B sails at $30\,km\,h^{-1}$ in the direction of the vector $3i + 4j$.
Write down
(a) the velocity vector of each ship,
(b) the velocity of B relative to A,
(c) the position vector of B relative to A at time t hours.
Given that visibility is $10\,km$, show that the ships are within sight of each other for 3 hours.

9) A and B are two ships which, at 1200 hours, are at P and Q respectively, where PQ = 39 km. A is steaming at $45 \, \text{km h}^{-1}$ in a direction perpendicular to PQ and B is steaming on a straight course at $30 \, \text{km h}^{-1}$ in such a direction as to approach A as closely as possible. Show that B steams at an angle arcsin $\frac{2}{3}$ with PQ.
Find when the ships are closest together.

10) A ship A is travelling due east at $24 \, \text{km h}^{-1}$. At noon a second ship B is 8 km away from A in a north-easterly direction, and one hour later B is again 8 km away, but in a south-easterly direction. Find the speed of B, which is to be assumed constant.
Calculate the minimum distance between A and B and show that when this position occurs B is due east of A.

11) Unit vectors in the directions east and north are **i** and **j** respectively. To a cyclist travelling due north at $8 \, \text{km h}^{-1}$ the direction of the wind appears to be $-\mathbf{i}$. He increases his speed to $15 \, \text{km h}^{-1}$ without altering course and the wind now appears to be in the direction $-\mathbf{i}-\mathbf{j}$. What is the true velocity vector of the wind?
The cyclist continues to cycle in a straight line at $15 \, \text{km h}^{-1}$ but changes direction and the wind now appears to blow in the direction **j**. Find the direction in which the cyclist is now travelling.

12) A river flows at $4 \, \text{m s}^{-1}$ from west to east between parallel banks which are at a distance 400 metres apart. A man rows a boat at a speed of $3 \, \text{m s}^{-1}$ in still water.
(a) State the direction in which the boat must be steered in order to cross the river from the southern bank to the northern bank in the shortest possible time. Find the time taken and the actual distance covered by the boat for this crossing.
(b) Find the direction in which the boat must be steered in order to cross the river from the southern bank to the northern bank by the shortest possible route. Find the time taken and the actual distance covered by the boat for this crossing.

INTERCEPTION

Interception, or collision, occurs if the relative line of motion of an object A, *passes through* the initial position of the reference object B (so that the shortest distance apart, B_0N, is zero).
Hence, if A intercepts B their relative velocity is parallel to the line joining their initial positions.
The time, t, that elapses before interception, is given by

$$t = \frac{\text{Initial distance apart}}{\text{Relative speed}}$$

EXAMPLES 13e

1) A cruiser is travelling due east at 15 knots. At 1200 hours a destroyer which is 12 nautical miles south west of the cruiser sets off at 20 knots to intercept the cruiser. At what time will interception occur and on what bearing should the destroyer travel?

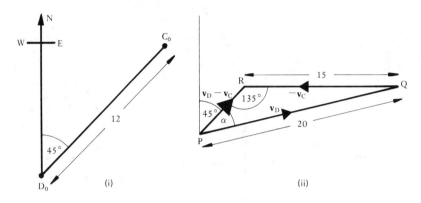

(i)   (ii)

Diagram (i) shows the positions at noon of the destroyer and cruiser.
In diagram (ii) the side $\overrightarrow{PR}$, of the velocity triangle PQR, represents the velocity of the destroyer relative to the cruiser.

For interception $\overrightarrow{PR}$ is parallel to D_0C_0, therefore $P\widehat{R}Q = 135°$.

In $\triangle PQR$, $\dfrac{\sin 135°}{20} = \dfrac{\sin \alpha}{15}$

$\Rightarrow$ $\alpha = 32°$

$\Rightarrow$ $P\widehat{Q}R = 13°$

And the destroyer's bearing is $\alpha + 45°$ i.e. $077°$

Then $\dfrac{PR}{\sin 13°} = \dfrac{20}{\sin 135°}$

Therefore the speed of D relative to C is 6.4 knots

Interception will take place after t hours where

$$t = \frac{12}{6.4} = 1.875$$

The destroyer will intercept the cruiser at 13.53 hours if it travels on a bearing $077°$.

2) Two aircraft, P and Q, are flying at the same height. P is moving in a direction $210°$ at $300 \, \text{km h}^{-1}$ and Q is flying north west. When Q is 5 km due south of P the pilots find that they are on a collision course. What is the speed of Q and after what time will collision occur if neither pilot changes course?

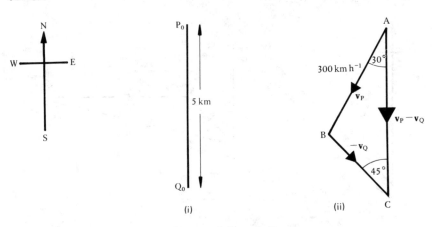

(i)   (ii)

Diagram (i) shows the initial positions of P and Q.

In diagram (ii), the side $\overrightarrow{AC}$ of the velocity triangle represents the velocity of P relative to Q.

For collision $\overrightarrow{AC}$ must be parallel to $\overrightarrow{P_0Q_0}$, i.e. $\overrightarrow{AC}$ runs due south.

In triangle ABC $\dfrac{BC}{\sin 30°} = \dfrac{300}{\sin 45°}$ $\Rightarrow$ $BC = 212$

Therefore the speed of Q is $212 \, \text{km h}^{-1}$

Also $\dfrac{AC}{\sin 105°} = \dfrac{300}{\sin 45°}$ $\Rightarrow$ $AC = 410$

But this represents the speed of P relative to Q, therefore the time before collision is expected is $\dfrac{5}{410}$ hours i.e. 44 seconds

Therefore Q is flying at $212 \, \text{km h}^{-1}$ and collision is expected after 44 seconds.

EXERCISE 13e

1) A destroyer moving on a bearing $030°$ at $50 \, \text{km h}^{-1}$ observes at noon a cruiser travelling due north at $20 \, \text{km h}^{-1}$. If the destroyer overtakes the cruiser one hour later find the distance and bearing of the cruiser from the destroyer at noon.

2) Two perpendicular roads intersect at P. Two cyclists are riding, one along each of the roads, towards P. One is 800 m from P and is riding at $18 \, km \, h^{-1}$ and the other has a speed of $20 \, km \, h^{-1}$ and is, at the same time, distant d from P. Find the value of d if:
(a) the cyclists meet at P,
(b) they are never nearer to each other than 50 m.

3) A yacht in distress is 8 km from a harbour in a direction $220°$ and is drifting on a course $070°$ at $4 \, km \, h^{-1}$. In what direction should a lifeboat travel to intercept the yacht if the speed of the lifeboat is $30 \, km \, h^{-1}$?

4) A runaway horse is galloping across a field in a direction $020°$ at $40 \, km \, h^{-1}$. It is already 300 m away in a direction due east, from a mounted rider who takes off in pursuit with a speed of $48 \, km \, h^{-1}$. In what direction should he ride to catch the runaway?

5) A particle P moves with velocity $(\mathbf{i} + \mathbf{j})$ whilst a particle Q moves with velocity $(-\mathbf{i} + 2\mathbf{j})$. Write down the velocity of Q relative to P.
Particle P is at the origin at the same instant as Q is at the point with position vector $(2\mathbf{i} + \mathbf{j})$. Find the shortest distance between P and Q in the subsequent motion.   (U of L)

6) Two aircraft A and B are flying at the same height in direction $030°$ and $350°$ respectively. At the instant when B is 10 km due eat of A it is realised that they are on a collision course. If the speed of A is $500 \, km \, h^{-1}$ find the speed of B.
If, at this instant, A changes course to $045°$ without altering speed, find the shortest distance between A and B.

7) Two straight roads intersect at O, one running north-south and the other west-east. A van A, travelling at constant velocity $32 \, km \, h^{-1}$ due south on one road, passes through O at the instant when a motor-cyclist B, moving towards O at constant velocity $40 \, km \, h^{-1}$ due east along the second road, is 5 km from O. Find:
(a) the distances AO and BO, to the nearest 0.1 km, when A and B are closest together,
(b) the time, to the nearest 0.1 minute, from the instant when A is at O until the instant of closest approach.
A helicopter is flying at constant height with constant velocity $96 \, km \, h^{-1}$ in the direction of $060°$. Find the velocity of the helicopter relative to A.

8) At noon, the position vectors of two ships A and B, relative to a lighthouse O, are $(5i + 20j)$ and $(-20i - 10j)$ respectively, where i and j are unit vectors due east and due north. The constant velocities of ships A and B are $(-21i - 5j)$ and $(15i + 25j)$. (Units are km and km h^{-1}.) Find the velocity of A relative to B. Find also the position vector of A relative to B at time t minutes after noon.
Determine, to the nearest minute, the time at which the two ships are closest together.   (U of L)

9) At noon an aircraft A is at a point with position vector $5i + j$ and is moving with constant velocity $-i + 3j$. A second plane B, whose constant velocity is $2i + 5j$, is simultaneously at the point with position vector $3i - 3j$. Show that, at noon, A and B are equidistant from any point on the line with vector equation $r = 4i - j + \lambda(2i - j)$ and find the point on this line which is also equidistant from the point $i - j$.
If $t = 0$ at noon find the value of t when A and B are closest together.

10) A cruiser is moving due east at 35 km h^{-1}. Relative to the cruiser a frigate is moving on a bearing of $210°$ at 56 km h^{-1}. Using a graphical method, or otherwise, find the magnitude and the direction of the velocity of the frigate relative to a coastguard who is recording the paths of these ships from a lighthouse.
At 1300 hours the frigate is 12 km due east of the cruiser. If both ships maintain their speeds and courses, find the time at which the distance between them is least and their actual distance apart at this instant.
Find also the time at which the frigate is due south of the cruiser.

SUMMARY

The motion of one object A relative to another object B is the motion it appears to have when viewed from B.

The velocity of A relative to B is $v_A - v_B$.

For interception or collision to occur, the relative velocity must be parallel to the initial displacement of A from B.

It is important to appreciate that several different methods are suitable for solving problems on relative motion. No one method is ideal for all problems and the student is advised to develop flexibility in choice of approach.

Further Problems

Although relative velocity is usually encountered in problems about moving vehicles, ships, aircraft etc., there are some questions of a less practical nature in which speeds are not necessarily constant and the paths are not always linear. The set of examples which follow are of this type.

EXAMPLES 13f

1) A particle P is moving in a clockwise sense at constant angular velocity ω round a circle whose equation is $x^2+y^2 = a^2$. When $t = 0$, P is at the point $(-a, 0)$. A second particle Q moves along the x axis with constant velocity $a\omega$ in the positive sense. Q is at the origin when $t = 0$. Find, in terms of a, ω and t the speed of P relative to Q at time t. Find also the direction of the velocity of P relative to Q when $t = \pi/\omega$

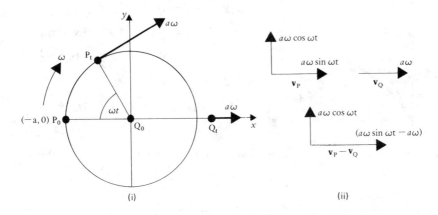

(i)   (ii)

Diagram (i) shows the positions of P and Q after t seconds. During this time, at angular velocity ω, P will describe an arc subtending an angle ωt at the centre, and will have a tangential speed of $a\omega$.

Diagram (ii) shows the components parallel to Ox and Oy of the velocities of P and Q and the velocity of P relative to Q at time t.

If V is the relative speed, then

$$V^2 = (a\omega \cos \omega t)^2 + (a\omega \sin \omega t - a\omega)^2$$
$$= a^2\omega^2 - 2a^2\omega^2 \sin \omega t + a^2\omega^2$$

The relative speed, $V = a\omega\sqrt{2(1-\sin \omega t)}$.

When $t = \dfrac{\pi}{\omega}$, the components of the relative velocity, parallel to Ox and Oy are:

$\rightarrow$ $a\omega \sin \pi - a\omega = -a\omega$

$\uparrow$ $a\omega \cos \pi = -a\omega$

Therefore the direction of the velocity of P relative to Q when $t = \dfrac{\pi}{\omega}$ is parallel to the line $y = x$.

2) Two particles P and Q are projected simultaneously from a point O in which **i** and **j** are unit vectors horizontally and vertically upwards respectively. P is projected with velocity $V\sqrt{3}\mathbf{j}$ and Q is projected with velocity $\frac{1}{2}V\mathbf{i} + \frac{1}{2}V\sqrt{3}\mathbf{j}$. Find the velocity and displacement of P relative to Q at any time t. Hence find the vertical displacement between P and Q when the horizontal displacement between them is of magnitude $2V$. Find also the distance between P and Q when P is at its highest point.

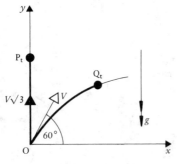

At time t,

for P $\ddot{x}_P = 0$ $\ddot{y}_P = -g$

$\dot{x}_P = 0$ $\dot{y}_P = V\sqrt{3} - gt$

$x_P = 0$ $y_P = Vt\sqrt{3} - \frac{1}{2}gt^2$

for Q $\ddot{x}_Q = 0$ $\ddot{y}_Q = -g$

$\dot{x}_Q = \frac{1}{2}V$ $\dot{y}_Q = \frac{1}{2}V\sqrt{3} - gt$

$x_Q = \frac{1}{2}Vt$ $y_Q = \frac{1}{2}Vt\sqrt{3} - \frac{1}{2}gt^2$

Hence $\mathbf{v}_P = (V\sqrt{3} - gt)\mathbf{j}$

$\mathbf{v}_Q = \frac{1}{2}V\mathbf{i} + (\frac{1}{2}V\sqrt{3} - gt)\mathbf{j}$

$\mathbf{r}_P = (Vt\sqrt{3} - \frac{1}{2}gt^2)\mathbf{j}$

$\mathbf{r}_Q = \frac{1}{2}Vt\mathbf{i} + (\frac{1}{2}Vt\sqrt{3} - \frac{1}{2}gt^2)\mathbf{j}$

The velocity of P relative to Q is $\mathbf{v}_P - \mathbf{v}_Q$ where

$$\mathbf{v}_P - \mathbf{v}_Q = -\tfrac{1}{2}V\mathbf{i} + \tfrac{1}{2}V\sqrt{3}\mathbf{j}$$

The displacement of P relative to Q is $\mathbf{r}_P - \mathbf{r}_Q$ where

$$\mathbf{r}_P - \mathbf{r}_Q = -\tfrac{1}{2}Vt\mathbf{i} + \tfrac{1}{2}Vt\sqrt{3}\mathbf{j}$$

The horizontal distance between P and Q is of magnitude $2V$ when

$$|-\tfrac{1}{2}Vt\mathbf{i}| = 2V$$

i.e. when $t = 4$

The vertical distance between P and Q is then

$$(\tfrac{1}{2}V)(4\sqrt{3}) = 2V\sqrt{3}$$

When P is at its highest point $\dot{y}_P = 0$ $\Rightarrow$ $t = \dfrac{V\sqrt{3}}{g}$

Then $\mathbf{r}_P - \mathbf{r}_Q = \dfrac{-V^2\sqrt{3}}{2g}\mathbf{i} + \dfrac{3V^2}{2g}\mathbf{j}$

The distance d between P and Q is given by

$$d^2 = \left(\frac{-V^2\sqrt{3}}{2g}\right)^2 + \left(\frac{3V^2}{2g}\right)^2$$

$\Rightarrow$
$$d = \frac{V^2\sqrt{3}}{g}$$

Therefore when P is at its highest point $\quad PQ = \dfrac{V^2\sqrt{3}}{g}$

EXERCISE 13f

1) Two particles P and Q start simultaneously in the same sense from the origin O and both have constant speed v. P moves on the circle $x^2 + y^2 - 2x = 0$ and Q moves on the tangent to the circle through O. Find the relative speed of the particles when P has rotated through an angle
(a) $\frac{1}{2}\pi$ (b) π (c) $\frac{2}{3}\pi$

2) A point P moves so that its coordinates at time t are $x = t$; $y = 2t^2$. A second point Q moves along the x axis so that at time t its position is $x = 2t$. A third point R, moving on the y axis, is such that $y = t^2$. Find:
(a) the velocity of P relative to R,
(b) the velocity of P relative to Q, when $t = 3$.

3) Two particles are travelling round the circle $x^2 + y^2 = 4$. One particle, A, is initially at the point $(2,0)$ and moves anticlockwise with constant angular velocity ω. The other particle, B, travels clockwise with constant angular velocity 2ω from its initial position at the point $(0,2)$. Find:
(a) the speed of A relative to B at time t,
(b) the value of t when the particles are first travelling in the same direction,
(c) the acceleration of A relative to B when $t = 1$.

4) A particle P is moving along the line $y = x$ so that its speed at time t is $\sqrt{2}\,ut$ where u is a constant. A second particle Q moves along the positive y axis with constant speed u. If, when $t = 0$, P is at the point $(-4, -4)$ moving towards O, and Q is at the origin, find:
(a) the velocity of P relative to Q at time t,
(b) the distance PQ when $t = 2$.

MISCELLANEOUS EXERCISE 13

1) A ship A is travelling due east at a speed of $8\,\mathrm{m\,s^{-1}}$, and a ship B is travelling due south at $10\,\mathrm{m\,s^{-1}}$. At an instant when A is 3 km from B in a direction $060°$, a motor boat leaves A and travels in a straight line to B with speed $14\,\mathrm{m\,s^{-1}}$. Show that it reaches B in 500 seconds. On reaching the ship B, the motor boat immediately turns and travels back to A in a straight line, again with speed $14\,\mathrm{m\,s^{-1}}$. Find graphically (or otherwise) the time taken for the return journey.   (C)

2) At 1000 hours a pilot boat leaves the jetty to join a ship which is 4 nautical miles from the jetty on a bearing of $315°$. The ship is steaming due east at a steady speed of 12 knots. Find the time at which the pilot boat reaches the ship and the distance and bearing of the ship from the jetty at that time if:
(a) the pilot boat travels at 15 knots,
(b) the pilot boat travels at the least possible speed.   (AEB)

3) A ship P steaming at 20 km/h in the direction $050°$ is 120 km due west of ship Q steaming at 12 km/h in the direction $330°$. If the ships do not alter course or speed, find by means of a scale drawing, or otherwise, the shortest distance between them in the subsequent motion. Find also the period of time during which the ships are within a range of 50 km of each other.   (U of L)

4) A ship is moving due West at 20 knots and the wind appears to blow from $22\frac{1}{2}°$ West of South. The ship then steams due South at the same speed and the wind then appears to blow from $22\frac{1}{2}°$ East of South. Find the speed of the wind and the true direction from which it blows, assuming that they remain constant.   (JMB)

5) The banks of a river 40 m wide are parallel and A and B are points on opposite banks. The distance AB is 50 m and B is downstream of A. There is a constant current of $4\,\mathrm{m\,s^{-1}}$ flowing. What is the minimum speed at which a motor boat must be able to move in still water in order to cross this river from A to B? If a boat sails from A to B with constant velocity in $7\frac{1}{2}$ seconds, find its speed relative to the water and the direction in which it is steered. Whilst this boat is sailing from A to B a man runs across a bridge which is at right angles to the banks of the river. To this man the boat appears to be travelling parallel to the banks of the river. Find the speed at which the man is running.
                                                                                      (AEB)

6) Relative to a ship which is travelling due north at a speed of $20\,\mathrm{km\,h^{-1}}$, the velocity of a speedboat is in the direction $045°$. Relative to a second ship which is travelling due south at a speed of $20\,\mathrm{km\,h^{-1}}$, the velocity of the speedboat is in the direction $030°$. Prove that the speedboat is travelling on the bearing $\theta°$ where $\tan\theta = \sqrt{3} - 1$,   and find its speed.

7) A cruiser sailing due north at $24 \, \text{km h}^{-1}$ sights a destroyer $48 \, \text{km}$ due east sailing at $56 \, \text{km h}^{-1}$ on a course $(360 - \alpha)°$ where $\cos \alpha = \frac{11}{14}$. Show that the destroyer's course relative to the cruiser is on the bearing $300°$ and find the relative speed. If the cruiser's guns have a maximum range of $30 \, \text{km}$ and both ships maintain course and speed, find for how long the destroyer will be within range. Immediately the destroyer is sighted an aircraft is despatched from the cruiser and flies in a straight line at a steady speed of $440 \, \text{km h}^{-1}$ on an intersection course with the destroyer. Find the course on which the aircraft flies.

8) A motorboat moving at $8 \, \text{km/h}$ relative to the water travels from a point A to a point B $10 \, \text{km}$ distant whose bearing from A is $150°$. It then travels to a point C, $10 \, \text{km}$ from B and due west of B. If there is a current of constant speed $4 \, \text{km/h}$ from north to south, find the two courses to be set, and prove that the total time taken to reach C is approximately 2 hours 20 minutes.

(U of L)

9) A port X is 18 nautical miles due north of another port Y. Steamers A, B leave X, Y respectively at the same time, A travelling at 12 knots due east and B at 8 knots in a direction $\arcsin \frac{1}{3}$ east of north. Find in magnitude and direction the velocity of B relative to A. Prove that subsequently the shortest distance between A and B is 14 nautical miles and find the time taken to reach this position.

If when the steamers are in this position a boat leaves A and travels due west so as to intercept B, find at what speed the boat must travel. (JMB)

10) Two aircraft are in horizontal flight at the same altitude. One is flying due north at $500 \, \text{km h}^{-1}$ whilst the other is flying due west at $600 \, \text{km h}^{-1}$. Realising that they are on collision courses the pilots take avoiding action simultaneously when the aircraft are $10 \, \text{km}$ apart. The pilot of the first plane changes his course to $345°$ (N $15°$ W) maintaining his speed of $500 \, \text{km h}^{-1}$ and the pilot of the second plane maintains his course but increases his speed to $V \, \text{km h}^{-1}$. Find the value of V if:
(a) the aircraft are still on collision courses,
(b) the change of speed is the least possible to ensure that the distance between the planes is never less than $2 \, \text{km}$. (AEB)

11) A ship is steaming at 15 knots due east, while the wind speed is 20 knots from due north. Find the magnitude and the direction, to the nearest degree, of the wind velocity relative to the ship.
Find also the course, between east and south, along which the ship would have to steer at 16 knots for the wind velocity relative to the ship to be at right angles to the course of the ship.
Obtain the magnitude of the velocity of the wind relative to the ship in this case. (U of L)

12) Two particles A and B are moving on a smooth horizontal plane in concentric circles with centre O. The lines OA and OB are rotating with constant angular velocities $+\omega$ and $+3\omega$ respectively and OA $= 2$OB $= 2r$. Find, in magnitude and direction, the velocity of B relative to A when the angle OB makes with OA is (a) $+90°$, (b) $+60°$.
When the angle AOB $= \theta$ the velocity of B relative to A is parallel to AO. Find the value of $\cos\theta$.
When OB is at an angle $-90°$ to OA the forces acting on the particles are removed so that each particle then moves in a straight line. Find the shortest distance between the particles in the subsequent motion.   (AEB)

13) An equilateral triangular course is marked out by buoys A, B, C in a broad straight reach of a river, the buoy C being upstream and the line AB perpendicular to the current. A motor launch follows the course ABCA. If V is the speed of the launch in still water and u the speed of the current, show that while the launch is moving along AB it is pointed at an angle θ to AB on the upstream side, where $\sin\theta = u/V$.
Find the angle between BC and the direction in which the launch is pointed while it is moving along BC. Show that when it reaches C the launch turns through $120°$.   (JMB)

14) A ship is moving at a constant speed of 10 km/h in the direction of the unit vector **i**. Initially, its position vector, relative to a fixed origin, is $10(-\mathbf{i}+\mathbf{j})$, where **i** and **j** are perpendicular vectors of length 1 km. Find its position vector relative to the origin at time t hours later.
A second ship is moving with constant speed u km/h parallel to the vector $\mathbf{i}+2\mathbf{j}$ and is initially at the origin.
(a) If $u = 10\sqrt{5}$, show that the minimum distance between the ships is 10 km.
(b) Find the value of u for which the ships are on a collision course and determine the value of t at which the collision would occur if no avoiding action were taken.   (AEB)

15) At a given instant, a ship P travelling due E at a speed of 30 km h^{-1} is 7 km due N of a second ship Q which is travelling N$\theta°$W at a speed of 14 km h^{-1}, where $\tan\theta = \frac{3}{4}$. Show that the speed of Q relative to P is 40 km h^{-1} and find the direction of the relative velocity.
The ships continue to move with uniform velocities. Find correct to three significant figures:
(a) the distance between the ships when they are nearest together,
(b) the time taken, in minutes, to attain this shortest distance.
If initially, the course of Q had been altered to bring the ships as close as possible, the speed of Q and the speed and course of P being unchanged, find the direction of this new course.   (JMB)

16) A particle is launched at time $t = 0$ so that it follows the path

$$\mathbf{r} = (-15 + 5t)\mathbf{i} + (70 + 30t - 5t^2)\mathbf{k}.$$

(Distances are measured in metres and time in seconds.)

Find:
(a) the position vector of the point of projection and the velocity vector of the
    particle at time $t = 0$.
(b) the speed of the particle at time t.
The particle meets the line which passes through the point with position vector
$5\mathbf{i}$, and whose gradient is $\mathbf{i} + 19\mathbf{k}$,   at a point A. Show that this occurs when
$t = 5$.
Find the position vector of the point A and its distance from the point of
projection.
Find also the time at which the particle is moving at right angles to its initial
direction of motion. (AEB)

17)

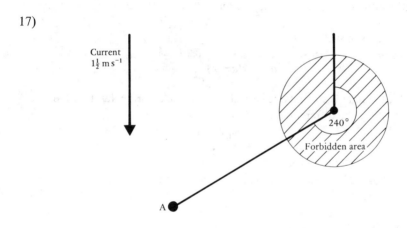

At a particular instant a dinghy is observed to be at A, 200 m from a
stationary buoy in a river estuary, and the bearing of A from the buoy is 240°
(see figure). The River Board's regulations state that it is forbidden to approach
within 50 m of the buoy. In this part of the estuary there is a steady current of
$1\frac{1}{2}$ m s^{-1} continuously flowing from due north. The dinghy, which can move at
a maximum speed of 4 m s^{-1} in still water, moves in a straight line so that it
passes as close to the buoy as the regulations allow. Show that there are two
possible directions in which the dinghy can be steered and find the shortest
time in each case for the dinghy to travel from A to the point where it is
nearest to the buoy. (AEB)

18) At time t two points P and Q have position vectors $\mathbf{p}$ and $\mathbf{q}$ respectively, where

$$\mathbf{p} = 2a\mathbf{i} + (a \cos \omega t)\mathbf{j} + (a \sin \omega t)\mathbf{k},$$
$$\mathbf{q} = (a \sin \omega t)\mathbf{i} - (a \cos \omega t)\mathbf{j} + 3a\mathbf{k}$$

and a, ω are constants. Find $\mathbf{r}$, the position vector of P relative to Q, and $\mathbf{v}$, the velocity of P relative to Q. Find also the values of t for which $\mathbf{r}$ and $\mathbf{v}$ are perpendicular.

Determine the smallest and greatest distances between P and Q. (U of L)

19) A river of width a m with straight parallel banks flows due north with speed u m s^{-1}. The points O and A are on opposite banks and A is due east of O. Co-ordinate axes Ox, Oy are taken in the east and north directions respectively. A boat, whose speed V m s^{-1} relative to the water is constant, starts from O and crosses the river.

(a) If u is constant and equal to $\frac{1}{6}V$ and the boat is steered so that it travels in a straight line towards A, find the time taken for the boat to travel from O to A.

(b) If u varies in such a way that

$$u = x(a-x)\frac{V}{a^2}$$

and if the boat is steered due east, show that the co-ordinates (x, y) of the boat satisfy the differential equation

$$\frac{dy}{dx} = \frac{x(a-x)}{a^2}$$

If the boat reaches the east bank at C, calculate the distance AC and find the time taken. (JMB)

20) The points X and Y are moving with the same speed u in the positive direction on the x axis and the y axis respectively. Find the velocity relative to X of the mid-point M of XY, and show that it is the reverse of the velocity of M relative to Y.

A particle P moves on the circle $x^2 + y^2 = 1$ with constant speed v. Show that at each instant when the acceleration of P is parallel to the line $x + y = 0$ the velocities of P relative to X and Y are equal in magnitude.

Find v in terms of u if the maximum value of the velocity of P relative to M is u. (U of L)

21) A river flows at a constant speed of $5\,\mathrm{m\,s^{-1}}$ between straight parallel banks which are $240\,\mathrm{m}$ apart. A boat crosses the river, travelling relative to the water at a constant speed of $12\,\mathrm{m\,s^{-1}}$. A man cycles at a constant speed of $4\,\mathrm{m\,s^{-1}}$ along the edge of one bank of the river in the direction opposite to the direction of flow of the river. At the instant when the boat leaves a point O on the opposite bank, the cyclist is $80\,\mathrm{m}$ downstream of O. The boat is steered relative to the water in a direction perpendicular to the banks. Taking $\mathbf{i}$ and $\mathbf{j}$ to be perpendicular horizontal unit vectors downstream and across the river from O respectively, express, in terms of $\mathbf{i}$ and $\mathbf{j}$, the velocities and the position vectors relative to O of the boat and the cyclist t seconds after the boat leaves O. Hence, or otherwise, calculate the time when the distance between the boat and the cyclist is least, giving this least distance.

If, instead, the boat were to be steered so that it crosses the river from O to a point on the other bank directly opposite to O, show that this crossing would take approximately 22 seconds.   (U of L)

22) To a motorist driving due South along a level road with constant speed u the wind appears to be blowing in a direction $W\theta°N$. When he is driving with th the same speed u due North the apparent direction of the wind is $W\phi°N$. Show that when he is driving at a speed $2u$ due North, the apparent direction of the wind is $W\psi°N$, where

$$2\tan\psi \;=\; 3\tan\phi - \tan\theta.$$

Determine the true direction of the wind.   (U of L)

CHAPTER 14

RESULTANTS OF COPLANAR FORCES.
EQUIVALENT FORCE SYSTEMS.

The resultant of a set of forces is the simplest possible force system which has the same effect in all respects as the original set.
The resultant of forces in one plane may be either a single force or a torque.

COPLANAR FORCES REDUCING TO A SINGLE FORCE

When the resultant of a set of coplanar forces is a single force, it is fully defined only when its magnitude, direction and line of action are known.
The *magnitude* and *direction* can be found by collecting the components, in each of two perpendicular directions, of the original forces (see Chapter 2).
The *position* of the resultant is determined by comparing its turning effect about a specified axis with that of the original forces.
In this way three independent equations are obtained.

EXAMPLES 14a

1) Find the magnitude and direction of the resultant of forces of magnitudes 6 N, 2 N, 2 N and 1 N which act along the sides $\overrightarrow{AB}$, $\overrightarrow{BC}$, $\overrightarrow{CD}$ and $\overrightarrow{AD}$ of a square ABCD and find where the line of action of the resultant cuts AB (produced if necessary).

Let the side of the square be a. Diagram (i) shows the original forces and diagram (ii) shows the resultant, represented by a pair of components X and Y parallel to AB and AD respectively and cutting AB at an unknown point P where $AP = d$.

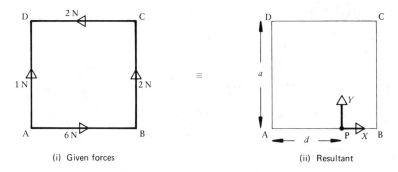

(i) Given forces

(ii) Resultant

Comparing the original forces with the resultant we have:

$$\rightarrow \qquad\qquad 6-2 = X$$

$$\uparrow \qquad\qquad 2+1 = Y$$

$$\text{A}\curvearrowright \qquad\qquad 2a + 2a = Yd$$

Hence $\qquad\qquad X = 4; \qquad Y = 3; \qquad d = \dfrac{4a}{3}$

Therefore the resultant is of magnitude $\quad \sqrt{(4^2 + 3^2)}\,\text{N} = 5\,\text{N}.$

Its line of action makes $\arctan \tfrac{3}{4}$ with AB
and cuts AB produced at P where $\quad 3\text{AP} = 4\text{AB}.$

2) Find the equation of the line of action of the resultant of forces of magnitudes $4\sqrt{2}\,\text{N}$, $13\,\text{N}$ and $3\,\text{N}$ which act as shown along lines whose vector equations are $\quad \mathbf{r} = \lambda(\mathbf{i}+\mathbf{j}), \quad \mathbf{r} = 2\mathbf{j}+\lambda(12\mathbf{i}+5\mathbf{j}) \quad$ and $\quad \mathbf{r} = 2\mathbf{i}+\lambda\mathbf{j} \quad$ respectively.

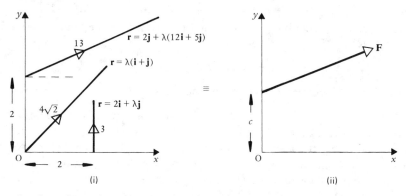

(i)

(ii)

Let the three forces be $\mathbf{F}_1$, $\mathbf{F}_2$ and $\mathbf{F}_3$, and let their resultant be $\mathbf{F}$.

$\mathbf{F}_1$ has magnitude $4\sqrt{2}$ and direction $\mathbf{i}+\mathbf{j}$, therefore

$$\mathbf{F}_1 = 4\sqrt{2}\left(\frac{\mathbf{i}+\mathbf{j}}{\sqrt{2}}\right) = 4\mathbf{i}+4\mathbf{j}$$

F_2 has magnitude 13 and direction $12i + 5j$, so

$$F_2 = 13\left(\frac{12i + 5j}{13}\right) = 12i + 5j$$

F_3 has magnitude 3 and direction j, so

$$F_3 = 3j$$

$$F = F_1 + F_2 + F_3 = 16i + 12j$$

Hence

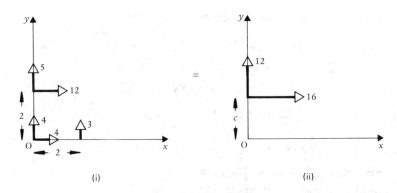

(i) $\equiv$ (ii)

Comparing clockwise moments about an axis through O we have,

$$(12)(2) - (3)(2) = (16)(c)$$

$$\Rightarrow \qquad c = \tfrac{9}{8}$$

The line of action of **F** therefore passes through the point with position vector $\tfrac{9}{8}j$ and is in the direction $16i + 12j$. Therefore its vector equation is

$$r = \tfrac{9}{8}j + \lambda(16i + 12j)$$

Note. The direction vector can be simplified to $4i + 3j$.

In this problem it would have been just as convenient to work with the line of action of **F** cutting the x axis, instead of the y axis, at an unknown point. If, however, the cartesian equation of the line of action is wanted it is best to take a point P on the y axis as the unknown point through which the resultant passes. In this way the distance OP is also the y intercept of the line of action of the resultant and can be used directly in the general equation $y = mx + c$.

3) ABCD is a square in which L bisects AB and M bisects BC. Forces of magnitudes 4, 8, P(newton) act respectively along $\overrightarrow{AB}$, $\overrightarrow{BC}$, $\overrightarrow{CD}$ and their resultant is parallel to $\overrightarrow{LM}$. Find the magnitude and position of the resultant and the value of P.

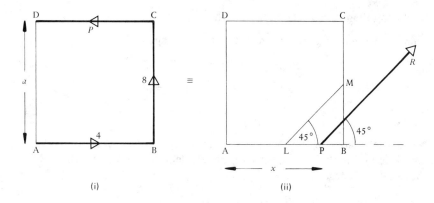

(i)   (ii)

Since LM makes an angle of $45°$ with AB, the resultant, of magnitude R is also at $45°$ to AB. Let the resultant cut AB at P where $AP = x$.

Comparing the resultant with the original forces,

$\rightarrow$ $4 - P = R \cos 45°$ [1]

$\uparrow$ $8 = R \sin 45°$ [2]

A$\}$ $8a + Pa = Rx \sin 45°$ [3]

From [2] $R = 8\sqrt{2}$

From [1] $P = 4 - 8 = -4$

From [3] $x = \dfrac{8a - 4a}{8} = \tfrac{1}{2}a$

Therefore the resultant is of magnitude $8\sqrt{2}$ N
and cuts AB at a point $\tfrac{1}{2}$AB from A, i.e. the resultant is along LM.

4) Forces $2P$, $3P$, $4P$ act respectively along the sides $\overrightarrow{AB}$, $\overrightarrow{BC}$, $\overrightarrow{CA}$ of an equilateral triangle ABC of side a. Find the magnitude and direction of their resultant and the distance from A of the point where it cuts AC.

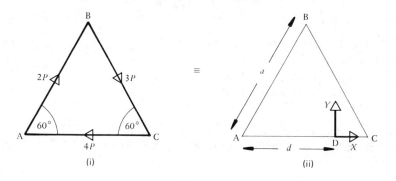

(i)   (ii)

Let the resultant force cut AC at D where AD $= d$.

Comparing the original three forces with the resultant we have:

$\rightarrow$ $\qquad$ $2P \cos 60° + 3P \cos 60° - 4P \; = \; X$ $\qquad$ [1]

$\uparrow$ $\qquad$ $2P \sin 60° - 3P \sin 60° \; = \; Y$ $\qquad$ [2]

A$\}$ $\qquad$ $3P(a \sin 60°) \; = \; -Yd$ $\qquad$ [3]

Note. When comparing torque about any axis, care must be taken to use the same sense for both force systems. In this problem the *clockwise* moment of the resultant is negative.

From [1] and [2] $\qquad X = -\dfrac{3P}{2}$ and $Y = -\dfrac{\sqrt{3}P}{2}$

In [3] $\qquad\qquad\qquad 3Pa\dfrac{\sqrt{3}}{2} = -\left(-\dfrac{\sqrt{3}P}{2}\right)d$

Giving $\qquad\qquad\qquad\qquad d = 3a$

The resultant is therefore of magnitude $\sqrt{X^2 + Y^2} = \sqrt{3}P$ and its direction

is at an angle α to AC where $\quad \tan\alpha = \dfrac{Y}{X} = \dfrac{1}{\sqrt{3}}$.

The line of action of the resultant passes through a point on AC produced, distant $3a$ from A and is at $30°$ to AC as shown below.

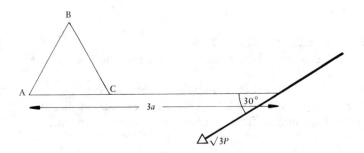

5) A, B and C are points with coordinates $(0,0)$, $(0,a)$ and $(a,0)$ referred to rectangular axes. The clockwise moments of a system of forces in the plane ABC about perpendicular axes through A, B and C are $6M$, $9M$ and $2M$ respectively. Find in terms of M and a the magnitude of the resultant of the system and the equation of its line of action.

Although in this problem the original forces are not specified individually, their resultant can still be determined by comparing its effect with that of the original system.

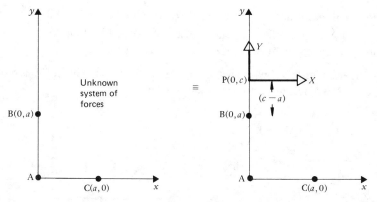

If the resultant has components X and Y and passes through a point $P(0,c)$ then comparing the moment of the original system with that of the resultant, about each of three axes through A, B and C (which are not collinear) we have:

A↻ $\qquad\qquad 6M = Xc$ $\qquad\qquad\qquad\qquad$ [1]

B↻ $\qquad\qquad 9M = X(c-a)$ $\qquad\qquad\qquad$ [2]

C↻ $\qquad\qquad 2M = Xc + Ya$ $\qquad\qquad\qquad$ [3]

[1] and [3] give $\qquad 2M = 6M + Ya \qquad \Rightarrow \qquad Y = -\dfrac{4M}{a}$

[1] and [2] give $\qquad 9M = 6M - Xa \qquad \Rightarrow \qquad X = -\dfrac{3M}{a}$

In [1] $\qquad\qquad 6M = \left(-\dfrac{3M}{a}\right)c \qquad \Rightarrow \qquad c = -2a$

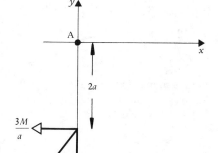

The magnitude R of the resultant is

$$\sqrt{X^2 + Y^2} = \frac{5M}{a}$$

Its line of action makes an angle α with the x axis where

$$\tan\alpha = \frac{Y}{X} = \frac{4}{3}$$

Therefore the equation of its line of action is

$$y = \tfrac{4}{3}x - 2a \quad \text{or} \quad 3y = 4x - 6a$$

6) Forces of magnitudes 3, 4, 2, 1, P, Q act along the sides $\overrightarrow{AB}$, $\overrightarrow{BC}$, $\overrightarrow{CD}$, $\overrightarrow{DE}$, $\overrightarrow{EF}$, $\overrightarrow{FA}$ respectively of a regular hexagon ABCDEF. Find the values of P and Q if the resultant of the six forces acts along CE.

Since the resultant is known to act along CE, a diagram in which CE is either horizontal or vertical makes the solution simpler.

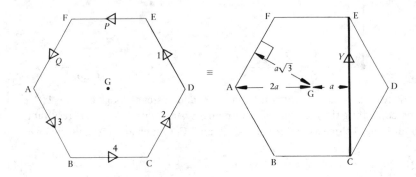

Taking G as the centre of the hexagon and $2a$ as the length of each side, comparison gives:

$\rightarrow$ $\qquad$ $4 - P + (2 - 1 - Q + 3)\cos 60° = 0$ $\qquad$ [1]

$\uparrow$ $\qquad$ $(2 + 1 - Q - 3)\sin 60° = Y$ $\qquad$ [2]

$G\curvearrowright$ $\qquad$ $(3 + 4 + 2 + 1 + P + Q)a\sqrt{3} = Ya$ $\qquad$ [3]

From [2] and [3] $\qquad$ $(P + Q + 10)\sqrt{3} = -Q\dfrac{\sqrt{3}}{2}$

Hence $\qquad$ $2P + 3Q + 20 = 0$

From [1] $\qquad$ $2P + Q - 12 = 0$

Therefore $\qquad$ $Q = -16$ and $P = 14$

Note. An alternative method of solution is to take moments about axes through C and E. The resultant moment is zero in both cases since the resultant force passes through both C and E.

EXERCISE 14a

In Questions 1–5, find the magnitude, direction and equation of the line of action of the resultant of the given forces (units are the newton and the metre throughout).

1)

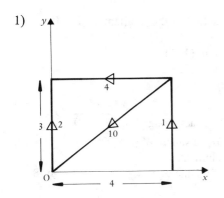

2)

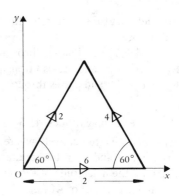

3)

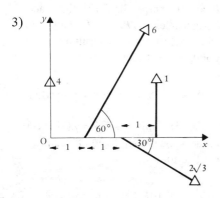

4)

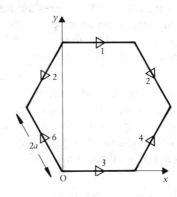

5)

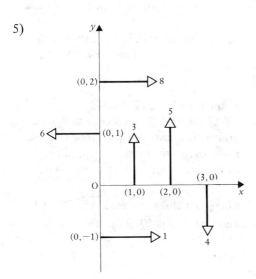

6) Find a vector equation for the line of action of the resultant of F_1, F_2 and F_3 if:
$F_1 = 3i + 7j$ and passes through the point $(1, 1)$
$F_2 = 5i - 4j$ and passes through the point $(7, -2)$
$F_3 = i - 6j$ and passes through the origin.

7) Forces of magnitudes 4, 3, 2, 1, P, Q act along $\overrightarrow{AB}$, $\overrightarrow{BC}$, $\overrightarrow{CD}$, $\overrightarrow{AD}$, $\overrightarrow{AC}$, $\overrightarrow{BD}$ respectively where ABCD is a square of side a.
(a) Find P and Q if the resultant acts along AB.
(b) Find the magnitude of the resultant if its line of action passes through B and is parallel to AC.

8) ABC is an equilateral triangle of side $2a$. A system of forces acts in the plane of the triangle. About axes through A, B and C perpendicular to this plane, the forces exert anticlockwise torques of magnitudes $+2Pa$, $+3Pa$ and $-Pa$ respectively. Find in terms of P and a, the magnitude of the resultant of the system and the distance from A of the point where it crosses AC.

9) Three forces of magnitudes $10\,N$, $3\sqrt{5}\,N$ and $25\,N$ act along lines whose vector equations are respectively
$r_1 = i - 2j + \lambda(4i + 3j)$, $r_2 = -2i + 4j + \lambda(2i - j)$ and $r_3 = 4i + \lambda(7i - 24j)$.
A fourth force F_4 is introduced, which reduces the system to equilibrium.
Find F_4 and a vector equation for its line of action.

10) Forces of magnitudes $9F$, $2F$, nF, mF and $10F$ act along the sides $\overrightarrow{AB}$, $\overrightarrow{BC}$, $\overrightarrow{CD}$, $\overrightarrow{DA}$ and the diagonal $\overrightarrow{DB}$ of a rectangle ABCD in which $AB = 4a$ and $BC = 3a$.
If AB and AD are taken as the x and y axes respectively and the equation of the line of action of the resultant is $12y + 5x = a$ find the values of n and m.

11) A, B and C are points with coordinates $(2, 0)$, $(2, 1)$ and $(0, 1)$ respectively referred to perpendicular axes Ox and Oy. Forces which act in the plane ABC have anticlockwise turning effects about axes through A, B and C of $+3$, $+5$ and $+4$ units respectively (the axes are perpendicular to the plane ABC). Find the equation of the line of action of their resultant.

12) Forces of magnitudes 2, 3, P and Q act along the sides $\overrightarrow{AB}$, $\overrightarrow{BC}$, $\overrightarrow{CD}$ and $\overrightarrow{DA}$ of a square. Find the magnitudes of P and Q if the line of action of the resultant of the four forces
(a) bisects AB and DC,
(b) bisects AB and passes through C.

RESULTANT OF PARALLEL FORCES

(a) Like Parallel Forces (i.e. forces in the same sense).

Consider two forces P and Q whose lines of action are parallel and are a distance d apart.

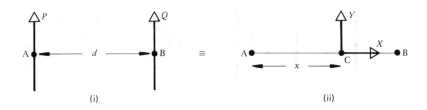

(i)   (ii)

If A and B are two points on the lines of action of P and Q respectively such that AB is perpendicular to both forces, then $AB = d$.

Diagram (ii) shows the resultant represented by components X and Y and passing through a point C on AB where $AC = x$.
Comparing the given forces with their resultant we have:

$\uparrow$ $\qquad\qquad\qquad\qquad P+Q \; = \; Y \qquad\qquad\qquad\qquad$ [1]

$\rightarrow$ $\qquad\qquad\qquad\qquad\quad 0 \; = \; X \qquad\qquad\qquad\qquad$ [2]

$A\;\curvearrowright$ $\qquad\qquad\qquad\qquad Qd \; = \; Yx \qquad\qquad\qquad\qquad$ [3]

From [3] $\qquad\qquad\qquad x \; = \; \left(\dfrac{Q}{P+Q}\right)d \; = \; AC$

Therefore $\qquad\qquad BC \; = \; d-x \; = \; \left(\dfrac{P}{P+Q}\right)d$

Hence the resultant of two like parallel forces P and Q is parallel to P and Q, is of magnitude $(P+Q)$ and divides AB (the distance between the parallel forces) in the ratio $Q:P$.

Note. Because of the geometric properties of parallel lines, it is not only AB but *any* transversal between P and Q which is divided by the resultant in the ratio $Q:P$.

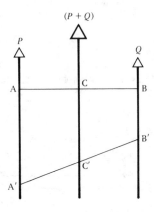

$$\frac{A'C'}{C'B'} = \frac{AC}{CB} = \frac{Q}{P}$$

Now let us consider what happens to the resultant if P and Q are each rotated in the same sense about A and B respectively through equal angles so that the forces are still parallel.

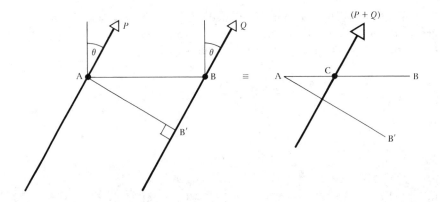

If AB' is perpendicular to P and Q in their new positions, the resultant, as we have just shown, is a force parallel to P and Q, of magnitude $(P+Q)$ and dividing AB' in the ratio $Q:P$.

But the line of action of the resultant also divides any other transversal, one of which is AB, in the ratio $Q:P$.

Therefore the new resultant passes through the same point C as the original resultant did (before P and Q were rotated).

This argument can be applied successively to include further forces and to establish the following general principle.

If for a set of like parallel forces, each force passes through a fixed point, the resultant also passes through a fixed point regardless of the orientation of those forces.

(b) Unlike Parallel Forces (i.e. forces in opposite senses)

Consider two forces P and Q whose lines of action are parallel and distant d apart and suppose that $Q > P$.

Again taking points A and B on the lines of action of P and Q respectively where $AB = d$ and representing the resultant by components X and Y as shown, comparison gives:

$\uparrow$ $Q - P = Y$

$\rightarrow$ $0 = X$

A$\uparrow$ $Qd = Yx$

This time $AC = x = \left(\dfrac{Q}{Q-P}\right)d$

so that $BC = d - x = \left(\dfrac{-P}{Q-P}\right)d$

Therefore $AC : CB = Q : -P$ showing that the resultant, which is of magnitude $Q - P$, divides AB *externally* in the ratio $Q : P$.

When parallel forces occur in problems it is frequently simpler to locate the resultant by using the principle of moments than to quote the results derived above.

(c) Equal Unlike Parallel Forces

This is a special case of (b) above when $P = Q$.
The magnitude of the resultant, $(Q - P)$, is now zero.
The turning effect however is not zero as can be seen by taking moments about an axis through A.

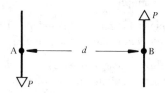

A pair of equal and opposite parallel forces therefore has a resultant which is pure torque. Such a pair of forces is known as a *couple*.

When a couple acts on a body there is no change in the linear movement of the body but there is a change in its rotation.

CONSTANT MOMENT OF A COUPLE

Consider a couple comprising two equal and opposite forces each of magnitude P whose lines of action are distant d apart.

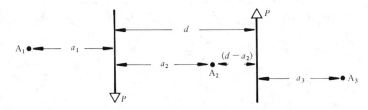

Axes perpendicular to the plane of action of the couple could be taken between the two forces (e.g. through A_2) or outside the lines of action of the two forces (e.g. through A_1 or A_3).

We shall now determine the torque exerted by the couple about each of these axes in turn.

A_1⟲   Anticlockwise torque $= P(a_1+d)-Pa_1 = Pd$

A_2⟲   Anticlockwise torque $= P(d-a_2)+Pa_2 = Pd$

A_3⟲   Anticlockwise torque $= P(d+a_3)-Pa_3 = Pd$

Therefore the moment of a couple is the same about all axes perpendicular to its plane.

The magnitude of the moment of a couple is often referred to as the magnitude of the couple.

Characteristics of a Couple

1. The *linear resultant* of a couple is *zero*.

2. The *moment* of a couple is *not zero* and is independent of the position of the axis so long as the axis is perpendicular to the plane in which the couple acts.

These characteristics are also those of a force system whose resultant is a couple, a property which can be used in solving many problems.

EXAMPLES 14b

1) ABCDEF is a regular hexagon of side $2a$. Forces of magnitudes $5P$, P, $3P$, $4P$, $2P$ and $2P$ act respectively along the sides $\overrightarrow{AB}$, $\overrightarrow{BC}$, $\overrightarrow{CD}$, $\overrightarrow{DE}$, $\overrightarrow{EF}$ and $\overrightarrow{FA}$. Prove that they reduce to a couple, and find its magnitude.

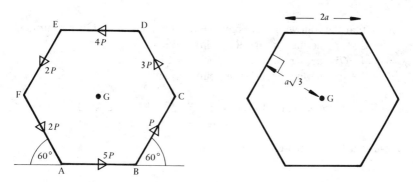

The resultant is a couple if the six forces have a linear resultant which is zero and a resultant moment which is not zero.

Resolving parallel and perpendicular to AB and taking moments about an axis through G we have:

$\rightarrow$ $\qquad\qquad 5P - 4P + (P - 3P - 2P + 2P) \cos 60° = 0$ $\qquad$ [1]

$\uparrow$ $\qquad\qquad\qquad (P + 3P - 2P - 2P) \sin 60° = 0$ $\qquad$ [2]

$G\!\downarrow$ $\qquad\quad (5P + P + 3P + 4P + 2P + 2P)a\sqrt{3} = 17Pa\sqrt{3}$ $\qquad$ [3]

Equations [1] and [2] show that the linear resultant is zero.
So the six forces reduce to a couple of magnitude $17Pa\sqrt{3}$ in the sense ABC.

2) ABCD is a square. Forces of magnitudes 1, 2, 3, P and Q units act along $\overrightarrow{AB}$, $\overrightarrow{BC}$, $\overrightarrow{CD}$, $\overrightarrow{DA}$ and $\overrightarrow{AC}$ respectively. Find values for P and Q so that the resultant of the five forces is a couple.

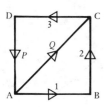

If the resultant is a couple, the linear resultant is zero. Hence the components in any direction total zero.

Resolving gives

$\rightarrow$ $\qquad\qquad 1 + Q \cos 45° - 3 = 0$

$\uparrow$ $\qquad\qquad 2 + Q \sin 45° - P = 0$

Hence, when $Q = 2\sqrt{2}$ and $P = 4$ the linear resultant of the given forces is zero.

This is *not sufficient* to ensure that the forces reduce to a couple. We must also show that their *turning effect is not zero*.

If $AB = a$,   the turning effect about A is $2a + 3a \neq 0$.

Therefore the forces reduce to a couple if $P = 4$ and $Q = 2\sqrt{2}$ units.

3) Show that the following forces reduce to a couple and find its magnitude.
$\mathbf{F_1} = -4\mathbf{i} + 3\mathbf{j}$ acting through the point $2\mathbf{i} - \mathbf{j}$
$\mathbf{F_2} = 6\mathbf{i} - 7\mathbf{j}$ acting through the point $-3\mathbf{i} + \mathbf{j}$
$\mathbf{F_3} = -2\mathbf{i} + 4\mathbf{j}$ acting through the point $4\mathbf{j}$

The resultant force is $X\mathbf{i} + Y\mathbf{j}$ where $X = -4 + 6 - 2 = 0$
and $Y = 3 - 7 + 4 = 0$

The resultant force is therefore zero.

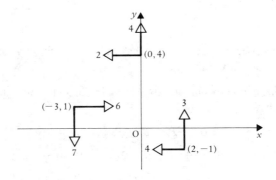

The resultant turning effect about an axis through O (taking anticlockwise as positive) is:
$$(3 \times 2 - 4 \times 1) + (7 \times 3 - 6 \times 1) + (2 \times 4) = 25$$

Since the resultant force is zero but the resultant turning effect is not zero, the forces reduce to a couple of magnitude 25 units anticlockwise.

4) Forces acting along the sides $\overrightarrow{AB}$, $\overrightarrow{BC}$ and $\overrightarrow{CA}$ of a triangle ABC have magnitudes proportional to the lengths of those sides. Prove that the three forces reduce to a couple.

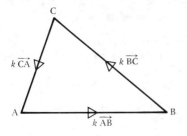
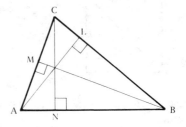

It is convenient in this problem to use the constant moment property of a couple.

Taking moments about axes through A, B and C we have:

A⤴
$$\text{Torque} = (AL)|k\,\overrightarrow{BC}|$$
$$= (k)(BC)(AL)$$
$$= 2k(\text{area of triangle ABC})$$

B⤴
$$\text{Torque} = (BM)|k\,\overrightarrow{CA}|$$
$$= 2k(\text{area of triangle ABC})$$

C⤴
$$\text{Torque} = (CN)|k\,\overrightarrow{AB}|$$
$$= 2k(\text{area of triangle ABC})$$

Since about each of three axes the turning effect of the given forces is the same, the forces reduce to a couple.

EXERCISE 14b

1) Show that forces of magnitudes $6F$, $7F$, F, $3F$, $4F$, $4F$ acting along the sides $\overrightarrow{AB}$, $\overrightarrow{CB}$, $\overrightarrow{DC}$, $\overrightarrow{DE}$, $\overrightarrow{FE}$, $\overrightarrow{AF}$ of a regular hexagon are equivalent to a couple and find its magnitude.

2) Forces 1, 2, 3, 4, P, Q act along the sides of a regular hexagon taken in order. Find values for P and Q for which the six forces reduce to a couple.

3) ABC is an equilateral triangle and D is the midpoint of BC. Forces P and $3P$ acting along $\overrightarrow{AB}$ and $\overrightarrow{AC}$ together with a third force in the plane ABC whose line of action passes through D, reduce to a couple. Find the magnitude and direction of the force through D.

4) Forces proportional to the sides of a quadrilateral taken in order act respectively along those sides. Prove that the resultant of the system is a couple whose magnitude is represented by twice the area of the quadrilateral.

In Questions 5-8, ABCD is a square of side $2a$. Forces of magnitudes F and $2F$ act along $\overrightarrow{AB}$ and $\overrightarrow{BC}$ respectively.

5) Find the magnitudes of two forces which, acting along AC and AD, combine with the two given forces to form a couple and find the magnitude of the couple.

6) Find the magnitude and direction of a force acting through D which, together with the given forces, form a couple.

7) A third force, together with the two given forces, reduce to a couple of magnitude $2Fa$. Find the magnitude and direction of the third force and the distance from A of the point where its line of action cuts AB (produced if necessary).

8) Two forces both of magnitude nF are added to the system. One acts along AC and the other passes through B.
Calculate n if the new system reduces to a couple.

9) Four forces are represented by $i-4j$, $3i+6j$, $-9i+j$ and $5i-3j$, and their points of application are given by $3i-j$, $2i+2j$, $-i-j$ and $-3i+4j$ respectively.
(a) Show that the forces reduce to a couple and find its magnitude.
(b) If the fourth force is removed and the first force is moved to the point $i-8j$ show that the system now reduces to a single force through the origin.

10) ABC is a right-angled triangle in which $AB = 4a$; $BC = 3a$. Forces of magnitudes P, Q and R act along the sides $\overrightarrow{AB}$, $\overrightarrow{BC}$ and $\overrightarrow{CA}$ respectively. Find the ratios of $P:Q:R$ if their resultant is a couple.
If the force along $\overrightarrow{AC}$ is now reversed, find in terms of P the magnitude of the resultant of the new system.

11) Forces of magnitudes 1, 6, 8, 2 and 5 units act along the sides $\overrightarrow{AB}$, $\overrightarrow{BC}$, $\overrightarrow{DC}$, $\overrightarrow{DE}$ and $\overrightarrow{EF}$ respectively of a regular hexagon and another force acts along FA. Give as much information as you can about the resultant of the six forces if the sixth force is:
(a) 1 unit along $\overrightarrow{FA}$,
(b) 7 units along $\overrightarrow{AF}$.

IDENTIFICATION OF FORCE SYSTEMS

A set of coplanar forces may:

    (a) be in equilibrium,
    (b) reduce to a couple,
    (c) reduce to a single force.

In order to establish which of these applies to a particular set of forces, *three independent facts* are needed (since coplanar forces have three degrees of freedom). These three facts are derived from various combinations of resolving and taking moments.

Suppose that X and Y represent the collected components in two perpendicular directions and that M_A, M_B and M_C represent the resultant moments about axes through any three non-collinear points A, B and C in the plane of the forces then:

(a) the system is in equilibrium if:

$$\text{(i)} \quad X = 0 \quad Y = 0 \quad M_A = 0$$

or (ii) $X = 0 \quad M_A = 0 \quad M_B = 0$ (provided that AB is not
perpendicular to X)

or (iii) $M_A = 0 \quad M_B = 0 \quad M_C = 0$

(b) the system reduces to a couple if:

$$\text{(i)} \quad X = 0 \quad Y = 0 \quad M_A \neq 0$$

or (ii) $M_A = M_B = M_C \neq 0$

(c) the system reduces to a single force if X and Y are not both zero.
The value of M_A is then required to locate this force.

Partial Identification

When less than three independent facts are given, the coplanar force system to
which they apply cannot be identified precisely.

EXAMPLES 14c

In these examples X, Y, M_A, M_B, M_C have the same significance as in the
preceding paragraph.

1) What is the state of a set of coplanar forces for which $X = 0$ and $Y = 0$?

If $X = 0$ and $Y = 0$ there is no linear resultant.
Therefore the set of forces is either in equilibrium or reduces to a couple.
(Without further information there is no way of differentiating between these
two possibilities.)

2) What is the resultant of a set of coplanar forces for which $M_A = M_B \neq 0$?

Since the turning effects about two different axes are equal the resultant could
be a couple.
On the other hand, points A and B could be equidistant from a linear resultant.

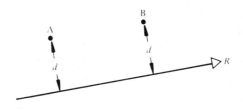

Therefore the set of forces reduces either to a couple or to a single force parallel
to AB.

3) A set of coplanar forces is such that $X = 0$ and $M_A = 0$. To what simple forms is it possible for the forces to reduce?

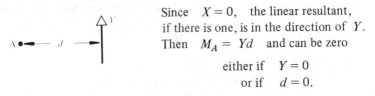

Since $X = 0$, the linear resultant, if there is one, is in the direction of Y. Then $M_A = Yd$ and can be zero

$$\text{either if} \quad Y = 0$$
$$\text{or if} \quad d = 0.$$

The resultant cannot be a couple since $M_A = 0$. Therefore,

either the system reduces to a single force in the direction of Y and passing through A (i.e. $d = 0$)

or the system is in equilibrium (i.e. $Y = 0$).

EXERCISE 14c

Describe carefully the resultant of a set of coplanar forces if:

1) The turning effect about each of three non-coplanar axes perpendicular to the plane of the forces is zero.

2) The turning effect about each of two axes perpendicular to the plane of the forces is zero.

3) The collected components of the forces are zero in the directions both of Ox and of Oy.

4) The collected components in Question 3 are not zero but the total moment about an axis through a point A in the plane of the forces is zero.

5) The system of forces causes a body to rotate while its centre of gravity remains stationary.

6) The forces are all parallel and in the same sense.

THE RESULTANT OF FORCES REPRESENTED BY LINE SEGMENTS

Suppose that two forces are represented completely (i.e. in magnitude, direction and *position*) by $p\overrightarrow{AB}$ and $q\overrightarrow{AC}$ where p and q are constants.

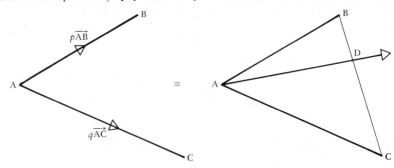

The resultant passes through A (the point of intersection of the given forces) and will cut the line through B and C at some unknown point D.

$p\overrightarrow{AB}$ can be replaced completely by components which intersect at A and are represented in magnitude and direction by $p\overrightarrow{AD}$ and $p\overrightarrow{DB}$ (treating ADB as a vector triangle).

Similarly $q\overrightarrow{AC}$ can be replaced completely by components through A represented in magnitude and direction by $q\overrightarrow{AD}$ and $q\overrightarrow{DC}$.

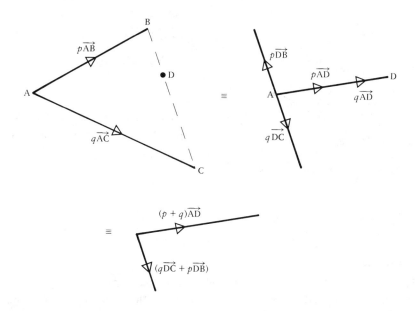

But if AD is to be the line along which the resultant force acts, the component which is not in this direction must be zero.

i.e. $$q\overrightarrow{DC}+p\overrightarrow{DB} \;=\; \overrightarrow{0}$$

Therefore $q\overrightarrow{DC}$ and $p\overrightarrow{DB}$ are equal and opposite and the position of D is such that

$$DB:DC \;=\; q:p$$

Forces represented completely by $p\overrightarrow{AB}$ and $q\overrightarrow{AC}$ have a resultant represented completely by $(p+q)\overrightarrow{AD}$ where D divides BC in the ratio $q:p$.

This important *Resultant Vector Theorem* applies to any two vectors which have the same sense relative to their point of intersection.

e.g.

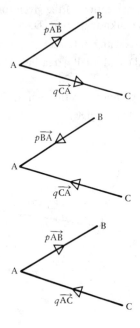

Both forces are *going away from* A therefore the theorem applies.

$$p\overrightarrow{AB} + q\overrightarrow{AC} = (p+q)\overrightarrow{AD}$$

where $BD : DC = q : p$.

Both forces are *going towards* A therefore the theorem applies.

$$p\overrightarrow{BA} + q\overrightarrow{CA} = (p+q)\overrightarrow{DA}$$

where $BD : DC = q : p$.

One force $(p\overrightarrow{AB})$ goes away from A and the other $(q\overrightarrow{CA})$ goes towards A so the theorem does not apply.

EXAMPLES 14d

1) In a triangle ABC forces represented by $2\overrightarrow{AB}$ and $3\overrightarrow{AC}$ act along the sides AB and AC respectively. Where does the line of action of the resultant force cut BC and what is its magnitude.

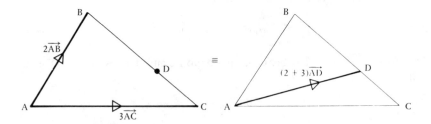

Using the resultant vector theorem:

$$2\overrightarrow{AB} + 3\overrightarrow{AC} = (2+3)\overrightarrow{AD} \quad \text{where} \quad BD : DC = 3 : 2$$

Therefore the resultant is represented in magnitude by 5AD and its line of action divides BC in the ratio $3 : 2$.

Sometimes a pair of forces whose resultant cannot at first be found by using this theorem, can be alternatively represented so that the theorem can be applied.

2) In a triangle ABC, M is the midpoint of AC. Two forces are represented completely by $2\overrightarrow{AC}$ and $3\overrightarrow{MB}$. Find the resultant.

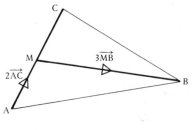

Since M is the point of intersection of the two forces, the resultant vector theorem can be used only if each force is represented by a line segment, one end of which is M. An alternative form must therefore be found for the force $2\overrightarrow{AC}$.

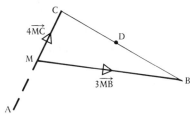

Now $AC = 2MC$ so $2\overrightarrow{AC} = 4\overrightarrow{MC}$. The theorem can now be applied giving:
$$4\overrightarrow{MC} + 3\overrightarrow{MB} = (4+3)\overrightarrow{MD}$$
where $CD:DB = 3:4$

Therefore the resultant of $2\overrightarrow{AC}$ and $3\overrightarrow{MB}$ is represented completely by $7\overrightarrow{MD}$ where D divides CB in the ratio $3:4$.

Successive applications of this theorem can be used to find the resultant of more than two forces given in line segment form, as is shown in some of the following examples.

3) Forces represented completely by $2\overrightarrow{AB}, \overrightarrow{CB}, 2\overrightarrow{CD}$ and $4\overrightarrow{AD}$ act along the sides of a quadrilateral ABCD. Find their resultant and find the points where its line of action intersects the diagonals of the quadrilateral.

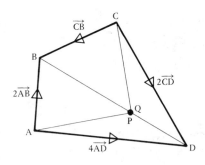

Applying the vector theorem we have:
$$2\overrightarrow{AB} + 4\overrightarrow{AD} = (2+4)\overrightarrow{AP}$$
where $BP:PD = 4:2$

and $\overrightarrow{CB} + 2\overrightarrow{CD} = (1+2)\overrightarrow{CQ}$

where $BQ:QD = 2:1$

P and Q divide BD in the same ratio, therefore they are the same point.

Therefore

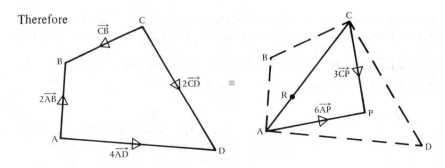

Again $3\overrightarrow{CP} + 6\overrightarrow{AP} = (3 + 6)\overrightarrow{RP}$ where   CR : RA $= 6 : 3 = 2 : 1$.

Therefore the resultant is represented completely by $9\overrightarrow{RP}$ where R is a point on the diagonal AC dividing it in the ratio $1 : 2$ and P is a point on the diagonal BD dividing it in the ratio $2 : 1$.

4) Forces represented completely by $2\overrightarrow{AB}$, $3\overrightarrow{BC}$, $4\overrightarrow{AC}$ act along the sides of a triangle ABC. Find their resultant and the point where its line of action cuts AB and BC.

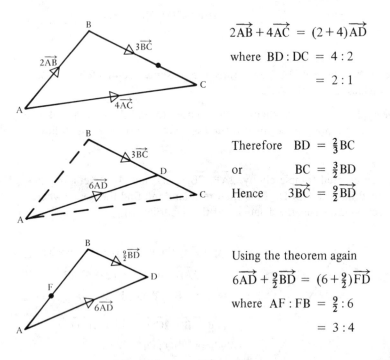

$$2\overrightarrow{AB} + 4\overrightarrow{AC} = (2 + 4)\overrightarrow{AD}$$

where BD : DC $= 4 : 2$

$$= 2 : 1$$

Therefore   BD $= \tfrac{2}{3}$BC

or   BC $= \tfrac{3}{2}$BD

Hence $3\overrightarrow{BC} = \tfrac{9}{2}\overrightarrow{BD}$

Using the theorem again

$$6\overrightarrow{AD} + \tfrac{9}{2}\overrightarrow{BD} = (6 + \tfrac{9}{2})\overrightarrow{FD}$$

where   AF : FB $= \tfrac{9}{2} : 6$

$$= 3 : 4$$

The resultant of $2\overrightarrow{AB}$, $3\overrightarrow{BC}$ and $4\overrightarrow{AC}$ is therefore represented by $\tfrac{21}{2}\overrightarrow{FD}$ where F divides AB in the ratio $3 : 4$ and D divides BC in the ratio $2 : 1$.

5) ABC is a triangle and G is its centroid. Show that forces represented completely by $\overrightarrow{PA}$, $\overrightarrow{PB}$, $\overrightarrow{PC}$, where P is any point in the plane of the triangle, have a resultant represented completely by $3\overrightarrow{PG}$.

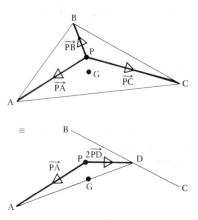

$$\overrightarrow{PB} + \overrightarrow{PC} = (1+1)\overrightarrow{PD}$$
where $BD : DC = 1 : 1$

Therefore AD is a median of $\triangle ABC$ and G is on AD
where $AG : GD = 2 : 1$

Now $\overrightarrow{PA} + 2\overrightarrow{PD} = (1+2)\overrightarrow{PG}$
since $AG : GD = 2 : 1$

Therefore the resultant of $\overrightarrow{PA}$, $\overrightarrow{PB}$ and $\overrightarrow{PC}$ is $3\overrightarrow{PG}$.

EXERCISE 14d

In Questions 1–4 find the resultant of the given forces. The positions of any additional points which are introduced must be carefully defined.

1)

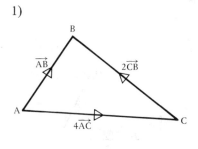

2)

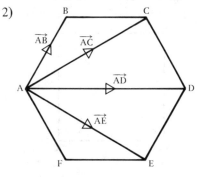

3)

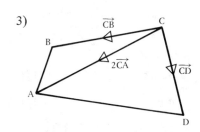

4)

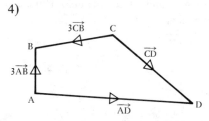

5) The circumscribed circle of an equilateral triangle ABC is drawn. From any point P on the circumference of the circle, forces $\overrightarrow{PA}$, $\overrightarrow{PB}$ and $\overrightarrow{PC}$ act along PA, PB and PC. Show that the magnitude of their resultant is independent of the position of P.

6) Forces represented completely by $\overrightarrow{AB}$, $\overrightarrow{AC}$ and $\overrightarrow{BM}$ act in the plane of a triangle ABC in which L and M are the midpoints of BC and AC respectively. Show that the resultant force is represented completely by $9\overrightarrow{GP}$ where P is on LM and divides it in the ratio $1:2$, and G is the centroid of the triangle.

GENERAL PROBLEMS ON COPLANAR FORCE SYSTEMS

1. Equivalent Force Systems

Two sets of forces are equivalent if, in all respects, they have the same effect. When the forces are coplanar their equivalence is defined by three independent relationships based on comparing components and/or torque.

EXAMPLES 14e

1) OABC is a square. Forces of magnitudes 3, 4, 2, 5 and $\sqrt{2}$ N act along $\overrightarrow{OA}$, $\overrightarrow{AB}$, $\overrightarrow{CB}$, $\overrightarrow{OC}$ and $\overrightarrow{OB}$ respectively. If this force system is to be replaced by two forces of equal magnitude acting along $\overrightarrow{OA}$ and $\overrightarrow{OC}$ and a third force whose line of action passes through A, find the magnitudes of these forces and the direction of the third force.

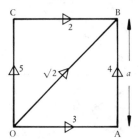 $\equiv$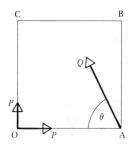

Using P and Q for the unknown magnitudes and θ as the unknown angle, comparison gives:

$\rightarrow$ $\qquad$ $3 + \sqrt{2}\cos 45° + 2 = P - Q\cos\theta$ $\qquad$ [1]

$\uparrow$ $\qquad$ $5 + \sqrt{2}\sin 45° + 4 = P + Q\sin\theta$ $\qquad$ [2]

$O\!\!\curvearrowright$ $\qquad$ $4a - 2a = Qa\sin\theta$ $\qquad$ [3]

From [3] $\qquad\qquad$ $Q = \dfrac{2}{\sin\theta}$

From [2] $\qquad\qquad$ $P = 10 - 2 = 8$

From [1] $\qquad\qquad$ $Q\cos\theta = 8 - 6 = 2$

Hence $\tan\theta = 1$

and $Q = 2\sqrt{2}$

The replacement force system therefore comprises two forces each of 8 N along $\overrightarrow{OA}$ and $\overrightarrow{OC}$ and a force of $2\sqrt{2}$ N passing through A and making an angle of $45°$ with AO.

2. The Combination of a Force and a Couple

Consider a force of magnitude F and a couple of moment M which act in one plane. With reference to perpendicular axes Ox and Oy which, for convenience, are chosen to be parallel and perpendicular to the given force, the original system and its resultant can be represented in a diagram as shown.

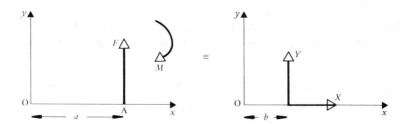

Note how the moment of the couple is shown as a curved arrow indicating turning effect. This must not be mistaken for a force.

Comparing in the usual way we have

$\rightarrow$ $\qquad\qquad\qquad 0 = X$ $\qquad\qquad$ [1]

$\uparrow$ $\qquad\qquad\qquad F = Y$ $\qquad\qquad$ [2]

$O\!\!\curvearrowright$ $\qquad\qquad Fa - M = Yb$ $\qquad\qquad$ [3]

From [1] and [2] we see that, in magnitude and direction, the resultant is identical to the original force.

From [2] and [3] $\qquad\qquad (a - b) = \dfrac{M}{F}$

i.e.

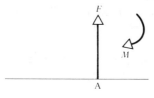 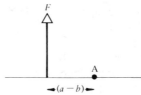

The very useful conclusion reached therefore is:

> A couple M together with a coplanar force F are equivalent to an equal force F displaced through a distance $\dfrac{M}{F}$

Because the direction of the displacement of the line of action depends on the sense of the couple it is advisable to calculate the displacement, rather than to quote it, in each problem.

SUMMARY

1) The resultant of any force system which is not in equilibrium is either a single force or a couple and has exactly the same linear and turning effects as the given system.

2) The resultant of two like parallel forces P and Q is of magnitude $P+Q$ and acts in a line parallel to P and Q dividing them internally in the ratio $Q:P$.

3) The resultant of two unlike, unequal, parallel forces P and Q is of magnitude $|P-Q|$ and acts in a line parallel to P and Q dividing them externally in the ratio $Q:P$.

4) If each member of a set of parallel forces passes through a fixed point, then their resultant also passes through a fixed point which is independent of their orientation.

5) A couple is a pair of equal and opposite non-collinear forces. It has zero linear resultant and produces pure rotation. The magnitude of a couple is its moment, which is Fd where F is the magnitude of each force and d is the distance between them.

6) The moment of a couple is the same about all axes perpendicular to its plane.

7) The combination of a force and a couple in the same plane is an equal force whose line of action is displaced.

8) The resultant of two forces represented completely by $p\overrightarrow{AB}$ and $q\overrightarrow{AC}$ is represented completely by $(p+q)\overrightarrow{AD}$ where D is on BC and $BD:DC = q:p$.

9) Complete specification of a force system in one plane requires three independent facts. When fewer than three are given or used, incomplete or ambiguous results arise.

EXAMPLES 14e (continued)

2) Forces P, $2P$, $3P$ act along the sides $\overrightarrow{AB}$, $\overrightarrow{BC}$, $\overrightarrow{CA}$ of an equilateral triangle of side a. Find the magnitude and direction of their resultant and the distance from A of the point where its line of action cuts AC (produced if necessary).

A couple of magnitude $\sqrt{3}Pa$ acting in the sense ABC and in the plane of the triangle is added to the system. Find the intersection with AC of the line of action of the resultant of the new system.

What single force must now be introduced to reduce the system to equilibrium?

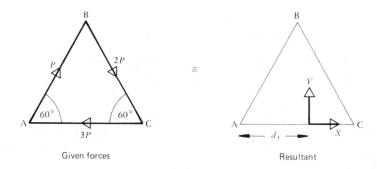

Given forces   Resultant

Comparing gives

$\rightarrow$ $$(P+2P)\cos 60° - 3P = X \qquad [1]$$

$\uparrow$ $$(P-2P)\sin 60° = Y \qquad [2]$$

$\text{A}\!\curvearrowright$ $$-2Pa\sin 60° = Yd_1 \qquad [3]$$

Hence $$X = -\frac{3P}{2}; \quad Y = -\frac{\sqrt{3}P}{2}; \quad d_1 = 2a$$

Therefore the resultant of the three forces has magnitude $\sqrt{X^2+Y^2} = \sqrt{3}P$; its direction makes an angle α with CA when $\alpha = \arctan\dfrac{Y}{X} = 30°$, and its line of action cuts AC produced at a distance $2a$ from A.

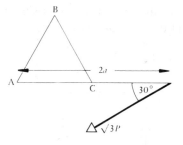

When a couple of magnitude $\sqrt{3}Pa$ is introduced, we have the combination of a force and a couple which is equivalent to an equal force in a different position. Let the new line of action cut AC at a point distant d_2 from A, then:

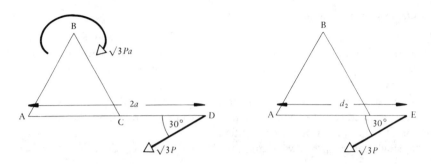

Comparing turning effect only (since the magnitude and direction of the new resultant are known to be the same as those of the old resultant),

$$\sqrt{3}P\,2a\sin 30° + \sqrt{3}Pa = \sqrt{3}P\,d_2\sin 30°$$

Hence

$$d_2 = 4a$$

Therefore the new resultant cuts AC produced at E, distant $4a$ from A.

To reduce the system to equilibrium, a force equal and opposite to, and collinear with, this resultant must be added, i.e. a force $\sqrt{3}P$ at $30°$ to AC and cutting AC produced at E.

3) Forces 7P, 5P, 3P and 2P act along the sides, $\overrightarrow{AB}$, $\overrightarrow{BC}$, $\overrightarrow{CD}$ and $\overrightarrow{DA}$ of a square ABCD of side a. Find the equation of the line of action of the resultant of the system using AB and AD as x and y axes respectively. A force F along AB and a couple of moment M are added to the system so that the new resultant passes through B and D. Find the magnitude and sense of the force and the couple.

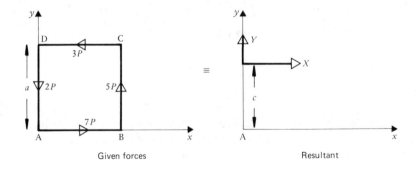

Given forces   Resultant

Comparing, we have:

$\rightarrow$
$$7P - 3P = X \tag{1}$$

$\uparrow$
$$5P - 2P = Y \tag{2}$$

$A \downarrow$
$$-5Pa - 3Pa = Xc \tag{3}$$

Therefore
$$X = 4P, \quad Y = 3P, \quad c = -2a$$

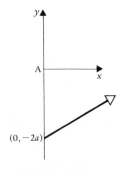

The gradient of the line of action of the resultant is $\dfrac{Y}{X} = \dfrac{3}{4}$ and the line of action cuts the y axis at $(0, -2a)$.

Its equation is therefore

$$y = \tfrac{3}{4}x - 2a$$

$\Rightarrow$
$$4y = 3x - 8a$$

Adding the force F and couple M to this resultant (which is equivalent to the original system) gives:

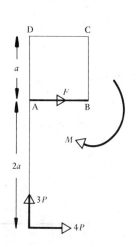
$\equiv$
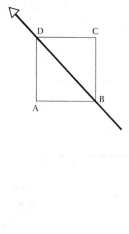

As the new resultant passes through B and D the turning effect of the system about axes through both B and D is zero.

$B \downarrow$
$$M + 3Pa - 4P(2a) = 0$$

$D \downarrow$
$$M - 4Pa(3a) - Fa = 0$$

Therefore
$$M = 5Pa \quad \text{and} \quad F = -7P$$

The force is of magnitude $7P$ in the sense $\overrightarrow{BA}$ and the couple is of magnitude $5Pa$ in the sense CBA.

4) Forces $3P$, $7P$, P, $2P$, mP and nP act along the sides $\overrightarrow{AB}$, $\overrightarrow{BC}$, $\overrightarrow{CD}$, $\overrightarrow{DE}$, $\overrightarrow{FE}$ and $\overrightarrow{FA}$ of a regular hexagon. Find the values of m and n if:
(a) the six forces reduce to a couple,
(b) the system reduces to a single force along AD.

(a)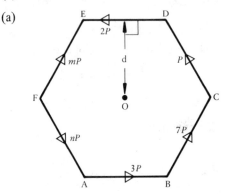

When the resultant is a couple the linear resultant is zero but the resultant moment is not.

Therefore → $3P - 2P + (7P - P + mP + nP) \cos 60° = 0$

and ↑ $(7P + P + mP - nP) \sin 60° = 0$

These give $m = -8$ and $n = 0$

With these values, and taking O as the centre of the hexagon,

O↻ $(3P + 7P + P + 2P + 8P)d \neq 0$

Therefore when $m = -8$ and $n = 0$ the system does reduce to a couple.

(b)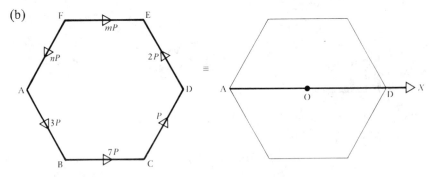

If the resultant is along AD, it is simpler if this line is horizontal (or vertical) in the diagram. Comparing gives

↑ $(P + 2P - nP - 3P) \sin 60° = 0$

O↻ $(3P + 7P + P + 2P - mP + nP)d = 0$

These give:　　　　　　　　$n = 0$　and　$m = 13$

With these values

→　　　　　　$X = 7P + 13P + (P - 2P + 3P) \cos 60° \neq 0$

Therefore when　$n = 0$　and　$m = 13$　the system does reduce to a single force along AD.

5) OABC is a rectangle in which　$OA = 2a$　and　$OC = a$.　Forces of magnitudes P, Q and R act along $\overrightarrow{OA}$, $\overrightarrow{AB}$ and $\overrightarrow{BC}$ respectively. When OA and OC are taken as x and y axes respectively, the line of action of the resultant of these forces has equation　$x = 4(y + a)$.
Find the ratio of the magnitudes of P, Q and R. Find also in terms of P and a, the moment of the couple necessary to transfer the line of action of the resultant to the line with equation　$4y = x + 2a$.

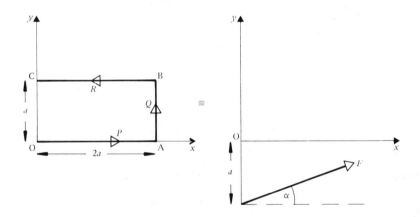

If the resultant makes an angle α with Ox then the gradient of its line of

action is　$\tan \alpha = \frac{1}{4}$　⇒　[diagram: right triangle with hypotenuse $\sqrt{17}$, base 4, height 1, angle α]

Comparing gives

→　　　　　　　　$P - R = F \cos \alpha$　　　　　　　[1]

↑　　　　　　　　　　$Q = F \sin \alpha$　　　　　　　[2]

O↻　　　　　$2aQ + aR = Fa \cos \alpha$　　　　　　　[3]

From [3]　　　　$R = F \cos \alpha - 2F \sin \alpha = \dfrac{F}{\sqrt{17}}(4 - 2)$

From [1]　　　　$P = F \cos \alpha + R = \dfrac{F}{\sqrt{17}}(4 + 2)$

Therefore $\qquad P:Q:R = \dfrac{6F}{\sqrt{17}}:\dfrac{F}{\sqrt{17}}:\dfrac{2F}{\sqrt{17}}$

i.e. $\qquad\qquad P:Q:R = 6:1:2.$

The resultant must now be transferred to act along a parallel line whose y intercept is the point $(0,\frac{1}{2}a)$.
If the necessary couple is of magnitude kPa then,

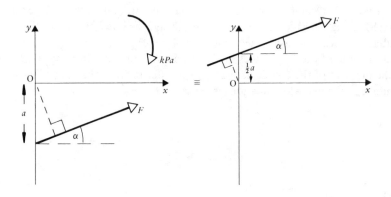

Comparing moments only,

$$kPa - Fa\cos\alpha = \tfrac{1}{2}Fa\cos\alpha$$

Hence $\qquad\qquad\qquad kP = \tfrac{3}{2}F\cos\alpha$

But $\quad P = \dfrac{6F}{\sqrt{17}} \quad$ so $\quad \dfrac{6Fk}{\sqrt{17}} = \left(\dfrac{3F}{2}\right)\!\left(\dfrac{4}{\sqrt{17}}\right) \;\Rightarrow\; k = 1$

Therefore the required couple is of magnitude Pa and acts in the sense CBA.

EXERCISE 14e

1) Forces of magnitudes $3F$, $4F$, $2F$, F act along the sides $\overrightarrow{AB}$, $\overrightarrow{BC}$, $\overrightarrow{CD}$, $\overrightarrow{DA}$ of a rectangle ABCD in which $AB = 4a$ and $AD = 3a$. If two more forces pF and qF act along $\overrightarrow{AC}$ and $\overrightarrow{BD}$ respectively, find the values of p and q for which the six forces:
(a) reduce to a couple,
(b) reduce to a force through B parallel to AC.
Explain why it is impossible to find values of p and q for which the system is in equilibrium.

2) Forces P, $2P$, $2P$ act along the sides $\overrightarrow{AB}$, $\overrightarrow{BC}$, $\overrightarrow{CA}$ of an equilateral triangle of side $2a$. Find the magnitude and direction of their resultant and find the point where its line of action cuts AC (produced if necessary).
The system is to be reduced to equilibrium by introducing a couple in the plane ABC and a force which acts through A. Find the magnitude and direction of the force and the magnitude and sense of the couple.

3) ABCD is a square of side 1 m. Forces F_1, F_2 and 4 N act along $\overrightarrow{AB}$, $\overrightarrow{BC}$ and $\overrightarrow{CD}$ respectively. The equation of the line of action of their resultant, referred to AB and AD as x and y axes respectively, is $3y = 2x + 6$. Calculate the values of F_1 and F_2.
A couple of magnitude 3 Nm in the plane of the square is now added to the system. Find the equation of the line of action of the new resultant.

4) Forces F, $2F$, $3F$ and $4F$ acting along the sides $\overrightarrow{AB}$, $\overrightarrow{BC}$, $\overrightarrow{CD}$ and $\overrightarrow{DA}$ of a square ABCD of side $2a$ are to be replaced by three forces acting along the sides of the triangle ABC. Find, in terms of F, the magnitude and sense of each of these forces. If the force acting along AC is now reversed find the distance from A of the point where the line of action of the resultant now cuts AB (produced if necessary).

5) Three forces which act along the sides $\overrightarrow{AB}$, $\overrightarrow{BC}$ and $\overrightarrow{CD}$ of a regular hexagon ABCDEF of side $2a$, have a resultant which acts along DF.
When a couple $4Pa$ in the sense CBA is added in the plane of the hexagon, the resultant acts along CA. Find the magnitudes of the three forces in terms of P.

6) Two forces in the same plane act as shown in the diagram.

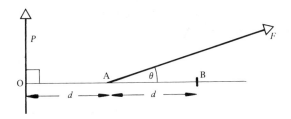

What can be added to the system in order to:
(a) reduce it to a single force equal in magnitude and direction to F but acting through (i) O   (ii) B,
(b) reduce it to equilibrium,
(c) reduce it to a clockwise couple of magnitude Pd.

MULTIPLE CHOICE EXERCISE 14

(The instructions for answering these questions are given on page x.)

TYPE I

1)

Forces act as shown round the sides of a square ABCD of side $2a$. The resultant force cuts AB at a point P.
(a) P is on AB produced and   AP $= 4a$.
(b) P bisects AB.
(c) P is on BA produced and   AP $= 2a$.
(d) P is on BA produced and   AP $= a$.

2) The resultant moment of a set of coplanar forces about each of two axes through points A and B is zero. The set of forces reduces to:
(a) equilibrium,
(b) a force through A and a couple,
(c) a couple,
(d) a force through A and B,
(e) either equilibrium or a force through A and B.

3)

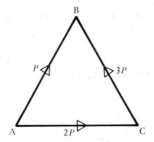

ABC is an equilateral triangle. The resultant of the three given forces intersects AC:
(a) on AC produced,
(b) on CA produced,
(c) between A and C,
(d) at C.

4)

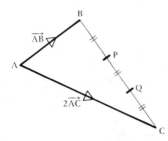

The resultant of $\overrightarrow{AB}$ and $2\overrightarrow{AC}$ is:
(a) $3\overrightarrow{AP}$,
(b) $3\overrightarrow{BC}$,
(c) $3\overrightarrow{AQ}$,
(d) $3\overrightarrow{PA}$.

5)

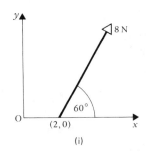

(i)

(ii)

The force in figure (i), together with a couple are equivalent to the force in figure (ii). The couple is:
(a) 4 N m clockwise,
(b) 8√3 N m anticlockwise,
(c) 4√3 N m clockwise,
(d) 16 N m anticlockwise.

TYPE II

6)

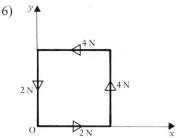

≡

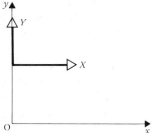

The diagrams represent a set of forces and their resultant.
(a) $X = -2$.
(b) The resultant is a couple.
(c) The resultant is a force at $45°$ to Oy.
(d) The resultant is a force at $45°$ to Ox.

7)

The resultant of the force of 4 N and the clockwise couple of 8 N m shown in the figure is:
(a) a force of magnitude 4 N,
(b) a force of magnitude -4 N,
(c) a force passing through O,
(d) a force passing through (4, 0).

TYPE III

8) (a) A set of coplanar forces has zero linear resultant.
    (b) A set of coplanar forces reduces to a couple.

9) (a) A set of coplanar forces is in equilibrium.
    (b) The moment of a set of coplanar forces about each of two different axes is zero.

10) (a) A set of coplanar forces reduces to a couple.
    (b) A set of like parallel forces acts in a plane.

11) (a) Forces represented by $2\overrightarrow{AB}$ and $3\overrightarrow{AC}$ have a resultant represented by $5\overrightarrow{AD}$.
    (b) In a triangle ABC, D is a point on BC where $BD:DC = 3:2$.

12) (a) The moment of a set of coplanar forces about each of three axes which are not in line, is zero.
    (b) A set of coplanar forces is in equilibrium.

TYPE IV

13) Find the magnitude and direction of the resultant of a set of coplanar forces.
    (a) The resultant anticlockwise torque about an axis through a point $2\mathbf{i}+3\mathbf{j}$ is 10 N m.
    (b) The resultant anticlockwise torque about an axis through a point $5\mathbf{i}-\mathbf{j}$ is 8 N m.
    (c) The resultant anticlockwise torque about an axis through a point $-4\mathbf{i}+\mathbf{j}$ is -4 N m.
    (d) The forces are not concurrent.

14) Find the resultant of forces represented by $\overrightarrow{AB}$, $2\overrightarrow{BC}$, $3\overrightarrow{AD}$ and $6\overrightarrow{DC}$.
    (a) ABCD is a quadrilateral.
    (b) AB = 2 m.
    (c) $B\widehat{A}C = 60°$.

15) Six forces act round the sides of a hexagon. Find the equation of the line of action of their resultant.
(a) Their magnitudes are P, $2P$, $4P$, $3P$, P, $2P$ along $\overrightarrow{AB}$, $\overrightarrow{BC}$, $\overrightarrow{CD}$, $\overrightarrow{ED}$, $\overrightarrow{FE}$, $\overrightarrow{AF}$ respectively.
(b) The hexagon is regular.
(c) The coordinates of vertex B are $(1, 1)$.

TYPE V

16) The resultant of a set of forces is a force **F**. When a couple is added to the system the new resultant also is **F**.

17) A set of forces whose linear resultant is zero must be in equilibrium.

18) The moment of a couple depends upon the axis of rotation.

19) If a set of coplanar forces is not in equilibrium they reduce either to a force or to a couple.

20) If an axis is chosen passing through a point on the resultant of a force system, the resultant torque of the system about that axis is zero.

MISCELLANEOUS EXERCISE 14

1) If ABC is any triangle and PQRS is a square of side $3a$, *write down* a complete specification of the resultant of each of the following sets of forces:
(a) Three forces which act on a particle and are represented in magnitude and direction by $\overrightarrow{AB}$, $\overrightarrow{BC}$ and $\overrightarrow{CA}$.
(b) Three forces represented completely by $\overrightarrow{AB}$, $\overrightarrow{BC}$ and $\overrightarrow{CA}$.
(c) Two forces of magnitudes F and $2F$ acting along $\overrightarrow{PQ}$ and $\overrightarrow{SR}$.
(d) Two forces of magnitudes F and $2F$ acting along $\overrightarrow{PQ}$ and $\overrightarrow{RS}$.
(e) Two forces each of magnitude F acting along $\overrightarrow{PQ}$ and $\overrightarrow{RS}$.
(f) Two forces represented completely by $\overrightarrow{AB}$ and $\overrightarrow{AC}$.
(g) Two forces represented completely by $\overrightarrow{AB}$ and $\overrightarrow{CA}$.

2) Prove that a couple, together with a force in the same plane, is equivalent to a single force. Describe completely the possible resultants of a force of 10 N acting in the same plane as a couple of magnitude 20 N m.

3)

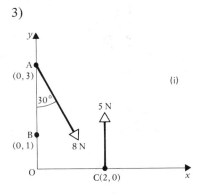
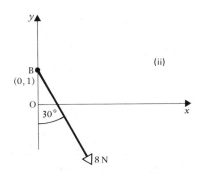

Two forces act as shown in diagram (i).
A third force is added to the system and the resultant of the three forces is shown in diagram (ii).
Find the magnitude, direction and position of the third force.

4) Replace forces F, $2F$, $3F$, $4F$ acting in order round the sides of a square ABCD of side a, by three forces acting along the sides of triangle AEB where E is the midpoint of CD.

5) Show that the resultant of forces $\overrightarrow{AB}$, $\overrightarrow{CB}$, $\overrightarrow{2CD}$ and $\overrightarrow{2AD}$ acting along the corresponding sides of a quadrilateral ABCD, is represented completely by $6\overrightarrow{QP}$ where P divides BD in the ratio $1:2$ and Q bisects AC.

6) A rod AB is loaded and supported as shown in the figure. Find the largest torque which can be applied to the rod in a vertical plane without causing the rod to overturn if the torque is:
(a) clockwise,
(b) anticlockwise.

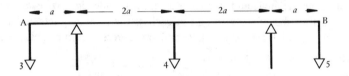

7) A system of coplanar forces has anticlockwise moments M, $2M$ and $5M$ respectively about the points $(a, 0)$, $(0, a)$ and (a, a) in the plane. Find the magnitude of the resultant of the system and the equation of its line of action.
(U of L)

8)

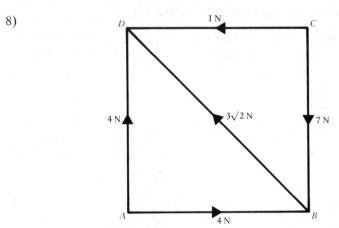

Forces of magnitude 4, 7, 1, 4 and $3\sqrt{2}$ newtons act along the sides AB, CB, CD, AD and the diagonal BD respectively of a square ABCD of side 0.1 m, as shown in the diagram. Show that the force system is equivalent to a couple and find the moment of this couple.   (U of L)

9) Three forces $7i + 5j$, $2i + 3j$ and λi act at the origin O, where i and j are unit vectors parallel to the x axis and the y axis respectively. The unit of force is the newton. If the magnitude of the resultant of the three forces is $17\,N$, calculate the two possible values of λ. Show that the two possible directions of the line of action of the resultant are equally inclined to Oy.   (AEB)

10) A non-uniform rigid beam AB, of length $3a$ and weight nW, rests on supports P and Q at the same level, where $AP = PQ = QB = a$. When a load of weight W is hung from A, the beam is on the point of tilting about P. Find the distance of the centre of gravity of the beam from A. When an additional load of weight W_1 is hung from B, the forces exerted on the supports at P and Q are equal. Find W_1 in terms of n and W.

If a couple, of moment L and acting in the vertical plane through AB, is now applied to the loaded beam, the reaction at P is increased in the ratio $3:2$.

Show that: $L = \frac{1}{3}(n+1)Wa$ (JMB)

11) All forces in this question act in the plane of a triangle ABC in which $AB = 4a$, $AC = 3a$ and the angle $A = 90°$.

Forces of magnitude $17P$, $15P$, $3P$ act along AB, BC, AC respectively in the directions indicated by the order of the letters. Calculate

(a) the magnitude of the resultant of these three forces and the tangent of the angle made by its line of action with AB,

(b) the distance from A of the point where the line of action of the resultant cuts AB.

A couple G is now added to the system and the resultant of this enlarged system acts through the point B. Calculate the magnitude and sense of G.

(U of L)

12) (a) In the regular hexagon $ABCDEF$, $\overrightarrow{AB} = \mathbf{a}$ and $\overrightarrow{BC} = \mathbf{b}$.
   Express in terms of $\mathbf{a}$ and $\mathbf{b}$, the vectors
   (i) $\overrightarrow{AC}$ (ii) $\overrightarrow{AD}$ (iii) $\overrightarrow{AE}$ (iv) $\overrightarrow{AF}$

(b) The origin O, the point A with position vector $4\mathbf{i} + 3\mathbf{j}$ and the point C with position vector $3\mathbf{i} - 4\mathbf{j}$ are three vertices of a square $OABC$. Calculate the position vector of B.
   Forces of magnitudes $5\,\text{N}$, $10\sqrt{2}\,\text{N}$ and $10\,\text{N}$ act along $\overrightarrow{OA}$, $\overrightarrow{OB}$ and $\overrightarrow{CO}$ respectively. Express each of these forces as a vector in terms of $\mathbf{i}$ and $\mathbf{j}$.
   Hence show that the resultant of these forces acts along $\overrightarrow{OA}$ and calculate the magnitude of this resultant.   (AEB)

13) Forces 2, 4, 6, $2p$, $2q$ and 18 newtons act along the sides AB, BC, CD, ED, EF and AF respectively of a regular hexagon $ABCDEF$, the directions of the forces being indicated by the order of the letters. If the system is in equilibrium, find, by resolving parallel and perpendicular to AB, the values of p and q. Check your result by finding the moment of the forces about O, the centre of the hexagon.

The forces along ED, EF and AF are now replaced by a coplanar force through O and a coplanar couple. If the resulting system is in equilibrium and if the length of each side of the hexagon is 2 metres, calculate

(a) the magnitude of this force through O,

(b) the magnitude of the couple.

14) A system of coplanar forces consists of forces of 4, 3, 2, 5 and 6 newton acting along the sides AB, BC, CD, DE and EF respectively of a regular hexagon ABCDEF of side 2 m, the forces acting in the directions indicated by the order of the letters. Find, in magnitude and direction, the force P newtons, acting at F, which will reduce the system to a couple and find the magnitude and sense of this couple. If the force P newtons is replaced by a force of 7 newtons along AF, show that the system now reduces to a single force and find the magnitude of this resultant and the point of intersection of its line of action with AB, produced if necessary.   (AEB)

15) Forces $i + 3j$, $-2i - j$, $i - 2j$ act through the points with position vectors $2i + 5j$, $4j$, $-i + j$ respectively. Prove that this system of forces is equivalent to a couple, and calculate the moment of this couple.   (U of L)

16) A system of forces acting in the plane of perpendicular axes Ox and Oy consists of:
a force $10P$ along Ox,
a force $-9P$ along Oy,
a force $13P$ along OA, where A is the point $(12a, 5a)$,
a force $20P$ along AB, where B is the point $(8a, 8a)$.
Find the magnitude, direction and equation of the line of action of the resultant of this system.
A clockwise coplanar couple of magnitude $240Pa$ is added to the system. Find the magnitude, direction and equation of the line of action of the resultant of the new system.   (AEB)

17) A rectangle ABCD has $AB = a$ and $AD = 2a$, and M is the midpoint of AD. Forces W, $2W$, $4W$, $6W$, $3W\sqrt{2}$, $W\sqrt{5}$ act along CB, DA, BA, CD, MB, DB respectively, the direction of the forces being indicated by the order of the letters. Reduce the system to a single force acting through A and a couple; state the magnitude and direction of the force, and show that the couple has moment $6aW$. Where does the resultant of the system cut AD? Find two parallel forces through B and D which are together equivalent to the system.   (C)

18) Find the magnitude and direction of the resultant of each of the following two systems of forces which act in the plane of a rectangle ABCD, in which $AB = 4a$ and $BC = 3a$.
(a) Forces $4P$ along AB, P along AD and $10P$ along DB.
(b) Forces which have total moment $-Pa$, $+15Pa$ and $-5Pa$ about A, B and D respectively ($+$ indicates the sense ABC).
Find also, in each case, the point of intersection of the line of action of the resultant with the line AB (produced if necessary).   (AEB)

19) Forces of magnitude $2P$, P, $2P$, $3P$, $2P$ and P act along the sides AB, BC, CD, ED, EF and AF respectively of a regular hexagon of side $2a$ in the directions indicated by the letters. Prove that this system of forces can be reduced to a single force of magnitude $2P\sqrt{3}$ acting along AC together with a couple. Find the magnitude of the couple.

Show that the system can be reduced to a single force without a couple. If the line of action of this force cuts FA produced at X, calculate the length of AX.

(U of L)

20) In the triangle ABC, $AB = AC = 10a$ and $BC = 12a$. The point E on AC is such that angle BEC is $90°$ and D is the midpoint of BC. Forces of magnitudes $2P$, $10P$, $5P$ and $10P$ act along $\overrightarrow{CB}$, $\overrightarrow{AD}$, $\overrightarrow{BE}$ and $\overrightarrow{AC}$ respectively. Calculate

(a) the sum of the resolved parts of these forces parallel to $\overrightarrow{BC}$,
(b) the sum of the resolved parts of these forces parallel to $\overrightarrow{AD}$,
(c) the magnitude of the resultant of these forces,
(d) the acute angle made by the line of action of the resultant with BC, giving your answer to the nearest degree.

The line of action of the resultant of these forces cuts BC at the point F. Find the distance BF in terms of a.   (AEB)

21) Unit vectors along the axes Ox and Oy are represented by $\mathbf{i}$ and $\mathbf{j}$ respectively. The position vectors of the points A and B are $8\mathbf{i} + 6\mathbf{j}$ and $5\mathbf{i} - 12\mathbf{j}$ respectively. The line AB crosses the x axis at the point C. Calculate

(a) the position vector of C,
(b) the position vector of the point D, the fourth vertex of the parallelogram $OADB$.

The force $\mathbf{F_1}$, of magnitude $40\,\text{N}$, acts at O along $\overrightarrow{OA}$ and the force $\mathbf{F_2}$, of magnitude $26\,\text{N}$, acts at O along $\overrightarrow{OB}$. By expressing $\mathbf{F_1}$ and $\mathbf{F_2}$ in terms of $\mathbf{i}$ and $\mathbf{j}$ calculate the magnitude of the resultant of these two forces and show that the line of action of the resultant passes through C.

The force $\mathbf{F_1}$ is replaced by another force $\mathbf{F_3}$, acting at O along OA. The resultant of $\mathbf{F_2}$ and $\mathbf{F_3}$ passes through D. Find $\mathbf{F_3}$ in terms of $\mathbf{i}$ and $\mathbf{j}$.   (AEB)

22) A lamina is in the shape of an equilateral triangle ABC, and D, E, F are the midpoints of BC, CA, AB respectively. Forces of magnitude $4\,\text{N}$, $8\,\text{N}$, $4\,\text{N}$, $3\,\text{N}$, $3\,\text{N}$ act along AB, BC, CA, BE, CF respectively, the direction of each force being indicated by the order of the letters. Find the magnitude of the resultant force on the lamina, and show that its line of action cuts AD produced at G, where $DG = AD$.

The lamina is kept in equilibrium by three forces acting along FE, DF, ED. Find the magnitudes of these forces.   (C)

23) The points A, B, C, D, E, F are the vertices of a regular hexagon. Forces each of 2 newtons act along AB and DC, and forces each of 1 newton act along BC and ED, in the directions indicated by the order of the letters. Forces P newtons and Q newtons act along EF and AF respectively. Find P and Q:
(a) if the system reduces to a couple,
(b) if the resultant of the system is a force acting along EB.   (U of L)

24) A system of forces in the plane of a triangle ABC has anticlockwise moments of G, $2G$ and $-2G$ about the points A, B and C respectively. State why the system reduces to a single force and not a couple. Find the point of intersection of the line of action of this force with the side BC, and calculate the moment about the centroid of the triangle ABC.   (JMB)p

25) State one set of conditions sufficient to ensure that a system of coplanar forces is in equilibrium.
Three points, A, B and C, have coordinates $(2a, 0)$, $(2a, 2a)$ and $(0, 2a)$ respectively referred to perpendicular axes Ox, Oy. A system of forces in the plane xOy has anti-clockwise moments of $40Pa$ and $60Pa$ about A and C respectively and a clockwise moment of $20Pa$ about B. Calculate the magnitude and direction of the resultant of this system and the equation of its line of action.   (AEB)

26) A triangle ABC has AB = 4 m, BC = 5 m, CA = 3 m, and D, E, F are the midpoints of BC, CA, AB respectively. Forces of magnitude 4 N, 5 N, 3 N, x N, y N act along AB, BC, CA, ED, CF respectively, the direction of the forces being indicated by the order of the letters. The resultant of the system acts along EF. Calculate x and y, and show that the magnitude of the resultant is 20 N.
The system is equivalent to a force P acting along AC, a force Q acting along CF and a couple of moment M. Find P, Q and M.   (C)

27) Forces $\lambda \overrightarrow{OA}$ and $\mu \overrightarrow{OB}$ act along the lines AO and OB respectively. Show that the resultant is a force $(\lambda + \mu)\overrightarrow{OC}$ where C lies on AB and $AC:CB = \mu:\lambda$. Forces $3\overrightarrow{AB}$, $2\overrightarrow{AC}$ and $\overrightarrow{CB}$ act along the sides AB, AC and CB respectively of a triangle ABC. Their resultant meets BC in P and AC in Q and its magnitude is kPQ. Find BP:PC, AQ:QC and k.   (U of L)

28) Prove that, if forces represented by $\lambda\overrightarrow{OP}$ and $\mu\overrightarrow{OQ}$ act along sides OP and OQ of triangle OPQ then the resultant force is $(\lambda+\mu)\overrightarrow{OX}$ where X is the point of PQ such that $\lambda PX = \mu XQ$.
Consider the case when $\lambda+\mu = 0$.

(a) Forces $6\overrightarrow{AB}$, $10\overrightarrow{AC}$, $3\overrightarrow{CB}$ act along the sides AB, AC and CB respectively of triangle ABC. The line of action of the resultant cuts AC at Y and BC at X. Find the ratios BX:XC and AY:YC and show that the magnitude of the resultant is 24YX.

(b) D, E and F are the midpoints of the sides QR, RP and PQ respectively of triangle PQR whose circumcentre is O. Forces of magnitude kQR, kRP and kPQ act at O in directions $\overrightarrow{OD}$, $\overrightarrow{OE}$ and $\overrightarrow{OF}$ respectively.
Prove that the forces are in equilibrium.

29) The diagonals of the plane quadrilateral ABCD intersect at O. X and Y are the midpoints of the diagonals AC and BD respectively (see figure).
Show that:
(a) $\overrightarrow{BA}+\overrightarrow{BC} = 2\overrightarrow{BX}$,
(b) $\overrightarrow{BA}+\overrightarrow{BC}+\overrightarrow{DA}+\overrightarrow{DC} = 4\overrightarrow{YX}$,
(c) $2\overrightarrow{AB}+2\overrightarrow{BC}+2\overrightarrow{CA}$ reduces to a couple, and state its magnitude in terms of the triangle ABC.
If $\overrightarrow{OA}+\overrightarrow{OB}+\overrightarrow{OC}+\overrightarrow{OD} = 4\overrightarrow{OM}$, find the location of the point M.

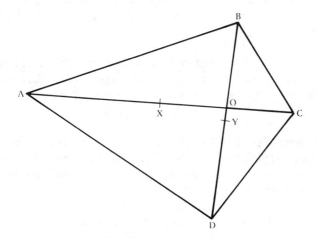

(AEB)

CHAPTER 15

CENTRE OF GRAVITY

WEIGHT AND CENTRE OF GRAVITY

A solid body is made up of a number of particles rigidly held together by forces of attraction, where each particle has a mass and therefore a weight which acts vertically downward. The weight of a solid body is the resultant of the weights of its constituent particles so, unless the body is of very great size, its weight is the resultant of a set of parallel forces. It was seen in Chapter 14 p. 464 that such a resultant passes through a fixed point whatever the orientation of the forces, so the weight of a body passes through a fixed point whatever the orientation of that body. This fixed point is called the centre of gravity of the body or (with certain limitations which are discussed later) the centre of mass of the body.

Thus the weight of a body is equal to the sum of the weights of its constituent particles and acts vertically downward through a fixed point in the body called the centre of gravity. The centre of gravity is independent of the orientation of the body.

To find the centre of gravity of a body we can use the fact that the *sum of the moments of the weights of the constituent particles about any axis is equal to the moment of the resultant weight about the same axis.* This will give the distance of the centre of gravity from that axis.
To locate the centre of gravity completely it may be necessary to take moments about two non-parallel lines or, for three dimensional problems about three non-parallel lines, but such problems do not concern us at this stage.

THE CENTRE OF GRAVITY OF A SET OF PARTICLES IN A PLANE

Consider three particles of weights $5g$ N, $2g$ N, $3g$ N which are at points $(3, -1)$, $(2, 3)$, $(-2, 5)$ referred to coordinate axes Ox and Oy.

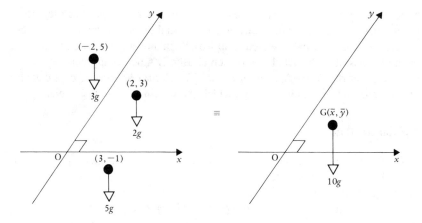

The centre of gravity of these particles is in the xy plane.

Let this point be $G(\bar{x}, \bar{y})$.

Suppose that the xy plane is horizontal so that the weights of the particles act vertically downward perpendicular to the xy plane and the total weight, $10g$, acts in the same direction through G.

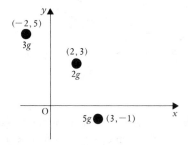

Using the principle of moments gives

$$(2g)2 + (5g)3 - (3g)2 = (10g)\bar{x}$$

$$\Rightarrow \qquad \bar{x} = \tfrac{13}{10}$$

$$(2g)3 + (3g)5 - (5g)1 = (10g)\bar{y}$$

$$\Rightarrow \qquad \bar{y} = \tfrac{8}{5}$$

So the centre of gravity is at the point $(\tfrac{13}{10}, \tfrac{8}{5})$

Note. When both coordinates of the centre of gravity are to be calculated, it is usually best to use a diagram drawn in a horizontal plane containing the x and y axes (as was done in the example above). Such a diagram allows the distances from the axes of each particle to be seen clearly. It must be appreciated, however, that the *lines of action of the weights cannot be marked* on a diagram of this type; only the point through which the weight passes can be seen.

The General Case

Consider particles of mass m_1, m_2, m_3 ... at the points (x_1, y_1), (x_2, y_2), (x_3, y_3) ... in the xy plane.
The weights of these particles are $m_1 g$, $m_2 g$, $m_3 g$ ...
The total weight is Σmg acting at a point $G(\bar{x}, \bar{y})$ in the xy plane.

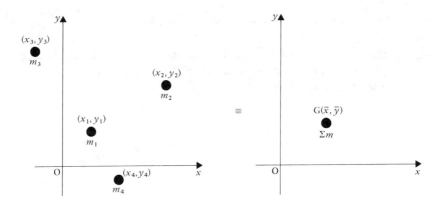

Taking the xy plane to be horizontal so that the weights of the particles are perpendicular to the xy plane, then using the principle of moments gives

$$(m_1 g)x_1 + (m_2 g)x_2 + (m_3 g)x_3 + \ldots = (m_1 + m_2 + m_3 + \ldots)g\bar{x}$$

$$\Rightarrow \qquad g\Sigma mx = \bar{x}g\Sigma m$$

Then, if we cancel g, $\qquad\qquad \bar{x} = \dfrac{\Sigma mx}{\Sigma m}$ (see Note on p. 501)

Similarly $\quad$ gives $\qquad \bar{y} = \dfrac{\Sigma my}{\Sigma m}$

This result may also be expressed in vector terms.
Let the particles be at the points whose position vectors are $\mathbf{r}_1$, $\mathbf{r}_2$, $\mathbf{r}_3$, ...

Then $\quad \mathbf{r}_1 = x_1\mathbf{i} + y_1\mathbf{j}$, $\quad \mathbf{r}_2 = x_2\mathbf{i} + y_2\mathbf{j}$, $\quad \mathbf{r}_3 = x_3\mathbf{i} + y_3\mathbf{j}$, ...

As before $\quad \bar{x} = \dfrac{\Sigma mx}{\Sigma m} \quad$ and $\quad \bar{y} = \dfrac{\Sigma my}{\Sigma m}$

The position vector of G is $\bar{\mathbf{r}}$ where $\quad \bar{\mathbf{r}} = \bar{x}\mathbf{i} + \bar{y}\mathbf{j}$

So $\qquad \bar{\mathbf{r}} = \dfrac{\Sigma mx\,\mathbf{i} + \Sigma my\,\mathbf{j}}{\Sigma m}$

$\qquad = \dfrac{(m_1x_1\mathbf{i} + m_2x_2\mathbf{i} + \ldots) + (m_1y_1\mathbf{j} + m_2y_2\mathbf{j} + \ldots)}{\Sigma m}$

$\qquad = \dfrac{m_1(x_1\mathbf{i} + y_1\mathbf{j}) + m_2(x_2\mathbf{i} + y_2\mathbf{j}) + \ldots}{\Sigma m}$

$\qquad = \dfrac{m_1\mathbf{r}_1 + m_2\mathbf{r}_2 + m_3\mathbf{r}_3 + \ldots}{\Sigma m}$

i.e. $\qquad\qquad\qquad \bar{\mathbf{r}} = \dfrac{\Sigma m\,\mathbf{r}}{\Sigma m}$

Reconsidering the first example in vector terms, we have particles of masses 2 kg, 5 kg and 3 kg at points whose position vectors are $2\mathbf{i} + 3\mathbf{j}$, $3\mathbf{i} - \mathbf{j}$ and $-2\mathbf{i} + 5\mathbf{j}$.

Using the result above, the position vector of G is

$$\frac{2(2\mathbf{i} + 3\mathbf{j}) + 5(3\mathbf{i} - \mathbf{j}) + 3(-2\mathbf{i} + 5\mathbf{j})}{10}$$

$$= \tfrac{1}{10}(13\mathbf{i} + 16\mathbf{j}).$$

Note. The formulae $\quad \bar{x} = \dfrac{\Sigma mx}{\Sigma m} \quad$ and $\quad \bar{y} = \dfrac{\Sigma my}{\Sigma m} \quad$ really give the coordinates of
the *centre of mass* of the set of particles.
We have used them to find the *centre of gravity* and it is correct to do this for all practical purposes.
These two points are *not* the same, however, if the set of particles occupies so large an area that the weights are not all parallel, or the value of g is not the same for all particles.

UNIFORM BODIES

A uniform body is made from uniform material, i.e. any given quantity of the material (measured by length, area or volume as appropriate) will have the same mass as any equal quantity of the same material.
It follows that a uniform body will have mass equally distributed about any line of symmetry; so

the centre of gravity of a uniform body lies on each line of symmetry that the body possesses.

For example, the centre of gravity of a uniform rod, circular lamina, sphere etc, lies at the centre of the body. The centre of gravity of a cylinder (hollow or solid) lies at the midpoint of its axis.
We can extend this argument to find the centre of gravity of some other simple bodies.

Centre of Gravity of a Uniform Triangular Lamina

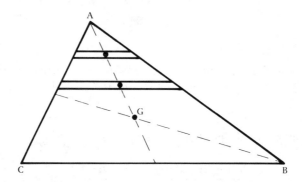

Consider the triangle as being made from a series of strips with sides parallel to the side BC. As each strip is uniform and is approximately a rectangle, its centre of gravity is at its midpoint.
So the centre of gravity of the triangle, G, must lie on the line joining the midpoints of these strips: i.e. on the median through A.
Similarly by considering the triangle as being made from a series of strips parallel to AC, G also lies on the median through B. Therefore

the position of the centre of gravity of a uniform triangle is at the point of intersection of the medians. This point is the centroid of the triangle and it is $\frac{2}{3}$ of the way along each median from the vertex.

Note. Centroid should not be regarded as another term for centre of gravity. The centroid of any body is its geometric centre and depends only on the shape of the body. When the body is uniform the centre of gravity is at the centroid but for non-uniform bodies the centre of gravity and centroid are unlikely to coincide.

Centre of Gravity of Some Special Uniform Triangular Laminas

(1) For a uniform isosceles triangular lamina ABC, in which AB = AC, the centre of gravity is on the line of symmetry AD and is $\frac{2}{3}$AD from A.

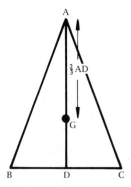

(2) For a uniform right-angled triangle lamina ABC, in which angle ABC is 90°, the centre of gravity is at distances $\frac{1}{3}$BA and $\frac{1}{3}$BC from the right angle, along BA and BC.

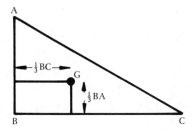

3) The centre of gravity of a uniform triangular lamina ABC coincides with the centre of gravity of three particles of equal mass placed at the vertices of the triangle. This property can be proved as follows.

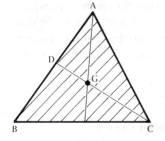

The centre of gravity G of the lamina
ABC is at the point of intersection of
the medians of △ABC

Let the mass of the particle at each vertex be m.
The resultant, $2mg$, of the weights at A and B passes through D, the midpoint of AB, i.e.

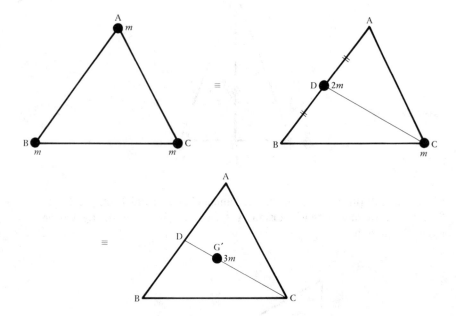

The resultant, $3mg$, of the weights $2mg$ at D and mg at C passes through
G′ where G′ is on DC such that   DG′:G′C = 1:2.
But CD is a median of the triangle, so G′ is the centroid of the triangle and so
coincides with G.
Hence the centre of gravity of the three equal mass particles at A, B and C
coincides with the centre of gravity of the uniform triangular lamina ABC.
(Incidentally, as it can also be shown that G divides the median through A and
the median through B in the ratio 2:1, this proves that the medians of a
triangle intersect at a point of trisection.)

EXERCISE 15a

1) Three particles A, B, C of mass 2, 3, 4 kg are at the points $(1, 4)$, $(3, 6)$, $(2, 1)$ in the xy plane. Find the coordinates of their centre of gravity.

2) Four particles A, B, C, D of mass 3, 5, 2, 4 kg are at the points $(1, 6)$, $(-1, 5)$, $(2, -3)$, $(-1, -4)$. Find the coordinates of their centre of gravity.

3) Three particles of mass 5, 3, 7 kg are at the points A, B, C, whose position vectors are $i - 2j$, $7i + j$, $-3i + 5j$. Find the position vector of their centre of mass. Find also the position vector of the centroid of the points A, B, C.

4) Four particles of mass 3, 2, 5 and 1 kg are at the points A, B, C, D whose position vectors are $2i - j$, $3i + 5j$, $-2i - j$, $i - 3j$. Find:
(a) the position vector of the centre of mass of the particles,
(b) the position vector of the centroid of the points A, B, C, D.

5) A uniform lamina is in the form of a trapezium ABCD where AB and DC are the parallel sides. Show that the centre of gravity of the trapezium lies on the line joining the midpoints of AB and DC.

6) The vertices of a triangle are at the points $i + j$, $3i - j$, $2i + j$. Find the position vector of the centre of gravity of the triangle, assuming it to be a uniform lamina.

7) Show that the centre of gravity of a uniform lamina in the form of a parallelogram is at the point of intersection of the diagonals.

8) By dividing a parallelogram into two triangles show that the centre of gravity of a lamina in the form of a parallelogram is the same point as the centre of gravity of four particles, two of mass m at one pair of opposite vertices and two of mass $2m$ at the other pair of opposite vertices.

COMPOSITE BODIES

Consider a body made up from two or more parts, each of which has a known weight and centre of gravity. As the weight of the complete body is the resultant of the weights of its parts, the principle of moments can again be used to find the centre of gravity of the body.

EXAMPLES 15b

1) A uniform lamina ABCDE is made from a square ABDE and an equilateral triangle BCD. Find the centre of gravity of the lamina.

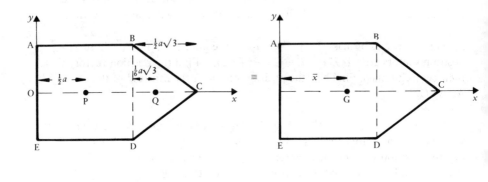

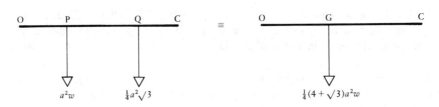

Because the body is made of uniform material, its centre of gravity is on the line of symmetry OC and the weight of any part of the body is proportional to the area of that part.

Taking a as the length of AB and w as the weight per unit area we see that

$\begin{cases}$ the weight of the square is $a^2 w$ and it acts at P, the centre of the square.

the weight of the triangle is $\frac{1}{4}a^2\sqrt{3}w$ acting at Q distant $\frac{1}{6}a\sqrt{3}$ from BD. $\end{cases}$

The position of G can now be found by taking moments about any line perpendicular to OC; in this solution we choose AE. The information required can be shown concisely by referring to axes Ox and Oy as shown, and tabulating the data.

Portion	Weight	x coordinate of centre of gravity
Square ABDE	$a^2 w$	$\frac{1}{2}a$
Triangle BCD	$\frac{1}{4}a^2\sqrt{3}w$	$a + \frac{1}{6}a\sqrt{3}$
Complete lamina	$\frac{1}{4}(4+\sqrt{3})a^2 w$	$\bar{x}$

$$(a^2w)(\tfrac{1}{2}a) + (\tfrac{1}{4}a^2w\sqrt{3})(a+\tfrac{1}{6}a\sqrt{3}) = \tfrac{1}{4}(4+\sqrt{3})a^2w\bar{x}$$

$$\Rightarrow \qquad \tfrac{1}{8}(5+2\sqrt{3})a = \tfrac{1}{4}(4+\sqrt{3})\bar{x}$$

$$\bar{x} = \tfrac{1}{26}(14+3\sqrt{3})$$

2) A thin uniform wire is bent to form the two equal sides AB and AC of triangle ABC, where AB = AC = 5 cm. The third side BC, of length 6 cm, is made from uniform wire of twice the density of the first. Find the centre of gravity of the framework.

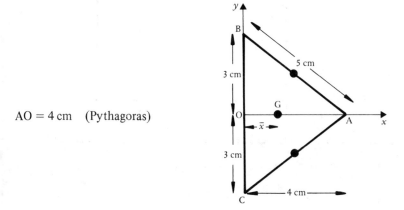

AO = 4 cm   (Pythagoras)

Let w be the weight per unit length of AB and AC so that the weight per unit length of BC is $2w$.

From symmetry the centre of gravity, G, of the body lies on OA, so we will take moments about BC.

Body	Weight	x coordinate of centre of gravity
Wire AB	$5w$	2
Wire AC	$5w$	2
Wire BC	$12w$	0
Framework ABC	$22w$	$\bar{x}$

$$(5w)2 + (5w)2 + (12w)0 = (22w)\bar{x}$$

$$\Rightarrow \qquad \bar{x} = \tfrac{5}{11}$$

The centre of gravity is $\tfrac{5}{11}$ cm from BC on the line of symmetry OA.

3) A uniform lamina is in the form of a rectangle ABCD where $AB = 2a$ and $BC = 4a$. E and F are points on BC and AD such that $BE = AF = a$, and H and J are the midpoints of EF and CD. A cut is made through the lamina along the line EH, and the rectangular section HECJ is folded along HJ so as to lie on top of FHJD. Find the centre of gravity of the resulting body.

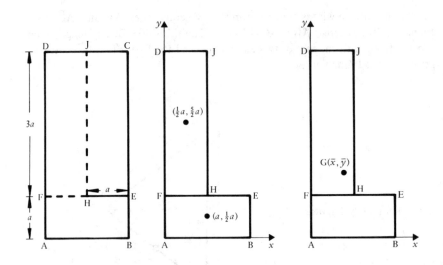

Let w be the weight per unit area of the rectangle ABEF.

Then $2w$ is the weight per unit area of the rectangle FHJD as it is of double thickness.

There are no lines of symmetry so we will have to take moments about two axes to find the position of G, the centre of gravity of the resulting lamina.

(Even if the lamina were symmetrical in shape it would be dangerous to use the properties of symmetry to locate G, because the different densities of the parts prevent the lamina from being *mechanically* symmetrical.)

Portion	Weight	Coordinates of centre of gravity	
		x	y
Rectangle ABEF	$2a^2w$	a	$\frac{1}{2}a$
Rectangle FHJD	$3a^2(2w)$	$\frac{1}{2}a$	$\frac{5}{2}a$
Complete body	$8a^2w$	$\bar{x}$	$\bar{y}$

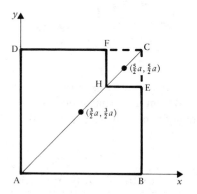

$$(2a^2 w)\tfrac{1}{2}a + (6a^2 w)\tfrac{5}{2}a = 8a^2 w\bar{y}$$

$$\Rightarrow \qquad \bar{y} = 2a$$

$$(2a^2 w)a + (6a^2 w)\tfrac{1}{2}a = 8a^2 w\bar{x}$$

$$\Rightarrow \qquad \bar{x} = \tfrac{5}{8}a$$

So the centre of gravity is $2a$ from AB and $\tfrac{5}{8}a$ from AD.

4) A uniform lamina is in the form of a square ABCD of side $3a$. E is a point on BC and F is a point on DC such that $CE = CF = a$. A square FCEH is removed from the lamina. Find the centre of gravity of the remainder.

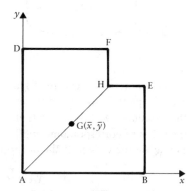

The figure is symmetrical about AHC so $\bar{x} = \bar{y}$ and it is sufficient to find only one coordinate of G.

The moment of the square ECFH *subtracted* from the moment of the square ABCD is equivalent to the moment of ABEHFD. Using w for the weight per unit area and taking moments about AD (the y axis) we have:

Portion	Weight	x coordinate of centre of gravity
Square ABCD	$9a^2 w$	$\tfrac{3}{2}a$
Square FHEC	$a^2 w$	$\tfrac{5}{2}a$
Remainder	$8a^2 w$	$\bar{x}$

$$(9a^2 w)(\tfrac{3}{2}a) - (a^2 w)(\tfrac{5}{2}a) = 8a^2 w\bar{x}$$

$$\Rightarrow \qquad \bar{x} = \tfrac{11}{8}a$$

The centre of gravity of the remainder is on AH distant $\tfrac{11}{8}a$ from AD.

5) A uniform solid is in the form of a cylinder of radius $2a$ and height $2h$ with a cylindrical hole of radius a and height h drilled centrally at one plane end. Find the centre of gravity of the solid.

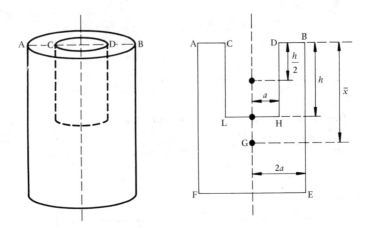

From symmetry the centre of gravity of the solid lies on the axis of the cylinder. The complete cylinder and the cylinder removed from it are similar bodies so their volumes (and therefore their weights) are in the ratio $8:1$, (the ratio of the cubes of corresponding lengths).
Let w be the weight of the portion removed.

Body	Weight	Distance of centre of gravity from AB
Solid cylinder ABEF	$8w$	h
Solid cylinder CDHL	w	$\frac{1}{2}h$
Remainder	$7w$	$\bar{x}$

A⟜B
$$(8w)(h) - w(\tfrac{1}{2}h) = (7w)\bar{x}$$
$$\Rightarrow \qquad \bar{x} = \tfrac{15}{14}h$$

Therefore the centre of gravity of the solid lies on the axis at a distance of $\frac{15}{14}h$ from the end with the hole in it.
Note. This method for determining the relationships between the weights of similar bodies is quicker than using 'weight per unit volume' and should be used whenever possible.

6) A uniform lamina is in the form of a triangle ABC where $AB = 3a$. D and E are points on AC and BC such that DE is parallel to AB and $DE = a$. The portion CDE is removed. Find the centre of gravity of the remainder.

The centre of gravity of the trapezium ABED can be found by the methods used in Examples 4 and 5 but an interesting alternative will be used this time.

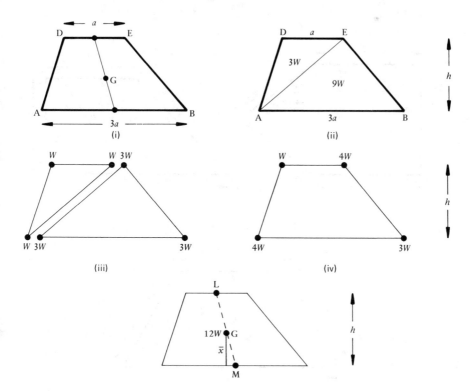

The line AE divides the trapezium into two triangles, ABE and ADE, with the same perpendicular height. Their areas and therefore their weights are proportional to their bases, i.e. in the ratio $3:1$.

Now each of these triangles can be replaced by three particles of equal weight placed at the vertices. As the weight of each triangle is thus going to be divided by three, their weights will be taken as $9W$ and $3W$ (ratio $3:1$).

The centre of gravity of triangle ABE is the same as the centre of gravity of three particles each of weight $3W$ at A, B and E.
For triangle AED we use three particles each of weight W at A, E and D

Now, taking h as the height of the trapezium, we have, from diagram (iv),

$$Wh + 4Wh + 4W(0) + 3W(0) = 12W\bar{x}$$

$$\Rightarrow \qquad \bar{x} = \tfrac{5}{12}h$$

But G lies on the line LM where L and M are the midpoints of DE and AB.

So G is on LM and is distant $\tfrac{5}{12}$LM from AB.

EXERCISE 15b

In Questions 1-3 find the position of the centre of gravity of each uniform lamina.

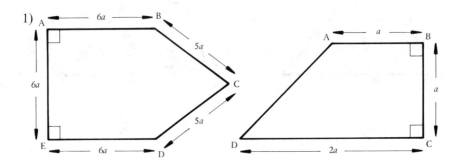

1)

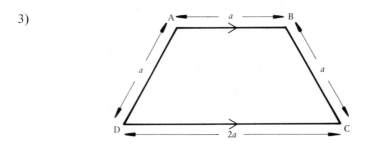

3)

4) A uniform solid body consists of a cylinder of radius $2a$ and height $2h$ with another cylinder of radius a and height h with one plane face placed centrally on one plane face of the first cylinder. Find the position of the centre of gravity of the solid.

5) A uniform wire is bent to form an equilateral triangle. Locate its centre of gravity.

6) A uniform wire is bent to form two adjacent sides of a square and another uniform wire of three times the density of the first is bent to form the other two adjacent sides of the square. Find the position of the centre of gravity of the complete square framework.

7) A uniform lamina is in the form of a square of side 2 m and has a weight of W per square metre. Two particles each of weight W are attached to two adjacent vertices. Find the position of the centre of gravity of the resulting body.

8) A uniform lamina is in the form of an isosceles right-angled triangle. The equal sides of the triangle are of length 4 m and the lamina has a weight W per unit area. A particle of weight $3W$ is attached to the right-angled vertex. Find the centre of gravity of the resulting body.

9) A uniform lamina consists of a square of side a with a circle of diameter a (made from the same material) glued on to the square so that a diameter of the circle coincides with one edge of the square. Locate the centre of gravity of the lamina.

10) A uniform lamina ABCD is in the form of a square and a uniform wire is placed round the circumference of the square. Locate the centre of gravity of the complete body.

The rectangular laminas illustrated in Questions 11 and 12 are uniform and part of the lamina has been folded back upon itself to form a section of double thickness. Locate the centre of gravity in each case.

11)

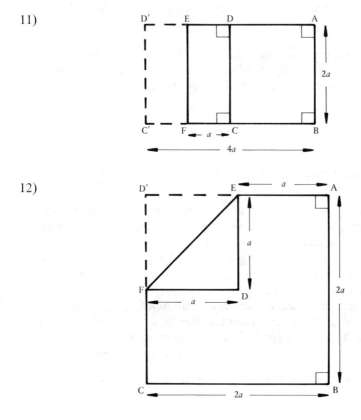

12)

Find the position of the centre of gravity of each of the uniform laminas in Questions 13 and 14.

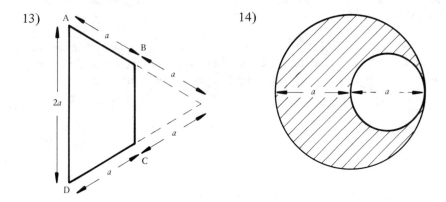

13)   14)

15) A uniform lamina is in the form of a rectangle of sides 2 m and 3 m. A circle of diameter 1 m with its centre equidistant from the sides of length 3 m, and $\frac{1}{2}$ m from one of the sides of length 2 m is cut from the lamina. Find the position of the centre of gravity of the remainder.

16) A uniform solid is in the form of a cylinder of radius a and height $2a$. A hole, whose cross section is a square of side a, is cut centrally from one end to a depth of a. Find the centre of gravity of the remainder.

CENTRE OF GRAVITY BY INTEGRATION

When a body cannot be divided into a small finite number of parts whose weights and centres of gravity are known, it may be divided into a large number of very small parts, called elements, whose weights and centres of gravity are known. The position of the centre of gravity of the body can then be found by taking moments about suitable axes although the summing of the moments of the parts may require integration.

Most bodies of this type belong to one of three categories,

(a) laminas, for which the usual element is a strip;

(b) solids of revolution, for which the usual element is a disc;

(c) surfaces of revolution for which the usual element is a cylindrical ring.

We will first consider each of these types in general and then examine a few special cases.

Laminas

Consider a uniform lamina bounded by the x axis, the ordinates $x = a$ and $x = b$ and a curve with equation $y = f(x)$.

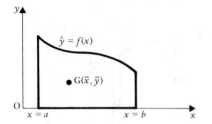 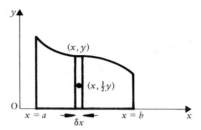

The chosen element is a vertical strip of height y and width δx.
As the strip is approximately rectangular, the coordinates of its centre of gravity are $(x, \frac{1}{2}y)$. If the weight per unit area is w and the area of the lamina is represented by A, the following table of data can be constructed.

Portion	Weight	Coordinates of centre of gravity	
		x	y
Element	$(y\,\delta x)w$	x	$\frac{1}{2}y$
Complete lamina	Aw	$\bar{x}$	$\bar{y}$

$$\sum_{x=a}^{x=b} (y\,\delta x)wx \simeq Aw\bar{x}$$

$$\Rightarrow \qquad \int_a^b xy\,dx = A\bar{x}$$

$$\sum_{x=a}^{x=b} (y\,\delta x)w(\tfrac{1}{2}y) \simeq Aw\bar{y}$$

$$\Rightarrow \qquad \int_a^b \tfrac{1}{2}y^2\,dx = A\bar{y}$$

If, for any particular lamina $f(x)$ is known, the necessary integration can be performed.
The value of A may, in some cases, be found from a standard formula.

Otherwise it can be evaluated using $\qquad A = \int_a^b y\,dx.$

Slight variations in the boundaries of the lamina do not affect the general method.

EXAMPLES 15c

1) Find the coordinates of the centre of gravity of a uniform lamina bounded by the axes and that part of the parabola $y^2 = 1-x$ which is in the first quadrant.

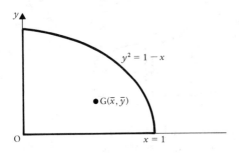
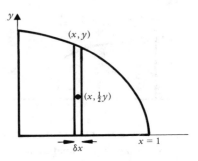

The curve cuts the x axis where $x = 1$ so, if the weight per unit area is w, we have

Portion	Weight	Coordinates of centre of gravity	
		x	y
Element	$(y\,\delta x)w$	x	$\tfrac{1}{2}y$
Complete lamina	Aw	$\bar{x}$	$\bar{y}$

$$\sum_{x=0}^{x=1} (y\,\delta x)wx \simeq Aw\bar{x}$$

$$\Rightarrow \qquad \int_0^1 xy\,dx = A\bar{x} \qquad\qquad [1]$$

$$\sum_{x=0}^{x=1} (y\,\delta x)w(\tfrac{1}{2}y) \simeq Aw\bar{y}$$

$$\Rightarrow \qquad \tfrac{1}{2}\int_0^1 y^2\,dx = A\bar{y} \qquad\qquad [2]$$

Now
$$A = \int_0^1 y\,dx = \int_0^1 (1-x)^{1/2}\,dx$$

$$= \left[-\tfrac{2}{3}(1-x)^{3/2}\right]_0^1$$

$$= \tfrac{2}{3}$$

So [1] gives
$$\tfrac{2}{3}\bar{x} = \int_0^1 x(1-x)^{1/2}\,dx$$

$$= \int_1^0 (1-u)u^{1/2}(-du) \qquad \text{where} \quad u = 1-x$$

$$= \left[-\tfrac{2}{3}u^{3/2} + \tfrac{2}{5}u^{5/2} \right]_1^0$$

$$= \tfrac{4}{15}$$

$\Rightarrow \qquad\qquad\qquad \bar{x} = \tfrac{2}{5}$

Then [2] gives
$$\tfrac{2}{3}\bar{y} = \tfrac{1}{2}\int_0^1 (1-x)\,dx$$

$$= \tfrac{1}{2}\left[x - \tfrac{1}{2}x^2 \right]_0^1$$

$$= \tfrac{1}{4}$$

$\Rightarrow \qquad\qquad\qquad \bar{y} = \tfrac{3}{8}$

So the coordinates of the centre of gravity of the lamina are $(\tfrac{2}{5}, \tfrac{3}{8})$.

2) Find the position of the centre of gravity of a uniform semicircular lamina of radius a.

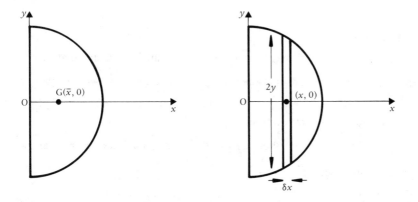

The element is an approximately rectangular strip of length $2y$ and width δx. Because the lamina is symmetrical about Ox, G is on Ox, so we need only to take moments about Oy.

Using w as the weight per unit area we have:

Portion	Weight	x coordinates of centre of gravity
Element	$(2y\, \delta x)w$	x
Semicircle	$Aw = \frac{1}{2}\pi a^2 w$	$\bar{x}$

$$\sum_{x=0}^{x=a} (2y\, \delta x)wx = \frac{1}{2}\pi a^2 w\bar{x}$$

$$\Rightarrow \qquad 2\int_0^a xy\, dx = \frac{1}{2}\pi a^2 \bar{x}$$

The semicircle is part of a circle, radius a, centre O, so its equation is $x^2 + y^2 = a^2$.

Hence $\qquad 2\int_0^a x\sqrt{a^2 - x^2}\, dx = \frac{1}{2}\pi a^2 \bar{x}$

$$\Rightarrow \qquad \bar{x} = \frac{4}{\pi a^2}\left[-\frac{1}{3}(a^2 - x^2)^{3/2}\right]_0^a = \frac{4a}{3\pi}$$

So the centre of gravity of a uniform semicircular lamina is on the radius of symmetry and distant $4a/3\pi$ from the centre.

EXERCISE 15c

1) Find the position of the centre of gravity of a uniform lamina that is:

a) in the form of the area between the x axis and the curve whose equation is $y = 1 - x^2$,

b) a quadrant of a circle of radius a,

c) in the shape of the area bounded by the x axis, the lines $x = 1$ and $x = 2$, and the curve $y = \dfrac{1}{x}$,

'd) in the form of the area between the y axis and the parabola $y^2 = x + 4$, (*Hint*. Use a horizontal strip as element.)

e) the section of a circle of radius a, cut off between two straight parallel lines at distances of $\frac{1}{2}a$ and a from the centre of the circle.

Centre of Gravity of a Solid of Revolution

A solid of revolution is formed when a given area rotates about a fixed axis, so the solid is always symmetrical about the axis of rotation.
The centre of gravity of a solid of revolution is therefore on the axis of rotation. Further, every section of the solid that is perpendicular to this axis, is circular. So if the solid is cut into slices with cuts perpendicular to the axis, each slice is approximately a circular disc.

Consider the solid formed when the area bounded by the x and y axes, the ordinate $x = a$ and part of the curve $y = f(x)$, is rotated through $360°$ about Ox.

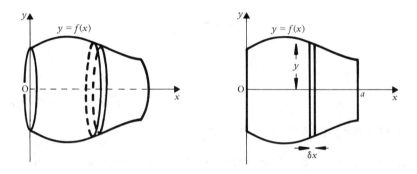

Let w be the weight per unit volume of the solid and let V be the total volume. Taking a disc-like slice, of radius y and thickness δx, as an element of volume we have:

Body	Weight	x coordinate of centre of gravity
Element	$\pi y^2 \delta x w$	x
Complete solid	Vw	$\bar{x}$

$$\sum_{x=0}^{x=a} (\pi y^2 \delta x w)x \simeq Vw\bar{x}$$

$$\Rightarrow \qquad \pi \int_0^a xy^2 \, dx = V\bar{x}$$

Now the integration on the left can be evaluated if $f(x)$ is given and V can be

calculated by using either a standard formula or $V = \int \pi y^2 \, dx$

EXAMPLES 15d

1) Find the position of the centre of gravity of a uniform solid right circular cone of base radius a and height h.

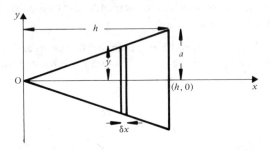

Referring the cone to x and y axes as shown, we see that the generator of the cone is the line with equation

$$y = \frac{a}{h}x$$

Taking w as the weight per unit volume of the cone and using a 'disc' element of radius y and thickness δx, we have:

Body	Weight	x coordinate of centre of gravity
Element	$\pi y^2 \delta x w$	x
Cone	$\frac{1}{3}\pi a^2 h w$	$\bar{x}$

$$\sum_{x=0}^{x=h} (\pi y^2 \delta x w)x \simeq \frac{1}{3}\pi a^2 h w \bar{x}$$

$$\Rightarrow \qquad \int_0^h xy^2 \, dx = \frac{1}{3}a^2 h \bar{x}$$

$$\Rightarrow \qquad \int_0^h x\left(\frac{ax}{h}\right)^2 dx = \frac{1}{3}a^2 h \bar{x}$$

$$\Rightarrow \qquad \bar{x} = \frac{3}{h^3}\left[\frac{x^4}{4}\right]_0^h = \frac{3h}{4}$$

So the centre of gravity of a uniform solid right circular cone is on the axis of symmetry, three-quarters of the way from the vertex to the base.

2) Find the position of the centre of gravity of the uniform solid obtained by rotating, about the x axis, the area bounded by the x axis, the line $x = 2a$ and the parabola $y^2 = 4ax$.

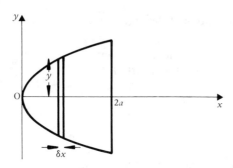

Taking w as the weight per unit volume and an element that is approximately a circular disc of volume $\pi y^2 \delta x$, we have:

Body	Weight	x coordinate of centre of gravity
Element	$\pi y^2 \delta x w$	x
Paraboloid	Vw	$\bar{x}$

$$\sum_{x=0}^{x=2a} (\pi y^2 \delta x w)x \simeq Vw\bar{x}$$

$$\Rightarrow \qquad \pi \int_0^{2a} xy^2 \, dx = V\bar{x}$$

This time there is no formula for V so we use $\qquad V = \int_0^{2a} \pi y^2 \, dx$

$$\Rightarrow \qquad \int_0^{2a} xy^2 \, dx = \bar{x} \int_0^{2a} y^2 \, dx$$

But $y^2 = 4ax$, so $\qquad \int_0^{2a} 4ax^2 \, dx = \bar{x} \int_0^{2a} 4ax \, dx$

$$\Rightarrow \qquad \tfrac{4}{3}a\left[x^3\right]_0^{2a} = 2a\bar{x}\left[x^2\right]_0^{2a} = \tfrac{4}{3}a$$

Hence the centre of gravity of the paraboloid is on the axis of symmetry and distant $\tfrac{2}{3}a$ from the plane face.

Note that when choosing the position of the x and y axes within a solid of revolution, the simplest equation of the generating curve should be considered.

In determining the position of the centre of gravity of a hemisphere, for instance, the centre of the plane face should be taken as the origin so that the generator is part of the circle with equation $x^2 + y^2 = r^2$

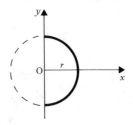

EXERCISE 15d

Find the position of the centre of gravity of the following uniform solid bodies.

1) A hemisphere of radius a.

2) A frustum of a cone formed by cutting a cone of base radius r, from the top of a cone of base radius $3r$ and height h. (*Hint.* Take the vertex of the large cone as origin.)

3) A solid sphere of radius a is cut into two sections by a plane. The maximum depth of the smaller section is h. Find the distance of the centre of gravity of the smaller cap from its plane face.

4) A section is cut from a uniform solid hemisphere of radius $3a$ by two cuts parallel to its plane face. If the radii of the plane faces of the section are $2a$ and a find the distance of its centre of gravity from the centre.

5) The solid formed by rotating, about the x axis, the area bounded by the x and y axes, the line $x = 1$ and the curve $y = e^x$.

Surfaces of Revolution

When a portion of a curve rotates about a fixed line, it traces out the surface of a three dimensional object, called a surface of revolution.
The location of the centre of gravity of a surface of revolution is, in general, beyond the scope of this book but there are two important cases that can be dealt with at this stage. These are:
(a) the surface of a cone without base, or hollow cone, formed when a straight line rotates about an axis to which it is inclined at an acute angle,
(b) the curved surface of a hemisphere, or hollow hemisphere, or hemispherical shell, formed when a circular quadrant rotates completely about a boundary radius.

EXAMPLES 15e

1) Find the distance from the vertex of the centre of gravity of a uniform hollow right circular cone.

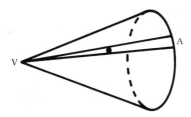

The conical surface can be divided completely into thin strips, from vertex to base. Each strip is approximately a triangular lamina. The centre of gravity of each such lamina is two thirds of the way from vertex to base. So the centre of gravity of the hollow cone must also be two thirds of the way from vertex to base and, from symmetry, on the axis of the cone.

2) Find the position of the centre of gravity of a uniform hemispherical shell of radius a.

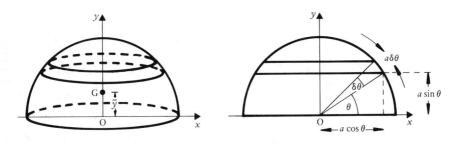

From symmetry the centre of gravity G of the hemisphere lies on Oy.
If we divide the hemisphere into slices parallel to its plane face then each slice is approximately a circular ring with its centre of gravity at its centre.
The ring shown in the diagram is approximately a cylinder of radius $a \cos \theta$ and width $a \, \delta\theta$ and so has a surface area of $(2\pi a \cos \theta)(a \, \delta\theta)$.
Let w be the weight per unit area of the hemisphere.

Body	Weight	y coordinate of centre of gravity
Element	$(2\pi a^2 \cos\theta\, \delta\theta)w$	$a \sin\theta$
Hemisphere	$2\pi a^2 w$	$\bar{y}$

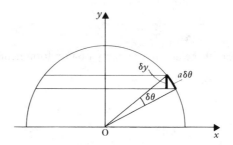

$$\sum_{\theta=0}^{\frac{1}{2}\pi} (2\pi a^2 \cos\theta\, \delta\theta w)a\sin\theta \simeq 2\pi a^2 w\bar{y}$$

Therefore

$$\int_0^{\frac{\pi}{2}} 2\pi a^3 w \cos\theta \sin\theta \, d\theta = 2\pi a^2 w\bar{y}$$

$\Rightarrow$

$$\bar{y} = \left[-\tfrac{1}{2} a \cos 2\theta \right]_0^{\frac{\pi}{2}} = \tfrac{1}{2}a$$

The temptation with this body is to take the ring of width δy and radius x, but this gives a bad approximation to its surface area as can be seen from the following cross section through the shell.

EXERCISE 15e

1) A uniform right hollow cone, without a base, has a height of $3h$ and its 'base' radius is $3r$. Its top is cut off at a distance h from the vertex. Find the position of the centre of gravity of the resulting right hollow frustum.

2) A uniform hollow sphere of radius a and centre O is cut into two sections by a plane distant b from O. Find the distance from O of the centre of gravity of the smaller section.

3) A section is cut from a uniform hollow sphere of radius $3a$, by two parallel planes distant a and $2a$ from the centre. Find the distance of the centre of gravity of this section from the first plane.

SPECIAL CASES

Certain uniform bodies require individual methods for locating their centres of gravity. The commonest of these are explained in the following examples.

EXAMPLES 15f

1) Find the position of the centre of gravity of a uniform wire bent into the form of an arc of a circle of radius a and subtending an angle 2α at the centre.

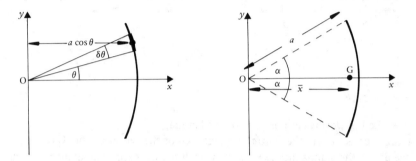

Let the weight per unit length of the wire be w.

Taking axes as shown, the centre of gravity of the arc lies on Ox.

If we divide the wire into small arcs subtending an angle $\delta\theta$ at O, then each element of length $a\delta\theta$ is approximately a particle.

Body	Weight	x coordinate of centre of gravity
Element	$(a\,\delta\theta)w$	$a\cos\theta$
Arc	$(a \times 2\alpha)w$	$\bar{x}$

$$\sum_{\theta=-\alpha}^{\alpha} (aw\,\delta\theta)a\cos\theta \simeq (a \times 2\alpha \times w)\bar{x}$$

$$\Rightarrow \qquad \int_{-\alpha}^{\alpha} a^2 w\cos\theta\,\mathrm{d}\theta = 2a\alpha w\bar{x}$$

$$\Rightarrow \qquad \frac{a}{2\alpha}\left[\sin\theta\right]_{-\alpha}^{\alpha} = \bar{x}$$

$$\Rightarrow \qquad \bar{x} = \frac{a\sin\alpha}{\alpha}$$

2) Find the position of the centre of gravity of a uniform lamina in the form of a sector of a circle of radius a subtending an angle 2α at the centre.

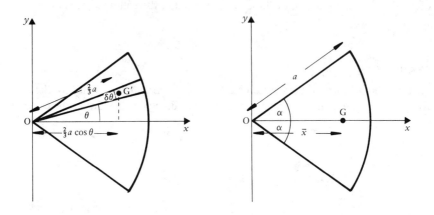

Let w be the weight per unit area of the lamina.

Taking axes as shown, the centre of gravity G of the sector lies on Ox.

If we divide the lamina into sectors, then each sector is approximately a triangle with centre of gravity G$'$ at a distance $\frac{2}{3}a$ from O.

Body	Weight	x coordinate of centre of gravity
Element	$(\frac{1}{2}a^2\delta\theta)w$	$\frac{2}{3}a\cos\theta$
Whole sector	$(\frac{1}{2}a^2 2\alpha)w$	$\bar{x}$

$$\sum_{\theta=-\alpha}^{+\alpha} (\tfrac{1}{2}a^2\delta\theta w)(\tfrac{2}{3}a\cos\theta) \simeq (\tfrac{1}{2}a^2 2\alpha w)\bar{x}$$

$$\Rightarrow \qquad \int_{-\alpha}^{+\alpha} \tfrac{1}{3}a^3 w\cos\theta\, d\theta = a^2\alpha w\bar{x}$$

$$\Rightarrow \qquad \bar{x} = \frac{a}{3\alpha}\Big[\sin\theta\Big]_{-\alpha}^{\alpha} = \frac{2a\sin\alpha}{3\alpha}$$

The position of the centre of gravity of a semi-circular lamina can be obtained from this result by substituting $\alpha = \pi/2$, thus giving an alternative method for No. 2 in examples 15c.

3) Find the position of the centre of gravity of a uniform solid tetrahedron.

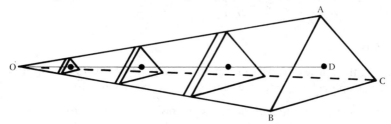

If we divide the tetrahedron into plane sections parallel to the base ABC these sections are approximately triangular laminas with their centres of gravity at the point of intersection of the medians. Thus the centre of gravity of the complete tetrahedron lies on the line joining O to D, the centroid of the base ABC.

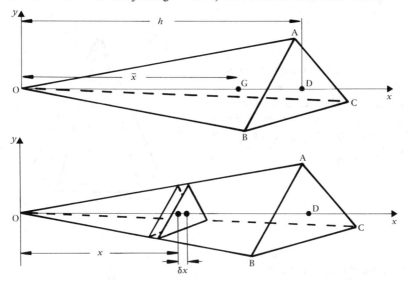

With axes as shown and taking the weight per unit volume as w, the height as h, and the area of $\triangle ABC$ as A then:

Body	Weight	Distance of centre of gravity from Oy
Element	$(x/h)^2 Aw\delta x$	x
Tetrahedron	$\frac{1}{3}Ahw$	$\bar{x}$

$$(\tfrac{1}{3}Ahw)\bar{x} \simeq \sum_{x=0}^{h}\left(\frac{x^2}{h^2}Aw\,\delta x\right)x$$

$$\Rightarrow \qquad \int_0^h \frac{x^2}{h^2}x Aw\,dx = \tfrac{1}{3}Ahw\bar{x}$$

Hence
$$\bar{x} = \frac{3}{h^3}\left[\frac{x^4}{4}\right]_0^h = \tfrac{3}{4}h$$

Therefore
$$OG = \tfrac{3}{4}OD$$

Therefore the centre of gravity of a uniform solid tetrahedron lies one quarter of the way up the line joining the centroid of the base to the vertex.

We can deduce the position of the centre of gravity of any uniform solid pyramid from this result. (The base of a pyramid can be any plane figure bounded by straight lines; the remaining faces of the pyramid are triangular and meet in a common vertex.)

If the pyramid is divided into sections parallel to the base, all such sections are similar so it can be seen that the centre of gravity G of the pyramid lies on the line joining the vertex V to O, the centroid of the base.

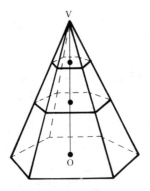

If the pyramid is divided into tetrahedrons each having the same height as the pyramid, the centre of gravity of each tetrahedron is at a point which is one quarter of the height of the pyramid above the base.

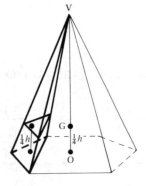

So the centre of gravity of a uniform solid pyramid lies on the line joining the vertex to the centroid of the base, at a point which is one quarter of the length of this line from the base.

Note. As the number of sides of a pyramid becomes infinitely large the sloping faces tend to form a curved surface and the pyramid becomes a cone thus confirming the position of the centre of gravity of a solid cone.

NON-UNIFORM BODIES

The centre of gravity of some non-uniform bodies can be found by using one of the methods already described but this can be done only if we know the way that the density varies. If this is the case, the weight per unit area or volume is no longer taken as a constant w.

EXAMPLES 15f (continued)

4) Find the position of the centre of gravity of a rod AB of length l where the weight per unit length of the rod at a point distant x from A is $(1+x)g$.

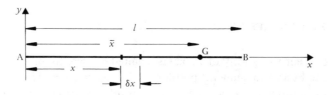

Consider a small section of the rod of length δx. This is approximately a particle of weight $(1+x)g\,\delta x$.

Body	Weight	Distance of centre of gravity from Oy
Element	$(1+x)g\,\delta x$	x
Rod	$\displaystyle\sum_{x=0}^{l}(1+x)g\,\delta x$	$\bar{x}$

$$\sum_{x=0}^{l}\left\{(1+x)g\,\delta x\right\}x \simeq \left[\sum_{x=0}^{l}(1+x)g\,\delta x\right]\bar{x}$$

$\Rightarrow$

$$\int_{0}^{l}x(1+x)g\,dx = \bar{x}\int_{0}^{l}(1+x)g\,dx$$

which gives

$$\bar{x} = \left(\frac{3+2l}{6+3l}\right)l$$

EXERCISE 15f

1) Find the position of the centre of gravity of a uniform semicircular lamina of radius a.

2) Find the position of the centre of gravity of a uniform wire bent into the shape of one quarter of a circle of radius r.

3) Find the position of the centre of gravity of a uniform sector of a circle of radius a if the angle at the centre of the sector is $\frac{2}{3}\pi$.

4) A rod AB is of length l and has a weight Wx per unit length at a point distant x from A. Find the distance of the centre of gravity from A.

5) A lamina in the form of a semicircle of radius a has a weight per unit area of Wr where W is a constant and r is the distance from the centre of the straight edge. By dividing the lamina into semicircular rings find the distance of the centre of gravity of the lamina from the centre of its straight edge.

STANDARD CENTRES OF GRAVITY

When the centre of gravity of a body is required in order to solve a problem it is useful to be able to quote the position of G (unless the problem specifically asks that the position of G be found). A list of the positions of the centres of gravity of some standard bodies follows.

Uniform body	Position of centre of gravity on axis of symmetry
Solid hemisphere	$\frac{3}{8}a$ from centre of sphere
Hollow hemisphere	$\frac{1}{2}a$ from centre of sphere
Arc subtending an angle 2α at the centre	$(a \sin \alpha)/\alpha$ from centre
Sector subtending an angle 2α at the centre	$\frac{2}{3}(a \sin \alpha)/\alpha$ from centre
Semicircular arc	$2a/\pi$ from centre
Semicircular lamina	$4a/3\pi$ from centre
Solid $\begin{cases}\text{tetrahedron}\\\text{pyramid}\\\text{cone}\end{cases}$	$\frac{1}{4}h$ from base
Hollow, without base, $\begin{cases}\text{tetrahedron}\\\text{pyramid}\\\text{cone}\end{cases}$	$\frac{1}{3}h$ from base

Bodies Hanging Freely from One Point

Consider a body freely suspended at one point A on the body.

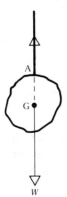

There are only two forces acting on the body, the tension in the tie at A and the weight acting through the centre of gravity G. If the body is in equilibrium under the action of these two forces then, as the weight acts vertically downward, the tension must act vertically upward. Then, as there is no torque, AG *must be vertical.*

Bodies Resting on Planes

Consider a body resting with its base in contact with a smooth horizontal plane.

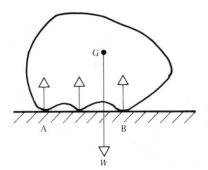 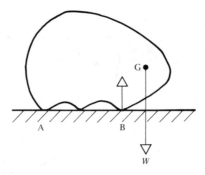

The forces acting on the body are its weight and the normal reaction forces at the points of contact between the body and the plane. These reaction forces are vertical and parallel, so the resultant normal reaction force must be between A and B, the extreme points of contact with the plane. If the body is resting in equilibrium the weight and the normal reaction force must be acting in opposite senses: therefore *the vertical through the centre of gravity must fall between A and B.*
If the vertical through G falls outside AB then the weight causes an overturning torque about A or B and the body will topple.

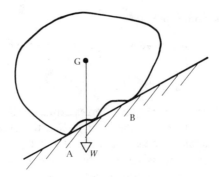

Similarly, if the only forces on a body on an inclined plane are the contact forces between the body and the plane (which may include friction) and the weight of the body, then again the vertical through G must fall between A and B to prevent toppling.

EXAMPLES 15g

1) A thin uniform wire AB is bent into the form of a semicircle. Find the inclination of AB to the vertical when the wire is freely suspended from A. A particle equal to the weight of the wire is now attached to B, find the new inclination of AB to the vertical.

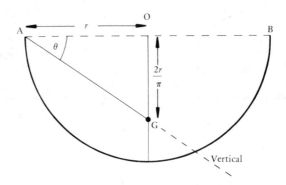

If O is the midpoint of AB and G is the centre of gravity of the wire then

$$OG = 2r/\pi \qquad \text{(quotable result)}$$

When the wire is freely suspended from A, AG is vertical.
So the angle between AB and AG is the angle made by AB with the vertical.

From the diagram $\tan \theta = 2/\pi$

Therefore AB makes an angle $\arctan(2/\pi)$ with the vertical .

When the particle is attached to B, the weight of the wire and the weight of the particle are a pair of equal, like, parallel forces. So their resultant, and hence the centre of gravity of the composite body, is midway between G and B.

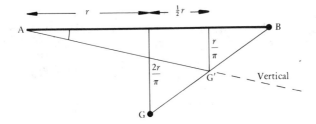

Now when this body is suspended from A, AG′ is vertical, so the inclination of AB to the vertical is the angle BÂG′.

But
$$\tan \widehat{BAG}' = \frac{r}{\pi} \div \frac{3r}{2} = \frac{2}{3\pi}$$

So AB makes an angle $\arctan 2/3\pi$ with the vertical.

2) A frustum of a uniform solid right circular cone is of height $3a$ and the radii of the plane faces are $2a$ and a. The frustum is freely suspended from a point on the edge of the smaller plane face and a particle is attached to the lowest point of this face so that the generator through the point of suspension is horizontal. If W is the weight of the frustum find the weight of the particle in terms of W.

We must first find the centre of gravity of the frustum.

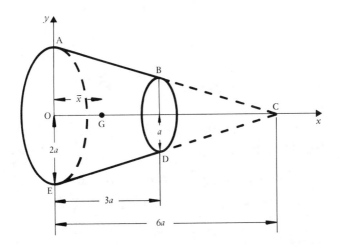

The complete cone and the cone removed are similar figures with corresponding lengths in the ratio $2:1$, so their volumes, and therefore weights, are in the ratio $8:1$.

Let W be the weight of the cone BCD.

Body	Weight	Distance of centre of gravity from Oy
Cone ACE	$8W$	$\frac{1}{4}(6a)$
Cone BCD	W	$(3a + \frac{3}{4}a)$
Frustum	$7W$	$\bar{x}$

$$8W(\tfrac{6}{4}a) - W(\tfrac{15}{4}a) = (7W)\bar{x}$$

$\Rightarrow$
$$\bar{x} = \tfrac{33}{28}a$$

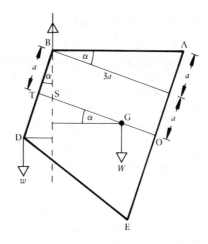

Let w be the weight of the particle at D.

From the diagram,
$$\tan \alpha = \tfrac{1}{3}, \quad TS = a \tan \alpha = \tfrac{1}{3}a \quad \text{and} \quad TG = \tfrac{51}{28}a,$$
so $\quad SG = TG - TS = \tfrac{125}{84}a$

$\overset{\rightarrow}{B)}$
$$(w)(2a \sin \alpha) - (W)(\tfrac{125}{84}a \cos \alpha) = 0$$

$\Rightarrow$
$$2w \tan \alpha = \tfrac{125}{84} W$$

$\Rightarrow$
$$w = \tfrac{125}{56} W$$

3) A uniform lamina is in the form of a square ABCD of side 2 m. E is a point on AD such that ED = x metre and the portion EDC is removed. Show that, if the lamina is placed in a vertical plane with AE on a rough horizontal surface, it will topple if $x > 3 - \sqrt{3}$.

If $x = 1\frac{1}{2}$ and the weight of the lamina is W find the least force which must be applied to the lamina to stop it toppling.

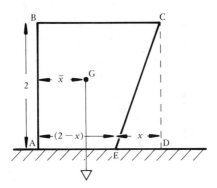

If G is the centre of gravity of the lamina, the lamina will rest in equilibrium in the position shown if the vertical through G falls within AE and it will topple about E if the line of action of the weight falls outside AE. So we must first find the distance of G from AB.

Let w be the weight per unit area.

Body	Weight	Distance of centre of gravity from AB
Square ABCD	$4w$	1
$\triangle$CDE	xw	$2 - \frac{1}{3}x$
Remainder	$(4-x)w$	$\bar{x}$

$$(4w)1 - xw(2 - \tfrac{1}{3}x) = (4-x)w\bar{x}$$

$$\Rightarrow \quad \frac{12 - 6x + x^2}{3(4-x)} = \bar{x}$$

The lamina will topple if $\bar{x} > AE$

i.e. if
$$\frac{12 - 6x + x^2}{3(4-x)} > 2 - x$$

$$\Rightarrow \quad x^2 - 6x + 6 < 0$$

$$\Rightarrow \quad [x - (3 + \sqrt{3})][x - (3 - \sqrt{3})] < 0$$

i.e. the lamina will topple if $x > 3 - \sqrt{3}$

To stop the lamina toppling about E a force must be applied to the lamina to counteract the moment of W about E. The minimum force necessary to do this is the one whose line of action is at the maximum possible distance from E, i.e. a force applied at C and perpendicular to CE.

When $x = 1\frac{1}{2}$, $\bar{x} = \frac{7}{10}$

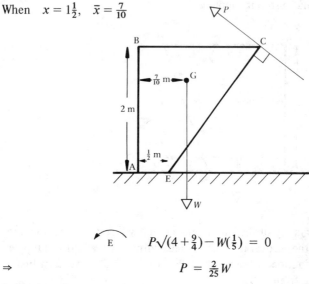

$$E \qquad P\sqrt{(4 + \tfrac{9}{4})} - W(\tfrac{1}{5}) = 0$$

$$\Rightarrow \qquad P = \tfrac{2}{25}W$$

So the least force which will stop the lamina toppling is $\frac{2}{25}W$ applied at C in a direction perpendicular to CE.

4) A uniform solid consists of a hemisphere of radius r and a right circular cone of base radius r fixed together so that their plane faces coincide. If the solid can rest in equilibrium with any point of the curved surface of the hemisphere in contact with a horizontal plane, find the height of the cone in terms of r.

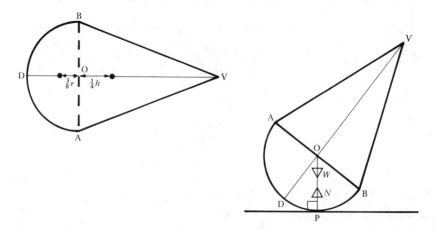

The only forces acting on the body are its weight and the normal reaction, N, acting at the point of contact, P, between the hemisphere and the horizontal plane. Now N is a vertical force which, for all positions of P, passes through the centre O of the hemisphere.

As the body can rest in equilibrium for all positions of P, the weight of the body must also always act through O, so O is the centre of gravity of the body.

Body	Weight	Distance of centre of gravity from AB
Hemisphere	$\frac{2}{3}\pi r^3 w$	$\frac{3}{8}r$
Cone	$\frac{1}{3}\pi r^2 hw$	$\frac{1}{4}h$
Complete body	$\frac{2}{3}\pi r^3 w + \frac{1}{3}\pi r^2 hw$	0

$$\tfrac{1}{4}h(\tfrac{1}{3}\pi r^2 hw) - \tfrac{3}{8}r(\tfrac{2}{3}\pi r^3 w) = 0$$

$$\Rightarrow \qquad h = r\sqrt{3}$$

So the height of the cone is $r\sqrt{3}$.

EXERCISE 15g

1) ABCD is a uniform rectangular lamina in which $AB = p$ and $BC = 3p$. The point E is on AD such that $ED = 3q$. Show that G, the centre of

gravity of the trapezium ABCE, is distant $\dfrac{3p^2 - 3pq + q^2}{2p - q}$ from AB

and find its distance from BC.

When the trapezium is suspended from E, the edge BC is horizontal.

Prove that $\qquad q = \tfrac{1}{2}p(3 - \sqrt{3})$

2) ABC is a uniform triangular lamina, right-angled at B. $AB = 2a$ and $BC = 3a$. Show that the centre of gravity of ABC is distant a from AB. The midpoints, P and Q, of CB and CA respectively are joined and the portion PQC is cut off. Find the distances from AB and BC of the centre of gravity of the lamina ABPQ.

When this lamina is suspended freely from the vertex A, AB is at an angle θ to the vertical. Find $\tan\theta$.

3) A child's toy consists of a solid uniform hemisphere of radius r and a solid uniform right circular cone of base radius r and height h. The bases of the two solids are glued together. If the density of the hemisphere is k times that of the cone, show that the distance from the vertex of the cone to the centre of gravity of the toy is

if the toy is
$$\frac{k(3r^2 + 8rh) + 3h^2}{4(2kr + h)}$$

(a) The toy is suspended from a point on the rim of the common base and rests in equilibrium with the axis of the cone inclined at an angle ϕ to the downward vertical. Find $\tan\phi$.

(b) If $h = 2r$, and the toy can rest in equilibrium with any point on the surface of the hemisphere in contact with a smooth horizontal plane, find the value of k.

4) A square lamina PQRS of side $2l$ is made of uniform thin material. When a semi-circular piece with PQ as diameter is removed from the square, show that the centre of mass of the remainder of the lamina is at a distance $\dfrac{20l}{3(8 - \pi)}$ from the line PQ.

The remainder of the lamina is suspended from a light string attached at R and hangs in equilibrium. Show that RS is inclined to the downward vertical at an angle θ, where

$$\tan\theta = \frac{2(14 - 3\pi)}{3(8 - \pi)}$$

(You may quote the position of the centre of gravity of a uniform semicircular lamina.)

5) ABCD is a uniform thin sheet of card of weight W and side $12a$. The centre of the card is the point P. A cut is made along AP and the section APB is folded over, along PB, and stuck to the section BPC. Find the distances from BC and CD of the centre of gravity of the resulting object APBCD.
If this object hangs freely from B, find the angle between BC and the vertical.
If a particle of weight kW is now attached at A so that the object rests in equilibrium with AC horizontal, find k.

SUMMARY

The weight of a body is the resultant of the weights of its parts.

The centre of gravity of a body is the fixed point through which the line of action of its weight passes whatever the orientation of the body.

The position of the centre of gravity of a body is found by using the fact that the sum of the moments of the weights of its parts about any axis is equal to the moment of the weight of the body about the same axis.

When a body whose centre of gravity is at a point G, is suspended freely from a point A in the body, AG is vertical.

MULTIPLE CHOICE EXERCISE 15
(The instructions for answering these questions are given on page x.)

TYPE I

1) Three particles of masses $1\,kg$, $2\,kg$, $1\,kg$ are at the points whose position vectors are $i+j$, $2i-j$, $3i+j$. The position vector of their centre of mass is:
(a) $\frac{1}{4}(6i+j)$ (b) $2i$ (c) $\frac{1}{3}(6i+j)$ (d) $8i$ (e) $2i+j$.

2) A lamina is in the shape of an isosceles trapezium. The two parallel sides are $5\,m$ apart and their lengths are $3\,m$ and $2\,m$. The distance of the centre of gravity of the trapezium from the longer of the parallel sides is:
(a) $\frac{8}{3}\,m$ (b) $\frac{8}{15}\,m$ (c) $6\,m$ (d) $\frac{5}{2}\,m$ (e) $\frac{7}{3}\,m$.

3)

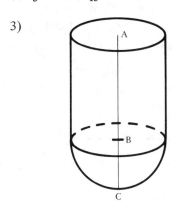

A child's drinking cup is made from a uniform solid hemisphere surmounted by a uniform hollow cylinder as shown in the diagram. If the cup is tilted on a horizontal surface it will always right itself (return to the position such that AC is vertical). The centre of gravity of the cup is:

(a) between B and C (b) at A (c) at B
(d) between B and A (e) at C.

4)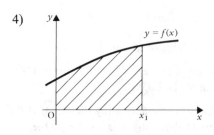

The area bounded by the curve $y = f(x)$, the x axis and the ordinates at O and x_1 represents a uniform lamina. The x coordinate of its centre of gravity is given by:

(a) $\dfrac{\displaystyle\int_0^{x_1} xy\,dx}{\displaystyle\int_0^{x_1} x\,dx}$ (b) $\dfrac{\displaystyle\int_0^{x_1} xy^2\,dx}{\displaystyle\int_0^{x_1} y^2\,dx}$ (c) $\dfrac{\displaystyle\int_0^{x_1} yx\,dx}{\displaystyle\int_0^{x_1} y\,dx}$ (d) $\displaystyle\int_0^{x_1} xy\,dx$

(e) $\frac{1}{2}x_1$

5) A uniform solid cone has a base radius r and height $4r$. It rests with its plane face on an inclined plane which is rough enough to prevent sliding. The cone will topple when the inclination of the plane to the horizontal is greater than:
(a) $45°$ (b) $\arctan\frac{1}{4}$ (c) $\arctan\frac{3}{4}$ (d) $90°$ (e) $\arctan\frac{1}{2}$.

TYPE V

6) The centre of mass of a non-uniform triangular lamina coincides with its centroid.

7) The centre of gravity of three particles of equal weight placed at the vertices of a triangle ABC coincides with the centroid of the triangle ABC.

8) A uniform wire is bent to form the sides of a triangle ABC. If the centre of gravity of the wire coincides with the centroid of the triangle ABC, triangle ABC must be equilateral.

9) The centre of gravity of a uniform lamina in the form of a quadrilateral coincides with the centre of gravity of four particles of equal weight placed at the vertices of the quadrilateral.

10) A uniform lamina in the form of a rectangle has one corner bent over as in the diagram. The centre of gravity of the resulting lamina lies on the diagonal AC.

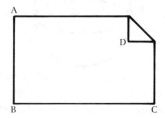

MISCELLANEOUS EXERCISE 15

1) A lamina ABCD is in the form of a trapezium in which DC is parallel to AB, $AB = 2a$, $CD = a$, $AD = h$ and the angle BAD is $90°$. Find the distance of the centroid of this lamina from the edges AD and AB.
The lamina is placed vertically with the edge BC on a horizontal plane. Find the minimum value of h for the lamina to remain in this position without toppling in its own vertical plane.   (AEB)

2) ABCD is a uniform square metal plate of side 3 m. Points E, F are taken on AB, BC respectively such that $BE = BF = x$ m and the portion BEF is removed. Find the distance of the centroid of the remainder from AD. Show that the remainder cannot stand in equilibrium on AE as base with AD vertical unless $2x^3 - 54x + 81 \geqslant 0$.
If the mass of the remainder is 14 kg, find in newtons the least horizontal force applied at C required to maintain it in equilibrium in this position when $x = 2$.   (U of L)

3) Show that the centre of mass of a uniform semi-circular lamina of radius a is at a distance $4a/3\pi$ from the mid point of the bounding diameter.
A uniform circular cone of height a and base radius a is cut in half by a plane passing through its axis. Find the distances of the centre of mass of one of the halves from its plane faces.

4) The diagonals AC, BD of a uniform quadrilateral lamina ABCD of weight W cross at right angles at O where $2AO = OC = 2b$ and $OB = OD = a$. Find the position of the centre of gravity of this lamina.
The lamina is placed in a vertical plane with CD resting on a horizontal table and a particle of weight kW is attached at A. If $a < b\sqrt{2}$ and the lamina is on the point of toppling in its own plane, find the value of k in terms of a and b.   (AEB)

5) Prove that the centre of mass of a uniform solid right circular cone, of height h and semi-vertical angle α is at a distance $\frac{3}{4}h$ from its vertex.
A frustum is cut from the cone by a plane parallel to the base at a distance $\frac{1}{2}h$ from the vertex. Show that the distance of the centre of mass of this frustum from its larger plane end is $11h/56$.
This frustum is placed with its curved surface in contact with a horizontal table. Show that equilibrium is not possible unless $45 \cos^2 \alpha \geqslant 28$.   (JMB)

6) Prove that the centre of gravity of a uniform thin hemispherical shell of radius r is at a distance $r/2$ from the centre.
The body of a cocktail shaker consists of a frustum of a right circular cone, the diameters of the ends being 4 cm and 8 cm and the height 12 cm. The lid is in the form of a hemisphere of diameter 8 cm. Both the body and the lid are made out of the same uniform thin material. Ignoring overlap find the position of the centre of gravity of the cocktail shaker with its lid on.   (AEB)

7) Show that the centroid of a uniform solid hemisphere of radius a is at a distance $3a/8$ from O, the centre of the plane face.

The figure below shows the central cross-section of a casting made in the form of a uniform solid hemisphere of radius a and centre O, with a hemispherical cavity of radius $\frac{1}{2}a$ and centre A. If this solid rests in equilibrium with its curved surface in contact with a horizontal plane, find the angle made by OA with the horizontal.

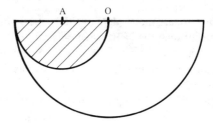

(U of L)

8) Prove that the centre of gravity of a uniform triangular lamina is the same as that of three equal particles placed at the vertices of the lamina.

A uniform lamina of weight W is in the shape of a quadrilateral ABCD. The diagonals AC, BD meet at P, where $AP < PC$, $BP < PD$, and O, R are points on AC, BD respectively such that $QC = AP$, $RD = BP$. By replacing triangles ABD, BCD by equivalent systems of particles, or otherwise, prove that the centre of gravity of the lamina is the same as that of a particle of weight $\frac{1}{3}W$ at Q and a particle of weight $\frac{2}{3}W$ at the midpoint of BD.

Deduce that the centre of gravity of the whole lamina is the same as that of the triangle PQR. (C)

9) Show that the centre of mass of a uniform right circular solid cone of height h is at a distance $3h/4$ from the vertex.

A uniform solid spinning top has the shape of an inverted right circular cone of radius $3r$ and height $4r$ surmounted by a cylinder of base radius $3r$ and height $6r$. Find the position of the centre of mass of the spinning top and hence show that if it is placed with the curved surface of the cone on a horizontal plane, the top will topple. (U of L)

10) In a uniform rectangular lamina ABCD the lengths AB and BC are $4a$ and $3a$ respectively and E is the point in CD such that $CE = \lambda a$. The portion BCE is removed. Find the distance of the centroid of the remainder from (i) AD, (ii) AB.

When this remainder is freely suspended from the corner A, the line AM, where M is the midpoint of BE, is vertical. Find the value of λ. (AEB)

11) A heavy uniform circular disc centre X and radius R has a circular hole centre Y and radius r cut from it, where $r < R$. If $XY = R - r$, and the centre of gravity of the crescent-shaped lamina is at a distance $\frac{4}{9}r$ from X, show that $R = \frac{5}{4}r$.

The lamina is now suspended from a point on its outer rim lying on the perpendicular to XY through X. Find the angle which XY makes with the vertical. If the weight of the crescent is W, find the smallest weight which must be attached to the lamina to maintain XY in a horizontal position.   (U of L)

12) A triangle ABC with $AB = BC = 2a$ and $AC = 2a\sqrt{2}$ is drawn on a uniform lamina. A semi-circle is drawn on BC as diameter, on the opposite side of BC from A, and the area enclosed by the triangle and the semi-circle is cut out. The resulting lamina is suspended freely from B. Show that AB makes an angle $\tan^{-1}(2 + \frac{3}{4}\pi)$ with the vertical. A point P is taken on AB and the triangle APC is cut off. If the remaining lamina hangs with BC vertical, find the distance BP.

[The centre of gravity of a uniform semi-circular lamina of radius a is at a distance $\frac{4}{3}(a/\pi)$ from the centre.]   (C)

13) Prove, by integration, that the distance of the centre of mass of a uniform solid right circular cone, of height h, from its plane base is $h/4$.

The cone is freely hinged at its vertex and is kept in equilibrium by a light rigid rod of length h joining the centre of the base to a point $h\sqrt{3}$ directly above the vertex. Show that the tension in the rod is $W\sqrt{3}/4$, where W is the weight of the cone.

Find the magnitude of the reaction at the hinge.   (U of L)

14) Find the coordinates of the centroid of a uniform lamina bounded by the curve $y^2 = x^3$ where $y > 0$, the x axis and the line $x = 4$. This lamina is suspended freely from the origin O. Find, to the nearest degree, the inclination to the vertical of the x axis.   (U of L)

15) Show that the distance of the centroid of a uniform circular sector AOB from the centre O is $(2a \sin\theta)/3\theta$, where 2θ is the angle AOB and a is the radius. Find the distance from O of the centroid of the segment of which AB is the chord, given that $\theta = \pi/6$. If a uniform lamina in the shape of this segment hangs at rest freely suspended from A, show that the tangent of the angle which AB makes with the downward vertical equals
$$(11 - 2\pi\sqrt{3})/(2\pi - 3\sqrt{3}).$$ (U of L)

16) PQRS is a uniform square lamina of side $2a$ and weight w per unit area. L is the midpoint of RS and M is the point on PS distant $\frac{1}{2}a$ from P. The triangular section SLM is removed.

Find the distances of the centre of gravity of the portion PQRLM from PQ and QR. This portion is suspended so that PR is horizontal, by vertical strings attached at P and R. Find the tensions in the strings.

17) A uniform lamina of weight W is in the shape of a triangle ABC with
AB = AC = $2a$ and the angle BAC equal to 2α. The side AB is fixed along a
diameter of a uniform solid hemisphere of radius a, the plane of the lamina being
perpendicular to the flat surface of the hemisphere. The body rests in equilibrium
with a point of the curved surface of the hemisphere in contact with a horizontal
table and with BC vertical. Show that the weight of the hemisphere is $\frac{8}{9}W\cot\alpha$.
A particle of weight W is attached to a point P of AB where AP $= \frac{2}{3}a$ and
the body now settles in equilibrium with the midpoint of BC vertically above A.
Prove that $\tan\alpha = \frac{1}{2}$.   (C)

18) Prove by integration that the centre of gravity of a uniform solid right
circular cone of vertical height h and base radius a is at a distance $3h/4$ from
the vertex of the cone. Such a cone is joined to a uniform solid right circular
cylinder of the same material and of height h and base radius a, so that the
plane base of the cone coincides with a plane face of the cylinder. Find the
distance of the centre of gravity of the solid from the centre of the base of the
cone.
When the solid hangs in equilibrium from a point A on the cirumference of the
base of the cone, the line joining A to the vertex of the cone is horizontal.
Prove that $4a = h\sqrt5$ and find the angle of inclination of the steepest
inclined plane on which the solid can stand in equilibrium on its plane face, the
plane being sufficiently rough to prevent sliding.   (JMB)

19) Show that the centre of mass of a uniform solid right circular cone of height
h is at a distance $\frac{1}{4}h$ from its base.
From a uniform solid right circular cylinder, of radius r and height h, a right
circular cone is bored out. The base of the cone coincides with one end of the
cylinder and the vertex O is at the centre of the other end. Show that the centre
of mass of the remainder of the cylinder is at a distance $3h/8$ from O.
The bored-out cylinder is placed with O uppermost on a horizontal plane which
is rough enough to prevent slipping; the plane is then gradually tilted. Show that
the cylinder topples when the inclination of the plane to the horizontal exceeds
$\tan^{-1}(8r/5h)$.   (JMB)

20) Prove that the centroid of a uniform solid hemisphere of radius a is at a
distance $3a/8$ from O, the centre of its plane face.
The hemisphere is suspended by two vertical strings, one fastened at O and the
other at a point P on the rim of the plane face. Given that the tension in one
string is three times the tension in the other string, find the two possible values
of the tangent of the angle made by OP with the horizontal.   (U of L)

21) A uniform lamina is bounded by that part of the parabola $y^2 = 4ax$,
$a > 0$,   which lies in the first quadrant, by the axis $y = 0$ of the parabola
and by the line $x = a$.   Find the coordinates of the centroid of the lamina.
This lamina is suspended freely from the vertex of the parabola. Find the tangent
of the angle of inclination to the vertical of the axis of the parabola.   (U of L)

CHAPTER 16

PROBLEMS INVOLVING RIGID BODIES

EQUILIBRIUM OF RIGID BODIES

There are several general considerations which are important when solving problems concerned with a rigid body which is in equilibrium under the action of a set of coplanar forces. These have all been explained in previous chapters and a summary of the main points is set out below.

1) When a body is in equilibrium under the action of three forces, the lines of action of the forces are concurrent. Useful methods for calculating unknown forces are Lami's Theorem and the Triangle of Forces. When determining angles the cotangent rule for a triangle can be useful (see p. 546).

2) When a body is in equilibrium under the action of more than three forces, only three independent equations can be found by various combinations of resolving and taking moments for the forces acting on that body. If more than three equations are needed they must come from other sources, such as the mensuration of the figure, Hooke's Law, etc.

3) The choice of axes about which moments are taken, or the direction in which forces are resolved, should be made with the following considerations in mind:
   (a) to keep the number of unknown quantities in any one equation down to a minimum,
   (b) to eliminate as many as possible of the unknown quantities that are *not* required.

4) In problems involving frictional forces, when equilibrium is about to be broken by slipping, friction is limiting at all points of contact at which slipping is about to occur.

5) If equilibrium is about to be broken by toppling the normal reaction force between the objects in contact acts through the point (or line) about which the body will topple.

Cotangent Rule for a Triangle

The general cotangent rule is given on p. ix.
It becomes particularly useful when $m = n$, as is the case in $\triangle ABC$ when D
bisects AC.

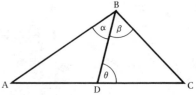

Then $2 \cot \theta = \cot \alpha - \cot \beta$

EXAMPLES 16a

1) A rod AB of length l has its centre of gravity at a point G where
$AG = \frac{1}{4}l$. The rod rests in equilibrium in a vertical plane at an angle β to
the horizontal, with its ends in contact with two inclined planes whose line of
intersection is perpendicular to the rod.
If the planes are smooth and are equally inclined at an angle α to the
horizontal show that $2 \tan \alpha \tan \beta = 1$.

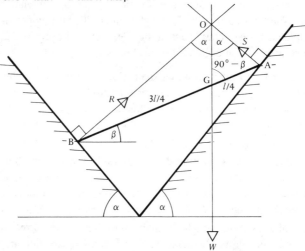

As the planes are smooth the forces acting on the rod are the normal reactions
at A and B and the weight at G. As only three forces act on the rod, they
must be concurrent at the point marked O.

In $\triangle OAB$, $\hat{BOG} = \alpha$, $\hat{AOG} = \alpha$, $\hat{OGA} = 90° - \beta$

Using the cotangent rule on this triangle gives

$$\tfrac{3}{4}l \cot \alpha - \tfrac{1}{4}l \cot \alpha = (\tfrac{3}{4} + \tfrac{1}{4})l \cot(90° - \beta)$$

$\Rightarrow \qquad \qquad \tfrac{1}{2} \cot \alpha = \tan \beta$

Therefore $\qquad \qquad 2 \tan \alpha \tan \beta = 1$

2) A ladder whose centre of gravity is at a point of trisection leans in a vertical plane with one end on rough horizontal ground and the other end against a rough vertical wall such that the centre of gravity of the ladder is nearer to the wall. If the coefficient of friction at each point of contact is μ and the ladder is on the point of slipping when it is inclined at an angle θ to the vertical prove that

$$\tan \theta = \frac{3\mu}{2-\mu^2}$$

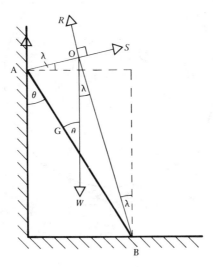

When the ladder is on the point of slipping, the end B will tend to slip away from the wall so the total reaction R at B makes an angle λ, where $\mu = \tan \lambda$, with the normal reaction at B as shown in the diagram. The end A will tend to slide down the wall so the total reaction S at A makes an angle λ with the normal reaction at the wall as shown in the diagram.

Considering the total reactions at A and B, the ladder is in equilibrium under the action of three forces only so these forces must be concurrent, say at O.

Now in triangle AOB, G divides AB in the ratio $1:2$ and we can use the cotangent rule in this triangle giving

$$(2+1)\cot \theta = 2 \cot \lambda - \cot (90° - \lambda)$$

$\Rightarrow$
$$3 \cot \theta = \frac{2}{\mu} - \mu$$

$\Rightarrow$
$$\tan \theta = \frac{3\mu}{2-\mu^2}$$

3) A uniform cylinder of radius a and weight W rests in equilibrium between two rough planes which are both inclined at $30°$ to the horizontal. The axis of the cylinder is parallel to the line joining the two planes and the coefficient of friction at the points of contact with both planes is $\frac{1}{2}$. Find the greatest couple that can be applied to the cylinder without making it rotate about its axis.

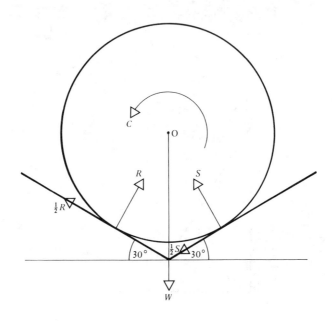

If a torque C is applied to the cylinder, and friction is limiting, then

$\rightarrow$ $\qquad R \sin 30° - \frac{1}{2}R \cos 30° - \frac{1}{2}S \cos 30° - S \sin 30° = 0$ $\qquad$ [1]

$\uparrow$ $\qquad \frac{1}{2}R \sin 30° + R \cos 30° + S \cos 30° - \frac{1}{2}S \sin 30° - W = 0$ $\qquad$ [2]

If the cylinder is not to rotate about its axis then

$\curvearrowright$ $\qquad C - \frac{1}{2}Sa - \frac{1}{2}Ra \leqslant 0 \quad \Rightarrow \quad 2C \leqslant (R + S)a$ $\qquad$ [3]

Simplifying [1] and [2] we have:

$$2(R - S) - \sqrt{3}(R + S) = 0$$

and $\qquad (R - S) + 2\sqrt{3}(R + S) = 4W$

Hence $\qquad\qquad\qquad (R + S) = \frac{8}{15} W\sqrt{3}$

Then in equation [3] $\qquad\qquad 2C \leqslant \frac{8}{15} Wa\sqrt{3}$

Therefore the greatest possible couple is $\frac{4}{15} Wa\sqrt{3}$.

Note. It is always wise to assemble *all the equations* which are to be used before beginning their solution. The form of equation [3] suggests that $(R+S)$ be found from equations [1] and [2] rather than R and S separately. In practice this is a much shorter process.

4) A uniform solid hemisphere of radius a rests with its curved surface in contact with a vertical wall. The hemisphere is supported by a light inextensible string of length a, one end of which is fixed to the wall and the other end to the highest point of the plane face of the hemisphere. If the hemisphere is on the point of slipping down the wall when its plane face is inclined at $\arctan\frac{4}{3}$ to the horizontal find the coefficient of friction between the hemisphere and the wall.

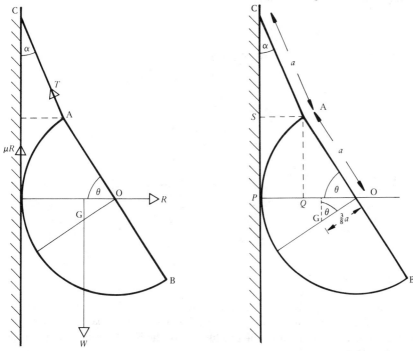

Let α be the inclination of the string to the wall.

From the diagram we see that $SA + QO = PO = a$

so $a \sin \alpha + a \cos \theta = a$

$\Rightarrow$ $\sin \alpha = 1 - \cos \theta$

But $\tan \theta = \frac{4}{3}$ $\Rightarrow$

So $\sin \alpha = 1 - \frac{3}{5} = \frac{2}{5}$ $\Rightarrow$

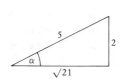

In this problem the tension, T, in the string is not asked for so, if we avoid introducing it into our solution, only two equations will be needed to determine the other two unknown quantities, μ and R.

T can be avoided if we take moments about axes through A and C.

$\widehat{C}$ $W(a - \frac{3}{8}a \sin \theta) - R(a \cos \alpha + a \sin \theta) = 0$ [1]

$\widehat{A}$ $\mu Ra \sin \alpha - Ra \sin \theta + W(a \cos \theta - \frac{3}{8}a \sin \theta) = 0$ [2]

All trig ratios for α and θ are known so

[1] becomes $7W = 2R(\sqrt{21} + 4)$

[2] becomes $3W = 2R(4 - 2\mu)$

Hence $\dfrac{3}{7} = \dfrac{4 - 2\mu}{\sqrt{21} + 4}$

$\Rightarrow$ $\mu = \dfrac{16 - 3\sqrt{21}}{14}$

Sliding and Overturning

Certain types of problems concerning a rigid body involve a variable quantity (such as a force or the inclination of a plane) which, as it increases, will eventually reach a point where it disturbs the equilibrium of the body. This equilibrium can be broken either by sliding or by overturning.

In order to determine the manner in which equilibrium is broken, each of these possibilities is considered separately and the results compared.

EXAMPLES 16a (continued)

5) A uniform solid cube of side $2a$ rests in rough contact with a horizontal plane, the coefficient of friction being $\frac{2}{5}$. A gradually increasing force, P, is applied at the midpoint of one top edge, perpendicular to the vertical face. Determine how the equilibrium will be broken.

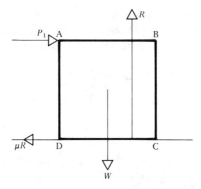

(i) Cube on the point of sliding

If the cube begins to slide, it will be about to do so when, from diagram (i),

$$P_1 = \mu R \quad \text{and} \quad R = W$$

$$\Rightarrow \qquad P_1 = \tfrac{2}{5}W \qquad\qquad\qquad [1]$$

(The line of action of R is not known in this case.)

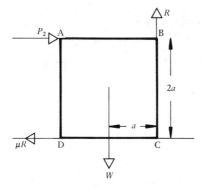

(ii) Cube on the point of overturning

If, on the other hand, the cube begins to overturn, it will rotate about the edge through C in diagram (ii). So the normal contact force, R, acts through this edge.

Taking moments about this edge in diagram (ii) gives

$$2aP_2 = aW$$

$$\Rightarrow \qquad P_2 = \tfrac{1}{2}W \qquad\qquad\qquad [2]$$

[1] and [2] show that $P_1 < P_2$

So, as P increases, the value of P_1 is reached before the value of P_2 can be reached.

Hence equilibrium is broken by sliding.

6) A uniform solid cylinder of radius a and height $3a$ is placed with one plane face in contact with a rough inclined plane. The inclination of the plane is slowly increased. Show that equilibrium will be broken by sliding if $\mu < \frac{2}{3}$

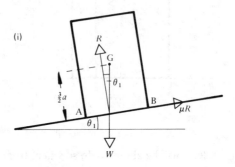

In diagram (i), the inclination of the plane to the horizontal is θ_1 and equilibrium is about to be broken by sliding.

Resolving perpendicular to the plane gives

$$R - W\cos\theta_1 = 0$$

resolving parallel to the plane gives

$$\mu R - W\sin\theta_1 = 0$$

Hence $$\mu = \tan\theta_1$$

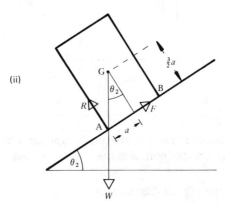

In diagram (ii) the plane is inclined to the horizontal at an angle θ_2 and equilibrium is about to be broken by overturning. So the line of action of W passes through A

Therefore $$\tan\theta_2 = \frac{2}{3}$$

If sliding is to occur before overturning, $\theta_1 < \theta_2$

i.e. $$\mu < \frac{2}{3}$$

EXERCISE 16a

1) A uniform rod rests in equilibrium with one end against a smooth vertical wall and the other end against a smooth plane inclined at $30°$ to the horizontal. Find the inclination of the rod to the horizontal.

2) A uniform ladder rests with one end against a rough wall and the other end on rough horizontal ground. When the ladder is inclined at $30°$ to the vertical it is on the point of slipping. The coefficient of friction between the ladder and the wall and the ladder and the ground is μ. Find the value of μ.

3) A smooth hemispherical bowl of radius a is fixed with its rim uppermost and horizontal. A smooth uniform rod of length $2l$ $(l > a)$ rests with one end inside the bowl and leaning on the rim. Find the length of the rod that overhangs the bowl.

4) A uniform cylinder of weight W rests with its axis horizontal and its curved surface in contact with a rough vertical wall and with a rough plane inclined at $45°$ to the horizontal. The coefficient of friction between the cylinder and the wall and the cylinder and the plane is μ. If the radius of the cylinder is a, find in terms of a, μ and W the greatest couple that will not rotate the cylinder.

5) A uniform solid cone of base radius a and height $2a$ is placed with its plane surface in contact with a rough plane which is initially horizontal. The coefficient of friction between the cone and the plane is $\frac{1}{4}$. Determine how equilibrium will be broken if:
(a) the plane is gradually tilted so that its inclination to the horizontal increases slowly,
(b) the plane is kept horizontal but a gradually increasing horizontal force is applied to the cone half-way up its height.

6) A uniform sphere of radius a rests against a vertical wall supported by a string of length $2a$ fixed to a point of its surface and to a point of the wall.
(a) If the wall is smooth find the inclination of the string to the vertical.
(b) If the wall is rough and the sphere is on the point of sliding down the wall when the string is inclined at $30°$ to the vertical, find the coefficient of friction between the sphere and the wall.

7) A uniform lamina in the form of a semicircle of radius a rests in a vertical plane with its curved edge in contact with a smooth vertical wall and rough horizontal ground. If the coefficient of friction between the lamina and the ground is $\frac{1}{6}$ find the inclination of its straight edge to the horizontal when it is on the point of slipping.

EQUILIBRIUM OF BODIES IN CONTACT

When two or more bodies in contact are in equilibrium under the action of a set of coplanar forces, the complete system is in equilibrium under the action of the external forces and each separate body is in equilibrium under the action of the forces acting on that body (these will include contact forces with other bodies). If the system is made up of two bodies, each body has three degrees of freedom so six independent equations may be derived for the system. The equilibrium either of the individual bodies or of the system as a whole may be considered when resolving or taking moments to form these six equations.
It must be remembered that six is the *maximum* number of independent equations but that many problems can be solved by using fewer than six. This occurs when some of the unknown quantities are not required and in this case their introduction into any equation should be avoided if this is possible. Careful choice of axes when taking moments, and direction when resolving, helps to keep the number of unknown quantities (and therefore equations) to a minimum. If there are more than two bodies in contact, the number of independent equations is three times the number of bodies in the system and these equations can be formed by considering the equilibrium of individual bodies or of two bodies or of any number of bodies, but the general principles mentioned above are important so that the number of equations is always kept to a minimum.

EXAMPLES 16b

1) A uniform rod of length $2a$ and weight W rests at an angle of $60°$ to the horizontal with one end hinged to a horizontal plane and resting on a cylinder of radius a and weight W which is itself resting on the horizontal plane. The axis of the cylinder is perpendicular to the vertical plane containing the rod. The contacts between the rod and the cylinder and between the cylinder and the ground are rough. Find the ratio of the frictional force to the normal reaction force at each point of contact.

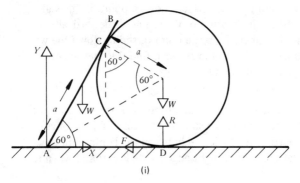

Diagram (i) shows the forces acting on the complete system.

(i)

Diagram (ii) shows separately the forces acting on the rod and the forces acting on the cylinder.

(**Note** that the contact forces between rod and cylinder are equal and opposite.)

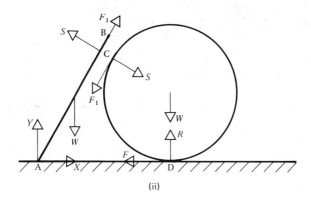

(ii)

If **C** is the point of contact of the rod with the cylinder

then
$$AC = a \tan 60°$$
$$= a\sqrt{3} = AD$$

$\widehat{A}$ for complete system $\qquad\qquad Wa \cos 60° + Wa\sqrt{3} - Ra\sqrt{3} = 0$ $\qquad$ [1]

$\widehat{C}$ for the cylinder only $\qquad\qquad (W-R)a \sin 60° + Fa\sqrt{3} \sin 60° = 0$ $\qquad$ [2]

[1] gives $\qquad\qquad \frac{1}{6}(\sqrt{3}+6)W$ $\Bigg\}$

$\qquad\qquad\qquad\qquad\qquad\qquad\qquad\qquad \Rightarrow\quad F:R = (6-\sqrt{3}):33$

Then [2] gives $\qquad F = \frac{1}{6}W$

$\widehat{D}$ for the cylinder only $\qquad Sa \sin 60° - F_1 a\sqrt{3} \sin 60° = 0$ $\qquad$ [3]

Therefore $\qquad\qquad\qquad F_1 : S = 1 : \sqrt{3}$

Note. By choosing to take moments about axes through **A**, **C** and **D**, we avoided introducing X and Y altogether and also kept the number of forces in each equation to a minimum.

2) A uniform rod AB of length $2l$ and weight $2W$ rests with the end A on rough ground. The rod is supported at an angle of $45°$ to the horizontal by a string of length l attached to the end B. A small ring of weight W is attached to the other end of the string and the ring is free to slide on a rough horizontal wire. The rod and the wire are both in the same vertical plane, and the coefficient of friction between the rod and the ground and between the ring and the wire is $\frac{1}{2}$. The wire is at a height h above the ground. Find the two possible values of h for the system to be in limiting equilibrium.

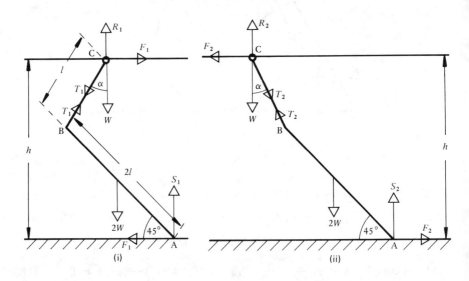

This is an example of a type of problem in which there are two possible geometric configurations, each leading to slightly different force systems which must be analysed individually.

Diagrams (i) and (ii) show the two possible positions of the string relative to the rod. In each position, resolving the forces acting on the system horizontally shows that the frictional force acting on the rod at A is equal to the frictional force acting on the ring at C.

First consider the position shown in diagram (i)

For the system as a whole, resolving vertically gives

$$S_1 + R_1 - 3W = 0 \qquad [1]$$

For the ring alone, taking moments about B (to avoid introducing T_1) gives

$$Wl \sin \alpha + F_1 l \cos \alpha - R_1 l \sin \alpha = 0$$

$\Rightarrow \qquad\qquad\qquad\qquad (R_1 - W) \tan \alpha = F_1 \qquad [2]$

For the rod alone, taking moments about B gives

$$2Wl \cos 45° + 2lF_1 \cos 45° - 2lS_1 \cos 45° = 0$$

$\Rightarrow$ $\qquad\qquad\qquad\qquad\qquad W + F_1 = S_1$ [3]

Solving equations [1], [2] and [3] gives

$$R_1 = \frac{W(\tan \alpha + 2)}{\tan \alpha + 1}$$

$$F_1 = \frac{W \tan \alpha}{\tan \alpha + 1}$$

$$S_1 = \frac{W(2 \tan \alpha + 1)}{\tan \alpha + 1}$$

Now for equilibrium there must be no slipping either at A or at C.

No slipping at A $\quad \Rightarrow \quad \dfrac{F_1}{S_1} \leqslant \tfrac{1}{2}$

$\Rightarrow \qquad \dfrac{\tan \alpha}{2 \tan \alpha + 1} \leqslant \tfrac{1}{2}$

This is always true, so slipping cannot occur at A whatever the value of α.

No slipping at C $\quad \Rightarrow \quad \dfrac{F_1}{R_1} \leqslant \tfrac{1}{2}$

$\Rightarrow \qquad \dfrac{\tan \alpha}{\tan \alpha + 2} \leqslant \tfrac{1}{2}$

$\Rightarrow \qquad \tan \alpha \leqslant 2$

So the system in position (i) is in limiting equilibrium when $\tan \alpha = 2$ and the *ring* is on the point of slipping.

In this case $\qquad\qquad h = 2l \sin 45° + l \cos \alpha$

$$= l\sqrt{2} + l/\sqrt{5} = \tfrac{1}{5}l(5\sqrt{2} + \sqrt{5})$$

When we consider the position shown in diagram (ii) it is clear that the same approach should be made, resulting in similar equations. These equations are

$$S_2 + R_2 - 3W = 0 \qquad\qquad \text{[1a]}$$

$$(R_2 - W) \tan \alpha = F_2 \qquad\qquad \text{[2a]}$$

$$W - F_2 = S_2 \qquad\qquad \text{[3a]}$$

Hence $\qquad \dfrac{F_2}{R_2} = \dfrac{\tan\alpha}{2-\tan\alpha}$ and $\dfrac{F_2}{S_2} = \dfrac{\tan\alpha}{1-2\tan\alpha}$

So, for no slipping at C,

$$\frac{\tan\alpha}{2-\tan\alpha} \leqslant \tfrac{1}{2} \quad \Rightarrow \quad \tan\alpha \leqslant \tfrac{2}{3}$$

and, for no slipping at A,

$$\frac{\tan\alpha}{1-2\tan\alpha} \leqslant \tfrac{1}{2} \quad \Rightarrow \quad \tan\alpha \leqslant \tfrac{1}{4}$$

Limiting friction is therefore reached at A before it can be reached at C, so this time the system is in limiting equilibrium when $\tan\alpha = \tfrac{1}{4}$ and the *rod* is about to slip.

In this case $\qquad h = l\sqrt{2} + 4l/\sqrt{17} = \tfrac{1}{17}l(17\sqrt{2} + 4\sqrt{17})$

EXERCISE 16b

1) A uniform rod AB of length $3l$ is freely hinged to level ground at A. The rod rests inclined at an angle of $30°$ to the ground resting against a uniform solid cube of edge l. Contact between the rod and cube is smooth and contact between the cube and the ground is rough. Find the reaction between the rod and cube and the coefficient of friction between the cube and the ground if the cube is on the point of slipping. The weight of the cube is twice the weight of the rod.

2) A uniform plank AB of length $4l$ and weight W rests with one end on level ground and leans against a cylinder of radius l such that the point of contact between the plank and cylinder is distant $3l$ from A. The cylinder is uniform and of weight W and rests on the ground with its axis perpendicular to the vertical plane containing the plank. Find the frictional force at each point of contact and if μ is the coefficient of friction at each point of contact show that for equilibrium to be possible $\mu \geqslant \tfrac{8}{21}$.

3) A uniform sphere of radius a and weight W has a light inelastic string of length a attached to a point on its circumference. The other end of the string has a small ring of weight W attached to it and the ring is free to slide on a rough horizontal wire. The sphere hangs below the wire and a horizontal force is applied to the sphere at a point level with its centre. The line of action of the force, the string and the centre of the sphere are all in the same vertical plane. If the coefficient of friction between the ring and wire is $\tfrac{2}{3}$ find the maximum force that can be applied to the sphere without upsetting equilibrium. Find also the inclination of the string to the vertical when the ring is about to slide along the wire.

4) Two uniform spheres of radius a and weight W rest on rough horizontal ground with their centres distant $2\sqrt{2}a$ apart. A third sphere of radius a and weight W is balanced on top of the other two spheres such that the centres of all three spheres lie in the same vertical plane. If the coefficient of friction, μ, is the same at all points of contact, find the minimum value of μ if equilibrium is to be maintained.

CONNECTED BODIES

When two bodies are connected by a smooth light hinge, which offers no resistance to their relative rotation, the bodies are said to be *freely jointed.*

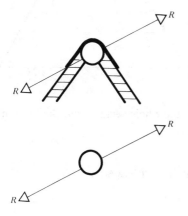

If the system is in equilibrium, the forces acting on the hinge are in equilibrium. Unless an external force acts at the hinge, the only forces affecting it are the reactions which the two jointed bodies exert on each other.

For equilibrium these forces are equal and opposite and so can be treated in the same way as contact forces.
(if there is also an external force acting at the hinge however, the internal forces are *not* equal and opposite.)

Because the directions of hinge forces are usually unknown it is most convenient to show these forces in component form as shown in the diagram.

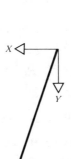
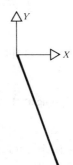

EXAMPLES 16c

1) Two uniform rods AB and BC of equal length but of weights W and $3W$ are freely jointed together at B. The rods stand in a vertical plane with the ends A and C on rough horizontal ground. If one rod is on the point of slipping when they are inclined at $60°$ to each other find the coefficient of friction μ between the rods and the ground, μ being the same at both points of contact. Find also the reaction at the hinge B when the rods are in this position.

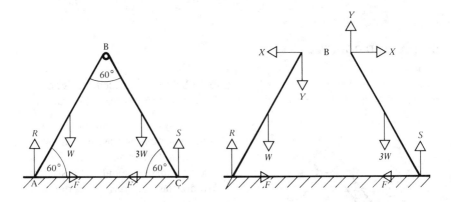

It is clear, from resolving horizontally for the whole system, that the frictional forces at A and C are equal and opposite.
Considering the whole system

A) $$S(4l\cos 60°) - 3W(3l\cos 60°) - W(l\cos 60°) = 0$$

$\Rightarrow$ $$S = \tfrac{5}{2}W \qquad\qquad [1]$$

C) $$R(4l\cos 60°) - W(3l\cos 60°) - 3W(l\cos 60°) = 0$$

$\Rightarrow$ $$R = \tfrac{3}{2}W \qquad\qquad [2]$$

Considering rod AB alone

B) $$F(2l\sin 60°) + W(l\cos 60°) - R(2l\cos 60°) = 0$$

Hence $$F = \tfrac{1}{3}W\sqrt{3} \qquad\qquad [3]$$

For no slipping at the end A,

$$F \leqslant \mu R \quad\Rightarrow\quad F \leqslant \tfrac{3}{2}\mu W$$

For no slipping at the end C,

$$F \leqslant \mu S \quad\Rightarrow\quad F \leqslant \tfrac{5}{2}\mu W$$

When the frictional force reaches the value $\tfrac{3}{2}\mu W$, slipping is about to occur at A but limiting friction has not yet been reached at C.

So it is the rod AB that is about to slip and this occurs when $F = \frac{3}{2}\mu R$

i.e. when $$\tfrac{1}{3}W\sqrt{3} \;=\; \tfrac{3}{2}\mu(\tfrac{3}{2}W)$$

$\Rightarrow$ $$\mu = \tfrac{2}{9}\sqrt{3}$$

To find the reaction at B we must consider the equilibrium of either rod alone.

For the rod AB

$\rightarrow$ $$F-X = 0 \;\Rightarrow\; X = \tfrac{1}{3}W\sqrt{3} \qquad\qquad [4]$$

$\uparrow$ $$R-W-Y = 0 \;\Rightarrow\; Y = \tfrac{1}{2}W \qquad\qquad [5]$$

So the magnitude, R, of the reaction at B is given by

$$R = \sqrt{(X^2 + Y^2)} = \tfrac{1}{6}W\sqrt{21}$$

and its line of action is at α to the vertical where

$$\tan\alpha = \frac{Y}{X} = \frac{\sqrt{3}}{2}$$

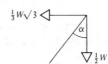

(In this problem the maximum number of independent equations (six) has been used. Five of them are numbered and the sixth was used in stating initially that the frictional forces at A and C are equal.)

2) Four uniform rods each of length l and weight W are freely jointed at their ends to form a framework. The ends of a light spring of modulus $3W$ are attached to two opposite vertices of the framework. The framework is freely suspended from one of the other vertices and, when hanging in equilibrium, takes the form of a square. Find the force in the spring and hence its natural length. Find also the reaction at the lowest joint.

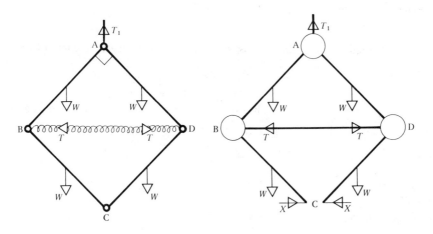

There are two points to consider in this problem:

(a) The external forces acting on the framework are symmetrical about the line AC, so the reactions at the hinges are also symmetrical about the line AC. Thus the reaction at C has no vertical component.

(b) There are external forces acting on the joints A, B and D, so the reactions on the ends of the rods at these joints are *not* equal and opposite.
It is usually possible to avoid introducing the internal forces at these joints into the analysis either
(1) by considering the equilibrium of sections of the framework which include the complete joint at A, B or D, or

(2) by choosing an axis through A, B or D when taking moments.

The forces at the joints A, B and D have not been entered but these joints have been circled to indicate that there are forces acting there.

For the forces acting on AB and BC taking moments about A gives

$$W(\tfrac{1}{2}l \cos 45°) + W(\tfrac{1}{2}l \cos 45°) - Tl \cos 45° + X(2l \cos 45°) = 0$$

$$\Rightarrow \qquad\qquad W - T + 2X = 0 \qquad\qquad [1]$$

For the forces acting on BC alone, taking moments about B gives

$$Xl \cos 45° - W(\tfrac{1}{2}l \cos 45°) = 0$$

$$\Rightarrow \qquad\qquad 2X - W = 0 \qquad\qquad [2]$$

Hence $X = \tfrac{1}{2}W$ and $T = 2W$

Now the length of the spring BD is $l\sqrt{2}$ so, if x is the natural length of the spring,

$$2W = \frac{3W(x - l\sqrt{2})}{x} \qquad\qquad \text{(Hooke's Law)}$$

$$\Rightarrow \qquad\qquad x = 3l\sqrt{2}$$

So the tension in the spring is $2W$ and its natural length is $3l\sqrt{2}$

The reaction at the joint C is $\tfrac{1}{2}W$ horizontally.

3) Two uniform rods AB and BC, each of length $2l$ and weight W are smoothly jointed at B. The rods rest in a vertical plane supported on two pegs P and Q which are distant l apart in a horizontal line. The coefficient of friction between each peg and the rod is $\frac{2}{3}$ and angle ABC is $90°$. If the rod AB is on the point of slipping find the angle it makes with the horizontal.

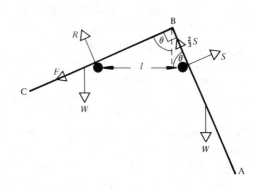

In this problem the components of reaction at B are marked parallel to the rods since the majority of the other forces act in these directions.

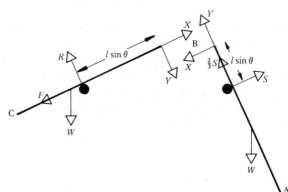

For the rod AB alone,

B)

$$Sl\cos\theta - Wl\cos\theta = 0 \qquad [1]$$

$$Y + \tfrac{2}{3}S - W\sin\theta = 0 \qquad [2]$$

For the rod BC alone,

P)

$$Wl(1 - \sin\theta)\sin\theta - Yl\sin\theta = 0 \qquad [3]$$

From [1] $S = W$

From [3] $Y = (1 - \sin\theta)W$

Then in [2] $\tfrac{2}{3}W = W\sin\theta - W(1 - \sin\theta)$

Hence $\sin\theta = \frac{5}{6}$ so the rod AB is at an angle of $56.4°$ to the horizontal.

EXERCISE 16c

1) Two uniform rods AB and BC of equal weight W but of lengths a and $2a$ are freely jointed together at B. The rods stand in a vertical plane with their ends A and C on rough horizontal ground, such that the angle ABC $= 90°$. If one of the rods is in limiting equilibrium find the minimum value of the coefficient of friction between the rods and the ground, it being the same for both rods. Find also the reaction at the hinge.

2) Two uniform rods AB and BC each of length l and weight W are freely jointed together at B. The rods rest in a vertical plane with A against a smooth vertical wall and C standing on rough horizontal ground. The coefficient of friction between the end C and the ground is $\frac{1}{2}$. Find the angle between the rods when they are resting in limiting equilibrium.

3) Three uniform rods each of length a and weight W are freely jointed together to form a triangle. The framework is freely suspended from one vertex. Find the reactions at the ends of the horizontal rod.

4) Four uniform rods of equal length l and weight W are freely jointed to form a framework ABCD. The joints A and C are connected by a light elastic string of natural length a. The framework is freely suspended from A and takes up the shape of a square. Find the modulus of elasticity of the string.

5) Two uniform rods AB and BC of lengths l and $2l$ and of weights W and $2W$ are freely jointed together at B. The rods rest in a vertical plane with BC horizontal and resting on a rough peg at a point which is distant $\frac{3}{2}l$ from B. The end A of the rod AB rests on a rough horizontal plane such that the angle ABC is $120°$. The coefficient of friction between BC and the peg and between A and the ground is μ. Find the minimum value of μ for equilibrium to be possible.

6) Three uniform rods AB, BC, CA of equal length a and weight W are freely jointed together to form a triangle ABC. The framework rests in a vertical plane on smooth supports at A and C so that AC is horizontal and B is above AC. A mass of weight W is attached to a point D on AB where AD $= a/3$. Find the reaction between the rods AB and BC.

MISCELLANEOUS EXERCISE 16

1) A uniform ladder of weight W rests with one end on rough horizontal ground and with the other end against a smooth vertical wall. The ladder is at an angle $\tan^{-1} 2$ to the ground and is in a vertical plane perpendicular to the wall. The coefficient of friction between the ladder and the ground is $\frac{1}{3}$. Find how far up the ladder a boy of weight $2W$ can climb without disturbing equilibrium. Find also the least horizontal force which must be applied to the foot of the ladder to enable the boy to climb to the top of the ladder without it slipping. (AEB)

2) A uniform rod AB of length $2l$ and weight W is in limiting equilibrium at an angle of $45°$ to the horizontal with its end A on a rough horizontal plane and with a point C in its length against a horizontal rail. This rail is at right angles to the vertical plane containing AB. The coefficient of friction between the rod and the plane is $\frac{1}{2}$ and between the rod and the rail is $\frac{1}{3}$. Calculate:
(a) the magnitude and direction of the resultant reaction at A,
(b) the length AC.   (AEB)

3) A uniform cylinder of radius a and weight W rests with its curved surface in contact with two fixed planes, each of which is inclined at $45°$ to the horizontal, the line of intersection of the planes being horizontal and parallel to the axis of the cylinder. A couple is applied to the cylinder in a plane perpendicular to its axis. If the angle of friction between the cylinder and each plane is $15°$ show that the cylinder will rotate if the moment of the couple exceeds $Wa/(2\sqrt{2})$.   (U of L)

4) Two points, A, B on a horizontal ceiling are at a distance $2a$ apart. A uniform rod CD of length a and weight W is suspended from A and B by two light strings AC, BD. A particle of weight $\frac{2}{5}W$ is attached to the rod at D, and the system hangs in equilibrium with the rod horizontal and AC inclined at an angle $\arctan \frac{4}{3}$ to the horizontal. Prove that the rod is at a distance $\frac{6}{7}a$ below the ceiling, and find the inclination of BD. If both strings are elastic and of natural length $\frac{1}{2}a$, find the modulus of each string in terms of W.   (C)

5) A heavy thin rod AB of length l can be made to balance across a small smooth peg C when a weight $2W$ is suspended from A. Alternatively, it can be made to balance across the peg with a weight $3W$ suspended from B. If the distance AC in the first case is the same as the distance BC in the second, show that the distance of the centre of gravity of the rod from A lies between $\frac{2}{5}l$ and $\frac{1}{2}l$. If the two equal distances above are each $\frac{1}{4}l$ and if the weights $2W$ and $3W$ are suspended from A and B respectively, find the distance from A to the peg when the rod balances.   (U of L)

6) A uniform block in the form of a cube stands on a plane inclined at an angle α to the horizontal in such a way that four of its edges are parallel to the line of greatest slope. A gradually increasing horizontal force is applied to the uppermost edge of the block at right angles to it and in a vertical plane through the centre of mass of the block, in the direction which would tend to move the block down the plane. If μ ($> \tan\alpha$) is the coefficient of friction between the block and the plane, show that the block will tilt without sliding provided that

$$\mu > \frac{2\tan^2\alpha + \tan\alpha + 1}{\tan^2\alpha + \tan\alpha + 2}.$$ (O)

7)

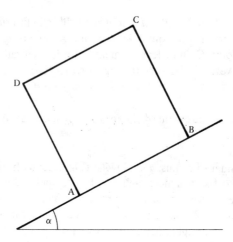

A uniform cube of weight W is placed as shown in the figure on a rough plane of inclination α $(< \frac{\pi}{4})$, the centre of the mass of the cube lying in the plane ABCD and the edges perpendicular to this plane being horizontal. If the coefficient of friction between the cube and the plane is μ show that the cube cannot remain in equilibrium unless $\mu \geqslant \tan \alpha$.

If $\tan \alpha = 1/2$, $\mu = 2/3$ and a horizontal force P, steadily increasing in magnitude from zero is applied at D (acting from left to right and with its line of action lying in the plane ABCD) show that equilibrium will be broken by the cube turning about the edge through B before it slides up the plane.   (U of L)

8) A rough heavy uniform sphere of radius a and centre C rests in contact with a horizontal floor at D. A uniform rod AB of length $2b$ and weight W is smoothly hinged at A to a fixed point on the floor and rests on the sphere, touching it at E. The rod is inclined at an angle 2θ to the horizontal (with $2b > a \cot \theta$) and is in the vertical plane ACD. If the contacts at D and E are rough enough to prevent slipping, prove that the mutual action and reaction at E act in the line ED and are each of magnitude $Wb \sin \theta (1 - \tan^2 \theta)/a$. The angle of friction at both D and E is λ. Prove that if $\lambda > \theta$ the friction is not limiting at either contact but that if $\lambda = \theta$ then the friction is limiting at E and not at D.   (JMB)

9) A uniform sphere of radius a, centre O and mass M rests on a rough horizontal plane. A uniform rod AB of length $2a$ and also of mass M rests with its end A on the plane and with a point C of the rod in contact with the sphere. The points C, O and A are in the same vertical plane and AB makes an angle of $60°$ with the horizontal.
(a) Show that the magnitude of the frictional force is the same at all three points of contact.
(b) Find the normal reaction between the rod and the sphere.

(c) The coefficient of friction μ is the same at all three points of contact and friction is limiting at one of them. Show that it must be at the point of contact between the rod and the sphere and find μ.

10)

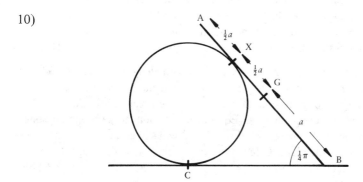

In the diagram, AB is a uniform ladder of length $2a$ and weight W, and G is the centre of mass of the ladder. The ladder is resting against a *fixed* cylindrical roller with circular cross-section whose axis is perpendicular to the vertical plane containing AB. The ladder is inclined at an angle $\frac{1}{4}\pi$ to the horizontal. The point of contact X of the ladder with the roller is at a distance $\frac{1}{2}a$ from the end A and the contact at X is smooth. Show that, in order that equilibrium be maintained in this position, the coefficient of friction μ at B must not be less than $\frac{1}{2}$.

A man of weight W stands at X and then starts walking slowly up the ladder. Show that if $\mu = \frac{11}{13}$ the ladder is on the point of slipping when he has moved a distance of $\frac{1}{4}a$. (O)

11) A uniform rod AB of weight W and length $2a$ is freely hinged at A to a fixed point on a rough horizontal table. A uniform rough sphere of radius a and weight $W\sqrt{3}$ rests on the table. The rod leans against the sphere so that the point of contact is at a distance $a\sqrt{3}$ from A and so that the rod and the centre of the sphere lie in a vertical plane. Show that the frictional force between the rod and the sphere is $\frac{1}{6}W$. If the coefficient of friction at each point of contact is μ find the smallest value of μ which makes equilibrium possible. (C)

12) Two equal uniform planks AB, CD have their lower ends B, D on rough horizontal ground and their upper ends A, C resting against one another. A third equal plank is now inserted between A and C and is held in a vertical position, not touching the ground, by friction at A and C. The coefficient of friction at A and C is μ, that at B and D is μ', and AB, CD are inclined to the horizontal at an angle θ. Find, in terms of μ and μ' the limits between which $\tan\theta$ must lie. Deduce that equilibrium in this position is possible only if $\mu\mu' \geqslant 1/3$. (JMB)

13) A uniform rod of weight $4W$ and length $2a$ is maintained in a horizontal position by two light inextensible strings each of length a attached to the ends of the rod. The other ends of the strings are attached to small rings each of weight W which can slide on a fixed rough horizontal bar with which the coefficients of friction are each $\frac{1}{2}$. Show that in equilibrium the distance between the bar and the rod cannot be less than $4a/5$, and find the greatest and least possible distances apart of the rings.   (U of L)

14) Two uniform rods, AB and BC are of the same length and weigh $3W$ and W respectively. They are smoothly jointed at B and stand in a vertical plane with A and C on a rough horizontal plane. The coefficient of friction between each rod and the plane is $\frac{2}{3}$. Equilibrium is about to be broken by one of the rods slipping on the plane. Find which rod will slip and calculate the angle each rod makes with the plane. Calculate also the reaction at the hinge B in magnitude and direction.   (AEB)

15) Two equal uniform rods AB, AC each of weight W and length $2a$ and a third uniform rod of weight W_1, are freely hinged together to form a triangle ABC in which the angle BAC is 2θ. The triangle hangs in a vertical plane from a smooth pivot at B, and a couple is applied to the rod AB so as to keep the triangle in equilibrium with BC horizontal and A below BC. Find:
(a) the moment of the couple, showing its sense in a diagram,
(b) the horizontal and vertical components of the forces exerted on AC by
   BC and AB.   (JMB)

16) The diagram shows two uniform rods AB, BC, each of length $2a$ and weight W which are smoothly hinged at B. The end A is smoothly hinged to a point on a fixed rough horizontal bar, the hinges allowing the rods to rotate in the vertical plane through the bar. The end C is fastened to a small ring of weight w which is threaded on the bar.

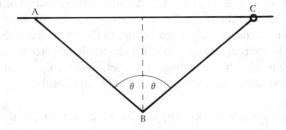

The rods are in equilibrium with each inclined at an angle θ to the vertical. Find the force of friction at C and the components of the reaction of the hinge on the rod AB at A.
Show that, when $W = 2w$ and the coefficient of friction at C is 1/4 the greatest possible distance AC in an equilibrium position of the rods is $12a/5$.
                    (JMB)

17)

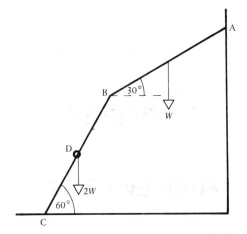

The diagram shows two uniform rods AB and BC smoothly jointed at B and resting in equilibrium with A against a smooth vertical wall, C on rough horizontal ground and BC passing through a fixed smooth ring at its mid-point D. The plane of the rods is perpendicular to both the wall and the ground. The rods have the same length; the rod AB is of weight W and inclined at $30°$ to the horizontal; the rod BC is of weight $2W$ and inclined at $60°$ to the horizontal. Prove that the reaction of the wall at A is $W\sqrt{3}/2$. Find:
(a) the reaction of the ring,
(b) the horizontal and vertical components of the reaction of the ground at C.
Show that the coefficient of friction at C must not be less than $3\sqrt{3}/11$.

(JMB)

18) Two straight uniform rods AB and BC, each of length $2a$ and weight W, are smoothly hinged together at B and are in equilibrium with A, B, C in the same horizontal line. The rod AB is simply supported at the point X in AB, where $BX = x$, and the rod BC is simply supported at the point Y in BC, where $BY = y$.
(a) By considering the equilibrium of the system, show that the reactions at

X and Y are $\dfrac{2yW}{x+y}$ and $\dfrac{2xW}{x+y}$ respectively.

(b) By considering the equilibrium of each rod separately, show that
  (i) if $x > a$, then $y < a$
  (ii) $2xy = a(x+y)$

  (iii) the mutual reaction between the rods at B has magnitude $\dfrac{W(x-y)}{x+y}$

(c) Find the value of y when $x = 2a$.

(AEB)

CHAPTER 17

FRAMEWORKS

A framework consists of a number of light rods which are smoothly jointed together at their ends to form a rigid construction.

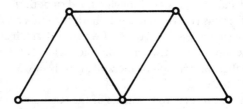

Note that the term 'light' rods means that the weights of the rods are negligible compared to the loads that they bear.

If a framework has external forces acting on it, each rod can perform one of two functions:

either they stop the framework from collapsing inwards

or they prevent the joints from flying apart.

A rod which is preventing a collapse exerts a push at either end. It is described as a strut and is said to be *in thrust or in compression*.

Rod in thrust

A rod which is preventing the framework from coming apart exerts a pull at either end. It is described as a tie and is said to be *in tension.*

Rod in tension

In both cases the forces exerted at the ends of the rod are equal and opposite. Consider a framework of three light rods smoothly jointed as shown in the diagram.

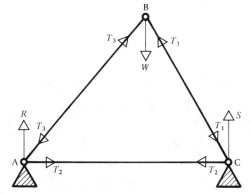

If the framework carries a load at B and is supported at A and C, then the forces acting at B are the weight W and the forces T_1 and T_3 in the rods BC and BA. The forces acting at A are the supporting force R and forces T_2 and T_3 in rods AC and AB. Similarly forces S, T_1, and T_2 act at C as shown.

If the whole system is in equilibrium *the forces acting at each joint are in equilibrium.*

As the forces in the rods occur in equal and opposite pairs they are internal forces, therefore *the external forces acting on the framework are in equilibrium.*

When solving problems it is not always as obvious as in the problem above which rods are in tension and which are in thrust, so we will adopt the policy of marking all rods in thrust so that negative answers indicate the rods which are in tension.

EXAMPLE 17a

A framework consists of three light rods each of length $2a$ smoothly jointed together to form a triangle ABC. The framework is smoothly hinged at B to a smooth vertical wall and carries a weight W at A, and rests in equilibrium with C below B. Find the reaction at B and the force in each rod.

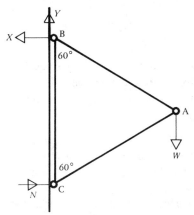

The reaction with the smooth wall at C is perpendicular to the wall.
The unknown reaction at the hinge B is made up of components X and Y.
The external forces are in equilibrium so resolving gives,

$\uparrow$ $\qquad\qquad Y = W$ $\qquad$ [1]

$\rightarrow$ $\qquad\qquad X = N$ $\qquad$ [2]

$\stackrel{\curvearrowleft}{C}$ $\qquad Wa\sqrt{3} = 2aX$ $\qquad$ [3]

Hence $\qquad X = W\sqrt{3}/2 \quad \text{and} \quad Y = W$

The reaction at B is $\sqrt{X^2 + Y^2} = \dfrac{W}{2}\sqrt{7}$

in a direction at $\quad \arctan\dfrac{X}{Y} \quad$ to CB, i.e. at $\quad \arctan\sqrt{3}/2 \quad$ to CB.

Each joint is in equilibrium

Considering first the forces acting at C, we have

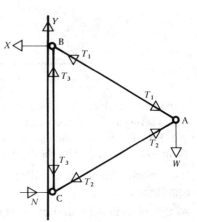

$\rightarrow \qquad\qquad T_2 \cos 30° = N$

$\downarrow \qquad\qquad T_3 + T_2 \cos 60° = 0$

But, from [2], $\quad N = W\sqrt{2}/2$

therefore $\qquad\qquad T_2 = W$

and $\qquad\qquad T_3 = -\tfrac{1}{2}W$

Considering the forces acting at A:

$\rightarrow \qquad T_2 \cos 30° + T_1 \cos 30° = 0$

But $\quad T_2 = W \quad$ so $\quad T_1 = -W.$

Therefore there is a tension W in AB, a tension $\tfrac{1}{2}W$ in BC and a thrust W in AC.

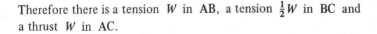

EXERCISE 17a

1) Two light rods AB and BC of length $2a$ and a respectively are smoothly jointed at B. The ends A and C are smoothly hinged to a vertical wall with A above C such that BC is horizontal, and a weight W is hung from B. Find the forces in the rods and the reaction at C.

2) The light rods AB, BC and CA of lengths $4a$, $3a$ and $5a$ respectively are smoothly jointed at their ends to form a triangle ABC. A weight W is hung from B and the triangle is supported at A and C, with AC horizontal and B vertically above AC. Find the reactions at A and C and the force in each rod.

3)

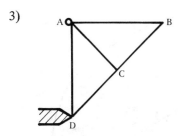

A framework consists of five light rods as shown in the diagram.
$AC = CB = CD = a$, $\quad AB = AD = \sqrt{2}a$.
The framework carries a weight W at B and is smoothly hinged at A with D resting against a smooth support. Find the reaction at D and show that there is no force in AC.

4)

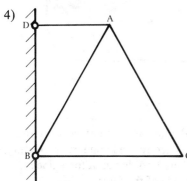

A framework consists of four light rods as shown in the diagram.
$AB = BC = CA = 2a$, and $AD = a$.
It is smoothly hinged to a vertical wall at B and D with BC horizontal, and carries a weight W at C. Find the reaction at D and the force in each rod.

The method for finding the force in the members of a framework used in the previous section is not practical for a large number of joints as the number of equations involved is too large to handle easily. There are two alternative methods which simplify the work, one is graphical and the other involves calculation.

GRAPHICAL METHOD   (BOW'S NOTATION)

This method is basically to draw a force polygon for each group of forces that are in equilibrium, i.e. the set of forces acting at each joint. A specialised notation makes this process easier by allowing each polygon to be superimposed on the previous one.

Consider a framework of three light rods as shown in the diagram.
The framework is smoothly jointed, rests in a vertical plane on smooth blocks at A and C and carries a weight 200 N at B. $AB = a$,
$AC = 2a$ and $BC = \sqrt{3}a$.

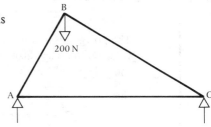

As the supports at A and C are smooth the forces at A and C are vertical.

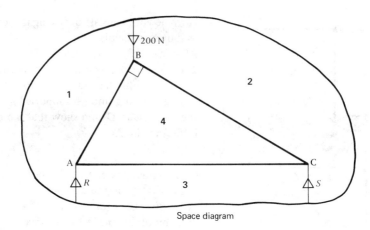

Space diagram

A boundary is drawn round the diagram and the line of action of each external force is drawn *outside* the framework and extended to the boundary so creating a number of closed spaces. Each space is numbered, so that each force line is identified by a pair of numbers, one on either side of the force.

Thus 1, 2 identifies the load at B, 2, 4 identifies the force in the rod BC, and so on.

Also each vertex of the framework can be identified by the set of numbers in the spaces around it.

Thus 1, 4, 2 identifies the vertex B, 2, 4, 3 the vertex C, and 1, 3, 4 the vertex A.

The force polygon for the external forces is drawn first. In this case the external forces are parallel so their magnitudes must be found by calculation:

$$\uparrow \qquad R + S = 200$$

$$\curvearrowright A \qquad S \times 2a = 200 \times \tfrac{1}{2}a \qquad \left.\right\} \qquad \text{therefore} \quad S = 50, \quad R = 150$$

As all the external forces are vertical, their force polygon is a straight line.

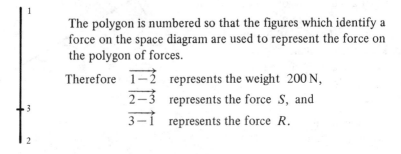

The polygon is numbered so that the figures which identify a force on the space diagram are used to represent the force on the polygon of forces.

Therefore $\overrightarrow{1-2}$ represents the weight 200 N,

$\overrightarrow{2-3}$ represents the force S, and

$\overrightarrow{3-1}$ represents the force R.

The next stage is to draw the force polygon for one of the vertices where an external force acts and not more than two forces are unknown.

Choosing A, we construct the triangle of forces for the forces acting at A.

The line $\overrightarrow{3-1}$, representing R, is already drawn.

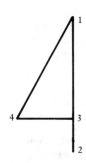

The force in AB is identified by the numbers 1, 4 in the space diagram, so starting at 1 we draw a line parallel to AB. The force in AC is identified by 3, 4, so starting at 3 a line is drawn parallel to AC.

The point of intersection of these two lines is the vertex 4.

As the triangle 1, 3, 4 represents three forces which are in equilibrium, the vertices of this triangle taken in order indicate the directions of the forces.

As $\overrightarrow{3-1}$ represents R, $\overrightarrow{1-4}$ represents the force in AB acting at A. This is towards the joint A, therefore rod AB is in thrust.

Similarly $\overrightarrow{4-3}$ represents the force in AC acting at A, and thus it is away from A. Therefore AC is in tension.

By measurement from the diagram: the force in AB is a thrust of 170 N
and the force in AC is a tension of 86 N.

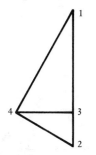

We have now introduced all four numbers in the diagram and by joining 4 to 2 the diagram is closed.

Thus 4, 2, 3 represents the triangle of forces for the joint C.

Now $\overrightarrow{2-3}$ represents the force S,

therefore $\overrightarrow{3-4}$ represents the force in AC at C

and $\overrightarrow{4-2}$ the force in BC at C: this is towards C.
Therefore BC is in thrust.

By measurement from the diagram the force in BC is a thrust of 100 N.

The triangle 1, 4, 2 represents the forces acting at B.

Thus the line $\overrightarrow{4-1}$ represents the force in the rod AB acting on the joint B.

The line $\overrightarrow{1-4}$ (in triangle 1, 4, 3) represents the force in the same rod but acting on A.

So the line joining 1 and 4 represents a pair of equal but opposite forces. For this reason the sense of each force along its line of action is *not* indicated in the construction.

Summing up, the steps to follow when using Bow's Notation are:
(1) Draw a boundary round the diagram and extend each external force line away from the framework to the boundary.
(2) Number each space. (Make sure there is only *one* number in each space.)
(3) Draw the polygon of forces for the external forces (these may have to be calculated first).
(4) Superimpose the force polygon for a joint where an external force acts and not more than two forces are unknown.
(5) Superimpose the force polygon for each remaining joint until the figure is complete. (When choosing the order in which to do this, make sure that there are not more than two unknown forces at any joint selected.)
We will now illustrate this method on a framework with more joints.

EXAMPLES 17b

1) A framework consists of seven light rods smoothly jointed together as shown in the diagram. The framework is smoothly hinged at A and carries a weight of 400 N at C. It is held in a vertical plane, with BC horizontal, by a horizontal force at B. Find the reaction at A and the force in each rod.

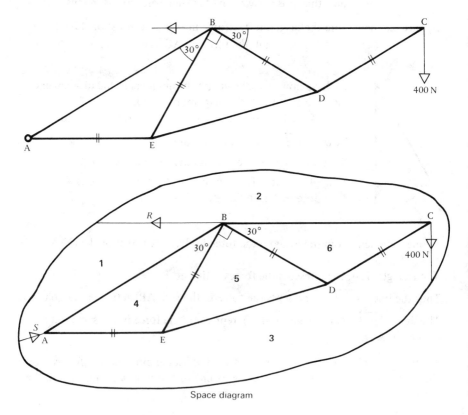

Space diagram

As the framework is in equilibrium under the action of three forces, their lines of action are concurrent: therefore the line of action of S is along AC (i.e. at $15°$ to the horizontal).

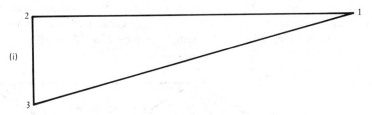

(i)

Diagram (i) shows the triangle of forces for the external forces:
the line $\overrightarrow{3-1}$ represents S.
By measurement the reaction S at A is 1550 N at $15°$ to the horizontal.

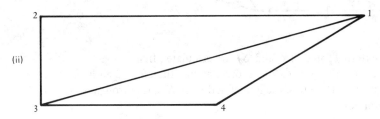

(ii)

In diagram (ii) the triangle of forces for the forces acting at A is superimposed.
As S acts along $\overrightarrow{3-1}$, the force in AB (1, 4) acts along $\overrightarrow{1-4}$ and the force in AE is represented by $\overrightarrow{4-3}$.
By measurement, the force in AB is a thrust of 800 N
and the force in AE is a thrust of 800 N.

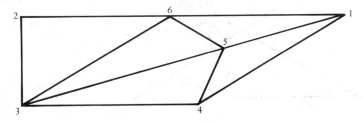

Superimposing the force triangles for the vertices E, then D, the figure is completed. By measurement from the diagram:

> the force in EB is a tension of 290 N
> the force in ED is a thrust of 970 N
> the force in DC is a thrust of 800 N
> the force in DB is a tension of 290 N
> the force in BC is a tension of 690 N.

METHOD OF SECTIONS

This method involves dividing the framework into two or more sections by drawing a line through *not more than three rods*. The forces in the *cut* rods are then treated as external forces for the section being considered. We will illustrate this method by working through the example on page 576.

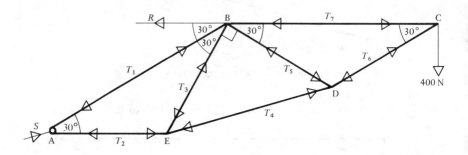

The external forces (R and S) are calculated first.

There are only three external forces acting, therefore their lines of action are concurrent. Therefore the line of action of S goes through C (i.e. at $15°$ to the horizontal).

$\uparrow$ $\qquad\qquad\qquad\qquad S \sin 15° = 400 \quad \Rightarrow \quad S = 1560\,\text{N}$

$\rightarrow$ $\qquad\qquad\qquad\qquad\qquad R = S \cos 15° = 1490\,\text{N}$

We now *cut* the framework through the rods AB, BE and ED and consider the section from A to this cut.

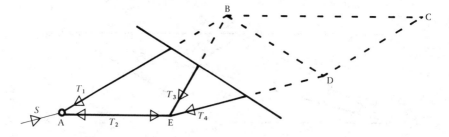

For this section T_2 is an internal force, so the section is in equilibrium under the action of external forces S, T_1, T_3, T_4. Let the length of the equal rods (AE, EB, BD, DC) be a.

Considering the equilibrium of these forces:

$\curvearrowright$E $\qquad\qquad\qquad T_1\, a \sin 30° - S\, a \sin 15° = 0$

$\Rightarrow$ $\qquad\qquad\qquad\qquad T_1 = 800 \quad (\text{AB is in thrust})$

$\widehat{B}$ $\qquad T_4 a \sin 45° - S\sqrt{3}a \sin 15° = 0$

$\Rightarrow \qquad\qquad T_4 = 980 \quad \text{(ED is in thrust)}$

$\widehat{A}$ $\qquad T_3 a \sin 60° + T_4 a \sin 15° = 0$

$\Rightarrow \qquad\qquad T_3 = -293 \quad \text{(EB is in tension)}$

The force in AE can be found easily by considering the equilibrium of the forces acting at A:

$\leftarrow \qquad\qquad T_2 + T_1 \cos 30° - S \cos 15° = 0$

$\Rightarrow \qquad\qquad T_2 = 800 \quad \text{(AE is in thrust)}$

This leaves the forces in BC, BD and DC to be found. If we cut the framework through BC, BD and DE and consider the section from C to this cut we can find the forces in BC and BD.

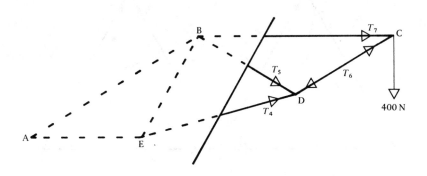

T_6 is an internal force, so this section is in equilibrium under the action of T_4, T_5, T_7 and the weight 400 N.
Considering the equilibrium of these forces

$\widehat{D}$ $\qquad\qquad 400 a \cos 30° + T_7 a \sin 30° = 0$

Therefore $\qquad\qquad T_7 = -693 \quad \text{(BC is in tension)}$

$\widehat{C}$ $\qquad\qquad T_4 a \sin 15° + T_5 a \sin 60° = 0$

$\Rightarrow \qquad\qquad T_5 = -293 \quad \text{(BD is in tension)}$

The remaining force, T_6, can be found by considering the equilibrium of the forces acting at C:

$\uparrow \qquad\qquad T_6 \cos 60° = 400$

$\Rightarrow \qquad\qquad T_6 = 800 \quad \text{(DC is in thrust)}$

The method of sections is particularly appropriate when forces in only a few rods are required. To find the force in one particular rod the framework is cut into sections by a line through that rod. It must be remembered, though, that the dividing line must not go through more than three rods whose forces are unknown.

EXAMPLES 17b (continued)

2) The framework in the diagram consists of seven equal light rods, each of length $2a$, smoothly jointed together. The framework rests in a vertical plane on smooth supports at A and D so that BC is horizontal. Loads of 500 N and 200 N are carried at B and C. Find the forces in the rods AB, BC and CE.

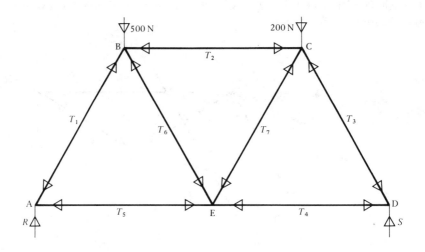

As the supports at A and D are smooth the reactions are vertical.
Considering the equilibrium of the external forces:

↑ $$R + S = 700$$

$\widehat{A}$ $$S(4a) = 500a + 200(3a)$$

Therefore $$S = 275 \quad \text{and} \quad R = 425$$

The stress in AB can be found easily by considering the equilibrium of the forces acting at A.

↑ (for joint A): $$425 = T_1 \sin 60° \implies T_1 = 491$$

The forces in BC and CE can be found by dividing the framework into two sections with a cut through BC, CE and ED and considering the left hand section.
(Analysing the right hand section works just as well.)

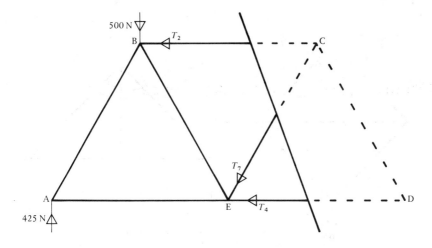

The forces in the rods AB, AE and BE are internal, so this section is in equilibrium under the action of the forces T_2, T_4, T_7, the reaction at A and the weight at B.

So for these forces: ↑ $\qquad T_7 \cos 30° + 500 - 425 = 0$

⇒ $\qquad\qquad\qquad T_7 = -87$

↶E $\qquad\qquad T_2 a\sqrt{3} + 500a - 425(2a) = 0$

⇒ $\qquad\qquad\qquad T_2 = 202$

Therefore the force in AB is a thrust of 491 N,
the force in BC is a thrust of 202 N,
the force in EC is a tension of 87 N.

SUMMARY

If a framework of light rods which are smoothly jointed together is in equilibrium then:
(a) the external forces acting on it are in equilibrium,
(b) the forces at each joint are in equilibrium.
When solving problems on light frameworks always find the external forces first. The method of sections will usually give the shortest solution unless the framework consists of many rods *and* all the forces are required.

EXERCISE 17b

The frameworks in Questions 1-4 consist of light rods smoothly jointed together and rest in a vertical plane as shown. The frameworks are either supported by forces as shown or smoothly hinged to a fixed support as shown. Find the external forces and calculate the force in each rod.

1)

2)

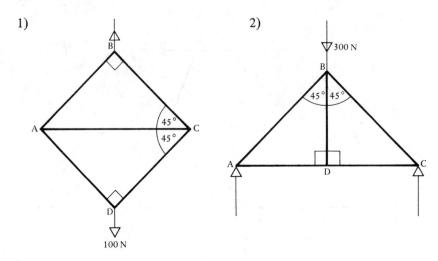

3)

4)

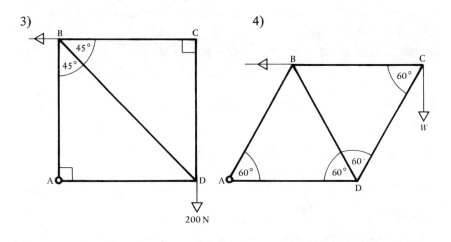

In Questions 5–10 find the external forces and find graphically the force in each rod.

5)

6)

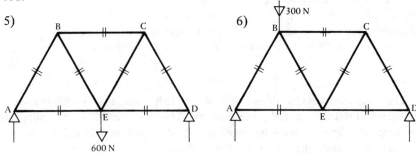

7)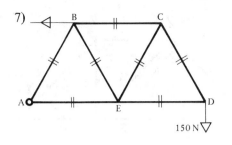

150 N

8)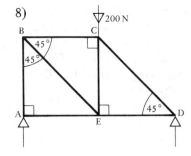

200 N

9)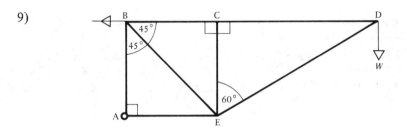

W

10)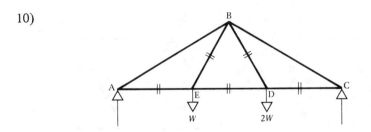

W   2W

11) The framework in the diagram is smoothly hinged at A and is held with AE vertical by a horizontal force at E. The rods AB, BC, BD, ED, EA are all equal and ABC is horizontal. The framework carries a load of 500 N at C. Find the reaction at A and the forces in the rods ED, BD and BC.

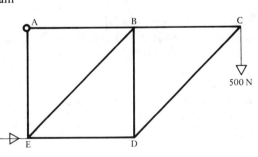

500 N

12) The framework ABCDEF
is smoothly supported at A and
D and carries weights of 200 N
and 100 N at B and C. Find
the forces in the rods FE, BE
and CD.

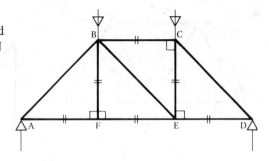

13) The framework BECDGFA is
smoothly supported at A and D
and carries weights W and 2W
at F and G. Find the forces in
the rods BE, BF and FG.

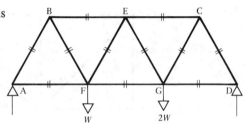

14) The framework ABCDE is smoothly
hinged at A and is held with AD horizontal by a vertical force at D. A force
of 200 N in the direction BE is applied
at B. Find the stresses in the rods BE,
EC and ED.

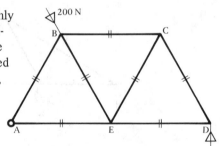

15) The framework ABCDE is
smoothly hinged at A and is held
with AED horizontal by a force at
B in the direction EB. The framework
carries a load W at D. Find the
reaction at A and the stresses in the
rods CE, AB and ED.

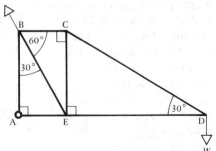

16) The framework ABCDEF is smoothly hinged at A and is held with BCD horizontal by a tie at B in the direction EB. A load of 600 N is carried at D. Find the reaction at A and the forces in rods BC, CE and ED.

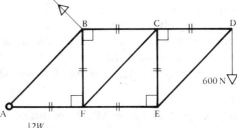

17)

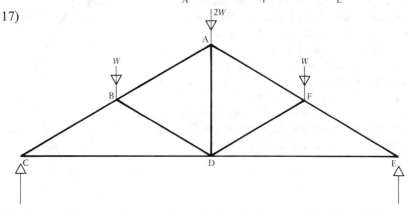

The figure represents a framework consisting of nine smoothly jointed light rods. AD is vertical, CD = DE and the acute angles in the figure are either 30° or 60°. The framework carries weights 2W at A, W at B and W at F and rests on smooth supports at C and E. Determine the stresses in the rods, specifying which are tensions and which are thrusts. (O)

18) The smoothly jointed framework ABCDEF consisting of eight light rods, is in equilibrium in a vertical plane, smoothly hinged to a vertical wall at A and B and carrying loads 2W and 3W at C and D respectively. The rod AF is of length a and all the other rods are of length $2a$. The rods AF, FE, BC and CD are horizontal. Calculate the force exerted by the framework on the wall at A. Find graphically, or otherwise, the forces in the rods CD, CE, CF and BC, stating which rods are in compression.

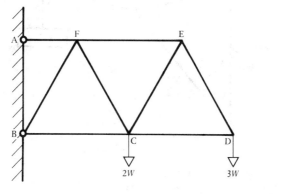

(AEB)

19) A framework consists of three light rods AB, BC, CA of lengths a, $a\sqrt{3}$, and a respectively, smoothly jointed at A, B, C. The framework is suspended freely from A and carries weights $2W$ at B and W at C. Show that, in the equilibrium position with B below A, the thrust in the rod BC is $2W$ and that the tensions in the rods AB, CA are $2W\sqrt{3}$, $W\sqrt{3}$ respectively.   (O)

20) A light framework ABCD consists of 5 smoothly jointed rods of equal length. The framework carries a load W at D and is smoothly hinged and fixed at A. The framework is kept in equilibrium in a vertical plane with AC horizontal by a force P applied at B in a direction parallel to CA. Find the magnitude of P and the magnitude and direction of the reaction at A. Find, graphically or otherwise, the forces in the five rods and state which rods are in compression.

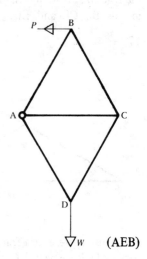

(AEB)

21) The light smoothly jointed framework shown is hinged to a vertical wall at A and B and carries a load of 400 N at D, AD being horizontal.
$AE = ED = AC = CD = 10 \, m,   EC = 5 \, m,   BC = 15 \, m.$
By means of a force diagram find the forces in all the members, stating which are in tension and which are in compression. Use the method of sections to check the magnitude of the force in AE.

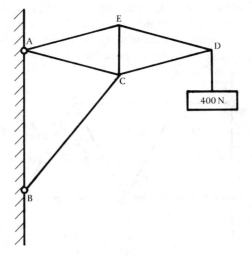

(AEB)

CHAPTER 18

PROBABILITY

Imagine that you have bought five tickets for a raffle and that 500 tickets altogether have been sold. Assuming that any one of the 500 tickets is as likely as any other to be drawn for first prize, you would say that you had 5 chances in 500, or a chance of 1 in 100, of winning first prize.

In this chapter we develop methods to deal with problems concerned with chance events.

Terminology and notation are introduced to enable us to refer to certain categories of situations precisely and more briefly.

Probability gives us a measure for the likelihood that something will happen. However it must be appreciated that probability can never predict the number of times that an occurence actually happens. But being able to quantify the likely occurrence of an event is important because most of the decisions that affect our daily lives are based on likelihoods and not on absolute certainties. For example, if it is known that it is likely to rain on two days out of five days at a place where you are taking a holiday, it does *not* mean that it *will* rain on four days out of a ten day holiday but that you would be wise to take a raincoat with you.

AN EVENT

An event is a defined occurrence or situation. For example:

(a) tossing a coin and the coin landing head up,

(b) scoring a six on the throw of a die,

(c) winning the first prize in a raffle,

(d) being dealt a hand of four cards which are all clubs.

A particular event is denoted by a capital letter, e.g. $A, B, \ldots$ etc.

POSSIBILITY SPACE

In each of the examples given there is an implied set of circumstances from which there are several possible outcomes, including the event(s) described. This set of possible outcomes is called the *possibility space*.
Considering the given examples, (a) to (d),

in (a) the event is one of the possible ways in which the coin can land, viz. head up, H, or tail up, T, i.e. the possibility space is H, T ;

in (b) the event is one of the possible ways of scoring on the throw of a die, i.e. the possibility space is 1, 2, 3, 4, 5, 6 ;

in (c) the possibility space is all the tickets in the draw ;

in (d) the possibility space is all the different combinations of four cards that can be obtained from fifty-two cards .

Now consider the following situation. A bag contains three white balls and two black balls, and one ball is removed from the bag. The possibility space is the set

$$\{\circ, \circ, \circ, \bullet, \bullet\}$$

If the event denoted by A is 'the removal of a white ball' the possibilities for A are the members of the set $\{\circ, \circ, \circ\}$.
Denoting 'the possibilities for the event A' as the set $\{A\}$ we can write $\{A\} = \{\circ, \circ, \circ\}$
and we note that $\{A\}$ is a subset of $\{\circ, \circ, \circ, \bullet, \bullet\}$.
In general, if E is an event then $\{E\}$ is a subset of {possibility space}.

PROBABILITY THAT AN EVENT OCCURS

The probability that an event A occurs is defined as

the number of ways in which A can happen expressed as a fraction of the number of ways in which all *equally likely* events, including A, occur.

The term 'equally likely' is important. For example, if a coin is bent so that when tossed it is more likely to land head up than tail up, then the events that the coin lands head up or lands tail up are *not* equally likely.

The *probability of an event A occurring* is denoted by $P(A)$

Hence

$$P(A) = \frac{\text{Number of ways in which } A \text{ occurs}}{\text{Number of ways in which all equally likely events, including } A, \text{ occur}}$$

or, when all members are equally likely,

$$P(A) = \frac{\text{Number of members of } \{A\}}{\text{Number of members of } \{\text{possibility space}\}}$$

This is the basic definition of probability. All other developments of probability theory are derived from this definition, and a large number of problems can be solved directly from it.

As $\{A\}$ is a subset of {possibility space} the numerator of this fraction is always less than, or equal to, the denominator so, for any event A,

$$0 \leqslant P(A) \leqslant 1$$

If $P(A) = 1$ the event is an absolute certainty.
If $P(A) = 0$ the event is an absolute impossibility.
For example, if one ball is taken from a bag containing only red balls

$$P(\text{ball is red}) = 1 \quad \text{and} \quad P(\text{ball is blue}) = 0$$

EXAMPLES 18a

1) A pack of felt tipped pens contains five red pens and four blue pens. If one pen is withdrawn at random what is the probability that it is blue?

The term 'at random' means that all possibilities are *equally likely*.

Thus the possibility space contains 9 equally likely events.
If A is the removal of a blue pen, then A can occur in 4 equally likely ways (i.e. $\{A\}$ has 4 members).
Thus $P(A) = 4/9.$

2) If one card is drawn at random from a pack of fifty-two playing cards what is the probability that it is an ace?

There are 52 equally likely events, i.e. the drawing of any one of the fifty-two playing cards.
An ace can be drawn in 4 equally likely ways.

Therefore $P(\text{ace}) = 4/52 = 1/13.$

3) Four cards are drawn at random from a pack of fifty-two playing cards. Find the probability that the four cards are all clubs.

Let A be the event 'the withdrawal of four clubs'.
As there are thirteen clubs in the pack, there are $^{13}C_4$ different combinations of four clubs.
So A can occur in $^{13}C_4$ ways, i.e. $\{A\}$ contains $^{13}C_4$ members.

Any distinct combination of four cards from the pack is equally likely and, as there are $^{52}C_4$ of these, the possibility space contains $^{52}C_4$ members.

Thus $\qquad P(A) = \dfrac{^{13}C_4}{^{52}C_4} = \dfrac{13!\,4!\,48!}{4!\,9!\,52!} = \dfrac{11}{4165} = 0.003$ to 3 d.p.

4) Four letters are chosen at random from the word DEALING.
Find the probability that:

(a) exactly two vowels are chosen,

(b) at least two vowels are chosen.

DEALING has three vowels and four consonants.
Four letters (without restriction) can be chosen in $^7C_4$ ways.
i.e. possibility space has $^7C_4$ members.

(a) A selection containing two vowels (out of E A I) also contains two consonants (out of D L N G).
As these are independent combinations, the number of ways of choosing four letters containing exactly two vowels is $^3C_2 \times {}^4C_2$.
Therefore the probability of selecting four letters, exactly two of which are vowels, is

$$\frac{^3C_2 \times {}^4C_2}{^7C_4} = \frac{18}{35}$$

(b) If the selection contains at least two vowels, then either it contains two vowels and two consonants or it contains three vowels and one consonant and these combinations are mutually exclusive. The number of combinations containing just two vowels is

$$^3C_2 \times {}^4C_2 = 18$$

The number of combinations containing three vowels is

$$^3C_3 \times {}^4C_1 = 4$$

Therefore the number of ways of selecting four letters containing at least two vowels is $18 + 4 = 22$.
Hence the probability of four letters chosen at random containing at least two vowels is

$$\frac{22}{^7C_4} = \frac{22}{35}$$

THE PROBABILITY THAT AN EVENT DOES NOT HAPPEN

If, in a possibility space of n equally likely occurences, the number of times an event A occurs is r, there are $n - r$ occasions when A does not happen.

'The event A does not happen' is denoted by $\bar{A}$ (and is read as 'not A').

Thus $\qquad P(A) = \dfrac{r}{n}$ and $P(\bar{A}) = \dfrac{n-r}{n} = 1 - \dfrac{r}{n}$

i.e. $\qquad\qquad\qquad\qquad P(\bar{A}) = 1 - P(A)$

or $\qquad\qquad\qquad\qquad P(A) + P(\bar{A}) = 1$

This relationship is most useful in the 'at least one' type of problem, as is illustrated below.

EXAMPLES 18a (continued)

5) If four cards are drawn at random from a pack of fifty-two playing cards find the probability that at least one of them is an ace.

If A is a combination of four cards containing at least one ace (i.e. either one ace, or two aces, or three aces or four aces)
then $\bar{A}$ is a combination of four cards containing *no* aces.

Now $\qquad P(\bar{A}) = \dfrac{\text{Number of combinations of four cards with no aces}}{\text{Total number of combinations of four cards}}$

$\qquad\qquad = {}^{48}C_4 / {}^{52}C_4 = 0.72$ to 2 d.p.

Using $P(A) + P(\bar{A}) = 1$ we have

$$P(A) = 1 - P(\bar{A}) = 1 - 0.72 = 0.28 \text{ to 2 d.p.}$$

6) Four balls are taken at random out of a box containing six red and four black balls. What is the probability that at least two red balls are removed?

The number of ways in which any four balls from the box of ten can be removed is ${}^{10}C_4$, i.e. the possibility space has ${}^{10}C_4$ members.
If A is a selection of four balls, at least two of which are red, then A contains either two, or three or four red balls.
Thus $\bar{A}$ is a selection containing either no red balls or one red ball.
As $\bar{A}$ involves two mutually exclusive combinations, while A involves three mutually exclusive combinations, we will consider $P(\bar{A})$.

The number of combinations of four balls containing either no red balls or one red ball is ${}^{4}C_4 + {}^{6}C_1 \times {}^{4}C_3$, i.e. $\{\bar{A}\}$ has ${}^{4}C_4 + {}^{6}C_1 \times {}^{4}C_3$ members.

So $\qquad P(\bar{A}) = \dfrac{{}^{4}C_4 + {}^{6}C_1 \times {}^{4}C_3}{{}^{10}C_4} = 0.119$ to 3 d.p.

Therefore $\quad P(A) = 1 - P(\bar{A}) = 1 - 0.119 = 0.88$ to 2 d.p.

Note that in each of the examples the word *random* is taken to mean that any choice is as likely as any other choice.

EXERCISE 18a

1) One integer is chosen at random from the set $\{1, 2, 3, 4, 5, 6, 7, 8\}$. What is the probability that it is a prime number?

2) Two books are taken at random from a shelf containing five paper backs and four hard backs. What is the probability that both are paper backs?

3) Three cards are drawn at random from a pack of fifty-two playing cards. What is the probability that at least one card is red?

4) Two balls are taken at random from a box containing three black, three red and three yellow balls. Find the probability that:
(a) neither of the balls removed is red,
(b) at least one is red,
(c) both are red.

5) If the letters of the word BOOK are arranged at random, what is the probability that the two O's are separated?

6) A two digit number is made by choosing two integers, at random, from the set $\{1, 2, 3, 4, 5, 6\}$. If each integer may be used more than once, what is the probability that the number is:
(a) divisible by 2   (b) not divisible by 5.

7) What is the probability that three letters chosen at random from the letters GREEN contain:
(a) the letter N   (b) two E's   (c) at least one E?

8) A team of four people is chosen at random from a group of three men and four women. Find the probability that there are:
(a) no men in the team,
(b) at least two men in the team.

9) A box contains four white counters and one red counter. If two counters are removed at random, what is the probability that the red counter is not removed?

10) A number is made by choosing two or three digits at random from the set $\{1, 2, 3, 4\}$. If each digit can be chosen more than once to make a number, what is the probability of a number less than 200 being made?

The solutions of the examples examined so far have used methods developed for permutations and combinations, and where this is possible it is usually the most direct approach. However the likely occurrence of some events cannot be worked out exactly, because the factors affecting whether that event does or does not occur cannot be measured or counted. For example, the probability that you would hit the bull's-eye on a dartboard with one throw of a dart would

depend on how much you had practised, how much natural talent for playing
darts you had, how tired you were, how much alcohol you had drunk, how
good a dart you were using etc., etc . . . all of which are impossible to quantify.

EMPIRICAL PROBABILITY

A method which can be adopted in the example given above is to throw the
dart several times (each throw is a trial) and count the number of times you hit
the bull's-eye (a success) and the number of times you miss (a failure). Then an
empirical value for the probability that you hit the bull's-eye with any one
throw is

$$\frac{\text{number of successes}}{\text{number of successes} + \text{number of failures}}$$

If the number of throws is small this does not give a particularly good estimate,
but for a large number of throws the result is more reliable.
When the probability of the occurrence of an event A cannot be worked out
exactly, an empirical value can be found by adopting the approach described
above, that is:

(a) making a *large number* of trials (i.e. set up an experiment in which the
    event may, or may not, occur and note the outcome),

(b) counting the number of times the event does occur, i.e. the number of
    successes,

(c) calculating the value of

$$\frac{\text{number of successes}}{\text{number of trials (i.e. successes} + \text{failures})} = \frac{r}{n}$$

The probability of the event A occuring is then defined as

$$P(A) = \lim_{n \to \infty} \left(\frac{r}{n} \right)$$

$n \to \infty$ means that the number of trials is large (but what should be taken as
'large' depends on the problem).

For some categories of events a theoretical probability can be found which may
or may not prove to be correct in practice. For example, if a coin is tossed and
we assume that it is *equally* likely to land head or tail up, the probability of a
head on any one toss is $\frac{1}{2}$. For a particular coin the empirical probability of a
head on any one toss can be found by experiment (i.e. tossing the coin several
times). If, by experiment, the coin is found to be equally likely to land head
up or tail up it is said to be *unbiased* or *fair*.

On the other hand if in 100 tosses, say, it is found that the coin lands head up 80 times it is reasonable to assume that the coin is *biased*, i.e. it is *not* equally likely to land head up or tail up.

Thus if a coin is known to be unbiased the probability of its landing head up on any one toss is $\frac{1}{2}$. Similarly if a die (numbered 1 to 6) is thrown, and it is known to be unbiased, the probability of throwing a six is $\frac{1}{6}$.

If a coin is known to be biased, so that it is twice as likely to land head up than tail up, then the number of *equally* likely results of tossing that coin are head up twice and tail up once.

So the probability of tossing a head with this coin is $\frac{2}{3}$.

More than One Event

We will now look at some problems involving the occurrence of two or more events. They can loosely be divided into two categories:

(a) 'either ... or' events such as the probability of scoring *either* 5 *or* 6 with one throw of a die,

(b) 'both ... and' events such as the probability of selecting *both* an orange *and* an apple from a bowl of mixed fruit.

Some events, such as the probability of obtaining at least one head when two coins are tossed, fall into both categories since this event involves *either* two heads *or* *both* one head *and* one tail.

At this stage however we will investigate the two categories separately.

MUTUALLY EXCLUSIVE EVENTS

Two events are mutually exclusive if the occurrence of either event excludes the possibility of the occurrence of the other event, i.e. *either* one event *or* the other event but *not both* can occur.

Consider, for example, choosing numbers at random from the set

$$\{3, 4, 5, 6, 7, 8, 9, 10, 11, 12\}$$

If A is the selection of a prime number,

           B is the selection of an odd number,

           C is the selection of an even number,

then A and C are mutually exclusive as none of the numbers in this set is both prime and even. But A and B are not mutually exclusive as some numbers are both prime and odd (viz. 3, 5, 7, 11).

The probability of either A or C can be found as follows: A can be selected in 4 ways out of 10 equally likely selections,

therefore $P(A) = \frac{4}{10}$.

C can be selected in 5 ways out of 10 equally likely selections,

therefore $P(C) = \frac{5}{10}$.

Out of the 10 equally likely choices the number of selections containing either A or C is $4 + 5$

$$\Rightarrow \qquad P(\text{either } A \text{ or } C) = \frac{4+5}{10} = \frac{4}{10} + \frac{5}{10} = P(A) + P(C)$$

'Either A or C' is denoted by $A \cup C$

So we can write the result above as $P(A \cup C) = \frac{9}{10}$.

In general, if E_1 and E_2 are mutually exclusive events and

$\begin{cases} E_1 \text{ occurs in } r \text{ out of } n \text{ equally likely occurrences} \\ E_2 \text{ occurs in } s \text{ out of } n \text{ equally likely occurrences} \end{cases}$

then $E_1 \cup E_2$ occurs in $r + s$ out of n equally likely occurrences.

Hence $P(E_1) = \dfrac{r}{n}, \quad P(E_2) = \dfrac{s}{n}, \quad P(E_1 \cup E_2) = \dfrac{r+s}{n}$

i.e.   if E_1 and E_2 are mutually exclusive events, then

$$P(E_1 \cup E_2) = P(E_1) + P(E_2)$$

EXAMPLES 18b

1) An unbiased die is in the form of an octahedron (eight faces), numbered 1, 2, 3, 3, 4, 5, 5, 6. When the die is thrown the score is taken from the face on which the die lands. What is the probability of obtaining a score of at least five from one throw?

A score of at least 5 means a score either of 5 or of 6 and these are mutually exclusive events.

A score of 5 can occur in two ways as the die is equally likely to land on any one of eight faces, two of which show 5.

i.e. $P(5) = \frac{2}{8}$

Similarly $P(6) = \frac{1}{8}$

Therefore $P(5 \cup 6) = \frac{2}{8} + \frac{1}{8} = \frac{3}{8}$

INDEPENDENT EVENTS

Two events are independent if the occurrence or non-occurrence of one event has no influence on the occurrence or non-occurrence of the other event,

For example if a coin is tossed and a die (numbered 1 to 6) is thrown, the way in which the coin lands in no way affects the possible ways in which the die can land (and vice versa) so throwing a head with the coin and a six with the die are independent events. If both are fair, then $P(\text{H}) = \frac{1}{2}$ and $P(6) = \frac{1}{6}$. Now for each of the two ways in which the coin can land there are six ways in which the die can land.

so
$$P(\text{H and } 6) = \frac{1 \times 1}{2 \times 6} = \frac{1}{2} \times \frac{1}{6} = P(\text{H}) \times P(6)$$

Now consider a bag which contains three white and two red balls. If a ball is removed at random, replaced, and then a second ball is removed, again we have two independent events.

If a red ball is taken out first (R_1) and a white ball is taken out second (W_2)

then
$$P(R_1) = \tfrac{2}{5} \quad \text{and} \quad P(W_2) = \tfrac{3}{5}$$

Also
$$P(R_1 \text{ followed by } W_2)$$

$$= \frac{2 \text{ ways for } R_1 \times 3 \text{ ways for } W_2}{5 \text{ possibilities for the first} \times 5 \text{ possibilities for the second}}$$

i.e.
$$P(R_1 \text{ followed by } W_2) = \frac{2 \times 3}{5 \times 5} = \frac{2}{5} \times \frac{3}{5} = P(R_1) \times P(W_2)$$

Denoting 'E_1 and E_2' by $E_1 \cap E_2$ we can say in general that

if E_1 and E_2 are independent events then
$$P(E_1 \cap E_2) = P(E_1) \times P(E_2)$$

EXAMPLES 18b (continued)

2) Three coins are tossed simultaneously. Two of the coins are fair and one is biased so that a head is twice as likely as a tail. Find the probability that all three coins turn up heads.

There are three coins involved so let them be a, b, c, and let H_a be the event of coin a landing head up and H_b and H_c the events that coins b and c land head up.

If a and b are the fair coins, and c is the biased coin

$$P(H_a) = \tfrac{1}{2}, \quad P(H_b) = \tfrac{1}{2}, \quad P(H_c) = \tfrac{2}{3}$$

The way in which any one of the coins lands has no influence on the way in which either of the others lands, i.e. H_a, H_b, H_c are independent events.

Therefore
$$P(H_a \cap H_b \cap H_c) = P(H_a) \times P(H_b) \times P(H_c)$$
$$= \tfrac{1}{2} \times \tfrac{1}{2} \times \tfrac{2}{3} = \tfrac{1}{6}$$

CONDITIONAL EVENTS

Consider a bag containing three white and two red balls. If the first ball removed is *not* replaced in the bag then the possibility space for the removal of a second ball has been reduced by one member, i.e. the events are no longer independent.

If the second ball taken out is red (R_2) then the number of ways in which this can occur depends on which ball was removed first.

If a white ball was removed, R_2 can happen in two ways out of four equally likely occurrences,

i.e. $P(R_2$ given that the first ball removed is white$) = \tfrac{2}{4}$

This is called the conditional probability that R_2 occurs when W_1 has occurred.

It is written as $P(R_2|W_1)$ and read as 'the probability that R_2 occurs given that W_1 has occurred' or more briefly as 'the probability of R_2 given W_1',

i.e. $P(R_2|W_1) = \tfrac{1}{2}$

If a red ball was removed first, R_2 can happen in only one out of four equally likely occurrences.

i.e. the conditional probability that R_2 occurs when R_1 has already occurred is $\tfrac{1}{4}$

i.e. $P(R_2|R_1) = \tfrac{1}{4}$

COMPOUND PROBABILITY

Now consider the probability of removing a white ball first (W_1) *and* then removing a red ball second (R_2).

There are 3×2 ways in which a white ball first and a red ball second can be removed.

There are 5×4 ways in which any one ball followed by another ball can be removed.

i.e.
$$P(W_1 \cap R_2) = \frac{3 \times 2}{5 \times 4} = \frac{3}{5} \times \frac{2}{4}$$

Now
$$P(W_1) = \tfrac{3}{5} \quad \text{and} \quad P(R_2|W_1) = \tfrac{2}{4}$$

i.e.
$$P(W_1 \cap R_2) = P(W_1) \times P(R_2|W_1)$$

This is called the *compound probability* of W_1 and R_2 occurring.

In general

> if E_1 and E_2 are two events, the compound probability of both E_1 and E_2 occurring is given by
>
> $$P(E_1 \cap E_2) = P(E_1) \times P(E_2|E_1)$$

Note that if E_1 and E_2 are independent events

then
$$P(E_1 \cap E_2) = P(E_1) \times P(E_2) \Rightarrow P(E_2|E_1) = P(E_2)$$

Summing up we have:

If A and B are two events

$$A \cap B \quad \text{means both } A \text{ and } B$$

$$A \cup B \quad \text{means either } A \text{ or } B$$

$$A \,|\, B \qquad \text{means } A \text{ given that } B \text{ has already occurred}$$

$P(A \cup B) = P(A) + P(B) \quad$ when A and B are mutually exclusive

$P(A \cap B) = P(A) \times P(B|A) \quad$ which reduces to

$$\left.\begin{aligned} P(A \cap B) &= P(A) \times P(B) \\ \Rightarrow \qquad P(B|A) &= P(B) \end{aligned}\right\} \quad \text{when } A \text{ and } B \text{ are independent}$$

EXAMPLES 18b (continued)

3) An unbiased die, marked 1 to 6, is rolled twice. Find the probability of:
(a) rolling two sixes,
(b) the second throw being a six, given that the first throw is a six,
(c) getting a score of ten from the two throws,
(d) throwing at least one six,
(e) throwing exactly one six.

If the die is unbiased it is equally likely to land on any face, so a score of 6 is just one of six equally likely scores, i.e. $P(6) = \tfrac{1}{6}$.
Also, each roll of the die is an independent event.

(a) As throwing six on the first roll (6_1) and throwing six on the second roll (6_2) of the die are independent events, the probability of throwing both a six at the first roll and a six at the second roll is

$$P(6_1) \times P(6_2) = \tfrac{1}{6} \times \tfrac{1}{6} = \tfrac{1}{36}$$

i.e.
$$P(6_1 \cap 6_2) = \tfrac{1}{36}$$

(b) The probability of the second throw being six, given that the first throw is six, is $P(6_2 \,|\, 6_1) = \tfrac{1}{6}$ $(= P(6_2))$.

(c) A score of ten is obtained either from two fives, or from six followed by four, or from four followed by six, and these are mutually exclusive events. Therefore

$$P(\text{score of ten}) = P(5_1 \cap 5_2) + P(6_1 \cap 4_2) + P(4_1 \cap 6_2)$$

$$\tfrac{1}{36} + \tfrac{1}{36} + \tfrac{1}{36} = \tfrac{1}{12}$$

(d) If A is the throwing of at least one six then $\bar{A}$ is not throwing a six (i.e. throwing 1, 2, 3, 4 or 5) on either of the throws.

The probability of not getting a six in one throw is $\tfrac{5}{6}$.

Hence
$$P(\bar{6}_1 \cap \bar{6}_2) = P(\bar{A}) = \tfrac{5}{6} \times \tfrac{5}{6} = \tfrac{25}{36}$$

Using
$$P(A) = 1 - P(\bar{A})$$

gives
$$P(A) = 1 - \tfrac{25}{36} = \tfrac{11}{36}$$

(e) If exactly one six is thrown then

    either   the first throw is six and the second throw is not six

    or   the first throw is not six and the second throw is six

and these are mutually exclusive events.

Now
$$P(6_1 \cap \bar{6}_2) \quad \text{is} \quad \tfrac{1}{6} \times \tfrac{5}{6} = \tfrac{5}{36}$$

and
$$P(\bar{6}_1 \cap 6_2) \quad \text{is} \quad \tfrac{5}{6} \times \tfrac{1}{6} = \tfrac{5}{36}$$

Therefore the probability of obtaining exactly one six is,

$$P(6_1 \cap \bar{6}_2) + P(\bar{6}_1 \cap 6_2) = \tfrac{5}{36} + \tfrac{5}{36} = \tfrac{5}{18}$$

4) A bag contains five red and six black counters. The counters are removed one at a time without replacement. If the counters are taken out at random find the probability that:

(a) the first two counters removed are red,

(b) the second counter removed is red.

Let R_1 and R_2 denote respectively the removal of a red counter first and a red counter second, and B_1 denote the removal of a black counter first.

(a) $P(R_1 \cap R_2) = P(R_1) \times P(R_2 | R_1)$

Now R_1 can happen in 5 out of 11 equally likely withdrawals,

i.e. $P(R_1) = \frac{5}{11}$

and $R_2 | R_1$ can happen in 4 out of 10 equally likely withdrawals,

i.e. $P(R_2 | R_1) = \frac{4}{10}$.

Therefore $P(R_1 \cap R_2) = \dfrac{5}{11} \times \dfrac{4}{10} = \dfrac{2}{11}$

(b) If the second counter is red, then either the first is red and the second is red, or the first is black and the second is red.

i.e.

$$P(R_2) = P[(R_1 \cap R_2) \cup (B_1 \cap R_2)]$$
$$= P(R_1)P(R_2 | R_1) + P(B_1)P(R_2 | B_1)$$
$$= \frac{2}{11} + \frac{6}{11} \times \frac{5}{10}$$
$$= \frac{5}{11}$$

Note that the result of (b) can be obtained by reasoning that any one of the eleven counters is equally likely to be the second counter removed, i.e. $P(R_2) = \frac{5}{11}$.

5) Three people A, B and C, gamble for a prize by rolling a die. The winner is the first person to roll a six. If the die is unbiased and they roll the die in the order A, then B, then C, find the probability that:

(a) A wins on the first throw, (b) C wins at his first attempt,

(c) B wins at his third attempt, (d) A wins.

Each throw of the die is an independent event and, on any one throw, the probability of a six is $\frac{1}{6}$ and the probability of not throwing a six is $\frac{5}{6}$.

(a) The probability that A wins on the first throw, $P(A_1)$, is $\frac{1}{6}$.

(b) A and B roll the die first so they must both fail at their first attempt ($\bar{A}_1$ and $\bar{B}_1$) if C is to win at his first attempt. These three events are independent, so the probability that C wins at his first attempt is

$$P(\bar{A}_1) \times P(\bar{B}_1) \times P(C_1) = \frac{5}{6} \times \frac{5}{6} \times \frac{1}{6} = \frac{25}{216}$$

(c) If B wins at his third attempt then A has had three failures, B two failures, and C two failures. Again these are independent events. Therefore the probability that B wins at his third attempt is

$$P(\bar{A}_1) \times P(\bar{B}_1) \times P(\bar{C}_1) \times P(\bar{A}_2) \times P(\bar{B}_2) \times P(\bar{C}_2) \times P(\bar{A}_3) \times P(B_3) = (\tfrac{5}{6})^7 \times \tfrac{1}{6}$$

(d) If A wins, then

either	A wins on his first throw
or	A wins on his second throw
or	A wins on his third throw
or	A wins on his fourth throw

and so on.

Now $P(A \text{ wins})$ on his

first throw is $\hspace{5em} P(A_1) = \tfrac{1}{6}$

second throw is $\hspace{2em} P(\bar{A}_1) \times P(\bar{B}_1) \times P(\bar{C}_1) \times P(A_2) = (\tfrac{5}{6})^3 \times \tfrac{1}{6}$

third throw is $\quad [P(\bar{A}_1 \cap \bar{B}_1 \cap \bar{C}_1) \times P(\bar{A}_2 \cap \bar{B}_2 \cap \bar{C}_2)] \times P(A_3) = (\tfrac{5}{6})^6 \times \tfrac{1}{6}$

fourth throw is $\hspace{8em} [(\tfrac{5}{6})^3]^3 \times P(A_4) = (\tfrac{5}{6})^9 \times \tfrac{1}{6}$

and so on.

These are mutually exclusive events, therefore

$$P(A) = \tfrac{1}{6} + \tfrac{1}{6}(\tfrac{5}{6})^3 + \tfrac{1}{6}(\tfrac{5}{6})^6 + \tfrac{1}{6}(\tfrac{5}{6})^9 + \ldots$$

This is an infinite GP with first term $\tfrac{1}{6}$ and common ratio $(\tfrac{5}{6})^3$ and so has

a sum to infinity of $\hspace{3em} \dfrac{\tfrac{1}{6}}{1-(\tfrac{5}{6})^3} = \dfrac{36}{91}$

Therefore the probability that A wins is $\tfrac{36}{91}$.

6) In a game of darts, the probability that a particular player aims at and hits the 'treble twenty' with one dart is 0.4. How many throws are necessary so that the probability of hitting the treble twenty at least once exceeds 0.9?

The probability of hitting the treble twenty, $P(A)$, is 0.4 on one throw, so the probability of not hitting the treble twenty, $P(\bar{A})$, is 0.6 on one throw, and $P(\bar{A})$ in two throws is $(0.6)^2$, etc.

The probability of hitting the treble twenty at least once in n throws

= $1 -$ (probability of not hitting the treble twenty on all n throws)

So in n throws $P(A$ at least once$) = 1 - (0.6)^n$.

For $P(A$ at least once$)$ to exceed 0.9 in n throws, we have

$$1 - (0.6)^n > 0.9$$

$\Rightarrow$ $$(0.6)^n < 0.1$$

$\Rightarrow$ $$n \log 0.6 < \log 0.1$$

$\Rightarrow$ $$n > \frac{\log 0.1}{\log 0.6} \qquad (\log 0.6 < 0)$$

$\Rightarrow$ $$n > 4.5$$

Therefore five throws are necessary.

7) In a group of students, 10% are left-handed, 8% are short-sighted and 2% are both left-handed and short-sighted.

(a) Given that a student is short-sighted, find the probability that he is left-handed.

(b) Find the probability that a left-handed student is also short-sighted.

If P(l.h.) represents the probability that a student is left-handed and if P(s.s.) represents the probability that a student is short-sighted then

$$P(\text{l.h.}) = 0.1, \quad P(\text{s.s.}) = 0.08 \quad \text{and} \quad P(\text{l.h.} \cap \text{s.s.}) = 0.02$$

a) Now $$P(\text{l.h.} \cap \text{s.s.}) = P(\text{l.h.}|\text{s.s.}) \times P(\text{s.s.})$$

$\Rightarrow$ $$0.02 = P(\text{l.h.}|\text{s.s.}) \times 0.08$$

$\Rightarrow$ $$P(\text{l.h.}|\text{s.s.}) = 0.25$$

b) $$P(\text{l.h.} \cap \text{s.s.}) = P(\text{s.s.}|\text{l.h.}) \times P(\text{l.h.})$$

$\Rightarrow$ $$0.02 = P(\text{s.s.}|\text{l.h.}) \times 0.1$$

$\Rightarrow$ $$P(\text{s.s.}|\text{l.h.}) = 0.2$$

EXERCISE 18b

1) Two unbiased coins are tossed. Find the probability of:
(a) two heads   (b) at least one head   (c) exactly one head.

2) Three unbiased coins are tossed. Find the probability of:
(a) three tails   (b) at least one tail.

3) The probability of an archer hitting the bull's-eye with any one shot is $\frac{1}{5}$.
Find the probability that:
(a) he hits the bull's-eye with his second shot,
(b) he hits the bull's-eye exactly once in three shots,
(c) he hits the bull's-eye at least once in four shots.

4) In a multiple choice examination each question has five possible answers,
only one of which is correct. If a candidate chooses his answers at random find
the probability that, in a test of ten such questions, he gets none right.

5) Two coins are tossed. One coin is fair and the other is biased so that throwing
a head is three times as likely as throwing a tail. Find the probability that:
(a) on one toss of both coins they both land head up,
(b) on two tosses of both coins, two tails are thrown both times,
(c) on two tosses, at least one head is thrown.

6) Two unbiased normal dice are thrown. On one throw find the probability of:
(a) two 1's   (b) a score of 3   (c) a score of at least 4.

7) An unbiased die in the shape of a tetrahedron has its faces numbered
1, 2, 3, 4.
The score is taken from the face on which it lands. Find the probability that:
(a) on one throw 4 is scored,
(b) on two throws a total of 2 is scored,
(c) on three throws a total of at least 4 is scored.

8) Two people, A and B, play a game by tossing a fair coin, and the first to
toss a head wins. If A tosses first find the probability that:
(a) A wins on his first toss,
(b) B wins on his first toss,
(c) A wins on his second toss.

9) Two people, A and B, play a game by rolling two fair dice; the first to roll
a double six wins. If A goes first, find the probability that:
(a) B wins on his first throw,
(b) A wins on his second throw.

10) Two people, A and B, play a game by tossing a fair coin and the first to
toss a head wins. If A goes first find the probability that A wins.

11) Three people, A, B and C play a game by rolling a fair die and the first
to roll a six wins. If they play in the order A then B then C, find the
probability that B wins.

12) Two people, A and B, play a game by drawing a card from a pack of fifty-two playing cards. The first to draw an ace wins. The cards drawn are not put back in the pack and they play in the order A, B. Find the probability that:
(a) A wins on his first draw,
(b) A wins on his second draw,
(c) A wins on his third draw.

13) A boy at a rifle range has a probability of $\frac{2}{5}$ of hitting a target with any one shot. Find the probability that he first hits a target with his third shot. How many shots are necessary for the probability of his hitting at least one target to be greater than $\frac{4}{5}$?

14) A box of screws contains 5% defective screws. If a screw is taken at random from the box, what is the probability that it is defective? How many times does this have to be repeated before the probability of removing at least one defective screw is 0.5?

15) In a card game for four players, a pack of fifty-two cards is dealt round so that each player receives thirteen cards. A hand that contains no card greater than nine is called a yarborough. How many deals are necessary for the probability of at least one hand being a yarborough to be greater than $\frac{1}{2}$? (Ace ranks high.)

16) A shelf has fifteen paperbacked and twelve hardbacked books on it. A book is taken at random and not replaced. A second and a third book are similarly removed. Find the probabiliy that:
(a) the first three books removed are paperbacks,
(b) the third book removed is a hardback.

17) Three balls are selected at random in order from a box containing 2 red, 3 yellow and 4 black balls. Find the probability that the third ball is yellow, given that the first is red and the second is black if:
(a) the balls are not put back in the box after selection,
(b) the balls are replaced in the box after each selection.

TREE DIAGRAMS

The number of ways in which an event A occurs and the number of occurrences of equally likely events is not always obvious from the statement of a problem. This is particularly true of compound events which can involve three or more separate events.

Consider, for example, tossing three coins. There are three ways in which the coins can land with 2 heads and a tail showing, because if the coins are numbered 1, 2, 3 for identification, they can land

$$H_1 H_2 T_3 \quad \text{or} \quad H_1 T_2 H_3 \quad \text{or} \quad T_1 H_2 H_3$$

Using the methods already developed, we have

$P(2H \text{ and } T)$ is given by

$$P[\text{either} (H_1 \cap H_2 \cap T_3) \quad \text{or} \quad (H_1 \cap T_2 \cap H_3) \quad \text{or} \quad (T_1 \cap H_2 \cap H_3)]$$

$$= P(H_1) \times P(H_2) \times P(T_3) + P(H_1) \times P(T_2) \times P(H_3) + P(T_1) \times P(H_2) \times P(H_3)$$

An alternative approach to problems such as this is to construct a diagram which shows all the likely outcomes. The probability of a particular outcome can then be found from the basic definition.

Consider again tossing three coins, numbered 1, 2 and 3. The likely outcomes of tossing coin 1 are a head or a tail. Starting at the left-hand side of the page we draw two branches, each branch being one of the possible events.

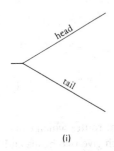

(i)

When coin 2 is tossed there are two possible events (head or tail) either of which may follow either of the possible outcomes of the toss of coin 1. To illustrate this we draw two branches at the end of each of the first two branches in diagram (i).

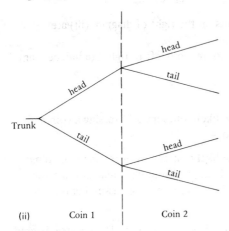

(ii)   Coin 1   Coin 2

Following the branches from the left (trunk) of the diagram through to the right we see that the likely events when tossing two coins are H_1H_2 or H_1T_2 or T_1H_2 or T_1T_2.

Any of these events is followed by two further likely occurrences when coin 3 is tossed. Branching again gives diagram (iii).

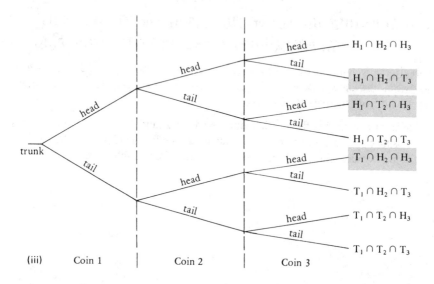

Starting from the trunk we see that there are eight different routes which can be followed, i.e. there are eight likely events, three of which give two heads and a tail.

If the coins are all *unbiased* then these eight events are *equally* likely.

Thus $$P(2\text{H and T}) = \frac{3 \text{ events}}{8 \text{ equally likely events}} = \frac{3}{8}$$

Note that (a) the eight compound events on the right of diagram (iii) are mutually exclusive,
(b) the events along any one route from left to right are independent.

EXERCISE 18c

1) Draw a tree diagram to represent the likely outcomes of tossing a coin and rolling a tetrahedral die numbered 1 to 4.

2) Draw a tree diagram to represent the likely outcomes of tossing two coins and rolling a tetrahedral die numbered 1 to 4. From your diagram find the probability of obtaining a head and a tail and a score of 4, assuming that the coins and the die are unbiased.

3) A die in the form of a cube is numbered 1, 1, 2, 2, 3, 4. Draw a tree diagram to illustrate the likely outcomes of rolling this die and tossing a coin. If both are unbiased, what is the probability of rolling a 2 on the die and tossing a head on the coin?

Tree diagrams can be used to find probabilities when the possible outcomes of an experiment are not equally likely.

Consider, for example, tossing two coins, one of which is fair and one of which is biased so that a tail is twice as likely as a head.

When the fair coin is tossed there are two *equally* likely events, viz. a head or a tail.

When the biased coin is tossed there are two distinct events but they occur in the proportion of one head to two tails, so there are three equally likely events, i.e. 1 head and 2 tails.

Drawing a tree diagram and starting with the fair coin we have

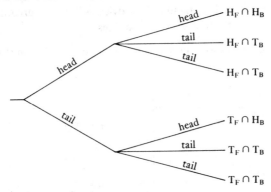

Hence there are six equally likely events

and
$$P(2 \text{ heads}) = \tfrac{1}{6}$$
$$P(\text{head and tail}) = \tfrac{3}{6} = \tfrac{1}{2}$$
$$P(2 \text{ tails}) = \tfrac{2}{6} = \tfrac{1}{3}$$

As consecutive branches represent independent events we can simplify this diagram by drawing branches for each distinct event (i.e. not for each equally likely event) and writing the probability of that event on the branch

i.e.

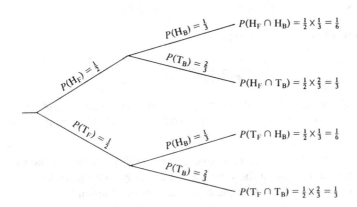

As the events at the right hand end of the figure are mutually exclusive we have

$$P(\text{head and tail}) = \tfrac{1}{3} + \tfrac{1}{6} = \tfrac{1}{2}$$

In most problems we are concerned only with the probability of one event, A, occurring. Tree diagrams may also be used to simplify the work in such problems by showing the probabilities of A and of $\bar{A}$. This is illustrated in the following examples.

EXAMPLES 18d

1) Three dice, each numbered 1 to 6 are rolled. One die is fair and the others are biased so that for each of them a six is twice as likely as any other score. Find the probability of rolling exactly two sixes.

Using a tree diagram to show the probabilities of 6 and $\bar{6}$ and starting with the fair die we have

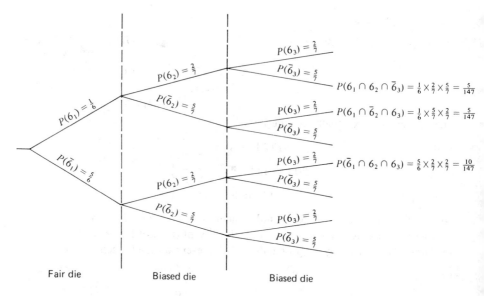

Therefore $P(\text{exactly two sixes})$ is

$$\frac{5}{147} + \frac{5}{147} + \frac{10}{147} = \frac{20}{147}$$

2) One of the dice described in Example 1 is chosen at random and on two throws it shows a six on each occasion. What is the probability that a biased die has been chosen?

There are two independent events to consider in this problem, i.e. choosing a die and rolling it twice. In the second event our only concern is whether a six shows up on both rolls or whether a six does not show up on both rolls.

Drawing a tree diagram and starting with a choice of die gives

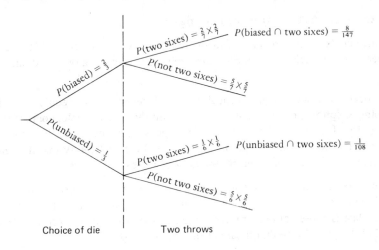

P(biased) = $\frac{2}{3}$

P(two sixes) = $\frac{2}{7} \times \frac{2}{7}$ P(biased ∩ two sixes) = $\frac{8}{147}$

P(not two sixes) = $\frac{5}{7} \times \frac{5}{7}$

P(unbiased) = $\frac{1}{3}$

P(two sixes) = $\frac{1}{6} \times \frac{1}{6}$ P(unbiased ∩ two sixes) = $\frac{1}{108}$

P(not two sixes) = $\frac{5}{6} \times \frac{5}{6}$

Choice of die   Two throws

If A is the rolling of two sixes and B is the selection of a biased die, the probability that the die is biased, given that two sixes are rolled, is $P(B|A)$. Using $P(A \cap B) = P(A)P(B|A)$ and the tree diagram above, we see that the probability of getting two sixes on any of the three dice is

$$\frac{8}{147} + \frac{1}{108} = \frac{337}{5292} = P(A)$$

But the probability of choosing a biased die and getting two sixes is

$$\frac{8}{147} = \frac{288}{5292} = P(A \cap B)$$

So the probability that the die is biased is $\frac{288}{337} = 0.85$ to 2 d.p.

Note that, after some practice, the reader may find that it is unnecessary to draw the complete tree diagram, indicating only those routes that are relevant to the problem.

EXERCISE 18d

Use a tree diagram to help in the solution of the following problems.

1) A tetrahedral die, marked 1, 2, 3, 4 is rolled twice. If the die is unbiased find the probability of getting a total score of three.

2) Two coins and a tetrahedral die numbered 1 to 4 are tossed. If all are unbiased, find the probability that a head, a tail and a 1 are tossed.

3) In a multiple choice test of three questions there are five alternative answers given to the first two questions and four alternative answers given to the last

question. If a candidate guesses answers at random, what is the probability that he will get:

(a) exactly one right   (b) at least one right?

4) Three coins are tossed. Two of them are fair and one is biased so that a head is three times as likely as a tail. Find the probability of getting two heads and a tail.

5) A local telephone call goes through three independent sets of equipment, the outgoing telephone, the automatic exchange and the receiving telephone. If the probability of failure on the outgoing telephone is 0.05, on the exchange is 0.01 and on the receiving telephone is 0.04, find the probability that if a call is not connected it is at least partly the fault of the exchange.

6) One box of chocolates contains five hard centres and three soft centres. Another box of chocolates contains eight hard centres and seven soft centres. A chocolate is chosen at random from either of the boxes. If it is a soft centred one find the probability that it came from the first box.

POSSIBILITY SPACE AND SAMPLE POINTS

The use of a tree diagram is helpful for dealing with a problem when the number of independent events is small and the outcome under consideration of each independent event is also small, otherwise we end up with a tree with so many branches that it is tedious to draw and difficult to use.

For example, if two dice, numbered 1 to 6, are thrown and *each* likely outcome has to be considered, the tree would have thirty six branches at the end. An alternative is to tabulate all the *equally* likely outcomes. Thus, if the dice are unbiased, we can list the equally likely outcomes as shown, where the left hand figure in each bracket is the score on one die and the right hand figure is the score on the other die.

(1, 1)	(2, 1)	(3, 1)	(4, 1)	(5, 1)	(6, 1)
(1, 2)	(2, 2)	(3, 2)	(4, 2)	(5, 2)	(6, 2)
(1, 3)	(2, 3)	(3, 3)	(4, 3)	(5, 3)	(6, 3)
(1, 4)	(2, 4)	(3, 4)	(4, 4)	(5, 4)	(6, 4)
(1, 5)	(2, 5)	(3, 5)	(4, 5)	(5, 5)	(6, 5)
(1, 6)	(2, 6)	(3, 6)	(4, 6)	(5, 6)	(6, 6)

This complete set of all the *equally likely* outcomes is called the *possibility space*. Each of the *equally likely* outcomes is called a *sample point*. (In this example there are thirty six sample points in the possibility space.)

From this possibility space we can find, for example, the probability of a score of at least 7.

The number of sample points for which the score is at least 7 (in the shaded area) is twenty one.

Hence
$$P(\text{at least } 7) = \tfrac{21}{36} = \tfrac{7}{12}$$

(The use of any other method would require consideration of the mutually exclusive events: either a score of 7 or of 8 or of 9 ... or of 12.)

EXAMPLES 18e

1) Two unbiased tetrahedral dice numbered 1 to 4 are thrown. Set up the possibility space and use it to find:
(a) the probability that at least one 4 is thrown,
(b) a total score of 5 is thrown.

In each sample point the left hand number is the score on one of the dice and the right hand number is the score on the other die.
Hence the possibility space is

$$
\begin{array}{llll}
(1,1) & (1,2) & (1,3) & (1,4) \quad B \\
(2,1) & (2,2) & (2,3) & (2,4) \quad A \\
(3,1) & (3,2) & (3,3) & (3,4) \\
(4,1) & (4,2) & (4,3) & (4,4)
\end{array}
$$

and we see that there are sixteen sample points.

(a) The subset of points with at least one 4, $\{A\}$, contains 7 points.
Hence $P(A) = \tfrac{7}{16}$.
(b) The subset of points giving a total score of 5, $\{B\}$, contains 4 points.
Hence $P(B) = \tfrac{4}{16} = \tfrac{1}{4}$.

'Either ... Or' Situations Involving Events that are Not Mutually Exclusive

Using the example above, let us now consider the probability that *either* at least one 4 is thrown *or* a total score of 5 is thrown, i.e. $P(A \cup B)$.
From the possibility space we see that

the subset of sample points in $\{A\}$ and the subset of sample points in $\{B\}$

are not mutually exclusive, because the sample points $(4,1)$ and $(1,4)$ are in both subsets.

The situation becomes clearer if we rearrange the sample points in the possibility space by placing the points in $\{A\}$ in one circle and the points in $\{B\}$ in a second overlapping circle so that the points in both $\{A\}$ and $\{B\}$, i.e. in $\{A \cap B\}$ are in the section common to both circles and the remaining points are outside both circles.

Such a diagram is called a *Venn Diagram.*

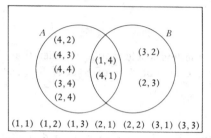

From this diagram we see that

the number of points in   either $\{A\}$ or $\{B\}$,   i.e. in $\{A \cup B\}$,
is *not* equal to

(the number of points in $\{A\}$) + (the number of points in $\{B\}$)

because this includes the points $(1, 4), (4, 1)$ twice.

Now the points $(1, 4)$ and $(4, 1)$ are in *both* $\{A\}$ *and* $\{B\}$, i.e. in $\{A \cap B\}$.

Hence,

(points in $\{A \cup B\}$) = (points in $\{A\}$) + (points in $\{B\}$) − (points in $\{A \cap B\}$)

$$= 7 + 4 - 2$$

As there are 16 sample points in total, we have

$$P(A \cup B) = \frac{7 + 4 - 2}{16}$$

$$= \frac{7}{16} + \frac{4}{16} - \frac{2}{16}$$

$$= P(A) + P(B) - P(A \cap B)$$

We can see that this is a general result by considering a possibility space containing n points in which,

the subset of possibilities for an event A contains r points,
the subset of possibilities for an event B contains s points
and t points are common to $\{A\}$ and $\{B\}$.

The Venn diagram illustrating this information is given below

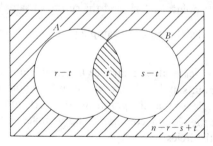

The circle A contains r sample points $\Rightarrow$ $P(A) = \dfrac{r}{n}$

The circle B contains s sample points $\Rightarrow$ $P(B) = \dfrac{s}{n}$

The intersection of the circles contains t points $\Rightarrow$ $P(A \cap B) = \dfrac{t}{n}$

Thus the number of points in   either $\{A\}$ or $\{B\}$,   i.e. in $\{A \cup B)\}$, is $r + s - t$

$\Rightarrow$ $$P(A \cup B) = \frac{r + s - t}{n}$$

Therefore $$P(A \cup B) = \frac{r}{n} + \frac{s}{n} - \frac{t}{n}$$

i.e. $$\boxed{P(A \cup B) = P(A) + P(B) - P(A \cap B)}$$

Note that the left hand lune (the unshaded part) contains $r - t$ points which are in $\{A\}$ but not in $\{B\}$, i.e. this lune contains the points in $\{A \cap \bar{B}\}$. Similarly the points in the right hand lune are those in $\{B\}$ but not in $\{A\}$, i.e. in $\{B \cap \bar{A}\}$.

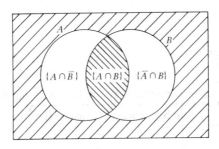

Note that, if A and B are mutually exclusive, $\{A \cap B\}$ contains no points, i.e.

$\Rightarrow$ $$P(A \cup B) = P(A) + P(B)$$

2) If A and B are two events such that $P(A) = \frac{1}{3}$, $P(B) = \frac{2}{9}$, $P(A \mid B) = \frac{1}{2}$. Find (a) $P(A \cap B)$ (b) $P(A \cup B)$ (c) $P(B \mid \bar{A})$.

Let   the number of points in the possibility space be n
            the number of points in $\{A\}$ be r
            the number of points in $\{B\}$ be s
and   the number of points in $\{A \cap B\}$ be t

Drawing a Venn diagram we have

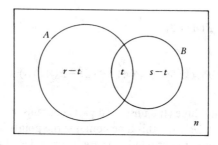

From the diagram

$$P(A) = \frac{r}{n} \qquad \text{i.e.} \quad \frac{r}{n} = \frac{1}{3} \qquad\qquad [1]$$

$$P(B) = \frac{s}{n} \qquad \text{i.e.} \quad \frac{s}{n} = \frac{2}{9} \qquad\qquad [2]$$

and $P(A \mid B) = \dfrac{\text{number of ways } A \text{ occurs, given that } B \text{ has occurred}}{\text{number of ways } B \text{ occurs (i.e. the equally likely events)}}$

$$= \frac{t}{s} \qquad \text{i.e.} \quad \frac{t}{s} = \frac{1}{2} \qquad\qquad [3]$$

(a) Now $P(A \cap B) = \dfrac{t}{n}$

$[3] \div [2] \quad \Rightarrow \qquad \dfrac{t}{n} = \dfrac{1}{9} \qquad\qquad [4]$

i.e. $P(A \cap B) = \dfrac{1}{9}$

(b) Using $$P(A \cup B) = P(A) + P(B) - P(A \cap B)$$

we have $$P(A \cup B) = \frac{1}{3} + \frac{2}{9} - \frac{1}{9}$$

$$= \frac{4}{9}$$

(c) $$P(B|\bar{A}) = \frac{\text{number of ways in which } B, \text{ and 'not } A\text{', occurs}}{\text{number of ways in which 'not } A\text{' occurs}}$$

$$= \frac{s - t}{n - r}$$

from [1], [2] and [4] we have

$$r = \tfrac{1}{3}n$$
$$s = \tfrac{2}{9}n$$
$$t = \tfrac{1}{9}n$$

Therefore $$\frac{s - t}{n - r} = \frac{\tfrac{2}{9}n - \tfrac{1}{9}n}{n - \tfrac{1}{3}n} = \tfrac{1}{9} \div \tfrac{2}{3} = \tfrac{1}{6}$$

i.e. $$P(B|\bar{A}) = \tfrac{1}{6}.$$

Note that:

(i) if two events E_1 and E_2 are independent then $P(E_1) = P(E_1|E_2)$.

In this problem $P(A) \neq P(A|B)$ so A and B are not independent.

(ii) if two events E_1 and E_2 are mutually exclusive then $P(E_1 \cap E_2) = 0$.

In this problem $P(A \cap B) \neq 0$ so A and B are not mutually exclusive.

EXERCISE 18e

1) Set up a possibility space for the toss of two fair coins and a fair tetrahedral die numbered 1 to 4. From your possibility space find the probability of obtaining:
(a) a head, a tail and a four.
(b) at least one head and a four.

2) Two cubical dice are tossed. Both dice are unbiased and one is numbered 1 to 6, the other is numbered 1, 2, 2, 3, 3, 4. Set up the possibility space and use it to find the probability of obtaining:
(a) a score of 5,
(b) a score of at least 5,
(c) a three on either of the two dice, but not on both.

3) Two tetrahedral dice, both numbered 1 to 4 are tossed. If one die is fair and the other is biased so that a four is twice as likely as any other score, set up the possibility space and use it to find the probability that:
(a) at least one four is thrown,
(b) a total score of four is obtained,
(c) either at least one four is thrown or at least one three is thrown.

4) A football match may be either won, drawn or lost by the home team, so there are three ways of forecasting the result of any one match, one correct and two incorrect. If random forecasts are made of the results of five matches, what is the probability of getting at least three correct results?

5) In a group of twenty students all of whom are studying Physics or Mathematics or both, ten are studying Physics and fifteen are studying Mathematics. Find the probability that a student chosen at random is:
(a) studying Physics,
(b) studying Physics and Mathematics,
(c) studying Physics but not Mathematics.
Illustrate your results on a Venn diagram.

6) Three unbiased dice, each numbered 1, 1, 2, 2, 3, 3 are tossed. Find the probability of throwing either at least one 2 or at least one 3.

7) Two normal fair dice, numbered 1 to 6, are tossed simultaneously. What is the probability of obtaining a total score greater than 7 if at least one of the dice scores 5.

8) A and B are two events such that $P(A) = \frac{1}{4}$ and $P(B) = \frac{1}{3}$ and $P(A \cup B) = \frac{1}{2}$. Find $P(A \cap B)$.

9) A and B are two events such that $P(A) = \frac{2}{7}$ and $P(A \cap B) = \frac{1}{5}$. If A and B are independent find $P(B)$ and $P(A \cup B)$.

10) A and B are two events such that $P(A) = \frac{2}{5}$, $P(A|B) = \frac{1}{3}$, $P(B|A) = \frac{1}{2}$.
Find $P(A \cup B)$ and state, with reasons, whether A and B are mutually exclusive.

EXPECTATION

The word 'expectation' or 'expected' is used to mean the most likely outcome of an experiment or the 'average' result in a series of experiments. The precise meaning of 'expectation' depends on the way it is used. The following examples illustrate its use in different situations.

EXAMPLES 18f

1) Two unbiased dice, numbered 1 to 6, are tossed one hundred and forty four times. Find the number of times that double 6 is expected.

$P(\text{double } 6) = \frac{1}{36}$,
i.e. as the dice are unbiased, a double 6 can occur in one way out of the thirty six equally likely ways in which the dice may land,
i.e. in thirty six throws we would expect one double 6 so in one hundred and forty four throws we would expect double 6 to appear on $144 \times \frac{1}{36}$ occasions,
i.e. the *expected* number of times that double 6 occurs, in one hundred and forty four throws, is four.

In general, if the probability of an event A is $P(A)$, then in n trials the expected number of times that A occurs is $nP(A)$.

2) The probability that it will snow on any one day in December is 0.05. On how many days is it expected to snow in December?

There are thirty one days in December.
So the number of days on which snow is expected is $31 \times 0.05 = 1.55$,
i.e. it is expected to snow on one or two days in December.

3) Three coins are tossed thirty times. Find the expected number of heads if two of the coins are fair and one is biased so that a tail is twice as likely as a head.

Tossing the three coins thirty times is equivalent to

$\Big\{$ tossing one fair coin sixty times
tossing the biased coin thirty times

$\Rightarrow$ $\Big\{$ the expected number of heads $= \frac{1}{2}(60) = 30$
the expected number of heads $= \frac{1}{3}(30) = 10$

Hence the total number of heads expected is 40.

4) Four counters are drawn at random from a bag containing five red and two black counters. Find the expected number of red counters.

In this context 'expected' means the average number of red counters expected to be drawn in any one trial.
If we find the total number of red counters that are likely in n trials (i.e. in n repeated drawings of four counters from the seven in the bag), then the average number per trial can be found.
The four counters can be

either   (2R and 2B) or (3R and 1B) or (4R)

$$P(2R \cap 2B) = \frac{^5C_2 \times 1}{^7C_4} = \frac{2}{7}$$

$$P(3R \cap 1B) = \frac{{}^5C_3 \times {}^2C_1}{{}^7C_4} = \frac{4}{7}$$

$$P(4R) = \frac{{}^5C_4}{{}^7C_4} = \frac{1}{7}$$

Therefore in n trials we would expect

two red counters to appear $\frac{2}{7} \times n$ times $\Rightarrow \frac{4n}{7}$ red counters

three red counters to appear $\frac{4}{7} \times n$ times $\Rightarrow \frac{12n}{7}$ red counters

four red counters to appear $\frac{1}{7} \times n$ times $\Rightarrow \frac{4n}{7}$ red counters

so we would expect a total of $(\frac{4}{7}n + \frac{12}{7}n + \frac{4}{7}n)$ red counters in n trials,

i.e. an average of $\frac{20}{7}$ counters per trial.

Expected Gain or Loss

We often encounter a situation in which the outcome involves either a gain or loss of money. If such a situation is repeated many times the average (expected) gain or loss can be found using the following definition.

> If there is a probability p of winning a sum of money £L the expected gain is £Lp.

EXAMPLES 18f (continued)

5) Two people, A and B, roll an unbiased die. The first to toss a 6 wins £10. Find A's expected winnings, if he goes first.

The probability that A wins, $P(A \text{ wins})$, is

either $P(A \text{ wins on his first throw}) = P(A_1)$

$$= \tfrac{1}{6}$$

or $P(A \text{ wins on his second throw}) = P(\bar{A}_1 \text{ and } \bar{B}_1 \text{ and } A_2)$

$$= (\tfrac{5}{6})^2 \times \tfrac{1}{6}$$

or $P(A \text{ wins on his third throw}) = P(\bar{A}_1 \cap \bar{B}_1 \cap \bar{A}_2 \cap \bar{B}_2 \cap A_3)$

$$= (\tfrac{5}{6})^4 \times \tfrac{1}{6}$$

and so on.

i.e. $P(A \text{ wins}) = \tfrac{1}{6} + (\tfrac{5}{6})^2(\tfrac{1}{6}) + (\tfrac{5}{6})^4(\tfrac{1}{6}) + \ldots$

This is a GP with first term $\frac{1}{6}$ and common ratio $(\frac{5}{6})^2$
and hence with a sum to infinity of

$$\frac{\frac{1}{6}}{1-(\frac{5}{6})^2} = \frac{6}{11}$$

Hence $P(A \text{ wins}) = \frac{6}{11}$

So A's expected winnings are $£10 \times \frac{6}{11} = £5.45$

This result is interpreted as meaning that if A and B played several times, with A going first each time, then on average A would expect to win £5.45 per game.

6) The probability of a candidate passing an examination at any one attempt is $\frac{3}{5}$. He carries on entering until he passes and each entry costs him £1. Find the expected cost of his passing the examination.

The probability of passing at the first attempt is $\frac{3}{5}$ and the cost is £1.

The probability of failing at the first attempt but passing at the second attempt is $(\frac{2}{5})(\frac{3}{5})$ and the cost of passing at the second attempt is £2.

The probability of failing at the first two attempts but passing at the third attempt is $(\frac{2}{5})^2(\frac{3}{5})$ and the cost is £3,

and so on.

Therefore the expected cost is

$$£[\tfrac{3}{5}(1) + \tfrac{3}{5}(\tfrac{2}{5})(2) + \tfrac{3}{5}(\tfrac{2}{5})^2(3) + \tfrac{3}{5}(\tfrac{2}{5})^3(4) + \cdots]$$

$$= £\tfrac{3}{5}[1 + 2(\tfrac{2}{5}) + 3(\tfrac{2}{5})^2 + 4(\tfrac{2}{5})^3 + \cdots]$$

Now $1 + 2x + 3x^2 + 4x^3 + \ldots = \dfrac{d}{dx}(x + x^2 + x^3 + x^4 + \ldots$

$$= \frac{d}{dx}[(1-x)^{-1} - 1] \qquad\qquad \text{if } |x| < 1$$

$$= \frac{1}{(1-x)^2} \qquad\qquad \text{if } |x| < 1$$

Therefore, replacing x by $\frac{2}{5}$,

$$1 + 2(\tfrac{2}{5}) + 3(\tfrac{2}{5})^2 + 4(\tfrac{2}{5})^3 + \ldots = \frac{1}{(1-\tfrac{2}{5})^2} = \tfrac{25}{9}$$

Hence the expected cost of passing the examination is

$$£\tfrac{3}{5} \times \tfrac{25}{9} = £\tfrac{5}{3} = £1.67$$

This result must be interpreted as being the cost per candidate averaged out for several candidates with the same probability $(\frac{3}{5})$ of passing at any one attempt. Obviously it will cost any one candidate an integral multiple of £1.

7) Three people A, B and C play a game of chance where the probability of A's winning is $\frac{3}{10}$. The winner gets a prize of £100. If a fourth person D wishes to buy A's place in the game, what would be a fair price for D to pay?

As the probability of A's winning is $\frac{3}{10}$, his expected gain is $\frac{3}{10} \times £100 = £30$. Therefore £30 is a fair price to pay for A's place in the game.

EXERCISE 18f

In this exercise you may assume, where necessary, that

$$1 + x + x^2 + x^3 + \ldots = (1-x)^{-1}$$

and

$$1 + 2x + 3x^2 + 4x^3 + \ldots = (1-x)^{-2}$$

1) Two unbiased dice, each numbered 1 to 6, are tossed. If this is repeated fifty times what is the expected number of times that a score of 11 will occur?

2) At a certain seaside resort the probability of rain on any one day in July is 0.02. If I take fourteen days holiday at that resort in July, on how many days should I expect it to rain?

3) In a class of thirty pupils, the probability that any one pupil is absent on any one day is 0.04. How many absence marks are expected in the class register for one week (five days)?

4) Two coins are tossed where one is fair and the other is biased so that a head is three times as likely as a tail. Find the probability that:
(a) two heads are tossed,
(b) one head and a tail are tossed,
In twenty such tosses, find the expected number of heads.

5) A pack of fifty-two playing cards is dealt round to four people so that each player gets thirteen cards. If a yarborough is a hand containing no card greater than a 9 (ace ranks high), find the expected number of yarboroughs in one thousand deals.

6) A 'lucky dip' box contains six tokens which can be exchanged for a prize. Four of the tokens are for books and two of the tokens are for records. A person selects three tokens at random, collects his prizes and then replaces the tokens in the box. If twenty people each have such a 'dip' in the box, what is the expected number of records to be given as prizes?

7) A team of four people is chosen at random from four men and three women. Find the expected number of women in the team.

8) Five books are chosen at random from a shelf of five paperbacks and four hardbacks. Find the expected number of hardbacks chosen.

9) Three people A, B, C gamble for a prize of £100 by rolling an unbiased die, numbered 1 to 6, in the order A, then B, then C and so on. The first

to roll a 6 wins the prize. If B wishes to sell his chance of winning to another person, what is a fair price to ask.

10) The probability of a person scoring at least 100 at a pintable is $\frac{1}{5}$. If it costs him 5 p for each attempt to score at least 100, and he carries on until he does score at least 100, how much is it expected to cost him?

11) At a shooting gallery, the probability that a boy hits a target with any one shot is $\frac{3}{5}$. If it costs him 5 p per shot, and he wins 50 p each time he hits a target, find his expected gain if he shoots until he does hit a target.

12) There is a probability of $\frac{1}{21}$ of getting the jackpot on a fruit machine. The jackpot pays out £1 and each go costs 10 p. If the machine is played until the jackpot pays out, what is the expected loss?

SUMMARY

For any event A

$$P(A) + P(\overline{A}) = 1$$

For any two events A, B

$$P(A \cap B) = P(A) \times P(B|A)$$
$$P(A \cup B) = P(A) + P(B) - P(A \cap B)$$

If A and B are independent (i.e. the occurrence of A has no influence on the likely occurrence of B and vice-versa) then

$$P(B|A) = P(B) \quad \Rightarrow \quad P(A \cap B) = P(A) \times P(B)$$

If A and B are mutually exclusive (i.e. A and B cannot both occur) then

$$P(A \cap B) = 0 \quad \Rightarrow \quad P(A \cup B) = P(A) + P(B)$$

MULTIPLE CHOICE EXERCISE 18

(Instructions for answering these questions are given on page x.)

TYPE I

1) A couple decide to have three children. Assuming that the birth of a boy or girl is equally likely, the probability that they have two girls and then a boy is:
(a) $\frac{3}{8}$　(b) $\frac{1}{2}$　(c) $\frac{1}{8}$　(d) $\frac{1}{6}$　(e) $\frac{1}{3}$.

2) A possibility space for the equally likely results of rolling one fair die and one biased die with a 6 twice as likely as any other score, contains the following number of sample points:
(a) 36　(b) 30　(c) 6　(d) 42　(e) 18.

3) Two books are chosen from three paperbacks and three hardbacks. The number of ways in which this can be done, given that at least one is a paperback, is:

(a) 24   (b) 15   (c) 9   (d) 12   (e) 3.

4) If A and B are events such that $P(A) = \frac{1}{2}$, $P(B) = \frac{1}{2}$, $P(A \cap B) = \frac{1}{4}$, then $P(A \cup B) =$

(a) 1   (b) $\frac{3}{4}$ (c) $\frac{1}{4}$ (d) $\frac{1}{16}$ (e) none of these.

5) A biased coin, such that a tail is twice as likely as a head, is tossed thirty times. The expected number of heads is:

(a) 15   (b) 20   (c) 10   (d) 1   (e) 30.

6) A and B are independent events and $P(A) = \frac{1}{4}$, $P(B) = \frac{1}{4}$. $P(\bar{A} \cap \bar{B})$ is:

(a) $\frac{3}{4}$ (b) $\frac{1}{16}$ (c) $\frac{1}{4}$ (d) $\frac{1}{2}$ (e) $\frac{9}{16}$

7) The number of ways in which two letters can be selected from the letters of the word POSSIBLE is:

(a) $^7C_2 + 1$ (b) $^8C_2$ (c) $^8P_2$ (d) $^7C_2$ (e) $^8P_2 + 1$.

8) The number of permutations of the letters of POSSIBILITY is:

(a) $^{11}P_{11}$ (b) $\dfrac{11!}{3! \, 2!}$ (c) $(^{11}P_3)(^{11}P_2)$ (d) $^{11}P_8$ (e) $\dfrac{11!}{5!}$

9) The shaded area in the Venn diagram represents:

(a) A (b) $\bar{B}$ (c) $A \cap \bar{B}$

(d) $A \cup \bar{B}$ (e) $A \mid B$.

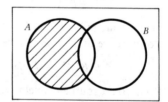

10) Six people are seated at a circular table. The number of ways in which this can be done is:

(a) 6!   (b) 5!   (c) $\dfrac{6!}{2}$ (d) $\dfrac{5!}{2}$ (e) $^6P_5$.

TYPE II

11) A and B are two independent events. $P(A) = 0.3$ and $P(B) = 0.4$.

(a) $P(A \cup B) = 0.7$ (b) $P(A \cap B) = 0.12$
(c) $P(A \mid B) = 0.3$ (d) $P(A \mid \bar{B}) = 0.4$.

12) Two different numbers are chosen at random from the set $\{1, 2, 3, 4, 5, 6\}$.

(a) If the choice is ordered, it can be made in $^6P_2$ ways.

(b) The probability of the second number chosen being 2 is $\frac{1}{6}$.

(c) The probability of choosing the ordered pair $(4, 5)$ is $\frac{1}{30}$.

13) A and B are mutually exclusive events.
(a) $P(A \cup B) = P(A) + P(B)$.
(b) $P(A \mid B) = P(A)$.
(c) $P(A \cap B) = 0$.

14) Two unbiased tetrahedral dice, each numbered one to four, are rolled.
(a) There are 16 ways in which the two dice can land.
(b) A total score of 4 and the throwing of at least one 1 are mutually exclusive events.
(c) The probability of not throwing a double 4 is the same as the probability of scoring at least 7.

15) Two people, A and B, toss a fair coin. Whoever tosses a head first wins 2 p, and they toss in the order A then B.
(a) The probability that A wins on his second toss is $\frac{1}{8}$.
(b) The probability that B wins on his second toss is $\frac{1}{8}$.
(c) If they carry on playing a large number of games, without changing the order of play, they each expect to win an average of 1 p per game.
(d) A wins and B wins are mutually exclusive events.

TYPE III

16) (a) A and B are independent events.
(b) $P(A \cap B) = P(A) \times P(B)$.

17) (a) $P(A) = a$, $P(B) = b$.
(b) $P(A \cup B) = a + b - ab$.

18) (a) $P(A \cap B) = 0$.
(b) $P(A \mid B) = \frac{1}{2}$.

19) (a) $P(E) = \dfrac{r}{n}$

(b) $P(\bar{E}) = \dfrac{n-r}{n}$

TYPE IV

20) Three people A, B and C draw a card at random from a pack of fifty-two playing cards. Find the probability that A is the first to draw an ace.
(a) A draws first.
(b) The cards are not replaced.
(c) B draws second.

21) Find $P(A \mid \bar{B})$.
(a) A and B are not independent events.
(b) $P(A) = \frac{1}{3}$.
(c) $P(A \cap B) = \frac{1}{5}$.

22) A committee is chosen at random from a group of ten people. Find the expected number of men on the committee.
(a) There are four members of the committee.
(b) There are six men in the group.
(c) The committee of four are seated at a round table.

23) Find the probability that a candidate who guesses at random obtains at least 40% in a multiple choice test.
(a) There are one hundred questions.
(b) Each question has five alternative answers, only one of which is correct.
(c) Each correct answer scores one mark, no marks are given for an incorrect answer.

TYPE V

24) The probability of tossing a head with a biased coin is $\frac{1}{2}$.

25) The number of ways of choosing two cards from a pack of fifty-two playing cards is $^{52}P_2$.

26) If A and B are mutually exclusive, $P(A|B) = 0$.

27) If $P(A) = \frac{1}{3}$, $P(\overline{A}) = \frac{2}{3}$.

28) If $P(A \text{ and } B) = 0$ then either $P(A) = 0$ or $P(B) = 0$.

29) The number of arrangements of the letters of the word EVERY is 24.

30) The number of ways of choosing two different letters from the set $\{A, B, C, D\}$ is 4.

MISCELLANEOUS EXERCISE 18

1) An unbiased die marked $1, 2, 2, 3, 3, 3$, is rolled three times. Find the probability of getting a total score of 4. (U of L)

2) A boy spins a coin three times and a girl spins a coin twice. Find the probability that the girl gets more heads than the boy. (U of L)

3) Two cards are to be drawn without replacement from a pack of playing cards. Find the probability that
(a) both will be diamonds,
(b) one card will be red and the other will be black. (U of L)

4) A boy and a girl spin a coin in turn, and the first to get a 'head' is the winner. The girl spins first. Find the probability that the boy wins. (U of L)

5) A train daily makes a journey which involves stopping at two stations. The probabilities of being delayed at these stations are 0.6 and 0.8 respectively and

any delays occur at the stations independently. Calculate (a) the probability of no delay and (b) the probability of one delay on the journey.   (U of L)

6) A box contains only four red balls and five white balls. Three balls are drawn successively at random from the box without replacement. Draw a tree diagram illustrating the various possibilities. Hence, or otherwise, find the probability that three white and three red balls are left in the box.   (U of L)

7) (a) A delegation of 4 persons is to be formed from 5 married couples. Find the number of ways in which the delegation can be chosen if it contains:
   (i) 2 married couples,
   (ii) at least one man and one woman,
   (iii) no married couple.
   (b) Three normal unbiased dice are thrown. Find the probability that there will be:
   (i) no sixes,
   (ii) at least one six,
   (iii) exactly one six.
Find also the probability that the three dice all show the same number when thrown.   (AEB)

8) A well-shuffled pack of 52 playing cards is dealt out to four players, each receiving 13 cards. Show that the probability that a particular player receives the four aces is 0.0026.
How many deals are necessary in order that the probability of a particular player receiving all four aces in at least one game exceeds 0.5?   (O)

9) If A and B are events and
$$p(A) = \tfrac{8}{15},$$
$$p(A \text{ and } B) = \tfrac{1}{3},$$
$$p(A|B) = \tfrac{4}{7},$$
calculate $p(B)$, $p(B|A)$ and $p(B|\bar{A})$ where $\bar{A}$ is the event 'A does not occur'.
State, with reasons, whether A and B are (a) independent, (b) mutually exclusive.   (C)

10) A committee of four people is chosen at random from a set of seven men and three women. Determine:
(a) the probability that there is at least one woman on the committee,
(b) the probability that there is at least one man on the committee,
(c) the expected number of women on the committee,
(d) the expected number of men on the committee.   (C)

11) An event has probability p of success and $q(= 1 - p)$ of failure. Independent trials are carried out until at least one success and at least one failure have occurred. Find the probability that r trials are necessary $(r \geqslant 2)$ and show that this probability equals $(\frac{1}{2})^{r-1}$ when $p = \frac{1}{2}$.
A couple decide that they will continue to have children until either they have both a boy and a girl in the family or they have four children. Assuming that boys and girls are equally likely to be born, what will be the expected size of their completed family?   (O)

12) (a) The events A and B are such that
$$P(A) = 0.4, \quad P(B) = 0.45, \quad P(A \cup B) = 0.68.$$
Show that the events A and B are neither mutually exclusive nor independent.

(b) A bag contains 12 red balls, 8 blue balls and 4 white balls. Three balls are taken from the bag at random and without replacement. Find the probability that all three balls are of the same colour.
Find also the probability that all three balls are of different colours.
                                                                 (U of L)

13) Two cards are drawn without replacement from a pack of playing cards. Using a tree diagram, or otherwise, calculate the probability
(a) that both cards are aces,
(b) that one (and only one) card is an ace,
(c) that the two cards are of different suits.
Given that at least one ace is drawn, find the probability that the two cards are of different suits.   (U of L)

14) A child throws two fair dice. If the numbers showing are unequal, he adds them together to get his final score. On the other hand, if the numbers showing are equal, he throws two more fair dice and adds all four numbers showing to get his final score. Calculate the probabilities that his final score is
(a) 2,   (b) 3,   (c) 4,   (d) 5,   (e) 6,   (f) more than 6.   (U of L)

15) A mother has found that 20% of the children who accept invitations to her children's birthday parties do not come. For a particular party she invites 12 children but has available only 10 party hats. What is the probability that there is not a hat for every child who comes to the party?
The mother knows that there is a probability of 0.1 that a child who comes to a party will refuse to wear a hat. If this is taken into account, what is the probability that the number of hats will not be adequate?   (O)

16) (a) Find the probability that the fourth power of any positive integer n ends in the digit 6.

   (b) In a certain tournament in which games cannot result in a draw A plays B until one of them has won a total of three games. If p is the probability that A wins any individual game he plays against B and if $q = 1 - p$, find in terms of p and q the probabilities that,

   (i) A wins the first three games,
   (ii) a decision is reached in the third game,
   (iii) A wins the match in the fourth game,
   (iv) a decision is reached in the fourth game.

If $p = \frac{2}{3}$, determine the probability of A winning the match before the sixth game. (AEB)

17) (a) Find how many numbers between 3000 and 4000 can be formed using only the digits 1, 2, 3 and 4, no digit being repeated.

   (b) A bag contains 4 red and 6 black balls. One ball is drawn at random; if it is black it is replaced in the bag, but if it is red it is not replaced. A second ball is then drawn. X denotes the event 'The first ball is red' and Y denotes the event 'The second ball is red'. Find the probabilities

   (i) $P(X)$,
   (ii) $P(Y$ given $X)$,
   (iii) $P(Y)$,
   (iv) P(either X or Y but not both). (C)

18) One of three coins is biased so that the probability of obtaining a head is twice as great as the probability of obtaining a tail. The other two coins are fair. One of the three coins is chosen at random and tossed three times, showing a head on each occasion. Using a tree diagram, or otherwise, find the probability that the chosen coin is biased. (U of L)

19) (a) In how many ways can a hand of 13 cards be dealt from a normal pack of 52 cards, all of which are different? Assuming that each deal is equally likely, what is the probability of being dealt 13 cards all of the same suit?
   [*Answers to both parts should be left in factorial form.*]

   (b) If A and B are independent events, the probabilities of which in a certain trial are a and b respectively, what are the probabilities of:
   (i) both A and B occurring,
   (ii) event A occurring but not B,
   (iii) neither A nor B occurring?

If these trials are repeated n times with no change in the values of a and b, what is the probability that neither A nor B will occur? If $a = b = 0.01$, find how many trials are required before this probability becomes less than 0.5. (AEB)

20) Eight trees are planted in a circle in random order. If two of the trees are diseased and later die, what is the probability that the two dead trees are next to each other?

If four of them are diseased find (a) the probability that at least two of them are next to each other, and (b) the probability that all four are next to each other.

(C)

21) When a boy fires an air-rifle the probability that he hits the target is p.
(a) Find the probability that, firing 5 shots, he scores at least 4 hits.
(b) Find the probability that, firing n shots $(n \geqslant 2)$, he scores at least two hits.

(C)p

22) (a) Four men, two women and a child sit at a round table. Find the number of ways of arranging the seven people if the child is seated (i) between the two women, (ii) between two men.

(b) A die with faces numbered 1 to 6 is biased so that
P (score is r) $= kr$, $(r = 1, \ldots, 6)$. Find the value of k.

If the die is thrown twice, calculate the probability that the total score exceeds 10.

(C)

23) (a) The results of eleven football matches (as win, lose or draw) are to be forecast. Out of all possible forecasts, find how many will have eight correct and three incorrect results.

(b) An unbiased die in the shape of a regular dodecahedron has twelve faces with the numbers 2, 2, 4, 4, 4, 6, 6, 10, 10, 10, 12, 12, showing separately on the faces. The result of a throw is the number showing on the uppermost face. Each of four players throws the die twice and scores the sum of the two results. What is the probability that all of the four players in succession will each obtain a score greater than six?

(c) An unbiased die in the shape of a cube shows 1, 2, 3, 4, 5, 6 on its six separate faces. It is tossed until it lands the same way up twice running. Find the probability that this requires r tosses.

(AEB)

24) The probabilities that a man makes a certain dangerous journey by car, motor cycle or on foot are $\frac{1}{2}$, $\frac{1}{6}$ and $\frac{1}{3}$ respectively. If the probabilities of an accident when he uses these means of transport are $\frac{1}{5}$, $\frac{2}{5}$ and $\frac{1}{10}$ respectively, find the probability of an accident occurring in a single journey.

If an accident is known to have happened, calculate the probabilities that the man was travelling

(a) by car,
(b) by motor cycle,
(c) on foot.

(U of L)

25) Four cards are drawn at random from a pack, one at a time with replacement. Find the probability that
(a) no heart is drawn,
(b) four hearts are drawn,
(c) two hearts and two diamonds are drawn (in any order),
(d) one card from each suit is drawn.   (U of L)

26) (a) Two cards are drawn without replacement from ten cards which are numbered from 1 to 10. Find the probability that
    (i) the numbers on both cards are even,
    (ii) the number on one card is odd and the number on the other card is even,
    (iii) the sum of the numbers on the two cards exceeds 4.
(b) Events A and C are independent. Probabilities relating to events A, B and C are as follows:
    $P(A) = 1/5$, $P(B) = 1/6$, $P(A \cap C) = 1/20$, $P(B \cup C) = 3/8$.
    Evaluate $P(C)$ and show that events B and C are independent.
                                                               (U of L)

27) (a) A box contains six dice, one of which is unfairly biased. If two dice are chosen at random simultaneously from this box, what is the probability that one of them will be biased?
(b) A uniform unbiased die is constructed in the shape of a regular tetrahedron with faces numbered 2, 2, 3 and 4, and the score is taken from the face on which the die lands. If two such dice are thrown together what total scores are possible at each throw and what is the probability of each score? What is expected to be the average score over a long series of throws?
    What is the probability of scoring:
    (i) exactly 6 on each of three successive throws,
    (ii) more than 4 on at least one of three successive throws?   (AEB)

28) (a) Show that it is more probable to get at least one six with a throw of three dice than to get two sixes with any one of fifteen throws of two dice.
(b) There are three identical boxes each containing a sum of money, no two boxes containing the same amount. A man chooses a box as follows: he first takes a box at random (call it A) and sees how much is in it. He then takes one of the other two boxes at random (call it B) and sees how much is in it. If box B contains more than box A, then the man chooses box B; if box B contains less than box A then he chooses the third box (call it C). Find the probability that he will choose:
    (i) the box containing the greatest value of money,
    (ii) the box containing the smallest value of money.   (AEB)

29) Suppose that letters sent by first and second class post have probabilities of being delivered a given number of days after posting according to the following table (weekends are ignored).

Days to delivery	1	2	3
1st class	0.9	0.1	0
2nd class	0.1	0.6	0.3

The secretary of a committee posts a letter to a committee member who replies immediately using the same class of post. What is the probability that four or more days are taken from the secretary posting the letter to receiving the reply if (a) first class, (b) second class post is used?
The secretary sends out four letters and each member replies immediately by the same class of post. Assuming the letters move independently, what is the probability that the secretary receives (a) all the replies within three days using first class post, (b) at least two replies within three days using second class post?

(O)

30) In a game of chance each player throws two unbiased dice and scores the difference between the larger and smaller numbers which arise. Two players compete and one or the other wins if, and only if, he scores at least 4 more than his opponent. Find the probability that neither player wins. (JMB)p

31) Six lines are drawn in a plane and produced to give all their points of intersection. If no three lines are concurrent, and no two parallel, show that there are 15 points of intersection. If three of these points are chosen at random show that the probability that they are all on one of the given lines is $\frac{12}{91}$. Find also the probability that if four points are chosen at random, they are not all on one of the given lines. (C)

32) In a certain examination paper there are 10 questions. Each question has 5 suggested answers, and the candidates have to choose the right one in each question. Suppose that candidate X chooses answers entirely at random, so that he is equally likely to choose any one of the 5 answers in each question. Calculate the probability that he will score at least 3 correct answers out of 10. (C)p

33) A tennis player A has a probability of $\frac{2}{3}$ of winning a set against a player B. A match is won by the player who first wins three sets. Find the probability that A wins the match.

34) (a) Three boys and three girls sit in a row of six seats.
Find the probability that
  (i) the three girls sit together,
  (ii) the girls and boys sit in alternate seats.
  (b) In an examination, one hundred candidates took papers in Physics and
Chemistry. Twenty five candidates failed in Physics only. Twenty
candidates failed in Chemistry only. Fifteen failed in both Physics and
Chemistry. A candidate is selected at random. Find the probability that
  (i) he failed in Chemistry if it is known that he failed in Physics,
  (ii) he failed in Physics if it is known that he failed in Chemistry,
  (iii) he failed either in Physics or in Chemistry but not in both.

35) A bag initially contains 1 red ball and 2 blue balls. A trial consists of
selecting a ball at random, noting its colour, and replacing it together with an
additional ball of the same colour. Given that three trials are made, draw a tree
diagram illustrating the various probabilities. Hence, or otherwise, find the
probability that
(a) at least one blue ball is drawn,
(b) exactly one blue ball is drawn.
Given that all three balls drawn are of the same colour find the probability that
they are all red.   (U of L)

APPENDIX

Quotable Formulae, Using Standard Symbols

MOTION WITH CONSTANT ACCELERATION

$$v = u + at$$
$$s = \tfrac{1}{2}(u + v)t$$
$$s = ut + \tfrac{1}{2}at^2$$
$$s = vt - \tfrac{1}{2}at^2$$
$$v^2 - u^2 = 2as$$

PROJECTILES

$$\ddot{x} = 0 \qquad \ddot{y} = -g$$
$$\dot{x} = V\cos\alpha \qquad \dot{y} = V\sin\alpha - gt$$
$$x = Vt\cos\alpha \qquad y = Vt\sin\alpha - \tfrac{1}{2}gt^2$$
$$y = x\tan\alpha - \frac{gx^2}{2V^2\cos^2\alpha}$$

SIMPLE HARMONIC MOTION

$$\ddot{x} = -n^2x$$
$$\dot{x} = n\sqrt{a^2 - x^2}$$
$$x = a\cos nt$$
$$\text{Period} = \frac{2\pi}{n}$$

CENTRES OF GRAVITY

Uniform Body	Position of G on axis of symmetry
Solid hemisphere	$\frac{3}{8}a$ from plane face
Solid $\begin{cases} \text{pyramid} \\ \text{cone} \end{cases}$	$\frac{1}{4}h$ from base
Hollow hemisphere	$\frac{1}{2}a$ from plane section
Hollow $\begin{cases} \text{pyramid} \\ \text{cone} \end{cases}$ (no base)	$\frac{1}{3}h$ from base
Circular arc subtending an angle 2α at centre	$\dfrac{a \sin \alpha}{\alpha}$ from centre
Circular sector subtending an angle 2α at centre	$\dfrac{2a \sin \alpha}{3\alpha}$ from centre

PROPERTIES OF MOTION ETC.

Newton's Law $\quad \mathbf{F} = m\mathbf{a}$

Momentum $\quad = m\mathbf{v}$

Kinetic Energy $\quad = \frac{1}{2}mv^2 \quad$ or $\quad \frac{1}{2}m\mathbf{v.v}$

Potential Energy $\quad = mgh$

Elastic Energy $\quad = \frac{1}{2}\dfrac{\lambda x^2}{l}$

Work done $\begin{cases} \text{by a constant force} = Fs \quad \text{or} \quad \mathbf{F.d} \\ \text{by a variable force} = \displaystyle\int \mathbf{F}\,ds \end{cases}$

Impulse $\begin{cases} \text{of a constant force} = \mathbf{F}t \\ \text{of a variable force} = \displaystyle\int \mathbf{F}\,dt \end{cases}$

ANSWERS

Most of the answers given here are quoted in an exact form (using surds, etc.). Students who have used a calculator in their solution can check their answers by converting an exact result to decimal form.

Exercise 1a — p. 4

1) a) 6 m $3\sqrt{3}$ m in the direction AC
   b) 10.5 m, 5.41 m from A to the midpoint of DE
2) $3\sqrt{3}$ m in the direction AC
3) a) $2\,\text{m s}^{-1}$ along DE
   b) $2\,\text{m s}^{-1}$ along AB
4) No
5) The straight sections AB and CD.

Exercise 2a — p. 18

1) $3\sqrt{2}$ m NE
2) a) $\overrightarrow{AC}$ b) $\overrightarrow{BD}$ c) $\overrightarrow{AD}$ d) $\overrightarrow{DB}$
3) a; $\mathbf{b}-\mathbf{a}$; $2(\mathbf{b}-\mathbf{a})$
6) b),   c),   e),   f)

Exercise 2b — p. 23

1) a) 5.64 N, 2.05 N
   b) $10\,\text{m s}^{-1}$, $17.3\,\text{m s}^{-1}$
   c) 6.4 N, 4.8 N
2) 2 N, 3.5 N
3) $P\sin 20°$, $W\cos 20°$, T; $P\cos 20°$, $W\sin 20°$
4) 4i; $3\sqrt{3}\mathbf{i}+3\mathbf{j}$; 3j; $-2\mathbf{i}$; $-2\sqrt{2}\mathbf{i}-2\sqrt{2}\mathbf{j}$
6) East: 7.07, -6 North: 7.07, 24

Exercise 2c — p. 26

1) $3\mathbf{i}+4\mathbf{j}$
2) $15\mathbf{i}-36\mathbf{j}$
3) $-14\mathbf{i}+14\sqrt{3}\mathbf{j}$
4) $48\mathbf{i}-14\mathbf{j}$
5) $-\frac{8}{5}\mathbf{i}-\frac{6}{5}\mathbf{j}$
6) $12\mathbf{i}+5\mathbf{j}$
7) $60\mathbf{i}-80\mathbf{j}$

8) $2\mathbf{i}-4\mathbf{j}$
9) $\pm(10\sqrt{2}\mathbf{i}-10\sqrt{2}\mathbf{j})$
10) $\frac{72}{5}\mathbf{i}-\frac{21}{5}\mathbf{j}$

Exercise 2d — p. 29

1) $\mathbf{r}=3\mathbf{i}+\lambda(2\mathbf{i}+4\mathbf{j})$
2) $\mathbf{r}=\mathbf{i}-\mathbf{j}+5\lambda\mathbf{i}$
3) $\mathbf{r}=5\mathbf{j}+\lambda(\mathbf{i}-5\mathbf{j})$
4) $\mathbf{r}=\lambda(3\mathbf{i}+4\mathbf{j}+2\mathbf{k})$
5) $\mathbf{r}=-4\mathbf{i}-\mathbf{j}+\mathbf{k}+\lambda(\mathbf{i}+\mathbf{j}-\mathbf{k})$

Note that the answers to the following questions can be given in other forms

6) $\mathbf{r}=2\mathbf{i}+3\mathbf{j}+\lambda(\mathbf{i}+10\mathbf{j})$
7) $\mathbf{r}=3\mathbf{i}+\lambda(4\mathbf{i}-9\mathbf{j})$
8) $\mathbf{r}=3\mathbf{j}+\lambda(\mathbf{i}-4\mathbf{j})$
9) $\mathbf{r}=5\mathbf{i}-7\mathbf{j}+\mathbf{k}+\lambda(3\mathbf{i}-8\mathbf{j}+3\mathbf{k})$
10) $\mathbf{r}=\mathbf{i}-3\mathbf{k}+\lambda(\mathbf{i}+\mathbf{j}-5\mathbf{k})$
11) $3\mathbf{i}+7\mathbf{j}$; $(\frac{25}{7},0)$, $(0,-\frac{25}{3})$
12) $\mathbf{i}-5\mathbf{j}$; $(3,-7)$
13) $\mathbf{i}-7\mathbf{j}$; $(1,-7)$, $(2,-14)$ etc.
14) j; $(2,1)$, $(2,4)$
15) $\mathbf{i}-\mathbf{j}$; $(0,4)$, $(0,4)$

Exercise 2e — p. 30

1) $\mathbf{r}=2\mathbf{i}-3\mathbf{j}+\lambda(8\mathbf{i}-7\mathbf{j})$
2) $\mathbf{r}=\lambda\mathbf{i}$
3) $\mathbf{r}=\mathbf{i}+\mathbf{j}+\lambda(4\mathbf{i}+10\mathbf{j})$
4) $\mathbf{r}=7\mathbf{i}+8\mathbf{j}+\lambda(\mathbf{i}-2\mathbf{j})$
5) $\mathbf{r}=\lambda(11\mathbf{i}-7\mathbf{j}+3\mathbf{k})$
6) a) $-\frac{10}{7}\mathbf{i}$ b) $-\frac{5}{4}\mathbf{j}$
7) a) $\frac{3}{5}\mathbf{i}$ b) $-\frac{3}{2}\mathbf{j}$
8) a) 11i   b) 22j
9) No
10) No
11) $\pm(25\mathbf{i}-60\mathbf{j})$

12) $\pm 4i$

13) $\pm (8i + 8j)$

14) $\pm 2\sqrt{10}(i + 3j)$

15) $\pm \sqrt{\frac{13}{5}}(4i - 7j)$

Exercise 2f — p. 31

1) $r = 4i - j + \lambda(i + 7j)$

2) $r = 3i - 2j - k + \lambda(-5i + 6j + 8k)$

3) $r = i + j + \lambda(4i - 3j)$

4) $r = -19j + \lambda(8i - 7j)$

5) $r = 4i + 4j + \lambda(9i - 2j)$

Exercise 2g — p. 37

1) a) 5 N; $\arctan \frac{4}{3}$ to the 3 N force

   b) 26 N; $\arctan \frac{5}{12}$ to the 24 N force

   c) $5\sqrt{2}$ N; $45°$ to each force

   d) $2\sqrt{10}$ N; $\arctan 3$ to the 2 N force

   e) 25 N; $\arctan \frac{24}{7}$ to the 7 N force

2) a) 13 N; $\arctan \frac{5}{12}$

   b) $2\sqrt{2}$ N; $45°$

   c) 25 N; $-\arctan \frac{7}{24}$

   d) 5 N; $\arctan (-\frac{3}{4})$

   e) $5\sqrt{2}$ N; $-\arctan (-\frac{1}{7})$

3) a) 14 N

   b) $(34 - 15\sqrt{3})^{1/2}$ N

   c) 9 N

   d) 5 N

   e) $2(13 + 6\sqrt{2})^{1/2}$ N

4) ± 5; $67.4°$, $112.6°$

5) 445 km h^{-1}

6) a) $75.5°$ b) $138.6°$

7) a) 15   b) 11.5

8) a) $104.5°$ b) 0

   c) $180°$

Exercise 2h — p. 43

1) 13 N; $\arctan \frac{12}{5}$ to i

2) 5 m s^{-1}; $\arctan \frac{4}{3}$ to i

3) a) $\sqrt{39}$ N; $\arctan \dfrac{\sqrt{3}}{6}$ to 4 N force

   b) $(46 + 16\sqrt{2})^{1/2}$;
      $\arctan \frac{1}{17}(14\sqrt{2} + 1)$ to force 3

4) $\frac{1}{5}\sqrt{1130}$ N;
   $\arctan \frac{13}{31}$ to AB outside ABCD

5) $\sqrt{7}$ N at $\arctan 3\sqrt{3}$ with BA

6) $9i + 5j$

7) 292 N at $6°$ to centre rope

8) 261 m on a bearing $305.1°$

9) $\sqrt{3}i \pm 6j$

10) 7.1 km h^{-1} S47$°$E

11) 139 km h^{-1}

12) a) 11.95 N at $3.5°$ to AD

    b) 12.13 N at $64.9°$ to AB

Exercise 2i — p. 46

1) $\frac{5}{2}i - j$

2) $7i + 2j$

3) $5i + j$

4) $6i - 2j$

5) $i + j$

6) $i + j$; No

7) $6i + j$

8) a) $r_1 = \lambda(24i - 7j)$;
      $r_2 = 5i + \mu(-2i + j)$

   b) $46i - 13j$

   c) $r = 12i - \frac{7}{2}j + \lambda(46i - 13j)$

Exercise 2j — p. 51

1) 0; 8 N m; -6 N m; 0

2) $6Fa\sqrt{3}$; $-2Fa\sqrt{3}$; $4Fa$

3) 0; 4 N m; $\sqrt{3}$ N m; -4 N m

4) $6Fa$; $-2Fa$; $2Fa$; $-Fa\sqrt{3}$

5) 1 N m anticlockwise

6) a) 460 N m   b) 345 N m

   c) -460 N m   d) 0

Exercise 2k — p. 57

1) Fa clockwise

2) $(7 - 4\sqrt{3})a$ N m anticlockwise

3) $\dfrac{Pa}{2}(12 - \sqrt{3})$ clockwise

4) $\frac{1}{2}(3 + \sqrt{3})$ N m anticlockwise

5) 23 units, 47 units, both clockwise

6) $-2, -7, -12, -6$ units

7) 11 N; -4 N; 3 N

Multiple Choice Exercise 2 — p. 59

1) c	2) c	3) a	4) d
5) c	6) c	7) a	8) d
9) a	10) c, d	11) b, d	12) a, c
13) a, b	14) B	15) A	16) B
17) E	18) c	19) I	20) A
21) I	22) I	23) A	24) F
25) T	26) F	27) F	28) F
29) F	30) F		

Miscellaneous Exercise 2 — p. 63

1) 24 N; $36.9°$

3) 8.1 N

4) $-3i - 3j$

5) $6.7°$

6) a) 8 m s^{-1} South West

 b) 4.3 m s^{-1}, $312°$

 c) 21 m s^{-1}, $262.3°$

7) a) i) $\overrightarrow{AC}$ ii) $\overrightarrow{EB}$

8) $\overrightarrow{BD}$

10) $2(\sqrt{3}-1) \text{ N}$

11) $P\sqrt{39}$ at $\arctan \sqrt{3}/7$ to AE

12) a) 12 b) 20 both clockwise

13) a) $\sqrt{3} \text{ N m}$

 b) $9\sqrt{3} \text{ N m}$ both in sense ABC

14) 2

15) $-8i + 10j$

16) $\dfrac{7\sqrt{3}-2}{13}$

17) a) $r_1 = i + 3j + \lambda(2i - j)$

 $r_2 = i - 2j + \mu(8i + 6j)$

 b) $10i + 5j$

 c) $r = 5i + j + \lambda(10i + 5j)$

18) a) $\sqrt{3}P$ b) $150°$ c) $120°, 60°$

19) $5.14P$ at $76.5°$ to Ox

20) Midpoint of XY

21) AB and CD bisect each other

22) a) $\frac{3}{2}a\sqrt{3}$ b) $\frac{3}{2}a\sqrt{3}$ c) $\frac{3}{2}a\sqrt{3}$
 all in sense CBA

23) $p = 5$ and $q = 1$ or
 $p = -7$ and $q = -11$

Exercise 3a — p. 69

1) $-2\sqrt{2}; 2$

2) 8.7 N at $46.7°$ to BA

3) $4i - 4j; 4\sqrt{2}; -4i + 4j$

4) $-10i - 4j$

5) $-12i - 3j$

6) 1.15 N or 0.35 N

Exercise 3b — p. 78

1) a) $26 \text{ N}; 10 \text{ N}$ b) $25.5 \text{ N}; 8.7 \text{ N}$

2) 5 N

3) $10 \text{ N}; 22.6°$

4) a) $30°$ b) $18.4°$

5) a) 5 N b) 5.77 N

6) $W; \sqrt{2}W$

7) $12\sqrt{3} \text{ N}; 24 \text{ N}$

8) $W/\sqrt{2}$ perp. to BC where W is the weight of the rod

Exercise 3c — p. 87

1) a) 0.364 b) $2(6 + 5\sqrt{3}) \text{ N}$

 c) $15°$

 d) 2.8 N at $13.4°$ to the horizontal

2) a) 5.72 N b) 19.34 N

3) 1009 N

4) $61.8°$

5) a) 1 N, no b) 4 N, no
 c) 4 N, yes

6) 2736 N

Exercise 3d — p. 90

1) $\frac{200}{19} \text{ N}$

2) 30 N

3) 1.35 m from the end

4) $\frac{180}{7}; \frac{100}{7}$

5) 1.39 m

6) $52; 66$

7) 10

8) $15; \frac{75}{2}$

Exercise 3e — p. 97

1) $\frac{9}{8}; 26\frac{2}{3} \text{ N}$

2) $60 \text{ N}; 180 \text{ N}; \arctan \frac{3}{2}$

3) $\frac{1}{2}W; \frac{1}{3}\sqrt{3}$

4) $\sqrt{3}; \frac{1}{3}W\sqrt{3}$

5) a) $3mg; mg\sqrt{13}$ at $\arctan \frac{2}{3}$ to PQ

 b) $3mg; mg$ vertically downwards

6) $2; 4; -\frac{9}{4}a$

7) $\frac{9}{2}; \frac{27}{2}$

8) $(5 + 4\sqrt{3}); 8; \frac{5}{12}\sqrt{3}$

9) $\frac{3}{4}a; \frac{1}{3}W\sqrt{3}$

10) $60°$

11) $173.2 \text{ N}, 60°$ or $86.6 \text{ N}, 19.1°$

Multiple Choice Exercise 3 — p. 100

1) c	2) b	3) b	4) d
5) d	6) b d	7) a b	8) c
9) a d	10) B	11) B	12) B
13) E	14) A	15) B	16) C
17) B	18) I	19) a	20) I
21) a c	22) I	23) d	24) F
25) F	26) T	27) F	28) T
29) T	30) F		

Miscellaneous Exercise 3 — p. 103

1) $\sqrt{10}$ units at $18.4°$ to BA;
 $\sqrt{10}$ units at $18.4°$ to BA produced

3) $45°; W\sqrt{5/2}$

4) Either $3W, 1/\sqrt{3}$ or $5W, \sqrt{3/5}$

5) 8640 N

7) $10^3/16 \text{ N}$

8) a) $10 \text{ N}, 10\sqrt{3} \text{ N}$

 b) $24 - 4\sqrt{3}, 12\sqrt{3} - 8$

 c) $5.73 \text{ N}, 8.73 \text{ N}$

 d) $51.9°, 33.04 \text{ N}$

9) $20\sqrt{3}$ N, 40 N

10) $\frac{10}{3}$ N; $\frac{25}{3}$ N

11) 0.8 N

12) 1.2 m; 140 N

13) $\frac{100}{9}\sqrt{3}$ N

14) $\frac{11}{3}$ m from A

15) $375g$ N m; $450g$ N m

17) a) 13 N   b) 12.8 N
    c) $3\sqrt{13}$ N   d) 3.6 N; 10.25 N

18) $100\sqrt{3}$; 200

19) $\frac{1}{2}F\sqrt{113}$ at $\arctan\frac{8}{7}$ to Ox; a

20) 1 m from A

21) 2 m from A; 100 N; 700 N

22) 70 kg; 14 kg

23) $\frac{1}{6}W\sqrt{3}$; W

24) $\frac{5}{2}W\cosec\theta$, $\frac{5}{2}W\cot\theta$, $\frac{1}{2}W$

25) a) $49.1°$ b) $58.4°$

26) $\frac{1}{4}$; $\frac{3}{2}l$

28) $W\sqrt{5/4}$ at $26.6°$ to vertical

29) a) $50\sqrt{3}$ b) 112.5

30) $\frac{1}{4}W$; $\frac{1}{8}W\sqrt{3}$; $\frac{7}{8}W$

31) $1.2W$; $36.9°$

32) $\arctan a/(h - \mu a)$

33) a) $2W$ b) $\arctan\sqrt{7}/7$
    c) $3\sqrt{2}W/2$

34) $60°$; $\sqrt{3}/3$; $\sqrt{3}W/3$

35) $\frac{3}{8}$; $\frac{5}{3}l$

36) $2M_1 - 3M_2 + 2M_3$; $2M_1 - 2M_2 + M_3$

37) $\frac{1}{2}$; $\frac{4}{3}W$

Exercise 4a — p. 113

1) 7.875 m s^{-1}

2) 1.481 m s^{-1}

3) 2.32 m s^{-1}, -0.387 m s^{-1}

4) 1.54 m s^{-1}, 0.769 m s^{-1}

5) a) 2 m s^{-1} b) 0
    c) -1.5 m s^{-1}

Exercise 4b — p. 116

1) a) 2 m s^{-1} b) -2 m s^{-1}

2) a) 0   b) 1 m s^{-1}

3) a) -3 m   b) 15 m
    c) 5 m s^{-1}
    d) -1 m s^{-1}, -16 m s^{-1}

4) a) -34 m s^{-1} b) -39 m s^{-1}
    c) $\frac{1}{10}$ s

5) a) 2.5 m   b) 6 m
    c) 1 m s^{-1} d) $t = +\frac{1}{2}$

Exercise 4c — p. 118

1) a) $4i + t(4\sqrt{5}i + 2\sqrt{5}j)$
    b) $(4 + 8\sqrt{5})i + 4\sqrt{5}j$

2) a) $3i + j + t(4\sqrt{2}i + 4\sqrt{2}j)$
    b) $(3 + 8\sqrt{2})i + (1 + 8\sqrt{2})j$

3) a) $j + t(4\sqrt{10}i - 12\sqrt{10}j)$
    b) $8\sqrt{10}i + (1 - 24\sqrt{10})j$

4) a) $2j + 5ti$
    b) $10i + 2j$

5) a) $i - j + t(5i - 12j)$
    b) $11i - 25j$

Exercise 4d — p. 119

1) -2 m s^{-2}

2) 8 m s^{-1}

3) a) 3 m s^{-1} b) 0
    c) -3 m s^{-1}

4) 2 m s^{-1}

5) 3 m s^{-2}

Exercise 4e — p. 123

1) 3 m s^{-2}, 250 m

2) 360 m

3) 96 m

4) -3 m s^{-2}, 114 m

5) a) -11 m s^{-1} b) 46.5 m
    c) 14 m

6) a) $+1.5$ m s^{-2} b) 16.5 m
    c) -4.5 m

Exercise 4f — p. 129

1) 17 m s^{-1}, 47.5 m

2) a) 12 m   b) 8 m

3) 2.5 m s^{-2}, 40 m

4) 2.5 m s^{-2}, 45 m

5) 5 m

6) 3 s later

7) 6.67 s

8) 5 m s^{-2}

9) $-\frac{1}{30}$ m s^{-2}

10) a) $5 \pm \sqrt{15}$ s   b) $5 + \sqrt{35}$ s

11) $6 + 3\sqrt{2}$ s

12) 5.71 m

13) 8 s

14) 360 m

15) 111 s

Exercise 4g — p. 133

1) $14\sqrt{10}$ m s^{-1}

2) 5.1 m

3) 1.43 s, 14 m s^{-1}

4) 4.08 s

5) 4.547 s

6) 26.1 m

7) 15.45 m s^{-1}

8) 6.8 s

9) 0.82 m

10) 1.275 m above the initial position

11) 60 m

Exercise 4h — p. 136

1) a) $v = 3t^2 i + 2t j; \ a = 6t i + 2j$
   b) $v = 27i + 6j; \ a = 18i + 2j; \ 3i + 2j$

2) a) $v = -4t^3 j; \ a = -12t^2 j$
   b) $v = -108j; \ a = -108j; \ -4j$

3) a) $v = i - 2t j; \ a = -2j$
   b) $v = i - 6j; \ a = -2j; \ i - 2j$

4) a) $v = 2t i - 2t j; \ a = 2i - 2j$
   b) $v = 6i - 6j; \ a = 2i - 2j; \ 2i - 2j$

5) $v = 4i + (3 - 10t)j; \ 4, \ 3;$
   $a = -10j$ (constant);
   acceleration due to gravity if j is
   vertically upwards

Exercise 4i — p. 139

1) $\dfrac{11\pi}{10} \text{rad s}^{-1}, \ \dfrac{3\pi}{2} \text{rad s}^{-1}$

2) $\dfrac{\pi}{30} \text{rad s}^{-1}$

3) 40 m s^{-1}

4) $1600\pi/3 \text{ km h}^{-1}$

5) 15.16 hours

Exercise 4j — p. 140

1) 6 rad s^{-1}

2) $\pi \text{ rad s}^{-2}$

3) $15 \text{ rad}, \frac{2}{5} \text{ rad s}^{-2}$

4) $-84\pi \text{ rad s}^{-2}$

5) $-\dfrac{10\pi}{9} \text{rad s}^{-2}$

6) $\dfrac{5\pi}{8}$

Multiple Choice Exercise 4 — p. 142

1) c   2) b   3) d   4) a
5) b   6) b   7) a, b 8) a, c
9) b   10) *A* 11) *B* 12) *D*
13) c   14) *A* 15) *I* 16) c
17) *F* 18) *T* 19) *T* 20) *F*
21) *T* 22) *T* 23) *F* 24) *F*

Miscellaneous Exercise 4 — p. 146

1) 0.591 s

2) $0.5 \text{ rad s}^{-2}, 24 \text{ m}$

3) $\dfrac{2\pi}{3} \text{m s}^{-1}, 2 \text{ m}$ at $60°$ to the vertical

4) 1.2 s

5) $10.8 \text{ s}, 37 \text{ m s}^{-1}$

6) 5 m s^{-2}

7) 20.6 m

8) 0.839 m

10) $2\sqrt{2} \text{ m s}^{-1}$

11) $-18i$

12) 9.64 m s^{-1}

14) 440 m

15) a) $l/24$ b) $4l/3$

16) $16 \text{ km/hr/min}, \frac{5}{3} \text{ km}$ beyond C

18) $40 \text{ rev}, 3 \text{ min}$

19) $\left(\dfrac{N - 300}{60}\right) \text{min}, 80 \text{ rev/min/min}, 150$

21) a) $\frac{1}{6}$ b) 800 m

22) $\dfrac{384}{4 + V}, \dfrac{120}{V}$
    a) 20 b) $1 \text{ m s}^{-2}, 3\frac{1}{3} \text{ m s}^{-2}$

Exercise 5a — p. 150

1) No

2) Yes

3) Yes

4) Yes

5) $2\sqrt{13} \text{ N}, 123.7°$

Exercise 5b — p. 155

1) 10 N

2) $\frac{8}{3} \text{ m s}^{-2}$

3) 15 N

4) $g(1 + 5\sqrt{3})$

5) $\dfrac{5\sqrt{3}}{8} \text{ m s}^{-2}$

6) $(25 - g)/5 \text{ m s}^{-2}$

7) $2\sqrt{35}/175$

8) $15(g - 4) \text{ N}$

9) $(3g - 5)/3 \text{ m s}^{-2}$ downwards

10) $16\,000 \text{ N}$

11) $750g, 500g, 0$

12) 1500 N

13) $50(5g - 1) \text{ N}$

14) $(11 - 3\sqrt{3})g/70 \text{ m s}^{-2}$

Exercise 5c — p. 163

1) $g/3, 20g/3$

2) $g/19, 180g/19$

3) $\dfrac{(M-m)g}{M+m}, \dfrac{2Mmg}{M+m}$

4) $\dfrac{g}{3}(\sqrt{3}-1), \dfrac{2g}{3}(2+\sqrt{3})$

5) $g/3, 4g/3$

6) $13g/33, 40g/11$

7) a) $2\sqrt{2}g/9, 20\sqrt{2}g/9$

   b) $\dfrac{g}{36}(6\sqrt{2}-5), \dfrac{5g}{9}(3\sqrt{2}+2)$

8) a) $g\sqrt{3}/6, 10g\sqrt{3}/3$

   b) $\dfrac{g}{60}(10\sqrt{3}-3), 10g\sqrt{3}/3$

9) $\dfrac{80g}{13}, \dfrac{80g}{13}$

10) $\dfrac{7g}{4}(\sqrt{6}+\sqrt{2})$

11) a) $\dfrac{11g}{36}$ b) $\dfrac{50g\sqrt{2}}{9}$

    c) $\dfrac{1}{2}\left(\sqrt{\dfrac{11g}{3}}\right)$

12) $2\sqrt{g/7}$

13) $\frac{13}{12}$ m

14) a) $\left(\dfrac{4\sqrt{2}g}{35}\right)^{\frac{1}{2}}$ b) $\dfrac{g}{\sqrt{2}}$

    c) $\frac{3}{35}$ m

Exercise 5d — p. 171

1) $8g/11, 15g/11$

2) $3g/19, 48g/19$

3) $13g/25, 48g/25$

4) $5g/11, 12g/11$

5) $g/5, 12g/5, 6g/5$

6) $11g/49, 120g/49, 240g/49$

7) $14g/29, 36g/29, 72g/29$

8) $g\sqrt{3}/17$

9) $\dfrac{g}{14}\sqrt{106}$

10) $\dfrac{g}{19}, \dfrac{15\sqrt{2}}{8}g$

11) $\dfrac{3g\sqrt{505}}{217}, \dfrac{10\sqrt{2}g}{7}$

Multiple Choice Exercise 5 — p. 172

1) b   2) a   3) e   4) c

5) d   6) b   7) a, b   8) a, c

9) a, b   10) a, b, c   11) C   12) D

13) E   14) A   15) A   16) c

17) I   18) b   19) c   20) a

21) I   22) T   23) T   24) F

25) F   26) T   27) F

Miscellaneous Exercise 5 — p. 176

1) $\dfrac{R}{2m}$

2) $\sqrt{3}/6$

3) $\dfrac{147\sqrt{2}}{8g}, \dfrac{21}{4g}(2+\sqrt{2})$

4) $-\dfrac{R}{m}, \dfrac{R}{M}$

5) $T=0$

6) 0.35

7) 1.2 kg; 5 m s^{-2}

8) $g/3, \frac{2}{3}mg$

9) $\dfrac{6}{17}$

10) $4\sqrt{\dfrac{2}{11g}}$

11) a) $m(g-a)$ b) $(M+m)(g-a)$

    c) $(M+m+X)(g-a)$;
       $M(g-a), (M+X)(g-a)$;
       $M(g-a), (m+M+X)(g-a)$

12) $\dfrac{g}{2}(\cos\theta-\sin\theta), \dfrac{mg}{2}(\cos\theta+\sin\theta)$,

    $Mg + \dfrac{mg}{2}(3+\sin 2\theta)$

13) $30°, mg\sqrt{3}$ at $30°$ to vertical;
    $\frac{3}{2}mg, \frac{1}{4}g, \frac{3}{2}\sqrt{3}mg$ at $30°$ to vertical

14) $\dfrac{g}{9}, \dfrac{40}{9}mg, \dfrac{5}{3}mg$

15) a) $\dfrac{6kMg}{k+8}$ b) $\dfrac{3kMg}{k+8}$

16) $28\frac{4}{7}$ s

17) a) $6mg/5\sqrt{2}$ b) $\frac{2}{5}$
    c) $\frac{6}{5}mg$ vertically downwards

18) $R_1 = \dfrac{m}{4a}(u^2-v^2), R_2 = \dfrac{mv^2}{2a}, \dfrac{5a}{4}$

20) $\dfrac{g}{8}$

21) a) $\frac{9}{2}$ m/s^2; 42 N, 24 N
    b) 2 m/s^2; 42 N, 24 N

Exercise 6a – p. 185

1) $Tx, 0, 0, -Fx$
2) $0, Tl \cos(\alpha + \beta), Wl \sin \alpha, -Fl$
3) 49 000 J
4) 126.8
5) 3×10^6 J
6) 6
7) $2\sqrt{106}$
8) 8844×10^3 J
9) 1400×10^3 J
10) 11 300 J, 17 300 J
11) 20 N
12) 250 J
13) 1330 N
14) 0.13

Exercise 6b – p. 192

1) 1110 kW
2) 1800 N
3) 4950 kW
4) 51.4 N
5) a) 37.5 m s^{-1} b) 19.5 m s^{-1}
   c) 461.5 m s^{-1}
6) 32.8 m s^{-1}
7) 60 N
8) 180 J, 32.9 W
9) 8 m s^{-2}
10) 5.51 m s^{-2}
11) 0.127 m s^{-2}
12) 3.3 m s^{-2}, 1420 N
13) 0.121 m s^{-2}
14) 6000 N

Multiple Choice Exercise 6 – p. 194

1) d   2) b   3) e   4) a
5) d   6) E 7) D 8) a
9) I 10) A 11) c   12) T
13) F 14) F 15) F 16) T
17) T

Miscellaneous Exercise 6 – p. 195

1) 125 kW
2) 4800 N, 35.7 m s^{-1}
3) 70 kW
4) 132 W, 0.275 m s^{-2}
5) $\dfrac{24\,000}{g} \text{ kg}, 9.14 \text{ m s}^{-2}$
6) $0.83 v^2, 5.34 \text{ m s}^{-2}$
7) 892.5 N, 81 800 N

8) 2.4 m s^{-2}, 13.9 kW
9) 45 m s^{-1}, 1.715 m s^{-2}
10) $73\frac{1}{3}$ kW, 50 km/h,
11) 3270 W,   a) 40 km/h   b) 24 km/h
12) 0.833 m s^{-2}, 86.2 km/h
13) 2160 N, 79.7 m
14) $\dfrac{3W}{n}, \dfrac{2g}{n}$
15) a) $\dfrac{10^3 H}{MV} - g \sin \alpha$
    b) $\dfrac{10^3 H}{MV} + g \sin \alpha$; $\dfrac{10^3 H}{3MVg}$; $\frac{3}{4} V$
16) 500 N; 15 kW
17) a) $23\frac{1}{3}$ kN   b) $\frac{7}{180} \text{ m/s}^2$
    c) $19\frac{5}{9}$ kN; 35×10^6 J
18) 450 N; 4.91 kW

Exercise 7a – p. 207

1) a) 23 m   b) 6 m   c) 4.5 m
2) 0.625 m
3) 40 N
4) $\dfrac{Mgl}{\lambda}$
5) $\dfrac{a_1 M_2 - a_2 M_1}{M_2 - M_1}, \dfrac{g(M_1 a_2 - M_2 a_1)}{a_1 - a_2}$
6) 1.5 kg
7) $\dfrac{9a}{4}$
8) 0.5 m
9) $\dfrac{16a}{7}$
10) $3mg, 3g$

Exercise 7b – p. 212

1) 9 J, 10 m
2) 2.4 m
3) $\frac{27}{14}$
4) $\pi \times 10^{-2}$ J

Exercise 7c – p. 218

1) 54 J, 5 m s^{-1}, 1 kg
2) a) 0.16 J   b) 0.25 J
3) 5.72 kJ
4) 3 J
5) $10m(2gh + v^2)$

Exercise 7d – p. 223

1) 2.5 m

2) $M\left(\dfrac{dg}{2}+4u^2\right)$

3) $\frac{1}{2}\sqrt{gl}$

4) $\sqrt{gl}$

5) 6 m

6) $(3+\sqrt{5})\dfrac{l}{2}$

7) $\dfrac{3l}{4}$

8) 0.45 m

Multiple Choice Exercise 7 – p. 224

1) c	2) a	3) c	4) c
5) d	6) b, c	7) c, d	8) d
9) B	10) C	11) B	12) D
13) I	14) I	15) A	16) b, c
17) F	18) F	19) T	20) F

Miscellaneous Exercise 7 – p. 226

1) $mgh-\frac{1}{2}mv^2$

2) 100 J

3) 680 J

4) 1500 W

5) $\sqrt{\dfrac{2gl}{3}}$

6) 0.96 m, 1.04 m

7) a) 3 m   b) $\sqrt{5}$ m

8) 3.17×10^5 J

9) 0.3 m

10) a) 30°   b) $W\sqrt{3}$, $\dfrac{W\sqrt{3}}{2}$, 30°

11) $\sqrt{\dfrac{5ga}{2}}$

12) a) 8g N   b) 0.128 m
    c) 0.36 m

13) 1.5 m; 2.82 m

14) 62.5 kJ, 10 kJ; $72\frac{1}{2}$ kW; 127.6 m

15) $\frac{5}{2}a$

16) a) $(2\sqrt{2ga})^{\frac{1}{2}}$ b) $2\sqrt{ga}$
    c) $2\sqrt{ga}(\cos\theta-\cos2\theta)$

17) $W\sqrt{3}/3$

18) a) $2a$ b) $\dfrac{3\sqrt{2ga}}{4}$

19) $5\sqrt{3}-8$

20) 2880 J

21) $\dfrac{W}{2}(2\sqrt{3}-3)$

22) mg

25) arctan 1/3, $\dfrac{2\sqrt{10}}{3}$, $\dfrac{3g\sqrt{10}}{10}$ N, $\dfrac{3\sqrt{10}}{5}$

Exercise 8a – p. 236

1) 17 m s^{-1}

2) $5\frac{5}{8}$ s

3) 18 N s

4) 24 N

5) 10.4 N s

6) $m(-4\mathbf{i}+9\mathbf{j})$

7) $4\mathbf{i}-7\mathbf{j}$

8) $3\mathbf{i}+\frac{9}{2}\mathbf{j}$

9) 40 N

10) $20\sqrt{5}$ N s at arctan $\frac{1}{2}$ to the direction of the initial velocity

11) a) $\dfrac{12}{5}\sqrt{7}$ N s   b) $\dfrac{12}{5}\sqrt{13-3\sqrt{3}}$ N s

12) 2000 litre

Exercise 8b – p. 241

1) a) $\frac{1}{2}$ m s^{-1} b) $\frac{7}{2}$ m s^{-1}

2) 600 kg

3) a) 486 m s^{-1} b) 480 m s^{-1}

4) 50 kg

6) a) $\frac{1}{50}u$ b) $\frac{2}{51}u$

7) $\dfrac{mv}{M+m}$; $\dfrac{m^2v^2+2gh(M+m)^2}{2h(M+m)}$

Exercise 8c – p. 248

1) a) $\dfrac{u}{2}$; $\dfrac{mu}{2}$ b) $\dfrac{u\sqrt{13}}{8}$; $\dfrac{mu\sqrt{13}}{8}$
   c) $\dfrac{u\sqrt{3}}{4}$; $\dfrac{mu\sqrt{3}}{4}$

2) 1.12 m s^{-1}; 3.36 N s

3) $\dfrac{J\sqrt{3}}{15}$; $\dfrac{4J\sqrt{3}}{15}$;

A: $\dfrac{J\sqrt{3}}{15m}$ along $\overrightarrow{AB}$;

B: $\dfrac{2J\sqrt{21}}{15m}$ at arctan $3\sqrt{3}$ to $\overrightarrow{AB}$;

C: $\dfrac{4J\sqrt{3}}{15m}$ along $\overrightarrow{CB}$

4) a) $\frac{3}{5}m\sqrt{6g}$ b) $\frac{1}{10}\sqrt{6g}$

5) a) $\frac{1}{2}mv$ b) $\frac{1}{2}v$ c) $\frac{1}{3}v$

6) a) 4.2 m s^{-1} b) 2.8 N s
   c) 1.4 m s^{-1} d) 0.99 m s^{-1}
   e) 0.99 N s; No

Exercise 8d — p. 255

1) 6 m s^{-1}; 16 m s^{-1}; 100 N s

2) 5.4 m s^{-1}; 3.9 m s^{-1}; 1.05 J

4) 0.2 kg; 2.5 m s^{-1}; 0.5 N s

5) $\dfrac{u}{5}$, $\dfrac{2u}{5}$, $\dfrac{8u}{5}$

6) a) $Mm(1+e)(V+v)/(M+m)$
   b) $Mm(1+e)(V-v)/(M+m)$

7) 2.5 m

8) $\sqrt{\dfrac{5}{6}}$; $\dfrac{2g}{5}\text{J}$

9) $44°$

10) e^2h, e^4h, e^6h; $h\left(\dfrac{1+e^2}{1-e^2}\right)$

Multiple Choice Exercise 8 — p. 256

1) d	2) d	3) c	4) c
5) c	6) a, d	7) a, d	8) c
9) c, b	10) b, c	11) B	12) C
13) B	14) B	15) D	16) A
17) c	18) a or b or c		19) I
20) d	21) T	22) F	23) T
24) T	25) F		

Miscellaneous Exercise 8 — p. 260

1) 65 m s^{-1}

2) 60 m s^{-1} upwards; 120 m s^{-1} downwards

3) $10^3 v^2 c \text{ N}$

4) 14.6 m s^{-1}

5) 1.2 m s^{-1}

6) $\dfrac{\sqrt{2}}{2}$; $m\sqrt{gh}\,(1+\sqrt{2})$; $\dfrac{mgh}{2}$

7) $\frac{1}{3}$

8) 8 m/s; $85 \times 10^4 \text{ N}$

11) $\dfrac{m_1 u}{m_2}$; $\dfrac{m_1}{m_2}$; $\dfrac{(m_2)^2}{m_1}$

12) $\dfrac{u(2-e)}{3}$; $\dfrac{2u(1+e)}{3}$; $\dfrac{u}{9}(e^2+8e-2)$

13) $\dfrac{V}{2}(1-e)$, $\dfrac{V}{4}(1-e^2)$; $\dfrac{V}{4}(1+e)^2$

14) 8175 J; 502.7 N

15) $\dfrac{V}{16}$, $\dfrac{3V}{16}$

16) $\dfrac{(1+e)(1-\lambda e)u}{(1+\lambda)^2}$; $\dfrac{(1+e)^2 u}{(1+\lambda)^2}$

17) $\frac{1}{3}V(1+e)$, $\frac{1}{3}V(1-2e)$; $\frac{1}{2}$

18) $\dfrac{15u^2}{32g}$

19) a) $2\sqrt{\dfrac{gh}{13}}$ b) $\dfrac{2h}{9}$ c) $\sqrt{\dfrac{13}{15}}$;
    $m\sqrt{\dfrac{2gh}{13}}(\sqrt{15}+\sqrt{13})$

20) $\dfrac{4a}{V}$; $\dfrac{V}{6}$; $\dfrac{5mV^2}{12}$

21) $\dfrac{m}{2}\sqrt{u^2-ga}$; $\sqrt{7ga}$; $\dfrac{mg}{4}$

22) $\dfrac{4V}{3}$; $\dfrac{4V}{3(n+1)}$

24) $\dfrac{(3-2\lambda)V}{3(\lambda+1)}$, $\dfrac{5V}{3(\lambda+1)}$

26) $\frac{1}{3}g$;   a) $3V/g$ b) $2V/g$
    c) $\frac{1}{3}V$ d) $2V/g$

28) $\frac{1}{2}\sqrt{2ga}$, $\frac{1}{2}\sqrt{2ga}$

29) $\frac{3}{5}u$, $\frac{1}{10}u$, $\frac{9}{5}mu$, $\frac{9}{20}mu^2$; $\frac{6}{5}mv$, $\frac{2}{5}v$

30) $\dfrac{3mg}{2}$; $\dfrac{g}{2}$; $\dfrac{3mgt}{14}$; $\dfrac{5gt}{7}$

32) $\dfrac{2\sqrt{2}J}{7}$

33) $\dfrac{20m}{7}$; $\dfrac{7u}{54}$

34) $4Mm(M+m)^2$; $4Mm(M-m)^2$;
    $(M-m)^4$

Exercise 9a — p. 270

1) 12.03

2) $10\sqrt{2}$, $5(2\sqrt{2}-1)$

3) 2; -10

4) 20; $15(2\sqrt{3}-3)$

5) $60°$, 45.31 m

6) 28 m s^{-1} at $44.5°$ above horizontal

7) 4.5 m

8) $9.6°$

9) 30 m s^{-1}

Exercise 9b — p. 277

1) 3.6 s

2) 1.76 s, 12.42 m

3) 2.6 sec, 1.3 sec

4) 28.7 m

5) 1.7 s, arctan (-0.716)

6) 22.8°

7) 70.5 m s^{-1}

8) 27.9 m s^{-1}

9) 1.28 s

10) 4.5 s, 179 m

11) $\mathbf{v} = \mathbf{i} + (2 - gt)\mathbf{j}$, $\mathbf{i} - 13\mathbf{j}$

$\mathbf{r} = t\mathbf{i} + (2t - \frac{1}{2}gt^2)\mathbf{j}$, $\frac{3}{4}(2\mathbf{i} - 11\mathbf{j})$

12) $\frac{1}{6}(16\mathbf{i} + 49\mathbf{j})$

13) $4\mathbf{i} + 4\mathbf{j}$, $3(4\mathbf{i} - 11\mathbf{j})$

14) arctan 7 below the horizontal;

$9y + 3x + 5x^2 = 0$

16) $\mathbf{r}_1 = 3t\mathbf{i} + (\sqrt{3}t - 5t^2)\mathbf{j}$

$\mathbf{r}_2 = \sqrt{3}t\mathbf{i} + (3t - 5t^2)\mathbf{j}$

$2(3\sqrt{2} - \sqrt{6})$

17) $\sqrt{2}$ s after projection; 20 m

18) 48.2 m s^{-1} at arctan $\frac{1}{12}$ below the horizontal

19) 2 s after projection of first particle; arctan $(-\frac{16}{63})$, arctan $(\frac{89}{252})$

Exercise 9c – p. 284

1) 44.7 m s^{-1} at 45° to the horizontal

2) 38.7 m s^{-1}, 37.5 m

3) 22.4 m s^{-1} at 45° to the horizontal, 12.5 m

4) 74.5 m s^{-1}

5) 9.8 m

6) 20.9°, 69.1°

7) 76.5°, 40.1°

8) 19.6°

9) 61 m s^{-1}

10) 5.1°, 178 m

11) 82.8°

13) arctan 4/5

15) 19.9°, 70.1°, 10 m

16) 25 m s^{-1} at arctan 4/3 to the horizontal

17) 2830 m, 14.1 s

18) arcsin $\frac{1}{4}\sqrt{2}$; $\dfrac{u^2}{18g}(4\sqrt{7} - 7)$

Multiple Choice Exercise 9 – p. 286

1) e   2) c   3) b   4) b

5) d   6) a   7) c   8) a, b

9) a, c   10) a, b, c   11) a, b   12) b

13) b   14) I 15) A 16) I

17) b

Miscellaneous Exercise 9 – p. 288

1) 4.74 m

5) 1 s; $5(2\sqrt{3} - 1)$ m

7) arctan $\left(\dfrac{u \sin \alpha - gt}{u \cos \alpha} \right)$

8) 10 m s^{-1}, arctan $\frac{3}{4}$ to the horizontal, 2.8 s, 9.6 m

9) arctan $\frac{1}{4}$, 1.13 s

10) 64 m, arcsin 4/5, 36 m, arcsin 3/5

11) 18.4°, 71.6°

12) 26.6°, 74.1°

14) 26.6° ⩽ α ⩽ 63.4°, 98 m, 10.7 m

15) b) $h\sqrt{\dfrac{1 + \sin \theta}{2}}$

17) a) 35.3°   b) 7h/3

18) $\dfrac{gT (\cos \alpha + \cos 2\alpha)}{2 \sin \alpha}$

19) 2/3

20) $20\sqrt{5}$ m s^{-1}; 120 m; 90 m

21) $3u^2/8g$; $\pm$ arctan $\sqrt{3/2}$ to horizontal

Exercise 10a – p. 296

1) 32 m s^{-2}; 6 m

2) 8 N

3) 0.63 ⩽ μ < 0.99

4) $7\sqrt{2}/2$

5) a) 42.7 N; 3.92 N   b) 14.4 rad s^{-1}

Exercise 10b – p. 302

1) $7\sqrt{3}/3$ rad s^{-1}

2) $5\sqrt{6}/3$

3) $\sqrt{g/l} \cos \theta$

4) a) $21\sqrt{5}/25$ b) 17.9 N

5) a) $2m\omega^2l$, mg b) $2m\omega^2l$, $m(g - \omega^2l)$

6) $M : m = 2 : 1$; $\omega^2 = g/l$

7) $7\sqrt{10}/5$ rad s^{-1}

8) $49m/4$ N

9) $3a/5$; $5/6$

Exercise 10c – p. 309

1) 11 m s^{-1}

2) 18.8°

3) 15.34 m s^{-1}

4) 21.8°

5) 44.27 m s^{-1}; 76.68 m s^{-1}

6) 8230 N; 0.0147 m

7) 32°

8) a) 88×10^3 N (inner)

b) 113×10^3 N (outer)

c) 202×10^3 N (inner)

Exercise 10d — p. 318

1) a) $\sqrt{2g}, 4g$ b) $\sqrt{3g}, 7g$
   c) $2\sqrt{g}, 10g$
2) a) $11g/2$ b) $15g/2$
   c) $19g/2$
3) $u > \sqrt{32gl}$
4) a) $2mg, \sqrt{2ga}, g\sqrt{5}$
   b) $7mg/2, \sqrt{3ga}, g\sqrt{39}/2$
   c) $5mg, 2\sqrt{ga}, 4g$
5) $5/6$ m
6) $a; a/4$

Exercise 10e — p. 327

1) $v \geqslant \sqrt{3g}$
2) $\frac{1}{2}\sqrt{ga}$
3) a) oscillates   b) loses contact
   c) describes complete circles
4) $7mg : mg$ a) $6g$ b) $2g$ c) $g\sqrt{17}$
5) a) $J \geqslant 21\sqrt{2}/4$ N s   b) $3\sqrt{7g}/4$
6) $a/2; 11 : 5$

Multiple Choice Exercise 10 — p. 328

1) c   2) b   3) c   4) c
5) d   6) a, c   7) c, d   8) a, c
9) a, b, d 10) D 11) C 12) D
13) I 14) b   15) b   16) F
17) F 18) F 19) F

Miscellaneous Exercise 10 — p. 330

1) 8.8 m s$^{-1} \leqslant v \leqslant 37.6$ m s^{-1}
2) $\frac{1}{2\pi}\sqrt{g/l}$
4) $\sqrt{2gr/11}$ to $\sqrt{2gr}$
5) $2a\sqrt{3}/3; 8a\sqrt{6}/9$
6) $\frac{3mg}{2}(2\cos\theta - 1)$
8) $3l/8; 4\sqrt{g/3l}$
9) $5a/4$
10) $n \geqslant 14$
12) $30°; \sqrt{2g/3l}$
15) $\sqrt{3ga}/2 \tan\alpha$
16) $\frac{1}{2}m(3g - a\omega^2)$
17) $12mg$
18) $mlv^2/(l^2 - h^2)$
   a) 15.85 N   b) 2.29 m s^{-1}; 32.7 N
19) $\frac{1}{2}l; \frac{1}{2}l; \frac{3}{2}mg; 3mg$
20) $\sqrt{g/3a}$
21) a) $m\sqrt{2ga \cos^3\alpha}$ b) $\sin\alpha\sqrt{2ga \cos\alpha}$
   c) $\cos^3\alpha$

22) $[u^2 - 2ga(1 + \cos\theta)]^{\frac{1}{2}}$;
   $mu^2/a - mg(2 + 3\cos\theta)$;
   $[ga/2(3\sqrt{2} + 4)]^{\frac{1}{2}}$
23) $\arccos(2g/l\omega^2)$
24) a) $10mg, 6mg$ c) $2\pi\sqrt{a/6g}$
25) $gb(1 - \sec\alpha + \frac{b}{a}\sec^2\alpha); gb(1 + \sec\alpha)$
26) $\sqrt{ga}$
27) $mg/2$
28) $m(r\omega^2 \cos\theta - g \sin\theta)$;
   $m(r\omega^2 \sin\theta + g \cos\theta); 4\pi\sqrt{3a/35g}$
29) $0.392; 21.4°; 35.5$ m s^{-1}
30) a) $\frac{15}{4}mg, \frac{9}{4}mg$ b) $\frac{1}{2}\sqrt{5ga}$
31) $2mg; 2mg, l\sqrt{3}, \sqrt{g/l}$

Exercise 11a — p. 342

1) $v = \left(\frac{t^2}{2} - 6t\right), -18$ m s^{-1},
   $s = \left(\frac{t^3}{6} - 3t^2\right); -72$ m
2) $v = t^2, s = \frac{t^3}{3}$
3) $v = \frac{3}{2}t^2 - t - 1, 31.5$ m s^{-1}
4) 18 m
5) 3 m
6) $v = \frac{1}{2} - \frac{1}{2t^2}, s = \frac{1}{2t} + \frac{t}{2} - 1, \frac{3}{8}$ m s$^{-1}, \frac{1}{4}$ m
7) 2 m s$^{-1}, s = 2t - \frac{1}{t} + c$
8) $v = \frac{1}{2}(1 - \cos 2t)$,
   $s = \frac{1}{2}(1 + t - \frac{1}{2}\sin 2t), \pi$ s
9) $\frac{9}{4}$ m s^{-1}
10) $\frac{32}{3}$ m s$^{-1}, 13\frac{1}{3}$ m
11) $\frac{1}{\omega}$
12) $0, 0, \frac{2}{\pi^2}$ m
13) $v = \frac{2}{5}t^2$
14) $s = \frac{32t^2}{15(t + 1)}$

Exercise 11b — p. 346

1) $v = \sqrt{6t}, s = \frac{2\sqrt{6}}{3}t^{\frac{3}{2}}, 45^{\frac{1}{3}}$ m s^{-1}
2) $\frac{2\sqrt{73}}{73}$ m s$^{-1}, \frac{1}{6}(\sqrt{73} - 1)$ m

3) -1 m

4) 8 m s^{-1}

Exercise 11c – p. 349

1) $a\sqrt{(2\lambda a/3)}$

2) $\dfrac{u^2}{6k}(2u + 3)$

3) a) $\dfrac{mu}{ke}(\sqrt{e}-1)$ b) $\dfrac{mu}{k\sqrt{e}}(\sqrt{e}-1)$

c) $\dfrac{mu^2}{ke}(e - 2)$

4) $\frac{20}{11}$ J; 8 m

5) $gT(1 - e^{-t/T}); gT^2(\ln 2 - \frac{1}{2})$

Exercise 11d – p. 353

1) a) 0.5 m s^{-2} b) 39.6 m

2) 5 s, 14.3 m

3) a) 8 m s^{-2} b) 2.46 s

4) a) 3.5 m s^{-2} b) 3.6 s

5) 1.2 m s^{-1}, 6.2 m s^{-1}

6) $113\frac{1}{3}$ m

Exercise 11e – p. 358

1) $6ti + 4j, 6i, 24i + 4j, 6i$

2) $(t^2 + 3)i + (1 - \frac{1}{2}t^2)j$

3) $18i + j, 27i + \frac{3}{2}j$

5) $3ti - 2tj$

6) $\sqrt{5}$ m s^{-1} at arctan $\frac{1}{2}$ to Ox

7) ω at $\left(\dfrac{\pi}{2} + \omega t\right)$ to Ox,

ω^2 at $-(\pi - \omega t)$ to Ox

8) $2\sqrt{10}$ m s^{-1} at arctan $\frac{1}{3}$ to Ox

10) $\dot{x} = \sqrt{(x^2 - 1)}, \dot{y} = 2\sqrt{y}$

11) $\dot{x} = 2t^{\frac{1}{2}}, \dot{y} = 3t^{\frac{1}{2}}$

Exercise 11f – p. 360

1) $a = 3i + 4j, v = (3i + 4j)t,$
$r = \frac{1}{2}(3i + 4j)t^2$

2) $r = \frac{1}{4}(t^3 i - t^2 j) + i + j; \frac{31}{4}i - \frac{5}{4}j$

3) $r = (2t - \sin t)i - \cos t j,$
$v = (2 - \cos t)i + \sin t j$

4) $r_0 = 2i - 3j, v = (3t^2 + 3)i - (4t^3 + 1)j,$
$v_0 = 3i - j, a = 6ti - 12t^2 j,$
$F = 24ti - 48t^2 j$

5) $v = (3i - j)t,$
$r(\text{rel to A}) = \frac{1}{2}(3i - j)t^2; 7i - 6j$

6) $(i + 2j)m$

Exercise 11g – p. 362

1) $r_0 = 0, v = 3t^2 i - 2(t + 1)j + 3k,$
$v_0 = -2j + 3k, a = 6ti - 2j$

2) $v = -\cos t i + tj + k,$
$r = -\sin t i + \frac{1}{2}t^2 j + tk$

3) $a = i + 2j + 3k, v = (i + 2j + 3k)t,$
$r = \frac{1}{2}(i + 2j + 3k)t^2; \sqrt{14}$

4) $r = e^t i + tj + \frac{1}{2}t^2 k, a = e^t i + k,$
$F = 2(e^t i + k)$

5) $F = -18tj - 3 \cos t k; 3\pi, 3\sqrt{(4 + \pi^4)}$

Exercise 11h – p. 363

1) $t = \frac{1}{2}; 5i + \frac{5}{2}j$

2) $t = 1; i + j + k$

3) No

4) $t = 3; 10i - j + 15k$

Exercise 11i – p. 365

1) $\frac{1}{5}\sqrt{5}, (t = \frac{3}{5})$

2) $(3 - 2\sqrt{2})^{\frac{1}{2}}, (t = \dfrac{\pi}{4})$

3) $2\sqrt{2}, (t = 3)$

4) $\sqrt{2}, (t = -1 \text{ or } 0)$

Exercise 11j – p. 367

1) a) 376 J   b) $130\sqrt{2}$ J

2) -27 J

3) 236 J

4) 3000 J

5) 51 J

6) 224 J (Note that it is not necessary to use the scalar product)

Exercise 11k – p. 370

1) a) 50 J   b) $41\frac{2}{3}$J

2) $11\frac{1}{4}$ m s^{-1}

3) $\frac{1}{20}d^2; \frac{1}{20}(20\,mgd - d^2)$

4) $\sqrt{2mu/k}$

5) a) $8mk$ b) $(V^2 - 16k)^{\frac{1}{2}}$

Multiple Choice Exercise 11 – p. 372

1) a	2) c	3) d	4) b
5) d	6) d)	7) e	8) c
9) a	10) d	11) a, b, c	12) b, c
13) a, b	14) b, c	15) a, b	16) c
17) B	18) C	19) A	20) C
21) D	22) a	23) c	24) A
25) I	26) b	27) T	28) F
29) T	30) T	31) F	

Miscellaneous Exercise 11 — p. 375

1) $-k \sin 3t, \frac{1}{3}k (\cos 3t - 1) + u,$
   $\frac{k}{9} (\sin 3t - 3t) + ut$

2) $(u^2 - a^2)^{\frac{1}{2}}$

3) $6m\,\mathbf{i}$

4) $\frac{1}{2}(t^2 + 2t + 2)\mathbf{i} + \frac{1}{2}(2 - 2t - 3t^2)\mathbf{j}$

5) $-54\mathbf{i}$

6) $10 \ln 2$

7) $10 - x$

8) $\frac{15}{32}u^4$

9) $g(t_2 - t_1)$

10) $2\mathbf{i} + 2\mathbf{j}$

11) $\frac{1}{m}[e^{-t}(mu + k) - k]$

12) 0.223 s, 1.61 s

13) 2.07 m s^{-1}, 5.84 m s^{-1}

14) a) 3 m s^{-2}, 0.5 m s^{-2}
    b) $\frac{1}{3}(24 + 13\sqrt{3})$ m s^{-2},
    $\frac{1}{3}(24 - 13\sqrt{3})$ m s^{-2},
    c) 258 m

15) 84.8 km h^{-1}

16) $2u$

17) gTe^{x/gT^2}

18) a) $1\frac{5}{27}$ m   b) 2 s   c) 4 m/s

21) 4 m, $2\lambda/(e^\lambda - 1)$ m s^{-1}, 5 m s^{-1}

22) $\frac{u}{k}(1 - e^{-kt}), ue^{-kt}, \frac{1}{k}\ln\left(\frac{g + ku}{g}\right)$

23) $\mathbf{r} = \frac{3}{2}t^2\mathbf{i} - 2t\mathbf{j}, \ 3y^2 = 8x$

24) $15\mathbf{i} + 50\mathbf{j} + 25\mathbf{k}$

26) $\mathbf{r} = (2T^2 - 1)\mathbf{i} + (T^4 + 1)\mathbf{j}, \ 7\mathbf{i} + 6\mathbf{j}$

27) $\frac{5mV}{2P}; \frac{17mV^2}{6P}$

28) a) $2uT$ b) $T \ln 3$
    c) $4mu^2$

30) 8

31) $\frac{\pi}{4}$ to Ox

32) $\frac{5}{v} - \frac{v}{80}, 70.2$ m

33) $\frac{m}{2k} \ln \left(\frac{4}{3}\right)$

34) $m\left[k^2 \ln\left(\frac{k}{k - u}\right) - ku\right]$

Exercise 12a — p. 388

1) a) $\pi\sqrt{2}$ s   b) $4\pi/3$

2) a) 6 m s^{-1} b) 24 m s^{-2}
   c) $\frac{\pi}{2}$ s

3) $2\sqrt{3}$ rad s^{-2}

4) $2\pi \left(\frac{x_2^2 - x_1^2}{v_1^2 - v_2^2}\right)^{\frac{1}{2}}$

5) $\frac{\pi}{3}; \frac{\pi\sqrt{3}}{3}$ rad s^{-1}

6) 1.2 m; 0.27 m s^{-1}; 0.18 m s^{-2}

7) 0.023 m; 3.7 m s^{-2}; 0.26 m s^{-1}

Exercise 12b — p. 392

1) a) $\frac{\pi\sqrt{3}}{12}$ s   b) $\frac{\pi\sqrt{3}}{8}$ s   c) $\frac{\pi\sqrt{3}}{12}$ s

2) a) $\frac{a\sqrt{3}}{2}$ b) $\frac{a}{2}$ c) $a\frac{\sqrt{3}}{2}$

3) $2T$

4) a) 38.2 s   b) 9.1 s

5) a) 1 m   b) 0.28 m s^{-2}
   c) $\frac{\pi\sqrt{3}}{12}$ m s^{-1}

Exercise 12c — p. 396

1) 0.0018 m

2) 9.803

3) 431 seconds in 24 hours in both cases

Exercise 12d — p. 400

2) $10g; E, \frac{2}{7}\pi\sqrt{2}$ s; $\frac{7}{10}\sqrt{2}$ m s^{-1}; 0.2 m

3) $6a; 2\pi\sqrt{\frac{2a}{5g}}$

4) $5a$

5) 800 N;   a) 80 m s^{-2}
   b) $\frac{\pi}{40}$ s   c) $2\sqrt{3}$ m s^{-1}

6) $2\pi\sqrt{\frac{ml}{\lambda}}; \frac{mgl}{\lambda}$

Exercise 12e — p. 411

1) $\frac{1}{3\sqrt{5g}}(2\pi + 3\sqrt{3})$

2) a) $\sqrt{5ga}$ b) $\sqrt{7ga}$

3) $2\sqrt{10}$ m s^{-1}; $\frac{1}{2\sqrt{10}}\left(\frac{\pi}{\sqrt{2}} + 2\sqrt{2}\right)$ s

4) a) $\dfrac{\pi}{2}\sqrt{\dfrac{a}{g}}$ b) $\sqrt{\dfrac{a}{g}}\left(\dfrac{\pi}{2}+1\right)$

  c) $\sqrt{\dfrac{a}{g}}\left(2\pi+4\right)$

5) $\dfrac{5a}{4};\dfrac{a}{4};\sqrt{\dfrac{a}{g}}\left(\dfrac{2\pi}{3}+\sqrt{3}\right)$

Multiple Choice Exercise 12 – p. 413

1) c   2) a   3) d   4) a, c
5) c, d   6) a, b, c 7) b, c   8) b
9) A 10) F 11) F 12) T
13) F 14) F 15) T

Miscellaneous Exercise 12 – p. 415

1) $\lambda\sqrt{d^2-x^2};\dfrac{\pi}{\lambda};\dfrac{\pi}{3\lambda}$

2) $\dfrac{3}{4}$ m; $\dfrac{\pi}{\sqrt{2g}}$

3) $2:7; 1.3$ s

4) $4\sqrt{\dfrac{2}{5}}$ m; $2\pi\sqrt{\dfrac{3}{5}}$ s; $4\sqrt{\dfrac{2}{3}}$ m s^{-1}

5) $4\sqrt{6}$ m s^{-1}; $12\sqrt{10}$ m s^{-2}
   a) 0.13 s   b) 225 J

6) 6 m/s, 2 m; 5.9 m/s

7) $2\pi\sqrt{\dfrac{ma}{\lambda}}; \sqrt{\left(2gc+\dfrac{\lambda c^2}{ma}\right)}$

8) $\left(3-\dfrac{3\sqrt{2}}{4}\right)l$

9) $\dfrac{2\pi}{3}\sqrt{\dfrac{b}{g\sin\theta}}; \sqrt{3bg\sin\theta}$

10) $\dfrac{a}{12}$;   a) $\dfrac{5a}{12}$ b) $5\sqrt{\dfrac{ag}{12}}; 5g$

11) $2\sqrt{2}$ m; $\frac{1}{2}\sqrt{2}$ m s^{-1} in direction PO

12) $3;\dfrac{l}{2}$

13) $3a$

14) $133\frac{1}{3}$ N; $\frac{2}{3}\sqrt{3}$ m/s

15) $\frac{40}{9}b; \frac{4}{3}\pi\sqrt{b/g}$

16) a) 2.75 b) 0.02 m   c) 0.06 m

17) $\sqrt{\dfrac{\lambda a}{3m}}$

18) $\dfrac{l}{4}$

19) $4\pi\sqrt{\dfrac{c}{g}}; \sqrt{cg}$

20) $2\pi\sqrt{\dfrac{6ml}{11\lambda}}; \sqrt{\dfrac{\lambda l}{22m}}$

21) $\pi\sqrt{\dfrac{a}{g}}; \dfrac{a}{4}$

Exercise 13a – p. 421

1) $8i-9j$
2) $\sqrt{26}$ m s^{-1}
3) $\arctan\frac{3}{4}$
4) $073.7°, 5.64$ m s^{-1}
5) 16.5 m s^{-1}; $110°$ or $160°$

Exercise 13b – p. 424

1) a) 665.7 s   b) 230 s
2) $032.8°, 237.2°; 64.4$ min
3) 89.3 s; 86.5 s; 117.2 s
4) 34.05 kmh^{-1}; 1 h 34 min
5) $098.1°$

Exercise 13c – p. 430

11) a) $-i-j$ b) $i+j$
2) 20
3) 23.4 km h^{-1}, N $\arctan\frac{7}{6}\sqrt{3}$ E
4) 5.83 km h^{-1}
5) 38.4 km h^{-1} in direction $167.7°$
6) $267.3°$ or $352.3°$
7) 13.3 km h^{-1}, 5.6 km h^{-1}
8) 12
9) 8.9 km h^{-1}
10) $210°$
11) $12\sqrt{3}$ km h^{-1}, $120°$
12) $193.9°; 166.1°; 20.8$ km h^{-1} due east

Exercise 13d – p. 438

1) 5 m s^{-1}, $126.9°$, 16 m
2) $34.3°$ with V_A produced, 2.66 s or
   $85.7°$ with V_A, 1.5 s
3) 5.32 km, 21.3 km h^{-1}, $138.2°$
4) 151 m
5) 12.27
6) 2.27 km
7) 6.94 km h^{-1}, 9.23 km h^{-1}
8) a) $16i+30j, 18i+24j$
   b) $2i-6j$
   c) $2ti+(10-6t)j$
9) 12.46 hours
10) $8\sqrt{11}$ km h^{-1}; $4\sqrt{2}$ km

11) $-7i + 8j; -7i \pm 4\sqrt{11}j$

12) a) $133\frac{1}{3}$ s, $666\frac{2}{3}$ m

b) Upstream at $\arccos\frac{3}{4}$ to the bank,
$\frac{1600}{21}\sqrt{7}$ s, $533\frac{1}{3}$ m

Exercise 13e — p. 442

1) $34.2, 047°$

2) 888.9 m, $d \leqslant 814.1$

3) $216.2°$

4) $038.4°$

5) $-2i + j; \frac{4}{5}\sqrt{5}$

6) 440 km h^{-1}, 1.8 km

7) a) 2.4 km, 2 km

b) 3.7 minutes,
144 km h^{-1} on a bearing $046°$

8) $-36i - 30j; (25 - 36t)i + (30 - 30t)j;$
12.49

9) $\frac{10}{3}i - \frac{2}{3}j; \frac{14}{13}$

10) 49 km h^{-1}, $172°$; $6\sqrt{3}$ km h^{-1} at 13.06;
13.26

Exercise 13f — p. 447

1) $v\sqrt{2}, 2v, v\sqrt{3}$

2) a) $\sqrt{37}$ at arctan 6 to Ox

b) $\sqrt{145}$ at arctan (-12) to Ox

3) $2\omega(5 + 4\sin 3\omega t)^{\frac{1}{2}}, \pi/2\omega,$
$2\omega^2(17 - 8\sin 3\omega)^{\frac{1}{2}}$

4) a) $u\sqrt{(2t^2 - 2t + 1)}$ at arctan $\dfrac{t-1}{t}$ to Ox

b) $2\sqrt{(u^2 - 4u + 8)}$

Miscellaneous Exercise 13 — p. 448

1) 1754 s

2) a) $11\frac{1}{2}$ minutes later, 2.9 nautical miles,
$349.6°$

b) 28 minutes later, 4 nautical miles,
north east

3) 13.75 km, 24.7 s

4) 20 knots, $315°$

5) 3.2 m s^{-1}, $5\frac{1}{3}$ m s^{-1} perpendicular to
the bank, $5\frac{1}{3}$ m s^{-1}

6) $10(11 + 6\sqrt{3})^{\frac{1}{2}}$

7) 40 km h^{-1}; 54 minutes; $084.3°$

8) $135.5°, 060°$

9) 12 knots, arcsin $7/9$ west of north,
$\dfrac{2\sqrt{2}}{3}$ hours, $24/7$ knots

10) a) 709 km h^{-1} b) 1029 km h^{-1}

11) 25 knots, $217°, 143°, 12$ knots

12) a) $\sqrt{13}\,\omega r$, arctan $3/2$ with OB produced

b) $\sqrt{7}\,\omega r$, arctan $3\sqrt{3}$ with BO,
$\cos\theta = 2/3, 7r/\sqrt{13}$

13) $\arcsin \dfrac{u}{2V}$

14) a) $10(t - 1)i + 10j$

b) $\frac{10}{3}\sqrt{5}$ km h^{-1}, $1\frac{1}{2}$ h

15) a) 6.72 km

b) 2.94, arcsin $7/15$ east of north

16) a) $-15i + 70k, 5i + 30k$

b) $\{25 + (30 - 5t)^2\}^{\frac{1}{2}}; 10i + 95k, 25\sqrt{2};$
$3\frac{1}{12}$ s

17) 69 s, 58 s

18) $(2a - a\sin\omega t)i + 2a\cos\omega t j$
$+ (a\sin\omega t - 3a)k;$
$-a\omega\cos\omega t i - 2a\omega\sin\omega t j$
$+ a\omega\cos\omega t k;$
$a\sqrt{5}, 5a$

19) a) $\dfrac{6a}{\sqrt{35}\,V}$ b) $a/6, a/V$

20) $u/\sqrt{2}, v = u(1 - 1/\sqrt{2})$

21) $v_B = 5i + 12j, v_E = -4i;$
$r_B = 5ti + 12tj, r_C = (80 - 4t)i + 240j;$
16 s, 80 m

22) $(270 + \alpha)°$ where $2\tan\alpha = \tan\theta + \tan\phi$

Exercise 14a — p. 460

1) $3\sqrt{17}$ at arctan $\frac{1}{4}$ to Ox; $12y = 3x + 16$

2) $2\sqrt{13}$ at arctan $\dfrac{3\sqrt{3}}{5}$ to Ox;
$5y = 3\sqrt{3}x - 4\sqrt{3}$

3) $10.4; y = 1.4x - 0.8$

4) $6; y = \sqrt{3}x$

5) $5; 3y = 4x + 8$

6) $r = \frac{14}{3}i + \lambda(9i - 3j)$

7) a) $P = \sqrt{2}; Q = -5\sqrt{2}$ b) $4\sqrt{2}$

8) $P\sqrt{13/3}; 4a/3$

9) $-21i + 21j; r = \frac{22}{21}i + \lambda(-i + j)$

10) $n = 5, m = 1$

11) $4y + x + 4 = 0$

12) a) $P = 2; Q = -7$

b) $P = -\frac{1}{2}; Q = -2$

Exercise 14b — p. 469

1) $7\sqrt{3}Fa$ where $2a$ is the length of one
side

2) $P = -1; Q = 6$

3) $\sqrt{13}P$; arctan $2\sqrt{3}$ with DB

5) $\sqrt{2}F$; F along CA and DA

6) $F\sqrt{5}$ at arctan $\frac{1}{2}$ to DA

7) $\sqrt{5}F$ at arctan 2 to BA; a

8) $-\dfrac{5\sqrt{2}}{6}$

9) 26 units

10) $4:3:5;\ \dfrac{35P}{12}$

11) a) A force of magnitude 8 units
    b) A couple

Exercise 14c — p. 472

1) Equilibrium
2) Either equilibrium or the resultant is a force passing through both axes
3) Either a couple or in equilibrium
4) A force passing through A
5) A couple
6) A force parallel to the given forces

Exercise 14d — p. 477

(N.B. There are alternative ways of expressing the answers to this exercise)

1) $15\overrightarrow{PQ}$ where AP : PC $= 2:1$ and BQ : QC $= 4:1$
2) $2\overrightarrow{AM} + 2\overrightarrow{AN} = 4\overrightarrow{AL}$; M bisects BC; N bisects DE; L bisects MN
3) $4\overrightarrow{CL}$ where L is the midpoint of MN, M bisects AB and N bisects AD
4) $8\overrightarrow{MN}$ where M bisects AC and BN : ND $= 1:3$

Exercise 14e — p. 486

1) a) $p = -25/8; q = -15/8$
   b) $p = 25/6; q = -15/8$
2) P parallel to BA cutting AC produced at D where AD $= 4a$; P parallel to AB; $2Pa\sqrt{3}$ in sense CBA
3) $5/2; -1; 3y = 2x$ or $3y = 2x + 12$
4) $5F$ along $\overrightarrow{AB}$; $5F$ along $\overrightarrow{BC}$; $7\sqrt{2}F$ along $\overrightarrow{CA}$; $5a/6$
5) $\dfrac{4P}{\sqrt{3}}(\overrightarrow{AB})$; $\dfrac{8P}{\sqrt{3}}(\overrightarrow{CB})$; $2P\sqrt{3}(\overrightarrow{CD})$

Multiple Choice Exercise 14 — p. 488

1) b	2) e	3) c	4) c
5) b	6) a, c	7) a, c	8) B
9) A	10) D	11) A	12) C
13) d	14) b, c	15) I	16) T
17) F	18) F	19) T	20) T

Miscellaneous Exercise 14 — p. 491

1) a) Equilibrium
   b) Couple of magnitude twice area ABC
   c) $3F$ parallel to $\overrightarrow{SR}$ and dividing SP in the ratio $1:2$
   d) F parallel to $\overrightarrow{RS}$ cutting PS produced $3a$ from S
   e) Couple of magnitude $3Fa$
   f) $2\overrightarrow{AD}$ where D bisects BC
   g) A force passing through A and represented by $\overrightarrow{CB}$

2) A force of 10 N parallel to the original force and distant 2 m from it on either side of it.

3) 5 N in a direction parallel to the negative y-axis and through $(2/5, 0)$.

4) $4F$ along AB; $\dfrac{5\sqrt{5}}{2}F$ along BE:
   $\dfrac{7\sqrt{5}}{2}F$ along EA

6) a) $18a$ b) $30a$
7) $5M/a$; $4y + 3x = 2a$
8) 0.3 N m
9) 6 or -24
10) $\dfrac{a(1 + n)}{n}$; $\dfrac{W(1 + n)}{3}$
11) a) $13P$, arctan 2.4
    b) $3a$; $12Pa$ in sense ABC
12) a) i) $a + b$ ii) $2b$ iii) $2b - a$
       iv) $b - a$
    b) $7i - j$; $4i + 3j$; $14i - 2j$; $-6i + 8j$; 15 N
13) $p = 11, q = 14$ a) $2\sqrt{19}$ b) $12\sqrt{3}$
14) $\sqrt{13}$; arctan $\sqrt{3}/7$ to AB; $19\sqrt{3}$ N m, ABC; $2\sqrt{19}$ N, distant $7\frac{2}{3}$ m from A
16) $10\overrightarrow{P}$ at arctan 4/3 to Ox;
    $3y = 4x - 112a$
    $10P$ at arctan 4/3 to Ox;
    $3y = 4x + 8a$
17) $10W$ at arctan 3/4 to DA produced at M; $7W$; $3W$
18) a) $13P$ at arctan 5/12 to AB;
       $4a/5$ from B on AB produced
    b) $\dfrac{4P}{3}\sqrt{10}$ at arctan 3 to BA;
       $a/4$ from A on AB
19) $Pa\sqrt{3}$; $a/2$
20) a) $8P$ b) $15P$
    c) $17P$ d) $62°, 10.4a$

21) a) $7\mathbf{i}$ b) $13\mathbf{i} - 6\mathbf{j}$
$\mathbf{F_1} = 32\mathbf{i} + 24\mathbf{j}$, $\mathbf{F_2} = 10\mathbf{i} - 24\mathbf{j}$;
$42\,\text{N}$; $16\mathbf{i} + 12\mathbf{j}$

22) $5; 6, 10 + \sqrt{3}, 10 - \sqrt{3}$

23) $P = 4; Q = 5; P = 4; Q = 4$

24) Midpoint of BC; G/3

25) $50P$; $3y + 4x = 12a$

26) $X = 8\,\text{N}$; $Y = 4\sqrt{13}\,\text{N}$; $M = 24\,\text{N m}$;
$P = 12\,\text{N}$; $Q = 8\sqrt{13}\,\text{N}$

27) $BP : PC = 2:3$; $AQ : QC = 1:3$;
$k = 20/3$

28) b) $5:3; 1:2$

29) c) $4\triangle ABC$
M is the midpoint of XY

Exercise 15a — p. 505

1) $\left(\dfrac{19}{9}, \dfrac{10}{3}\right)$

2) $\left(-\dfrac{1}{7}, \dfrac{3}{2}\right)$

3) $\dfrac{1}{15}(5\mathbf{i} + 28\mathbf{j})$, $\dfrac{1}{3}(5\mathbf{i} + 4\mathbf{j})$

4) $\dfrac{1}{11}(3\mathbf{i} - \mathbf{j})$, $\mathbf{i}$

6) $2\mathbf{i} + \tfrac{1}{3}\mathbf{j}$

Exercise 15b — p. 512

1) $\dfrac{71}{12}a$ from C

2) $\dfrac{7}{9}a$ from BC, $\dfrac{4}{9}a$ from DC

3) $\dfrac{5a\sqrt{3}}{18}$ from AB

4) $\dfrac{7h}{6}$ from the base of the larger cylinder

5) centroid of the triangle

6) $\tfrac{3}{8}$ of the side of the square from each of the heavier sides

7) $\tfrac{2}{3}$ m from the edge joining the particles

8) $\dfrac{32\sqrt{2}}{33}$ m along the median through the right angled vertex

9) $\left(\dfrac{2 + \pi}{4 + \pi}\right)a$ from the straight edge

10) centre of the square

11) $\dfrac{a}{4}$ from DC

12) $\dfrac{a\sqrt{2}}{24}$ from D on BD

13) $\dfrac{2a\sqrt{3}}{9}$ from AD

14) $\dfrac{a}{6}$ from the centre of the largest circle

15) $\dfrac{12}{24 - \pi}$ from the centre of the hole

16) $a\left(\dfrac{4\pi - 3}{4\pi - 2}\right)$ from the solid base

Exercise 15c — p. 518

1) a) $(0, \tfrac{2}{5})$
   b) $4a\sqrt{2}/3\pi$ from centre along radius of symmetry
   c) $\left(\dfrac{1}{\ln 2}, \dfrac{1}{\ln 16}\right)$
   d) $(-\tfrac{3}{5}, 0)$
   e) $\dfrac{6a\sqrt{3}}{8\pi - 6\sqrt{3}}$ from centre

Exercise 15d — p. 522

1) $\tfrac{3}{8}a$ from plane face

2) $\tfrac{3}{13}h$ from base

3) $\dfrac{h(4a - h)}{4(3a - h)}$

4) $\dfrac{45a}{4(19\sqrt{8} - 22\sqrt{5})}$

5) $\left(\tfrac{1}{2}\left(\dfrac{e^2 + 1}{e^2 - 1}\right), 0\right)$

Exercise 15e — p. 524

1) $\tfrac{5}{8}h$ from base

2) $\tfrac{1}{2}(a + b)$

3) $\tfrac{1}{4}a$

Exercise 15f — p. 530

1) $\dfrac{4a}{3\pi}$ from diameter

2) $\dfrac{2r\sqrt{2}}{\pi}$ from centre along radius of symmetry

3) $\dfrac{a\sqrt{3}}{\pi}$ from centre along radius of

symmetry

4) $\frac{2}{3}l$

5) $\dfrac{3a}{2\pi}$

Exercise 15g – p. 537

1) $\dfrac{p(3p-2q)}{3(2p-q)}$

2) $\frac{2}{3}a, \frac{7}{9}a; \frac{6}{11}$

3) a) $\dfrac{4r(2kr+h)}{h^2-3kr^2}$ b) $\frac{4}{3}$

5) $5a, 5a; \arctan \frac{5}{7}; \frac{1}{6}$

Multiple Choice Exercise 15 – p. 539

1) b   2) e   3) a   4) c
5) a   6) F   7) T   8) T
9) F   10) F

Miscellaneous Exercise 15 – p. 541

1) $\dfrac{7a}{9}, \dfrac{4h}{9}, \dfrac{a\sqrt{10}}{5}$

2) 12.2 N

3) $\dfrac{a}{4}, \dfrac{a}{\pi}$

4) $\dfrac{b}{3}$ from O on OC, $\dfrac{3a^2+2b^2}{6b^2-3a^2}$

6) 8.57 cm from the base

7) 10.1°

9) $\dfrac{73r}{33}$ from the joint face

10) $\dfrac{(\lambda^2-12\lambda+48)a}{3(8-\lambda)}, \dfrac{2(6-\lambda)a}{8-\lambda}, 4$

11) 70.4°, $\dfrac{16W}{45}$

12) $a\sqrt{2}$

13) $\frac{1}{4}W\sqrt{7}$

14) $(\frac{20}{7}, \frac{5}{2}); 41°$

15) $\dfrac{a}{(2\pi-3\sqrt{3})}$

16) $\frac{23}{26}a, \frac{11}{13}a; \frac{51}{32}a^2w$ at P, $\frac{53}{32}a^2w$ at Q

18) $\dfrac{5h}{16}, \arctan \dfrac{4\sqrt{5}}{11}$

20) $\frac{2}{3}, 2$

21) $(\frac{3}{5}a, \frac{3}{4}a); \frac{5}{4}$

Exercise 16a – p. 553

1) 40.9°

2) $2-\sqrt{3}$

3) $\dfrac{7l-\sqrt{l^2+32a^2}}{4}$

4) $\dfrac{\mu(1+\sqrt{2}-\mu)aW}{1+\mu^2}$

5) a) by sliding   b) by sliding
6) a) $\arcsin \frac{1}{3}$ b) 1

7) $\arcsin \dfrac{\pi}{8}$

Exercise 16b – p. 558

1) $\dfrac{3\sqrt{3}W}{8}$ where W is the weight of the

rod, $3\sqrt{3}/41$

2) $\dfrac{8W}{45}$ at all points of contact

3) $\dfrac{4W}{3}, \arctan \frac{4}{3}$

4) $\sqrt{2}-1$

Exercise 16c – p. 564

1) $\dfrac{4}{7}, \dfrac{W}{2}$ at $\arctan \frac{3}{4}$ to the horizontal

2) 150.3°

3) $\dfrac{\sqrt{21}W}{6}$ at $\arctan \dfrac{\sqrt{3}}{2}$ to the horizontal

4) $\dfrac{2aW}{l\sqrt{2}-a}$

5) $\dfrac{7\sqrt{3}}{24}$

6) $\dfrac{W\sqrt{57}}{18}$ at $\arctan \dfrac{\sqrt{3}}{4}$ to the horizontal

Miscellaneous Exercise 16 – p. 564

1) $\dfrac{3}{4}, \dfrac{W}{4}$

2) a) $\dfrac{\sqrt{5}}{4}W$ at $\arctan \frac{1}{2}$ to the vertical

b) $\dfrac{4l}{3}$

4) $\arctan \dfrac{12}{5}$ to the horizontal, $\dfrac{35}{64}W, \dfrac{91}{80}W$

5) $\dfrac{11l}{20}$

9) b) $Mg/2\sqrt{3}$ c) $1/\sqrt{3}$

11) $\dfrac{1}{\sqrt{3}}$

12) $\dfrac{2}{3\mu'} \leqslant \tan\theta \leqslant 2\mu$

13) $\dfrac{16a}{5}, \dfrac{4a}{5}$

14) BC, $45°$, $\dfrac{\sqrt{5}W}{2}$ at $\arctan\frac{1}{2}$ to the horizontal

15) a) $2a(2W + W_1)\sin\theta$
   b) $\frac{1}{2}(W + W_1)\tan\theta, \frac{1}{2}W_1$,
      $\frac{1}{2}(W + W_1)\tan\theta, \frac{1}{2}(2W + W_1)$

16) $\frac{1}{2}W\tan\theta$, W vertically,
    $\frac{1}{2}W\tan\theta$ horizontally

17) a) $\dfrac{W}{2}$ b) $\dfrac{3\sqrt{3}W}{4}, \dfrac{11W}{4}$

18) c) $\frac{2}{3}a$

Exercise 17a – p. 572

1) AB $-\dfrac{2\sqrt{3}}{3}W$, BC $\dfrac{\sqrt{3}}{3}W$,

   $\dfrac{\sqrt{3}}{3}W$ in the direction CB

2) $9W/25, 16W/25$, AB $3W/5$, BC $4W/5$,
   AC $-12W/25$

3) W in the direction AB

4) $2\sqrt{3}W/3$ in the direction AD;
   AB $2\sqrt{3}W/3$, BC $\sqrt{3}W/3$;
   CA $-2\sqrt{3}W/3$, AD $-4\sqrt{3}W/3$

Exercise 17b – p. 581

1) 100 N at B,
   AB, BC, CD, AD $-50\sqrt{2}$ N,
   AC 100 N

2) 150 N, 150 N, AB, BC $150\sqrt{2}$ N;
   AD, DC -150 N; BD 0

3) 200 N at B, $200\sqrt{2}$ N at A at $45°$ to AD;
   AB, AD 200 N; BD $-200\sqrt{2}$ N;
   BC, CD 0

4) $W\sqrt{3}$ at B, $2W$ at A at $30°$ to AD;
   AB, AD, CD $2W\sqrt{3}/3$;
   BD $-2W\sqrt{3}/3$; BC $-W\sqrt{3}/3$

5) 300 N, 300 N, AB, BC, CD $200\sqrt{3}$ N.
   AE, ED$-100\sqrt{3}$ N; BE, EC$-200\sqrt{3}$ N

6) 225 N at A, 75 N at D, AB 260 N;
   BC, BE, CD 87 N; AE -130 N,
   CE -87 N, ED -43 N

7) 378 N at $23.3°$ to AD at A, 346 N at B;
   CD, BC, BE -173 N; CE, AB 173 N,
   ED 87 N, AE 260 N

8) 100 N at A and D; AB, BC, CE 100 N,
   ED -100 N, CD 141 N, AE 0,
   BE -141 N

9) $2.7W$ at B, $2.9W$ at A at $20.1°$ to AE;
   CD, BC $-1.7W$, ED $2W$, CE 0
   BE $-1.4W$, AB W, AE $2.7W$

10) $5W/3$ at C, $4W/3$ at A, AB $8W/3$,
    AE $-4\sqrt{3}W/3$, BE $-2\sqrt{3}W/3$,
    DE $-\sqrt{3}W$, BC $10W/3$,
    DC $-5\sqrt{3}W/3$, BD $-4\sqrt{3}W/3$

11) 112 N at $26.6°$ below the horizontal
    500 N, -500 N, -500 N

12) -167 N, 47.1 N, 186 N

13) $4\sqrt{3}W/9, -8\sqrt{3}W/9, -\sqrt{3}W$

14) 100 N, -100 N, -50 N

15) $3.80W$ at $52.4°$ below AD, W,
    $-3.01W$, $1.73W$

16) 948 N at $18.4°$ below AE, -1200 N,
    -600 N, $600\sqrt{2}$ N

17) Thrusts: AB, FA $3W$; BC, EF $4W$;
    BD, DF W
    Tensions: CD, DE $2W\sqrt{3}$; AD W

18) $\frac{16}{3}W\sqrt{3}$ horizontally, $W\sqrt{3}, 2W\sqrt{3}$,
    $-\frac{10}{3}W\sqrt{3}, \frac{11}{3}W\sqrt{3}$

20) $\sqrt{3}W/3, 2\sqrt{3}W/3$ along AB;
    AD, DC $-\sqrt{3}W/3$, AB $\sqrt{3}W/3$
    BC $-\sqrt{3}W/3$, AC $\sqrt{3}W/3$

21) CD 800 N; ED, AE -800 N,
    EC 400 N, BC 860 N, AC 230 N

Exercise 18a – p. 592

1) $\frac{1}{2}$

2) $\frac{5}{18}$

3) $\frac{15}{17}$

4) a) $\frac{5}{12}$ b) $\frac{7}{12}$ c) $\frac{1}{12}$

5) $\frac{1}{2}$

6) a) $\frac{1}{2}$ b) $\frac{5}{6}$

7) a) $\frac{3}{5}$ b) $\frac{3}{10}$ c) $\frac{9}{10}$

8) a) $\frac{1}{35}$ b) $\frac{22}{35}$

9) $\frac{3}{5}$

10) $\frac{2}{5}$

Exercise 18b – p. 602

1) a) $\frac{1}{4}$ b) $\frac{3}{4}$ c) $\frac{1}{2}$

2) a) $\frac{1}{8}$ b) $\frac{7}{8}$

3) a) $\frac{1}{5}$ b) $\frac{48}{125}$ c) $\frac{369}{625}$

4) $(0.8)^{10} = 0.1074$

5) a) $\frac{3}{8}$ b) $\frac{1}{64}$ c) $\frac{63}{64}$

6) a) $\frac{1}{36}$ b) $\frac{1}{18}$ c) $\frac{11}{12}$

7) a) $\frac{1}{4}$ b) $\frac{1}{16}$ c) $\frac{63}{64}$

8) a) $\frac{1}{2}$ b) $\frac{1}{4}$ c) $\frac{1}{8}$

9) a) $\dfrac{35}{(36)^2} = 0.027$ b) $\dfrac{35^2}{36^3} = 0.026$

10) $\frac{2}{3}$

11) $\frac{30}{91} = 0.330$

12) a) $\frac{1}{13}$ b) 0.068 c) 0.0599

13) $\frac{18}{125}, 4$

14) $\frac{1}{20}, 14$

15) 1267

16) a) $\frac{7}{45}$ b) $\frac{4}{9}$

17) a) $\frac{3}{7}$ b) $\frac{1}{3}$

Exercise 18c – p. 606

2) $\frac{1}{8}$

3) $\frac{1}{6}$

Exercise 18d – p. 609

1) $\frac{1}{8}$

2) $\frac{1}{8}$

3) a) $\frac{2}{5}$ b) $\frac{13}{25}$

4) $\frac{7}{16}$

5) 0.01

6) $\frac{45}{101}$

Exercise 18e – p. 615

1) a) $\frac{1}{8}$ b) $\frac{3}{16}$

2) a) $\frac{1}{6}$ b) $\frac{3}{4}$ c) $\frac{7}{18}$

3) a) $\frac{11}{20}$ b) $\frac{3}{20}$ c) $\frac{4}{5}$

4) $\frac{17}{81}$

5) a) $\frac{1}{2}$ b) $\frac{1}{4}$ c) $\frac{1}{4}$

6) $\frac{26}{27}$

7) $\frac{7}{11}$

8) $\frac{1}{12}$

9) $\frac{7}{10}, \frac{11}{14}$

10) $\frac{4}{5}$, no as $P(A \cap B) \neq 0$

Exercise 18f – p. 620

1) 2.78

2) 0.28

3) 6

4) a) $\frac{3}{8}$ b) $\frac{1}{2}, 25$

5) 2.19

6) 20

7) 1.7

8) 2.2

9) £32.97

10) 25 p

11) 42 p

12) £1.10

Multiple Choice Exercise 18 – p. 621

1) c   2) d   3) d   4) b

5) c   6) e   7) a   8) b

9) c   10) b   11) b, c   12) a, b, c

13) a, c   14) a   15) a, d   16) C

17) E   18) D   19) C   20) c

21) I   22) c   23) A   24) F

25) F   26) T   27) T   28) F

29) F   30) F

Miscellaneous Exercise 18 – p. 624

1) $\frac{1}{36}$

2) $\frac{3}{16}$

3) a) $\frac{1}{17}$ b) $\frac{26}{51}$

4) $\frac{1}{3}$

5) a) 0.08 b) 0.44

6) $\frac{10}{21}$

7) a) i) 10   ii) 200   iii) 80
   b) i) $\frac{125}{216}$ ii) $\frac{91}{216}$ iii) $\frac{25}{72}, \frac{1}{36}$

8) 267 (274 from tables)

9) $p(B) = \frac{7}{12}, p(B|A) = \frac{5}{8}, p(B|\bar{A}) = \frac{15}{28}$, not independent and not mutually exclusive

10) a) $\frac{5}{6}$ b) 1   c) $\frac{6}{5}$ d) $\frac{14}{5}$

11) $pq(p^{r-2} + q^{r-2}), 2\frac{3}{4}$

12) b) $35/253; 48/253$

13) a) $\frac{1}{221}$ b) $\frac{32}{221}$ c) $\frac{13}{17}; \frac{25}{33}$

14) a) 0   b) $\frac{1}{18}$
    c) $73/1296$ d) $73/648$
    e) $37/324$ f) $857/1296$

15) $0.28, 0.11$

16) a) $\frac{2}{5}$
    b) i) p^3,   ii) $p^3 + q^3$,   iii) $3p^3q$
       iv) $3p^3q + 3pq^3, \frac{64}{81}$

17) a) 6
    b) i) $\frac{2}{5}$ ii) $\frac{1}{3}$ iii) $\frac{28}{75}$ iv) $\frac{38}{75}$

18) $\frac{32}{59}$

19) a) $\dfrac{52!}{39!\,13!}, \dfrac{4(39!\,13!)}{52!}$
    b) i) ab ii) $a(1-b)$
       iii) $(1-a)(1-b)$
       iv) $(1-a)^n(1-b)^n, 35$

20) $\frac{2}{7},$ a) $\frac{34}{35}$ b) $\frac{4}{35}$

21) a) $5p^4 - 4p^5$
    b) $1 - np(1-p)^{n-1} - (1-p)^n$

22) a) i) 48   ii) 288
   b) $\frac{1}{21}$, $\frac{32}{147}$

23) a) 1320   b) $(\frac{8}{9})^4$ c) $\frac{1}{6}(\frac{5}{6})^{r-2}$

24) $\frac{1}{5}$;   a) $\frac{1}{2}$ b) $\frac{1}{3}$ c) $\frac{1}{6}$

25) a) $\frac{81}{256}$ b) $\frac{1}{256}$ c) $\frac{3}{128}$ d) $\frac{3}{32}$

26) a) i) $\frac{2}{9}$ ii) $\frac{5}{9}$ iii) $\frac{43}{45}$;   b) $\frac{1}{4}$

27) a) $\frac{1}{3}$
   b) $\{4, 5, 6, 7, 8\}$, $\frac{1}{4}$, $\frac{1}{4}$, $\frac{5}{16}$, $\frac{1}{8}$, $\frac{1}{16}$, 5.5

28) b) i) $\frac{1}{2}$ ii) $\frac{1}{6}$

29) 0.01, 0.87, 0.96, 0.085

30) 0.914

31) $\frac{82}{91}$

32) 0.322

33) $\frac{64}{81}$

34) a) i) $\frac{1}{5}$ ii) $\frac{1}{10}$ b) i) $\frac{3}{8}$ ii) $\frac{3}{7}$ iii) $\frac{9}{20}$

35) a) $\frac{9}{10}$ b) $\frac{1}{5}$; $\frac{1}{5}$

INDEX

Acceleration 3, 118, 293, 338
  angular 139
  as a change in direction 293
  as a change in speed 293
  as a function of displacement 345
  as a function of time 338
  as a function of velocity 344
  constant 123
  due to gravity 131
  radial 294
  related 165
Air resistance 1
Amplitude of simple harmonic motion 384
Angle of friction 83
Angular acceleration 139
Angular velocity 136
  relation to linear velocity 138
Associated circular motion for SHM 389
Average speed 112
Average velocity 112
Axis of rotation 519

Banked tracks 303
Biased 594
Bob 1
Body
  hanging from a point 531
  resting on a plane 531
Bow's Notation 573

Centre of gravity 498
  of a set of particles 498
  of a solid pyramid 528
  of a triangular lamina 502
  of composite bodies 505
  of non-uniform bodies 529
  standard results 530
  using calculus to find 514, 519, 522,
    525, 526
Centre of mass 501
Centroid 503
Circular motion 294
  constant speed 294
  variable speed 310
  radial acceleration 294
  tangential acceleration 310

Closest approach 435
Coefficient of friction 82
Coefficient of restitution 250
Collision of moving particles 362
Components
  Cartesian 21
  of acceleration 267, 355
  of displacement 268, 355
  of a force 20
  of a vector 15, 19
  of a velocity 268, 355
Compound probability 597
Compression
  light rods 570
  springs 200
Concurrent forces 73
Conditional events 597
Conditional probability 597
Conditions for equilibrium 92, 94
Conical pendulum 297
Connected bodies 559
Connected particles 157
Conservation of mechanical energy 218
  use in problem solving 219
Conservation of linear momentum 237, 250
Contact forces 79
Contact
  rough 82
  smooth 82
Coplanar vectors 16
Coplanar forces 92, 454, 478
Cotangent Rule ix, 546
Couple 466
  characteristics of 466
  combination with a force 479
  constant moment of 466
Course 424

Degrees of freedom 92
Direct impact 250
  elastic 250
  inelastic 250
Direction of motion 114
  resultant 420
Displacement 3
  relative 432

655

Displacement–time graph 111
Distance 2
Distance apart of moving particles 364

Elastic impact 250
Elastic limit 200
Elastic strings 199
    work done in stretching 208
Elasticity, modulus of 200
Energy 213
    conservation of 218
    elastic potential 215
    gravitational potential 214
    kinetic 213
    relation to work 213
Equation (vector)
    of a line 27
    of a line through two points 28
    of motion 117, 123
    of path of a particle 31, 117
Equilibrant 69
Equilibrium 66
    conditions for 92, 94
    limiting 82
    of bodies in contact 554
    of concurrent forces 66
    of coplanar forces 92
    of connected bodies 559
    of three forces 70
Equivalent sets of forces 478
Event 587
Expectation 616
Expected gain or loss 618
Extension 199
External
    contact 81
    forces 81

Fixed objects 82
Force 5
    components of 20
    equivalent to a couple and a force 479
    external 81
    frictional 82
    internal 81
line of action of 30
    moment of 48
    position of resultant 44, 454
    resultant (and see resultant vector)
        44, 454, 463, 465
    turning effect of 46
Forces
    coplanar systems of 454
    contact 79
    equivalent systems of 478
    in equilibrium 66, 70, 73, 88, 92
    in light rods 570
    parallel 463

polygon of 15
    triangle of 15, 70
Force systems
    equivalent 478
    identification of 470
Frame of reference 82, 425
Frameworks 570
    light 570
    heavy 560
Free vector 15
Freely jointed bodies 559
Friction 82
    angle of 83
    coefficient of 82
    limiting 82

Graphical methods
    Bow's notation for light frameworks
        573
    for constant acceleration 125
    for relative velocity 426
Gravitation, acceleration due to 131

Hinge 559
Hollow 2
Hooke's Law 199

Identification of force systems 470
Impact
    direct 250
    elastic 250
    inelastic 250
    internal 237
    perfectly elastic 250
Impulse 232
    instantaneous 233
    of a constant force 232
    of a variable force 368
    relation to momentum 232
Impulsive tension 242
Independent events 596
Interception 440
Internal
    contact 81
    forces 81
    impact 237
Intersection of two lines 44

Jointed rods
    heavy 560
    light 570

Kinetic energy 213
    relation to work 213
    using scalar product 366

Lami's Theorem 72
Lamina 1
    centre of gravity of 515

Light 1
Light rods, framework of 570
Limiting friction 82
Line, vector equation of 27
Lines, intersection of two 44
Line of action
    of a force 30
    of a resultant force 44
Load 571

Mass 6, 152
Mechanical energy 218, 254
Method of sections 578
Modulus of elasticity 200
Moment
    of a couple 466
    of a force 48
    resultant 53, 88
    zero 49
Moments, principle of 54
Momentum 232
    conservation of 237, 250
    relation to impulse 232
Motion in a circle 294
    radial acceleration 294
    tangential acceleration 310
    with constant speed 294
    with variable speed 310
Motion in a straight line 110, 338
Motion in a vertical circle 310
    restricted to a circular path 314
    not restricted to a circular path 318
Motion in three dimensions 360
Motion in two dimensions 134, 355, 359
Motion, Newton's Laws of 149, 151, 157,
    347, 359

Motion of connected particles 157
Moving particles
    collision of 362
    distance apart 364
    least distance apart 364, 435
Mutually exclusive events 594

Natural length 199
Newton 5
Newton's laws of motion 149, 151, 157,
    347, 359
Newton's law of restitution 250
Normal contact force 79
Normal reaction 79

Occurrence 587
Oscillations 385, 404
    incomplete 401
Overturning 550

Parabolic flight 279

Parallel forces
    resultant of like 463
    resultant of unlike 465
Particle 1
Perfectly elastic impact 250
Period of oscillation (SHM) 385
Polygon of vectors 15
Position of a resultant force 44
Position vector 27
Possibility space 588, 610
Potential energy
    gravitational 214
    elastic 215
Power 186
    of a moving vehicle 187
Principles
    conservation of mechanical energy 218
    conservation of momentum 237, 250
    impulse–momentum 232
    moments 54
    work–energy 213
Probability 587
    compound 597
    conditional 597
    empirical 593
    that an event occurs 588
    that an event does not occur 590
Projectiles 267
    angle of projection 281
    equation of path 271
    greatest height 280
    maximum range on a horizontal plane
        280
    range on a horizontal plane 280
    time of flight 279
Pulley systems 157

Radial acceleration 294
Range on a horizontal plane 280
Reaction 6
    normal 6
    total 83
Recoil of guns 239
Relative
    displacement 432
    position 432
    velocity 426
Resolving 15, 19
Resultant 15, 32, 38
    force 454
    moment 53
    of forces represented by line segments
        472
    of parallel forces 463, 465
    torque 53
    vector 15
    velocity 420
Resultant Vector Theorem 472

Restitution
  coefficient of 250
  Newton's law of 250
Retardation 121
Rigid body
  centre of gravity of 498
  equilibrium of 92, 94
Rough contact 82

Sample points 610
Scalar 12
Seconds pendulum 394
Sections, method of 578
Sideslip of a vehicle 304
Simple harmonic motion 382
  amplitude 384
  angular 383, 385
  centre 384
  equations of motion 388
  forces causing 396
  incomplete oscillations 401
  linear 383, 384
  period of 385
  relation to motion in a circle 389
Simple pendulum 393
Situation 587
Sliding and overturning 550
Space diagram 574
Speed 3
  average 112
Smooth 2
  contact 82
Spherical shell 2
Spring 200
Systems of connected particles 157
Strut 570

Tension
  impulsive 242
  in a light rod 570
  in a string 7
  in elastic strings 199
  in springs 201
Three forces in equilibrium 70
Thrust
  in a light rod 570
  in a spring 201
Tie 570
Tied vector 15
Toppling 550
Torque 48, 469
  direction of 48
  graphical representation of 49
  resultant 53
Trajectory 271
Tree diagram 604
Triangle
  of forces 70
  of vectors 15

Turning effect 46

Uniform
  acceleration 123
  body 502
  velocity 110
Variable acceleration 339, 345, 346, 382
Vector 12
  addition 15
  Cartesian components of 21
  components of 15
  differentiation with respect to time 136
  direction 25
  equation of a line 27
  free 15
  integration with respect to time 339
  magnitude of 22
  modulus of 22
  negative 14
  position 27
  representation 12
  resultant 15, 32, 38
  symbols 13
  tied 15
  unit 24
Vector quantity 12
Vectors
  angle between 32
  coplanar 16
  equal 13
  equal and opposite 14
  equivalent 15
  parallel 14
  polygon of 15
  resolving 19
  triangle of 15
Velocity 3, 338
  angular 136
  at an instant 114
  average 112
  constant 117
  relative 426
  resultant 420
  uniform 110
Velocity–displacement graph 351
Velocity–time graph 119, 350
Venn diagram 612
Vertical motion under gravity 131

Weight 5, 152
Work 181
  relation to mechanical energy 213
  done against gravity 183
  done by a constant force 366
  done by a variable force 368
  done in stretching an elastic string 208
  done by a moving vehicle 183
  negative 182
Wind direction 429